Processes, Systems, and Information

An Introduction to MIS

David M. Kroenke

Earl McKinney Jr.
Bowling Green State University

PEARSON

Boston   Columbus   Indianapolis   New York   San Francisco
Upper Saddle River   Amsterdam   Cape Town   Dubai   London
Madrid   Milan   Munich   Paris   Montreal   Toronto   Delhi
Mexico City   Sao Paulo   Sydney   Hong Kong   Seoul   Singapore
Taipei   Tokyo

Editorial Director: Sally Yagan
Executive Editor: Bob Horan
Director of Development: Steve Deitmer
Development Editor: Laura Town
Editorial Project Manager: Kelly Loftus
Editorial Assistant: Ashlee Bradbury
Director of Marketing: Maggie Moylan
Senior Marketing Manager: Anne Fahlgren
Senior Managing Editor: Judy Leale
Senior Operations Supervisor: Arnold Vila
Operations Specialist: Maura Zaldivar
Creative Director: Blair Brown

Sr. Art Director/Design Supervisor: Janet Slowik
Interior and Cover Designer: Karen Quigley
Interior Illustrations: Simon Alicea
Cover Art: Shutterstock/Stacie Stauff Smith Photography
Editorial Media Project Manager: Allison Longley
Production Media Project Manager: Lisa Rinaldi
Full-Service Project Management: Jennifer Welsch/Bookmasters, Inc.
Composition: Integra Software Services Pvt. Ltd.
Printer/Binder: Courier/Kendallville
Cover Printer: Lehigh-Phoenix Color/Hagerstown
Text Font: 10/12 Times

Credits and acknowledgments borrowed from other sources and reproduced, with permission, in this textbook appear on the appropriate page within text.

Microsoft® and Windows® are registered trademarks of the Microsoft Corporation in the U.S.A. and other countries. Screen shots and icons reprinted with permission from the Microsoft Corporation. This book is not sponsored or endorsed by or affiliated with the Microsoft Corporation.

This publication contains references to the products of SAP AG. SAP, R/3, SAP NetWeaver, Duet, PartnerEdge, ByDesign, SAP BusinessObjects Explorer, StreamWork, and other SAP products and services mentioned herein as well as their respective logos are trademarks or registered trademarks of SAP AG in Germany and other countries.

Business Objects and the Business Objects logo, BusinessObjects, Crystal Reports, Crystal Decisions, Web Intelligence, Xcelsius, and other Business Objects products and services mentioned herein as well as their respective logos are trademarks or registered trademarks of Business Objects Software Ltd. Business Objects is an SAP company.

Sybase and Adaptive Server, iAnywhere, Sybase 365, SQL Anywhere, and other Sybase products and services mentioned herein as well as their respective logos are trademarks or registered trademarks of Sybase, Inc. Sybase is an SAP company.

SAP AG is neither the author nor the publisher of this publication and is not responsible for its content. SAP Group shall not be liable for errors or omissions with respect to the materials. The only warranties for SAP Group products and services are those that are set forth in the express warranty statements accompanying such products and services, if any. Nothing herein should be construed as constituting an additional warranty.

Many of the designations by manufacturers and sellers to distinguish their products are claimed as trademarks. Where those designations appear in this book, and the publisher was aware of a trademark claim, the designations have been printed in initial caps or all caps.

Library of Congress Cataloging-in-Publication Data

Kroenke, David.
   Processes, systems, and information : an introduction to MIS / David M. Kroenke, Earl McKinney Jr.
     p. cm.
   Includes bibliographical references and index.
   ISBN-13: 978-0-13-278347-7 (pbk.: alk. paper)
   ISBN-10: 0-13-278347-9 (pbk.: alk. paper)
     1. Management information systems.   I. McKinney, Earl.   II. Title.
   T58.6.K7733 2013
   658.4'038011—dc23
                                                          2011035614

10 9 8 7 6 5 4 3 2 1

ISBN 10:   0-13-278347-9
ISBN 13: 978-0-13-278347-7

Brief Contents

PART 1   MIS and You   2

Chapter 1   Introduction to MIS   4
Chapter 2   Business Processes, Information Systems, and Information   26

PART 2   Information Technology   52

Chapter 3   Hardware, Software, and Networks   54
Chapter 4   Database Processing   90

PART 3   Operational Processes   128

Chapter 5   Using IS to Improve Processes   130
Chapter 6   Supporting Processes with ERP Systems   156
Chapter 7   Supporting the Procurement Process with SAP   184
Appendix 7   SAP Procurement Tutorial   212
Chapter 8   Supporting the Sales Process with SAP   228
Appendix 8   SAP Sales Tutorial   254

PART 4   Dynamic Processes and Information Systems   270

Chapter 9   Collaboration Processes and Information Systems   272
Chapter 10   The Impact of Web 2.0 and Social Media on Business Processes   312
Chapter 11   Business Intelligence   340

PART 5   MIS Management Processes   374

Chapter 12   MIS Management Processes: Process Management, Systems Development, and Security   376

Application Exercises   418
Glossary   437
Index   449

Contents

Preface   *xii*
About the Authors   *xix*

PART 1   MIS and You   2

Chapter 1   Introduction to MIS   4

Q1 Why Is Introduction to MIS the Most Important Class in the Business School?   6
Are There Cost-Effective Business Applications of Facebook and Twitter?   7
How Can I Attain Job Security?   7
How Can Intro to MIS Help You Learn Nonroutine Skills?   8

Q2 What Is MIS?   10
Processes, Information Systems, and Information   10
Management and Use   10
Achieve Organizational Strategy   11

Q3 How Does MIS Relate to Organizational Strategy?   12

Q4 What Five Forces Determine Industry Structure?   12

Q5 What Is Competitive Strategy?   14

Q6 How Does Competitive Strategy Determine Value Chain Structure?   15
Primary Activities in the Value Chain   15
Support Activities in the Value Chain   16
■ MIS INCLASS 1: Industry Structure → Competitive Strategy → Value Chains → Business Processes ↔ Information Systems   17
Value Chain Linkages   17

Q7 How Do Value Chains Determine Business Processes and Information Systems?   18
■ ETHICS GUIDE: Yikes! Bikes   20
■ CASE STUDY 1: Getty Images Serves up Profit and YouTube Grows Exponentially   24

Chapter 2   Business Processes, Information Systems, and Information   26

Q1 What Is a Business Process?   28
An Example Business Process   28
Why Do Organizations Standardize Business Processes?   30

Q2 What Is an Information System?   31
■ MIS INCLASS 2: Recognizing Processes Close to Home   32

Q3 How Do Business Processes and Information Systems Relate?   32
Information Systems in the Context of Business Processes   33
Business Processes and Information Systems Have Different Scope   35

Q4 What Is Information?   36
Where Is Information?   37

Q5 What Factors Drive Information Quality?   38
Data Factors   38
Human Factors   39
How Do Groups Conceive Information?   40

Q6 How Do Structured and Dynamic Processes Vary?   41
Characteristics of Structured Processes   41
Characteristics of Dynamic Processes   41
■ ETHICS GUIDE: Egocentric Versus Empathetic Thinking   44
■ CASE STUDY 2: An Amazon of Innovation   49

PART 2   Information Technology   52

Chapter 3   Hardware, Software, and Networks   54

Q1 What Do Business Professionals Need to Know About Computer Hardware?   56

Computer Data   57

In Fewer Than 300 Words, How Does a Computer Work?   58

Why Does a Manager Care How a Computer Works?   59

What Is the Difference Between a Client and a Server?   59

Q2 What Do Business Professionals Need to Know About Software?   61

What Are the Major Operating Systems?   61

Own Versus License   63

What Types of Applications Exist, and How Do Organizations Obtain Them?   64

How Do Organizations Acquire Application Software?   66

Is Open Source a Viable Alternative?   66

Q3 What Types of Computer Networks Exist?   68

What Are the Components of a LAN?   68

What Are the Alternatives for Connecting to a WAN?   71

Q4 What Do Business Professionals Need to Know About the Internet?   73

An Internet Example   73

The TCP/IP Architecture   74

Application Layer Protocols   74

TCP and IP Protocols   75

IP Addressing   76

Q5 What Happens on a Typical Web Server?   77

■ **MIS INCLASS 3: Opening Pandora's Box   78**

Three-Tier Architecture   79

Watch the Three Tiers in Action!   79

Hypertext Markup Language (HTML)   80

XML, Flash, Silverlight, and HTML5   82

Q6 How Do Organizations Benefit from Virtual Private Networks (VPNs)?   82

■ **ETHICS GUIDE: Churn and Burn   84**

■ **CASE STUDY 3: Keeping Up with Wireless   89**

Chapter 4   Database Processing   90

Q1 What Is the Purpose of a Database?   92

Q2 What Are the Contents of a Database?   93

What Are Relationships Among Rows?   94

Metadata   96

Q3 What Are the Components of a Database Application System?   97

What Is a Database Management System?   97

Creating the Database and Its Structures   98

Processing the Database   98

Administering the Database   99

What Are the Components of a Database Application?   100

What Are Forms, Reports, Queries, and Application Programs?   100

Why Are Database Application Programs Needed?   101

Multi-User Processing   102

■ **MIS INCLASS 4: How Much Is a Database Worth?   103**

Enterprise DBMS Versus Personal DBMS   103

Q4 How Do Data Models Facilitate Database Design?   104

What Is the Entity-Relationship Data Model?   105

Entities   105

Relationships   106

Q5 How Is a Data Model Transformed into a Database Design?   108

Normalization   108

Data Integrity Problems   109

Normalizing for Data Integrity   109

Summary of Normalization   110

Representing Relationships   110

Q6 What Is the Users' Role in the Development of Databases?   112

Q7 How Can the Intramural League Improve Its Database?   113

League Database, Revision 1   114

League Database, Revision 2   115

■ ETHICS GUIDE: Nobody Said I Shouldn't   118

■ CASE STUDY 4: Aviation Safety Network   125

PART 3   Operational Processes   128

Chapter 5   Using IS to Improve Processes   130

Q1 What Are the Fundamental Types of Processes in Organizations?   132

Examples of Processes   132

Scope of Processes   133

Objectives of Processes   134

Q2 What Are Examples of Common Business Processes?   135

Inbound Logistics Processes   135

Operations Processes   135

Outbound Logistics Processes   136

Sales and Marketing Processes   136

Service Processes   136

Human Resources Processes   137

Technology Development Processes   137

Q3 How Can Organizations Improve Processes?   137

Process Objectives   137

Process Measures   138

Q4 How Can Organizations Use IS to Improve Processes?   139

Three Ways IS Improve Processes   139

Non-IS Process Improvements   140

Participants and Diagrams in Process Improvement   141

Q5 How Can an IS Hinder a Process?   143

Information Silos   143

Why Information Silos Exist   143

Q6 How Can SOA Improve Processes?   144

Service   144

■ MIS INCLASS 5: Improving the Process of Making Paper Airplanes   145

Encapsulation   147

Standards   147

■ ETHICS GUIDE: Process Improvement or Privacy Problem?   148

■ CASE STUDY 5: Process Cast in Stone   154

Chapter 6   Supporting Processes with ERP Systems   156

Q1 What Problem Does an ERP System Solve?   158

Enterprise Application Integration (EAI)   158

Enterprise Resource Planning (ERP)   159

ERP Implementation: Before and After Examples   160

Q2 What Are the Elements of an ERP System?   163

The Five Components of an ERP System: Software, Hardware, Data, Procedures, and People   164

Q3 What Are the Benefits of an ERP System?   167

Q4 What Are the Challenges of Implementing an ERP Solution?   168

■ MIS INCLASS 6: Building a Model   169

Implementation Decisions   169

People Issues   170

Q5 What Types of Organizations Use ERP?   171

ERP by Industry Type   171

ERP by Organization Size   171

International ERP   172

Q6 Who Are the Major ERP Vendors?   172

ERP Vendor Market Share   173

ERP Products   173

Q7 What Makes SAP Different from Other ERP Products?   174

SAP Inputs and Outputs   175

SAP Software   176

■ ETHICS GUIDE: ERP Estimation   178

■ CASE STUDY 6: The Sudden End of the U.S. Air Force   182

Chapter 7   Supporting the Procurement Process with SAP   184

Q1 What Are the Fundamentals of a Procurement Process?   186

Q2 How Did the Procurement Process at CBI Work Before SAP?   188

Q3 What Were the Problems with the Procurement Process Before SAP?   190

Warehouse Problems   190

Accounting Problems   191

Purchasing Problems   191

Q4 How Does CBI Implement SAP?   192

Q5 How Does the Procurement Process Work at CBI After SAP?   193

Purchasing   194

Warehouse   195

Accounting   196

The Benefits of SAP for the CBI Procurement Process   196

Q6 How Can SAP Improve the Integration of Supply Chain Processes at CBI?   197

Supply Chain Processes   198

Supply Chain Process Integration   198

Improving Supply Chain Process Integration by Sharing Data   198

Improving Supply Chain Process Integration by Increasing Process Synergy   199

SAP Integration Problems with Emerging Technologies   200

■ MIS INCLASS 7: The Bicycle Supply Game   202

Q7 How Does the Use of SAP Change CBI?   204

Wally's Job Change   205

■ ETHICS GUIDE: Procurement Ethics   206

■ ACTIVE CASE 7: SAP Procurement Process Tutorial   211

Appendix 7   SAP Procurement Tutorial   212

Chapter 8   Supporting the Sales Process with SAP   228

Q1 What Are the Fundamentals of a Sales Process?   230

Q2 How Did the Sales Process at CBI Work Before SAP?   231

Q3 What Were the Problems with the Sales Process Before SAP?   233

Sales Problems   233

Warehouse Problems   233

Accounting Problems   234

Q4 How Does CBI Implement SAP?   234

Q5 How Does the Sales Process Work at CBI After SAP?   235

Sales   235

Warehouse   236

Accounting   238

Benefits of SAP for the CBI Sales Process   239

■ **MIS INCLASS 8: Phones and Processes   239**

Q6 How Can SAP Improve the Integration of Customer-Facing Processes at CBI?   240

Integration of Customer-Facing Processes   240

Improving Customer-Facing Process Integration by Sharing Data   240

Improving Customer-Facing Process Integration by Increasing Process Synergy   241

SAP Integration Problems with Emerging Technologies   242

Integration Challenges and Lessons   243

Process Integration Lessons   244

Q7 How Does E-Commerce Integrate Firms in an Industry?   244

E-Commerce Merchant Companies   246

Nonmerchant E-Commerce   246

How Does E-Commerce Improve Market Efficiency?   246

Process Integration and Your Business Future   247

■ **ETHICS GUIDE: Are My Ethics for Sale?   248**

■ **ACTIVE CASE 8: SAP Sales Process Tutorial   253**

Chapter 8A   SAP Sales Tutorial   254

PART 4   Dynamic Processes and Information Systems   270

Chapter 9   Collaboration Processes and Information Systems   272

Q1 What Makes for Effective Collaboration?   274

Warning!   275

What Are Critical Collaboration Skills?   275

What Is a Successful Collaborative Team?   276

Q2 What Are Characteristics of Fundamental Collaboration Processes?   277

Decision-Making Collaboration   277

Decision-Making Collaboration Processes   278

Problem-Solving Collaboration   280

Problem-Solving Collaboration Processes   280

Project Management Collaboration Processes   281

Q3 How Can Collaboration Systems Improve Team Communication?   283

Q4 How Can Collaboration Systems Manage Content?   285

Shared Content with No Control   285

Shared Content with Version Management   286

Shared Content with Version Control   288

■ **MIS INCLASS 9: Virtual Practice!   290**

Q5 How Can You Use Microsoft SharePoint for Student Team Projects?   291

SharePoint Features Recommended for Student Teams   291

What Are Recommended Uses for Particular SharePoint Tools?   294

Q6 How Can Collaboration Systems Control Workflow?   296

The Workflow Problem Requirements   296

Implementing the Workflow   297

■ **ETHICS GUIDE: Virtual Ethics?   302**

■ **CASE STUDY 9: Eating Our Own Dog Food   307**

Chapter 10   The Impact of Web 2.0 and Social Media on Business Processes   312

Q1 What Are Web 2.0 and Social Media?   314

Web 2.0   314

Social Media   316

Q2 How Can Web 2.0 Improve Business Processes?   318
The Promotion Process   318
The Online Advertising Sales Process   319
The Market Research Process   319
The B2C Sales Process   320
Supporting New Processes with Web 2.0   320
Process Integration with Web 2.0   320

Q3 How Can Social Media Improve Business Processes?   320
Sharing Social Media   321
Networking Social Media   322
Collaboration Social Media   324
Supporting New Processes with Social Media   325
Process Integration with Social Media   325
Tips for Conducting Social Media Promotions   325

Q4 How Can Web 2.0 Improve the Process of Building Social Capital?   326
What Is Social Capital?   326
How an Organization Can Use Social Media to Increase the Number of Relationships   326
How an Organization Can Use Social Media to Increase the Strength of Relationships   328
■ MIS INCLASS 10: Using Twitter to Support the Class Discussion Process   329
How an Organization Can Use Social Media to Connect to Those with More Assets   329

Q5 What Are the Challenges for Businesses Using Web 2.0?   330
Management Problems   330
User Content Problems   330
Responding to User Content Problems   331

Q6 What Is on the Horizon That Will Have a Significant Impact on Web 2.0?   332
■ ETHICS GUIDE: Ethics, Social Media, and Stretching the Truth   334
■ CASE STUDY 10: Tourism Holdings Limited (THL)   338

Chapter 11   Business Intelligence   340

Q1 Why Do Organizations Need Business Intelligence (BI)?   342

Q2 How Does BI Support the Informing Process?   343
The Informing Process in the Sales Process   344
Standardizing the Informing Process   344
Versions of the Informing Processes   345

Q3 What Are Examples of the Reporting Process?   347
Noninteractive Reports   348
Interactive Reports   351

Q4 What Are Examples of the Data Mining Process?   354
Cluster Analysis   354
Regression Analysis   355
Market Basket Analysis   355
Decision Trees   356
■ MIS INCLASS 11: I Know That, I Think   357
Supervised and Unsupervised Data Mining Analysis   358

Q5 What Are the Components of a BI System?   358
Hardware   358
Software   358
Data   358
Procedures   359
People   359

Q6 What Are the Potential Problems with BI Systems?   359
Data Problems   359
People Problems   360

Q7 What Future Technological Advances Will Affect BI Use? 362
Technology 362
Technology Backlash 362

Q8 Who Are the Key BI Vendors and How Does SAP Accomplish BI? 363
Vendors 363
SAP BI 364
■ **ETHICS GUIDE: The Ethics of Profiling Customers 366**
■ **CASE STUDY 11: Tourism Holdings Limited (THL) (continued) 370**

PART 5 MIS Management Processes 374

Chapter 12 MIS Management Processes: Process Management, Systems Development, and Security 376

Q1 What Are the Activities of Business Process Management? 378
The BPM Monitoring Activity 379
The BPM Modeling Activity 380
The BPM Create Components Activity 380
The BPM Implement Process Activity 382

Q2 What Are the Activities of Systems Development Life Cycle (SDLC) Development Process? 384
Define the System 384
Determine Requirements 386
Design Components 387
Implement the System 388
Maintain the System 389

Q3 Which Comes First: Process or Systems Development? 390
Business Processes First 390
Information System First 391
Another Factor: Off-the-Shelf Software 392
And the Answer Is . . . 392

Q4 What Is Information Systems Security? 392
What Are the Sources of Vulnerabilities? 392
What Are the Types of Security Threats? 393
■ **MIS INCLASS 12: Phishing for Credit Cards, Identifying Numbers, and Bank Accounts 395**

Q5 What Are the Components of an Organization's Security Program? 396
What Is Management's Security Role? 397
The *NIST Handbook* of Security Elements 397

Q6 What Technical Safeguards Are Available? 398
Identification and Authentication 398
Encryption 399
Firewalls 401
Malware Protection 401
Design Secure Applications 403
Data Safeguards 403

Q7 What Human Security Safeguards Are Available? 403
Human Resources 404
Account Administration 405
Systems Procedures 406
Security Monitoring 407
Organizational Response to Security Incidents 407
■ **ETHICS GUIDE: Security Privacy 410**
■ **CASE STUDY 12: Slow Learners, or What? 416**

Application Exercises 418
Glossary 437
Index 449

Preface

Since the emergence of ERP and EAI systems in the early 1990s, the MIS discipline has undergone a slow but persistent change. Whereas the early emphasis of MIS was on the management and use of information systems, *per se,* emerging cross-functional systems began to place the focus on processes that utilize such systems. We believe that existing MIS textbooks, particularly those at the introductory level, do not sufficiently recognize this change in emphasis. Hence, we offer this textbook that provides a strong process orientation.

Background

The relationship of business processes and information systems is complex. They are not one and the same; a given process might use several different information systems, and, at the same time, a given information system might support many different processes. So, we cannot say that a process encapsulates all of its information systems, nor can we say that an information system encapsulates all of its processes.

In part because of this complex relationship, we define *MIS* as the management and use of *processes, information systems, and information* to help organizations achieve their strategy (Chapter 1). We further define *management* not in the traditional sense of plan, organize, control, and staff, but rather as the *creation, monitoring, and adaptation of processes, systems, and information*. The fabric of this text is woven around and through these definitions.

Potential adopters of this textbook are departments that make business processes a key component or thread throughout their curricula. This group includes all of the universities that are part of the SAP University Alliance, those that are part of the Microsoft Dynamics Academic Alliance, and other institutions for which a business process orientation is important. Chapters 7 and 8 provide specific examples of the use of SAP, and the cases that conclude each of those chapters provide tutorial exercises that use the SAP University Alliance's Global Bikes Inc. (GBI) simulation.

In our opinion, a text must go beyond the operational processes that comprise Chapters 7 and 8. Of course, operational processes are most important, and five chapters of our text include or are devoted to them. However, other dynamic processes, such as collaboration, project management, problem solving, business intelligence, and social networking, are also important. Hence, we believe that this text should include much more than SAP-oriented processes.

Text Features

A challenge of teaching the introduction to MIS course from a process orientation is the lack of business knowledge and experience on the part of most students. Many universities offer the introduction to MIS course at the sophomore and even freshmen levels. Most of these students have completed few business courses. Even when this course is taught to higher-level students, however, few of them have significant business or process experience. They have been lifeguards or baristas. When we attempt to talk about, for example, the impact of process change on departmental power, that discussion goes over the heads of the students. They may memorize the terms, but they often lose the essence of the discussion. The features of this text are designed, in part, to address this problem.

Opening Vignettes

Each chapter opens with a short vignette of a business situation and problem that necessitates knowledge of that chapter. We use three different fictitious organizational settings:

1. FlexTime, a popular workout studio
2. Central Colorado State, a university
3. Chuck's Bikes, a bicycle manufacturer that competes with Global Bikes

Each of these vignettes presents a situation that illustrates the use of the chapter's contents in an applied setting. Most contain a problem that requires knowledge of the chapter to understand and solve.

MIS InClass Exercises

Every chapter includes a student group exercise that is intended to be completed during class. The purpose of the exercise is to engage the student with the chapter's knowledge. These exercises are part lab and part case study in nature and are included within the chapter. In our experience, some of them lead to spirited discussions, and we could have let them run on for two or three class periods, had we had that luxury.

SAP Tutorial Exercises

The appendices to Chapters 7 and 8 contain process exercises that involve the SAP Alliance's GBI simulation. Professors at institutions that are members of the Alliance will be able to use these with their students. Because not every department that might want to use this book is a member of that alliance, we have made these exercises optional appendices. You can omit the exercises without any loss of continuity.

The exercises are, we hope, purposeful yet simple to do. Our goal was to make it possible for them to be conducted by teaching assistants and faculty who have not been able to attend the SAP university training. To that end, we provide extensive instructor support materials.

Earl McKinney, the author of the tutorial exercises, has been teaching SAP for 5 years at Bowling Green State University. The tutorial exercises included in this book have been tested extensively with introduction to MIS students in a BGSU lab setting. In addition to the exercises, Earl has written a detailed teaching guide on how best to use the exercises as well as tips and pointers about their use and his experience about where students are most likely to struggle.

Over these years, Earl learned that when doing SAP exercises, it is far too easy for the students to slip into "monkey-see, monkey-do" mode without any clear understanding of what they are doing, or why. Based on this classroom experience, we believe that the setup to procurement and sales in Chapters 7 and 8, together with the exercises themselves, help the student move beyond simple copy mode to learn, in addition to SAP keystrokes, the nature of process-oriented software and its role in organizations.

Like all who have used the GBI simulation, we are grateful to the SAP Alliance and to the simulation's authors. In accordance with both the letter and spirit of the SAP Alliance community's policy, we have placed these exercises out on the SAP University Alliance Web site. We hope you will find sufficient value in this text to use it in your classroom, but please feel free to use these exercises even if you do not adopt this text.

By the way, the body of Chapters 7 and 8 use the example of Chuck's Bikes International, rather than GBI. We made this change at the request of the SAP Alliance. The Alliance prefers that authors not add new material to GBI, change any characters, make videos, and so forth. We created CBI so as to comply with that request while at the same time providing more detailed business scenarios that are compatible with GBI.

Question-Based Pedagogy

Research by Marilla Svinicki in the Psychology Department of the University of Texas indicates that today's students need help managing their time. She asserts that we should never give homework assignments such as "read pages 75–95." The problem, she says, is that students will fiddle with those pages for 30 minutes and not know when they're done. Instead, she recommends that we give our students a list of questions and the assignment that they be able to answer those questions. When they can answer the questions, they're done studying.

We have used this approach in our classrooms, and we believe that it is most effective. Students like it as well. Hence, we have organized each chapter as a list of questions.

Ethics Guides

We believe that business ethics are a critically important component of the introduction to MIS course, and that the best way to teach ethics is in the context of case-like situations. We also believe that ethics ought not to be relegated to a single chapter or chapter section. Including ethics in one place leads to the inoculation theory of education: "We don't need to discuss ethics, we've already done that." Accordingly, each chapter contains one two-page spread called an Ethics Guide. They are shown in the table of contents; to sample just one of them, turn to page 366.

Collaboration Exercises

As stated in Chapter 1, collaboration is a key skill for today's business professionals. Accordingly, we believe that teaching collaboration, collaboration processes, and collaboration information systems is an important component of this course. To that end, each chapter includes a collaboration exercise to be accomplished by a student team. In our opinion, it is not possible for students to complete all of these in one term. Instead, we recommend using three or four of them throughout the term.

In doing these exercises, we recommend that students not meet face-to-face, at least not most of the time, but use modern collaboration tools for their meetings. Google Docs and related tools are one possibility. We prefer requiring the students to use Office 365 and Microsoft SharePoint. Pearson Education will host SharePoint for adopters of this text, if you choose to do so. Contact your local Pearson Sales Representative to learn more about using SharePoint in your class.

End-of-Chapter Cases

The chapter opening vignettes are based on real-life experience, but the organizations they describe are fictitious. We use fictitious companies because we want the students to be able to learn from organizational mistakes and, at times, even organizational foolishness. We have not found many real companies that will allow us to share their laundry in this way, and, in any case, it seems to us unfair to ask for an organization's cooperation and then turn around and publish its problems.

However, we do believe students need to see examples of the role of MIS in actual organizations to help them bridge the chapter content to the real world. Hence, each chapter concludes with a case that illustrates some aspect of the chapter's contents in a real-world company. Unlike the introductory vignettes, the cases all have happy endings.

Active Reviews

Each chapter includes an Active Review at the end. These reviews help students ensure that they have learned the most essential material. They also serve as a list of potential exam questions and thus help students prepare for exams.

Application Exercises

For courses that involve a Microsoft Office component, we have developed a set of Excel and Access exercises for all chapters. These exercises, which assume the student has beginner's level expertise with these products, appear beginning on page 418. They are listed approximately in increasing order of difficulty.

What We Left Out

We chose to keep this book to the traditional 12-chapter length because we find that this number of chapters fits best into the number of class lessons of most courses. Because we are adding substantial process-oriented material, however, that meant that we needed to remove some content from the typical introduction to MIS text.

In this text, we have reduced and simplified the discussions of hardware, software, and data communications to fit into a single chapter. Furthermore, we simplified and shortened the discussion of information systems development. Finally, you will find no mention of IS departmental management in this text. It is not that we believe the shortened and omitted content is unimportant, rather, we think the opportunity cost is the least for these topics.

This text includes some material that has been previously published in David Kroenke's text, *Using MIS*. The two texts differ in that *Using MIS* makes information systems primary, whereas this text makes business processes primary. Both texts will continue to be published. Because of this difference, however, every sentence that was brought over was examined from the perspective of business processes and much of that content was changed in both minor and major ways. The discussion of collaboration, for example, is reframed into the context of dynamic business processes. That said, the majority of the material in this text is new.

Chapter Outline

This text is organized into five parts: Introduction, Technology, Structured Processes, Dynamic Processes, and Management.

Introduction

Chapter 1 sets the stage by illustrating the need for this course and especially for the behaviors and skills that students gain in the course. It defines *MIS* and summarizes the means by which organizations obtain goals and objectives. Porter's Industry, Five Forces, and Value Chain models are presented.

Chapter 2 defines and illustrates processes, information systems, and information. It uses the university intramural league to illustrate the relationship of processes and information systems. It also defines information using the Gregory Bateson definition that *information* is a difference that makes a difference.

Technology

Chapters 3 and 4 address technology. Chapter 3 provides a quick summary of hardware, software, and network products and technologies. Chapter 4 discusses database processing. These chapters serve as a technology platform for the discussions in the remaining chapters.

Structured Processes

Chapters 5 through 8 discuss structured processes and related information systems and information. Chapter 5 provides an overview of the scope and objectives of business processes. It also discusses process adaptation and improvement and the use of process objectives and measures in making process changes. Chapter 6 is a survey of EAI and ERP information systems, their benefits, and their challenges.

Chapters 7 and 8 are "applied" chapters. They show how SAP is used in two representative processes—procurement and sales. Two processes were chosen so that students could begin to see what is common to all processes and what might differ between processes. These two processes, buying and selling, are fundamental to business and both are widely used. Each chapter includes a student lab exercise appendix that uses the SAP Alliance's GBI simulation.

Dynamic Processes

Chapters 9 through 11 address what we term *dynamic processes*. Such processes are not as structured nor as rigid as the more structured operational processes. We dislike the term *unstructured processes*, because we believe that such processes do have structure, at least at a meta-level. Hence, we use the term *dynamic processes*.

Chapter 9 discusses collaboration processes for both problem-solving and project management applications. We discuss modern collaboration IS and give particular attention to Microsoft's Office 365 suite, which includes Office, Outlook, Lync, and SharePoint Online.

Chapter 10 addresses the use of Web 2.0 and social media in organizations. We discuss Lin's theory of social capital, apply that theory to organizational use of social media systems, and survey the processes supported by social media systems. Chapter 11 considers processes supported by business intelligence (BI) systems and discusses BI systems, data warehouses, and data mining.

IS Management Processes

Part 5 consists of a single chapter, Chapter 12, that addresses IS management processes. It includes business process management (BPM), the systems development life cycle (SDLC), and security. It includes a discussion of processes involved in creating and using an organizational security program.

Supplements

The following supplements are available at the Online Instructor Resource Center, accessible through *www.pearsonhighered.com/kroenke:*

Instructor's Manual

The instructor's manual, prepared by Timothy O'Keefe of the University of North Dakota, includes a chapter outline, list of key terms, suggested answers to the MIS InClass questions, and answers to all end-of-chapter questions.

Test Item File

This Test Item File, prepared by ANSR Source, Inc., contains over 1,500 questions, including multiple-choice, true/false, and essay questions. Each question is followed by the correct answer, the learning objective it ties to, page reference, AACSB category, and difficulty rating.

PowerPoint Presentations

The PowerPoints, prepared by Robert Szymanski of Georgia Southern University, highlight text learning objectives and key topics and serve as an excellent aid for classroom presentations and lectures.

Image Library

This collection of the figures and tables from the text offers another aid for classroom presentations and PowerPoint slides.

TestGen

Pearson Education's test-generating software is available from *www.pearsonhighered.com/irc*. The software is PC/MAC compatible and preloaded with all of the Test Item File questions. You can manually or randomly view test questions and drag and drop to create a test. You can add or modify test bank questions as needed. Our TestGens are converted for use in BlackBoard and WebCT. These conversions can be found on the Instructor's Resource Center. Conversions to Moodle, D2L, or Angel can be requested through your local Pearson sales representative.

MyMISLab (www.mymislab.com)

MyMISLab is an easy-to-use online tool that personalizes course content and provides robust assessment and reporting to measure individual and class performance. All of the resources you need for course success are in one place—flexible and easily adapted for your course experience. Students can purchase access to MyMISLab with a Pearson eText of all chapters or without a Pearson eText by visiting *www.mymislab.com*. They can also purchase an access card packaged with the text from *www.pearsonhighered.com* at a reduced price.

Microsoft SharePoint

Pearson Education is pleased to host Microsoft SharePoint sites for use by your students. At your request, we will create a site collection for you to use with your students. You will be given administrator privileges for that collection, and you can create subsites for sections, teams, and projects. Each collection will include templates for students to use when answering the collaboration exercises at the end of each chapter. Contact your local Pearson sales representative to learn more about using SharePoint in your class.

CourseSmart

CourseSmart eTextbooks were developed for students looking to save on required or recommended textbooks. Students simply select their eText by title or author and purchase immediate access to the content for the duration of the course using any major credit card. With a CourseSmart eText, students can search for specific keywords or page numbers, take notes online, print out reading assignments that incorporate lecture notes, and bookmark important passages for later review. For more information or to purchase a CourseSmart eTextbook, visit *www.coursesmart.com*.

Acknowledgments

First, we thank the numerous fellow-traveler professors and professionals who encouraged the development of this text and who have helped us in many ways along our path. In particular, we thank:

Yvonne Antonucci, *Widener University*

Cynthia Barnes, *Lamar University*

John Baxter, *SAP*

William Cantor, *Pennsylvania State University–York Campus*

Gail Corbitt, *SAP*

Darice Corey, *Albertus Magnus College*

Mike Curry, *Oregon State University*

Heather Czech, *SAP*

Janelle Daugherty, *Microsoft Dynamics*

Peter DeVries, *University of Houston, Downtown*

Lauren Eder, *Rider University*

Kevin Elder, *Georgia Southern University*

John Erickson, *University of Nebraska at Omaha*

Donna Everett, *Morehead State University*

David Firth, *The University of Montana*

Jerry Flatto, *University of Indianapolis*

Kent Foster, *Microsoft*

Biswadip Ghosh, *Metropolitan State College of Denver*

Bin Gu, *University of Texas at Austin*

William Haseman, *University of Wisconsin–Milwaukee*

Jun He, *University of Michigan–Dearborn*

Mark Hwang, *Central Michigan University*

Gerald Isaacs, *Carroll University*

Stephen Klein, *Ramapo University*

Ben Martz, *University of Northern Kentucky*

William McMillan, *Madonna University*

Natalie Nazarenko, *SUNY College at Fredonia*

Timothy O'Keefe, *University of North Dakota*

Tony Pittarese, *East Tennessee State University*

Martin Ruddy, *Bowling Green State University*

James Sager, *California State University–Chico*

Narcissus Shambare, *College of Saint Mary*

Robert Szymanski, *Georgia Southern University*

Lou Thompson, *University of Texas, Dallas*

Ming Wang, *California State University*

We wish to thank the incredible production team that helped us to bring this book into existence. First and foremost, we thank Bob Horan, our editor, for his long-standing encouragement for a process-oriented introductory MIS text and for his untiring support throughout the process. Thanks too, to Laura Town, our developmental editor, whose direction, guidance, and patient efforts to help us improve the book paid, we believe, great dividends. Laura's a joy to work with and exceedingly competent. We especially thank Kelly Loftus for returning to the fold to help us marshal this text and all its supplements through the Pearson production process and to Jen Welsch of Bookmasters for her management of the project as well. We also thank Janet Slowik, art director, and her team for designing this book.

We thank our friend and colleague, Chuck Yoos, of Fort Lewis College, for hours and hours and hours of conversation on the meaning of information and the role of information in organizations today. Chuck is responsible for the helpful distinction between *perceiving data* and *conceiving information* and many other insights that have shaped this text's material. Chuck's Bikes is named in honor of him.

I (David) am especially grateful to Harold Wise at East Carolina University for long and fruitful discussions on ways of teaching processes and ERP in the introductory MIS class. Harold has extensive experience working with SAP in industry and provided clear guidance to me as I thought about this text. Harold and I looked at adding process-like supplements to my text *Experiencing MIS* and ultimately decided that to do justice to the topic the material needed to be reworked from the ground up, using a new definition of MIS that included processes.

Finally, we are most grateful to our wives and families who have lovingly supported us through these processes.

David Kroenke
Seattle, Washington

Earl McKinney Jr.
Bowling Green, Ohio

About the Authors

David Kroenke David Kroenke has many years of teaching experience at Colorado State University, Seattle University, and the University of Washington. He has led dozens of seminars for college professors on the teaching of information systems and technology; in 1991 the International Association of Information Systems named him Computer Educator of the Year. In 2009, David was named Educator of the Year by the Association of Information Technology Professionals-Education Special Interest Group (AITP-EDSIG).

David worked for the U.S. Air Force and Boeing Computer Services. He was a principal in the start-up of three companies. He also was vice president of product marketing and development for the Microrim Corporation and was chief of technologies for the database division of Wall Data, Inc. He is the father of the semantic object data model. David's consulting clients have included IBM, Microsoft, and Computer Sciences Corporations, as well as numerous smaller companies. Recently, David has focused on using information systems for collaboration in education and industry.

His text *Database Processing* was first published in 1977 and is now in its 12th edition. He has published many other textbooks, including *Database Concepts,* 5th ed. (2011), *Using MIS,* 5th ed. (2013), *Experiencing MIS,* 3rd ed. (2012), *MIS Essentials,* 2nd ed. (2012), *SharePoint for Students* (2012), and *Office 365 in Business* (2012). David lives in Seattle. He is married and has two children and three grandchildren.

Earl McKinney Jr. Teaching the introduction to MIS course has been Earl McKinney's passion for 20 years. He first caught the bug at his alma mater the U.S. Air Force Academy and has continued his addiction during his tenure at Bowling Green State University. While teaching that class and other undergraduate and graduate classes, Earl has also introduced a half dozen new courses on security, social media, ERP, and information. He has been awarded a number of department and college teaching awards by students and fellow faculty. His interest in the broader context of the business curriculum is reflected in several of his publications and by the Decision Science Institute's National Instructional Innovation Award.

Earl's research in e-commerce, small team communication during a crisis, and theoretical work on the notion of information has been published in *Behaviour and Information Technology, Human Factors, Information and Management,* and *MIS Quarterly.* He consults with James Hall, the former head of the NTSB for British Petroleum, the U.S. Forest Service, and several Air Force agencies on human factors and aviation communication issues.

He holds an undergraduate economics degree from the Air Force Academy, a Master's of Engineering from Cornell University, and a PhD in MIS from the University of Texas. A former Air Force fighter pilot, Earl lives in Bowling Green with his wife and has two grown sons.

PART 1

MIS AND YOU

Knowledge of information systems will be critical to your success in business. If you major in accounting, marketing, management, or in another major, you may not yet know how important such knowledge will be to you. The purposes of Part 1 of this textbook are to demonstrate why this subject is so important to every business professional today and to introduce important terms and concepts that you will need to succeed.

Chapter 1 lays the foundation. First, we discuss why this course is of critical importance to every business student today. We claim, in fact, that it is the most important course you will take. Then, we define *MIS* and explain how organizational strategy determines the structure and functions of MIS components.

In Chapter 2, we will define and illustrate business processes, information systems, and information. As you will see, these three constructs are closely interwoven. Understanding the relationships among them sets the foundation for the rest of this text.

We begin each chapter with a short business vignette to help you relate the chapter's concepts to the business world. Chapter 1 begins with FlexTime, a hip, urban, sophisticated workout studio located in downtown Indianapolis. Kelly Summers started

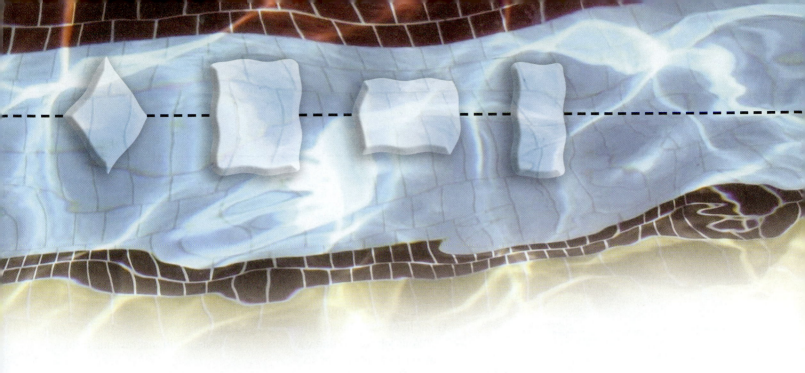

FlexTime 20 years ago after teaching aerobics at another firm. She began modestly, teaching a few classes a week at a small facility in the back of a downtown Indianapolis office building. Over time, she grew the business, until back office record keeping became unmanageable. At that point, she hired Neil West to help her install information systems. Over the past 5 years, they have created information systems that enable them to track members, send bills, collect payments, and so forth, as well as systems that generate a database that Neil claims is FlexTime's most important asset. In Chapter 1, we see Kelly terminating an employee, for reasons that you will soon learn.

In Chapter 2, we will turn to the intramural athletic department at a fictitious, but typical, university named Central Colorado State. That department uses two information systems—one that supports just the intramural department and a second that is used university-wide. One of the department's part-time employees makes a mistake that causes customer service problems, as you will see.

"**F**ired? You're firing me?"

"Well, *fired* is a harsh word, but . . . well, FlexTime has no further need for your services."

"But, Kelly, I don't get it. I really don't. I worked hard, and I did everything you told me to do."

"Jennifer, that's just it. You did everything *I* told you to do."

"I put in so many hours. How could you fire me????"

"Your job was to find ways we can generate additional revenue from our existing club members."

"Right! And I did that."

"No, you didn't. You followed up on ideas *that I gave you*. But we don't need someone who can follow up on my plans. We need someone who can figure out what we need to do, create her own plans, and bring them back to me. . . . And others."

"How could you expect me to do that? I've only been here 4 months!!!"

"It's called teamwork. Sure, you're just learning our business, but I made sure all of our senior staff would be available to you . . ."

"I didn't want to bother them."

"Well, you succeeded. I asked Jason what he thought of the plans you're working on. 'Who's Jennifer?' he asked."

"But, doesn't he work at night?"

"Right. He's the night staff manager . . . and 37 percent of our weekday business occurs after 7 P.M. Probably worth talking to him."

"I'll go do that!"

"Jennifer, do you see what just happened? I gave you an idea and you said you'll do it. That's not what I need. I need you to find solutions on your own."

"I worked really hard. I put in a lot of hours. I've got all these reports written."

"Has anyone seen them?"

"I talked to you about some of them. But, I was waiting until I was satisfied with them."

"Right. That's not how we do things here. We develop ideas and then kick them around with each other. Nobody has all the answers. Our plans get better when we comment and rework them . . . I think I told you that."

"Maybe you did. But I'm just not comfortable with that."

"Well, it's a required skill here."

"I know I can do this job."

"Jennifer, you've been here almost 4 months; you have a degree in business. Several weeks ago, I asked you for your first idea about how to upsell our customers. Do you remember what you said?"

"Yes, I wasn't sure how to proceed. I didn't want to just throw something out that might not work."

"But how would you find out if it would work?"

"I don't want to waste money . . ."

"No, you don't. So, when you didn't get very far with that task, I backed up and asked you to send me a diagram of the life cycle for one of our clients . . . how we get them in the door, how we enroll them in their first classes, how we continue to sell to them . . ."

"Yes, I sent you that diagram."

"Jennifer, it made no sense. Your diagram had people talking to Neil in accounts receivable before they were even customers."

"I know that process, I just couldn't put it down on paper. But, I'll try again!"

"Well, I appreciate that attitude, but times are tight. We don't have room for trainees. When the economy was strong, I'd have been able to look for a spot for you, see if we can bring you along. But, we can't afford to do that now."

"What about my references?"

"I'll be happy to tell anyone that you're reliable, that you work 40 to 45 hours a week, and that you're honest and have integrity."

"Those are important!"

"Yes, they are. But today, they're not enough."

See also *www.youtube.com/watch?v=8UQx-zUuGf4*.

Q1. Why is Introduction to MIS the most important class in the business school?

Q2. What is MIS?

Q3. How does MIS relate to organizational strategy?

Q4. What five forces determine industry structure?

Q5. What is competitive strategy?

Q6. How does competitive strategy determine value chain structure?

Q7. How do value chains determine business processes and information systems?

Chapter Preview

"But today, they're not enough."

Do you find that statement sobering? And if timely hard work isn't enough, what is? We will begin this book by discussing the key skills that Jennifer (and you) need and explain why this course is the single best course in all of the business school for teaching you those key skills.

You may find that last statement surprising. If you are like most students, you have no clear idea of what your MIS class will be about. If someone were to ask you, "What do you study in that class?" you might respond that the class has something to do with computers and maybe computer programming. Beyond that, you might be hard-pressed to say more. You might add, "Well, it has something to do with computers in business," or maybe, "We are going to learn to solve business problems with computers using spreadsheets and other programs." So, how could this course be the most important one in the business school?

We begin with that question. Once you have gained an understanding of how important this class will be to your career, we will discuss fundamental concepts. We will wrap up with some practice on one of the key skills you need to learn.

Q1. Why Is Introduction to MIS the Most Important Class in the Business School?

Introduction to MIS is the most important class in the business school. That statement was not true in 2005, and it may not be true in 2022. But it is true in 2012.

Why?

The ultimate reason lies in a principle known as **Moore's Law**. In 1965, Gordon Moore, cofounder of Intel Corporation, stated that because of technology improvements in electronic chip design and manufacturing, "The number of transistors per square inch on an integrated chip doubles every 18 months." His statement has been commonly misunderstood to be, "The speed of a computer doubles every 18 months," which is incorrect but captures the sense of his principle.

Because of Moore's Law, the ratio of price to performance of computers has fallen from something like $4,000 for a standard computing device to something around a penny for that same computing device.[1] See Figure 1-1.

FIGURE 1-1

Changes in Price/ Performance of Processors

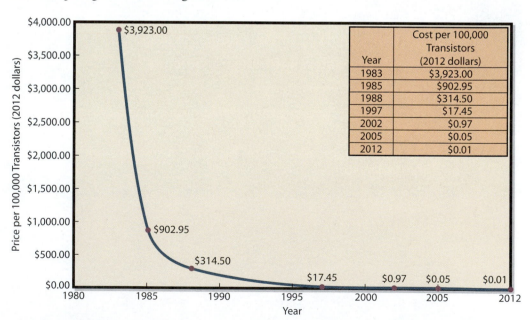

Year	Cost per 100,000 Transistors (2012 dollars)
1983	$3,923.00
1985	$902.95
1988	$314.50
1997	$17.45
2002	$0.97
2005	$0.05
2012	$0.01

[1] These figures represent the cost of 100,000 transistors, which can roughly be translated into a unit of a computing device. For our purposes, the details don't matter. If you doubt any of this, just look at your $49 cell phone and realize that you pay $40 a month to use it.

As a future business professional, however, you needn't care how fast a computer your company can buy for $100. That's not the point. Here's the point:

> Because of Moore's Law, the cost of data communications and data storage is essentially zero.

Think about that statement before you hurry to the next paragraph. What happens when those costs are essentially zero? Here are some consequences:

- YouTube
- iPhone
- Facebook
- Second Life
- Pandora
- Twitter
- LinkedIn
- foursquare
- Google+

None of these were prominent in 2005, and, in fact, most didn't exist in 2005.

Are There Cost-Effective Business Applications of Facebook and Twitter?

Of course. FlexTime is profitably using them today. Fitness instructors post announcements via Twitter. FlexTime collects those tweets and posts them on its Facebook page. Total software cost to FlexTime? Zero.

But ask another question: Are there wasteful, harmful, useless business applications of Facebook and Twitter? Of course. Do I care to follow the tweets of the mechanic who changes the oil in my car? I don't think so.

But there's the point. Maybe I'm not being creative enough. Maybe there are great reasons for the mechanic to tweet customers and I'm just not able to think of them. Which leads us to the first reason Introduction to MIS is the most important course in the business school today:

> Future business professionals need to be able to assess, evaluate, and apply emerging information technology to business.

You need the knowledge of this course to attain that skill, and having that skill will lead to greater job security.

How Can I Attain Job Security?

A wise and experienced business executive once said that the only job security that exists is "a marketable skill and the courage to use it." He continued, "There is no security in our company, there is no security in any government program, there is no security in your investments, and there is no security in Social Security." Alas, how right he turned out to be.

So what is a marketable skill? It used to be that one could name particular skills, such as computer programming, tax accounting, or marketing. But today, because of Moore's Law, because the cost of data storage and data communications is essentially zero, any routine skill can and will be outsourced to the lowest bidder. And if you live in the United States, Canada, Australia, Europe, and so on, that is unlikely to be you. Numerous organizations and experts have studied the question of what skills will be marketable during your career. Consider two of them.

First, the RAND Corporation, a think tank located in Santa Monica, California, has published innovative and groundbreaking ideas for more than 60 years, including the initial design for the Internet. In 2004, RAND published a description of the skills that workers in the twenty-first century will need:

Rapid technological change and increased international competition place the spotlight on the skills and preparation of the workforce, particularly the ability to adapt to changing technology and shifting demand. Shifts in the nature of organizations . . . favor strong nonroutine cognitive skills.[2]

Whether you are majoring in accounting or marketing or finance or information systems, you need to develop strong nonroutine cognitive skills.

What are such skills? Robert Reich, former Secretary of Labor, enumerates four components:[3]

- Abstract reasoning
- Systems thinking
- Collaboration
- Ability to experiment

Figure 1-2 shows an example of each. Reread the FlexTime case that started this chapter, and you will see that Jennifer lost her job because of her inability to practice these skills.

How Can Intro to MIS Help You Learn Nonroutine Skills?

Introduction to MIS is the best course in the business school for learning these four key skills, because every topic will require you to apply and practice them. Here's how.

ABSTRACT REASONING   **Abstract reasoning** is the ability to make and manipulate models. You will work with one or more models in every course topic and book chapter. For example, in Chapter 2 you will learn ways to *model* business processes and you will also learn a *model* of the five components of an information system.

In this course, you will not just manipulate models in this text or a model that your instructor has developed, you will also be asked to construct models of your own. In Chapter 4, for example, you will learn how to create data models and in Chapter 5 you will learn how to make process models.

SYSTEMS THINKING   Can you go to a grocery store, look at a can of green beans, and connect that can to U.S. immigration policy? Can you watch tractors dig up a forest of pulpwood trees and connect that woody trash to Moore's Law? Do you know why one of the major beneficiaries of YouTube is Cisco Systems?

Answers to all of these questions require systems thinking. **Systems thinking** is the ability to model the components of the system and to connect the inputs and outputs among those components into a sensible whole, one that explains the phenomenon observed. For example, how do all of those items get on the shelves at Walmart? It involves the supply chain, business processes, and computer networks, but how?

As you are about to learn, this class is about information *systems*. We will discuss and illustrate systems; you will be asked to critique systems; you will be asked to compare alternative

FIGURE 1-2

Need for Reich's Four Critical Skills

Skill	Example	Jennifer's Problem
Abstraction	Construct a model or representation.	Inability to model the customer life cycle.
Systems thinking	Model system components and show how components' inputs and outputs relate to one another.	Confusion about when/how customers contact accounts payable.
Collaboration	Develop ideas and plans with others. Provide and receive critical feedback.	Unwilling to work with others with work-in-progress.
Experimentation	Create and test promising new alternatives, consistent with available resources.	Fear of failure prohibited discussion of new ideas.

---

[2] Lynn A. Karoly and Constantijn W. A. Panis, *The 21st Century at Work* (Santa Monica, CA: RAND Corporation, 2004), p. xiv.
[3] Robert B. Reich, *The Work of Nations* (New York: Alfred A. Knopf, 1991), p. 229.

systems; you will be asked to apply different systems to different situations. All of those tasks will prepare you for systems thinking as a professional.

COLLABORATION   Chapter 9 will teach you collaboration skills and illustrate several sample collaboration information systems. Every chapter of this book includes collaboration exercises that you may be assigned in class or as homework.

Here's a fact that surprises many students: Effective collaboration isn't about being nice. In fact, surveys indicate the single most important skill for effective collaboration is to give and receive critical feedback. Advance a proposal in business that challenges the cherished program of the VP of marketing, and you will quickly learn that effective collaboration skills differ from party manners at the neighborhood barbeque. So, how do you advance your idea in the face of the VP's resistance? And without losing your job? In this course, you can learn both skills and information systems for such collaboration. Even better, you will have many opportunities to practice them.

ABILITY TO EXPERIMENT

"I've never done this before."

"I don't know how to do it."

"But will it work?"

"Is it too weird for the market?"

Fear of failure: the fear that paralyzes so many good people and so many good ideas. In the days when business was stable, when new ideas were just different verses of the same song, professionals could allow themselves to be limited by fear of failure.

But think again about the application of social networking to the oil change business. Is there a legitimate application of social networking there? If so, has anyone ever done it? Is there anyone in the world who can tell you what to do? How to proceed? No. As Reich says, professionals in the twenty-first century need to be able to experiment.

Successful experimentation is not throwing buckets of money at every crazy idea that enters your head. **Experimentation** is, however, making a careful and reasoned analysis of an opportunity, envisioning potential products or solutions or applications of technology, and then developing those ideas that seem to have the most promise, consistent with the resources you have. Successful experimentation also means learning from the experience; if it worked, why? If not, why not?

In this course, you will be asked to use products with which you have no familiarity. Those products might be Microsoft Access, Visio, or something called SAP, or they might be features and functions of Blackboard that you have not used. Or, you may be asked to collaborate using Microsoft Office 365 or Google Docs with Google +. Will your instructor explain and show every feature of those products that you will need? You should hope not. You should hope your instructor will leave it up to you to experiment, to envision new possibilities on your own, and to experiment with those possibilities, consistent with the time you have available.

The bottom line? This course is the most important course in the business school because:

> 1. It will give you the background you need to assess, evaluate, and apply emerging information systems technology to business.
> 2. It can give you the ultimate in job security—marketable skills—by helping you learn abstraction, systems thinking, collaboration, and experimentation.

With that introduction, let's get started![4]

---

[4] For another perspective on the importance of these skills, read *http://www.nytimes.com/2011/07/13/opinion/13friedman.html?_r=1.*

Q2. What Is MIS?

In this text, we define **management information systems**, or **MIS**, as the management and use of processes, information systems, and information to help organizations achieve their strategies. This definition has three key elements:

- Processes, information systems, and information
- Management and use
- Organizational strategies

Consider each, starting with processes, information systems, and information.

Processes, Information Systems, and Information

Chapter 2 discusses these three terms and their interrelationships in detail. For now, however, consider the following intuitive definitions. A *process,* or as it is sometimes called, a *business process,* is a way of doing something. FlexTime has a process for enrolling new members at the studio. The process involves gathering data about the new members, collecting dues, entering the members' data into a computer database, and so forth. Because organizations accomplish work via processes, focusing on them is key to improving organizational effectiveness and efficiency, as you will learn throughout this book.

An *information system* is a collection of components, including a computer, that stores and retrieves data and produces information. Business processes and information systems are not the same things. A process may use multiple information systems. And, an information system may touch many different processes. You can avoid considerable confusion by differentiating between those two concepts. Finally, *information* is some form of knowledge that helps employees to do their jobs.

But, we're getting ahead of the story. In Chapter 2, we will formalize these definitions, explore them in detail, and investigate their relationships. Use these informal definitions as placeholders just to get started.

Management and Use

For the purposes of this text, we do not define *management* in the classical sense; that is, something like "plan, organize, control, and staff." Rather, because of the nature of MIS, we will define **management (of MIS)** as the creation, monitoring, and adapting of processes, information systems, and information.

Consider FlexTime's process for enrolling new members at the workout studio. That process did not just pop up like a mushroom after a hard rain; it was constructed by someone to meet FlexTime's needs. Over time, requirements for that process will change; perhaps FlexTime will introduce a new class of membership that necessitates additional process steps. FlexTime needs to monitor its processes to detect when this situation has occurred. When it does, the process will need to be adapted to meet the new requirements.

Similar statements apply to information systems. Information systems need to be created; computers, programs, databases, and other elements need to be constructed in such a way that they meet the requirements of the business processes that they serve. Like processes, they need to be monitored to ensure that they continue to meet their requirements, and they need to be adapted when they do not.

The same comments pertain to information. For example, managers at FlexTime have a set of reports that show frequency of member visits. Over time, monitoring of manager decisions about class offerings may indicate that new information is needed to help managers improve those decisions. If so, the information system will need to be adapted to produce that new information.

Figure 1-3 shows the scope of MIS, but the cells are blank. One of the major purposes of this text is to help you fill in those cells.

At this point, you might be saying, "Wait a minute. I'm a finance (or accounting, or management) major, not an information systems major. I don't need to know how to build or adapt processes or information systems."

	Process	Information Systems	Information
Create			
Monitor			
Adapt			

FIGURE 1-3
Scope of MIS

If you are saying that, you are like a lamb headed for fleecing. Like Jennifer, throughout your career, in whatever field you choose, you will work with processes, information systems, and information. To ensure these elements meet your needs, you need to take an *active role* in their management. Even if you are not a business analyst, a programmer, a database designer, or some other IS professional, you must take an active role in specifying process, system, and information requirements and in helping manage development projects to create or adapt them. Without active involvement on your part, it will only be good luck that causes processes, information systems, or information to meet your needs.

In addition to development tasks, you will also have important roles to play in the *use* of MIS. Of course, you will need to learn how to follow processes and employ information systems to accomplish your goals. But you will also have important ancillary functions as well. For example, when using an information system, you will have responsibilities for protecting the security of the system and its data. You may also have tasks for backing up data. When the system fails (most do, at some point), you will have tasks to perform while the system is down as well as tasks to accomplish to help recover the system correctly and quickly.

Achieve Organizational Strategy

The last part of the definition of MIS is that MIS exists to help organizations achieve their *strategies*. First, realize that this statement hides an important fact: Businesses themselves do not "do" anything. A business is not alive, and it cannot act. It is the people within a business who sell, buy, design, produce, finance, market, account, and manage. So, MIS exists to help people who work in a business to achieve the strategies of that business.

At times, it can be difficult for organizations to stay focused on business strategy because information technology is seductive: "Our competitor is using Twitter to announce products; we better do the same." Because of the rapid pace of technology development, it can be tempting to construct information systems just to be "modern" or so that the company can claim to be an "Enterprise 2.0 company" or for some other reason. Constructing systems for such reasons is unwise and wasteful of both time and money. Processes, systems, and information need to be created for the purpose of achieving the organization's strategy. Period. They are not created because the IS department thinks it needs to be created or because the company is "falling behind the technology curve."

This point may seem so obvious that you wonder why we mention it. Every day, however, some business somewhere is developing an information system for the wrong reasons. Right now, somewhere in the world, a company is deciding to create a social networking site for the sole reason that "every other business has one." This company is not asking questions like, "What is the purpose of the social networking site?" or, "What is it going to do for our strategic goals?" or, "Are the costs of the site sufficiently offset by the benefits?"—but it should be!

Even more serious, somewhere right now an IS manager has been convinced by some vendor's sales team or by an article in a business magazine that his or her company must upgrade to the latest, greatest high-tech gizmo. This IS manager is attempting to convince his or her manager that this expensive upgrade is a good idea. We hope that someone somewhere in the company is asking questions like, "What strategic goal or objective will be served by the investment in the gizmo?"

As a future business professional, you need to learn to look at information systems and technologies only through the lens of *business need*. Learn to ask, "All of this technology may be great, in and of itself, but what will it do for us? What will it do for our business and our particular strategy?"

Because strategy is so important to MIS, we will discuss the relationship of MIS and strategy in the next question, and then, in the balance of this chapter, explore the relationship of MIS to value chains and related concepts.

FIGURE 1-4

Organizational Strategy Determines MIS

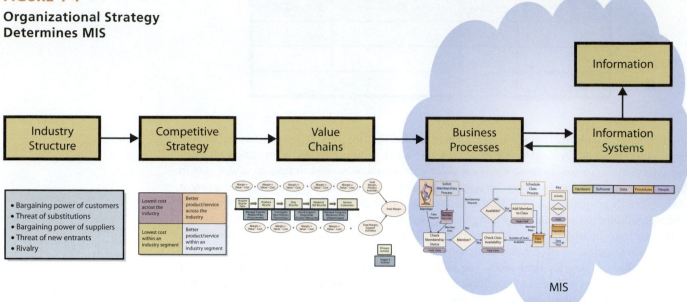

Q3. How Does MIS Relate to Organizational Strategy?

As stated, MIS exists to help organizations achieve their strategy. But, where does that strategy come from? You will learn theories and techniques for creating, managing, and adapting organization strategy in your management and business strategy classes. That discussion is beyond the scope of an MIS text. However, because of the intimate relationship between strategy and MIS, we need to have some grounding, some starting point. Accordingly, we will use what is considered to be the gold standard of business strategy, and that is the set of business models developed by Michael Porter. In particular, we will use Porter's models of industry structure, competitive strategy, and value chains. These models are not the only relevant strategy models, but they are widely known and will give us a good grounding for your study of MIS.

Figure 1-4 summarizes the ways these models relate to MIS. In short, organizations examine the structure of their industry and from that develop a competitive strategy. That strategy determines the organization's value chains, which, in turn, determine business processes. Business processes can, in turn, determine information systems. However, as you will learn in Chapter 2, the relationship between business processes and information systems is complex; in some cases, the information system's capabilities will be constrained. If so, the information system's features and functions may determine the structure of business processes as well. Finally, as shown in Figure 1-4, information systems produce information.

To understand this figure, we begin with Porter's five forces model.

Q4. What Five Forces Determine Industry Structure?

Porter developed the **five forces model**[5] as a model for determining the potential profitability of an industry. Over the years, this model has been applied for another purpose; that is, as a way of understanding organizations' competitive environments. That understanding is then used to formulate a competitive strategy, as you will see.

---

[5] Michael Porter, *Competitive Strategy: Techniques for Analyzing Industries and Competitors* (New York: Free Press, 1980).

Porter's five competitive forces can be grouped into two types: forces related to competition and forces related to supply chain bargaining power.

Competitive forces:

- Competition from vendors of substitutes
- Competition from new competitors
- Competition from existing rivals

Bargaining power forces:

- Bargaining power of suppliers
- Bargaining power of customers

Porter assesses these five forces to determine the characteristics of an industry, how profitable it is, and how sustainable that profitability will be. Here, we will use this model for a different purpose: to identify sources of strong competition and to use this knowledge to create a competitive strategy to combat those strong forces. To help you relate to this model, consider how it applies to the workout studio market in general and to FlexTime in particular.

Each of the three competitive forces concerns the danger of customers taking their business elsewhere. As shown in the first column of Figure 1-5, two strength factors that relate to all three of these forces are switching costs and customer loyalty. If the costs of switching to another vendor are high, then the strength of the competitive forces is low. Similarly, if customers are loyal to the company or brand, then the strength of the competitive forces is low.

Now consider each of the three competitive forces individually. The threat of a substitute is stronger if the substitute's price is lower and if the perceived benefits of the substitute are similar. As shown in Figure 1-5, FlexTime views home workouts and athletic and country clubs

FIGURE 1-5

Five Forces at FlexTime

Type (Strength Factors)	Competitive Force (Strength Factors)	FlexTime Threat (Factors Assessment)	FlexTime's Strength Assessment
	Substitutes (Lower price and perceived benefits the same)	**Home workouts** (Low switching costs, cheap, but not the same experience at all) **Athletic clubs** (Expensive, high switching costs, substitute not as familiar)	**Home workouts threat:** medium **Athletic club threat:** weak
Competitve (Switching costs, customer loyalty)	**New entrants** (Barriers to entry, capital requirements, noncapital resources)	**New copycats** (Medium switching costs, customers loyal to FlexTime, capital requirements medium, customer database is barrier to entry)	**New copycat threat:** weak
	Rivalry (Price, quality, innovation, marketing)	**Rivals** (Medium switching costs, customers loyal to FlexTime, customers influenced by price/quality/innovation/marketing)	**Rivals threat:** strong
Supply chain bargaining power (Availabilty of substitutes, relative size)	**Supplier**	**Landlord** (Few suitable buildings with parking, FlexTime switching costs high, multiyear contract) **Equipment & supply vendors** (Many substitutes, low switching costs, brand not important)	**Landlord bargaining power threat:** strong **Equipment & supply vendors bargaining power threat:** weak
	Customer	**Club members** (Relative size: bargaining power of a single customer is weak)	**Club member bargaining power:** weak

as substitution threats. FlexTime judges the threat from home workouts to be medium, because although switching costs are low and working out a home is cheap, the experience of a home workout is not as motivating as a FlexTime workout. To manage this threat, FlexTime needs to ensure that members have a vastly superior workout experience as compared to the one that they can have at home.

The threat from athletic and country clubs is weak because it is expensive, the switching costs are high (people have to apply for membership and pay annual fees), and the experience is less familial. To manage this threat, FlexTime needs to keep its familial atmosphere.

Figure 1-5 also shows how FlexTime views threats from new entrants and industry rivals (called copycats). It judges the competitive threat of new entrants to be weak for the reasons shown. Note that the cost of developing a large database of active customers is high and it requires months or years to do. Thus, FlexTime's customer database is a barrier to new entrants.

FlexTime judges the threat to rivals as strong, the strongest of all the competitive threats. FlexTime needs to ensure that it develops a competitive strategy to combat such rivals.

The last two rows of Figure 1-5 concern bargaining power forces from suppliers or from customers. As shown, the strength of these forces depends on the availability of substitutes and the relative size of the firm (here, FlexTime) compared to the size of suppliers or customers. A Nobel prize–winning scientist has strong bargaining supplier power at your university, because such scientists are rare. In contrast, a temporary part-time instructor has little bargaining power, because many people can fill that role. If such instructors were to form a union, however, then that union would have greater bargaining power because of its relative size.

Similarly, you, as an individual, have little bargaining power as a customer to your university. Your application is readily replaced with another, and you are an individual attempting to bargain with a large organization. However, a large organization like Oracle or Microsoft or Google would have much stronger bargaining power for its employees at your university.

Examine Figure 1-5 to learn why FlexTime views the bargaining power of its landlord to be strong, but the power of equipment and supply vendors to be weak. It also views the bargaining power of any single customer to be weak as well.

To summarize, FlexTime concludes that, whatever it does with regard to MIS, it needs to proceed in such a way that it does not weaken its ability to combat the threats from rivals or further reduce its bargaining power with the owner of the building it occupies. Furthermore, any new MIS component (process, information system, or information) that enables it to better combat threats from rivals or bargaining power with the owner is particularly desirable.

Q5. What Is Competitive Strategy?

An organization responds to the structure of its industry by choosing a **competitive strategy**. Porter followed his five forces model with the model of four competitive strategies shown in Figure 1-6.[6] According to Porter, a firm can engage in one of four fundamental competitive strategies. An organization can be the cost leader and provide products at the lowest prices in the industry, or it can focus on adding value to its products to differentiate them from those of the

FIGURE 1-6

Porter's Four Competitive Strategies

	Cost	Differentiation
Industry-wide	Lowest cost across the industry	Better product/service across the industry
Focus	Lowest cost within an industry segment	Better product/service within an industry segment

[6] Michael Porter, *Competitive Strategy* (New York: Free Press, 1980).

competition. Further, the organization can employ the cost or differentiation strategy across an industry, or it can focus its strategy on a particular industry segment.

Consider the car rental industry, for example. According to the first column of Figure 1-6, a car rental company can strive to provide the lowest-cost car rentals across the industry, or it can seek to provide the lowest-cost car rentals to a "focused" industry segment—say, U.S. domestic business travelers.

As shown in the second column, a car rental company can seek to differentiate its products from the competition. It can do so in various ways—for example, by providing a wide range of high-quality cars, by providing the best reservation system, by having the cleanest cars or the fastest check-in, or by some other means. The company can strive to provide product differentiation across the industry or within particular segments of the industry, such as U.S. domestic business travelers.

According to Porter, to be effective the organization's goals, objectives, culture, and activities must be consistent with the organization's strategy. Regarding MIS, this means that all processes, information systems, and information must be constructed to facilitate the organization's competitive strategy. It also means that processes need to be set up to monitor the degree to which MIS continues to support competitive strategy.

Consider competitive strategy at FlexTime. As a hip, urban, mostly adult facility, it has a focused strategy. As you just learned, its primary competitive threat is from rivals in that market segment. FlexTime can meet that threat by having the lowest prices or by adding something to the workout experience that differentiates it from the competition. FlexTime differentiates itself on the intensity of its workouts. As Neil says, "People leave here pumped and upbeat!"

FlexTime is not as profitable as its owners want it to be. To increase profitability, the owners seek ways to reduce costs. But whatever cost savings FlexTime implements, it cannot lose workout intensity, its competitive advantage over rivals.

Q6. How Does Competitive Strategy Determine Value Chain Structure?

Organizations analyze the structure of their industry, and, using that analysis, they formulate a competitive strategy. They then need to organize and structure the organization to implement that strategy. If, for example, the competitive strategy is to be the *cost leader*, then business activities need to be developed to provide essential functions at the lowest possible cost.

A business that selects a *differentiation* strategy would not necessarily structure itself around least-cost activities. Instead, such a business might choose to develop more costly processes, but it would do so only if those processes provided benefits that outweighed their risks. Porter defined **value** as the amount of money that a customer is willing to pay for a resource, product, or service. The difference between the value that an activity generates and the cost of the activity is called the **margin**. A business with a differentiation strategy will add cost to an activity only as long as the activity has a positive margin.

A **value chain** is a network of value-creating activities. According to Porter, that generic chain consists of five **primary activities** and four **support activities**.

Value chain analysis is most easily understood in the context of manufacturing, so we will leave the FlexTime case for now and switch to the example of a bicycle manufacturer.

Primary Activities in the Value Chain

Figure 1-7 summarizes the primary activities of the value chain. Raw materials are obtained using inbound logistics activity, products and goods are produced in operations/manufacturing activity, and those products and goods are shipped to customers using outbound logistics activity. Additionally, organizations have sales and marketing as well as customer service activity.

To understand the essence of these activities, consider a small bicycle manufacturer (see Figure 1-8). First, the manufacturer acquires bicycle parts (inbound logistics). This activity concerns the receiving and handling of raw materials and other inputs. The accumulation of those materials adds value in the sense that even a pile of unassembled parts is worth something

FIGURE 1-7

Primary Activities in the Value Chain

Primary Activity	Description
Inbound Logistics	Receiving, storing, and disseminating inputs to products
Operations/manufacturing	Transforming inputs into final products
Outbound logistics	Collecting, storing, and physically distributing products to buyers
Sales and marketing	Inducing buyers to purchase products and providing a means for them to do so
Customer service	Assisting customer's use of products and thus maintaining and enhancing the products' value

to some customer. A collection of the parts needed to build a bicycle is worth more than an empty space on a shelf. The value is not only the parts themselves, but also the time required to contact vendors for those parts, to maintain business relationships with those vendors, to order the parts, to receive the shipment, and so forth.

In the produce bicycle (operations/manufacturing) activity, the bicycle maker transforms raw materials into a finished bicycle, a process that adds more value. Next, the company ships bicycles (outbound logistics) to customers. Of course, there is no customer to send the bicycle to without the marketing and sales activity. Finally, the service activity provides customer support to the bicycle users.

Each stage of this generic chain accumulates costs and adds value to the product. The net result is the total margin of the chain, which is the difference between the total value added and the total costs incurred.

Support Activities in the Value Chain

The support activities in the generic value chain contribute indirectly to all of the primary value chain activities. They include procurement, which consists of the processes of finding vendors, setting up contractual arrangements, and negotiating prices. (This differs from inbound logistics, which is concerned with ordering and receiving in accordance with agreements set up by procurement.)

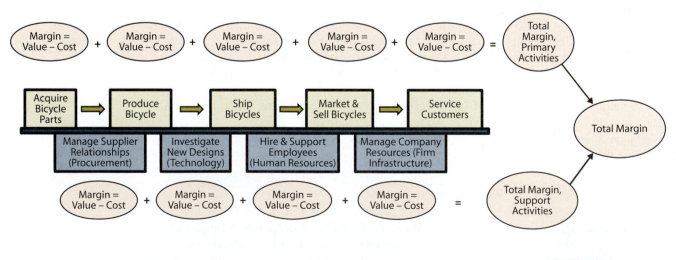

FIGURE 1-8

Value Chain for Bicycle Manufacturer

MIS InClass 1

Industry Structure → Competitive Strategy → Value Chains → Business Processes ←→ Information Systems

As shown in Figure 1-4, information systems are a logical consequence of an organization's analysis of industry structure via the chain of models shown in the title above. Consequently, you should be able to combine your knowledge of an organization's industry, together with observations of the structure and content of its Web storefront, to infer the organization's competitive strategy and possibly make inferences about its activities and business processes. The process you use here also can be useful in preparing for job interviews.

Form a team of three (or as directed by your professor) and perform the following exercises. Divide work, as appropriate, but create common answers for the team.

Source: monticello/Shutterstock; Eric Isselée/Shutterstock; Denis Pepin/Shutterstock; gresei/Shutterstock.

1. The following pairs of Web storefronts have industry segments that overlap in some way. Briefly visit each site of each pair:

   www.sportsauthority.com vs. www.soccer.com
   www.target.com vs. www.sephora.com
   www.woot.com vs. www.amazon.com
   www.petco.com vs. www.healthyfoodforpets.com
   www.llbean.com vs. www.rei.com

2. Select two pairs from the list in item 1. For each pair of companies, answer the following questions:
   a. How do the companies' markets/market segments differ?
   b. How do their competitive pressures differ?
   c. How do their competitive strategies differ?
   d. How does the "feel" of their Web sites differ?
   e. How does the "feel" of the user interface of their Web sites differ?
   f. How could either company change its Web site to better accomplish its competitive strategy?
   g. Would the change you recommend in item f necessitate a change in one or more of the companies' activities? Explain your answer.

3. Use your answers in item 2 to explain the following statement: "The structure of an organization's information system (here, a Web storefront) is determined by its competitive strategy." Structure your answer so that you could use it in a job interview to demonstrate your overall knowledge of business planning.

4. Present your team's answer to the rest of the class.

Porter defined *technology* broadly. It includes research and development, but it also includes other activities within the firm for developing new techniques, methods, and procedures. He defined *human resources* as recruiting, compensation, evaluation, and training of full- and part-time employees. Finally, *firm infrastructure* includes general management, finance, accounting, legal, and government affairs.

Supporting functions add value, albeit indirectly, and they also have costs. Hence, as shown in Figure 1-8, supporting activities contribute to a margin. In the case of supporting activities, it would be difficult to calculate the margin because the specific value added of, say, the manufacturer's lobbyists in Washington, D.C., is difficult to know. But there is a value added, there are costs, and there is a margin, even if it is only in concept.

Value Chain Linkages

Porter's model of business activities includes **linkages**, which are interactions across value activities. For example, manufacturing systems use linkages to reduce inventory costs. Such a system uses sales forecasts to plan production; it then uses the production plan to determine raw material needs and then uses the material needs to schedule purchases. The end result is just-in-time inventory, which reduces inventory sizes and costs.

Value chain analysis has a direct application to manufacturing businesses like the bicycle manufacturer. However, value chains also exist in service-oriented companies like FlexTime.

Before leaving the topic of competitive strategy, consider the issues raised in the Ethics Guide on pages 20–21. This guide discusses a company's competitive strategy and its possible impact on employees.

The difference is that most of the value in a service company is generated by the operations, marketing and sales, and service activities. Inbound and outbound logistics are not typically as important.

Q7. How Do Value Chains Determine Business Processes and Information Systems?

The answer to this question requires more knowledge than you currently have. You should be able to answer it well by the end of this course, however. In the meantime, you can gain an intuitive understanding of the way that competitive strategy drives value chains and MIS by considering processes and information systems at two bicycle rental companies. While both focus on a particular market segment, one has a low-cost strategy, and the other differentiates on service quality.

Consider Figure 1-9. The top part of this figure shows four activities in the operations activity. The next section illustrates business processes for a company with the competitive

FIGURE 1-9

Example Processes for Two Bike Rental Companies

Value Chain Activity		Greet Customer	Determine Needs	Rent Bike	Return Bike & Pay
Low-Cost Rental to Students	**Message that implements competitive strategy**	"You wanna bike?"	"Bikes are over there. Help yourself."	"Fill out this form, and bring it to me over here when you're done."	"Show me the bike." "OK, you owe $23.50. Pay up."
	Supporting business process	None.	Physical controls and procedures to prevent bike theft.	Printed forms and a shoebox to store them in.	Shoebox with rental form. Minimal credit card and cash receipt system.
High-Service Rental to Business Executives at Conference Resort	**Message that implements competitive strategy**	"Hello, Ms. Henry. Wonderful to see you again. Would you like to rent the WonderBike 4.5 that you rented last time?"	"You know, I think the WonderBike Supreme would be a better choice for you. It has …"	"Let me just scan the bike's number into our system, and then I'll adjust the seat for you."	"How was your ride?" "Here, let me help you. I'll just scan the bike's tag again and have your paperwork in a second." "Would you like a beverage?" "Would you like me to put this on your hotel bill, or would you prefer to pay now?"
	Supporting business process	Customer tracking and past sales activity system.	Employee training and information system to match customer and bikes, biased to upsell customer.	Automated inventory system to check bike out of inventory.	Automated inventory system to place bike back in inventory. Prepare payment documents. Integrate with resort's billing system.

strategy of providing low-cost rentals to college students. Notice that none of the supporting business processes involve information systems.

The bottom section shows how a company with a competitive strategy of providing high-quality rentals to business executives at a conference resort might implement this portion of that same value chain.

Note that the value chain activities are the same for both companies. Both greet the customer, determine the customer's needs, rent a bike, and return the bike. However, each company implements these activities in ways that are consistent with its competitive strategy.

The low-cost vendor has created barebones, minimum processes to support its value chain. The high-service customer service vendor has created more elaborate business processes (supported by information systems) that are necessary to differentiate its service from that of other vendors. As Porter says, however, these processes and systems must create sufficient value that they will more than cover their costs. If not, the margin of those systems will be negative.

If a value chain's margin is negative, the company must make some change. Either the value must be increased, or the costs of the value chain need to be reduced.

Ethics Guide

Yikes! Bikes

Suppose you are an operations manager for Yikes! Bikes, a manufacturer of high-end mountain bicycles with $20 million in annual sales. Yikes! has been in business over 25 years, and the founder and sole owner recently sold the business to an investment group, Major Capital. You know nothing about the sale until your boss introduces you to Andrea Parks, a partner at Major Capital, who is in charge of the acquisition. Parks explains to you that Yikes! has been sold to Major Capital and that she will be the temporary general manager. She explains that the new owners see great potential in you, and they want to enlist your cooperation during the transition. She hints that if your potential is what she thinks it is, you will be made general manager of Yikes!

Parks explains that the new owners have decided there are too many players in the high-end mountain bike business, and they plan to change the competitive strategy of Yikes! from high-end differentiation to lowest-cost vendor.

Accordingly, they will eliminate local manufacturing, fire most of the manufacturing department, and import bikes from China. Further, Major Capital sees a need to reduce expenses and plans a 10 percent across-the-board staff reduction and a cut of two-thirds of the customer support department. The new bikes will be of lesser quality than current Yikes! bikes, but the price will be substantially less. The new ownership group believes it will take a few years for the market to realize that Yikes! bikes are not the same quality as they were. Finally, Parks asks you to attend an all-employee meeting with the founder and her.

At the meeting, the founder explains that due to his age and personal situation, he decided to sell Yikes! to Major Capital and that starting today Andrea Parks is the general manager. He thanks the employees for their many years of service, wishes them well, and leaves the building. Parks introduces herself to the employees and states that Major Capital is

very excited to own such a great company with a strong, quality brand. She says she will take a few weeks to orient herself to the business and its environment and plans no major changes to the company.

You are reeling from all this news when Parks calls you into her office and explains that she needs you to prepare two reports. In one, she wants a list of all the employees in the manufacturing department, sorted by their salary (or wage for hourly employees). She explains that she intends to cut the most costly employees first. "I don't want to be inflexible about this, though," she says. "If there is someone whom you think we should keep, let me know, and we can talk about it."

She also wants a list of the employees in the customer support department, sorted by the average amount of time each support rep spends with customers. She explains, "I'm not so concerned with payroll expense in customer support. It's not how much we're paying someone; it's how much time they're wasting with customers. We're going to have a bare-bones support department, and we want to get rid of the gabby chatters first."

You are, understandably, shocked and surprised . . . not only at the speed with which the transaction has occurred, but also because you wouldn't think the founder would do this to the employees. You call him at home and tell him what is going on.

"Look," he explains, "when I sold the company, I asked them to be sure to take care of the employees. They said they would. I'll call Andrea, but there's really nothing I can do at this point; they own the show."

In a black mood of depression, you realize you don't want to work for Yikes! anymore, but your wife is 6 months pregnant with your first child. You need medical insurance for her at least until the baby is born. But what miserable tasks are you going to be asked to do before then? And you suspect that if you balk at any task, Parks won't hesitate to fire you, too.

As you leave that night you run into Lori, the most popular customer support representative and one of your favorite employees. "Hey," Lori asks you, "what did you think of that meeting? Do you believe Andrea? Do you think they'll let us continue to make great bikes?"

DISCUSSION QUESTIONS

1. In your opinion, did the new owners take any illegal action? Is there evidence of a crime in this scenario?

2. Was the statement that Parks made to all of the employees unethical? Why or why not? If you questioned her about the ethics of her statement, how do you think she would justify herself?

3. What do you think Parks will tell the founder if he calls as a result of your conversation with him? Does he have any legal recourse? Is Major Capital's behavior toward him unethical? Why or why not?

4. Parks is going to use information to perform staff cuts. What do you think about her rationale? Ethically, should she consider other factors, such as number of years of service, past employee reviews, or other criteria?

5. How do you respond to Lori? What are the consequences if you tell her what you know? What are the consequences of lying to her? What are the consequences of saying something noncommittal?

6. If you actually were in this situation, would you leave the company? Why or why not?

7. In business school, we talk of principles like competitive strategy as interesting academic topics. But, as you can see from the Yikes! case, competitive strategy decisions have human consequences. How do you plan to resolve conflicts between human needs and tough business decisions?

8. How do you define job security?

Active Review

Use this Active Review to verify that you understand the material in the chapter. You can read the entire chapter and then perform the tasks in this review, or you can read the text material for just one question and perform the tasks in this review for that question before moving on to the next one.

Q1. Why is Introduction to MIS the most important class in the business school?

Define *Moore's Law* and explain why its consequences are important to business professionals today. State how business professionals should relate to emerging information technology. Give the text's definition of *job security* and use Reich's enumeration of four key skills to explain how this course will help you attain that security.

Q2. What is MIS?

Define *MIS*. Describe, in the intuitive manner used in this chapter, the meaning of processes, information systems, and information. Define the term *management* (of MIS), and summarize the reasons why this text claims it is important to all businesspeople, not just MIS professionals. Explain the confusion in the statement "organizations achieve their strategies." Summarize why it can be difficult for organizations to focus MIS on organizational strategy.

Q3. How does MIS relate to organizational strategy?

Summarize the reasons that the Porter models are relevant to MIS. Diagram and explain the relationship among industry structure, competitive strategy, value chains, business processes, information systems, and information. Explain why it is not possible to say that business processes always determine information systems.

Q4. What five forces determine industry structure?

Describe the original purpose of the five forces model and the different purpose for which this chapter uses it. Name two types of forces and describe strength factors for each. Name three competitive forces and describe strength factors for each. Name two supply chain forces. Summarize the strong forces operating on FlexTime.

Q5. What is competitive strategy?

Describe four different strategies, as defined by Porter. Give an example of four different companies that have implemented each of the strategies.

Q6. How does competitive strategy determine value chain structure?

Define the terms *value*, *margin*, and *value chain*. Explain why organizations that choose a differentiation strategy can use value to determine a limit on the amount of extra cost to pay for differentiation. Name the primary and support activities in the value chain and explain the purpose of each. Explain the concept of linkages.

Q7. How do value chains determine business processes and information systems?

What is the relationship between a value chain and a business process? How do business processes relate to competitive strategy? How do information systems relate to competitive strategy? Justify the comments in the two rows labeled "Supporting business process" in Figure 1-9.

Key Terms and Concepts

Abstract reasoning   *8*
Competitive strategy   *14*
Experimentation   *9*
Five forces model   *12*
Linkages   *17*

Management information
  systems (MIS)   *10*
Management (of MIS)   *10*
Margin   *15*
Moore's Law   *6*

Primary activities   *15*
Support activities   *15*
Systems thinking   *8*
Value   *15*
Value chain   *15*

Using Your Knowledge

1. Do you agree that this course is the most important course in the business school? Isn't accounting more important? No business can exist without accounting. Or, isn't management more important? After all, if you can manage people, why do you need to know how to innovate with technology? You can hire others to think innovatively for you.

   However, what single factor will impact all business more than IS? And, isn't knowledge and proficiency with IS and IT key to future employment and success?

   Give serious thought to this question and write a single-page argument as to why you agree or disagree.

2. Describe three to five personal goals for this class. None of these goals should include anything about your GPA. Be as specific as possible, and make the goals personal to your major, interests, and career aspirations. Assume that you are going to evaluate yourself on these goals at the end of the quarter or semester. The more specific you make these goals, the easier it will be to perform the evaluation.

3. Suppose you decide to start a business that recruits students for summer jobs. You will match available students with available jobs. You need to learn what positions are available and what students are available for filling those positions. In starting your business, you know you will be competing with local newspapers, Craigslist (www.craigslist.org), and with your college. You will probably have other local competitors as well.
   a. Analyze the structure of this industry according to Porter's five forces model.
   b. Given your analysis in part a, recommend a competitive strategy.
   c. Describe the primary value chain activities as they apply to this business.
   d. Describe a business process for recruiting students.
   e. Describe information systems that could be used to support the business process in part d.
   f. Explain how the process you described in part d and the system you described in part e reflect your competitive strategy.

4. Consider the two different bike rental companies in Figure 1-9. Think about the bikes that they rent. Clearly, the student bikes will be just about anything that can be ridden out of the shop. The bikes for the business executives, however, must be new, shiny, clean, and in tiptop shape.
   a. Compare and contrast the operations value chains of these two businesses as they pertain to the management of bicycles.
   b. Describe a business process for maintaining bicycles for both businesses.
   c. Describe a business process for acquiring bicycles for both businesses.
   d. Describe a business process for disposing of bicycles for both businesses.
   e. What roles do you see for information systems in your answers to the earlier questions? The information systems can be those you develop within your company or they can be those developed by others, such as Craigslist.

5. Samantha Green owns and operates Twigs Tree Trimming Service. Samantha graduated from the forestry program of a nearby university and worked for a large landscape design firm, performing tree trimming and removal. After several years of experience, she bought her own truck, stump grinder, and other equipment and opened her own business in St. Louis, Missouri.

   Although many of her jobs are one-time operations to remove a tree or stump, others are recurring, such as trimming a tree or groups of trees every year or every other year. When business is slow, she calls former clients to remind them of her services and of the need to trim their trees on a regular basis.

   Samantha has never heard of Michael Porter or any of his theories. She operates her business "by the seat of her pants."
   a. Explain how an analysis of the five competitive forces could help Samantha.
   b. Do you think Samantha has a competitive strategy? What competitive strategy would seem to make sense for her?
   c. How would knowledge of her competitive strategy help her sales and marketing efforts?
   d. Describe, in general terms, the kind of information system that she needs to support sales and marketing efforts.

Collaboration Exercise 1

Collaborate with a group of fellow students to answer the following questions. For this exercise do not meet face to face. Your task will be easier if you coordinate your work with SharePoint, Office 365, Google Docs with Google + or equivalent collaboration tools. (See Chapter 9 for a discussion of collaboration tools and processes.) Your answers should reflect the thinking of the entire group, and not just that of one or two individuals.

1. Abstract reasoning.
   a. Define *abstract reasoning,* and explain why it is an important skill for business professionals.

b. Explain how a list of items in inventory and their quantity on hand is an abstraction of a physical inventory.

c. Give three other examples of abstractions commonly used in business.

d. Explain how Jennifer failed to demonstrate effective abstract-reasoning skills.

e. Can people increase their abstract-reasoning skills? If so, how? If not, why not?

2. Systems thinking.

a. Define *systems thinking,* and explain why it is an important skill for business professionals.

b. Explain how you would use systems thinking to explain why Moore's Law caused a farmer to dig up a field of pulpwood trees. Name each of the elements in the system, and explain their relationships to each other.

c. Give three other examples of the use of systems thinking with regard to consequences of Moore's Law.

d. Explain how Jennifer failed to demonstrate effective systems-thinking skills.

e. Can people improve their systems-thinking skills? If so, how? If not, why not?

3. Collaboration.

a. Define *collaboration,* and explain why it is an important skill for business professionals.

b. Explain how you are using collaboration to answer these questions. Describe what is working with regards to your group's process and what is not working.

c. Is the work product of your team better than any one of you could have done separately? If not, your collaboration is ineffective. If that is the case, explain why.

d. Does the fact that you cannot meet face to face hamper your ability to collaborate? If so, how?

e. Explain how Jennifer failed to demonstrate effective collaboration skills.

f. Can people increase their collaboration skills? If so, how? If not, why not?

4. Experimentation.

a. Define *experimentation,* and explain why it is an important skill for business professionals.

b. Explain several creative ways you could use experimentation to answer this question.

c. How does the fear of failure influence your willingness to engage in any of the ideas you identified in part b.

d. Explain how Jennifer failed to demonstrate effective experimentation skills.

e. Can people increase their willingness to take risks? If so, how? If not, why not?

f. Do you think IS make experimentation easier or harder?

5. Job security.

a. State the text's definition of *job security*.

b. Evaluate the text's definition of job security. Is it effective? If you think not, offer a better definition of job security.

c. As a team, do you agree that improving your skills on the four dimensions in Collaboration Exercise 1 will increase your job security?

d. Do you think technical skills (accounting proficiency, financial analysis proficiency, etc.) provide job security? Why or why not. Do you think you would have answered this question differently in 1980? Why or why not?

CASE STUDY 1

Getty Images Serves Up Profit and YouTube Grows Exponentially

Chapter 1 stated that near-free data communication and data storage have created unprecedented opportunities for highly profitable businesses. Here we will consider two: Getty Images and YouTube.

Getty Images was founded in 1995 with the goal of consolidating the fragmented photography market by acquiring many small companies, applying business discipline to the merged entity, and developing modern information systems. The advent of the Web drove the company to e-commerce and in the process enabled Getty to change the workflow and business practices of the professional visual-content industry. Getty Images had grown from a startup to become, by 2004, a global, $600 million plus, publicly traded, very profitable company. By 2007, Getty had increased its revenue to more than $880 million. More recent financial information is unavailable, because in July 2008 Getty was purchased by the private equity firm Hellman & Friedman, LLC, for $2.4 billion.

Getty Images obtains its imagery (still, video, and audio) from photographers and other artists under contract, and it owns the world's largest private archive of imagery. Getty also employs staff photographers to shoot the world's news, sport, and entertainment events. In the case of photography and film that it does not own, it provides a share of the revenue generated to the content owner. Getty Images is both a producer and a distributor of imagery, and all of its products are sold via e-commerce on the Web.

Getty Images employs three licensing models: The first is *subscription*, by which customers contract to use as many images as they want as often as they want (this applies to the news, sport, and entertainment imagery). The second model is *royalty-free*. In this model, customers pay a fee based on the file size of the image and can use the image any way they want and as many times as they want. However, under this model, customers have no exclusivity or ability to prevent a competitor from using the same image at the same time.

The third model, *rights managed*, also licenses creative imagery. In this model, which is the largest in revenue terms, users pay fees according to the rights that they wish to use—size, industry, geography, prominence, frequency, exclusivity, and so forth.

According to its Web site:

Getty Images has been credited with the introduction of royalty-free photography and was the first company to license imagery via the Web, subsequently moving the entire industry online. The company was also the first to employ creative researchers to anticipate the visual content needs of the world's communicators (http://corporate.gettyimages.com/source/company.html, accessed December 2007).

Because Getty Images licenses photos in digital format, its variable cost of production is essentially zero. Once the company has obtained a photo and placed it in the commerce server database, the cost of sending it to a customer is zero. Getty Images does have the overhead costs of setting up and operating the e-commerce site, and it does pay some costs for its images—either the cost of employing the photographer or the cost of setting up and maintaining the relationship with out-of-house photographers. For some images, it also pays a royalty to the owner. Once these costs are paid, however, the cost of producing a photo is nil. This means that Getty Images' profitability increases substantially with increased volume.

Why did Hellman & Friedman purchase Getty Images? According to its Web site, Hellman & Friedman, "focuses on investing in businesses with strong, defensible franchises and predictable revenue and earnings growth and which generate high levels of free cash flow or attractive returns on the capital reinvested in the business." With a near zero cost of production, it is likely that Getty Images does indeed generate high levels of free cash flow!

At the same time that Getty Images was achieving its peak as a public company, another team of entrepreneurs found a different way to take advantage of near-free data communications and data storage. On February 15, 2005, Chad Hurley, Steve Chen, and Jawed Karim registered the domain "YouTube" and by April 23 had posted their first video. By November, YouTube had 200,000 registered users and was showing 2 million videos per day. In 9 months, YouTube had grown from nothing to 200,000 users.

By January 2006, when YouTube had just 20 employees, it was showing 25 million videos per day. By May 2006, YouTube was showing 43 percent of all videos viewed over the Internet. By July 2006, users were viewing 100 million videos and uploading 65,000 new videos per day. Think about that: 30 employees were serving 100 million videos per day. That's 3.33 million videos *per employee*, all accomplished in just over 1 year.

Today, YouTube has more than 2 billion views per day, and 24 hours of video is uploaded every minute. According to Viralblog, 70 percent of YouTube's traffic comes from outside the United States.

That phenomenal success was capped by Google's $1.65 billion acquisition of YouTube in October 2006. In just 20 months, YouTube's founders had turned nothing but an idea into $1.65 billion. That's a rate of $2,750,000 of equity per day.

What's the point of these examples? The opportunities were there in 1995, in 2005, and they are still there today. Although it is unlikely that you, too, will have such success, think about it: How can you use free data communications and data storage in your business? Or, in a job interview, how might you suggest that your prospective employer use such resources?

Questions

1. Visit www.gettyimages.com and select "Images/Creative/Search royalty-free." Search for an image of a major city of interest to you. Select a photo and determine its default price. Follow the link on the photographer's name to find other images by that photographer.
2. Explain how Getty Images' business model takes advantage of the opportunities created by IT, as described in Chapter 1.
3. Evaluate the photography market using Porter's five forces. Do you think Getty Images' marginal cost is sustainable? Are its prices sustainable? What is the key to its continued success?
4. What seems to be Getty Images' competitive strategy?
5. Explain how Getty Images' use of information systems contributed to the company's value when it was acquired.
6. How did the availability of near-free data communication and data storage facilitate YouTube's success? Would YouTube have been possible without them?
7. Even though the cost of data communication and data storage is very low, for the volume at which YouTube operates they are still substantial expenses. How did YouTube fund these expenses? (Search the Internet for "History of YouTube" to find information to answer this question.)
8. How does YouTube (now owned by Google) earn revenue?

Using the cases of Getty Images and YouTube as a guide, answer the following questions:

9. Choose a corporation located in the geographic vicinity of your college or university. In what ways is it already taking advantage of the low cost of data communication and data storage?
10. Using the corporation you identified in question 9, identify three innovative ways that the corporation could take advantage of the low cost of data communication and storage.
11. Create an outline of a statement about the importance of near–zero-cost data storage and data communication that you could use in a job interview. Assume you wish to demonstrate that you have knowledge of the power of emerging technology as well as the capacity to think innovatively. Incorporate the example you used in your answers to questions 9 and 10 in your statement.

Sources: www.gettyimages.com (accessed December 2004, May 2007, June 2009, May 2011); www.hf.com (accessed June 2009); www.youtube.com/watch?v=x2NQiVcdZRY (accessed May 2011); and www.viralblog.com/research/youtube-statistics (accessed May 2011).

"What do you mean I'm not a valid student?" Carter Jackson, a student at Central Colorado State, is trying to check out soccer equipment from the university intramural center and is talking with Dirk Johansen, one of the center's part-time employees.

"Valid? Yeah, I did say that. Sorry. Look, you might be a fine student for all I know, but this computer is telling me you haven't paid your bill." Dirk looks at the long line forming behind Carter.

"What bill?"

"I don't know. It doesn't tell me."

"Look," Carter is trying to be patient, "I'm the coach of the Helicopters, the best soccer team in the league. The team will be here in 30 minutes. We need to practice. I need the soccer gear, the shirts, the cones, all the stuff to get started."

"Yeah, I've heard of the Helicopters. Good team . . . at least last year."

"So, gimme the gear and I'll get out of here," Carter sees a ray of hope.

"Can't do it. I can't check out any gear to anyone who's not in good standing with university accounting . . . or whoever is on the other end of this computer." Dirk is adamant.

"Look, accounting is closed. I can't fix this problem now."

"Right. You should have paid your bill earlier."

"I did pay my bill. I don't know what this is about. Just *loan* me the gear."

"I can't." Dirk looks at the even longer line of people behind Carter.

"OK. I see one of our players coming in from the lot. Let me call her over here and you can check it out to her."

"Is her name Carter Jackson?"

"No, you idiot. *My* name is Carter Jackson. I already told you that." Carter is angry now.

"Hey, don't get snippy. I'll call security."

"OK, sorry. My name is Carter Jackson. Her name is Heather Nealey."

"I'm sure she's a nice person, but she's not getting any soccer gear. The only person on the Helicopters who can check out equipment is the team captain, someone named Carter Jackson." Dirk sounds like he's talking to a 2-year-old.

"That's me!"

"Right. And you haven't paid your bill, so, no equipment until you do."

"I'm sure I've paid all my bills. I don't know what's going on, but I'll fix it tomorrow. How about if I give you a credit card?" Carter's getting desperate.

"We don't take credit cards here. Just university IDs."

"I already gave you my ID."

"Right. The bogus one."

"IT ISN'T BOGUS, YOU NITWIT!"

"Carter, Heather, whatever your name is, get out of here. There's 10 people in line behind you. Move on and let me get these people their equipment."

"Yeah, buddy, stop yelling and let us get our stuff," says someone waiting in line.

"Oh, he's the Helicopters' coach. Probably complaining that he didn't get new balls. Thinks he can get away with anything," says another person in line.

The next day at the accounting office . . .

"Hi, my name's Carter Jackson. I'm here to take care of whatever problem there is on my account."

"OK. Give me your student card." June Marble has been working in the accounting office for 30 years.

"Sure."

June scans the card and looks at her computer. "What problem are you here about?" June asks.

"I'm not sure. I was trying to check out equipment for the Helicopters last night. . ."

"Helicopters? You in the right place?" June can't resist teasing him.

"It's an intramural soccer team. OK? Anyway, I was trying to check out equipment and this nitwit told me that I have a past due bill."

"Hmmm. I don't see any problem with your account. You've got a few charges this month, but we haven't sent out this month's bills. Don't worry about it." June starts to turn away from the counter.

"But he thinks my account is bad or something."

"Tell him to call me."

"He doesn't come in till 6:30 tonight."

"Oh, I leave at 5:00." June looks back at her computer screen. "Hey, wait. There's another Carter Jackson who left . . . oh, I can't tell you the story, but I suspect they confused your accounts somehow."

Q1. What is a business process?

Q2. What is an information system?

Q3. How do business processes and information systems relate?

Q4. What is information?

Q5. What factors drive information quality?

Q6. How do structured and dynamic processes vary?

Chapter Preview

In Chapter 1, we defined MIS as the management and use of business processes, information systems, and information to help organizations achieve their strategies. This chapter extends that discussion by defining and describing that definition's three fundamental terms: business process, information system, and information. We begin with business processes, describing their components, and then introduce you to BPMN, the standard way of documenting business processes. Next we will define information systems and describe their components. Then we will explain how business processes and information systems relate. Following that, we will present several different definitions of information and ask where and how information is created. Finally, we will discuss factors that influence information quality and then return to the question of how organizations use information systems. We will wrap up by explaining how these concepts will be treated in the rest of this text.

Q1. What Is a Business Process?

A **business process** is a sequence of activities for accomplishing a function. For example, your university has business processes to:

- Add a class to the business curriculum
- Add a new section to a class schedule
- Assign a class section to a classroom
- Drop a class section
- Record final grades

An **activity** is a task within a business process. Examples of activities that are part of the record final grades process are:

- Compute final grades
- Fill out grade reporting form
- Submit the grade recording form to the departmental administrator

Business processes also involve resources, such as people, computers, data and document collections, and so forth. To understand those, consider the business process for checking out equipment that opened this chapter.

An Example Business Process

Dirk, the student who was issuing sports equipment at the start of this chapter, was following a business process. As yet, we don't know exactly what the process was, but clearly it involved checking out equipment only to team captains and ensuring that those captains were in good standing with the university's accounting office.

DOCUMENTING BUSINESS PROCESSES To talk meaningfully about business processes, we need some way of documenting them. Or, using Reich's term in Chapter 1, we need to create an *abstraction* of business processes. The computer industry has created dozens of techniques for documenting business processes over the years, and this text will use one of them known as the **Business Process Management Notation (BPMN) standard.** We use this technique both because it is a global standard and also because it is widely used in industry. Microsoft Visio Premium,[1] for example, includes templates for creating process drawings using BPMN symbols.

---

[1] Visio is a diagram-drawing product licensed by Microsoft. If your university belongs to the Microsoft Academic Alliance (which is likely), you can obtain a copy of Visio for free. If you want to draw diagrams that use BPMN symbols, be certain that you obtain the Premium version of this product, which is available from the Academic Alliance.

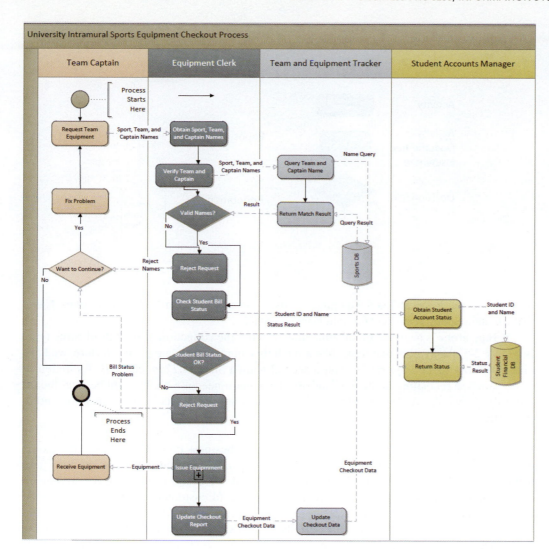

FIGURE 2-1

University Intramural Sports Equipment Checkout Process

Figure 2-1 is a BPMN model, or abstraction, of the business process used by the intramural sports league. Each of the long columns is headed by a name such as *Team Captain* and *Equipment Clerk*. That name identifies a **role,** which is a subset of the activities in a business process that is performed by a particular actor. **Actors** can be people; in the opening vignette, Dirk was fulfilling the role of Equipment Clerk. As you will learn, actors can also be computers, but that's getting ahead of the story.

The long columns in Figure 2-1 are called **swimlanes**; each such lane contains all the activities for a particular role. Swimlanes make it easy to determine which roles do what. According to the BPMN standard, the process starts at a circle with a narrow border and ends at a circle with a heavy border. Thus, in Figure 2-1, the business process starts at the top of the *Team Captain* swimlane and ends at the heavy-bordered circle near the end of that swimlane. The BPMN standard defines dozens of symbols; the symbols we will use in this text are summarized in Figure 2-2.

Activities are shown in rectangles with rounded corners, and decisions are shown by diamonds. A solid arrow shows the flow of action; the solid arrow between the Obtain Sport, Team, and Captain Names and Verify Team and Captain activities means that once the Equipment Clerk has obtained the names, the next task in the process is to verify them.

Dotted arrows show the flow of the data that is named on the arrow. Thus, the dotted arrow between the Request Team Equipment activity and the Obtain Sport, Team, and Captain Names activity means that the data items named on that arrow are sent from one activity to another.

FIGURE 2-2

Summary of BPMN Symbols

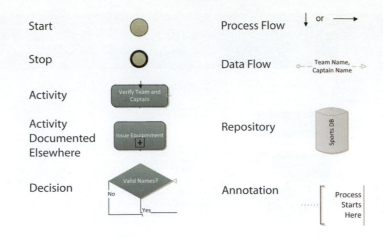

In this case, the Request Team Equipment activity is sending Team Name and Captain Name to the Obtain Sport, Team, and Captain Names activity.

A **repository** is a collection of something, usually the collection of records of some type. In Figure 2-1, the symbol that looks like a small tin can represents a repository. Here, we have one repository named *Sports DB* and a second named *Student Financial DB*. As hinted in those names, a repository is often a database (DB), but it need not be. It might be a cardboard box full of records. And some repositories, like inventories, are collections of things other than data.

HOW MUCH DETAIL IS ENOUGH? As an abstraction, a business process diagram shows some details and omits others. It has to, otherwise it would be hundreds of pages long and needlessly so because many details are obvious. We don't need to show that the equipment clerk should open the checkout window before talking to customers or that he or she must turn on a computer before using it. However, we need to show sufficient detail so as to avoid ambiguity. The process with one big activity named Check Out Equipment leaves out too much detail. Such a diagram would not show, for example, that only authorized team captains can check out equipment.

To simplify process diagrams, the details of some activities are documented separately. In Figure 2-1 examine the activity Issue Equipment (near the bottom of the Equipment Clerk swimlane). The activity is shown with a plus sign enclosed in a small box. That notation signifies that the details of the Issue Equipment activity are documented elsewhere. As stated, such external documentation is used to simplify a diagram; it is also used when the details of the subprocess are unimportant to the process under study or when those details are unknown. For example, the details of an activity that is performed by an external agency like a credit bureau would be unknown.

Why Do Organizations Standardize Business Processes?

Other than very small businesses, most businesses choose to standardize business processes. For one, standard processes enable the business to enforce policies. The intramural sports league has decided that equipment is to be checked out only to authorized and identified team captains and that those captains must have a problem-free account with the university's accounting's office. If every equipment clerk had a different process, there would be no way to enforce those policies.

Second, standardized business processes produce consistent results. When every employee follows the same process steps, the results will be the same, regardless of who is staffing the window. Third, standardized processes are scalable. If the intramural sports league decides to open a third or fourth center at a remote campus, it can do so more easily if its business processes are standardized.

Finally, standardized business processes reduce risk. When every employee follows the same process, the opportunities for error and serious mistakes are greatly reduced.

You might be wondering that if such standardized processes are so great, why didn't Carter get his team's equipment? To answer that question, you need to understand information systems and their relationship to business processes, so we will consider them next. Be patient, you will see what happened to Carter very soon.

Q2. What Is an Information System?

A **system** is a group of components that interact to achieve some purpose. As you might guess, an **information system (IS)** is a group of components that interact to produce information. That sentence, although true, raises another question: What are these components that interact to produce information?

Figure 2-3 shows the **five-component framework**—a model of the components of an information system: **computer hardware, software, data, procedures**, and **people**. These five components are present in every information system, from the simplest to the most complex. For example, when you use a computer to write a class report, you are using hardware (the computer, storage disk, keyboard, and monitor), software (Word, WordPerfect, or some other word-processing program), data (the words, sentences, and paragraphs in your report), procedures (the methods you use to start the program, enter your report, print it, and save and back up your file), and people (you).

Consider a more complex example, say an airline reservation system. It, too, consists of these five components, even though each one is far more complicated. The hardware consists of dozens or more computers linked together by telecommunications hardware. Furthermore, hundreds of different programs coordinate communications among the computers, and still other programs perform the reservations and related services. Additionally, the system must store millions upon millions of characters of data about flights, customers, reservations, and other facts. Hundreds of different procedures are followed by airline personnel, travel agents, and customers. Finally, the information system includes people, not only the users of the system, but also those who operate and service the computers, those who maintain the data, and those who support the networks of computers.

Notice the symmetry in these five components. Hardware and people are actors; they do things. Programs and procedures are instructions. Programs tell the hardware what to do, and procedures tell the humans what to do. Data is the bridge between the machine side (hardware and software) and the human side (procedures and people).

The important point here is that the five components in Figure 2-3 are common to all information systems, from the smallest to the largest. As you think about any information system, including a new one like social networking by mechanics discussed in Chapter 1, learn to look for these five components. Realize, too, that an information system is not just a computer and a program, but rather an assembly of computers, software, data, procedures, and people.

Also, problems develop if any one of these five components is overlooked. A common mistake is to assume that hardware and software are the only costs of a new system. In fact, the costs of designing and documenting procedures and the labor costs of training employees to use those procedures can far exceed the hardware and software costs for a new system.

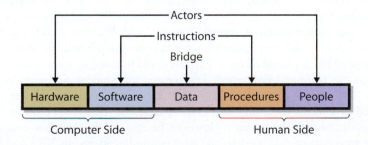

FIGURE 2-3

Five Components of an Information System

MIS InClass 2

Recognizing Processes Close to Home

The management and use of business processes is crucial to your success as a business professional. Although you may not realize it, business processes are all around us. To help you understand this fact, work with a group of students to complete the following tasks:

1. Identify three important business processes used at your university. Choose one process that involves finances, one process that involves operations, and one process that involves marketing.
2. Complete the following for each process:
   a. Name the process.
   b. Identify and briefly describe three to five key activities for the process.
   c. Describe performance measures that management can use to assess the process.
   d. If the process is assisted with information systems, describe how. If you don't know if the process is assisted

Source: © Jinlide/Dreamstime.com.

by information systems, describe how you think information systems could be used.

3. Present the results of your group's work to the rest of the class.

These five components also mean that many different skills are required besides those of hardware technicians or computer programmers when building or using an information system. People are needed who can design the databases that hold the data and who can develop procedures for people to follow. Managers are needed to train and staff the personnel for using and operating the system. We will return to this five-component framework later in this chapter, as well as many other times throughout this book.

Before we move forward, note that we have defined an information system to include a computer. Some people would say that such a system is a **computer-based information system**. They would note that there are information systems that do not include computers, such as a calendar hanging on the wall outside of a conference room that is used to schedule the room's use. Such systems have been used by businesses for centuries. Although this point is true, in this book we focus on computer-based information systems. To simplify and shorten the book, we will use the term *information system* as a synonym for *computer-based information system*.

Q3. How Do Business Processes and Information Systems Relate?

To understand this crucial question, look again at Figure 2-1. Who are the actors playing the roles in that diagram? The team captain role is a human who is recognized by the league as a captain of a sports team in the league. What about equipment clerk? From the opening vignette, and from the discussion in this chapter, the equipment clerk role is played by one or more part-time employees. But, does this role have to be performed by a human? Could it be performed by some computer-based system? Yes, it could. It could all be done in a browser. The only activity that is likely to require a human is Issue Equipment, and that is a subactivity that could be placed into a role of its own. The rest could be done by a computer-based system.

What about the Team and Equipment Tracker and the Student Accounts Manager roles? Could they be performed by humans? Of course, and in the 1950s and earlier all such roles were performed by humans accessing data in filing cabinets. Thus, the entire business process in Figure 2-1 could be done by humans. However, because of the very low cost of computers and the nearly zero cost of data storage and data communications, in 2012 and beyond most such roles are performed by computers, following instructions in software. Grocery stores have a similar example. It used to be that a human was required for checkout. Now, at many stores, you can scan your groceries yourself; the role of checker has been taken over by scanners and computers.

Information Systems in the Context of Business Processes

Let's assume that the Team and Equipment Tracker and the Student Accounts Manager roles are performed by computers. To understand them, consider Figure 2-4, which extracts those two roles along with the activities that access them from Figure 2-1. Consider the activity Check Student Bill Status in the Equipment Clerk role. It generates and sends Student ID and Name to the Obtain Student Account Status activity.

Check Student Bill Status uses a computer-based system, and procedures need to be written to instruct the clerk how to invoke that system and transmit the data. Let's assume those procedures tell the clerk how to access and fill out the data entry form in Figure 2-5. The Obtain Student Bill Status activity is performed by a computer, which means that the activity is encoded in a computer program. That program accesses the Student Financial DB to obtain the student's account status.

Notice how the five components are integrated into the business process. Computers and humans are actors who play roles in the business process. The particular techniques for using the computer system to perform an activity are encoded in procedures for human actors, and they are encoded in programs for computer actors. Data is bridging the two types of actors.

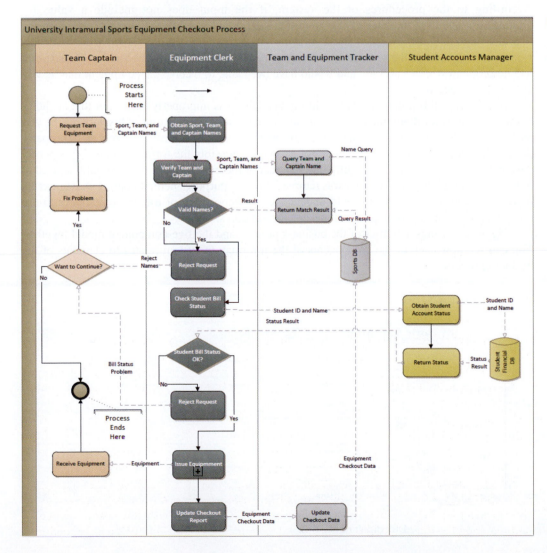

FIGURE 2-4

Activities That Involve Computer Actors

FIGURE 2-5

Account Status Request Data Input Form

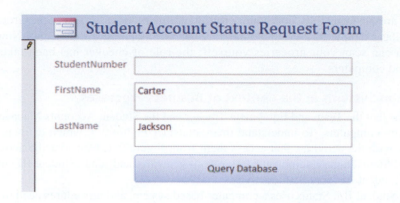

All of this brings us to why the Helicopters' equipment request was denied. The procedures for using the information system to check student account status include two modes of access. If the form shown in Figure 2-5 includes a value for *StudentNumber* (what *Student ID* is called within the information system), then the Obtain Student Bill Status program returns one account (or none if there is no match). However, if the form in Figure 2-5 does not include a *StudentNumber*, then that program returns all accounts that match values for first and last name.

Figure 2-6 shows the data that were returned from the program executing the Return Status activity. As you can see, the bottom of the form indicates that two records were returned. According to the procedures of the system, if the input does not include a value for *StudentNumber*, then the user of the system is supposed to verify the student's ID with the returned value of *StudentNumber*. Had Dirk done so, he would have seen that two student records were returned, and that the second one belonged to the Carter in front of his window. That Carter had no problem with his account and would have been able to receive the equipment that he was authorized to receive.

What caused this problem? One could say that Dirk was improperly trained, or that he didn't know procedures for doing his job. Or, maybe, given the long line in front of his window, he was hasty and made a mistake. Or, one could say the system that performs this role is improperly designed; it ought not to have two modes of access. Or possibly the form in Figure 2-6 is poorly designed. Something other than a tiny little number at the bottom of the form should be used to indicate that more than one account was returned. For our purposes here, it doesn't matter, except that, as a future manager, you should understand the importance of training employees to use information systems according to their designed procedures.

Figure 2-7 brings activities of the business process and the five-component model together. You can see how each of the components of the information system relates to elements of the business process.

FIGURE 2-6

Student Account Status Return Form

Student Account Status Return Form	
StudentNumber	100020015
FirstName	Carter
LastName	Jackson
Status	Problem

Record: ◄ ◄ 1 of 2 ► ►► ►✱ No Filter Search

Dirk didn't notice this.

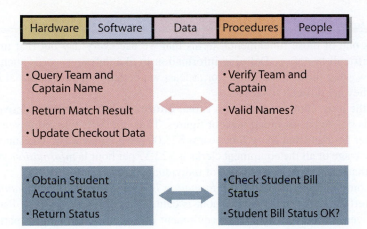

FIGURE 2-7

Five Components and Activities

This example also shows an aggravating reality. The intramural sports league refers to student identifiers as *Student ID*s. The university's student accounting system refers to student identifiers as *StudentNumbers*. These entities have two names for the same thing. Why? There could be many different reasons. Perhaps they were developed by different teams of people at different times; or, they have different cultures, the manager of the intramural sports used the term Student ID where he worked as a graduate student, and she used that term with the team that built the intramural sports information system. Whatever the reason, such synonyms are common when using different information systems. You and the people you manage may find such multiplicity of names frustrating and confusing, but rest assured that you will find them.

Business Processes and Information Systems Have Different Scope

Before we move on, notice something that is very confusing to many students and that, in fact, is misunderstood by many business professionals. The scope of business processes and the scope of information systems are different. The business process in Figure 2-1 uses two different information systems: a local one and a university-wide one. In general, a business process may use zero, one, or many different information systems.

Similarly, although not shown, each of the two information systems in Figure 2-1 is used by many other business processes. The system that plays the Team and Equipment Tracker role also plays a role in other business processes, such as the Check In Equipment process and the Schedule Teams process. The system that plays the Students Account Manager role also plays a role in processes such as the Buy Athletic Tickets process and the Pay Dorm Bill process, and so forth. In general, an information system plays a role in from one to many business processes.

Thus, the scope of business processes and information systems that support them overlap, but they are different, as shown in Figure 2-8.

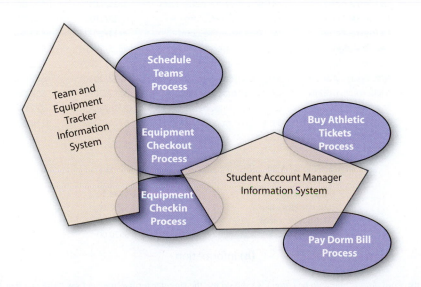

FIGURE 2-8

Overlap of Process and IS Scope

Q4. What Is Information?

Information is one of those fundamental terms that we use every day but that turns out to be surprisingly difficult to define. Defining information is like defining words such as *alive* and *truth*. We know what those words mean, or at least we pretend we do in normal conversation. Nonetheless, they are difficult to define.

Probably the most common definition is that **information** is knowledge derived from data, whereas *data* is defined as recorded facts or figures. Thus, the facts that employee James Smith earns $17.50 per hour and that Mary Jones earns $25.00 per hour are *data*. The statement that the average hourly wage of all the equipment clerks is $22.37 per hour is *information*. Average wage is knowledge that is derived from the data of individual wages.

Another common definition is that *information is data presented in a meaningful context*. The fact that Jeff Parks earns $10.00 per hour is data.[2] The statement that Jeff Parks earns less than half the average hourly wage of the equipment clerks, however, is information. It is data presented in a meaningful context.

Another definition is that *information is processed data,* or sometimes, *information is data processed by sorting, filtering, grouping, comparing, summing, averaging, and other similar operations.* The fundamental idea of this definition is that we do something to data to produce information. The list of orders in Figure 2-9(a) is data; that data has been sorted,

FIGURE 2-9

Information Produced by Processing

Adams, James	JA3@somewhere.com	1/15/2012	$145.00
Angel, Kathy	KA@righthere.com	9/15/2012	$195.00
Ashley, Jane	JA@somewhere.com	5/5/2012	$110.00
Austin, James	JA7@somewhere.com	1/15/2011	$55.00
Bernard, Steven	SB@ourcompany.com	9/17/2012	$78.00
Casimiro, Amanda	AC@somewhere.com	12/7/2011	$52.00
Ching, Kam Hoong	KHC@somewhere.com	5/17/2012	$55.00
Corning,Sandra	KD@somewhereelse.com	7/7/2012	$375.00
Corning,Sandra	SC@somewhereelse.com	2/4/2011	$195.00
Corovic,Jose	JC@somewhere.com	11/12/2012	$55.00
Daniel, James	JD@somewhere.com	1/18/2012	$52.00
Dixon, James T	JTD@somewhere.com	4/3/2011	$285.00
Dixon,Eleonor	ED@somewhere.com	5/17/2012	$108.00
Drew, Richard	RD@righthere.com	10/3/2011	$42.00
Duong,Linda	LD@righthere.com	5/17/2011	$485.00
Garrett, James	JG@ourcompany.com	3/14/2012	$38.00
Jordan, Matthew	MJ@righthere.com	3/14/2011	$645.00
La Pierre,Anna	DJ@righthere.com	12/7/2011	$175.00
La Pierre,Anna	SG@righthere.com	9/22/2012	$120.00
La Pierre,Anna	TR@righthere.com	9/22/2011	$580.00
La Pierre,Anna	ALP@somewhereelse.com	3/15/2011	$52.00
La Pierre,Anna	JQ@somewhere.com	4/12/2012	$44.00
La Pierre,Anna	WS@somewhere.com	3/14/2011	$47.50
Lee,Brandon	BL@somewhereelse.com	5/5/2010	$74.00
Lunden,Haley	HL@somewhere.com	11/17/2009	$52.00
McGovern, Adrian	BL@righthere.com	11/12/2010	$47.00
McGovern, Adrian	AM@ourcompany.com	3/17/2011	$52.00
Menstell,Lori Lee	LLM@ourcompany.com	10/18/2012	$72.00
Menstell,Lori Lee	VB@ourcompany.com	9/24/2012	$120.00

(a) Data

CustomerName	Number of Orders	TotalPurchases
La Pierre,Anna	6	$1,018.50
Rikki, Nicole	2	$330.00
Menstell,Lori Lee	2	$192.00
McGovern, Adrian	2	$99.00
Corning,Sandra	2	$570.00

(b) Information

---

[2] Actually the word *data* is plural; to be correct we should use the singular form *datum* and say "The fact that Jeff Parks earns $10 per hour is a datum." The word *datum* however, sounds pedantic and fussy, and we will avoid it in this text.

filtered, grouped, and computations have been made upon it to create the information in Figure 2-9(b).

A fourth definition, created by the psychologist George Bateson, is that information is *a difference that makes a difference*. At the start of this chapter, Dirk perceived that Carter's account was in arrears or had some other problem. That perception was a difference. Now, because of the intramural sport's league's policy, encoded in its business process, that difference made a difference.

None of these definitions is perfect; each can be useful in certain circumstance, and they all have problems. For now, consider the four of them as four sides of a boundary of what the term *information* means.

However, one characteristic of information may surprise you. Understanding this characteristic will make you a far better consumer of MIS. We begin by asking the question "Where is information?"

Where Is Information?

Examine the data in Figure 2-10. Put that data in front of your family dog. Does this information mean anything to your dog? No. They mean nothing to Fido. Fido may perceive information, but it will have to do with scents on the book, as in "someone had tacos for lunch."

Now, put that same data in front of someone who leads a weekly Weight Watcher's group. Ask that person to interpret the data. He will most likely say that the first column contains the name of a person, the second the person's current weight, and the third the number of pounds lost. If that person looks closely, he may also find information: People who weigh the most tend to lose the most. (In this data, for the most part, the bigger the value in the second column, the bigger the value in the third.)

Now, put that same data in front of someone who manages an IQ testing center for adults. Ask that person to interpret the data. She will most likely say the first column contains the name of a person, the second the person's IQ test score, and the third the person's age. Furthermore, she may also find the information that, according to this data, IQ increases with age.

We can continue this thought experiment to the manager of a bowling league, but you get the point: At least in these cases, the information resides in the head of the person who perceives the data. Does this occur here only because the data are not labeled? Had we put labels on the

Christianson	140	42
Abernathy	107	25
Green	98	21
Moss	137	38
Baker	118	32
Jackson	127	38
Lloyd	119	29
Dudley	111	22
McPherson	128	33
Jefferson	107	24
Nielsen	112	33
Thomas	118	29

FIGURE 2-10
Sample Data

FIGURE 2-11

**Data Processing and
Information**

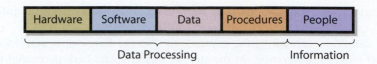

columns of data in Figure 2-10 would the information have been on the piece of paper? No. Labeled columns of data are still just marks on a paper. All the interpretation, and any information constructed, will occur in the mind of the person confronted with the data. In this text, we will say humans *perceive* data but *conceive* information.

Look at Figure 2-11, which again shows the five components of an information system. According to this figure, hardware runs software that processes data to produce a data display. That display is then perceived by a human and is conceived into information by the thinking process of that human. That conceiving process is guided by procedures, but involves critical-thinking skills that go beyond basic procedures.

Thus, for our purposes, it is only the human component of an information system that produces and understands information. Perhaps within the next 30 years the field of artificial intelligence will create machines that emulate humans' ability to conceive information. However, even if such systems exist today, they are rare and we can safely ignore them in mainstream commerce.

Q5. What Factors Drive Information Quality?

Figure 2-12 summarizes the factors that influence information quality. Some of the factors concern the data that is used to conceive the information, and some concern the abilities and characteristics of the human creating the information.

Data Factors

First, data must be accurate. It must be a correct and complete measure of whatever it is supposed to measure. If the data has been processed, it must have been processed correctly, in accordance with expectations and standards.

Second, data must be timely. A monthly report that arrives 6 weeks late is most likely useless. The data arrives long after the decisions have been made that needed related information. An information system that tells you about poor credit of a customer to which you have already shipped goods is unhelpful and frustrating. Notice that timeliness can be measured against a calendar (6 weeks late) or against events (before we ship).

When you participate in the development of an information system, timeliness will be part of the requirements that you specify. You need to give appropriate and realistic timeliness needs. In some cases, developing systems that provide data in near real time is much more difficult and expensive than producing data a few hours later. If you can get by with data that is a few hours old, say so during the requirements specification phase.

Consider an example. Suppose you work in marketing and you need to be able to assess the effectiveness of new online ad programs. You want an information system that not only will deliver ads over the Web, but that also will enable you to determine how frequently customers click on those ads. Determining click ratios in near real time will be very expensive;

FIGURE 2-12

**Factors That Affect
Information Quality**

Data	**Human**
• Accurate	• Knowledge
• Timely	• Criteria
• Correct granularity	
• Easy to use	

saving the data in a batch and processing it some hours later will be much easier and cheaper. If you can live with data that is a day or two old, the system will be easier and cheaper to implement.

Third, data must be of the appropriate granularity. Data that is too fine-grained has too many details; data that is too coarse is too highly summarized. A file that contains records of millions of clicks on a Web page is too fine-grained for an analysis of revenue generated by different page designs. A file of national sales data is too coarse-grained for an analysis of the relative performance of city sales regions. Ideally, data is detailed enough to serve the purpose at hand, but just barely so.

It is possible to group data that is too fine into appropriate granularity; however, data that is too coarse cannot be subdivided into its constituents. Hence, when specifying requirements, if you are going to err, err on the side of being too fine-grained.

Finally, data needs to be easy to use. The data in Figure 2-6 is correct, timely, and at the right level of granularity, but it is not easy to use. The 2 is presented subtly and is difficult to find. An easier-to-use presentation would show, for example, a picture of the two students named Carter Jackson so that it would be obvious that two different student records have been returned.

Human Factors

Again, in this text we will say that humans perceive data and conceive information. Thus, the quality of the information produced is at least as much determined by characteristics of the human involved than it is by the data utilized.

The first factor of importance when conceiving information is knowledge. Decades of psychological research indicate that what humans know greatly influences what they perceive. So, the data that you pay attention to is determined, in part, by your knowledge. Additionally, once you have perceived a difference, your knowledge will help you determine which differences make a difference to the problem at hand. So, what you know about a domain will determine the quality of the information you conceive.

A second human factor that affects information quality is the **criteria** used to interpret the data. To understand this, consider a marketing analyst who wants to conceive information from the sales data in Figure 2-9(a). Figure 2-13 shows data that has been filtered, grouped, and summed from that raw data.

The analyst has used several criteria to construct the report. First, customers with only one purchase have been filtered out of this report, so one criterion is "Consider only repeat customers."

FIGURE 2-13

Applying Criteria to Data

Customer Name	Number of Orders	Total Purchases
La Pierre, Anna	6	$1,018.50
Corning, Sandra	2	$570.00
Rikki, Nicole	2	$330.00
Menstell, Lori Lee	2	$192.00
McGovern, Adrian	2	$99.00

(a) Data Sorted by Total Purchase Amount

Customer Name	Number of Orders	Total Purchases	Average Order Total
La Pierre, Anna	6	$1,018.50	$169.75
Corning, Sandra	2	$570.00	$285.00
Rikki, Nicole	2	$330.00	$165.00
Menstell, Lori Lee	2	$192.00	$96.00
McGovern, Adrian	2	$99.00	$49.50

(b) Data with Average Order Total

Given that the report is shown in descending order of total purchases, it would appear that another criterion in use is "Consider customers with the largest order total first." Now suppose that the marketing analyst notices there seems to be only one male name in this list. That suggests another criterion: "Consider sales grouped by sex of customer."

Figure 2-13 (b) shows this same data, but includes the computation of the average order total. Notice that the order of customers has changed. Considering average order total, Sandra Corning is the top customer; considering only total purchases, Anna La Pierre is the top customer. So, average order seems to make a difference in the relative merit of customers. If the analyst is concerned with increasing the total number of orders, then he or she might use the criteria "average." At this point, we have four criteria for determining which differences make a difference:

- Include only repeat customers
- Consider order of total or average purchases
- Group customers by sex
- Use average order total

Is this a good set of criteria? It is if it helps the business professional to be more successful. It will be if it helps her to make better decisions, to deal more effectively with employees and customers, or to construct better strategies and tactics.

This subject is both rich and deep, and there is a good deal more to explore.[3] Alas, we need to move on. For now, the most important point for you to remember is that data is external, objective, and similar for all. Information is internal, depends on the person, and can be different for all. Thus, two people can perceive the same data, but conceive different information from that data.

How Do Groups Conceive Information?

"Wait a minute," you may be saying. "Hold on. If every human conceives his or her own version of information from a personal perspective, how do we ever get anything done? Why aren't groups constantly disagreeing about everything? How could I ever manage a group like that?"

Because information is conceived personally, it might be that everyone always disagrees about everything. It is, however, unlikely. Why? Because we all share the same mental apparatus. In fact, the biologist Humberto Maturana claims that cognition and communication evolved only to allow us to organize our collective behavior.[4] He believes that because we have the same hardware, we will conceive information the same way, and thus be able to organize ourselves into groups that have a selective advantage over other groups.

So, given that we share the same mental apparatus, perceive the same data, and use the same criteria, we will tend to conceive information in the same way. Often, however, the more interesting case occurs when we do not conceive information in the same way. If everyone is engaged in the process and communicating honestly, then that can only occur when people perceive the data differently (someone notices something that others have not) or when people are using different criteria. The latter case may occur because they have found a criterion that others have not found or that they stress on one criterion more than others do.

You can apply this insight the next time you are in a group that is having a discussion that is going round and round and getting nowhere. Ask the group members what data they perceive. Ask them what criteria they are using to make their statements. If you can start a discussion about criteria, it will often lead to a discussion of why you are using those criteria. This

See the Guide on pages 44–45 to learn one technique that business professionals use to obtain a common definition of a problem.

---

[3] See, for example, Earl McKinney and Chuck Yoos, "Information About Information, a Taxonomy of Views," *MIS Quarterly*, 2010, Volume 24, pp. 329–344.
[4] Humberto R. Maturana, *The Tree of Knowledge* (Boston: Shambhala Publications, 1992).

technique is a useful and valuable way of getting a group unstuck. Try it. See also the discussion of collaboration and collaboration information systems in Chapter 9.

Q6. How Do Structured and Dynamic Processes Vary?

Businesses have dozens, hundreds, even thousands of different processes. Some processes are stable, almost fixed, in the flow among their activities. For example, the process of a sales clerk accepting a return at Nordstrom, or other quality retail store, is fixed. If the customer has a receipt, take these steps. . . . If the customer has no receipt, take these other steps. . . . The process needs to be standardized so that customers are treated correctly, so that returned goods are accounted for appropriately, and so that sales commissions are reduced in a way that is fair to the sales staff.

Other processes are less structured, less rigid, and sometimes creative. For example, how does Nordstrom's management decide what women's clothes to carry next spring? They can look at past sales, consider current economic conditions, and make assessments about women's acceptance of new styles at recent fashion shows, but the process for combining all those factors into orders of specific garments in specific quantities and colors is not nearly as structured as that for accepting the return of goods.

In this text, we divide processes into two broad categories. **Structured processes** are formally defined, standardized processes. Most structured processes support day-to-day operations: accepting a return, placing an order, computing a sales commission, and so forth. **Dynamic processes** are less specific, more adaptive, and even intuitive. Using Twitter to generate buzz about next season's product line is an example of a dynamic process. Deciding whether to open a new store location or how best to solve a problem of excessive returns are other examples of dynamic processes.

Characteristics of Structured Processes

Figure 2-14 summarizes the major differences between structured and dynamic processes. Structured processes are formally defined with specific detailed activities arranged into fixed, predefined sequences, like that shown in the BPMN diagram in Figure 2-4. Changes to structured processes are slow, made with deliberation, and are difficult to implement. Control is critical in structured processes. For example, at Nordstrom's item returns must be done in a consistent, controlled fashion so that, among other reasons, sales commissions are reduced appropriately. Innovation of structured processes is not expected, nor is it generally appreciated or rewarded. "Wow, I've got four different ways of returning items" is not a positive accomplishment in retail sales.

For structured processes, both efficiency and effectiveness are important, and we will define them in Chapter 5. For now, assume that *efficiency* means accomplishing the process with minimum resources, and *effectiveness* means that the process contributes directly to the organization's strategy. Reducing time required to sell an item at a grocery store by 1 second would be a huge efficiency gain. If, at Nordstrom's, the competitive strategy is to treat customers as royalty, then a return process that humiliates customers is ineffective.

Finally, information systems for structured processes are prescriptive. They clearly delimit what the users of the system can do and under what conditions they can do it. In Chapters 7 and 8, you will see how information systems based on SAP, an enterprise-wide IS, constrain human activity to specific tasks at specific points in procurement, sales, or other processes. Variations on those tasks will not be tolerated, as you will learn.

Characteristics of Dynamic Processes

The second column of the table in Figure 2-14 summarizes characteristics of dynamic processes. First, such processes tend to be informal. This does not mean that they are unstructured; rather it means that the process cannot be reduced to fixed steps taken in a specific control flow every time. BPMN diagrams of dynamic processes are always highly generic. They have activities with

FIGURE 2-14

**Differences Between
Structured and Dynamic
Processes**

Structured Processes	Dynamic Processes
Formally defined process	Informal process
Process change slow and difficult	Process change rapid and expected
Control is critical	Adaptation is critical
Innovation not expected	Innovation required
Efficiency and effectiveness are important	Effectiveness is important
IS are prescriptive	IS are supportive

generalized names like "gather data," "analyze past sales," and "assess fashion shows." Human intuition plays a big role in a dynamic process.

Dynamic processes, as their name implies, change rapidly. If structured processes are cast in stone, dynamic processes are written in sand on a windy beach. "We'll try it this way. If it works, great, if not, we'll do something else." A good example is the process for using Twitter to generate buzz for the spring fashions. Which employees tweet? And how? And what? And how frequently? The team will measure results and change their process as needed. Such rapid change is expected. By the way, this need to try and revise reinforces the need to be able to experiment—one of the four key skills for success, as discussed in Chapter 1.

Rather than controlled, dynamic processes are adaptive; they must be so to evolve with experience. Dynamic process actors collaborate; they give feedback to each other, and over time the process evolves into one that no single person might have envisioned, and one that works better than anyone could have created on their own ahead of time.

Adaptation requires innovation. Whereas innovation on a structured process like computing commissions is likely to get you fired, innovating with Twitter to forecast sales will be highly rewarded.

For the most part, dynamic processes are evaluated on effectiveness more than efficiency. Did the process help us accomplish our strategy? This is not to say that efficient use of resources does not matter; rather, dynamic processes change so fast that it is not possible to measure efficiency over time. Typically, costs are controlled by budget: "Get the best result you can with these resources."

Finally, information systems for dynamic processes are supportive rather than prescriptive. Information systems provide a platform, an infrastructure, to facilitate dynamic processes. Microsoft's Office 365, for example, includes a videoconferencing product named Lync and a resource-sharing product called SharePoint, as you will learn in Chapter 9. IS that use those products provide a forum for group work. They enable team members to easily communicate and share documents, files, wikis, and so on, and thus support whatever process the team is engaged upon. Business intelligence systems enable teams to gather intelligence needed to support decisions within a dynamic process.

This structured–dynamic distinction is important. For one, the behavior you choose as a business professional depends on the type of process in which you are involved. Innovation will be expected in dynamic processes, but discouraged in structured processes. Rigid structure will be appreciated in critical manufacturing processes, but disdained in collaboration.

For information systems, this distinction is important in the nature and character of the system. As stated, when SAP is used to support structured processes it will restrict your behavior and readily (and successfully) frustrate any attempts at innovation. In contrast, SharePoint is an open book. Put anything in it you want; control that content in whatever way you think is appropriate. As you learn about these products, understand that their nature and character is a direct reflection of the kind of process they are intended to support.

Ethics Guide

Egocentric Versus Empathetic Thinking

As stated earlier, a problem is a perceived difference between what is and what ought to be. When developing information systems, it is critical for the development team to have a common definition and understanding of the problem. This common understanding can be difficult to achieve, however.

Cognitive scientists distinguish between egocentric and empathetic thinking. Egocentric thinking centers on the self; someone who engages in egocentric thinking considers his or her view as "the real view" or "what really is." In contrast, those who engage in empathetic thinking consider their view as one possible interpretation of the situation and actively work to learn what other people are thinking.

Different experts recommend empathetic thinking for different reasons. Religious leaders say that such thinking is morally superior; psychologists say that empathetic thinking leads to richer, more fulfilling relationships. In business, empathetic thinking is recommended because it is smart. Business is a social endeavor, and those who can understand others' points of view are always more effective. Even if you do not agree with others' perspectives, you will be much better able to work with them if you understand their views.

Consider an example. Suppose you say to your MIS professor, "Professor Jones, I couldn't come to class last Monday. Did we do anything important?" Such a statement is a prime example of egocentric thinking. It takes no account of your professor's point of view and implies that your professor talked about nothing important. As a professor, it is tempting to say, "No, when I noticed you weren't there, I took out all the important material."

To engage in empathetic thinking, consider this situation from the professor's point of view. Students who do not come to class cause extra work for their professors. It does not matter how valid your reason for not attending class; you may actually have been contagious with a fever of 102. But, no matter what, your not coming to class is more work for your professor. He or she must do something extra to help you recover from the lost class time.

Using empathetic thinking, you would do all you can to minimize the impact of your absence on your professor. For example, you could say, "I couldn't come to class, but I got the class notes from Mary. I read through them, and I have a question about establishing alliances as competitive advantage. . . . Oh, by the way, I'm sorry to trouble you with my problem."

Before we go on, let's consider a corollary to this scenario: Never, ever, send an e-mail to your boss that says, "I couldn't come to the staff meeting on Wednesday. Did we do anything important?" Avoid this for the same reasons as those for missing class. Instead, find a way to minimize the impact of your absence on your boss.

Empathetic thinking is an important skill in all business activities. Skilled negotiators always know what the other side wants; effective salespeople understand their customers'

Source: Rob Byron/Shutterstock.

needs. Buyers who understand the problems of their vendors get better service. And students who understand the perspective of their professors get better. . . .

DISCUSSION QUESTIONS

1. In your own words, explain how egocentric and empathetic thinking differ.
2. Suppose you miss a staff meeting. Using empathetic thinking, explain how you can get needed information about what took place in the meeting.
3. How does empathetic thinking relate to problem definition?
4. Suppose you and another person differ substantially on a problem definition. Suppose she says to you, "No, the real problem is that . . ." followed by her definition of the problem. How do you respond?
5. Again, suppose you and another person differ substantially on a problem definition. Assume you understand his definition. How can you make that fact clear?
6. Explain the following statement: "In business, empathetic thinking is smart." Do you agree?

Source: Artur Bogacki/Shutterstock.

Active Review

Use this Active Review to verify that you understand the material in the chapter. You can read the entire chapter and then perform the tasks in this review, or you can read the text material for just one question and perform the tasks in this review for that question before moving on to the next one.

Q1. What is a business process?

Define *business process* and give an example of two business processes not in this text. Define *activity* and give examples of five activities. Explain the need for an abstraction of a business process and describe the purpose of the BPMN notation. Define *role* and *actor* and explain their relationship. Identify four swimlanes in Figure 2-1 and explain their utility. Explain the meaning of each of the symbols in Figure 2-2. Give an example of two repositories. Describe criteria for deciding how much detail is enough in a process diagram. Describe four reasons that organizations standardize business processes.

Q2. What is an information system?

Define *system* and *information system*. Name and describe the five components of an information system. Describe, as best you know at this time, the five components of an information system required to buy a product online. Explain why a variety of skills are required to develop an information system.

Q3. How do business processes and information systems relate?

Using Figure 2-1 as an example, explain how all of the roles in that process could be played by human actors. Explain which of the roles could be played by computer actors. Explain where procedures appear in a business process diagram. In general, how many information systems can a business process use? In general, in how many business processes does a particular IS appear. Explain Figure 2-8.

Q4. What is information?

Give four different definitions for *information* and explain the problem of each. According to this text, explain where information resides. Do you agree? Why or why not? Which definition of information will be used in this text, and why? Summarize the data factors that drive information quality.

Q5. What factors drive information quality?

Summarize the human factors that drive information quality. Define *criteria* and explain how they pertain to information. Explain why this definition of information does not necessarily lead different people to different information. Describe a practical application of criteria for group discussions that are stuck in a discussion rut.

Q6. How do structured and dynamic processes vary?

In your own words, describe and characterize structured processes. Describe and characterize dynamic processes. Describe the differences in expected employee behavior for each type of process. Summarize differences in the character of IS that support each category of process.

Key Terms and Concepts

Activity *28*
Actor *29*
Business process *28*
Business Process Management
  Notation (BPMN) standard *28*
Computer-based information
  system *32*
Computer hardware *31*

Criteria *39*
Data *31*
Dynamic processes *41*
Five-component framework *31*
Information *36*
Information system (IS) *31*
People *31*
Procedures *31*

Repository *30*
Role *29*
Software *31*
Structured processes *41*
Swimlane *29*
System *31*

Using Your Knowledge

1. Consider Dirk's error in the opening vignette of this chapter.
   a. List four possible solutions to this problem.
   b. Of your four solutions, which is the most effective? Why?
   c. Of your four solutions, which is the cheapest? Which is the easiest to implement? Explain.
   d. Describe the cost of Dirk's error to the intramural league and to each of the actors in the story.

2. Explain, in your own words, the relationship between business processes and information systems. Assume you are going to give your explanation to a business professional who knows little about information systems.

3. In Figure 2-8, the team and equipment tracker information system is used exclusively by processes within the intramural sports organization. The student account manager information system is used university-wide. Given these two different scopes:
   a. Which will be the easier system to change? Why?
   b. If problems occur with either of these systems, which system is more likely to provide a rapid fix?
   c. If the intramural sports league wants a change to the form in Figure 2-6, how do you think they should proceed?
   d. If the university IS department decides to change the student account manager information system, how might that change affect the business process in Figure 2-1? Is it likely that the intramural sports organization can stop any change that will adversely impact its processes? Why or why not?

4. Consider some of the ramifications of the way in which information is defined in this chapter.

   a. Why, according to this chapter, is it incorrect to say, "Consider the information in Figure 2-10?" Where is the information?
   b. When you read a news article on the Web, where is the news? When you and a friend read the same news, is it the same news? What is going on here?
   c. Suppose you are having a glass of orange juice for breakfast. As you look at the juice, where is it? Is the thing that you know as orange juice on the table, or is it in your mind? After you drink the orange juice, where is it?
   d. Suppose I say that a glass of orange juice is a collection of molecules arranged into structures. When pressed, suppose I say a molecule is a collection of atoms, arranged according to certain principles. When further pressed, suppose I say that atoms are collections of electrons and neutrons, and, when pressed even more, I say, well, electrons are assemblies of quarks and leptons, and so on, and that they, in turn, are collections of differential equations. In saying all this, have I said anything about the orange juice? Or, have I just made statements about constructs in my mind? What do you think?
   e. Consider the statement, "Words are just tokens that we exchange to organize our behavior; we don't know anything, really, about what it is they refer to, but they help us organize our social behavior. Reality is a mutual hallucination. It only looks the way it does because all of us have the same, more or less, mental apparatus, and we act as if it's there." Do you agree with this statement? Why or why not?

f. Describe how you might use insights from this sequence of questions to become a better business professional.

5. Using Figure 2-14 as a guide, identify two structured processes and two dynamic processes at your university. Explain how the degree of structure varies in these processes. How do you think change to these processes is managed? Describe how the nature of the work performed in these processes varies. Explain how information systems are used to facilitate these processes. How do you think the character of the information systems supporting these processes varies?

Collaboration Exercise 2

Collaborate with a group of fellow students to answer the following questions. For this exercise do not meet face to face. Your task will be easier if you coordinate your work with SharePoint, Office 365, Google Docs with Google + or equivalent collaboration tools. (See Chapter 9 for a discussion of collaboration tools and processes.) Your answers should reflect the thinking of the entire group, and not just that of one or two individuals.

The purpose of this exercise is to compute the cost of class registration. To do so, we will consider both class registration processes as well as information systems that support them.

1. Class registration processes:
    a. List as many processes involved in class registration as you can. Consider class registration from the standpoint of students, faculty, departments, and the university. Consider resources such as classrooms, classroom sizes, and requirements for special facilities, such as audiovisual equipment, labs, and similar needs. Also consider the need for departments to ensure that classes are offered in such a manner that students can complete a major within a 4- or 5-year time period. For this exercise, ignore graduate schools.
    b. For each process, identify human actors. Estimate the number of hours each actor spends in the roles that he or she plays per enrollment period. Interview, if possible, two or three actors in each role to determine the time they spend in that role, per term.
    c. Estimate the labor cost of the processes involved in class registration. Assume the fully burdened (wages plus benefits plus applicable taxes) hourly rate of clerical staff is $50 per hour, that of professorial staff is $80. Determine the number of departments involved in registration, and estimate the number of clerical and professional actors involved in each. Use averages, but realize that some departments are much larger than others.
2. Information systems:
    a. For each process identified in question 1, list supporting information systems. Consider information systems that are used university-wide, those used by departments, and those used by individuals.
    b. For each information system identified in part a, above, describe the five components of that information system.
    c. List sources of cost for each of the five components identified in your answer to part a. Consider both development and operational costs. Explain how some of the personnel costs in your answer here may overlap with the costs of actors in processes. Why will only some of those costs overlap? Do all of the costs of class registration information systems apply to the cost of class registration business processes? Why or why not?
    d. As a student, you have no reasonable way to estimate particular information systems costs in your answer to part c, above. However, using your best judgment, estimate the range of total costs. Would it be closer to $10,000? $100,000? $1,000,000? More? Justify your answer.
3. Effectiveness and efficiency:
    a. What does the term *effectiveness* mean when applied to business processes? List as many pertinent effectiveness objectives for class registration as possible. List possible measures for each objective.
    b. What does the term *efficiency* mean when applied to business processes? List as many pertinent efficiency objectives for class registration as possible. List possible measures for each objective.
4. The quarter system. Many universities operate on a four-term quarter system that requires class registration four times per year as opposed to semester systems that require class registration just three times per year. As of 2011, the state of Washington has experienced large tax revenue reductions and has severely cut the budget of state universities, resulting in substantial increases in student tuition and fees, yet the University of Washington continues to operate on a quarter system.
    a. Assume that you work for a university using a quarter system. Justify that system. Can your argument be based upon registration process efficiency? Why or why not? Can it be based on registration process effectiveness? Why or why not?
    b. Assume you attend a university on a quarter system. Using your answers to questions 1 and 2, write a two-page memo explaining the advantages of converting to a semester system.
    c. Considering your answers to questions 1 and 2, do you think it would be wise for universities to convert to semester systems? Why or why not? Would

you recommend a national policy for universities to use the semester system?

d. If converting from a quarter system to a semester system is advantageous, why not convert to a one-term system? What would be the advantages and disadvantages of such a system? Would you recommend one if it reduced your tuition by 25 percent? 50 percent? 75 percent?

e. At present, there has been no public outcry to convert the University of Washington to a semester system. There has been, however, considerable public anguish about the increasing costs of tuition. Why do you suppose this situation exists?

f. Given all of your answers to these questions, which type of term system (e.g., quarter, semester, year) does your team believe is best? Justify your answer.

CASE STUDY 2

An Amazon of Innovation

On November 29, 2010, Amazon.com customers ordered 13.7 million items worldwide, an average of 158 items per second. On its peak order fulfillment day, Amazon.com shipped more than 9 million units, and over the entire 2010 holiday season it shipped to 178 countries.[5] Such performance is only possible because of Amazon.com's innovative use of information systems. Some of Amazon.com's major innovations are listed in Figure 2-15.

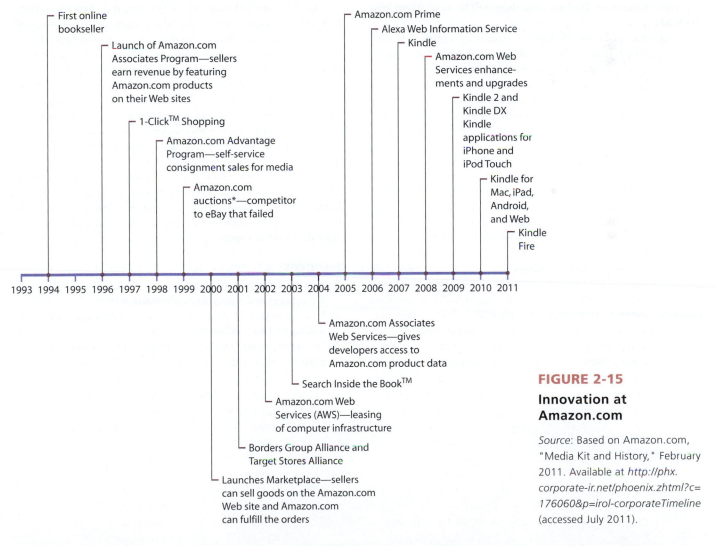

FIGURE 2-15

Innovation at Amazon.com

Source: Based on Amazon.com, "Media Kit and History," February 2011. Available at *http://phx. corporate-ir.net/phoenix.zhtml?c= 176060&p=irol-corporateTimeline* (accessed July 2011).

---

[5] Amazon.com, "Third-Generation Kindle Now the Bestselling Product of All Time on Amazon Worldwide," News release, December 27, 2010. Available at *http://phx.corporate-ir.net/phoenix.zhtml?c=176060&p=irol-newsArticle&ID=1510745&highlight=* (accessed June 2011).

You may think of Amazon.com as simply an online retailer, and that is indeed where the company has achieved most of its success. To achieve that success, Amazon.com had to build enormous supporting infrastructure—just imagine the information systems, processes, and infrastructure needed to ship 9 million items on a single day. That infrastructure, however, is only needed during the busy holiday season. Most of the year, Amazon.com is left with excess infrastructure capacity. Starting in 2000, Amazon.com began to lease some of that capacity to other companies. In the process, it played a key role in the creation of what is termed *the cloud* and *cloud services*, which you will learn about in Chapter 3. For now, just think of cloud services as Internet-based computer resources that are leased on flexible terms. Today, Amazon.com's business can be grouped into three major categories:

- Online retailing
- Order fulfillment services
- Cloud services

Consider each.

Amazon.com created the business model for online retailing. It began as an online bookstore, but every year since 1998 it has added new product categories. In 2011, the company sold goods in 29 product categories. Undoubtedly, there will be more by the time you read this.

Amazon.com is involved in all aspects of online retailing. It sells its own inventory. It incentivizes you, via its Associates program, to sell its inventory as well. Or, it will help you sell your own inventory within its product pages or through one of its consignment venues. Online auctions are the only major aspect of online sales in which Amazon.com does not participate. It tried auctions in 1999, but it could never make inroads against eBay.[6]

Today, it's hard to remember how much of what we take for granted was pioneered by Amazon.com. "Customers who bought this, also bought"; online customer reviews; customer ranking of customer reviews; book lists; Look Inside the Book; automatic free shipping for certain orders or frequent customers; and Kindle books and devices were all novel concepts when Amazon.com introduced them.

Amazon.com's retailing business operates on very thin margins. Products are usually sold at discounts from the stated retail price, and 2-day shipping is free for Amazon Prime members (frequent buyers). How does Amazon.com do it? For one, Amazon.com drives its employees incredibly hard. Former employees complain of long hours, severe pressure, and a heavy workload. But a company can only drive its employees so hard.

What else explains those thin margins? Another major factor is efficient business processes. When you are shipping 13 million items a day, saving a tenth of a cent in operations expense on each item saves $130,000 a day! Amazon.com also has been able to find ways to use the benefits of Moore's Law and the innovative use of nearly free data processing, storage, and communication to improve its business processes.

The second major category of Amazon.com products is order fulfillment services. You can ship your inventory to an Amazon.com warehouse and have Amazon.com manage it and ship to your customers. Amazon.com also can handle your customers' returns. All for a small processing fee. Your information systems can access Amazon.com's information systems just as if they were your own. Using a technology known as Web services (discussed in Chapter 5), your order processing information systems can directly integrate, over the Web, with Amazon.com's inventory, fulfillment, and shipping applications. Your customers need not know that Amazon.com played any role at all.

Why is Amazon.com able to do all this for a small fee? Because it uses the same, highly tuned and efficient business processes for fulfilling your orders as it does its own. Amazon.com is, in essence, leasing its process expertise to you.

The third product category is Amazon Web Services (AWS). With AWS, organizations can lease time on Amazon.com's computer equipment in very flexible ways. Amazon.com's Elastic Cloud 2 enables organizations to expand and contract the computer resources they need within minutes. Amazon.com has a variety of payment plans, and it is possible to buy computer time for less than a penny an hour. This dynamic, elastic leasing is only possible because the leasing organization's computer programs interface directly with Amazon.com's computer programs to programmatically scale up and scale down the resources leased. For example, if a news site publishes a story that causes a sudden surge of traffic, that news site can, programmatically, request, configure, and use more computing resources for an hour, a day, a month, whatever. Amazon.com also uses its cloud to support Silk, the innovative browser on the Kindle Fire. You will learn more about the cloud in Chapter 3.

Questions

1. In what ways does Amazon.com, as a company, evidence the willingness and ability to collaborate?
2. In what ways does Amazon.com, as a company, evidence the willingness and ability to experiment?
3. In what ways do you think the employees at Amazon.com must be able to perform systems and abstract thinking?

---

[6] For a fascinating glimpse of this story from someone inside the company, see "Early Amazon: Auctions" at *http://glinden.blogspot.com/2006/04/early-Amazon.com-auctions.html* (accessed June 2011).

4. Describe, at a high level, the principal roles played by each of the five components of an information system that supports Amazon.com's order fulfillment information systems.
5. Summarize the importance of business processes to Amazon.com's success.
6. Choose any five of the innovations in Figure 2-15 and explain how you think Moore's Law facilitated that innovation.

7. Suppose you work for Amazon.com or a company that takes innovation as seriously as Amazon does. What do you suppose is the likely reaction to an employee who says to his or her boss, "But, I don't know how to do that!"?
8. Using your own words and based on your own experience, what skills and abilities do you think you need to have to thrive at an organization like Amazon.com?

INFORMATION TECHNOLOGY

The two chapters in Part 2 address the idea that information technology is the foundation for MIS. You may think that such technology is unimportant to you as a business professional. However, as demonstrated by FlexTime and the university's intramural sports league, today's managers and business professionals work with information technology all the time as consumers, if not in a more involved way.

Chapter 3 discusses hardware, software, and computer networks. It defines basic terms and fundamental computing concepts. You will need these terms so that, for example, when we refer to thin-client or thick-client applications later in this text, you will know what those terms mean. Also, you may, like Neil and Kelly, someday work in a small business and have important decisions to make about what computing equipment and software that you need.

Chapter 4 describes database processing. You will learn the purpose and roles for databases and database applications. You will also learn how to create simple

entity-relationship data models, which are abstractions from which you can create database structure. We will illustrate database modeling and design using the database employed by the intramural sports league.

The purpose of these two chapters is to teach you technology sufficient for you to be an effective IT consumer, like Neil at FlexTime. You will learn basic terms, fundamental concepts, and useful frameworks so that you will have the knowledge to ask good questions and make appropriate requests of the IS professionals who will serve you. Those concepts and frameworks will be far more useful to you than the latest technology trend, which may be outdated by the time you graduate.

"Neil, I don't want to put the condo up as collateral."

"Kelly, you were there. We heard him together: Our house appraisal came in too low, and they want more collateral. It's either the condo or take another $150,000 out of the building budget."

"If this economy doesn't improve and if FlexTime can't support the new mortgage, we could lose it all. The business, our house, everything. The condo would be all we have left."

"OK, Kelly, let's look at the costs again."

Neil opens his file on a computer. They look at it together.

"The land, the basic building construction, the parking lots . . . I don't see how we get those costs down, but I'll talk to the contractor again. What about the locker rooms? Can we do anything to bring the locker room costs down?"

"Neil, I've been thinking about that. Maybe we go to a warehouse look. Of course we have to have showers, toilets, sinks, and mirrors . . . and the lockers, but what if we go radically industrial? We could save on tile and fixtures."

"OK, Kelly, that's a start. What else?"

"Hey, Neil, what's this $175,000 for network infrastructure? What do we need that for?"

"Hooking up all the computers."

"$175,000 to hook up a computer? Come on, Neil, get real."

"Kelly, it's not just one computer, it's all of our computers. Plus all the new gear."

"Speaking of new gear!" Felix sticks his head into Neil's office, "Check out my new shoes. They talk to my wristband and, if I have a wireless network nearby, the wristband talks to the network and stores my workout data on my workout Web site. Cool! This gonna work in the new building?"

Felix heads down the hall.

"See what I mean, Kelly? Plus all the new machines have network adapters—either wired or wireless. And this is just the tip of the iceberg. Everybody wants to have their workout data collected, stored, and processed. We're going to have to store more and more personal workout data. And it's got to get from the spinning machine, or the shoes, or the whatever, to the network somehow."

"Neil, I can understand spending money on wires; they're made of something and they have to be installed. But wireless? How come the air costs $175,000?"

"That's not fair, Kelly. The $175,000 includes wires installed in the walls, but actually, that's not a big expense. The major expenses are equipment items like switches, routers, and other equipment that can give us the performance we need."

"Neil, this stuff is expensive. Cisco router??? Why do we need four of them? Or, hey, what is a VPN/firewall appliance? Appliance? Like a toaster? Pricey little number. Can we get by without it? There must be some fat in here we can remove."

Neil grimaces.

"Neil, why don't we just use iPhones? They talk to shoes, too. Like Felix."

"You mean have our clients use an iPhone app?"

"Yeah. I tried one last week, Neil, and it was great. I was out running and it worked just like my cell phone. I didn't have a wireless network anywhere near me. When I got back here I used the app to download the data to our computer. Why don't our clients do that?"

"Kelly, where is FlexTime in that transaction?"

"FlexTime? Nowhere. It was just me and the shoes and the iPhone and the app and, ah Neil, I get the picture. Why would they need us?"

"Plus we have to do all we can to support whatever devices are coming down the road in the next 10 years."

"Neil, I'm in over my head on this. I don't even know the difference between a LAN and a WAN. But, I'll talk to our architect and try to get the locker room costs down. Meanwhile, can you take a look at this $175,000? Do we need all of it? Do we need all of it now? Can we shave even $20,000 off?"

Q1. What do business professionals need to know about computer hardware?

Q2. What do business professionals need to know about software?

Q3. What types of computer networks exist?

Q4. What do business professionals need to know about the Internet?

Q5. What happens on a typical Web server?

Q6. How do organizations benefit from virtual private networks (VPNs)?

Chapter Preview

This chapter presents the minimum essential knowledge you'll need to be an effective consumer of today's hardware, software, and network technology. You may be asking, why? What should it matter to me? The answer is that if you work for a small organization, you will likely be in a position like Kelly's and Neil's at FlexTime. You will need to make decisions, or at least approve recommendations about what you need and how much it should cost. At FlexTime, how much do they need to pay for network infrastructure in their new building? Making that decision requires at least the knowledge in this chapter. Or, what if you work in product management for a large company? Does your product "talk" to some network? If not, could it? Should it? Does it require a LAN or a WAN? And what are those, anyway?

You may say, "Well, I'll just rely on outside experts to tell me what to do." But, that strategy may not work in the twenty-first century. Many of your competitors will be able to ask and understand technology questions—and use the money and time their knowledge saves them for other business investments, like building locker rooms and parking lots. In fact, today, basic knowledge of technology is a key component of any business professional's toolkit. So, let's get started with hardware.

Q1. What Do Business Professionals Need to Know About Computer Hardware?

As discussed in the five-component framework, **hardware** consists of electronic components and related gadgetry that input, process, output, and store data according to instructions encoded in computer programs or software. Figure 3-1 shows the components of a generic computer. This computer could be a large one at a corporate data center, it could be your PC, or it could be your iPad.

Typical **input hardware** devices are the keyboard, mouse, touch pad/screen, document scanners, and bar-code (Universal Product Code) scanners like those used in grocery stores. Microphones also are input devices. Finally, both wired and wireless data communication devices provide input data to the computer.

Processing devices include the **central processing unit (CPU)**, which is sometimes called "the brain" of the computer. Although the design of the CPU has nothing in common with the anatomy of a brain, this description is helpful, because the CPU does have the "smarts" of the machine. The CPU selects instructions, processes them, performs arithmetic and logical comparisons, and stores results of operations in memory. Some computers have two or more CPUs. A computer with two CPUs is called a **dual-processor** computer. Quad-processor computers have four CPUs. Some high-end computers have 16 or more CPUs.

FIGURE 3-1

Categories of Computer Hardware

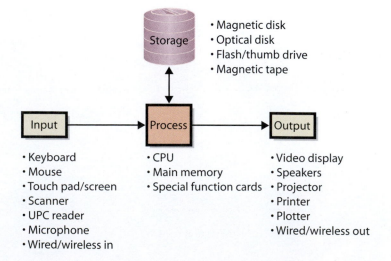

- Magnetic disk
- Optical disk
- Flash/thumb drive
- Magnetic tape

Storage

Input → Process → Output

Input:
- Keyboard
- Mouse
- Touch pad/screen
- Scanner
- UPC reader
- Microphone
- Wired/wireless in

Process:
- CPU
- Main memory
- Special function cards

Output:
- Video display
- Speakers
- Projector
- Printer
- Plotter
- Wired/wireless out

CPUs vary in speed, function, and cost. Because of Moore's Law, hardware vendors such as Intel, Advanced Micro Devices, and National Semiconductor continually improve CPU speed and capabilities while reducing CPU costs (as discussed under Moore's Law in Chapter 1). Whether you or your department needs the latest, greatest CPU depends on the nature of your work, as you will learn.

The CPU works in conjunction with **main memory**, sometimes called **RAM (random access memory)**. The CPU reads data and instructions only from main memory, processes that data, and places it back into main memory. Data on an external device, say, a DVD, must be brought into main memory before it can be processed.

Finally, computers also can have special function cards that can be added to augment its basic capabilities. A common example is a card that provides enhanced clarity and speed for the computer's video display.

Output hardware, devices that are externally connected to the computer, consist of video displays, speakers, projectors, printers, and other special-purpose devices, such as the large flatbed plotters used for making maps and other large printed displays. Wired and wireless signals are also produced by communication devices.

Storage hardware saves data and programs. Magnetic disk is by far the most common storage device, although optical disks such as CDs and DVDs also are popular. Flash drives, or as you may know them, thumb drives, are also storage devices. In large corporate data centers, data is sometimes stored on magnetic tape.

Computer Data

Before we can further describe hardware, we need to define several important terms. We begin with binary digits.

BINARY DIGITS   Computers represent data using **binary digits** called **bits**. A bit is either a zero or a one. Bits are used for computer data because they are easy to represent electronically. For example, as shown in Figure 3-2, a switch can be either closed or open. A computer can be designed so that an open switch represents zero and a closed switch represents one. Or the orientation of a magnetic field can represent a bit; magnetism in one direction represents a zero, magnetism in the opposite direction represents a one. Or, for optical media, small pits are burned onto the surface of the disk so that they will reflect light. In a given spot, a reflection means a one; no reflection means a zero.

SIZING COMPUTER DATA   All computer data are represented by bits. The data can be numbers, characters, currency amounts, photos, recordings, or whatever. All are simply a string of bits.

For reasons that interest many but are irrelevant for future managers, bits are grouped into 8-bit chunks called **bytes**. For character data, such as the letters in a person's name, one character will fit into one byte. Thus, when you read a specification that a computing device has 100 million bytes of memory, you know that the device can hold up to 100 million characters.

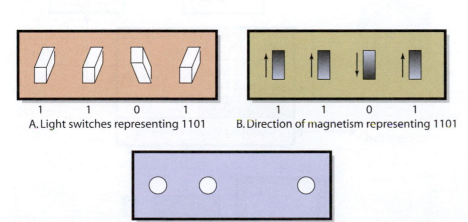

A. Light switches representing 1101   B. Direction of magnetism representing 1101

C. Reflection/no reflection representing 1101

FIGURE 3-2

Binary Digit Representations

FIGURE 3-3

Units of Data for Computer Memory

Term	Definition	Abbreviation
Byte	Number of bits to represent one character	
Kilobyte	1,024 bytes	K
Megabyte	1,024 K = 1,048,576 bytes	MB
Gigabyte	1,024 MB = 1,073,741,824 bytes	GB
Terabyte	1,024 GB = 1,099,511,627,776 bytes	TB
Petabyte	1,024 TB = 1,125,899,906,842,624 bytes	PB
Exabyte	1,024 PB = 1,152,921,504,606,846,976 bytes	EB

Bytes are used to measure sizes of noncharacter data as well. Someone might say, for example, that a given picture is 100,000 bytes in size. This statement means the length of the bit string that represents the picture is 100,000 bytes or 800,000 bits (because there are 8 bits per byte).

The specifications for the size of main memory, disk, and other computer devices are expressed in bytes. Figure 3-3 shows the set of abbreviations that are used to represent computer memory sizes. A **kilobyte**, abbreviated **K**, is a collection of 1,024 bytes. A **megabyte**, or **MB**, is 1,024 kilobytes. A **gigabyte**, or **GB**, is 1,024 megabytes, and a **terabyte**, or **TB**, is 1,024 gigabytes. A **petabyte**, or **PB**, is 1,024 terabytes, and an **exabyte**, or **EB**, is 1,024 petabytes.

How much hardware do you need? The Ethics Guide on pages 84–85 features a contrarian who sees consumers as being trapped between hardware and software vendors.

Sometimes you will see these definitions simplified as 1K equals 1,000 bytes and 1MB equals 1,000K. Such simplifications are incorrect, but they do ease the math. Also, disk and computer manufacturers have an incentive to propagate this misconception. If a disk maker defines 1MB to be 1 million bytes—and not the correct 1,024K—the manufacturer can use its own definition of MB when specifying drive capacities. A buyer may think that a disk advertised as 100MB has space for 100 × 1,024K bytes, but, in truth, the drive will have space for only 100 × 1,000,000 bytes. Normally, the distinction is not too important, but be aware of the two possible interpretations of these abbreviations.

In Fewer Than 300 Words, How Does a Computer Work?

Figure 3-4 shows a snapshot of a computer in use. The CPU is the major actor. To run a program or process data, the computer first transfers the program or data from disk to *main memory*. Then, to execute an instruction, it moves the instruction from main memory into the CPU via the data channel or bus. The CPU has a small amount of very fast memory called a cache, in which it keeps frequently used instructions. Having a large cache makes the computer faster, but cache is expensive.

FIGURE 3-4

Computer Components

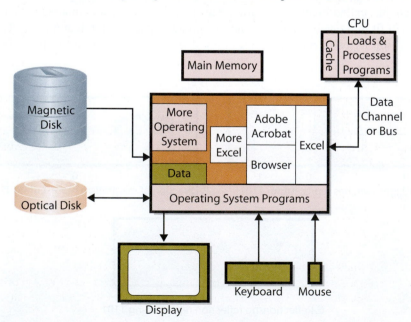

Main memory of the computer in Figure 3-4 contains program instructions for Microsoft Excel, Adobe Acrobat, and a browser (say, Google Chrome). It also contains a block of data and instructions for the **operating system (OS)**, which is a program that controls the computer's resources.

Main memory is too small to hold all of the programs and data that a user might want to process. For example, no personal computer has enough memory to hold all of the code in Microsoft Word, Excel, and Access. Consequently, the CPU loads programs into memory in chunks. In Figure 3-4, one portion of Excel was loaded into memory. When the user requested additional processing (say, to sort the spreadsheet), the CPU loaded another piece of Excel.

If the user opens another program (say, Word) or needs to load more data (say, a picture), the operating system will direct the CPU to attempt to place the new program or data into unused memory. If there is not enough memory, it will remove something, perhaps the block of memory labeled "More Excel," and then it will place the just-requested program or data into the vacated space. This process is called **memory swapping**.

Why Does a Manager Care How a Computer Works?

You can order computers with varying sizes of main memory. An employee who runs only one program at a time and who processes small amounts of data requires very little memory—1GB will be adequate. However, an employee who processes many programs at the same time (say, Word, Excel, Firefox, Access, Acrobat, and other programs) or an employee who processes very large files (pictures, movies, or sound files) needs lots of main memory, perhaps 3GB or more. If that employee's computer has too little memory, then the computer will constantly be swapping memory, and it will be slow. (This means, by the way, that if your computer is slow and if you have many programs open, you likely can improve performance by closing one or more programs. Depending on your computer and the amount of memory it has, you might also improve performance by adding more memory.)

You can also order computers with CPUs of different speeds. CPU speed is expressed in cycles called *hertz*. In 2012, a slow personal computer has a speed of 1.5 Gigahertz. A fast personal computer has a speed of 3+ Gigahertz, with dual processing. As predicted by Moore's Law, CPU speeds continually increase.

Additionally, CPUs today are classified as 32-bit or 64-bit. Without delving into the particulars, a 32-bit is less capable and cheaper than a 64-bit CPU. The latter can address more main memory; you need a 64-bit processor to effectively utilize more than 4GB of memory. The 64-bit processors have other advantages as well; as you'd expect, they are more expensive than 32-bit processors.

An employee who does only simple tasks such as word processing does not need a fast CPU; a 32-bit, 1.5 Gigahertz CPU will be fine. However, an employee who processes large, complicated spreadsheets; manipulates large database files; or edits large picture, sound, or movie files needs a fast computer like a 64-bit, dual processor with 3.5 Gigahertz or more.

One last comment: The cache and main memory are **volatile**, meaning that their contents are lost when power is off. Magnetic and optical disks and flash drives are **nonvolatile**, meaning that their contents survive when power is off. If you suddenly lose power, the contents of unsaved memory—say, documents that have been altered—will be lost. Therefore, on a desktop computer, get into the habit of frequently (every few minutes or so) saving documents or files that you are changing. Save your documents before your roommate trips over the power cord.

What Is the Difference Between a Client and a Server?

Before we can discuss computer software, you need to understand the difference between a client and a server. Figure 3-5 shows the computing environment of the typical user. Users employ **client** computers for deskwork like word processing and spreadsheet analysis. You are also using a client computer when you install a game or an application on your iPad.

Client computers also have software that enables them to connect to a network. It could be a private network at their company or school, or it could be the Internet, which is a public network.

FIGURE 3-5
Client and Server
Computers

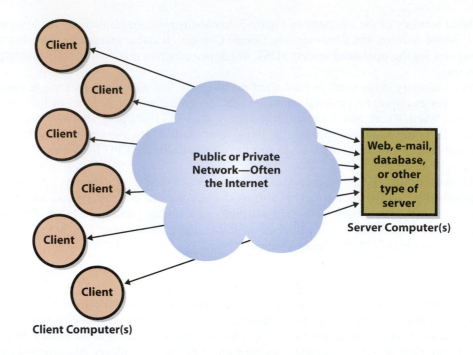

Client

Client

Client

Client

Client

Client

Public or Private Network—Often the Internet

Web, e-mail, database, or other type of server

Server Computer(s)

Client Computer(s)

Servers, as their name implies, provide some service. Some servers process e-mail; others process Web sites; others process large, shared databases; some process multiuser games; and some process iPad or other device applications.

A server is just a computer, but, as you might expect, server computers must be fast, and they usually have multiple CPUs. They need lots of main memory, say 16GB or more, and they require very large disks—often a terabyte or more. Because servers are almost always accessed from another computer via a network, they have limited video displays, or even no display at all. For the same reason, many have no keyboard. Most servers today have 64-bit processors.

For sites with large numbers of users (e.g., Amazon.com), servers are organized into a collection of servers called a **server farm**, like the one shown in Figure 3-6. Servers in a farm coordinate their activities in an incredibly sophisticated and fascinating technology dance. They receive and process hundreds, possibly thousands, of service requests per minute.

FIGURE 3-6
An Example Server Farm

As stated in Case 2, in November 29, 2010, Amazon.com processed an average of 158 order items per second for 24 hours straight. In such a dance, computers hand off partially processed requests to each other while keeping track of the current status of each request. They can pick up the pieces when a computer in the farm fails. All of this is done in the blink of an eye, with the user never knowing any part of the miracle underway. It is absolutely gorgeous engineering!

Q2. What Do Business Professionals Need to Know About Software?

As a future manager or business professional, you need to know the essential terminology and software concepts that will enable you to be an intelligent software consumer. To begin, consider the basic categories of software shown in Figure 3-7.

Every computer has an *operating system,* which is a program that controls that computer's resources. Some of the functions of an operating system are to read and write data, allocate main memory, perform memory swapping, start and stop programs, respond to error conditions, and facilitate backup and recovery. In addition, the operating system creates and manages the user interface, including the display, keyboard, mouse, and other devices.

Although the operating system makes the computer usable, it does little application-specific work. If you want to write a document or access a database, you need *application programs,* such as an iPad weather forecasting application or Oracle's customer relationship management (CRM) application.

Both client and server computers need an operating system, though they need not be the same. Further, both clients and servers can process application programs. The application's design determines whether the client, the server, or both, process it.

You need to understand two important software constraints. First, a particular version of an operating system is written for a particular type of hardware. For example, Microsoft Windows works only on processors from Intel and companies that make processors that conform to the Intel instruction set (the commands that a CPU can process). Furthermore, the 32-bit version of Windows runs only on Intel computers with 32-bit CPUs and the 64-bit version of Windows runs only on Intel computers with 64-bit CPUs. In other operating systems, such as Linux, many versions exist for many different instruction sets and for both 32- and 64-bit computers.

Second, application programs are written to use a particular operating system. Microsoft Access, for example, will only run on the Windows operating system. Some applications come in multiple versions. For example, there are Windows and Macintosh versions of Microsoft Word. But unless informed otherwise, assume that a particular application runs on just one operating system.

We will next consider the operating system and application program categories of software.

What Are the Major Operating Systems?

The major operating systems are listed in Figure 3-8. Consider each.

NONMOBILE CLIENT OPERATING SYSTEMS For nonmobile business use, the most important operating system is Microsoft **Windows**. Some version of Windows resides on more than 85 percent of the world's desktops, and, if we consider just business users, the figure is more

	Operating System	Application Programs
Client	Programs that control the client computer's resources	Applications that are processed on client computers
Server	Programs that control the server computer's resources	Applications that are processed on server computers

FIGURE 3-7

Types of Software

Category	Operating System	Used for	Remarks
Nonmobile clients	Windows	Personal computer clients	Most widely used operating system in business. Current version is Windows 7. Since 2006, can also run on Macintosh hardware.
	Mac OS Lion	Macintosh clients	Used by graphic artists and gaining popularity in other communities.
	Unix	Workstation clients	Popular on powerful client computers used in engineering, computer-assisted design, architecture. Difficult for the nontechnical user.
	Linux	Just about anything	Open source variant of Unix. Adapted to almost every type of computing device. On a PC, used with Open Office application software.
Mobile clients	Symbian	Nokia, Samsung, and other phones	Popular worldwide, but less so in North America. Market share in decline.
	BlackBerry OS	Research In Motion BlackBerries	Device and OS developed for use by business. Very popular in beginning, but strongly challenged by iPhone and others.
	iOS	iPhone, iPod Touch, iPad	Rapidly increasing installed base with success of the iPhone and iPad.
	Android	T-Mobile and other phones and devices	Linux-based phone operating system from Google. Rapidly increasing market share.
Servers	Windows Server	Servers	Businesses with a strong commitment to Microsoft.
	Unix	Servers	Fading from use. Replaced by Linux.
	Linux	Servers	Very popular. Aggressively pushed by IBM.

FIGURE 3-8

Major Operating Systems

than 95 percent. Many different versions of client Windows are available: Windows 7, Windows Vista, and Windows XP run on client computers.

Apple Computer, Inc., developed its own operating system for the Macintosh, **Mac OS**. The current version is Mac OS Lion. Macintosh computers are used primarily by graphic artists and workers in the arts community. Mac OS was designed originally to run the line of CPU processors from Motorola. In 1994, Mac switched to the PowerPC processor line from IBM. As of 2006, Macintosh computers are available for both PowerPC and Intel CPUs. A Macintosh with an Intel processor is able to run both Windows and the Mac OS.

Unix is an operating system that was developed at Bell Labs in the 1970s. It has been the workhorse of the scientific and engineering communities since then. Unix is generally regarded as being more difficult to use than either Windows or the Macintosh. Many Unix users know and employ an arcane language for manipulating files and data. However, once they surmount the rather steep learning curve, most Unix users become fanatic supporters of the system. Sun Microsystems and other vendors of computers for scientific and engineering applications are the major proponents of Unix. In general, Unix is not for the business user.

Linux is a version of Unix that was developed by the open source community (discussed on page 63). This community is a loosely coupled group of programmers who mostly volunteer their time to contribute code to develop and maintain Linux. The open source community owns Linux, and there is no fee to use it. Linux can run on client computers, but usually only when budget is of paramount concern.

MOBILE CLIENT OPERATING SYSTEMS Figure 3-8 lists four principal mobile operating systems. Symbian was popular in Europe and the Far East, less so in North America. Its popularity is in decline. BlackBerry OS was one of the most successful, early mobile operating systems; it is used on BlackBerry devices, primarily by business users. It is now losing market share to iOS and Android.

iOS is the operating system used on the iPhone, iPad, and iPod Touch. When first released, it broke new ground on ease of use and compelling display, features that are being copied by the BlackBerry OS and Android. With the popularity the iPhone and iPad, Apple has been increasing the market share of iOS. In 2011, iOS had 44% of the mobile market.

Android is a mobile operating system licensed by Google. Android devices have a very loyal following, especially among technical users. Recently, Android has been gaining market share over the BlackBerry OS.

Most industry observers would agree that Apple has led the way, both with the Mac OS and iOS, in creating easy-to-use interfaces. Certainly, many innovative ideas have first appeared in a Macintosh or iSomething and then later been added, in one form or another, to Windows or one of the mobile operating systems.

SERVER OPERATING SYSTEMS The last three rows of Figure 3-8 show the three most popular server operating systems. Windows Server is a version of Windows that has been specially designed and configured for server use. It has much more stringent and restrictive security procedures than other versions of Windows and is popular on servers in organizations that have made a strong commitment to Microsoft.

Unix can also be used on servers, but it is gradually being replaced by Linux.

Linux is frequently used on servers by organizations that want, for whatever reason, to avoid a server commitment to Microsoft. IBM is the primary proponent of Linux, and in the past it has used it as means to better compete against Microsoft. Although IBM does not own Linux, IBM has developed many business systems solutions that use Linux. By using Linux, IBM does not have to pay a license fee to Microsoft or another OS vendor.

Own Versus License

When you buy a computer program, whether an operating system or an application, you are not actually buying that program. Instead, you are buying a **license** to use that program. For example, when you buy a Windows license, Microsoft is selling you the right to use Windows. Microsoft continues to own the Windows program. Large organizations do not buy a license for each computer user. Instead, they negotiate a site license, which is a flat fee that authorizes the company to install the product (operating system or application) on many or all of that company's computers, or on all of the computers at a specific site.

In the case of Linux, no company can sell you a license to use it. It is owned by the open source community, which states that Linux has no license fee (with certain reasonable restrictions). Large companies such as IBM and smaller companies such as RedHat can make money by providing customer support for and education about Linux, but no company makes money selling Linux licenses.

CLOUD COMPUTING AND VIRTUALIZATION You may hear two new terms that have become popular with regard to server computer hardware and software: cloud computing and virtualization. **Cloud computing** is a form of hardware/software leasing in which organizations obtain server resources from vendors that specialize in server processing. The amount of server time and the resources leased is flexible and can change dynamically (and dramatically). Customers pay only for resources used. Major companies that offer cloud computing products include Amazon.com, IBM, Microsoft, Oracle, and RackSpace.

Your university is a prime candidate to use cloud computing for systems like class registration. If you are on a semester program, registration occurs only three times a year, so any servers that are dedicated solely to registration will be idle most of the year. With cloud computing, your university could lease server resources when it needs them from a cloud vendor like IBM. Your university will use substantial computing resources to support registration in August, January, and June, but nearly none in other months. It will pay just for the services that it uses.

Cloud computing enables multiple organizations to utilize the same computing infrastructure. Tax preparation firms can use the same IBM servers in April that your university uses in August, January, and June. In a sense, cloud computing is a form of CPU-cycle inventory consolidation.

Cloud computing is feasible because cloud vendors harness the power of virtualization. Virtualization is the process whereby multiple operating systems share the same hardware. Thus, with virtualization one server can support, say, two instances of Windows Server, one instance of Linux, and three instances of Windows 7. Because these instances are isolated, it will appear to each that it has exclusive control over the server computer.

Because of virtualization, it is quite easy for cloud vendors to reconfigure servers to support changes in workload. If your university needs another 100 servers in August, IBM need only add 100 instances of your university's server environment to its virtual computers. If, 2 days later, your school needs another 100 instances, IBM allocates another 100. Behind the scenes, IBM is likely moving these instances among servers, balancing its workload on the computers that run the virtual operating systems. None of that activity is visible to your university, or to the students who are registering for class.

What Types of Applications Exist, and How Do Organizations Obtain Them?

Application software performs a service or function. Some application programs are general purpose, such as Microsoft Excel or Word. Other application programs provide specific functions. QuickBooks, for example, is an application program that provides general ledger and other accounting functions. We begin by describing categories of application programs and then describe sources for them as shown in Figure 3-9.

WHAT CATEGORIES OF APPLICATION PROGRAMS EXIST? **Horizontal-market application** software provides capabilities common across all organizations and industries. Word processors, graphics programs, spreadsheets, and presentation programs are all horizontal-market application software.

Examples of such software are Microsoft Word, Excel, and PowerPoint. Examples from other vendors are Adobe's Acrobat, Photoshop, and PageMaker and Jasc Corporation's Paint Shop Pro. iPhone and iPad e-mail and texting applications are other examples. Horizontal-market applications are used in a wide variety of businesses across all industries. They are purchased off-the-shelf, and little customization of features is necessary (or possible).

Vertical-market application software serves the needs of a specific industry. Examples of such programs are those used by dental offices to schedule appointments and bill patients; those used by auto mechanics to keep track of customer data and customers' automobile repairs; and those used by parts warehouses to track inventory, purchases, and sales. The iPad application FitnessBuilder, one that Felix and Kelly might use at FlexTime, is another vertical-market application that tracks workouts.

Some vertical applications can be altered or customized. If so, the company that licenses the application software will provide such services for a fee or offer referrals to qualified consultants who can provide this service.

One-of-a-kind application software is developed for a specific, unique need. The IRS develops such software, for example, because it has needs that no other organization has.

HOW DO THIN CLIENTS COMPARE TO THICK CLIENTS? When you use an application such as Adobe Acrobat, it runs only on your computer and does not need to connect to any server to run. Such programs are called desktop programs and are not considered clients.

Applications that process code on both the client and the server are called **client-server applications**. A **thick-client** application is an application program that must be preinstalled on the client. A **thin-client** application is one that runs within a browser and need not be preinstalled. When the user of a thin-client application starts that application, if any code is needed, the browser loads that code dynamically from the server. No one needs to preinstall any client code. To see a

FIGURE 3-9

Application Software Sources and Types

Software Type	Software Source		
	Off-the-shelf	Off-the-shelf and then customized	Custom-developed
Horizontal applications	■		
Vertical applications	■	■	
One-of-a-kind applications			■

thin-client in action, open a browser and go to *www.LearningMIS.com*. When you do so, the browser starts by downloading needed code from the server that hosts that site.

To summarize, the relationship of application types is as follows:

- Desktop application
- Client-server application
    - Thick client
    - Thin client

Thick and thin clients each have their own advantages and disadvantages. Because thick clients can be larger (they do not have to be downloaded while the user waits), they can have more features and functions. However, they do have to be installed, such as when you buy a new application for your iPhone or other mobile device. Periodically, you update to new versions when you sync your phone or otherwise connect to the source of the application. To you as an individual, this isn't much of a problem. However, in a large organization, where it is important that everyone use the same version of the same application, such installation and version management is an expensive administrative burden.

Thin-client applications are preferred to thick-client applications because they require only a browser; no special client software needs to be installed. This also means that when a new version of a thin-client application is created, the browser automatically downloads that new code. However, because the code is downloaded during use, thin clients need to be smaller.

Today, organizations use a wide mixture of applications and operating systems. Figure 3-10 shows a typical situation. Two computers are running Windows, one is running Mac OS and one is running iOS on an iPhone. The first two client computers use thin-client applications in a

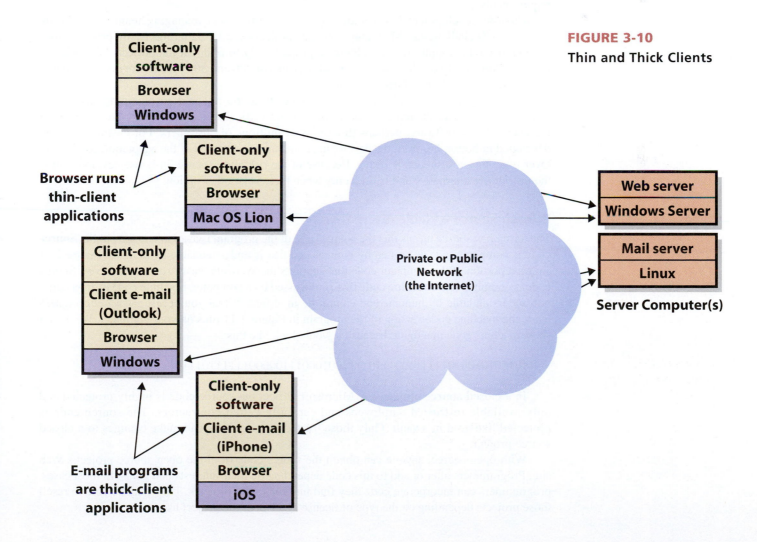

FIGURE 3-10
Thin and Thick Clients

browser. The third and fourth client computers each have a thick-client e-mail application installed; one is running Microsoft Office Outlook and the second is running Apple's iPhone e-mail application.

Figure 3-10 shows two servers; the Windows Server computer is supporting a Web server and the Linux server is supporting e-mail.

How Do Organizations Acquire Application Software?

You can acquire application software in exactly the same ways that you can buy a new suit. The quickest and least risky option is to buy your suit off-the-rack. With this method, you get your suit immediately, and you know exactly what it will cost. You may not, however, get a good fit. Alternately, you can buy your suit off-the-rack and have it altered. This will take more time, it may cost more, and there's some possibility that the alteration will result in a poor fit. Most likely, however, an altered suit will fit better than an off-the-rack one.

Finally, you can hire a tailor to make a custom suit. In this case, you will have to describe what you want, be available for multiple fittings, and be willing to pay considerably more. Although there is an excellent chance of a great fit, there is also the possibility of a disaster. Still, if you want a yellow and orange polka-dot silk suit with a hissing rattlesnake on the back, tailor-made is the only way to go. You can buy computer software in exactly the same ways: off-the-shelf software, off-the-shelf with alterations software, or tailor-made. Tailor-made software is called **custom-developed software**.

Organizations develop custom application software themselves or hire a development vendor. Like buying the yellow and orange polka-dot suit, such development is done in situations in which the needs of the organization are so unique that no horizontal or vertical applications are available. By developing custom software, the organization can tailor its application to fit its requirements.

Custom development is difficult and risky. Staffing and managing teams of software developers is challenging. Managing software projects can be daunting. Many organizations have embarked on application development projects only to find that the projects take twice as long—or longer—to finish as planned. Cost overruns of 200 and 300 percent are not uncommon. We will discuss such risks further in Chapter 12.

In addition, every application program needs to be adapted to changing needs and technologies. The adaptation costs of horizontal and vertical software are amortized over all of the users of that software, perhaps thousands or millions of customers. For custom software developed in-house, however, the developing company must pay all of the adaptation costs itself. Over time, this cost burden is heavy. Because of the risk and expense, in-house development is the last-choice alternative and is used only when there is no other option.

Is Open Source a Viable Alternative?

The term *open source* means that the source code of the program is available to the public. **Source code** is computer code as written by humans and that is understandable by humans. Figure 3-11 shows a portion of the computer code that supports the Web site *www.LearningMIS.com*. Source code is compiled into **machine code** that is processed by a computer. Machine code is, in general, not understandable by humans and cannot be modified. When you access *www.LearningMIS .com*, the machine code version of the program in Figure 3-11 runs on your computer. We do not show machine code in a figure because it would look like this:

```
1101001010010111111001110111100100011100000111111011101111110011 . . .
```

In a **closed source** project, say Microsoft Office, the source code is highly protected and only available to trusted employees and carefully vetted contractors. The source code is protected like gold in a vault. Only those trusted programmers can make changes to a closed source project.

With open source, anyone can obtain the source code from the open source project's Web site. Programmers alter or add to this code depending on their interests and goals. In most cases, programmers can incorporate code they find into their own projects. They may be able to resell those projects depending on the type of license agreement the project uses.

```
#region Dependency Properties

public static readonly DependencyProperty
    LessonIDProperty = DependencyProperty.Register(
        "LessonID",
        typeof(int),
        typeof(Lesson),
        new PropertyMetadata(new PropertyChangedCallback(Lesson.OnLessonDataChanged)));

public int LessonID
{
    get { return (int)GetValue(LessonIDProperty); }
    set { SetValue(LessonIDProperty, value); }
}

private static void OnLessonDataChanged(DependencyObject d, DependencyPropertyChangedEventArgs e)
{

    // reload the stage for the new TopicID property
    Lesson thisLesson = d as Lesson;

    lessonObject = thisLesson; // there is only one lesson object ... this is a static ref to it

    thisLesson.LoadLessonData(); // get data from xml file on server
    //call to thisLesson.CreateLessonForm(); must be done after load b/c of asynchronous read
}

#endregion
```

FIGURE 3-11

Example Source Code

Open source succeeds because of collaboration. A programmer examines the source code and identifies a need or project that seems interesting. He or she then creates a new feature, redesigns or reprograms an existing feature, or fixes a known problem. That code is then sent to others in the open source project who then evaluate the quality and merits of the work and add it to the product, if appropriate.

Typically, there is a lot of give and take; there are many cycles of iteration and feedback. Because of this iteration, a well-managed project with strong peer reviews can result in very high-quality code, like that in Linux.

The Internet proved to be a great asset for open source, and many open source projects became successful, including:

- Open Office (a Microsoft Office look-alike)
- Firefox (a browser)
- MySQL (a DBMS, see Chapter 5)
- Apache (a Web server, see Chapter 4)
- Ubuntu (a Windows-like desktop operating system)
- Android (a mobile-device operating system)

WHY DO PROGRAMMERS VOLUNTEER THEIR SERVICES? To anyone who has never enjoyed writing computer programs, it is difficult to understand why anyone would donate their time and skills to contribute to open source projects. Programming is, however, an intense combination of art and logic, and designing and writing a complicated computer program is exceedingly pleasurable (and addictive). If you have an artistic and logical mind, you ought to try it.

Anyway, the first reason that people contribute to open source is that it is great fun! Additionally, some people contribute to open source because it gives them the freedom to choose the projects upon which they work. They may have a programming day job that is not terribly interesting, say, writing a program to manage a computer printer. Their job pays the bills, but it is not fulfilling.

In the 1950s, Hollywood studio musicians suffered as they recorded the same style of music over and over for a long string of uninteresting movies. To keep their sanity, those musicians would gather on Sundays to play jazz, and a number of high-quality jazz clubs resulted. That's what open source is to programmers: A place where they can exercise their creativity while working on projects they find interesting and fulfilling.

Another reason for contributing to open source is to exhibit one's skill, both for pride as well as to find a job or employment as a consultant. A final reason is to start a business selling services to support an open source product.

SO, IS OPEN SOURCE VIABLE? The answer depends on the individual company or business, and its needs. Open source has certainly become legitimate. According to *The Economist,* "It is now generally accepted that the future will involve a blend of both proprietary and open-source software."[1] During your career, open source will likely take a greater and greater role in software. However, whether open source works for a particular situation depends on the requirements and constraints of that situation.

Q3. What Types of Computer Networks Exist?

A computer **network** is a collection of computers that communicate with one another over transmission lines or wireless connections. As shown in Figure 3-12, the three basic types of networks are local area networks, wide area networks, and internets.

A **local area network (LAN)** connects computers that reside in a single geographic location on the premises of the company that operates the LAN. The number of connected computers can range from two to several hundred. The distinguishing characteristic of a LAN is *a single location*. **Wide area networks (WANs)** connect computers at different geographic locations. The computers in two separated company sites must be connected using a WAN. To illustrate, the computers for a College of Business located on a single campus can be connected via a LAN. The computers for a College of Business located on multiple campuses must be connected via a WAN.

The single- versus multiple-site distinction is important. With a LAN, an organization can place communication lines wherever it wants, because all lines reside on its premises. The same is not true for a WAN. A company with offices in Chicago and Atlanta cannot run a wire down the freeway to connect computers in the two cities. Instead, the company contracts with a communications vendor that is licensed by the government and that already has lines, or has the authority to run new lines, between the two cities.

An internet is a network of networks. Internets connect LANs, WANs, and other internets. The most famous internet is **"the Internet"** (with an uppercase letter *I*), the collection of networks that you use when you send e-mail or access a Web site. In addition to the Internet, private networks of networks, called *internets*, also exist.

The networks that comprise an internet use a large variety of communication methods and conventions, and data must flow seamlessly across them. To provide seamless flow, an elaborate scheme called a *layered protocol* is used. The details of protocols are beyond the scope of this text. Just understand that a **protocol** is a set of rules that two communicating devices follow. There are many different protocols; some are used for LANs, some are used for WANs, some are used for internets and the Internet, and some are used for all of these. We will identify several common protocols in this chapter.

What Are the Components of a LAN?

A LAN is a group of computers connected together on a single site. Usually the computers are located within a half mile or so of each other. The key distinction, however, is that all of the

FIGURE 3-12

Three Types of Computer Networks

Type	Characteristic
Local area network (LAN)	Computers connected at a single physical site
Wide area network (WAN)	Computers connected among two or more geographically separated sites
The Internet and internets	Networks of networks

---

[1] "Unlocking the Cloud," *The Economist,* May 28, 2009. Available at *www.economist.com/opinion/displaystory.cfm? story_id=13740181* (accessed June 2009).

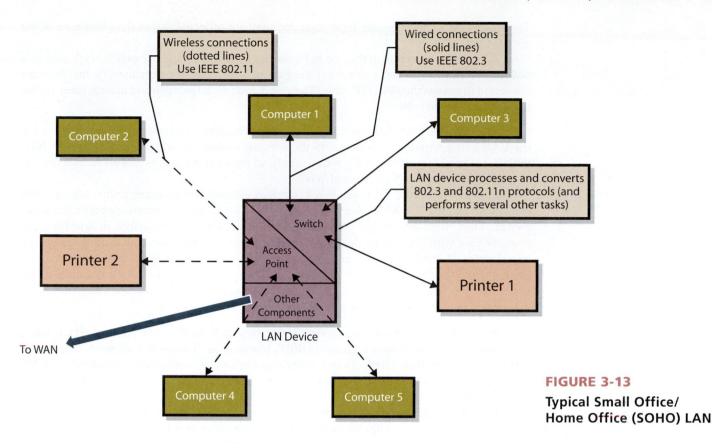

FIGURE 3-13

Typical Small Office/ Home Office (SOHO) LAN

computers are located on property controlled by the organization that operates the LAN. This means that the organization can run cables wherever needed to connect the computers.

A TYPICAL SOHO LAN Figure 3-13 shows a LAN that is typical of those in a **small office or a home office (SOHO)**. Typically such LANs have fewer than a dozen or so computers and printers. Many businesses, of course, operate LANs that are much larger than this one. The principles are the same for a larger LAN, but the additional complexity is beyond the scope of this text.

The computers and printers in Figure 3-13 communicate via a mixture of wired and wireless connections. Computers 1 and 3 and Printer 1 use wired connections; Computers 2, 4, and 5 as well as Printer 2 use wireless connections. The devices and protocols used differ for wired and wireless connectivity.

WIRED CONNECTIVITY Computers 1 and 3 and Printer 1 are connected to a **switch**, which is a special-purpose computer that receives and transmits wired traffic on the LAN. In Figure 3-13, the switch is contained within a box labeled "LAN device." When either of these two computers communicates with each other or with Printer 1, it does so by sending the traffic to the switch, which redirects the traffic to the other computer or Printer 1.

The **LAN device** contains several important networking components. It has a switch, as just described, and, as you are about to learn, it also has a device for wireless communication. In most cases, it has devices for connecting to a WAN and via the WAN to the Internet, and numerous other elements. For SOHO applications, LAN devices are usually provided by the phone or cable vendor. They have many different names, depending on their brand.

Each wired computer or printer on the LAN has a **network interface card (NIC)**, which is a device that connects the computer's or printer's circuitry to the network cables. The NIC works with programs in each device to implement the protocols necessary for communication. Most computers today ship from the factory with an onboard NIC, which is a NIC built into the computer's circuitry.

The computers, printers, and switch on a wired LAN are connected using one of two wired media. Most LAN connections are made using **unshielded twisted pair (UTP) cable**. This cable contains sets of wires that are twisted together to improve signal quality. However, if the connection carries a lot of traffic, the UTP cable may be replaced by **optical fiber cables**.

The signals on such cables are light rays, and they are reflected inside the glass core of the optical fiber cable.

LANs that are larger than the one in Figure 3-13 use more than one switch. Typically, in a building with several floors, a switch is placed on each floor, and the computers on that floor are connected to the switch with UTP cable. The switches on each floor connect to each other via the faster-speed optical cable.

WIRELESS CONNECTIONS In Figure 3-13, three of the computers and one printer are connected to the LAN using wireless technology. In the wireless computers and printer, a **wireless NIC (WNIC)** is used instead of a NIC. Today, nearly all personal computers and all mobile devices ship from the factory with an onboard WNIC.

As shown in Figure 3-13, the WNIC devices connect to an **access point**, which is the component of the LAN device that processes wireless traffic and communicates with the wired switch. Thus, with this design, every device on the LAN, whether wired or wireless, can communicate with every other device. Wireless devices communicate with each other via the access point. If wireless devices need to connect to a wired device, they do so via the access point, then to the switch, and then to the wired devices. Similarly, wired devices communicate with each other via the switch. If the wired devices need to connect to wireless ones, they do so via the switch, then to the access point, and then to the wireless devices.

LAN PROTOCOLS For two devices to communicate, they must use the same protocol. The Institute for Electrical and Electronics Engineers (IEEE, pronounced "I triple E") sponsors committees that create and publish protocols and other standards. The committee that addresses LAN standards is called the *IEEE 802 Committee*. Thus, IEEE LAN protocols always start with the numbers 802.

The **IEEE 802.3 protocol** is used for wired LAN connections. This protocol standard, also called **Ethernet**, specifies hardware characteristics, such as which wire carries which signals. It also describes how messages are to be packaged and processed for wired transmission over the LAN.

The NIC in most personal computers today supports what is called **10/100/1000 Ethernet**. These products conform to the 802.3 specification and allow for transmission at a rate of 10, 100, or 1,000 Mbps (megabits per second). Switches detect the speed that a given device can handle and communicate with it at that speed. If you check computer listings at Dell, HP, Lenovo, and other manufacturers, you will see PCs advertised as having 10/100/1000 Ethernet. Today, speeds of up to 1Gbps are possible on wired LANs.

By the way, the abbreviations used for communications speeds differ from those used for computer memory. For communications equipment, k stands for 1,000, not 1,024 as it does for memory. Similarly, M stands for 1,000,000, not 1,024 times 1,024; G stands for 1,000,000,000, not 1,024 times 1,024 times 1,024. Thus, 100 Mbps is 100,000,000 bits per second. Also, communications speeds are expressed in *bits*, whereas memory sizes are expressed in *bytes*.

Wireless LAN connections use the **IEEE 802.11 protocol**. Several versions of 802.11 exist, and, as of 2012, the most current is IEEE 802.11n. The differences among the variations are beyond the scope of this discussion. Just note that the current standard, 802.11n, allows speeds of up to 600 Mbps.

Observe that the LAN in Figure 3-13 uses both the 802.3 and 802.11 protocols. The NICs operate according to the 802.3 protocol and connect directly to the switch, which also operates on the 802.3 standard. The WNICs operate according to the 802.11 protocol and connect the wireless access point. The access point must process messages using both the 802.3 and 802.11 standards; it sends and receives wireless traffic using the 802.11 protocol, and then communicates with the switch using the 802.3 protocol. Characteristics of LANs are summarized in the top two rows of Figure 3-14.

Bluetooth is another common wireless protocol. It is designed for transmitting data over short distances, replacing cables. Some devices, such as wireless mice and keyboards, use Bluetooth to connect to the computer. Cell phones use Bluetooth to connect to automobile entertainment systems.

FlexTime has a LAN that connects computer workstations together and to the server. That network also makes Internet connections using a DSL modem (on the next page). Fixed desktop

Type	Topology	Transmission Line	Transmission Speed	Equipment Used	Protocol Commonly Used	Remarks
Local area network	Local area network	UTP or optical fiber	Common: 10/100/1000 Mbps Possible: 1 Gbps	Switch NIC UTP or optical	IEEE 802.3 (Ethernet)	Switches connect devices, multiple switches on all but small LANs.
	Local area network with wireless	UTP or optical for non-wireless connections	Up to 600 Mbps	Wireless access point Wireless NIC	IEEE 802.11n	Access point transforms wired LAN (802.3) to wireless LAN (802.11).
Connections to the Internet	DSL modem to ISP	DSL telephone	Personal: Upstream to 1 Mbps downstream to 40 Mbps (max 10 likely in most areas)	DSL modem DSL-capable telephone line	DSL	Can have computer and phone use simultaneously. Always connected.
	Cable modem to ISP	Cable TV lines to optical cable	Upstream to 1 Mbps Downstream 300 Kbs to 10 Mbps	Cable modem Cable TV cable	Cable	Capacity is shared with other sites; performance varies depending on others' use.
	WAN wireless	Wireless connection to WAN	500 Kbps to 1.7 Mbps	Wireless WAN modem	One of several wireless standards.	Sophisticated protocol enables several devices to use the same wireless frequency.

FIGURE 3-14

Summary of LAN Networks

computers and some of the stationary workout equipment use wires and Ethernet. Laptops and some of the other workout equipment are wireless and use a version of IEEE 802.11. Some of the devices used at FlexTime, like Kelly's and Felix's talking shoes, connect using Bluetooth.

What Are the Alternatives for Connecting to a WAN?

As stated, a WAN connects computers located at physically separated sites. Although you may not have realized it, when you connect your personal computer, iPhone, or Kindle to the Internet, you are connecting to a WAN. You are connecting to computers, owned and operated by an **Internet service provider (ISP)**, that are not physically located at your site.

An ISP has three important functions. First, it provides you with a legitimate Internet address. Second, it serves as your gateway to the Internet. The ISP receives the communications from your computer and passes them on to the Internet, and it receives communications from the Internet and passes them on to you. Finally, ISPs pay for the Internet. They collect money from their customers and pay access fees and other charges on your behalf.

Figure 3-14 shows the three common WAN alternatives for connecting to the Internet. Notice that we are discussing how your computer connects to a WAN; we are not discussing the structure of the WAN itself. WAN architectures and their protocols are beyond the scope of this discussion. Search the Web for *leased lines* or *PSDN* if you want to learn more about WAN architectures.

SOHO LANs (like that in Figure 3-13) and individual home and office computers are commonly connected to an ISP in one of three ways: a special telephone line called a DSL line, a cable TV line, or a wireless-phone-like connection. All three of these alternatives require that the *digital data* in the computer be converted to a wavy, or analog signal. A device called a modem, or modulator/demodulator, performs this conversion.

As shown in Figure 3-15, once the modem converts your computer's digital data to analog, that analog signal is then sent over the telephone line, TV cable, or air. If sent by telephone line, the first telephone switch that your signal reaches converts the signal into the form used by the international telephone system.

DSL MODEMS A **DSL modem** is the first modem type. DSL stands for **digital subscriber line**. DSL modems operate on the same lines as voice telephones, but they operate so that their signals do not interfere with voice telephone service. Because DSL signals do not interfere with telephone signals, DSL data transmission and telephone conversations can occur

FIGURE 3-15

Signal Modulation for Accessing the Internet

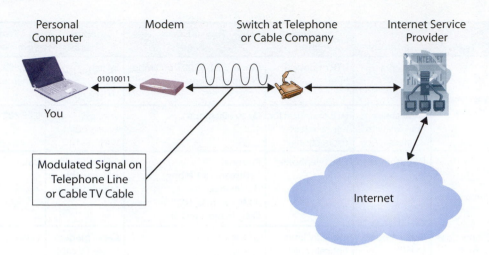

simultaneously. A device at the telephone company separates the phone signals from the computer signals and sends the latter signal to the ISP. DSL modems use their own protocols for data transmission.

There are gradations of DSL service and speed. Most home DSL lines can download data at speeds ranging from 256 kbps to 10 Mbps and can upload data at slower speeds—for example, 512 kbps. DSL lines that have different upload and download speeds are called asymmetric digital subscriber lines (ADSL). Most homes and small businesses can use ADSL because they receive more data than they transmit (e.g., pictures in news stories), and hence they do not need to transmit as fast as they receive.

Some users and larger businesses, however, need DSL lines that have the same receiving and transmitting speeds. They also need performance-level guarantees. Symmetrical digital subscriber lines (SDSL) meet this need by offering the same fast speed in both directions.

CABLE MODEMS A **cable modem** is a second modem type. Cable modems provide high-speed data transmission using cable television lines. The cable company installs a fast, high-capacity optical fiber cable to a distribution center in each neighborhood that it serves. At the distribution center, the optical fiber cable connects to regular cable-television cables that run to subscribers' homes or businesses. Cable modems modulate in such a way that their signals do not interfere with TV signals.

Because up to 500 user sites can share these facilities, performance varies depending on how many other users are sending and receiving data. At the maximum, users can download data up to 50 Mbps and can upload data at 512 kbps. Typically, performance is much lower than this, but still, in most cases, the download speed of cable modems is considerably higher than that for DSL lines.

WAN WIRELESS CONNECTION A third way that you can connect your computer, iPhone, Kindle, iPad, or other communicating device is via a **WAN wireless** connection. Such connections use cell phone technology. Amazon's Kindle, for example, uses a Sprint wireless network to provide wireless data connections. The iPhone uses a LAN-based wireless network if one is available and a WAN wireless network if one is not. The LAN-based network is preferred because performance is considerably higher. As of 2012, WAN wireless provides average performance of 500 kbps, with peaks of up to 1.7 Mbps, as opposed to the typical 50 Mbps for LAN wireless.

A variety of WAN wireless protocols exist. Sprint and Verizon use a protocol called EVDO; AT&T, which supports the iPhone, and T-Mobile use one called HSDPA. Another protocol, **WiMax**, has been implemented by Clearwire and is available on Sprint's XOHM network (see Case 3 on page 89). The meaning of these acronyms and their particulars are unimportant to us; just realize that a marketing and technology battle is underway for WAN wireless. WiMax has the greatest potential for speed, but it is currently the least available. Figure 3-14 (page 71) summarizes these alternatives.

When Kelly and Felix used their shoes to communicate their workout data, those shoes used the Bluetooth wireless protocol to communicate to the iPhone, and the iPhone used a wireless

WAN to transfer the data to the server. When they are inside the FlexTime building, to increase performance the iPhone will use the FlexTime wireless LAN rather than the wireless WAN to connect to the server.

You will sometimes hear the terms *narrowband* and *broadband* with regard to communications speeds. Narrowband lines typically have transmission speeds less than 56 kbps. Broadband lines have speeds in excess of 256 kbps. Today, all popular communication technologies provide broadband capability, and so these terms are likely to fade from use.

Q4. What Do Business Professionals Need to Know About the Internet?

As discussed in Q3, the Internet is an *internet*, meaning that it is a network of networks. As you might guess, the technology that underlies the Internet is complicated and beyond the scope of this text. However, because of the popularity of the Internet, certain terms have become ubiquitous in twenty-first-century business society. In this question, we will define and explain terms that you need to know to be an informed business professional and consumer of Internet services.

An Internet Example

Figure 3-16 illustrates one use of the Internet. Suppose you are sitting in snowbound Minneapolis and you want to communicate with a hotel in sunny, tropical, northern New Zealand. Maybe you are making a reservation using the hotel's Web site, or maybe you are sending an e-mail to a reservations clerk inquiring about facilities or services.

To begin, note that this example is an internet because it is a network of networks. It consists of two LANs (yours and the hotel's) and four WANs. (In truth, the real Internet consists of tens of thousands of WANs and LANs, but to conserve paper we don't show all of them here.)

Your communication to the hotel involves nearly unimaginable complexity. Somehow, your computer communicates with a server in the New Zealand hotel, a computer that it has never "met" before and knows nothing about. Further, your transmission, which is too big to travel in

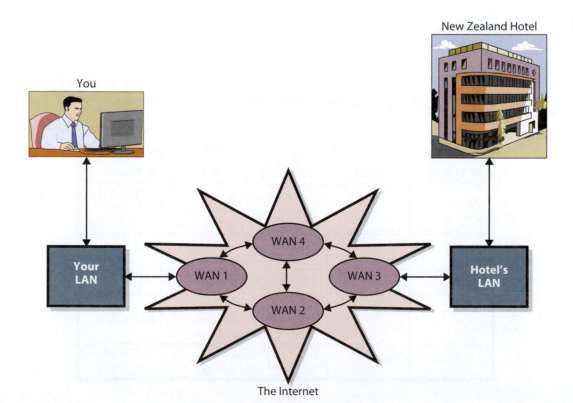

FIGURE 3-16

Making Hotel Reservation Using the Internet

one piece, is broken up into parts and each part passed along from WAN to WAN in such a way that it arrives intact. Then your original message is reassembled, any parts that were lost or damaged (this happens) are resent, and the reconstructed message is delivered to the server for processing. All of this is accomplished by computers and data communications devices that most likely have not interacted before.

What all these devices do know, however, is that they process the same set of protocols. Thus, we need to begin with Internet protocols.

The TCP/IP Architecture

The protocols used on the Internet are arranged according to a structure known as the **TCP/IP architecture**, which is a scheme of five protocol types arranged in layers. As shown in Figure 3-17, the top layer concerns protocols for applications like browsers and Web servers. The next two layers concern protocols about data communications across any inter-net (note small *i*; this means any network of networks), including the Internet. The bottom two layers involve protocols that concern data transmission within a network. For example, the IEEE 802.3 and 802.11 LAN protocols and the cell phone protocols operate at the bottom two layers.

As stated, a protocol is a set of rules and data structures for organizing communication. One or more protocols is defined at each layer. Data communications and software vendors write computer programs that implement the rules of a particular protocol. (For protocols at the bottom layer, the physical layer, they build hardware devices that implement the protocol.)

You are probably wondering, "Why should I know about this?" The reason for knowing about this is to understand terms you will hear and products you will use, buy, or possibly invest in, that relate to each other via this architecture.

Application Layer Protocols

You will directly encounter at least three application layer protocols in your professional life. (In fact, you have used two of them already). **Hyper Text Transport Protocol (HTTP)** is the protocol used between browsers and Web servers. When you use a browser like Internet Explorer, Safari, or Chrome, you are using a program that implements the HTTP protocol. At the other end, at the New Zealand Hotel, for example, there is a server that also processes HTTP, as you will learn in Q5. Even though your browser and the server at the hotel have never "met" before, they can communicate with one another because they both follow the rules of HTTP. Your browser sends requests for service encoded in a predefined HTTP *request format*: The server receives that request; processes the request, say, reserves a room for you; and formats a response in a predefined HTTP *response format*.

As you will learn in Chapter 12, a secure version of HTTP is available called **HTTPS**. Whenever you see *https* in your browser's address bar, you have a secure transmission and you

FIGURE 3-17

TCP/IP Architecture

Layer	Name	Scope	Purpose	Example Protocol
5	Application	Program to program	Enable communication among programs	HTTP; HTTPS; SMTP; FTP
4	Transport	Internets	Reliable internet transport	TCP
3	Internet	Internets	Internet routing	IP
2	Data Link	Network	Flow among switches and access points	IEEE 802.3 IEEE 802.11
1	Physical	Two devices	Hardware specifications	IEEE 802.3 IEEE 802.11

can safely send sensitive data like credit card numbers. However, when you are on the Internet, unless you are using HTTPS, you should assume that all of your communication is open and could be published on the front page of your campus newspaper tomorrow morning.

Hence, when you are using HTTP, e-mail, text messaging, chat, videoconferencing, or anything other than HTTPS, know that whatever you are typing or saying could be known by anyone else. Thus, in your classroom, when you send a text message to a fellow student, that message can be intercepted and read by anyone in your class, including your professor. The same is true of people at a coffee shop, an airport, or anywhere.

Two additional TCP/IP application layer protocols are common. **SMTP**, or **Simple Mail Transfer Protocol** is used for e-mail transmissions (along with other protocols as well). **FTP**, or **File Transfer Protocol**, is used to move files over the Internet. One very common use for FTP is to maintain Web sites. When a Web site administrator wishes to post a new picture or story on a Web server, the administrator will often use FTP to move the picture or other item to the server. Like HTTP, FTP has a secure version as well, but do not assume you are using it.

With this knowledge, we can clear up one common misconception. You are using the Internet when you use any of these protocols. However, you are using the Web only when you use either HTTP or HTTPS. Thus, the **Web** is the Internet-based network of browsers and servers that process HTTP or HTTPS. When you send e-mail, you are using the Internet, but not the Web. It is incorrect to say you are using the Web to send e-mail or text messages.

TCP and IP Protocols

You have some idea of the protocols used at the application (top) layer in Figure 3-17, and from the discussion in Q3, you have some idea of the LAN protocols used at the bottom two layers. But what is the purpose of the layers in between, the transport and internet layers? You know these two layers must be important because the TCP/IP architecture is named after them.

These protocols manage traffic as it passes across an internet (including the Internet) from one network to another. The most important protocol in the transport layer is **TCP**, or **Transmission Control Protocol**. As a transport protocol, TCP has many functions, most of which are beyond the scope of our discussion. One easily understood function, however, is that TCP programs break your traffic up into pieces and send each piece along its way. It then works with TCP programs on other devices in the internet to ensure that all of the pieces arrive at their destination. If one or more pieces is lost or damaged, TCP programs detect that condition and cause retransmission of that piece. Hence, the TCP layer is said to provide *reliable internet transport.*

The primary protocol of the internet layer is called **IP (Internet Protocol)**, which is a protocol that specifies the routing of the pieces of your data communication through the networks that comprise any internet (including the Internet). In Figure 3-16, applications on devices at each of the networks (the two LANs and the four WANs) receive a portion of your message and route it to another computer in its network, or to another network altogether. A **packet** is a piece of a message that is handled by programs that implement IP. A **router** is a special purpose computer that moves packet traffic according to the rules of the IP protocol.

Your message is broken into packets (for simplicity, we are leaving a LOT out here), and each packet is sent out onto the Internet. The packet contains the address of where it is supposed to go. Routers along the way receive the packet, examine the destination IP address, and send it either to the desired destination or to another router that is closer to the desired destination.

When your message starts on its way to the New Zealand hotel, no device knows what route the pieces will take. Until the last hop, a router just sends the packet to another router that it determines to be closer to the final destination. In fact, the packets that make up your message may take different pathways through the Internet (this is rare, but it does occur). Because of this routing scheme, the Internet is very robust. For example, in Figure 3-16 either WAN 2 or WAN 4 could fail and your packets will still get to the hotel.

To summarize, TCP provides reliable internet transport and IP provides internet routing.

IP Addressing

An **IP address** is a number that identifies a particular device. **Public IP addresses** identify a particular device on the public Internet. Because public IP addresses must be unique, worldwide, their assignment is controlled by a public agency known as **ICANN (Internet Corporation for Assigned Names and Numbers)**.

Private IP addresses identify a particular device on a private network, usually on a LAN. Their assignment is controlled within the LAN, usually by the device labeled LAN Device in Figure 3-13. When you sign on to a LAN at a coffee shop, for example, the LAN device loans you a private IP address to use while you are connected to the LAN. When you leave the LAN, it reuses that address.

USE OF PRIVATE IP ADDRESSES When your computer uses TCP/IP within a LAN, say to access a private Web server within the LAN, it uses a private IP address. However, and this is far more common, when you access a public site, say *www.pearsonhighered.com* from within the LAN, your traffic uses your internal IP address until it gets to the LAN device. At that point, the LAN device substitutes your private IP address for its public IP address and sends your traffic out on the Internet.

This private/public IP address scheme has two major benefits. First, public IP addresses are conserved. All of the computers on the LAN use only one public IP address. Second, by using private IP addresses, you need not register a public IP address for your computer with ICANN-approved agencies. Furthermore, if you had a public IP address for your computer, every time you moved it, say from home to school, the Internet would have to update its addressing mechanisms to route traffic to your new location. Such updating would be a massive burden (and a mess)!

PUBLIC IP ADDRESSES AND DOMAIN NAMES IP addresses have two formats. The most common format, called **IPv4**, has a four-decimal dotted notation like 165.193.123.253; the second, called **IPv6**, has a longer format. Both are used today. In your browser, if you enter *http://165.193.123.253*, your browser will connect with the device on the public Internet that has been assigned to this address. Try it to find out who has this address.

Nobody wants to type IP addresses like *http://165.193.123.253* to find a particular site. Instead, we want to enter names like *www.Pandora.com* or *www.Woot.com*. To facilitate that desire, ICANN administers a system for assigning names to IP addresses. First, a **domain name** is a worldwide-unique name that is affiliated with a public IP address. When an organization or individual wants to register a domain name, it goes to a company that applies to an ICANN-approved agency to do so. *www.GoDaddy.com*, shown in Figure 3-18, is an example of such a company.

GoDaddy (or other, similar companies) will first determine if the desired name is unique, worldwide. If so, then it will apply to register that name to the applicant. Once the registration is

FIGURE 3-18

GoDaddy.com Registers Domain Names

Source: www.GoDaddy.com.

completed, the applicant can affiliate a public IP address with the domain name. From that point onward, traffic for the new domain name will be routed to the affiliated IP address.

Note two important points: First, several (or many) domain names can point to the same IP address. Right now, *www.MyMISProf.com* and *www.MyMISTutor.com* both point to the same public IP address. Second, the affiliation of domain names with IP addresses is dynamic. The owner of the domain name can change the affiliated IP addresses at its discretion.

Before we leave the Internet, you need to know one more term. A **URL (Uniform Resource Locator)** is an address on the Internet. Commonly, it consists of a protocol (like http:// or ftp://) followed by a domain name or public IP address. A URL is actually considerably more complicated than this description, but that detailed knowledge won't get you a good date, so we'll hurry along. The preferred pronunciation of URL is the sound of the letters U, R, L.

Q5. What Happens on a Typical Web Server?

In this question, we will apply the knowledge from this chapter to investigate what happens on a typical Web server. We will use the example of a Web storefront, which is a server on the Web from which you can buy products. Web storefronts are one type of e-commerce, which we will discuss in Chapter 8. Here, just consider the Web storefront as an example Web server.

Suppose you want to buy climbing equipment from REI, a co-op that sells outdoor clothing and equipment. To do so, you go to *www.REI.com* and navigate to the product(s) that you want to buy (see Figure 3-19). When you find something you want, you add it to your shopping cart and keep shopping. At some point you check out by supplying credit card data.

In Q4, we discussed how your traffic crosses over the Internet to arrive at a server. The next question is: What happens at that server when it arrives? Or, from another perspective, if you want to set up a Web storefront for your company, what facilities do you need?

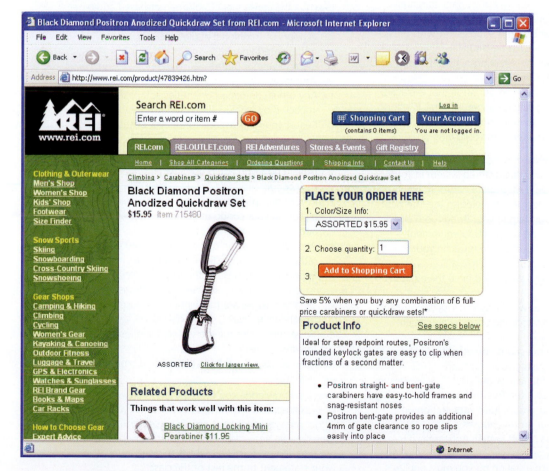

FIGURE 3-19

Sample Retail Web Page

Source: Used with permission of REI and Black Diamond.

MIS InClass 3

Opening Pandora's Box

Nearly free data communications and data storage have created unprecedented opportunities for businesses, as we have described numerous times. Inevitably, such technology will have a revolutionary impact in the home as well.

Sonos (and related companies) is a good example. Sonos has leveraged emerging technologies, especially wireless technology, to develop easily installed, high-quality wireless audio systems. Customers hook one of several different Sonos devices into their home LAN device using a wired Ethernet connection. That device then connects wirelessly to up to 32 other Sonos audio devices around the home. Each device can play its own music or other audio, all independently; some can play the same program, or all can be forced to play the same audio program.

Some Sonos devices provide wireless stereo to existing stereo systems; other devices include the wireless receiver and an amplifier and the customer provides the speakers. Still other devices provide wireless capabilities, an amplifier, and the speakers in one unit.

Each Sonos device includes a computer running Linux. Those computers communicate wirelessly using a proprietary Sonos protocol. Because every device communicates with every other device, Sonos refers to its network of equipment as a *wireless mesh*. The benefit of this mesh to the consumer is flexibility and ease of installation. The devices find each other and determine their own data communications pathways (akin to, but different from, IP routing on the Internet).

Sonos works with any Internet radio source and with music services such as Pandora. With Pandora (and similar services), you establish a personal radio station by selecting a favorite song or musical work. Pandora then plays music based on your selection. You can vote thumbs up or thumbs down on music that is played. Based on your ratings Pandora selects other music that Pandora algorithms determine are similar to music you like.

Form a group of students and answer the following questions:

1. Imagine that you have graduated, have the job of your dreams, and want to install a wireless stereo system in your new condo. Assume that you have a spare bedroom you use as an office that has a LAN device connected to the Internet. You have an existing stereo system in your living room and a pair of unused speakers, but no other stereo equipment. Assume that you want to play audio and music in your office, your living room, and your bedroom.
   a. Go to *www.Sonos.com* and select and price the equipment you will need.
   b. Go to Sonos' competitors at *www.LogitechSqueezeBox.com* and *www.apple.com* and select and price the equipment you will need.
   c. Recommend one of the selections you identified in your answers to a and b and justify your selection.
   d. Report your findings to the rest of the class.
2. Visit *www.Pandora.com*. Using the free trial membership, build a radio station for your group. Base your station on whatever song or music your group chooses.
3. The Sonos equipment has no on-off switch. Apparently it is designed to be permanently on, like your LAN device. You can mute each station, but to turn a station off you must unplug it,

Source: Richard Levine/Alamy Images.

an action few people take. Suppose you have tuned a Sonos device to a Pandora station and you mute that device. Because the Sonos equipment is still on, it will continues downloading packets over the Internet to a device that no one is listening to.
   a. Describe the consequences of this situation on the Internet.
   b. You pay a flat fee for your Internet connection. In what ways does such a fee structure discourage efficiency?
4. Using your group's imagination, curiosity, and experience, describe the consequences of Internet-based audio on:
   a. Existing radio stations
   b. Vendors of traditional audio receivers
   c. Audio entertainment
   d. Cisco (a vendor of Internet routers)
   e. Your local ISP
   f. Any other companies or entities you believe will be impacted by wireless audio systems
   Report your conclusions to the rest of the class.
5. Using history as a guide, we can imagine that audio leads the way for video.
   a. Explain how you could use a wireless video system in your new condo.
   b. In your group's opinion, is having multiple wireless video players in your condo more or less desirable than wireless audio? Explain your response.
   c. Answer items a–f in question 4, but use wireless video rather than audio as the driving factor.
   Report your answers to the rest of the class.
6. Considering all of your answers to questions 1–5:
   a. What industries are the winners and losers with regards to wireless media?
   b. What companies are the winners and losers with regards to wireless media?
   c. How do your answers to items a and b guide your job search?
7. Use the knowledge you have gained in answering questions 1–6 to prepare a 1-minute statement that you could make in a job interview about the emerging opportunities in Internet-based audio and video. Assume that with this statement you wish to demonstrate your ability to think innovatively. Deliver your statement to the rest of the class.

Three-Tier Architecture

Almost all e-commerce applications use the **three-tier architecture**, which is an arrangement of user computers and servers into three categories or tiers, as shown in Figure 3-20. The **user tier** consists of computers, phones, and other devices that have browsers that request and process Web pages. The **server tier** consists of computers that run Web servers and process application programs. The **database tier** consists of computers that run a DBMS that processes SQL requests to retrieve and store data. Figure 3-20 shows only one computer at the database tier. Some sites have multicomputer database tiers as well.

When you enter *http://www.REI.com* in your browser, the browser sends a request that travels over the Internet to a computer in the server tier at the REI site. That request is formatted and processed according to the rules of HTTP. (Notice, by the way, that if you just type *www.REI.com*, your browser will add the *http://* to signify that it is using HTTP.) In response to your request, a server tier computer sends back a **Web page**, which is a document that is coded in one of the standard page markup languages. The most popular page markup language is the *Hypertext Markup Language (HTML)*, which is described later in this section.

Web servers are programs that run on a server tier computer and that manage HTTP traffic by sending and receiving Web pages to and from clients. A commerce server is an application program that runs on a server tier computer. A commerce server receives requests from users via the Web server, takes some action, and returns a response to the users via the Web server. Typical commerce server functions are to obtain product data from a database, manage the items in a shopping cart, and coordinate the checkout process. In Figure 3-20, the server tier computers are running a Web server program, a commerce server application, and other applications having an unspecified purpose.

To ensure acceptable performance, commercial Web sites usually are supported by several or even many Web server computers in a facility called a **Web farm**. Work is distributed among the computers in a Web farm so as to minimize customer delays. The coordination among multiple Web server computers is a fascinating engineering, but, alas, we do not have space to tell that story here. Just imagine the coordination that must occur as you add items to an online order when, to improve performance, different Web server computers receive and process each addition to your order.

Watch the Three Tiers in Action!

To see a three-tier example in action, go to your favorite Web storefront site, place something in a shopping cart, and consider Figure 3-20 as you do so. When you enter an address into your browser, the browser sends a request for the default page to a server computer at that address. A Web server and possibly a commerce server process your request and send back the default page.

As you click Web pages to find products you want, the commerce server accesses the database to retrieve data about those products. It creates pages according to your selections and

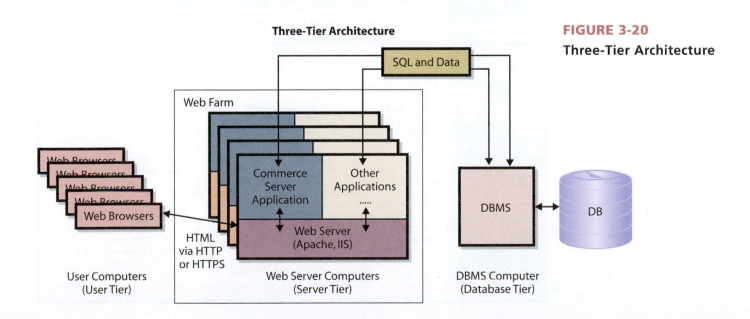

Three-Tier Architecture

FIGURE 3-20

Three-Tier Architecture

sends the results back to your browser via the Web server. Again, different computers on the server tier may process your series of requests and must constantly communicate about your activities. You can follow this process in Figure 3-20.

In Figure 3-19, the user has navigated through climbing equipment at REI.com to find a particular item. To produce this page, the commerce server accessed a database to obtain the product picture, price, special terms (a 5 percent discount for buying six or more), product information, and related products.

The user placed six items in her basket, and you can see the response in Figure 3-21. Again, trace the action in Figure 3-20 and imagine what occurred to produce the second page. Notice that the discount was applied correctly.

When the customer checks out, the commerce server program will be called to process payment, schedule inventory processing, and arrange for shipping. Truly this is an amazing capability!

Because this chapter concerns technology, we won't mention the business processes that underlie and integrate with this processing. But, in passing, realize that there will be dozens of business processes for finding vendors, ordering merchandise, receiving and stocking merchandise, picking items for order fulfillment, shipping merchandise, billing buyers, and managing accounts payable and receivable, and so forth.

Hypertext Markup Language (HTML)

Hypertext Markup Language (HTML) is the most common language for defining the structure and layout of Web pages. An HTML **tag** is a notation used to define a data element for display or other purposes. The following HTML is a typical heading tag:

```
<h2>Price of Item</h2>
```

Notice that tags are enclosed in < > (called *angle brackets*) and that they occur in pairs. The start of this tag is indicated by <h2>, and the end of the tag is indicated by </h2>. The words

FIGURE 3-21

Shopping Cart Page

Source: Used with permission of REI and Black Diamond.

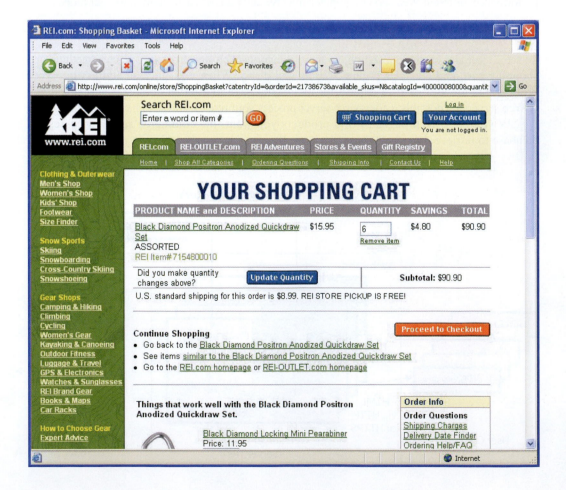

```html
<h1 class="style4"><span class="style6">Management Information Systems (MIS)</span>:</h1>
<h2>Definition:</h2>
<p> </p>
<table style="width: 100%">
    <tr>
        <td style="width: 177px"> </td>
        <td class="style7" style="width: 133px">Processes</td>
        <td class="style7" style="width: 140px">Information Systems</td>
        <td class="style7" style="width: 134px">Information</td>
    </tr>
    <tr>
        <td class="style1" style="width: 177px">Create</td>
        <td class="style8" style="width: 133px">XX</td>
        <td class="style8" style="width: 140px">XX</td>
        <td class="style8" style="width: 134px">XX</td>
    </tr>
    <tr>
        <td class="style2" style="width: 177px">Monitor</td>
        <td class="style8" style="width: 133px">XX</td>
        <td class="style8" style="width: 140px">XX</td>
        <td class="style8" style="width: 134px">XX</td>
    </tr>
    <tr>
        <td class="style3" style="width: 177px; height: 28px">Adapt</td>
        <td class="style8" style="width: 133px; height: 28px">XX</td>
        <td class="style8" style="width: 140px; height: 28px">XX</td>
        <td class="style8" style="width: 134px; height: 28px">XX</td>
    </tr>
</table>
<p> </p>
<p><a href="http://www.LearningMIS.com">Link to Class WebSite</a></p>

</body>
```

FIGURE 3-22
Example HTML

between the tags are the value of the tag. This HTML tag means to place the words "Price of Item" on a Web page in the style of a level-two heading. The creator of the Web page will define the style (font size, color, and so forth) for h2 headings and the other tags to be used.

Web pages include **hyperlinks**, which are pointers to other Web pages. A hyperlink contains the URL of the Web page to find when the user clicks the hyperlink. The URL can reference a page on the server that generated the page containing the hyperlink or it can reference a page on another server.

Figure 3-22 shows sample HTML code. The tag <h1> means to format the indicated text as a level-one heading; <h2> means a level-two heading. The tag <table> defines a table, and the tag <a> defines a hyperlink. This tag has an attribute, which is a variable used to provide properties about a tag. Not all tags have attributes, but many do. Each attribute has a standard name. The attribute for a hyperlink is *href*, and its value indicates which Web page is to be displayed when the user clicks the link. Here, the page *http://www.LearningMIS.com* is to be returned when the user clicks the hyperlink. Figure 3-23 shows this page as rendered by Internet Explorer.

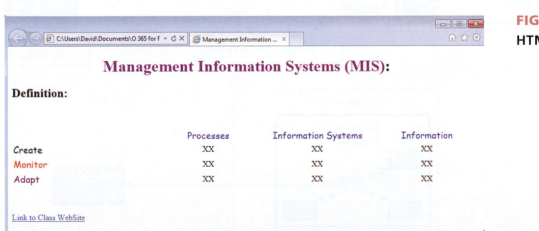

FIGURE 3-23
HTML in Browser

XML, Flash, Silverlight, and HTML5

HTML has been the workhorse of the Web for more than 15 years. However, it has problems and limitations that have been overcome by newer technologies. **XML (eXtensible Markup Language)** is a markup language that fixes several HTML deficiencies and is commonly used for program-to-program interaction over the Web. **Flash** is an add-on to browsers that was developed by Adobe and is useful for providing animation, movies, and other advanced graphics inside a browser. **Silverlight** is a browser add-on that was developed by Microsoft for the same purposes as Flash. Silverlight has newer technology and more functionality than Flash but is less frequently used. Finally, HTML5 is a new version of HTML that also supports animation, movies, and graphics.

Almost all experts agree that XML will continue to be the most important technology for interprogram communication on the Web. Some people believe that HTML5 will replace standard HTML and Flash and possibly Silverlight as well.

Q6. How Do Organizations Benefit from Virtual Private Networks (VPNs)?

A **virtual private network (VPN)** uses the Internet to create the appearance of private point-to-point connections. In the IT world, the term **virtual** means something that appears to exist that does not in fact exist. Here, a VPN uses the public Internet to create the appearance of a private connection.

A TYPICAL VPN Figure 3-24 shows one way to create a VPN to connect a remote computer, perhaps an employee working at a hotel in Miami to a LAN at a Chicago site. The remote user is the VPN client. That client first establishes a connection to the Internet. The connection can be obtained by accessing a local ISP, as shown in the figure; or, in some hotels, the hotel itself provides a direct Internet connection.

In either case, once the Internet connection is made, VPN software on the remote user's computer establishes a connection with the VPN server in Chicago. The VPN client and VPN server then have a connection. That connection, called a *tunnel*, is a virtual, private pathway over the public, shared network from the VPN client to the VPN server. Figure 3-25 illustrates the connection as it appears to the remote user.

FIGURE 3-24

VPN: Actual Connections

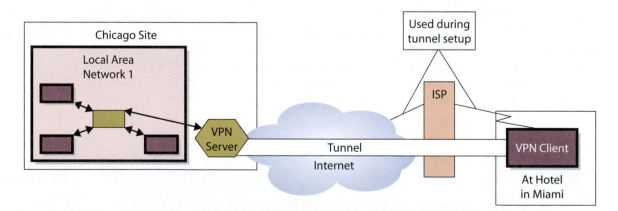

FIGURE 3-25

VPN: Apparent Connection

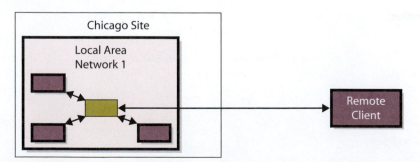

VPN communications are secure, even though they are transmitted over the public Internet. To ensure security, VPN client software *encrypts*, or codes (see Chapter 12, page 395), the original message so that its contents are protected from snooping. Then the VPN client attaches the Internet address of the VPN server to the message and sends that package over the Internet to the VPN server. When the VPN server receives the message, it strips its address off the front of the message, *decrypts* the coded message, and sends the plain text message to the original address on the LAN. In this way, secure private messages are delivered over the public Internet.

VPNs offer the benefit of point-to-point leased lines, and they enable remote access, both by employees and by any others who have been registered with the VPN server. For example, if customers or vendors are registered with the VPN server, they can use the VPN from their own sites. Figure 3-26 shows three tunnels: one supports a point-to-point connection between the Atlanta and Chicago sites, and the other two support remote connections.

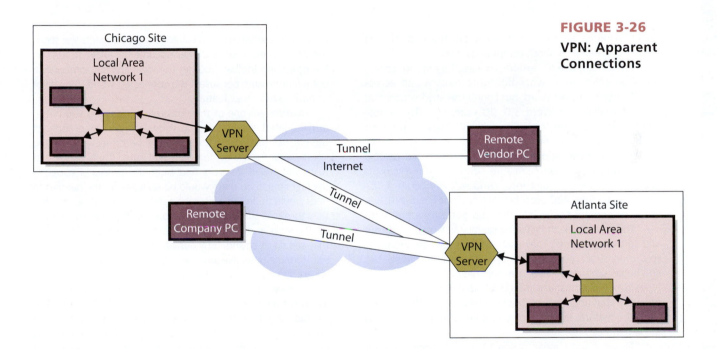

FIGURE 3-26

VPN: Apparent Connections

Ethics Guide

Churn and Burn

An anonymous source, whom we'll call Mark, made the following statements about computing devices:

"I never upgrade my system. At least, I try not to. Look, I don't do anything at work but write memos and access e-mail. I use Microsoft Word, but I don't use any features that weren't available in Word 3.0, 20 years ago. This whole industry is based on 'churn and burn': They churn their products so we'll burn our cash.

"All this hype about 3.0GHz processors and 500GB disks—who needs them? I'm sure I don't. And if Microsoft hadn't put so much junk into Windows, we could all be happy on an Intel 486 processor like the one I had in 1993. We're suckers for falling into the 'you gotta have this' trap.

"Frankly, I think there's a conspiracy between hardware and software vendors. They both want to sell new products, so the hardware people come up with these incredibly fast and huge computers. Then, given all that power, the software types develop monster products bloated with features and functions that nobody uses. It would take me months to learn all of the features in Word, only to find out that I don't need those features.

"To see what I mean, open Microsoft Word, click on View, then select Toolbars. In my version of Word, there are 19 toolbars to select, plus one more to customize my own toolbar. Now what in the world do I need with 19 toolbars? I write all the time, and I have two selected: Standard and Formatting. Two out of 19! Could I pay Microsoft 2/19 of the price of Word, because that's all I want or use?

"Here's how they get you, though. Because we live in a connected world, they don't have to get all of us to use those 19 toolbars, just one of us. Take Bridgette, over in Legal, for example. Bridgette likes to use the redlining features, and she likes me to use them when I change draft contracts she sends me. So if I want to work on her documents, I have to turn on the Reviewing toolbar. You get the idea; just get someone to use a feature and, because it is a connected world, then all of us have to have that feature.

"Viruses are one of their best ploys. They say you better buy the latest and greatest in software—and then apply all the patches that follow so that you'll be protected from the latest zinger from the computer 'bad guys.' Think about that for a minute. If vendors had built the products correctly the first time, then there would be no holes for the baddies to find, would there? So they have a defect in their products that they turn to a sales advantage. You see, they get us to focus on the virus and not on the hole in their product. In truth, they should be saying, 'Buy our latest product to protect yourself from the defective junk we sold you last year.' But truth in advertising hasn't come that far.

"Besides that, users are their own worst enemies as far as viruses are concerned. If I'm down on 17th Street at 4 in the morning, half drunk and with a bundle of cash hanging out of my pocket, what's likely to happen to me? I'm gonna get mugged. So if I'm out in some weirdo chat room—you know, out where you get pictures of weird sex acts and whatnot—and download and run a file, then of course I'm gonna get a virus. Viruses are brought on by user stupidity, that's all.

"One of these days, users are going to rise up and say, 'That's enough. I don't need any more versions . . . any more version SPAM. I'll stay with what I have, thank you very much.' In fact, maybe that's happening right now. Maybe that's why software sales aren't growing like they were. Maybe people have finally said, 'No more toolbars!'"

DISCUSSION QUESTIONS

1. Summarize Mark's view of the computer industry. Is there merit to his argument? Why or why not?
2. What holes do you see in the logic of his argument?
3. Someone could take the position that these statements are just empty rantings—that Mark can say all he wants, but the computer industry is going to keep on doing as it has been. Is there any point in Mark sharing his criticisms?
4. Comment on Mark's statement—"Viruses are brought on by user stupidity, that's all."
5. All software products ship with known problems. Microsoft, Adobe, and Apple all ship software that they know has failures. Is it unethical for them to do so? Do software vendors have an ethical responsibility to openly publish the problems in their software? How do these organizations protect themselves from lawsuits for damages caused by known problems in software?
6. Suppose a vendor licenses and ships a software product that has both known and unknown failures. As the vendor learns of the unknown failures, does it have an ethical responsibility to inform the users about them? Does the vendor have an ethical responsibility to fix the problems? Is it ethical for the vendor to require users to pay an upgrade fee for a new version of software that fixes problems in an existing version?

Active Review

Use this Active Review to verify that you understand the material in the chapter. You can read the entire chapter and then perform the tasks in this review, or you can read the text material for just one question and perform the tasks in this review for that question before moving on to the next one.

Q1. What do business professionals need to know about computer hardware?

List categories of hardware and explain the purpose of each. Define *bit* and *byte*. Explain why bits are used to represent computer data. Define the units of bytes used to size memory. In general terms, explain how a computer works. Explain how a manager can use this knowledge. Explain why you should save your work from time to time while you are using your computer.

Explain the functions of client and server computers. Describe how the hardware requirements vary between the two types. Define *server farm* and describe the technology dance that occurs on a server farm.

Q2. What do business professionals need to know about software?

Review Figure 3-7 and explain the meaning of each cell in this table. Explain the difference between software ownership and software licenses. Explain the differences among horizontal-market, vertical-market, and one-of-a-kind applications. Describe the three ways that organizations can acquire software.

Define *client-server application* and differentiate it from, say, Adobe Acrobat. Explain the difference between thin and thick clients. Describe the advantages and disadvantage of each. Name the operating system on the mobile device you use and identify one thick-client on that device.

Name three successful open source projects. Describe four reasons programmers contribute to open source projects. Define *open source, closed source, source code,* and *machine code.* In your own words, explain why open source is a legitimate alternative but may or may not be appropriate for a given application.

Q3. What types of computer networks exist?

Define *computer network*. Explain the differences among LANs, WANs, internets, and the Internet. Describe the purpose of a protocol. Explain the key distinction of a LAN. Describe the purpose of each component in Figure 3-13. Define *IEEE 802.3* and *802.11* and differentiate them. Explain why your connection to an ISP is a WAN and not a LAN. Name three functions of an ISP. Explain three ways you can connect to the Internet. Describe the differences among DSL, cable, and WAN wireless alternatives.

Q4. What do business professionals need to know about the Internet?

Explain the statement, "The Internet is an internet." Define *TCP/IP* and name its layers. Explain, in general terms, the purpose of each layer. Explain the purpose of HTTP, HTTPS, SMTP, and FTP. Explain why TCP is said to provide *reliable internet transport*. Define *IP, packet,* and *router*. Explain why IP is said to provide internet routing. Describe the advantages of private and public IP addresses. List the purposes of the LAN device. Explain, in general terms, how you would obtain a domain name. Describe the relationship of a domain name and public IP addresses. Define *URL*.

Q5. What happens on a typical Web server?

Explain *Web storefront*. Define three-tier architecture and name and describe each tier. Explain the function of a Web page, a Web server, and a commerce server. Explain the purpose of a Web farm. Explain the function of each tier in Figure 3-20 as the pages in Figures 3-19 and 3-21 are processed. Define *HTML* and explain its purpose. Define *href* and *attribute*. Explain the purpose of XML, Flash, Silverlight, and HTML5.

Q6. How do organizations benefit from virtual private networks (VPNs)?

Describe the problem that a VPN solves. Use Figure 3-26 to explain one way that a VPN is set up and used. Define *tunnel*. Describe how encryption is used in a VPN. Explain why a Windows user does not need to license or install other software to use a VPN.

Key Terms and Concepts

10/100/1000 Ethernet *70*
Access point (AP) *70*
Application software *64*
Binary digit (bits) *57*
Bluetooth *70*
Bytes *57*
Cable modem *72*
Central processing unit (CPU) *56*
Client *59*
Client-server applications *64*
Closed source *66*
Cloud computing *63*
Custom-developed software *66*
Database tier *79*
Digital subscriber line (DSL) *71*
Domain name *76*
DSL modem *71*
Dual-processor *56*
Ethernet *70*
Exabyte *58*
File Transfer Protocol (FTP) *75*
Flash *82*
Gigabyte (GB) *58*
Hardware *56*
Horizontal-market application *64*
HTML (Hypertext Markup
   Language) *80*
HTTP (Hypertext Transport
   Protocol) *74*
HTTPS *74*
Hyperlinks *81*
ICANN (Internet Corporation for
   Assigned Names and Numbers) *76*
IEEE 802.11 protocol *70*

IEEE 802.3 protocol *70*
Input hardware *56*
Internet *68*
Internet service provider (ISP) *71*
iOS *62*
IP (Internet Protocol) *75*
IP address *76*
IPv4 *76*
IPv6 *76*
Kilobyte (K) *58*
LAN device *69*
License *63*
Linux *62*
Local area network (LAN) *68*
Mac OS *62*
Machine code *66*
Main memory *57*
Megabyte (MB) *58*
Memory swapping *59*
Network *68*
Network interface card (NIC) *69*
Nonvolatile *59*
Operating system (OS) *59*
Optical fiber cables *69*
Output hardware *57*
Packet *75*
Petabyte *58*
Private IP address *76*
Protocol *68*
Public IP address *76*
RAM (random access memory) *57*
Router *75*
Server farm *60*
Server tier *79*

Servers *60*
Silverlight *82*
Small office/home office (SOHO) *69*
SMTP (Simple Mail Transfer
   Protocol) *75*
Source code *66*
Switch *69*
Tag *80*
TCP (Transmission Control
   Protocol) *75*
TCP/IP architecture *74*
Terabyte (TB) *58*
Thick client *64*
Thin client *64*
Three-tier architecture *79*
Unix *62*
Unshielded twisted pair (UTP) cable *69*
URL (Uniform Resource Locator) *77*
User tier *79*
Vertical-market application *64*
Virtual *82*
Virtual private network (VPN) *82*
Volatile *59*
WAN wireless *72*
Web *75*
Web farm *79*
Web page *79*
Web server *79*
Wide area network (WAN) *68*
WiMax *72*
Windows *61*
Wireless NIC (WNIC) *70*
XML (eXtensible Markup
   Language) *82*

Using Your Knowledge

1. Microsoft offers free licenses of certain software products to students at colleges and universities that participate in the Microsoft Developer Network (MSDN) Academic Alliance (AA). If your college or university participates in this program, you have the opportunity to obtain hundreds of dollars of software, for free. Here is a partial list of the software you can obtain:

   - Microsoft Access 2010
   - OneNote
   - Expression Studio
   - Windows 2008 Server
   - Microsoft Project 2010
   - Visual Studio Developer
   - SQL Server 2008
   - Microsoft Visio

   a. Search *www.microsoft.com*, *www.google.com*, or *www.bing.com* and determine the function of each of these software products.
   b. Which of these software products are operating systems and which are application programs?
   c. Which of these programs should you download and install tonight?
   d. Either (1) download and install the programs in your answer to part c, or (2) explain why you would not choose to do so.
   e. Does the MSDN AA provide an unfair advantage to Microsoft? Why or why not?

2. Suppose you work at FlexTime and Neil has asked you to help analyze a software-selection decision. In particular, he wants you to prepare a list of the

advantages and disadvantages of the following three thin-client application alternatives:
  i. An open source application that FlexTime runs on its own servers
  ii. A licensed application that FlexTime runs on its own servers
  iii. A licensed application that FlexTime runs in the cloud

a. List the criteria that you would use in comparing the advantages and disadvantages.

b. Summarize the advantages and disadvantages of these alternatives that you can determine without knowledge of specific costs and features and functions.

c. List and describe the data, other than that in item b, that you need to obtain in order to evaluate the criteria in your answer to item a.

d. If you provide your answers to items a–c to Neil, have you helped him? What value exists in your answers?

3. Suppose you manage a group of seven employees in a small business. Each of your employees wants to be connected to the Internet. Consider two alternatives:
   Alternative A: Each employee has his or her own modem and connects individually to the Internet.
   Alternative B: The employees' computers are connected using a LAN, and the network uses a single modem to connect.

a. Sketch the equipment and lines required for each alternative.

b. Explain the actions you need to take to create each alternative.

c. Which of these two alternatives do you recommend?

4. Suppose that you have a consulting practice implementing LANs for fraternities and sororities on your campus.

a. Consider a fraternity house. Explain how a LAN could be used to connect all of the computers in the house. Would you recommend an Ethernet LAN, an 802.11 LAN, or a combination? Justify your answer.

b. This chapter did not provide enough detail for you to determine how many switches the fraternity house might need. However, in general terms, describe how the fraternity could use a multiple-switch system.

c. Considering the connection to the Internet, would you recommend that the fraternity house use a DSL, cable modem, or WAN wireless? Although you can rule out at least one of these alternatives with the knowledge you already have, what additional detail do you need in order to make a specific recommendation?

d. Should you develop a standard package solution for each of your customers? What advantages accrue from a standard solution? What are the disadvantages?

5. Consider the needs for network infrastructure at FlexTime. Neil wants to carefully review the $175,000 network infrastructure proposal and eliminate any equipment or services that he can. At the same time, while the building is being remodeled the walls will be open, and this will be the best possible time to add cabling and any other equipment that FlexTime may eventually need.

   Assume you have Neil's task. How would you proceed? We don't have enough information to analyze that proposal in detail. Instead, answer the following questions that concern how Neil might go about making this analysis.

a. Describe FlexTime equipment that is likely to have a wired connection to a LAN.

b. Describe FlexTime equipment that is likely to have a wireless connection to a LAN.

c. Describe customer equipment that is likely to have a wireless connection to a FlexTime LAN.

d. Neil (and you) needs to plan for the future. How are your answers to items a–c likely to change in the next 5 years? In the next 10 years?

e. Describe a process for determining the total wireless demand for a room that contains 50 spinning bicycles.

f. Using the knowledge you have gained from this chapter, list all of the equipment and cabling that FlexTime will need for its new building. Just list equipment categories; you do not have sufficient information to specify particular brands or models of equipment.

g. Suppose Neil receives three different bids for the network infrastructure. Does he necessarily choose the lowest-cost one? Why or why not? What process should Neil use to analyze the three proposals?

Collaboration Exercise 3

Collaborate with a group of fellow students to answer the following questions. For this exercise do not meet face to face. Your task will be easier if you coordinate your work with SharePoint, Office 365, Google Docs with Google + or equivalent collaboration tools. (See Chapter 9 for a discussion of collaboration tools and processes.) Your answers should reflect the thinking of the entire group, and not just that of one or two individuals.

Consider the information technology skills and needs of your parents, relatives, family friends, and others in the Baby Boomer generation. Though you may not know it, you possess many skills that generation wants but does not have. You know how to text, how to download music from iTunes, how to buy and sell items on eBay, how to use Craigslist, and how to use a PDA, an iPhone, and so forth.

You probably can even run the navigation system in your parents' car.

1. Thinking about Baby Boomers whom you know, brainstorm with your team the skills you possess that they do not. Consider all of the items just described and others that come to mind. If you have not read Using MIS InClass 3 (page 78), do so now. Make a common, team list of all those skills.
2. Interview, survey, or informally discuss the items on your list in part 1 with your parents and other Baby Boomers. As a team, determine the five most frustrating and important skills that these people do not possess.
3. The Baby Boomer market has both money and time, but not as much information technology capability as they need, and they do not like it.

With your team, brainstorm products that you could sell to this market that would address the Baby Boomers' techno-ignorance. For example, you might create a video of necessary skills, or you might provide a consulting service setting up Microsoft Home Server computers. Consider other ideas and describe them as specifically as you can. You should consider at least five different product concepts.

4. Develop sales material that describes your services, the benefits they provide, and why your target market should buy those products. Try your sales pitch on friends and family.
5. How viable is your concept? Do you think you can make money with these products? If so, summarize an implementation plan. If not, explain why not.

CASE STUDY 3

Keeping Up with Wireless

Data communications technology is one of the fastest-changing technologies, if not *the* fastest changing, in all of IT. Substantial portions of the knowledge you gain from this chapter will be obsolete within the first 5 years of your career. Unfortunately, we do not know which portions that will be.

Consider the example of WAN wireless technology. Three protocol standards are in competition: EVDO, HSDPA, and WiMax. Because WiMax has the greatest potential performance, we will consider it further in this case.

Craig McCaw built one of the world's first cellular networks in the early 1980s and brought cells phones to the masses. In the 1990s, he sold his company to AT&T for $11.5 billion. In 2003, McCaw started a new venture, Clearwire, by buying rights to technology based on WiMax, to address what is called the "problem of the last mile." Will WiMax defeat the other WAN wireless technologies? We do not know. But, when someone with McCaw's knowledge, experience, and wealth starts a new venture based on that new technology, we should pay attention.

To begin, what is the problem of the last mile? The bottleneck on data communications into homes, and into smaller businesses, is the last mile. Fast optical-fiber transmission lines lie in the street in front of your apartment or office; the problem is getting that capacity into the building and to your computer or TV. Digging up the street and backyard of every residence and small business to install optical fiber is not an affordable proposition. Even if that could be done, such infrastructure cannot be used by mobile devices. You cannot watch a downloaded movie on a commuter train using an optical fiber line.

The WiMax standard, IEEE 802.16, could be implemented by many companies, but only if those companies own wireless frequencies for data transmission. Hence, the interest of people like McCaw and other cellular players such as Sprint. The WiMax standard includes two usage models: *fixed* and *mobile*. The former is akin to LAN wireless in existence today; mobile access allows users to move around, as they do with cell phones, staying connected.

On December 1, 2008, Clearwire merged with Sprint Nextel and received a $3.2 billion outside investment. In the process, Clearwire gained access to Sprint Nextel's spectrum holdings (authority to use certain frequencies for cellular signals). The merged company is called Clearwire, and the products are marketed as Sprint Xohm.

Clearwire already provides fixed use in many cities. As of June 2010, mobile WiMax services were available only in selected cities, but rollout to many more cities is planned in the near future.

Questions

1. List five possible commercial applications for mobile WiMax. Consider applications that necessitate mobility.
2. Evaluate each of the possible applications in your answer to question 1. Select the three most promising applications and justify your selection.
3. Clearwire went public in March 2007 at an initial price of $27.25. As of October 2010, the price was $6.50. Go online and research the company to find out what happened to its share price. Explain why its share price has dropped.
4. AT&T and T-Mobile have endorsed HSDPA, but it does not have the same potential maximum transmission rates. Rather than jump on the WiMax bandwagon, those companies plan to deploy a different technology called Long Term Evolution (LTE). Search the Web for LTE versus WiMax comparisons and compare and contrast these two technologies.
5. Where will this end? In which of these technologies would you be willing to invest $100 million? Why?

C arter Jackson is standing at the counter of the University Intramural Sports League, the same counter he stood in front of at the start of Chapter 2.

"What is this?" Carter asks the counter attendant, Jeremy Bates, pointing to his student account billing statement.

"This what?" It's 2:30 in the afternoon and Jeremy is still waking up.

"This bill . . . $187.78. What's it for? It's on my university account for last month."

"Don't know. Did you buy something here?" Jeremy's rubbing his eyes.

"No. I have absolutely no idea what this is for. And I'm on a tight budget. I need to get this fixed."

"Well, let me take a look. Give me your ID card."

"Last time I did this, I was told that I owed money that I didn't owe."

"I didn't do that . . . I've never even seen you before." Jeremy's not liking the tone of this conversation, and so early in his day.

"Sure, *you* didn't tell me that. But whoever was standing there last fall did."

"Whatever. In any case, it looks like you were billed $187.78 for soccer equipment that you didn't return."

"What are you talking about? I'm not supposed to return it until the end of the season, which is 3 weeks from now."

"Not for this year. For last year." Jeremy wishes he were still asleep.

"But I wasn't coach last year. Someone else was." Carter's got a bad feeling about where this is going.

"That's not what it says here. It says here that you're the coach of the Helicopters . . . by the way, great game on Saturday. I never thought you guys would pull it out, but you did. How's your goalie, by the way?" Jeremy hopes to calm Carter down.

"She's fine . . . sore, but fine. So, look, I'm the coach of the Helicopters this year, but I wasn't last year."

"Maybe not. I don't know. All it says here is, Helicopters, Coach, Carter Jackson. Here, look at my screen."

Carter looks over the counter at Jeremy's screen.

"So, where does it show I owe 187 bucks?"

"It doesn't . . . that comes from another report. But like it shows, you checked out soccer balls and jerseys back in 2010 that were never checked in."

"I did not. I was in New Zealand in 2010!"

"Well, your team did."

"Don't you have another screen, another form, that shows who was coach back then?"

"Not that I know about. To tell you the truth, you're not the first person to complain about this." Jeremy's thinking this is too much . . . maybe he shouldn't stay up so late on Tuesday nights, especially if he has to work. "Give me your name and somebody will contact you."

"You've already got my name. Right there on your screen." Carter's wondering where they find these guys.

"Oh, yeah."

"But I can't wait. I need to get this fixed NOW. I can't afford any more problems."

"OK, let me see if Dawn is here."

Enter Dawn Jenkins, Intramural Director. In contrast to Jeremy, Dawn's full of enthusiasm and energy.

"Hi, Jeremy, what seems to be the problem?" she asks.

"I was billed 187, no wait, almost 188 bucks for soccer equipment that wasn't returned last year," Carter interrupts.

"Yeah, you have to return all the equipment. . . ." Dawn starts to give her standard pitch.

"But I wasn't coach last year," Carter interrupts.

"Oh, one of those. OK. I get it." Some of the energy seeps out of her voice. "Here's the problem. Our computer doesn't tell us who was coach last year. But it does remember that the team didn't return its soccer gear. Do you know last year's coach?" she asks hopefully.

"Yeah, Fred Dillingham. He graduated."

"Oh, dear. Well, we need our equipment back."

"Look, Dawn, I never met the guy. I heard he was a great coach, but he's gone. I can't call him up, wherever he is, and ask for your equipment back. Why didn't you bill him before he left?" Carter thought to himself, "These people are idiots."

"Well, we had a little problem. Mary Anne, who normally does that each year, had her baby and was gone. Nobody knew to run the missing equipment report."

"So how come I get billed now?"

"Because I figured it out and ran the report last month."

"Dawn, this is a mess."

"What do we do? We need to replace missing gear."

Q1. What is the purpose of a database?

Q2. What are the contents of a database?

Q3. What are the components of a database application system?

Q4. How do data models facilitate database design?

Q5. How is a data model transformed into a database design?

Q6. What is the users' role in the development of databases?

Q7. How can the intramural league improve its database?

Chapter Preview

Clearly, the intramural sports league has problems. At least one problem is a *process* problem. The fact that one of the league's employees took maternity leave should not mean that it doesn't send out bills for missing equipment. The league management has confused an *employee*, Mary Anne, with a *role* in a business process. We will address problems like this in Chapters 5 through 8.

For now, we will focus on the problems in their database. Something is not quite right; the database should contain the name of the coaches of past years, at least. But how should they change it? We will address this issue in Q7 of this chapter.

But to begin, realize that businesses of every size organize data records into collections called *databases*. At one extreme, small businesses use databases to keep track of customers; at the other extreme, huge corporations such as Dell and Amazon.com use databases to support complex sales, marketing, and operations activities. In between, we have businesses like FlexTime that use databases as a crucial part of their operations but that lack the trained and experienced staff to manage and support their databases. To obtain answers to the one-of-a-kind queries he needs, Neil needs to be creative and adaptable in the way that he accesses and uses his database.

This chapter discusses the why, what, and how of database processing. We begin by describing the purpose of databases and then explain the important components of database systems. We then overview the process of creating a database system and summarize your role as a future user of such systems.

Users have a crucial role in the development of database applications. Specifically, the structure and content of the database depends entirely on how users view their business activity. To build the database, the developers will create a model of that view using a tool called the entity-relationship model. You need to understand how to interpret such models, because the development team might ask you to validate the correctness of such a model when building a system for your use. Finally, we describe the various database administration tasks.

This chapter focuses on database technology. Here we consider the basic components of a database and their functions. You will learn about the use of database reporting and data mining in Chapter 11.

Q1. What Is the Purpose of a Database?

The purpose of a database is to keep track of things. When most students learn that, they wonder why we need a special technology for such a simple task. Why not just use a list? If the list is long, put it into a spreadsheet. In fact, many professionals do keep track of things using spreadsheets. If the structure of the list is simple enough, there is no need to use database technology. The list of student grades in Figure 4-1, for example, works perfectly well in a spreadsheet.

FIGURE 4-1

List of Student Grades in a Spreadsheet

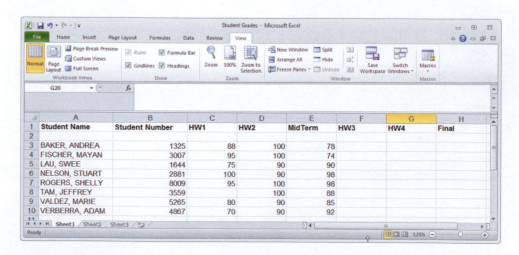

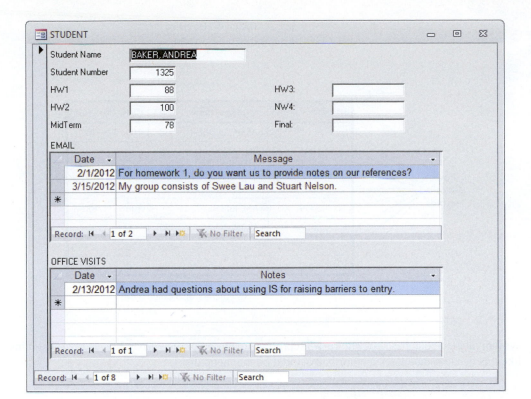

FIGURE 4-2

Student Data in a Form, Data from a Database

Suppose, however, that the professor wants to track more than just grades. Say that the professor wants to record e-mail messages as well. Or, perhaps the professor wants to record both e-mail messages and office visits. There is no place in Figure 4-1 to record that additional data. Of course, the professor could set up a separate spreadsheet for e-mail messages and another one for office visits, but that awkward solution would be difficult to use because it does not provide all of the data in one place.

Instead, the professor wants a form like that in Figure 4-2. With it, the professor can record student grades, e-mails, and office visits all in one place. A form like the one in Figure 4-2 is difficult, if not impossible, to produce from a spreadsheet. Such a form is easily produced, however, from a database.

The key distinction between Figures 4-1 and 4-2 is that the data in Figure 4-1 is about a single theme or concept. It is about student grades only. The data in Figure 4-2 has multiple themes; it shows student grades, student e-mails, and student office visits. We can make a general rule from these examples: Lists of data involving a single theme can be stored in a spreadsheet; lists that involve data with multiple themes require a database. We will say more about this general rule as this chapter proceeds.

Q2. What Are the Contents of a Database?

A **database** is a self-describing collection of integrated records. To understand the terms in this definition, you first need to understand the terms illustrated in Figure 4-3. As you learned in Chapter 3, a **byte** is a character of data. In databases, bytes are grouped into **columns**, such as *Student Number* and *Student Name*. Columns are also called **fields**. Columns or fields, in turn, are grouped into **rows**, which are also called **records**. In Figure 4-3, the collection of data for all columns (*Student Number*, *Student Name*, *HW1*, *HW2*, and *MidTerm*) is called a *row* or a *record*. Finally, a group of similar rows or records is called a **table** or a **file**. From these definitions, you can see that there is a hierarchy of data elements, as shown in Figure 4-4.

It is tempting to continue this grouping process by saying that a database is a group of tables or files. This statement, although true, does not go far enough. As shown in Figure 4-5, a database is a collection of tables *plus* relationships among the rows in those tables, *plus* special data, called metadata, that describes the structure of the database. By the way, the cylindrical

FIGURE 4-3

Elements of the Student Table (also called a file)

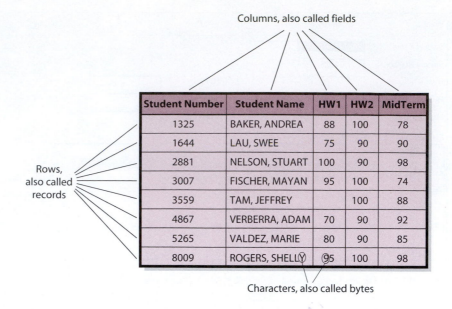

Columns, also called fields

Student Number	Student Name	HW1	HW2	MidTerm
1325	BAKER, ANDREA	88	100	78
1644	LAU, SWEE	75	90	90
2881	NELSON, STUART	100	90	98
3007	FISCHER, MAYAN	95	100	74
3559	TAM, JEFFREY		100	88
4867	VERBERRA, ADAM	70	90	92
5265	VALDEZ, MARIE	80	90	85
8009	ROGERS, SHELLY	95	100	98

Rows, also called records

Characters, also called bytes

symbol labeled "database" in Figure 4-5 represents a computer disk drive. It is used in diagrams like this because databases are normally stored on magnetic disks.

What Are Relationships Among Rows?

Consider the terms on the left-hand side of Figure 4-5. You know what tables are. To understand what is meant by *relationships among rows in tables*, examine Figure 4-6. It shows sample data from the three tables *Email*, *Student*, and *Office_Visit*. Notice the column named *Student Number* in the *Email* table. That column indicates the row in *Student* to which a row of *Email* is connected. In the first row of *Email*, the *Student Number* value is 1325. This indicates that this particular e-mail was received from the student whose *Student Number* is 1325. If you examine the *Student* table, you will see that the row for Andrea Baker has this value. Thus, the first row of the *Email* table is related to Andrea Baker.

Now consider the last row of the *Office_Visit* table at the bottom of the figure. The value of *Student Number* in that row is 4867. This value indicates that the last row in *Office_Visit* belongs to Adam Verberra.

From these examples, you can see that values in one table relate the rows in that table to rows in a second table. Several special terms are used to express these ideas. A **key** (also called a

FIGURE 4-4

Hierarchy of Data Elements

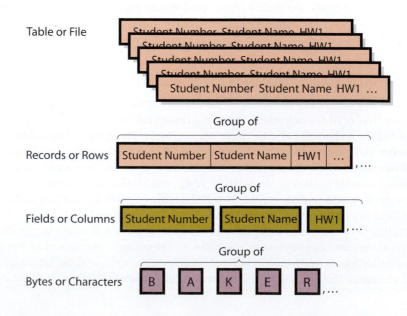

Table or File

Records or Rows

Fields or Columns

Bytes or Characters

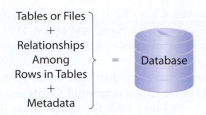

FIGURE 4-5

Contents of a Database

primary key) is a column or group of columns that identifies a unique row in a table. *Student Number* is the key of the *Student* table. Given a value of *Student Number*, you can determine one and only one row in *Student*. Only one student has the number 1325, for example.

Every table must have a key. The key of the *Email* table is *EmailNum*, and the key of the *Office_Visit* table is *VisitID*. Sometimes more than one column is needed to form a unique identifier. In a table called *City*, for example, the key would consist of the combination of columns (*City, State*), because a given city name can appear in more than one state.

Student Number is not the key of the *Email* or the *Office_Visit* tables. We know that about *Email* because there are two rows in *Email* that have the *Student Number* value 1325. The value 1325 does not identify a unique row, therefore *Student Number* cannot be the key of *Email*. Nor is *Student Number* a key of *Office_Visit*, although you cannot tell that from the data in Figure 4-6. If you think about it, however, there is nothing to prevent a student from visiting a professor more than once. If that were to happen, there would be two rows in *Office_Visit* with the same value of *Student Number*. It just happens that no student has visited twice in the limited data in Figure 4-6.

FIGURE 4-6

Examples of Relationships

Email Table

EmailNum	Date	Message	Student Number
1	2/1/2012	For homework 1, do you want us to provide notes on our references?	1325
2	3/15/2012	My group consists of Swee Lau and Stuart Nelson.	1325
3	3/15/2012	Could you please assign me to a group?	1644

Student Table

Student Number	Student Name	HW1	HW2	MidTerm
1325	BAKER, ANDREA	88	100	78
1644	LAU, SWEE	75	90	90
2881	NELSON, STUART	100	90	98
3007	FISCHER, MAYAN	95	100	74
3559	TAM, JEFFREY		100	88
4867	VERBERRA, ADAM	70	90	92
5265	VALDEZ, MARIE	80	90	85
8009	ROGERS, SHELLY	95	100	98

Office_Visit Table

VisitID	Date	Notes	Student Number
2	2/13/2012	Andrea had questions about using IS for raising barriers to entry.	1325
3	2/17/2012	Jeffrey is considering an IS major. Wanted to talk about career opportunities.	3559
4	2/17/2012	Will miss class Friday due to job conflict.	4867

Student Number is, however, a key, but it is a key of a different table, namely *Student*. Hence, the column *Student Number* in the *Email* and *Office_Visit* is called a **foreign key**. This term is used because such columns are keys of a different (foreign) table than the one in which they reside.

Before we go on, databases that carry their data in the form of tables and that represent relationships using foreign keys are called **relational databases**. (The term *relational* is used because another, more formal name for a table like those we are discussing is **relation**.) In the past, there were databases that were not relational in format, but such databases have nearly disappeared. Chances are you will never encounter one, and we will not consider them further.[1]

Metadata

Recall the definition of database: A database is a self-describing collection of integrated records. The records are integrated because, as you just learned, rows can be tied together by their key/foreign key relationship. But what does *self-describing* mean?

It means that a database contains, within itself, a description of its contents. Think of a library. A library is a self-describing collection of books and other materials. It is self-describing because the library contains a catalog that describes the library's contents. The same idea also pertains to a database. Databases are self-describing because they contain not only data, but also data about the data in the database.

Metadata are data that describe data. Figure 4-7 shows metadata for the *Email* table. The format of metadata depends on the software product that is processing the database. Figure 4-7 shows the metadata as they appear in Microsoft Access. Each row of the top part of this form describes a column of the *Email* table. The columns of these descriptions are *Field Name*, *Data Type*, and *Description*. *Field Name* contains the name of the column, *Data Type* shows the type of data the column may hold, and *Description* contains notes that explain the source or use of the column. As you can see, there is one row of metadata for each of the four columns of the *Email* table: *EmailNum*, *Date*, *Message*, and *Student Number*.

FIGURE 4-7

Metadata for Email Table

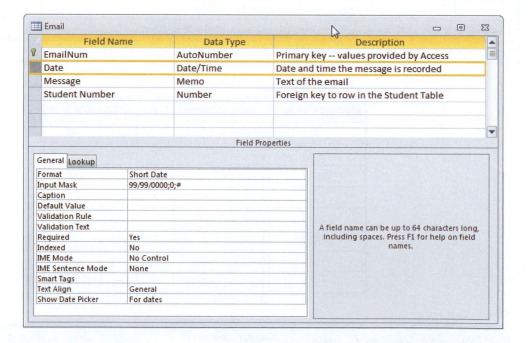

[1] Another type of database, the **object-relational database**, is rarely used in commercial applications. Search the Web if you are interested in learning more about object-relational databases. In this book, we will describe only relational databases.

The bottom part of this form provides more metadata, which Access calls *Field Properties*, for each column. In Figure 4-7, the focus is on the *Date* column (note the light rectangle drawn around the *Date* row). Because the focus is on *Date* in the top pane, the details in the bottom pane pertain to the *Date* column. The Field Properties describe formats, a default value for Access to supply when a new row is created, and the constraint that a value is required for this column. It is not important for you to remember these details. Instead, just understand that metadata are data about data and that such metadata are always a part of a database.

The presence of metadata makes databases much more useful. Because of metadata, no one needs to guess, remember, or even record what is in the database. To find out what a database contains, we just look at the metadata inside the database.

Q3. What Are the Components of a Database Application System?

Figure 4-8 shows the three major components of a **database application system**: a database, a DBMS, and one or more database applications. We have already described the contents of the database. We will next describe the DBMS and then, finally, discuss database applications, which include computer programs.

Of course, as an information system, database application systems also have the other three components: hardware, people and procedures. Because the purpose of this chapter is to discuss database technology, we will omit them from this discussion.

What Is a Database Management System?

A **database management system (DBMS)** is a program used to create, process, and administer a database. As with operating systems, almost no organization develops its own DBMS. Instead, companies license DBMS products from vendors such as IBM, Microsoft, Oracle, and others. Popular DBMS products are **DB2** from IBM, **Access** and **SQL Server** from Microsoft, and **Oracle Database** from the Oracle Corporation. Another popular DBMS is **MySQL**, an open

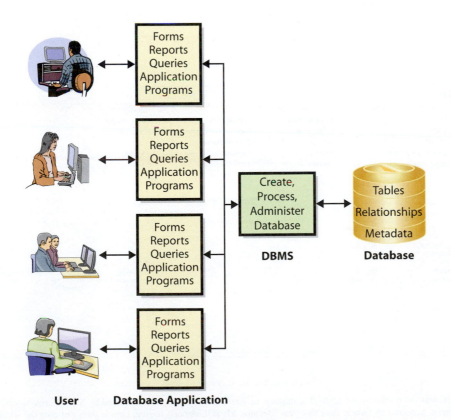

FIGURE 4-8

Components of a Database Application System

source DBMS product that is license-free for most applications.[2] Other DBMS products are available, but these five process the bulk of databases today.

Note that a DBMS and a database are two different things. For some reason, the trade press and even some books confuse the two. A DBMS is a software program; a database is a collection of tables of data, relationships, and metadata. The two are very different in nature.

Creating the Database and Its Structures

Database developers use the DBMS to create tables, relationships, and other structures in the database. The form in Figure 4-7 can be used to define a new table or to modify an existing one. To create a new table, the developer just fills the new table's metadata into the form.

To modify an existing table—say, to add a new column—the developer opens the metadata form for that table and adds a new row of metadata. For example, in Figure 4-9 the developer has added a new column called *Response?*. This new column has the data type *Yes/No*, which means that the column can contain only one value—*Yes* or *No*. The professor will use this column to indicate whether he has responded to the student's e-mail. A column can be removed by deleting its row in this table, though doing so will lose its existing data.

Processing the Database

The second function of the DBMS is to process the database. Such processing can be quite complex, but, fundamentally, the DBMS provides four processing operations: *read*, *insert*, *modify*, or *delete* data. These operations are requested in different ways. From a form, when the user enters new or changed data, a computer program behind the form calls the DBMS to make the necessary database changes. From a Web application, a program on the client or on the server calls the DBMS to make the change.

Structured Query Language (SQL) is an international standard language for processing a database. All five of the DBMS products mentioned earlier accept and process SQL (pronounced "see-quell") statements. As an example, the following SQL statement inserts a new row into the *Student* table:

```
INSERT INTO Student
([Student Number], [Student Name], HW1, HW2, MidTerm)
VALUES
(1000, 'Franklin, Benjamin', 90, 95, 100);
```

FIGURE 4-9

Adding a New Column to a Table (Microsoft Access)

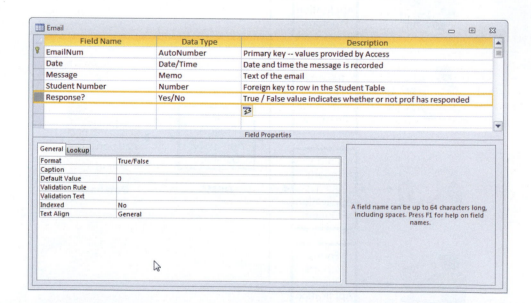

[2] MySQL was supported by the MySQL company. In 2008, that company was acquired by Sun Microsystems, which was, in turn, acquired by Oracle later that year. Because MySQL is open source, Oracle does not own the source code, however.

As stated, statements like this one are issued "behind the scenes" by programs that process forms. Alternatively, they can be issued directly to the DBMS by an application program.

You do not need to understand or remember SQL language syntax. Instead, just realize that SQL is an international standard for processing a database. SQL can also be used to create databases and database structures. You will learn more about SQL if you take a database management class.

Administering the Database

A third DBMS function is to provide tools to assist in the administration of the database. Database administration involves a wide variety of activities. For example, the DBMS can be used to set up a security system involving user accounts, passwords, permissions, and limits for processing the database. To provide database security, a user must sign on using a valid user account before she can process the database.

Permissions can be limited in very specific ways. In the Student database example, it is possible to limit a particular user to reading only *Student Name* from the *Student* table. A different user could be given permission to read the entire *Student* table, but limited to update only the *HW1*, *HW2*, and *MidTerm* columns. Other users can be given still other permissions.

In addition to security, DBMS administrative functions include backing up database data, adding structures to improve the performance of database applications, removing data that are no longer wanted or needed, and similar tasks.

For important databases, most organizations dedicate one or more employees to the role of **database administration (DBA)**, which is defined by the major responsibilities listed in Figure 4-10. You will learn more about this topic if you take a database management course.

> Databases can contain valuable information that can be used for both authorized and unauthorized purposes, as described in the Ethics Guide on pages 118–119.

FIGURE 4-10

Summary of Database Administration Tasks

Category	Database Administration Task	Description
Development	Create and staff DBA function	Size of DBA group depends on size and complexity of database. Groups range from one part-time person to small group.
	Form steering committee	Consists of representatives of all user groups. Forum for community-wide discussions and decisions.
	Specify requirements	Ensure that all appropriate user input is considered.
	Validate data model	Check data model for accuracy and completeness.
	Evaluate application design	Verify that all necessary forms, reports, queries, and applications are developed. Validate design and usability of application components.
Operation	Manage processing rights and responsibilities	Determine processing rights/restrictions on each table and column.
	Manage security	Add and delete users and user groups as necessary; ensure that security system works.
	Track problems and manage resolution	Develop system to record and manage resolution of problems.
	Monitor database performance	Provide expertise/solutions for performance improvements.
	Manage DBMS	Evaluate new features and functions.
Backup and Recovery	Monitor backup procedures	Verify that database backup procedures are followed.
	Conduct training	Ensure that users and operations personnel know and understand recovery procedures.
	Manage recovery	Manage recovery process.
Adaptation	Set up request tracking system	Develop system to record and prioritize requests for change.
	Manage configuration change	Manage impact of database structure changes on applications and users.

FIGURE 4-11

FlexTime's Database Application System

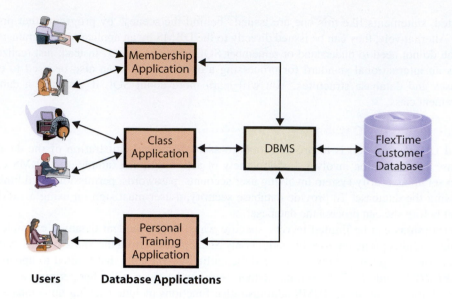

Users   Database Applications

What Are the Components of a Database Application?

A database, all by itself, is not very useful. The tables in Figure 4-6 have all of the data the professor wants, but the format is unwieldy. The professor wants to see the data in a form like that in Figure 4-2 and also as a formatted report. Pure database data are valuable, but in raw form they are not pertinent or useful. In terms of information, it is difficult to conceive differences that make a difference among rows of data in tables.

A **database application** is a collection of forms, reports, queries, and application programs that use the DBMS to process a database. A database may have one or more applications, and each application may have one or more users. As stated, the database application(s), the DBMS, and the database comprise the database application system.

Figure 4-11 shows three applications used at FlexTime. The first one is used to bill and manage FlexTime memberships; the second schedules and bills scheduled classes; and the third tracks and supports personal training sessions. These applications have different purposes, features, and functions, but they all process the same FlexTime customer database.

What Are Forms, Reports, Queries, and Application Programs?

Figure 4-2 shows a typical database application data entry **form**. Data entry forms are used to read, insert, modify, and delete data. **Reports** show data in a structured context. Some reports, like the one in Figure 4-12, also compute values as they present the data. An example is the computation of *Mid Term Total* in Figure 4-12. If forms and reports are well designed, they allow users to readily identify *differences that make a difference*. Thus, they enable users to conceive information.

FIGURE 4-12

Example Report

Student Report with Emails

Student Name	HW1	HW2	MidTerm	Mid Term Total	Date	Message
BAKER, ANDREA	88	100	78	266		
					2/1/2012	For homework 1, do you want us to provide notes on our references?
					3/15/2012	My group consists of Swee Lau and Stuart Nelson.
LAU, SWEE	75	90	90	255		
					3/15/2012	Could you please assign me to a group?
NELSON, STUART	100	90	98	288		
FISCHER, MAYAN	95	100	74	269		
TAM, JEFFREY		100	88			

FIGURE 4-13

Example Database Query

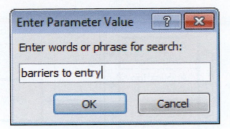

(a) Query Form for Search

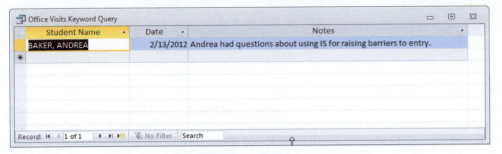

(b) Query Result

But, there's more. DBMS products provide comprehensive and robust features for querying database data. For example, suppose the professor who uses the Student database remembers that one of the students referred to the topic *barriers to entry* in an office visit, but cannot remember which student or when. If there are hundreds of students and visits recorded in the database, it will take some effort and time for the professor to search through all office visit records to find that event. The DBMS, however, can find any such record quickly. Figure 4-13(a) shows a **query** form in which the professor types in the keyword for which she is looking. Figure 4-13(b) shows the results of the query in the *Notes* field of the *Email* table.

Why Are Database Application Programs Needed?

Forms, reports, and queries work well for standard functions. However, most applications have unique requirements that a simple form, report, or query cannot meet. For example, at the university intramural center, what should be done if only a portion of a team's need can be met? If a coach requests 10 soccer balls and only 3 are available, should a backorder for 7 more be generated automatically? Or, should some other action be taken?

Application programs process logic that is specific to a given business need. In the Student database, an example application is one that assigns grades at the end of the term. If the professor grades on a curve, the application reads the breakpoints for each grade from a form, and then processes each row in the *Student* table, allocating a grade based on the breakpoints and the total number of points earned.

Another important use of application programs is to enable database processing over the Internet. For this use, the application program serves as an intermediary between the Web server and the DBMS and database. The application program responds to events, such as when a user presses a submit button; it also reads, inserts, modifies, and deletes database data.

For example, Figure 4-14 shows four different database application programs running on a Web server computer. Users with browsers connect to the Web server via the Internet. The Web server directs user requests to the appropriate application program. Each program then processes the database via the DBMS.

FIGURE 4-14

Applications Running on a Web Server

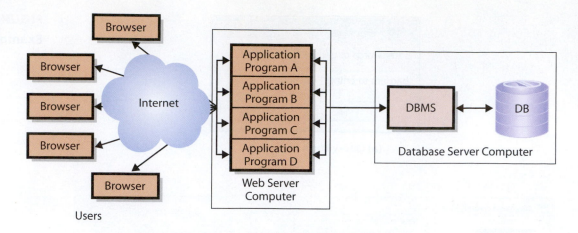

Multi-User Processing

Figures 4-8, 4-11, and 4-14 show multiple users processing the database. Such multi-user processing is common, but it does pose unique problems that you, as a future manager, should know about. To understand the nature of those problems, consider the following scenario.

Suppose two of the users are FlexTime employees using the Class application in Figure 4-11. For convenience, let's call them Andrea and Jeffrey. Assume that Andrea is on the phone with a customer who wants to enroll in a particular spinning class. At the same time, Jeffrey is talking with another customer who wants to enroll in that same class. Andrea reads the database to determine how many vacancies that class has. While doing this, she unknowingly invokes the Class application when she types in her data entry form. The DBMS returns a row showing there is one slot left in that class.

Meanwhile, just after Andrea accesses the database, Jeffrey's customer says she wants to be in that class, and so he also reads the database (via the Class application program) to determine how many slots are available. The DBMS returns the same row to him, indicating that one slot is left.

Andrea's customer now says that he will enroll in the class, and Andrea records this fact in her form. The application rewrites that class row back to the database, indicating that there are no slots left.

Meanwhile, Jeffrey's customer says that she will take the class. Jeffrey records this fact in his form, and the application (which is still using the row it read indicating that a slot is available) rewrites that class row to the database, indicating there are no openings left. Jeffrey's application knows nothing about Andrea's work and hence does not know that her customer has already taken the last slot.

Clearly, there is a problem. Both customers have been assigned the same last slot in the class. When they attend the class, one of them will not have a bike to ride, which will be frustrating to the customers as well as the instructor.

This problem, known as the **lost update problem**, exemplifies one of the special characteristics of multi-user database processing. To prevent this problem, some type of locking must be used to coordinate the activities of users who know nothing about one another. Locking brings its own set of problems, however, and those problems must be addressed as well. We will not delve further into this topic here, however.

Realize from this example that converting a single-user database to a multi-user database requires more than simply connecting another computer. The logic of the underlying application processing needs to be adjusted as well. Be aware of possible data conflicts when you manage business activities that involve multi-user processing. If you find inaccurate results that seem not to have a cause, you may be experiencing multi-user data conflicts. Contact your IS department for assistance.

MIS InClass 4

How Much Is a Database Worth?

FlexTime realizes over 15,000 person-visits a year, an average of 500 visits per day. Neil, one of the two business partners, believes that FlexTime's database is its single most important asset. According to Neil:

> **Take away anything else—the building, the equipment, the inventory—anything else, and we'd be back in business 6 months or less. Take away our customer database, however, and we'd have to start all over. It would take us another 8 years to get back to where we are.**
>
> **Why is the database so crucial? It records everything the company's customers do.**

If FlexTime decides to offer an early morning kickboxing class featuring a particular trainer, it can use its database to offer that class to everyone who ever took an early morning class, a kickboxing class, or a class by that trainer. Customers receive targeted solicitations for offerings they care about and, maybe equally important, they don't receive solicitations for those they don't care about. Clearly, the FlexTime database has value and, if it wanted to, FlexTime could sell that data.

In this exercise, you and a group of your fellow students will be asked to consider the value of a database to organizations other than FlexTime.

Source: Alamy Images Royalty Free.

1. Many small business owners have found it financially advantageous to purchase their own building. As one owner remarked upon his retirement, "We did well with the business, but we made our real money by buying the building." Explain why this might be so.

2. To what extent does the dynamic you identified in your answer to item 1 pertain to databases? Do you think it likely that, in 2050, some small businesspeople will retire and make statements like, "We did well with the business, but we made our real money from the database we generated?" Why or why not? In what ways is real estate different from database data? Are these differences significant to your answer?

3. Suppose you had a national database of student data. Assume your database includes the name, e-mail address, university, grade level, and major for each student. Name five companies that would find that data valuable, and explain how they might use it. (For example, Pizza Hut could solicit orders from students during finals week.)

4. Describe a product or service that you could develop that would induce students to provide the data in item 3.

5. Considering your answers to items 1 through 4, identify two organizations in your community that could generate a database that would potentially be more valuable than the organization itself. Consider businesses, but also think about social organizations and government offices.

   For each organization, describe the content of the database and how you could entice customers or clients to provide that data. Also, explain why the data would be valuable and who might use it.

6. Prepare a 1-minute statement of what you have learned from this exercise that you could use in a job interview to illustrate your ability to innovate the use of technology in business.

7. Present your answers to items 1–6 to the rest of the class.

Enterprise DBMS Versus Personal DBMS

DBMS products fall into two broad categories. **Enterprise DBMS** products process large organizational and workgroup databases. These products support many, possibly thousands, of users and many different database applications. Such DBMS products support 24/7 operations and can manage databases that span dozens of different magnetic disks with hundreds of gigabytes or more of data. IBM's DB2, Microsoft's SQL Server, and Oracle's Oracle Database are examples of enterprise DBMS products.

Personal DBMS products are designed for smaller, simpler database applications. Such products are used for personal or small workgroup applications that involve fewer than

FIGURE 4-15

Microsoft Access as
Application Generator
and DBMS

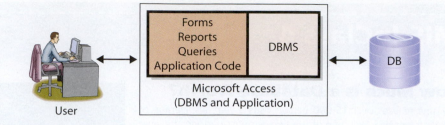

100 users, and normally fewer than 15. In fact, the great bulk of databases in this category have only a single user. The professor's Student database is an example of a database that is processed by a personal DBMS product.

In the past, there were many personal DBMS products—Paradox, dBase, R:base, and FoxPro. Microsoft put these products out of business when it developed Access and included it in the Microsoft Office suite. Today, about the only remaining personal DBMS is Microsoft Access.

To avoid one point of confusion for you in the future, the separation of application programs and the DBMS shown in Figure 4-11 is true only for enterprise DBMS products. Microsoft Access includes features and functions for application processing along with the DBMS itself. For example, Access has a form generator and a report generator. Thus, as shown in Figure 4-15, Access is both a DBMS *and* an application development product.

Q4. How Do Data Models Facilitate Database Design?

In Chapter 12, we will describe the process for developing information systems in more detail. However, business professionals have such a critical role in the development of database applications that we need to anticipate part of that discussion here by introducing two topics—data modeling and database design.

Because the design of the database depends entirely on how users view their business environment, user involvement is critical for database development. Think about the Student database. What data should it contain? Possibilities are: *Students, Classes, Grades, Emails, Office_Visits, Majors, Advisers, Student_Organizations*—the list could go on and on. Further, how much detail should be included in each? Should the database include campus addresses? Home addresses? Billing addresses?

In fact, there are dozens of possibilities, and the database developers do not, and cannot, know what to include. They do know, however, that a database must include all the data necessary for the users to perform their jobs. Ideally, it contains that amount of data and no more. So, during database development the developers must rely on the users to tell them what to include in the database.

Database structures can be complex, in some cases very complex. So, before building the database the developers construct a logical representation of a database data called a **data model**. This model describes the data and relationships that will be stored in the database; it is akin to a blueprint. Just as building architects create a blueprint before they start building, database developers create a data model before they start designing the database.

Figure 4-16 summarizes the database design process. Interviews with users lead to database requirements, which are summarized in a data model. Once the users have approved (validated) the data model, it is transformed into a database design. That design is then implemented into database structures. We will consider data modeling and database design briefly in the next two sections. Again, your goal should be to learn the process so that you can be an effective user representative for a development effort. Also, Figure 4-16 is just part of the systems development process; other requirements are used to develop application programs and features beyond the scope of this book.

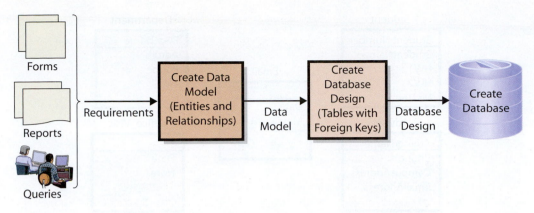

FIGURE 4-16

Database Design Process

What Is the Entity-Relationship Data Model?

The **entity-relationship (E-R) data model** is a tool for constructing data models. Developers use it to describe the content of a data model by defining the things (*entities*) that will be stored in the database and the *relationships* among those entities. A second, less popular, tool for data modeling is the Unified Modeling Language (UML). We will not describe that tool here. However, if you learn how to interpret E-R models, with a bit of study you will be able to understand UML models as well.

Entities

An **entity** is something that the users want to track. Examples of entities are *Order*, *Customer*, *Salesperson*, and *Item*. Some entities represent a physical object, such as *Item* or *Salesperson*; others represent a logical construct or transaction, such as *Order* or *Contract*. For reasons beyond this discussion, entity names are always singular. We use *Order*, not *Orders*; *Salesperson*, not *Salespersons*.

Entities have **attributes** that describe characteristics of the entity. Example attributes of *Order* are *OrderNumber*, *OrderDate*, *SubTotal*, *Tax*, *Total*, and so forth. Example attributes of *Salesperson* are *SalespersonName*, *Email*, *Phone*, and so forth. Entities also have an **identifier**, which is an attribute (or group of attributes) whose value is associated with one and only one entity instance. For example, *OrderNumber* is an identifier of *Order*, because only one *Order* instance has a given value of *OrderNumber*. For the same reason, *CustomerNumber* is an identifier of *Customer*. If each member of the sales staff has a unique name, then *SalespersonName* is an identifier of *Salesperson*.

Before we continue, consider that last sentence. Is the salesperson's name unique among the sales staff? Both now and in the future? Who decides the answer to such a question? Only the users know whether this is true; the database developers cannot know. This example underlines why it is important for you to be able to interpret data models, because only users like you will know for sure.

Figure 4-17 shows examples of entities for the Student database. Each entity is shown in a rectangle. The name of the entity is just above the rectangle, and the identifier is shown in a section at the top of the entity. Entity attributes are shown in the remainder of the rectangle. In Figure 4-17, the *Adviser* entity has an identifier called *AdviserName* and the attributes *Phone*, *CampusAddress*, and *EmailAddress*.

Observe that the entities *Email* and *Office_Visit* do not have an identifier. Unlike *Student* or *Adviser*, the users do not have an attribute that identifies a particular e-mail. *Student Number* will not work because a student could send several e-mails. We *could* make one up. For example, we could say that the identifier of *Email* is *EmailNumber*, but if we do so we are not modeling how the users view their world. Instead, we are forcing something onto the users. Be aware of this possibility when you review data models about your business. Do not allow the database developers to create something in the data model that is not part of your business world.

FIGURE 4-17

Example Entities

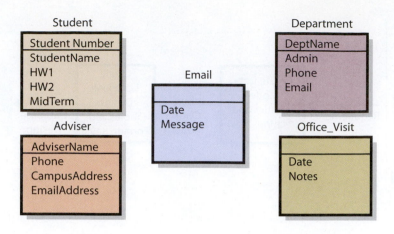

Relationships

Entities have **relationships** to each other. An *Order*, for example, has a relationship to a *Customer* entity and also to a *Salesperson* entity. In the Student database, a *Student* has a relationship to an *Adviser*, and an *Adviser* has a relationship to a *Department*.

Figure 4-18 shows sample *Department*, *Adviser*, and *Student* entity instances and their relationships. For simplicity, this figure shows just the identifier of the entities and not the other attributes. For this sample data, *Accounting* has a relationship to three professors—Jones, Wu, and Lopez—and *Finance* has relationships to two professors—Smith and Greene.

The relationship between *Advisers* and *Students* is more complicated, because in this example an adviser is allowed to advise many students, and a student is allowed to have many advisers. Perhaps this happens because students can have multiple majors. In any case, note that Professor Jones advises students 100 and 400 and that student 100 is advised by both Professors Jones and Smith.

Diagrams like the one in Figure 4-18 are too cumbersome for use in database design discussions. Instead, database designers use diagrams called **entity-relationship (E-R) diagrams**. Figure 4-19 shows an E-R diagram for the data in Figure 4-18. In this figure, all of the entity instances of one type are represented by a single rectangle. Thus, there are rectangles for the *Department*, *Adviser*, and *Student* entities. Attributes are shown as before in Figure 4-17.

Additionally, a line is used to represent a relationship between two entities. Notice the line between *Department* and *Adviser*, for example. The forked lines on the right side of that line

FIGURE 4-18

Example Entity Instances and Relationships

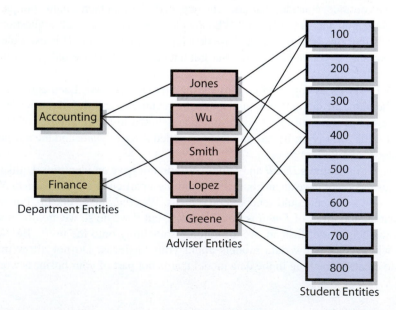

FIGURE 4-19

Entity Relationships, Version 1

signify that a department may have more than one adviser. The little lines, which are referred to as **crow's feet**, are shorthand for the multiple lines between *Department* and *Adviser* in Figure 4-18. Relationships like this one are called **1:N**, or **one-to-many relationships**, because one department can have many advisers, but an adviser has at most one department.

Now examine the line between *Adviser* and *Student*. Notice the short lines that appear at each end of the line. These lines are the crow's feet, and this notation signifies that an adviser can be related to many students and that a student can be related to many advisers, which is the situation in Figure 4-18. Relationships like this one are called **N:M**, or **many-to-many relationships**, because one adviser can have many students and one student can have many advisers.

Students sometimes find the notation N:M confusing. Just interpret the *N* and *M* to mean that a variable number, greater than one, is allowed on each side of the relationship. Such a relationship is not written *N:N*, because that notation would imply that there are the same number of entities on each side of the relationship, which is not necessarily true. *N:M* means that more than one entity is allowed on each side of the relationship and that the number of entities on each side can be different.

Figure 4-20 shows the same entities with different assumptions. Here, advisers may advise in more than one department, but a student may have only one adviser, representing a policy that students may not have multiple majors.

Which, if either, of these versions is correct? Only the users know. These alternatives illustrate the kinds of questions you will need to answer when a database designer asks you to check a data model for correctness.

Figures 4-19 and 4-20 are typical examples of an entity-relationship diagram. Unfortunately, there are several different styles of entity-relationship diagrams. This one is called, not surprisingly, a **crow's-foot diagram** version. You may learn other versions if you take a database management class. These diagrams were created in PowerPoint, which works fine for simple models. More complex models can be created in Microsoft Visio and other products that were purpose-built for creating E-R models.

The crow's-foot notation shows the maximum number of entities that can be involved in a relationship. Accordingly, they are called the relationship's **maximum cardinality**. Common examples of maximum cardinality are 1:N, N:M, and 1:1 (not shown).

Another important question is, "What is the minimum number of entities required in the relationship?" Must an adviser have a student to advise, and must a student have an adviser? Constraints on minimum requirements are called **minimum cardinalities**.

Figure 4-21 presents a third version of this E-R diagram that shows both maximum and minimum cardinalities. The vertical bar on a line means that at least one entity of that type is required. The small oval means that the entity is optional; the relationship *need not* have an entity of that type.

Thus, in Figure 4-21 a department is not required to have a relationship to any adviser, but an adviser is required to belong to a department. Similarly, an adviser is not required to

FIGURE 4-20

Entity Relationships, Version 2

have a relationship to a student, but a student is required to have a relationship to an adviser. Note, also, that the maximum cardinalities in Figure 4-21 have been changed so that both are 1:N.

Is the model in Figure 4-21 a good one? It depends on the policy of the university. Again, only the users know for sure.

Q5. How Is a Data Model Transformed into a Database Design?

Database design is the process of converting a data model into tables, relationships, and data constraints. The database design team transforms entities into tables and expresses relationships by defining foreign keys. Database design is a complicated subject; as with data modeling, it occupies weeks in a database management class. In this section, however, we will introduce two important database design concepts: normalization and the representation of two kinds of relationships. The first concept is a foundation of database design, and the second will help you understand important design considerations.

Normalization

Normalization is the process of converting a poorly structured table into two or more well-structured tables. A table is such a simple construct that you may wonder how one could possibly be poorly structured. In truth, there are many ways that tables can be malformed—so many, in fact, that researchers have published hundreds of papers on this topic alone.

Consider the *Employee* table in Figure 4-22(a). It lists employee names, hire dates, e-mail addresses, and the name and number of the department in which the employee works. This

FIGURE 4-22

Table with Problematic Structure

Employee

Name	HireDate	Email	DeptNo	DeptName
Jones	Feb 1, 2009	Jones@ourcompany.com	100	Accounting
Smith	Dec 3, 2011	Smith@ourcompany.com	200	Marketing
Chau	March 7, 2011	Chau@ourcompany.com	100	Accounting
Greene	July 17, 2010	Greene@ourcompany.com	100	Accounting

(a) Table Before Update

Employee

Name	HireDate	Email	DeptNo	DeptName
Jones	Feb 1, 2009	Jones@ourcompany.com	100	Accounting and Finance
Smith	Dec 3, 2011	Smith@ourcompany.com	200	Marketing
Chau	March 7, 2011	Chau@ourcompany.com	100	Accounting and Finance
Greene	July 17, 2010	Greene@ourcompany.com	100	Accounting

(b) Table with Incomplete Update

table seems innocent enough. But consider what happens when the Accounting department changes its name to Accounting and Finance. Because department names are duplicated in this table, every row that has a value of "Accounting" must be changed to "Accounting and Finance."

Data Integrity Problems

Suppose the Accounting name change is correctly made in two rows, but not in the third. The result is shown in Figure 4-22(b). This table has what is called a **data integrity problem**, which is the situation that exists when the database contains inconsistent data. Here, two rows indicate that the name of Department 100 is "Accounting and Finance," and another row indicates that the name of Department 100 is "Accounting."

This problem is easy to spot in this small table. But consider a table like the *Customer* table in the Amazon.com database or the eBay database. Those databases may have hundreds of millions of rows. Once a table that large develops serious data integrity problems, months of labor will be required to remove them.

Data integrity problems are serious. A table that has data integrity problems will produce incorrect and inconsistent data. Users will lose confidence in their ability to conceive information from that data, and the system will develop a poor reputation. Information systems with poor reputations become serious burdens to the organizations that use them.

Normalizing for Data Integrity

The data integrity problem can occur only if data are duplicated. Because of this, one easy way to eliminate the problem is to eliminate the duplicated data. We can do this by transforming the table in Figure 4-22 into two tables, as shown in Figure 4-23. Here, the name of the department is stored just once; therefore no data inconsistencies can occur.

Of course, to produce an employee report that includes the department name, the two tables in Figure 4-23 will need to be joined back together. Because such joining of tables is common, DBMS products have been programmed to perform it efficiently, but it still requires work. From this example, you can see a trade-off in database design: Normalized tables eliminate data duplication, but they can be slower to process. Dealing with such trade-offs is an important consideration in database design.

The general goal of normalization is to construct tables such that every table has a *single* topic or theme. In good writing, every paragraph should have a single theme. This is true of databases as well; every table should have a single theme. The problem with the table in Figure 4-22 is that it has two independent themes: employees and departments. The way to correct the problem is to split the table into two tables, each with its own

Employee

Name	HireDate	Email	DeptNo
Jones	Feb 1, 2009	Jones@ourcompany.com	100
Smith	Dec 3, 2011	Smith@ourcompany.com	200
Chau	March 7, 2011	Chau@ourcompany.com	100
Greene	July 17, 2010	Greene@ourcompany.com	100

Department

DeptNo	DeptName
100	Accounting
200	Marketing
300	Information Systems

FIGURE 4-23

Two Normalized Tables

theme. In this case, we create an *Employee* table and a *Department* table, as shown in Figure 4-23.

As mentioned, there are dozens of ways that tables can be poorly formed. Database practitioners classify tables into various **normal forms**, which are classifications of tables according to the kinds of problems they have. Transforming a table into a normal form to remove duplicated data and other problems is called *normalizing* the table.[3] Thus, when you hear a database designer say, "Those tables are not normalized," she does not mean that the tables have irregular, not-normal data. Instead, she means that the tables have a format that could cause data integrity problems.

Summary of Normalization

As a future user of databases, you do not need to know the details of normalization. Instead, understand the general principle that every normalized (well-formed) table has one and only one theme. Further, tables that are not normalized are subject to data integrity problems.

Be aware, too, that normalization is just one criterion for evaluating database designs. Because normalized designs can be slower to process, database designers sometimes choose to accept non-normalized tables. The best design depends on the users' processing requirements.

Representing Relationships

Figure 4-24 shows the steps involved in transforming a data model into a relational database design. First, the database designer creates a table for each entity. The identifier of the entity becomes the key of the table. Each attribute of the entity becomes a column of the table. Next, the resulting tables are normalized so that each table has a single theme. Once that has been done, the next step is to represent relationship among those tables.

For example, consider the E-R diagram in Figure 4-25(a). The *Adviser* entity has a 1:N relationship to the *Student* entity. To create the database design, we construct a table for *Adviser* and a second table for *Student*, as shown in Figure 4-25(b). The key of the *Adviser* table is *AdviserName*, and the key of the *Student* table is *StudentNumber*. Further, the *EmailAddress* attribute of the *Adviser* entity becomes the *EmailAddress* column of the *Adviser* table, and the *StudentName* and *MidTerm* attributes of the *Student* entity become the *StudentName* and *MidTerm* columns of the *Student* table.

The next task is to represent relationships. Because we are using the relational model, we know that we must add a foreign key to one of the two tables. The possibilities are: (1) place the foreign key *StudentNumber* in the *Adviser* table or (2) place the foreign key *AdviserName* in the *Student* table.

The correct choice is to place *AdviserName* in the *Student* table, as shown in Figure 4-25(c). To determine a student's adviser, we just look into the *AdviserName* column of that student's row. To determine the adviser's students, we search the *AdviserName* column in the *Student* table to determine which rows have that adviser's name. If a student changes advisers, we simply change the value in the *AdviserName* column. Changing *Jackson* to *Jones* in the first row, for example, will assign student 100 to Professor Jones.

For this data model, placing *StudentNumber* in *Adviser* would be incorrect. If we were to do that, we could assign only one student to an adviser. There is no place to assign a second adviser.

FIGURE 4-24

Summary of Database Design Process

- Represent each entity with a table
  – Entity identifier becomes table key
  – Entity attributes become table columns
- Normalize tables as necessary
- Represent relationships
  – Use foreign keys
  – Add additional tables for N:M relationships

---

[3] See David Kroenke and David Auer, *Database Processing*, 12th ed. (Upper Saddle River, NJ: Prentice Hall, 2012) for more information.

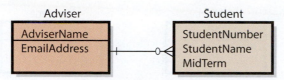

FIGURE 4-25

Representing a 1:N Relationship

(a) 1:N Relationship Between Adviser and Student Entities

Adviser Table—Key is AdviserName

AdviserName	EmailAddress
Jones	Jones@myuniv.edu
Choi	Choi@myuniv.edu
Jackson	Jackson@myuniv.edu

Student Table—Key is StudentNumber

StudentNumber	StudentName	MidTerm
100	Lisa	90
200	Jennie	85
300	Jason	82
400	Terry	95

(b) Creating a Table for Each Entity

Adviser Table—Key is AdviserName

AdviserName	EmailAddress
Jones	Jones@myuniv.edu
Choi	Choi@myuniv.edu
Jackson	Jackson@myuniv.edu

Foreign Key Column Represents Relationship

Student—Key is StudentNumber

StudentNumber	StudentName	MidTerm	AdviserName
100	Lisa	90	Jackson
200	Jennie	85	Jackson
300	Jason	82	Choi
400	Terry	95	Jackson

(c) Using the *AdviserName* Foreign Key to Represent the 1:N Relationship

This strategy for placing foreign keys will not work for all relationships, however. Consider the data model in Figure 4-26(a); here advisers and students have a many-to-many relationship. An adviser may have many students, and a student may have multiple advisers (for multiple majors).

The foreign key strategy we used for the 1:N data model will not work here. To see why, examine Figure 4-26(b). If student 100 has more than one adviser, there is no place to record second or subsequent advisers.

To represent an N:M relationship, we need to create a third table, as shown in Figure 4-26(c). The third table has two columns, *AdviserName* and *StudentNumber*. Each row of the table means that the given adviser advises the student with the given number.

As you can imagine, there is a great deal more to database design than we have presented here. Still, this section should give you an idea of the tasks that need to be accomplished to create a database. You should also realize that the database design is a direct consequence of decisions made in the data model. If the data model is wrong, the database design will be wrong as well.

FIGURE 4-26

Representing an N:M Relationship

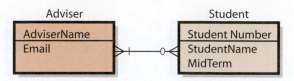

(a) N:M Relationship Between Adviser and Student

Adviser—Key is AdviserName

AdviserName	Email
Jones	Jones@myuniv.edu
Choi	Choi@myuniv.edu
Jackson	Jackson@myuniv.edu

No room to place second or third AdviserName

Student—Key is StudentNumber

StudentNumber	StudentName	MidTerm	AdviserName
100	Lisa	90	Jackson
200	Jennie	85	Jackson
300	Jason	82	Choi
400	Terry	95	Jackson

(b) Incorrect Representation of N:M Relationship

Adviser—Key is AdviserName

AdviserName	Email
Jones	Jones@myuniv.edu
Choi	Choi@myuniv.edu
Jackson	Jackson@myuniv.edu

Student—Key is StudentNumber

StudentNumber	StudentName	MidTerm
100	Lisa	90
200	Jennie	85
300	Jason	82
400	Terry	95

Adviser_Student_Intersection

AdviserName	StudentNumber
Jackson	100
Jackson	200
Choi	300
Jackson	400
Choi	100
Jones	100

Student 100 has three advisers.

(c) Adviser_Student_Intersection Table Represents the N:M Relationship

Q6. What Is the Users' Role in the Development of Databases?

As stated, a database is a model of how the users view their business world. This means that the users are the final judges as to what data the database should contain and how the records in that database should be related to one another.

The easiest time to change the database structure is during the data modeling stage. Changing a relationship from one-to-many to many-to-many in a data model is simply a matter of changing the 1:N notation to N:M. However, once the database has been constructed, loaded with data, and application forms, reports, queries, and application programs have been created, changing a one-to-many relationship to many-to-many means weeks of work.

You can glean some idea of why this might be true by contrasting Figure 4-25(c) with Figure 4-26(c). Suppose that instead of having just a few rows, each table has thousands of rows; in that case, transforming the database from one format to the other involves considerable work. Even worse, however, is that someone must change application components as well. For example, if students have at most one adviser, then a single text box can be used to enter *AdviserName*. If students can have multiple advisers, then a multiple-row table will need to be used to enter *AdviserName* and a program will need to be written to store the values of *AdviserName* into the *Adviser_Student_Intersection* table. There are dozens of other consequences, consequences that will translate into wasted labor and wasted expense.

Thus, *user review of the data model is crucial.* When a database is developed for your use, you must carefully review the data model. If you do not understand any aspect of it, you should ask for clarification until you do. *Entities must contain all of the data you and your employees need to do your jobs, and relationships must accurately reflect your view of the business.* If the data model is wrong, the database will be designed incorrectly, and the applications will be difficult to use, if not worthless. Do not proceed unless the data model is accurate.

As a corollary, when asked to review a data model, take that review seriously. Devote the time necessary to perform a thorough review. Any mistakes you miss will come back to haunt you, and by then the cost of correction may be very high with regard to both time and expense. This brief introduction to data modeling shows why databases can be more difficult to develop than spreadsheets.

Q7. How Can the Intramural League Improve Its Database?

We conclude this chapter by returning to the intramural league and its database. As you saw in the opening vignette, the league has at least two problems: a process problem that caused the missing equipment report not to have been produced on time and a database problem that allocates equipment to teams, but not to coaches, the people who are responsible for returning the equipment. We will address process problems starting in the next chapter. For now, let's consider the database problem.

Figure 4-27 shows the tables in the League database. Each rectangle represents a table, and the items in the rectangles are fields in the table. The key symbol ⚷ means that ID is the primary key of each table. In fact, the design of these tables uses what are called **surrogate keys**, which are unique identifiers assigned by the DBMS. Every time a new row is created, the DBMS, here Microsoft Access, creates a unique identifier for that row. That identifier has no meaning to the users, but it is guaranteed to be unique. The primary key of all three tables is a surrogate key named *ID*. (These are three different fields; they are just named the same thing in their respective tables.)

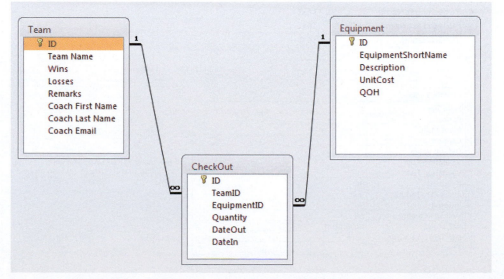

FIGURE 4-27

Tables in the League Database

There are several ways of solving the league's problem. In the following explanation, we will proceed in a way that avoids messy pitfalls and results in an acceptable result. It will also give you a taste of what database designers do. If you take a database class, you will approach problems like this in a systematic way, based on sound theory. Here, we will just work our way through to a solution.

League Database, Revision 1

The problem is that equipment is checked out to teams, and teams can have different coaches in different years. So, one way to solve that problem is to add a new field to the *Team* table that indicates the year of the data. Figure 4-28 shows the structure of a new table with a new field called *Season*. It will have values like "2010–2011."

Now, consider the implications of that change. When we add *Season*, we are actually changing the theme of the table. It is no longer about a team; it is about a team's situation (i.e., performance, coach) in a given season. Consequently, we really should change the name of the table from *Team* to something like *Team_Season*. Note this was done in Figure 4-28.

Figure 4-29 shows a report that reflects this change. It makes sense; we are now recording the win/loss record for a particular year as well as the coach for that year. The *Remarks* also pertain to a given team in a given season. By making this change, we have made the table's structure less ambiguous.

However, we've lost something. Where can we store an item of data that belongs to a team, but not to a particular season? If the league wants to record, say, the first season a team played, where would that be stored? If we store *FirstSeasonPlayed* in this table, we will create a data integrity problem (you will have a chance to verify this in Using Your Knowledge Exercise 3 on page 121.) In fact, we have no place to store anything else about the team that does not change from year to year, maybe jersey color (if that is fixed).

If this is a problem for the league, it will need to define a new table, called *Team,* and store the data that does not change from year to year in that new table. It would then need to define a new relationship from *Team* to *Team_Season*. (See Using Your Knowledge Exercise 4 on page 121.) For now, let's assume that the league has no need for such overall team data and ignore this problem.

FIGURE 4-28

League Database, Revision1, Team_Season Table

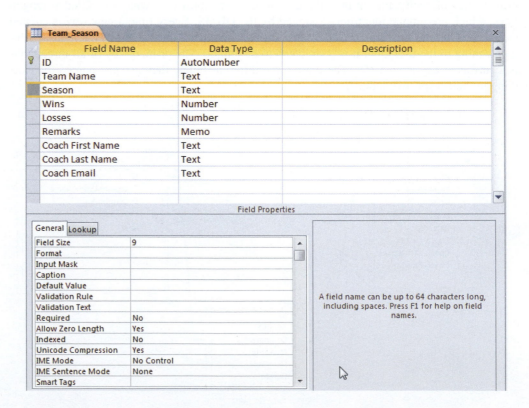

Team History Report, Revision 1

Team Name	Season	Wins	Losses	Remarks	Coach First Name	Coach Last Name	Coach Email
Helicopters	2009-2010	7	0	Won the tournament first year.	Fred	Dillingham	FD@ourschool.edu
Helicopters	2010-2011	7	0	Won the tournament last year.	Fred	Dillingham	FD@ourschool.edu
Helicopters	2011-2012	7	0	Won the tournament last year, again.	Carter	Jackson	CJ@ourschool.edu
Huskies	2009-2010	1	5	Nearly won tournament.	Sark	Justin	SJ@ourschool.edu
Huskies	2010-2011	1	5	Lost several games by forefeit.	Sark	Justin	SJ@ourschool.edu
Huskies	2011-2012	1	5	Improving ...	Sark	Justin	SJ@ourschool.edu
Wolverines	2011-2012	5	2	Off to good start.	Daniel	Smith	DS@SmithFamily.com

FIGURE 4-29

Report for League DB, Revision 1

However, by solving the problem in this way we have created a new problem. Notice in the report in Figure 4-29 that by storing a row for each team, each season, that we have duplicated the e-mail addresses for those who have coached more than once. For the data shown, if, for example, Sark Justin, changes his or her e-mail, three rows will need to be changed. Hence, this new table is vulnerable to data integrity problems; it is not normalized. We need to fix it in the next revision.

League Database, Revision 2

Consider Figure 4-30, which shows an E-R model of the League database after the revision just described. The changed entity is shown in brown, and the new attribute, *Season,* is shown in blue. Neither the *Checkout* nor *Equipment* entities have been changed, so their attributes are omitted for simplicity.

ADDING THE COACH ENTITY Examining the model in Figure 4-30, we can see that *Team_Season* has two themes; one is about the team in a given season and the second is about a coach and his or her e-mail. Using our normalization criterion, we know that each entity should have a single theme. So, we decide to move the *Coach* attributes from *Team_Season* into a new entity called *Coach*, as shown in Figure 4-31.

OK so far, but what is the relationship between *Coach* and *Team*? If we look at the data in Figure 4-29, it appears that a given coach can coach many teams, in the same or different seasons (note Fred Dillingham, the coach who took off with the gear). It also appears that a team has at most one coach. Thus, the relationship from *Coach* to *Team_Season* seems to be 1:N.

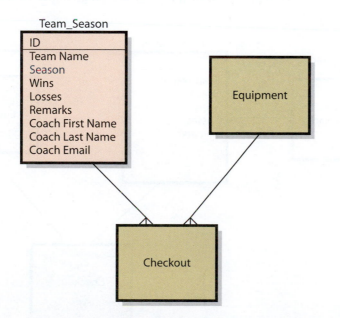

FIGURE 4-30

League E-R Diagram, Revision 1

FIGURE 4-31

**League E-R Diagram with
Coach Entity**

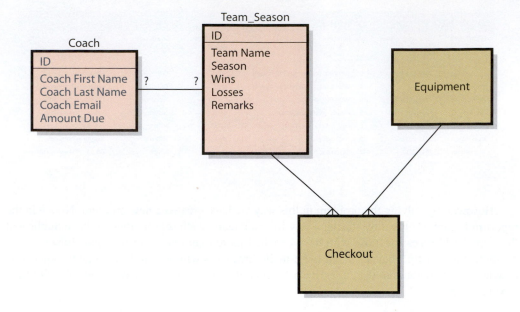

However, and this is where you, as a business professional, come into the picture; it is dangerous to make such conclusions from sample data. We might just have an odd set of data. An experienced database design team knows to interview users (which could be you) to find out. In this case, let's assume that the 1:N relationship is correct.

The decisions yield the E-R diagram in Figure 4-32. Before we continue, notice we've added *Amount Due* to the *Coach* entity. The idea behind this addition is that at the end of the sport's season, an application program will compute the amount due based on the current cost of equipment that has not been returned. As equipment is returned, this amount will be decremented appropriately.

REPRESENTING THE RELATIONSHIP IN THE DATABASE DESIGN As described in Q5, we represent a 1:N relationship by adding the key of the parent (the entity on the 1 side) to the child (the entity on the many side). Here, we need to add the key of *Coach* to *Team_Season*. Figure 4-33 shows the result; *CoachID* in *Team_Season* is a foreign key that references *ID* in *Coach*.

With this design, every table has a single theme and is normalized. This design is therefore not subject to data integrity problems. Note, however, that it will be necessary to join rows in the table together to produce reports. DBMS products are programmed to do that efficiently,

FIGURE 4-32

**League E-R Diagram,
Revision 2**

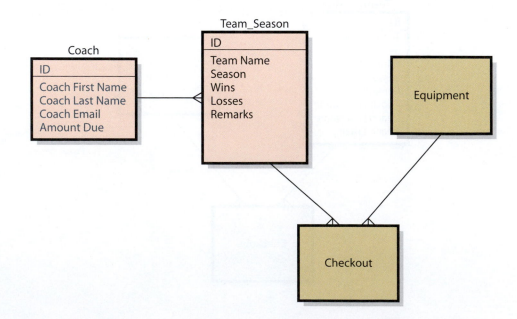

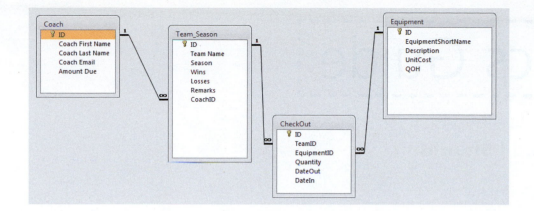

FIGURE 4-33

League Database Design, Revision 2

however. The report in Figure 4-34 shows equipment that has been checked out by coaches, but that has not yet been returned. This report was created by joining data in all four of the tables in Figure 4-33 together.

With these two changes, the intramural league can now allocate equipment checkouts to specific coaches. These changes, in and of themselves, will not solve the league's problem, but it will at least allow the league to know definitively who checked out what equipment. The complete solution to the problem requires a change in process as well.

Coach Equipment Report -- Items Checked Out as of 10/17/2012

Coach First Name	Coach Last Name	Coach Email	Team Name	Season	DateOut	Equipment	Quantity
Fred	Dillingham	FD@ourschool.edu					
			Helicopters	2009-2010			
					11/6/2010	Soccer Jerseys	12
					11/6/2010	Soccer Balls	3
Sark	Justin	SJ@ourschool.edu					
			Huskies	2009-2010			
					10/4/2009	Soccer Balls	3
			Huskies	2011-2012			
					9/6/2012	Soccer Balls	2
					9/6/2012	Soccer Jerseys	12
					9/6/2012	Soccer Balls	1
Daniel	Smith	DS@SmithFamily.com					
			Wolverines	2011-2012			
					9/6/2012	Soccer Balls	3
					9/6/2012	Soccer Jerseys	14
					9/6/2012	Soccer Balls	2
Carter	Jackson	CJ@ourschool.edu					
			Helicopters	2011-2012			
					9/4/2012	Soccer Balls	2
					9/4/2012	Soccer Jerseys	17
					9/4/2012	Soccer Balls	3

FIGURE 4-34

Report Showing Equipment Still Checked Out to Coaches

Ethics Guide

Nobody Said I Shouldn't

"My name is Chris and I do systems support for our group. I configure the new computers, set up the network, make sure the servers are operating, and so forth. I also do all of the database backups. I've always liked computers. After high school, I worked odd jobs to make some money, then I got an associate degree in information technology from our local community college.

"Anyway, as I said, I make backup copies of our databases. One weekend, I didn't have much going on, so I copied one of the database backups to a DVD and took it home. I had taken a class on database processing as part of my associate degree, and we used SQL Server (our database management system) in my class. In fact, I suppose that's part of the reason I got the job. Anyway, it was easy to restore the database on my computer at home, and I did.

"Of course, as they'll tell you in your database class, one of the big advantages of database processing is that databases have metadata, or data that describe the content of the database. So, although I didn't know what tables were in our database, I did know how to access the SQL Server metadata. I just queried a table called *sysTables* to learn the names of our tables. From there it was easy to find out what columns each table had.

"I found tables with data about orders, customers, salespeople, and so forth, and, just to amuse myself, and to see how much of the query language SQL that I could remember, I started playing around with the data. I was curious to know which order entry clerk was the best, so I started querying each clerk's order data, the total number of orders, total order amounts, things like that. It was easy to do and fun.

"I know one of the order entry clerks, Jason, pretty well, so I started looking at the data for his orders. I was just curious, and it was very simple SQL. I was just playing around with the data when I noticed something odd. All of his biggest orders were with one company, Valley Appliances, and even stranger, every one of its orders had a huge discount. I thought, well, maybe that's typical. Out of curiosity, I started looking at data for the other clerks, and very few of them had an order with Valley Appliances. But, when they did, Valley didn't get a big discount. Then I looked at the rest of Jason's orders, and none of them had much in the way of discounts, either.

"The next Friday, a bunch of us went out for a beer after work. I happened to see Jason, so I asked him about Valley Appliances and made a joke about the discounts. He asked me what I meant, and then I told him that I'd been looking at the data for fun and that I saw this odd pattern. He just laughed, said he just 'did his job,' and then changed the subject.

"Well, to make a long story short, when I got to work on Monday morning, my office was cleaned out. There was nothing there except a note telling me to go see my boss. The bottom line was, I was fired. The company also threatened that if I didn't return all of its data, I'd be in court for the next 5 years . . . things like that. I was so mad I didn't even tell them about Jason. Now my problem is that I'm out of a job, and I can't exactly use my last company for a reference."

DISCUSSION QUESTIONS

1. Where did Chris go wrong?
2. Do you think it was illegal, unethical, or neither for Chris to take the database home and query the data?
3. Does the company share culpability with Chris?
4. What do you think Chris should have done upon discovering the odd pattern in Jason's orders?
5. What should the company have done before firing Chris?
6. Is it possible that someone other than Jason is involved in the arrangement with Valley Appliances? What should Chris have done in light of that possibility?
7. What should Chris do now?
8. "Metadata make databases easy to use, for both authorized and unauthorized purposes." Explain what organizations should do in light of this fact.

Active Review

Use this Active Review to verify that you understand the material in the chapter. You can read the entire chapter and then perform the tasks in this review, or you can read the text material for just one question and perform the tasks in this review for that question before moving on to the next one.

Q1. What is the purpose of a database?

State the purpose of a database. Explain the circumstances in which a database is preferred to a spreadsheet. Describe the key difference between Figures 4-1 and 4-2.

Q2. What are the contents of a database?

Define the term *database*. Explain the hierarchy of data and name three elements of a database. Define *metadata*. Using the example of *Student* and *Office_Visit* tables, show how relationships among rows are represented in a database. Define the terms *key, foreign key*, and *relational database*.

Q3. What are the components of a database application system?

Explain why a database, by itself, is not very useful to business users. Name the components of a database application system and sketch their relationship. Explain the acronym DBMS and name its functions. List five popular DBMS products. Explain the difference between a DBMS and a database. Summarize the functions of a DBMS. Define *SQL*. Describe the major functions of database administration.

Name and describe the components of a database application. Explain the need for application programs. For multi-user processing, describe one way in which one user's work can interfere with another's. Explain why multi-user database processing involves more than just connecting another computer to the network. Define two broad categories of DBMS and explain their differences.

Q4. How do data models facilitate database design?

Explain why user involvement is critical during database development. Describe the function of a data model. Sketch the

database development process. Define *E-R model, entity, relationship, attribute*, and *identifier*. Give an example, other than one in this text, of an E-R diagram. Define *maximum cardinality* and *minimum cardinality*. Give an example of three maximum cardinalities and two minimum cardinalities. Explain the notation in Figures 4-18 and 4-19.

Q5. How is a data model transformed into a database design?

Name the three components of a database design. Define *normalization* and explain why it is important. Define *data integrity problem* and describe its consequences. Give an example of a table from this chapter with data integrity problems and show how it can be normalized into two or more tables that do not have such problems. Describe two steps in transforming a data model into a database design. Using an example not in this chapter, show how 1:N and N:M relationships are represented in a relational database.

Q6. What is the users' role in the development of databases?

Describe the users' role in database development. Explain why it is easier and cheaper to change a data model than to change an existing database. Use the examples of Figures 4-25(c) and 4-26(c) in your answer. Describe two criteria for judging a data model. Explain why it is important to devote time to understanding a data model.

Q7. How can the intramural league improve its database?

What two factors caused the problem at the intramural league? Explain the first revision to the database. Explain what was lost in this revision. Explain why the revision caused a data integrity problem. Describe the need for the *Coach* table and justify the decision to model the relationship from *Coach* to *Team_Season* as 1:N. Explain how that relationship was represented in the database.

Key Terms and Concepts

Access   *97*
Attributes   *105*
Byte   *93*
Columns   *93*
Crow's feet   *107*
Crow's-foot diagram   *107*
Data integrity problem   *109*
Data model   *104*
Database   *93*
Database administration (DBA)   *99*
Database application   *100*
Database application system   *97*
Database management system
  (DBMS)   *97*
DB2   *97*
Enterprise DBMS   *103*
Entity   *105*

Entity-relationship (E-R) data
  model   *105*
Entity-relationship (E-R)
  diagrams   *106*
Fields   *93*
File   *93*
Foreign keys   *96*
Form   *100*
Identifier   *105*
Key   *94*
Lost update problem   *102*
Many-to-many (N:M) relationships   *107*
Maximum cardinality   *107*
Metadata   *96*
Minimum cardinality   *107*
MySQL   *97*
Normal forms   *110*

Normalization   *108*
Object-relational database   *96*
One-to-many (1:N) relationships   *107*
Oracle Database   *97*
Personal DBMS   *103*
Primary key   *95*
Query   *101*
Records   *93*
Relation   *96*
Relational databases   *96*
Relationships   *106*
Report   *100*
Rows   *93*
SQL Server   *97*
Structured Query Language (SQL)   *98*
Surrogate key   *113*
Table   *93*

Using Your Knowledge

1. Draw an entity-relationship diagram that shows the relationships among a database, database applications, and users.
2. Consider the relationship between *Adviser* and *Student* in Figure 4-20. Explain what it means if the maximum cardinality of this relationship is:
   a. N:1
   b. 1:1
   c. 5:1
   d. 1:5
3. Suppose the intramural league wants to keep track of the first season that a team played in the league. Make that addition to *Team_Season* for the data shown in Figure 4-29. Explain why the table now has duplicated data. Explain potential data integrity problems from that data.
4. To solve the problem in Exercise 3, create a new entity named *Team*. Extend the E-R diagram in Figure 4-32 to include the *Team* entity. State the cardinality of the relationship between *Team* and *Team_Season*. Show how the database structure in Figure 4-33 will need to be changed to accommodate this new table.
5. Identify possible entities in the data entry form in Figure 4-35. What attributes are shown for each? What do you think are the identifiers?
6. Using your answer to Exercise 5, draw an E-R diagram for the data entry form in Figure 4-35. Specify cardinalities. State your assumptions.
7. The partial E-R diagram in Figure 4-36 is for a sales order. Assume there is only one *Salesperson* per *SalesOrder*.

FIGURE 4-35

Sample Data Entry Form

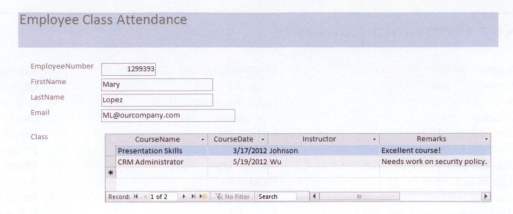

FIGURE 4-36

Partial E-R Diagram for Sales Order

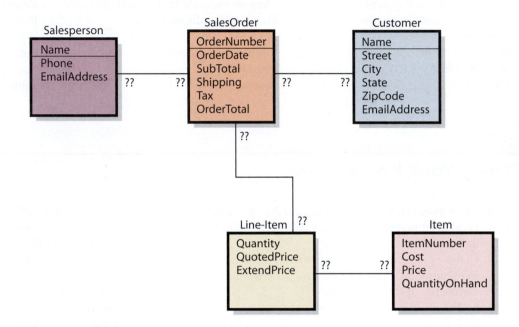

a. Specify the maximum cardinalities for each relationship. State your assumptions, if necessary.

b. Specify the minimum cardinalities for each relationship. State your assumptions, if necessary.

8. Consider the report in Figure 4-12 in the context of information as a *difference that makes a difference.*

What differences does the structure of this report show? Describe five ways that this report could be changed that would make it easier for humans to conceive information. Name the criteria you used in suggesting these five changes.

Collaboration Exercise 4

Collaborate with a group of fellow students to answer the following questions. For this exercise do not meet face to face. Your task will be easier if you coordinate your work with SharePoint, Office 365, Google Docs with Google + or equivalent collaboration tools. (See Chapter 9 for a discussion of collaboration tools and processes.) Your answers should reflect the thinking of the entire group, and not just that of one or two individuals.

The purpose of this exercise is to compute the cost of class registration. To do so, we will consider both class registration processes as well as information systems that support them.

Figure 4-37 shows a spreadsheet that is used to track the assignment of sheet music to a choir—it could be a church choir or school or community choir. The type of choir does not matter, because the problem is universal. Sheet music is expensive, choir members need to be able to take sheet music away for practice at home, and not all of the music gets back to the inventory. (Sheet music can be purchased or rented, but either way, lost music is an expense.)

Look closely at this data and you will see some data integrity problems—or at least some possible data integrity problems. For one, do Sandra Corning and Linda Duong really have the same copy of music checked out? Second, did Mozart and J. S. Bach both write a Requiem, or in row 15 should J. S. Bach actually be Mozart? Also, there is a problem with Eleanor Dixon's phone number; several phone numbers are the same as well, which seems suspicious.

Additionally, this spreadsheet is confusing and hard to use. The column labeled *First Name* includes both people names and the names of choruses. *Email* has both e-mail addresses and composer names, and *Phone* has both phone numbers and copy identifiers. Furthermore, to record a checkout of music the user must first add a new row and then reenter the name of the work, the composer's name, and the copy to be checked out. Finally, consider what happens when the user wants to find all copies of a particular work: The user will have to examine the rows in each of four spreadsheets for the four voice parts.

In fact, a spreadsheet is ill-suited for this application. A database would be a far better tool, and situations like this are obvious candidates for innovation.

1. Analyze the spreadsheet shown in Figure 4-37 and list all of the problems that occur when trying to track the assignment of sheet music using this spreadsheet.
2. Figure 4-38(a) shows a two-entity data model for the sheet-music-tracking problem.
   a. Select identifiers for the *ChoirMember* and *Work* entities. Justify your selection.
   b. This design does not eliminate the potential for data integrity problems that occur in the spreadsheet. Explain why not.
   c. Design a database for this data model. Specify key and foreign key columns.

⊿	A	B	C	D	E
1	Last Name	First Name	Email	Phone	Part
2	Ashley	Jane	JA@somewhere.com	703.555.1234	Soprano
3	Davidson	Kaye	KD@somewhere.com	703.555.2236	Soprano
4	Ching	Kam Hoong	KHC@overhere.com	703.555.2236	Soprano
5	Menstell	Lori Lee	LLM@somewhere.com	703.555.1237	Soprano
6	Corning	Sandra	SC2@overhere.com	703.555.1234	Soprano
7		B-minor mass	J.S. Bach	Soprano Copy 7	
8		Requiem	Mozart	Soprano Copy 17	
9		9th Symphony Chorus	Beethoven	Soprano Copy 9	
10	Wei	Guang	GW1@somewhere.com	703.555.9936	Soprano
11	Dixon	Eleanor	ED@thisplace.com	703.555.12379	Soprano
12		B-minor mass	J.S. Bach	Soprano Copy 11	
13	Duong	Linda	LD2@overhere.com	703.555.8736	Soprano
14		B-minor mass	J.S. Bach	Soprano Copy 7	
15		Requiem	J.S. Bach	Soprano Copy 19	
16	Lunden	Haley	HL@somewhere.com	703.555.0836	Soprano
17	Utran	Diem Thi	DTU@somewhere.com	703.555.1089	Soprano

FIGURE 4-37

Sheet Music Spreadsheet

FIGURE 4-38

Three Data Model Alternatives

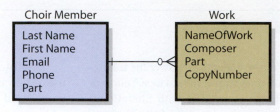

(a) Data Model Alternative 1

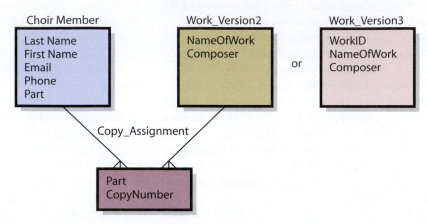

(b) Data Model Alternative 2

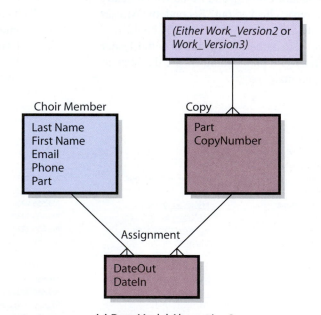

(c) Data Model Alternative 3

3. Figure 4-38(b) shows a second alternative data model for the sheet-music-tracking problem. This alternative shows two variations on the *Work* entity. In the second variation, an attribute named *WorkID* has been added to *Work_Version3*. This attribute is a unique identifier for the work; the DBMS will assign a unique value to *WorkID* when a new row is added to the *Work* table.

a. Select identifiers for *ChoirMember, Work_Version2, Work_Version3,* and *Copy_Assignment.* Justify your selection.
b. Does this design eliminate the potential for data integrity problems that occur in the spreadsheet? Why or why not?
c. Design a database for the data model that uses *Work_Version2*. Specify key and foreign key columns.

d. Design a database for the data models that uses *Work_Version3*. Specify key and foreign key columns.

e. Is the design with *Work_Version2* better than the design for *Work_Version3*? Why or why not?

4. Figure 4-38(c) shows a third alternative data model for the sheet-music-tracking problem. In this data model, use either *Work_Version2* or *Work_Version3*, whichever you think is better.

a. Select identifiers for each entity in your data model. Justify your selection.

b. Summarize the differences between this data model and that in Figure 4-38(b). Which data model is better? Why?

c. Design a database for this data model. Specify key and foreign key columns.

5. Which of the three data models is the best? Justify your answer.

CASE STUDY 4

Aviation Safety Network

The mission of the Aviation Safety Network (ASN) is to provide up-to-date, complete, and reliable data on airliner accidents and safety issues to those with a professional interest in aviation. ASN defines an *airliner* as an aircraft capable of carrying 14 or more passengers. ASN data include data on commercial, military, and corporate airplanes.

ASN gathers data from a variety of sources, including the International Civil Aviation Board, the National Transportation Safety Board, and the Civil Aviation Authority. Data are also taken from magazines, such as *Air Safety Week* and *Aviation Week and Space Technology*; from a variety of books; and from prominent individuals in the aviation safety industry.

ASN compiles the source data into a Microsoft Access database. The core table contains over 10,000 rows of data concerning incident and accident descriptions. This table is linked to several other tables that store data about airports, airlines, aircraft types, countries, and so forth. Periodically, the Access data are reformatted and exported to a MySQL database, which is used by programs that support queries on ASN's Web site (*http://aviation-safety.net/database*).

On that site, incident and accident data can be accessed by year, by airline, by aircraft, by nation, and in other ways. For example, Figure 4-39 shows a list of incidents and accidents that involved the Airbus 320. When the user clicks on a particular accident, such as the one on January 15, 2009, a summary of the incident is presented, as shown in Figure 4-40.

In addition to descriptions of incidents and accidents, ASN also summarizes the data to help its users determine airliner accident trends. For example, Figure 4-41 shows the geographic locations of fatal accidents for 2007. Notice that there were almost no such accidents in Australia, Russia, or China. Either these countries are particularly vigilant about aircraft safety, were lucky, or not all accidents were reported.

Hugo Ranter of the Netherlands started the ASN Web site in 1995. Fabian I. Lujan of Argentina has maintained the site since 1998. ASN has nearly 10,000 e-mail subscribers in 170 countries, and the site receives over 50,000 visits per week. For more information about this site, go to *http://aviation-safety.net/about*.

Questions

1. All of the data included in this database are available in public documents. Because this is the case, what is the value of the Aviation Safety Network? Why don't users just consult the online version of the underlying references? In your answer, consider the difference between data and information.

2. What was the cause of the incident shown in Figure 4-40? That incident, in which no one was fatally injured, was caused by geese that struck an Airbus 320 that was flown by US Airways out of La Guardia Airport, New York. It would be illogical to conclude from this one incident that it is dangerous to fly where there are geese or Airbus 320s, US Airways, or out of La Guardia. Or would it be illogical? Suppose that you wanted to determine whether there is a systematic pattern of flights downed by geese, or with the A320, US Airways, or La Guardia. How would you proceed? How would you use the resources of *http://aviation-saftey.net* to make this determination?

3. The ASN database and Web site were created and are maintained by two individuals. The database might be complete and accurate, or it might not be. To what extent should you rely on these data? What can you do to decide whether you should rely on the data at this site?

4. Consider the data in Figure 4-41. Describe indications you see that indicate this figure may not include all accident data. If you believe that not all data is included, what value does this figure have to you? What would be legitimate uses for this data and what uses are likely to be erroneous?

5. Suppose you work in the marketing department for an airline. Can you use these data in your marketing efforts? If so, how? What are the dangers of basing a marketing campaign on safety?

6. Suppose you are a maintenance manager for a major airline. How can you use these data? Would it be wise to develop your own, similar database? Why or why not?

FIGURE 4-39

Incidents and Accidents Involving the Airbus 320

Source: Reprinted by permission of Aviation Safety Network, © 2009 ASN. *www.aviation-safety.net*.

FIGURE 4-40

Incident Description Summary

Source: Reprinted by permission of Aviation Safety Network, © 2009 ASN. *www.aviation-safety.net*.

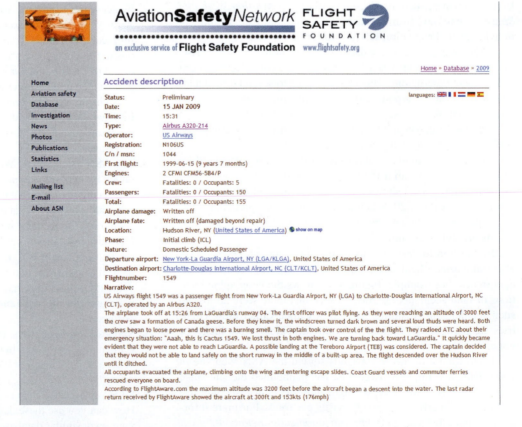

FIGURE 4-41

**Fatal Accidents,
Worldwide, 2007**

Source: Reprinted by permission of
Aviation Safety Network, © 2009
ASN. *www.aviation-safety.net.*

OPERATIONAL PROCESSES

Chapters 1 and 2 introduced the idea of business processes and their relationship to information systems. In Chapters 3 and 4, we diverted from the process topic to discuss the fundamental technologies that you need to know to understand the relationship of processes and information systems in greater depth. With that background, we are now able to return to the topic of business processes. Although we will discuss processes in business, processes are common in every type of organization, as well as in your everyday life—you have a process for starting a car, for doing laundry, and for balancing your checkbook.

Chapters 5 through 8 discuss structured processes and related information systems and information. Chapter 5 provides an overview of business processes and how they

can be improved with information systems. Chapter 6 introduces ERP information systems. ERP systems support many business processes by consolidating all the data for the business in one large and complex database. The chapter also discusses SAP, a particular ERP system, and describes the fundamentals of how it works.

Chapters 7 and 8 are "applied" chapters. They show how SAP is used in two representative business processes—procurement and sales. Two specific processes were chosen in order to show what is common to all processes and what might differ between processes. These two processes, buying and selling, are fundamental to business and both are widely used.

Sarah sits in the student union at Central Colorado State drinking coffee and eating her morning bagel when the question suddenly occurs to her, "How did this stuff get here? The milk? The coffee? The bagel? How did it get here?"

Somewhere there must be a cow that produced the milk that's in her coffee. Where is that cow? Who owns that cow? Who milked that cow? Who decided to ship that particular milk to the union that morning? Who delivered the milk? On what truck? How was the truck routed to customers? Who trained the truck driver?

For that matter, how did the coffee get there? It was grown in Kenya, shipped to the United States, roasted in New Jersey, packaged by a vendor, and delivered to the union. How did all of that happen?

What about the bagel? Who baked it? When? How many bagels did they bake? How did they make that decision?

What about the chair she is sitting on? The wood was grown in Brazil and shipped to China, where the chair was manufactured, and then it was delivered to an import/export business in San Francisco. How did it get here? Who bought it? For whom did they work? Who paid them? How?

The more Sarah thinks about it, the more she realizes that a near miracle occurred just to bring her to this experience. Hundreds, if not thousands, of different processes had successfully interacted just to bring her a simple bagel and coffee.

It's truly amazing. And those processes had to do more than just work. They had to work in such a way that all of the economic entities involved obtained a payment to cover their costs and make a profit. How did that occur? Who set the prices? Who computed the quantity of nonfat milk to be shipped in the night before? How does all of this come about about?

In truth, all of this activity comes about through the interaction of business processes. The union has a process for ordering, receiving, storing, and paying for ingredients like milk and coffee. The coffee roaster has a process for assembling demand, ordering its raw materials, and making deliveries. All of the other businesses have processes for conducting their affairs as well.

Q1. What are the fundamental types of processes in organizations?

Q2. What are examples of common business processes?

Q3. How can organizations improve processes?

Q4. How can organizations use IS to improve processes?

Q5. How can an IS hinder a process?

Q6. How can SOA improve processes?

Chapter Preview

Although processes help explain Sarah's miracle, they go largely unnoticed. Processes are not exciting—no one makes a movie, creates a Facebook page, writes a bestseller, or says to a friend, "Hey, check out that process." Many IS professionals once took them for granted, too. After all, computers were going to change everything—the new tricks, rapidly improving performance, and mind-numbing speeds made them the star, not the processes they supported. Those days are over.

Processes are now the most common way to think of business. Further, processes, along with IS and information, are now the foundation of MIS. Because processes are so central to business and MIS, we devote this chapter to processes and how they can be improved. We strongly believe that it is vital for you to be able to see business operations as processes and learn how IS can make these processes better. In the previous chapters, you learned about information systems and their components; here you will learn *how* to apply them to business processes.

To grasp why processes have become so important, let's look at another example. Sarah has a part-time job at a pizza place that is part of a larger pizza chain. Each month, employees are asked to submit suggestions for process improvement. Such improvements are important. If that national pizza chain sells a million pizzas a month, and if Sarah finds a way to improve that process a single penny each time, the company would save $10,000 a month, every month, on that improvement alone.

Q1. What Are the Fundamental Types of Processes in Organizations?

Let's review what we already know about processes. In Chapter 2, we defined a **business process** as a sequence of activities for accomplishing a function. We also defined an **activity** as a task within a business process and **resources** as the items, such as people, computers, data, and document collections, necessary to accomplish an activity. **Actors** are resources who are either humans or computers. Finally, a **role** is a subset of the activities in a business process that is performed by a particular actor.

Examples of Processes

At Sarah's pizza restaurant, five processes are needed to fulfill a pizza order. These five, shown in Figure 5-1, are Order, Assemble, Bake, Package, and Deliver.[1] For each of the five processes, activities, roles, resources, and actors can be specified. The five processes are accomplished by the Cashier, Chef, and Driver roles, as shown. Further, each process can be deconstructed into activities. For example, the Assemble process has three main activities—Prepare Dough, Add Sauces, and Add Toppings. Within the Prepare Dough activity, Sarah, an actor, plays the role of Chef and uses resources such as a Recipe and Utensils. Processes and their activities are both depicted by rectangles, because in practice the terms are sometimes used interchangeably. For example, Add Sauces could be considered a process with activities Add Tomato Sauce and Sprinkle on Spices.

A student's life is full of processes. Some of these processes, similar to making a pizza, occur in the same sequence. For example, making it to class might include the processes of getting to the bus stop, taking the bus, getting off the bus, and walking to class. Other processes, such as planning parties, paying bills, doing laundry, or reading MIS textbooks, are not as sequential.

IS can be used to improve processes. For example, students use IS to improve both sequential processes and independent processes. In the past, you used to call people to invite them to an

---

[1] From Larry Pervin, "Manufacturing and Work Processes," University of Illinois at Urbana-Champaign, September 2009. Available at *http://www.ler.illinois.edu/sociotech/*.

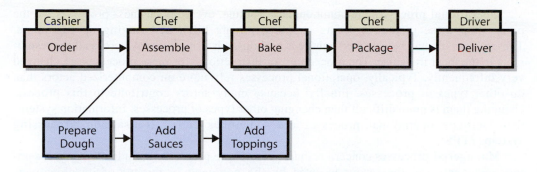

Assemble Process Activities	Resources	Role
Prepare Dough	People, Recipe, Utensils, etc.	Chef
Add Sauces	People, Measuring Cup, Scales, etc.	Chef
Add Toppings	People, Quantity of Toppings, Sequence List, etc.	Chef

FIGURE 5-1

Five Sequential Processes, Resources, Actors, and Roles at the Pizza Shop

event, now Facebook makes that easier; you used to do your taxes by hand, now TurboTax makes that more accurate; and you used to buy greeting cards at a store and mail them at the post office, now e-cards make that process faster.

Although you manage a few important processes in your life, the manager of the pizza shop may have a dozen key processes to oversee, such as hiring employees, closing the store at night, depositing receipts at the bank, taking deliveries, and running promotions. Next door, Walmart managers operate many of the same processes and thousands of others. In both companies, business professionals constantly look for ways to improve or correct process deficiencies. As you will see in this and the next six chapters, IS can help improve business processes much as they have helped you improve your personal processes.

Scope of Processes

Before we can discuss how IS can improve processes, let's organize the landscape of business processes. That way, we can better understand the wide variety of processes in common use in organizations today. We organize processes in Figure 5-2 into the three categories first introduced in Chapter 2: strategic, managerial, and operational.

FIGURE 5-2

Scope and Characteristics of Processes

Scope	Characteristics	Mix of Actors	Frequency	Examples	IS Supporting This Type of Process
Strategic	Broad-scope, organizational issues	More people than other processes	Low	Decide on new restaurant location, corporate budgeting	Executive support system (ESS)
Managerial	Allocation and use of resources	Mix	Medium	Assess seasonal promotions, plan and schedule cashiers	Management information system (MIS)
Operational	Common, routine, day-to-day	More computers than other processes	High	Order supplies, pay bills, check out customers	Transaction processing system (TPS)

Operational processes are commonplace, routine, everyday business processes. At the pizza shop these include ordering supplies, paying bills, and ringing up customers. These processes may be executed hundreds or thousands of times a day across all the restaurants in the local franchise. The procedures, or instructions, for these processes are changed very infrequently. Typically, operational processes rely more on computerized actors than do other types of processes. Finally, because many actors contribute to this process, changing them is more difficult than changing other types of processes. Information systems that facilitate operational processes are sometimes called **transaction processing systems (TPS)**.

Managerial processes concern resource use. These processes include planning, assessing, and analyzing the resources used by the company in pursuit of its objectives. Managerial processes occur much less frequently and with many fewer computerized actors than operational processes have. At the pizza franchise, these processes include assessing seasonal promotions, planning and scheduling cashiers, and determining which personnel to promote. Information systems that facilitate managerial processes are sometimes called **management information systems (MIS)**, which, by the way, is a second meaning for the term *MIS*.

Strategic processes seek to resolve issues that have long-range impact on the organization. These processes have broad scope and impact most of the firm. Because judgment and a tolerance for ambiguity are important, strategic processes typically have more human actors than do operational or managerial processes. Examples of strategic processes include determining where to locate a new restaurant, setting a business's budget, and introducing a new product. Information systems that support strategic processes are sometimes called **executive support systems (ESS)**.

Objectives of Processes

The operational–managerial–strategic distinction is an important way to classify a process. A second valuable way to understand how processes differ is to consider their objectives, as shown in Figure 5-3. An **objective** is a desired goal an organization has decided to pursue. These objectives can be classified as effective or efficient.

An **effective** objective helps achieve organizational strategy. Sarah's pizza shop depends heavily on pizza sales to college students. As a result, one objective of the Sales process is to sell to freshmen.

A second type of objective is efficiency. An **efficient** objective seeks more output with the same inputs or the same output with fewer inputs. The pizza shop might try to improve the efficiency of the Deliver process. To do so, the shop may specify an objective of reducing unnecessary delays.

To summarize effective objectives help achieve company strategy and efficient objectives seek to conserve limited resources. In other words, efficiency is doing things right, whereas effectiveness is doing the right things.

These two categories of process objectives—efficiency and effectiveness—can occur at any of the three levels of processes—operational, managerial, or strategic. That said, the most common combinations are operational processes with efficiency objectives and strategic processes with effectiveness objectives.

FIGURE 5-3

Process Objectives and Measures

Objective Category	Definition	Example Process and Objective at Pizza Shop
Effectiveness	Achieve organizational strategy	Sales process: Sell to freshmen
Efficiency	Create more output with same input or same output with fewer inputs	Deliver process: Reduce unnecessary delays

Primary Activity	Description	Support Activity		
Inbound Logistics	Receiving, storing, and disseminating inputs to products	Human Resources	Technology	Infrastructure
Operations	Transforming inputs into final products			
Outbound logistics	Collecting, storing, and physically distributing products to buyers			
Sales and marketing	Inducing buyers to purchase products and providing a means for them to do so			
Customer service	Assisting customer's use of products and thus maintaining and enhancing the products' value			

FIGURE 5-4

The Value Chain

Q2. What Are Examples of Common Business Processes?

So far, we have classified processes by their scope—strategic, managerial, and operational, and by their objectives—effectiveness and efficiency. A third characteristic of processes is their place within the value chain. Recall from Chapter 1 that a value chain is a series of value-adding activities.[2] As shown in Figure 5-4, a value chain is composed of five primary activities and several support activities. The primary activities are inbound logistics, operations, outbound logistics, sales and marketing, and service. The support activites include human resources, technology, and infrastructure (which includes legal, finance, general management, and other functions). The supporting activites support each of the primary activities.

Figure 5-5 highlights a variety of processes in each of the primary activities and two of the support activities. This overview of business processes will help you see the variety of processes at a typical firm within the context of the value chain—a framework that is common in business. You will learn more about these business processes and value chains in other business school courses.

Inbound Logistics Processes

Inbound logistics receives, stores, and disseminates product input.[3] Processes in inbound logistics listed in Figure 5-5 include Procurement, Manage Inventory, and Evaluate Potential Suppliers. **Procurement** is an operational process that acquires goods and services. Procurement activities at the pizza shop include ordering ingredients and boxes, as well as receiving and paying for those items. This Procurement process is the subject of Chapter 7. Inventory management processes use past data to compute stocking levels, reorder levels, and reorder quantities in accordance with inventory policy. An example of a strategic inbound logistics process is the evaluation of potential suppliers. When the pizza shop orders ingredients, it only uses suppliers who were previously approved by the strategic process called Supplier Selection.

Operations Processes

Operations transform inputs into outputs. Operations processes schedule the equipment, people, and facilities necessary to build or assemble a product or provide a service. Assembling and baking pizzas are two operational operations processes. An example of a management operations process is scheduling maintenance on the ovens. Strategic processes evaluate if the pizza company should open another restaurant or change its menu.

---

[2] Warning: Porter uses the term *activities* to describe these categories. We use the term *activity* in our definition of a process as a series of activities.

[3] Definitions of value chain activities are from Michael Porter's *Competitive Advantage* (New York: Simon and Schuster, 1998).

FIGURE 5-5
Value Chain Activities
and Process Examples

Value Chain Activity	Operational Process	Managerial Process	Strategic Processes
Primary Activities			
Inbound logistics	Procurement (*Chapter 7*)	Manage inventory	Evaluate potential suppliers
Operations	Assemble product	Schedule maintenance	Open new restaurant
Outbound logistics	Sales (*Chapter 8*)	Award refund	Determine payment policy
Sales & marketing	Mail promotion	Evaluate promotional discounts	Launch new product
Service	Track orders	Evaluate complaint patterns	Evaluate outsourcing options
Support Activities			
Human resources	Recruit employees	Plan future needs	Determine pay scales
Technology development	Test software	Estimate milestones	Evaluate acquisition options

Outbound Logistics Processes

Outbound logistics processes collect, store, and distribute products to buyers. Outbound logistics processes concern the management of finished-goods inventory and the movement of goods from that inventory to the customer. Outbound logistics processes are especially prominent for nonmanufacturers, such as distributors, wholesalers, and retailers.

An operational outbound process is the **Sales process** that records the sales order, ships the product, and bills the customer. Other operational outbound logistics processes at the pizza shop include the Order, Package, and Deliver processes. A managerial outbound logistics process is Award a Refund. A strategic outbound logistics process is Determine Payment Policy, such as deciding if the shop will accept personal checks.

Sales and Marketing Processes

Sales and marketing provide the means and incentives for customers to purchase a product or service. The primary objective of sales and marketing processes is to find prospects and transform them into customers by selling them something. The end of the sales and marketing process is the beginning of the Sales process mentioned earlier. When the pizza chain mails promotions to prospects it is executing its operational Promotion process. Evaluate Promotional Discounts is a managerial marketing process. Examples of strategic marketing processes are Launch New Product or Open New Restaurant.

Service Processes

Providing after-sales support to enhance or maintain the value of a product is called *service*. Operational **customer service processes** include Track Orders, Customer Support, and Customer Support Training. Customers call customer service to ask questions about their order status, to query and report problems with their accounts, and to receive assistance with product use. When a customer calls the pizza shop about a late delivery, the store manager initiates a service process. This process records some of the key circumstances for later analysis and awards the customer a discount on a future purchase or the immediate delivery of another pizza. A management service process evaluates customer complaints to determine if there are patterns to the complaints, such as day of the week or a particular delivery person. Evaluating outsourcing service options is a strategic service process.

Human Resources Processes

Human resources processes assess the motivations and skills of employees; create job positions; investigate employee complaints; and staff, train, and evaluate personnel. Operational human resources processes recruit, compensate, and assess employee performance for the organization. In a small company such as the pizza shop, posting a job may be a simple process requiring one or two approvals. In a larger, more formal organization, posting a new job may involve multiple levels of approval requiring use of a tightly controlled and standardized process. Management processes address the development and training of the organization's workforce and planning for future needs. Strategic processes in human resources determine pay scales, authorize types of incentives, and decide organizational structure.

Technology Development Processes

Technology development processes include designing, testing, and developing technology in support of the primary activities. An operational technology development process tests whether newly developed software can handle tens of thousands of possible keystroke entries. A managerial technology development process is a milestone development process that estimates time required for each step in a software development process. A strategic technology development process decides if a particular technology will be purchased or developed by the company.

Q3. How Can Organizations Improve Processes?

You can fill a library with books on the topic of improving processes. Here we simplify some of these suggestions into general categories. Then, in Q4, we add to this list several ways that IS can help improve a process. Figure 5-6 shows three fundamental steps in a process for improving processes. We call this process the **OMIS model**, for **O**bjectives, **M**easures, and **I**nformation **S**ystems.

Process Objectives

Each process has one or more objectives. The first step in the OMIS model, as shown in Figure 5-7, is to specify and, if possible, improve the objectives for the process.

As mentioned earlier, process objectives can be classified as either efficient or effective. For example, the Sales process at the pizza shop has two objectives. One is an efficiency objective—reduce the time needed to place an order by phone—and the other is an effectiveness objective—sell to freshman.

Often a process will have unstated objectives. The OMIS model requires that each process have explicitly stated objectives. At other times, businesspeople may disagree about the objectives, and this step will force them to resolve these differences. Finally, processes may have stated objectives that are vague or inappropriate. For example, a vague objective would be to have a great sales process. Inappropriate objectives are objectives not matched to strategy. If the strategic plan of the pizza shop is to target freshman, but the only two promotional process objectives are to promote multitopping pizzas and salad orders, the promotional process objectives are inappropriate for the stated strategy.

In today's Information Age, process improvement can cross over a line into evading someone's personal privacy. Read the Ethics Guide on pages 148–149 to consider this dilemma.

To improve a process:
• **O**bjectives: Specify and improve
• **M**easures: Specify and improve
• **IS**: Implement IS improvements

FIGURE 5-6

Steps in the OMIS Model

FIGURE 5-7

Options for Improving the Objectives of a Process

To improve a process:

• **O**bjectives: Specify and improve
          Classify objectives as effectiveness or efficiency
          Make objectives explicit
          Obtain agreement about objectives
          Ensure that objectives are not vague or inappropriate

• **M**easures: Specify and improve
• **IS**: Implement IS improvements

FIGURE 5-7

Options for Improving the Objectives of a Process

Process Measures

The second step in the OMIS model, as shown in Figure 5-8, is to specify and, if possible, improve how each objective is measured. **Measures**, also called **metrics**, are quantities assigned to attributes. For example, a measure of the deliver process is the elapsed time from leaving the store until arrival at the customer's location. This attribute is measured using the quantity of minutes and seconds.

Some measures are common, others can be unique. Some processes have commonly accepted ways to measure them, like delivery time for a pizza. Other processes have measures that are created by managers for that particular process. In either case, the second step of the OMIS model requires that the measures be clearly identified and improved, if possible.

Selecting and creating measures can be difficult. Many of the objectives of a process are difficult to quantify. For example, the pizza shop wants to sell to freshmen so that these students become frequent customers over their time at the university. However, it is hard to know which customers are freshmen. As a result, the pizza shop decides to measure the number of deliveries to the dorms as an approximation. Freshmen are not the only dorm residents, but this is the only measure that is available to the pizza shop.

Although measuring dorm sales is clearly not a perfect measure of freshmen sales, the pizza shop owner realizes that all measures are imperfect to some degree. Einstein once said, "Not everything that can be counted counts, and not everything that counts can be counted." When considering measures, recognize they all have limitations and that the key business challenge is to select the best ones available and to know their limits.

The best measures are reasonable, accurate, and consistent. A reasonable measure is a measure that is valid and compelling. It is reasonable to approximate freshmen pizza orders with dorm orders. Accurate measures are exact and precise. An accurate measure is 26 pizzas, a less accurate one is "more than last week." To accurately assess an objective, it may be appropriate to have multiple measures. For example, to assess selling to freshmen the pizza shop might also record the number of pizzas delivered to campus during the freshmen orientation weekend. A final characteristic of a good measurement is consistency. A business should develop measures of processes that are reliable; that is, the measure returns the same value if the same situation reoccurs.

Having specified and improved the stated objectives and measures, we can now consider how to improve a process with IS. The results of the improvement will be apparent in the specified measures.

FIGURE 5-8

Options for Improving the Measures of a Process

To improve a process:
• **O**bjectives: Specify and improve

• **M**easures: Specify and improve
          Ensure that measures are:
              –Reasonable
              –Accurate
              –Consistent

• **IS**: Implement IS improvements

Q4. How Can Organizations Use IS to Improve Processes?

Today, information systems are playing an increasingly important role in business processes. Think about Sarah in the student union, virtually all the organizational processes she is considering depend heavily on IS. Look around you. Did any man-made item in your sight get there without an IS helping that process along? Probably not.

An IS can support a process in a number of ways. Here we consider three ways, as shown in Figure 5-9.

Three Ways IS Improve Processes

One way to improve a process with IS is to improve the efficiency or effectiveness of the activities. Earlier in this chapter we suggested that Facebook, TurboTax, and e-cards are examples of improving an activity with an IS. Similarly, the pizza shop can equip each delivery vehicle with a GPS with traffic updates. This would help to reduce unnecessary delays in this activity in the Deliver process. As a result, the measure of this objective—delivery time—is improved.

At Central Colorado State one strategic objective is to expand the use of education technology. In one process, the Teaching process, the classroom teaching activity is improved with a new IS in the classroom that can display online material, DVD resources, and other content. One measure of the Teaching process is frequency of use of educational technology.

Information systems can also improve a process by improving the links among activities either in the same process or among activities in different processes. The impact of one activity on another activity is called a **linkage**. This definition of linkage is more broad than in Chapter 1 where a linkage was the interaction across value chain activities. There the interaction was among value chain activities, here it is the interaction among any activities in a process. For example, consider the new IS the pizza shop installed to record pizza orders as they are phoned in. This IS improved an activity in the Order process, and it improved the link between Order activities and Deliver activities. The system displays new orders in real time on all the drivers' GPS displays. Using this data, drivers can make better plans about when to stop for gas or when to wait for one more pizza to finish cooking before heading out on deliveries. As a result, delivery time is again improved with this IS.

At Sarah's university, Moodle, a learning management IS, was implemented to improve the linkage among a variety of educational processes. For example, students can collaborate on the system using the discussion board and submit the results of their collaboration for evaluation without leaving Moodle. The processes of Collaboration and Evaluation are jointly improved—the objective of increasing collaboration and reducing time spent submitting evaluation material are both improved.

A third way that IS can improve a process is to improve control of the process. In general, **control** limits behavior. A process is like a river; controls are like dams and sidewalls that limit and direct the flow of the river. Like a dam that maintains a steady flow for the river, controls

---

To improve a process:

- **O**bjectives: Specify and improve

- **M**easures: Specify and improve

- **IS:** Implement IS improvements.
  Improvements can enhance:
  - An activity
    Pizza shop: GPS improves offsite Deliver process

  - Linkages among activities
    Pizza shop: Order display improves offsite Deliver process

  - Control of an activity
    Pizza shop: Order input control improves in restaurant Deliver process

FIGURE 5-9

Options for Improving the Use of IS in a Process

help reduce wide variations in a process so that it runs consistently and smoothly. In other words, the process provides consistent results. One common control used in organizations is standardization, another is IS.

Control is vital to business processes. Controls at the pizza shop help make every pizza the same size, keep the oven at a consistent temperature, and allow only the manager to void sales on the cash register. An example of an IS control is the computer added recently to the in-restaurant Order process. Waiters and waitresses now input orders on the computer rather than on handwritten slips. One control on this process is that incomplete orders are not sent to the kitchen. For example, if a waiter fails to enter three pizza toppings for a three-topping pizza or a dressing is not specified for a salad, the system alerts the waiter to enter the missing data. The kitchen is not given the order until it is corrected by the waiter. This control helps reduce delivery time, in this case, for in-restaurant orders.

At Central Colorado State an example of using an IS to improve control is the recent procedural change to the Login process. The old procedure required users to login with both a username and password; now the procedure takes the user's e-mail as the username. With fewer inputs, there are fewer errors. Fewer errors are a sign of improved control. The objectives of the Login process—accurate authentication and reducing time—are both improved.

These examples show some of the possibilities for improving processes with information systems. IS support of processes will continue to grow as the price–performance ratio of computers continues to plummet, new technologies and ideas continue to enter the business world, and young professionals join the workforce who are more comfortable with technology than any previous generation. The most significant technology for improving business processes has emerged over the past decade. These are multimillion-dollar ERP systems that are designed to support and coordinate a wide range of company processes.

For you to be able to contribute in such an environment, hone your ability to visualize and assess business processes. That is, once you isolate a particular process, determine its objectives, assess the quality of its measures, and determine if IS can support that process. To this end, the OMIS model is designed to equip you with a series of questions you can ask to better understand a current process and to make suggestions for improvement.

Non-IS Process Improvements

We would be remiss if we did not include a discussion of how processes can be improved by non-IS means. In Figure 5-10, we present the two general categories: add more resources and change the structure of the process.

A business can improve a process by adding resources to a given process without changing its structure. One way to reduce delays in the Delivery process is to simply add more drivers. Similarly, some processes can be improved by reducing resources. If the pizza shop has drivers sitting around talking, their productivity may increase by reducing the driving staff.

A second way of altering a business process is to change its structure. Process designers can change the arrangement of the activities of a process without changing resource allocations. An example of changing a structure can be seen in the Assemble process. Currently, each chef rolls dough, adds toppings, then loads his or her own pizza into the oven and takes it out when it is finished. On busy nights, a better structure to the process would be to specialize the jobs. That

FIGURE 5-10

Non-IS Process Improvements

Improvement Category	Process	Examples in Pizza Shop	Objective	Measure
Add more resources	Delivery	Hire more drivers	Reduce unnecessary delays	Average time in minutes
Change the structure	Make	Specialize cooks	Reduce unnecessary delays	Average time in minutes

is, one chef rolls dough for all the pizzas, another adds ingredients, and a third moves pizzas in and out. This helps reduce delays, an objective of the Assemble process.

Although it is convenient to describe process improvement as IS and non IS, in practice the two frequently overlap. Often a process structure is redesigned to take advantage of new IS. For example, the process of sharing academic content with students has changed structure with online content. Once the process was for students to buy a textbook at the college bookstore; now the process includes that activity but also includes online supplements.

Keep in mind that there are always ways to improve processes. The issue is whether it is worth the cost and if the improvements help the process better achieve the firm's strategy. For example, the pizza shop can always add more drivers or use Twitter to take orders, but managers must decide if these improvements are better than other choices that might be less expensive or time consuming and achieve the strategy better.

Although our OMIS model is a good way to begin your process education, the most common approach to process improvement, particularly in the manufacturing industry, is called Six Sigma. **Six Sigma** seeks to improve process outputs by removing causes of defects and minimizing variability in the process. Each Six Sigma project follows a very structured sequence of steps with quantified financial measures. Six Sigma gets its name from its goal that 99.99966 percent of process outputs will be free from defects. Without such high quality processes, Six Sigma proponents argue that we would be without electricity 10 minutes each week, 810 commercial airliners would crash every month, and 50 newborn babies would be dropped at birth by a doctor every day.[4]

Participants and Diagrams in Process Improvement

Whether achieved through Six Sigma, the OMIS model, or other approaches, process improvement at medium-to-large organizations always involves a team. Typically, the process includes the users who are the actors in the process, managers, and business analysts. Managers help by coordinating the changes, acquiring the necessary resources, and motivating participants. Business analysts contribute by understanding the fundamentals of process change and by creating diagrams of processes.

Unless the process is very simple, like assembling or baking a pizza, diagramming a process is typically necessary in order for team members to understand the process and to identify activities that must be changed. It is necessary for the redesign team to understand how the current process works and what the intended process should look like. Diagrams of the current process are typically called **as-is diagrams** and diagrams of suggested improvements **ought-to-be diagrams**. Diagrams can take many forms, but as mentioned in Chapter 2, we will use the current gold standard, BPMN.

To better understand BPMN diagramming, consider the Select New Supplier process for Sarah's pizza shop. This is the process used by the pizza franchise company that owns and operates Sarah's pizza shop and a dozen other outlets in the same region. The company must find and select suppliers for fresh pizza items, cleaning supplies, uniform cleaning, office supplies, and waste removal. The objectives of this managerial process are to find low-cost but good-quality suppliers. The measures for these objectives are shown in Figure 5-11.

Objectives	Measures
Good Quality Effectiveness	Difference in scheduled and actual delivery time Number of returned purchases
Low Cost Efficiency	Supplier price at or below industry average

FIGURE 5-11

Objectives and Measures of the New Supplier Process

[4] J. Harrington and K. Lomax, *Performance Improvement Methods: Fighting the War on Waste* (New York: McGraw-Hill), p. 57.

The Select New Supplier process is shown in Figure 5-12. It begins when the franchise communicates a request for proposal (RFP) to potential suppliers (the Request Proposal from Supplier activity). This activity, completed by the warehouse manager, finds potential suppliers, performs a cursory investigation of their products, and contacts the potential supplier's sales office. If the supplier responds positively, the next step is the Receive Proposal from Supplier activity. In this activity, a supplier provides address and contract data and a list of products the supplier expects to sell to the franchise if the supplier is approved. This application data and product data are inserted as new supplier data in a resource labeled Warehouse DB. Once this activity is complete, the warehouse manager evaluates the potential supplier's product list to determine items that may be appropriate. While this activity is happening, an accountant is also evaluating the supplier's credit policies in the Evaluate Supplier Credit Policies activity. The data generated about the supplier's credit policies is stored in the Accounting DB. This data will be used later by the accounting department in payment processes. Accounting also collects other data on the supplier in order to reach an approve/disapprove supplier decision. This activity is called Evaluate Supplier Financial Strength. If the accountants approve the potential supplier, a Complete the Application activity is initiated that specifies the potential products to be ordered. Finally, after the first month, the final activity, Evaluate Supplier Performance, is accomplished. The franchise strives to determine quickly whether a supplier is working out.

FIGURE 5-12

BPMN Diagram of the New Supplier Process

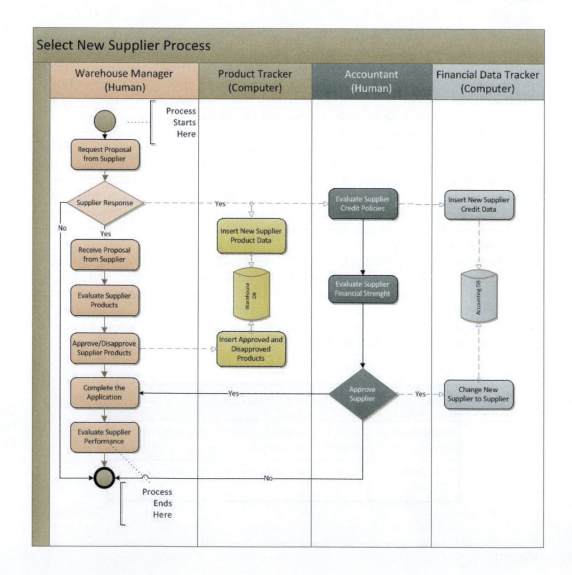

Q5. How Can an IS Hinder a Process?

As we have seen, an IS can be used to improve a process. However, an IS can also reduce process efficiency and effectiveness and limit its improvement. Notice that the objectives of the Select New Supplier process are to select suppliers that are low cost and good quality. The final activity in the Select New Supplier process is Evaluate New Supplier Performance. To evaluate the new supplier, an analyst must obtain data on the new supplier's deliveries to the pizza shops. One measure of good quality is the timeliness of delivery—the difference in time between scheduled delivery and actual delivery. Unfortunately, the scheduled delivery times are stored in the franchise database system, but actual delivery times are stored in spreadsheets at the different shops. Storing data in multiple places can hinder a process and make it difficult to improve. The data could be stored in multiple places for a number of reasons, and we will consider these shortly.

Information Silos

Sharing data is essential to improving a process. The key disadvantage of maintaining data in multiple places is that the data are difficult to share. This situation is called **information silos**, a condition that exists when data are isolated in separated information systems or when data are duplicated in various files and databases. When duplicated, the data can become inconsistent if changes are made to just one copy. Stated from a process point of view, the data needed by one process are stored in an information system designed and used in another process. (Isolated systems are referred to as *silos* because when drawn in diagrams they appear as long vertical columns—like silos.) Because they operate in isolation from one another, they create islands of automation or information silos that can diminish the efficiency and effectiveness of a process and limit the opportunities to improve it.

Information silos can make processes inefficient. For example, the Evaluate New Supplier activity is very inefficient. An analyst must first find the actual delivery times and then enter these times into the same database that tracks scheduled delivery times in order to calculate the timeliness of delivery. The same situation occurs when the franchise runs the Evaluate Promotional Campaign process. Redeemed promotional coupons are collected at each store. However, the number of pizzas sold during the campaign is kept in the franchise sales database.

Information silos can also make processes ineffective. Anytime data is transcribed from one place to another or entered in two places errors can occur. With errors, the measures calculated for some new suppliers and promotions will be incorrect, making these processes less effective than if the data were in one place.

The most obvious fix to eliminate information silos is to store a single copy of data in a shared database and revising business processes to use that database. A single-copy database solution is a feature of the ERP systems that we will discuss in the next three chapters.

Why Information Silos Exist

Information silos at the pizza franchise are caused, in part, by the physical separation of the stores from the franchise headquarters. However, this information silo problem occurs even when all the data is under the same roof. For example, at the franchise office, one database stores data on restaurant sales while another database keeps track of the inventory and deliveries. In each database, the data are compiled at the end of the day and shared with the other database. This delay normally does not impact the franchise; however, several times a year sales are quite unusual, and this delay leads to running out of items at the restaurants or unneeded deliveries. If the data were all in one system, these problems would be less likely to occur.

If the problems of information silos are so evident and the ERP solution so clear, why does this issue ever arise? Organizations store data in separate databases for several reasons.

First, organizational departments prefer to control the systems they use. Departmental personnel like to control how databases are set up, what the data will look like, and how the database will be updated. Also, one department may have very different objectives than other departments in the firm. These objectives might be to minimize inventory or serve customers. Therefore, a department system that helps accomplish this one objective might be deemed better by the department than an enterprise system that does not support that objective as well.

Another reason departments set up their own databases is that they analyze the costs and benefits of the system using their own, fairly narrow measures. Using their own narrow department measures, the advantages of an enterprise system may not be evident. Only when many processes in many departments all rely on the same IS do the savings really accumulate.

There are also more legitimate reasons for a department to use its own database. Some processes use sensitive data not needed in other processes, such as tax data for accounting processes and health care claims data for the HR department. Also, a department system can be purchased and implemented more quickly than most enterprise solutions. Finally, departmental IS are much more affordable; enterprise systems can cost as much as 10 to 50 times as much as a single-department application.

In the past, the choice was frequently to use a department IS to support a department process, because cross-department IS were rare. Today, the expectation is to share data among departments as organizations seek to improve their processes, not just in one pizza franchise, but across a global enterprise.

Q6. How Can SOA Improve Processes?

Data trapped in silos limit process improvements. Although enterprise systems can address this problem, another approach is SOA, or *services-oriented architecture*. SOA is a new IS approach designed to make it easier to share data among process activities.

Earlier we stated that an IS can improve process activities, linkages, and control. SOA, like an IS, improves a process by facilitating data sharing and by improving control by enforcing standards. We close the chapter with this topic because it is a valuable approach to combat information silos and an interesting current example of how IS can improve processes.

SOA was originally used to design interacting, widely distributed, Internet-based computer programs. SOA enables the development of *middleware*, software that sits between two computer programs and facilitates interprogram communication and data sharing. More recently, systems designers have applied SOA principles to business process activities, whether those activities are manual, partly automated, or fully automated. SOA offers great flexibility, ease of use, and adaptability, and we can expect that it will see even greater use as organizations continue the trend toward integrating processes.

To begin, SOA is not a piece of software or hardware. It is a design philosophy. Two previous design philosophies were standalone computers and client-server architecture. **Service-oriented architecture (SOA)** is a design in which every activity is modeled as an encapsulated service and exchanges among those services are governed by standards. This definition has three key terms: *service, encapsulation,* and *standards*. Consider each.

Service

First, a **service** is a repeatable task that a business needs to perform. A service is similar to an activity in a process, a very common activity that may be used by many processes. A service needs access to data to be efficient. At a bookstore, the following are examples of services:

- Calculate a tax amount.
- Pay another business.
- Check inventory of a book.

Each of these services is performed frequently at the bookstore, and each requires data. Further, each of these services is an activity in several processes. Prior to SOA, checking inventory might be hardwired into each process in a slightly different fashion, making the code and activity difficult to use in different processes. If the process designers treat these services as standalone, independent activities, these activities can be plugged into various processes without rewriting code.

MIS InClass 5

Improving the Process of Making Paper Airplanes[5]

The purpose of this exercise is to demonstrate process concepts. In this exercise, students will form assembly lines to create paper airplanes. Each assembly line will have the same four activities, each called a Work Center (WC), as shown in Figure 5-13. Raw material is a stack of plain paper, finished goods are the folded airplanes, and WIP is "Work in Progress," which is the output of the WC prior to the next WC.

One student is assigned to each of the four WCs in the assembly line. Student 1 (in WC 1) creates the first fold, as shown at the top of Figure 5-14. Student 2, at WC 2, folds the corners, also shown in Figure 5-14. The location and assembly instructions for Students 3 and 4 are also shown in Figure 5-14. In addition to the four students who fold the planes, seven other students observe, time, and record each assembly line, as listed below, using the three forms in Figure 5-15:

Observer 1: Use Form 1, record WC 1 task times.

Observer 2: Use Form 1, record WC 2 task times.

Observer 3: Use Form 1, record WC 3 task times.

Observer 4: Use Form 1, record WC 4 task times.

Observer 5: Use Form 2, record cycle time at the end of the line.

Observer 6: Use Form 3, record colored sheet throughput time.

Observer 7: Count WIP at the end of each run.

Each assembly line is run to construct 20 airplanes. Prior to beginning the process, each line will run a practice session of four or five planes. Then, clear the line, start the clock, and make the 20 airplanes. Each WC continues to work until the 20th plane is finished, which means that more than 20 will be started because there will be WIP when the 20th is finished. About halfway through the run, the instructor will insert a colored piece of paper as raw material. Each student assembler works at his or her own pace. As workers build planes, they should work at a comfortable pace and not speed. This is not a contest for maximum output, but for quality.

After the first run is completed, make a second run of 20 planes with all the same roles. However, each student can work

Source: Benis Arapovic/Shutterstock.

only when there is an airplane in their inbox (WIP) and no airplane in their outbox (WIP). Again, midway through the run the instructor will insert a colored sheet of paper.

After the runs:

1. In teams, diagram the process using BPMN symbols such as roles, swimlanes, activities, and decisions. Name resources assigned to roles.
2. Apply the OMIS model to improve this process. Discuss the objectives of the assembly line. If you were in charge of the assembly line like this one, do you think your objectives would be efficiency or effectiveness? Specify the measures used to monitor progress toward your objective(s).
3. Assume that the WC folding is done by four machines. In that scenario, the second run uses different software than the first run. Does this new IS improve an activity, linkage, or control?
4. Are any data in an information silo on the first or second runs?
5. Which measure changed most significantly from the first to the second run? Did you anticipate this? Are other processes with other measures just as subject to change with a similar minor change in information?
6. Were there any controls on the assembly process? Could an IS improve the process by improving control? On which measure(s) will this improvement appear?

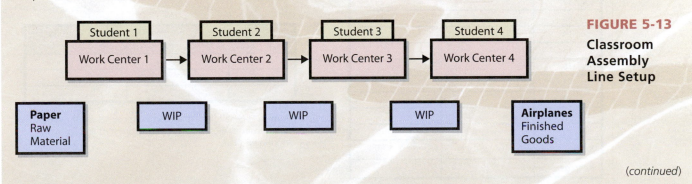

FIGURE 5-13

Classroom Assembly Line Setup

(continued)

[5] Based on "A Classroom Exercise to Illustrate Lean Manufacturing Pull Concepts," by Peter J. Billington, in *Decision Sciences Journal of Innovative Education*, 2(1), 2004, pp. 71–77.

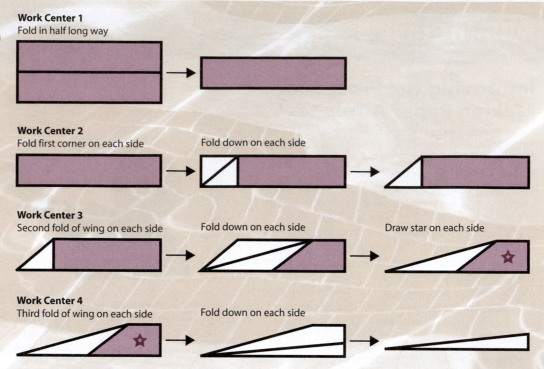

FIGURE 5-14

Assembly (Folding) Instructions

Work Center 1
Fold in half long way

Work Center 2
Fold first corner on each side   Fold down on each side

Work Center 3
Second fold of wing on each side   Fold down on each side   Draw star on each side

Work Center 4
Third fold of wing on each side   Fold down on each side

FIGURE 5-15

Airplane Folding Recording Forms

Work Center _____ (1, 2, 3, or 4)

Unit	Run 1 (seconds)	Run 2 (seconds)
1		
2		
3		
4		
5		
6		
7		
8		
9		
10		
11		
12		
13		
14		
15		
16		
17		
18		
19		
20		
Sum		
Average		

Form 1: Airplane manufacturing task time. Observers 1, 2, 3, and 4 use this form to record assembly times for each Work Center.

System	Throughput Time for 20 Sheets Run 1	Throughput Time for 20 Sheets Run 2
Run 1		
Run 2		

Form 2: Airplane manufacturing cycle time for 20 airplanes. Observer 5 uses this form to record start and finish time for entire run of 20 planes.

System	Throughput Time for Colored Sheets Run 1	Throughput Time for Colored Sheets Run 2
Run 1		
Run 2		

Form 3: Paper airplane manufacturing color sheet throughput time. Observer 6 uses this form to record start and finish time for colored sheet.

Encapsulation

Now consider *encapsulation,* the second key term in the SOA definition. **Encapsulation** hides details inside a container. In networks, encapsulation is used to allow devices to communicate containers (packets) of data without being concerned about the data inside. SOA uses encapsulation in much the same way, hiding data within containers so that services can communicate. Figure 5-16 shows the interactions of two services at Hard Books, Inc., a book supplier for the bookstore. The Process Credit Order service is part of a business Order process. Authorize Credit is a second service that is part of a different business process called Credit Authorization. Using SOA principles, each service will be designed to be independent; neither will be aware of how the other does its work and neither will need to know. Instead, these services need only agree on how they will exchange data and what that exchange means.

The Process Credit Order service sends customer credit data to the Authorize Credit service. It receives back a credit authorization that contains an approval or rejection and other data. The Credit Authorization process could involve flipping a coin, throwing darts, or performing some sophisticated data mining analysis on the customer's data. Process Credit Order does not know, nor does it need to know, how that authorization is made.

When the logic for some service is isolated in this way, the logic is said to be encapsulated in the service. Encapsulation places the logic in one place, which is exceedingly desirable. For one, all other services know to go to that one place for that service. Even more important, if the managers of the credit department decide to change how they make credit authorizations, Process Credit Order is not affected. As long as the structure and meaning of customer credit data and credit authorization data do not change, Process Credit Order is completely isolated from changes in Authorize Credit or any other service in the Credit Authorization process.

Because of encapsulation, service implementations can be readily adapted to new requirements, technologies, and methodologies. In fact, it does not matter who performs the services or where they are performed. Credit authorization could be done by a single company department on a single computer. Later, it could be changed to be performed by a different company, on different computers, in another part of the world. As long as the interface between Process Credit Order and Authorize Credit does not change, Authorize Credit is free to change its implementation.

Standards

The third key term in the SOA definition is *standards*. Data, and more generically, messages, are exchanged among services using standardized formats and techniques, which are referred to as **SOA standards**. In the past, the programmers of the Process Credit Order program would meet with the programmers of the Authorize Credit program and design a unique, proprietary means for exchanging data via this interface. Such a design is expensive and time consuming. Consequently, the computer industry developed standard ways for formatting messages and describing services and standard protocols for managing the exchanges among services. Those standards eliminated the need for proprietary designs and expanded the scope and importance of SOA.

SOA can improve the efficiency and effectiveness of a process in the same ways an IS improves processes. SOA makes activities easier and hence less costly to access. Further, SOA improves control because it limits the messages exchanged by using standards. Standards help control the exchange of messages.

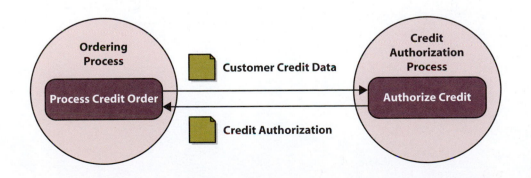

FIGURE 5-16

Example of Two Independent Encapsulated Services

Ethics Guide

Process Improvement or Privacy Problem?

A new type of IS, a vehicle tracking system is improving many company processes, and at the same time, raising privacy issues. These vehicle tracking systems are typically used by companies on their fleet of vehicles. They are becoming increasingly common in food delivery and car rental companies.

These companies use the systems to better track their fleet of vehicles, improve routing and dispatch, prevent theft, and improve vehicle retrieval. Some hotel companies are using the systems to ensure that special guests are appropriately welcomed upon arrival at the hotel.

These systems typically include the wireless device attached to the vehicle and some type of GPS tracking server that receives data from the device, stores it and creates reports for analysis. Two types of systems are in use. Active systems collect data and transmit the data to the server in real time via cellular networks. Passive systems store the data on board for later download to the server.

Automobile insurance companies are beginning to offer discounts to drivers willing to install a wireless computer device on their cars. This device can measure distance traveled, acceleration, speed, turning forces, and braking. If these measures indicate a cautious driver, some insurance companies give 20 to 30 percent discounts. Many cautious drivers hail this improvement as a just reward for their good driving. They also might like to see this device on all vehicles in order to increase public safety on the roads. Others, particularly privacy advocates, see it as yet another example of an invasion of privacy.

DISCUSSION QUESTIONS

1. Would you install such a device to get a discount? What if the discount was 50 percent? 70 percent?

2. Is it appropriate for parents not to tell their 16-year-old driver that they installed this device on their cars in order to secretly learn from the insurance company how cautiously the teen drives?

3. Is it ethical for a company to sell this data to a car manufacturer? The insurance company never specifically asked its customers if it could share this data, and the car company does not want any customer-identifying data, just the driver's age and the measures for each driver.

4. Should the legal system be able to subpoena this data from the insurance company as evidence in a court case? Would your answer change if you were being falsely accused of a hit-and-run accident?

5. Car rental and food delivery companies are required to tell their drivers when these systems are in place. In what ways can these systems lead to abuse and how could the systems be designed to limit these abuses?

6. Should Sarah's pizza franchise require this device for all vehicles used by its drivers? It would not be used for insurance purposes, but to determine better delivery routes and to encourage delivery drivers to be more cautious.

7. For the pizza franchise, this device is an IS that improves a process. The business process is Delivery.

What are the objectives of the Delivery process? What measures would the IS improvement make available?

8. Is this IS improvement an improvement in activity, linkage, or control?

9. In this scenario, improving a process with IS reduces privacy. Do all IS improvements involving processes with employees or customers reduce privacy? Can you think of processes with sensitive employee or customer data in health care, finance, or social media where improving the process with IS does not threaten privacy?

Active Review

Use this Active Review to verify that you understand the material in the chapter. You can read the entire chapter and then perform the tasks in this review, or you can read the text material for just one question and perform the tasks in this review for that question before moving on to the next one.

Q1. What are the fundamental types of processes in organizations?

Define *business process* and the key terms that describe business processes: *activity, resource, role,* and *actor*. Name the term that can be fulfilled by either a human or computer. Explain what business professionals constantly seek to do with their processes. List the three main categories of process scope, and explain how each one is different from the others. Give examples of processes in each of the categories. Define *efficiency* and *effectiveness*. What things are efficient and effective?

Q2. What are examples of common business processes?

Explain a process in each of the primary activities of the value chain. Explain a support activity process in HR and accounting. Specify if that process is operational, managerial, or strategic and explain why you classified it that way. Describe a procurement process and a sales and marketing process.

Q3. How can organizations improve processes?

Explain the OMIS model. Explain vague and inappropriate objectives. Explain measures and discuss why they are difficult to develop. Give examples of reasonable, accurate, and consistent process measures.

Q4. How can organizations use IS to improve processes?

Explain the three ways IS can be used to improve a particular process. Specify a process and explain how an IS can improve that process. Specify measures and objectives for the process. Give an example of a process where an activity can be improved using an IS. Define *linkage* and explain how IS can improve linkage in a process. Explain why control is important for a business process. Describe an example of how IS can improve control in a process. Explain the two categories of non-IS process improvement and give an example of each. Describe why, in practice, IS and non-IS improvements frequently overlap. State the goal of Six Sigma. Identify common participants in a process improvement team. Describe the two types of BPMN diagrams.

Q5. How can an IS hinder a process?

Describe how IS configuration in a company can hamper a process and limit its improvement. Describe an information silo. Explain the impact of silos on process objectives. Explain the most common fix to the silo problem. Describe why departments like to control the systems they use. Explain why a department may legitimately seek to keep its data in multiple databases.

Q6. How can SOA improve processes?

Describe, in general, the two ways that SOA can improve a process (e.g., improve an activity, supply a linkage, or implement a control). Explain the term *service*. Give examples of services in an example process. Describe encapsulation. Give an example of two encapsulated services in a process. Explain how the independence of each encapsulated service makes process improvement possible. Describe how messages used to be exchanged between services and the role standards play in making this exchange better. Give an example of an SOA standard.

Key Terms and Concepts

Activity *132*
Actor *132*
As-is diagram *141*
Business process *132*
Control *139*
Customer service processes *136*
Effective *134*
Efficient *134*
Encapsulation *147*
Executive support system
   (ESS) *134*
Human resource processes *137*
Information silo *143*

Linkage *139*
Management information system
   (MIS) *134*
Managerial processes *134*
Measures *138*
Metrics *138*
Objective *134*
OMIS model *137*
Operational processes *134*
Ought-to-be diagram *141*
Outbound logistics processes *136*
Procurement process *135*
Resources *132*

Role *132*
Sales processes *136*
Service *144*
Service-oriented architecture
   (SOA) *144*
Six Sigma *141*
SOA standards *147*
Strategic processes *134*
Technology development
   processes *137*
Transaction processing system
   (TPS) *134*

Using Your Knowledge

1. Use OMIS to improve the following processes. That is, specify objectives and measures and an IS that will improve the process.
   a. Selecting a job after college
   b. Planning and executing a wedding or a funeral
   c. Taking photos at college, uploading the photos to Facebook, then showing the photos to relatives on their TV using a Wii or Xbox for Internet access.
   d. The process the pizza shop uses to buy supplies

2. For the processes presented in question 1, suggest how each could be improved by non-IS means; that is, by adding resources or changing the process structure.

3. For the processes presented in question 1, classify each IS improvement as improving an activity, improving the linkages among activities, or improving control.

4. When you go to a restaurant, that restaurant must execute several operational processes. Apply the OMIS model to several of these processes. These processes might include seating, ordering, cooking, delivering, and paying. For each process specify objectives and measures and an IS that will improve the process.

5. How can your college use IS to make its processes better? Can you think of ways to use new IS tools, such as smartphones and social media, to make college processes better? Specify the objectives and measures that these IS help improve. Does your college have information silos? Which departments keep data needed by processes outside the department?

6. When you order a meal at McDonald's that data is stored in an enterprise IS to be used by various processes. Make a list of the McDonald's processes your Happy Meal purchase will appear in. You may want to review the value chain processes discussed in Q2.

7. Make a Facebook cause (*www.facebook.com/causes*). Invite several friends to join. Using paper and pencil or diagramming software, make a BPMN diagram of the three or four key activities in this promotional process. Specify objectives and measures for this process and explain how Facebook (IS) improves the promotional process.

8. Create a BPMN diagram of the five to seven key activities in the process of getting your suitcase to its destination. Specify objectives and measures for this process.

Collaboration Exercise 5

Collaborate with a group of fellow students to answer the following questions. For this exercise do not meet face to face. Your task will be easier if you coordinate your work with SharePoint, Office 365, Google Docs with Google+ or equivalent collaboration tools. (See Chapter 9 for a discussion of collaboration tools and processes.) Your answers should reflect the thinking of the entire group, and not just that of one or two individuals.

The county planning office issues building permits, septic system permits, and county road access permits for all building projects in an eastern state. The planning office issues permits to homeowners and builders for the construction of new homes and buildings and for any remodeling projects that involve electrical, gas, plumbing, and other utilities, as well as the conversion of unoccupied spaces such as garages into living or working space. The office also issues permits for new or upgraded septic systems and permits to provide driveway entrances to county roads.

Figure 5-17 shows the permit process that the county used for many years. Contractors and homeowners found this

FIGURE 5-17

Sequential Permit Review Process

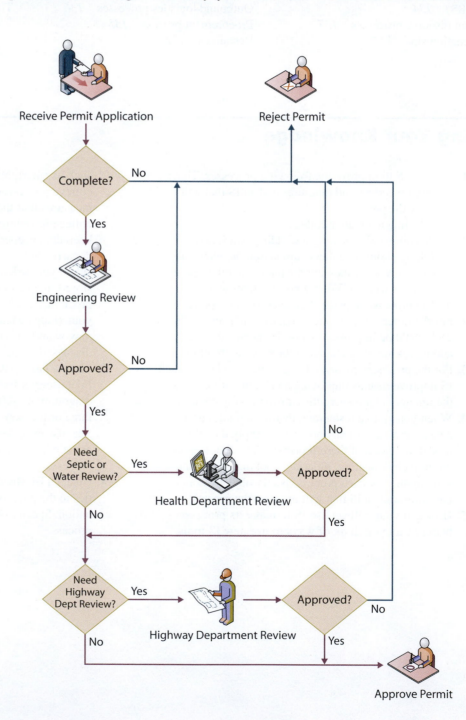

process to be slow and very frustrating. For one, they did not like its sequential nature. Only after a permit had been approved or rejected by the engineering review process would they find out that a health or highway review was also needed. Because each of these reviews could take 3 or 4 weeks, applicants requesting permits wanted the review processes to be concurrent rather than serial. Also, both the permit applicants and county personnel were frustrated because they never knew where a particular application was in the permit process. A contractor would call to ask how much longer, and it might take an hour or more just to find which desk the permits were on.

Accordingly, the county changed the permit process to that shown in Figure 5-18. In this second process, the permit office made three copies of the permit and distributed one to each department. The departments reviewed the permits in parallel; a clerk would analyze the results and, if there were no rejections, approve the permit.

Unfortunately, this process had a number of problems, too. For one, some of the permit applications were lengthy; some included as many as 40 to 50 pages of large architectural drawings. The labor and copy expense to the county was considerable.

Second, in some cases departments reviewed documents unnecessarily. If, for example, the highway department rejected an application, then neither the engineering nor health departments needed to continue their reviews. At first, the county responded to this problem by having the clerk who analyzed results cancel the reviews of other departments when he or she received a rejection. However, that policy was exceedingly unpopular with the permit applicants, because once an application was rejected and the problem corrected, the permit had to go back through the other departments. The permit would go to the end of the line and work its way back into the departments from which it had been pulled. Sometimes this resulted in a delay of 5 or 6 weeks.

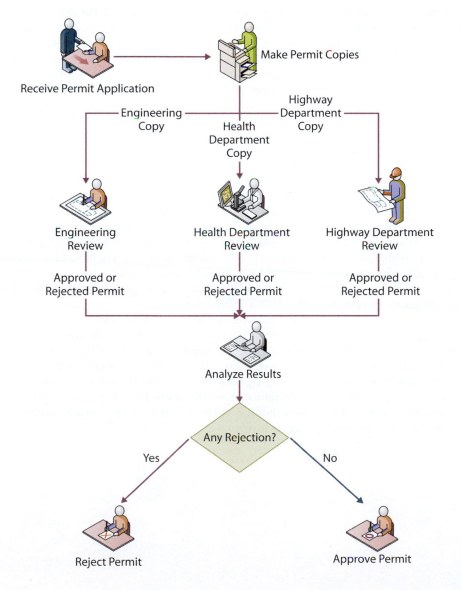

FIGURE 5-18

Parallel Permit Review Process

Canceling reviews was unpopular with the departments as well, because permit-review work had to be repeated. An application might have been nearly completed when it was cancelled due to a rejection in another department. When the application came through again, the partial work results from the earlier review were lost.

1. Is this process an operational, managerial, or strategic process?

2. Apply the OMIS model to the parallel permit process. Identify at least one flaw in each measure.

3. For your proposed IS improvements, specify if they are activity, linkage, or control improvements.

4. Where are the information silos? Why did these silos develop over the years? Are there good reasons to convert to an enterprise system?

5. Draw the new process using BPMN.

CASE STUDY 5

Process Cast in Stone

Bill Gates and Microsoft were exceedingly generous in the allocation of stock options to Microsoft employees, especially during Microsoft's first 20 years. Because of that generosity, Microsoft created 4 billionaires and an estimated 12,000 millionaires as Microsoft succeeded and the value of employee stock options soared. Not all of those millionaires stayed in the Seattle/Redmond/Bellevue, Washington, area, but thousands did. These thousands of millionaires were joined by a lesser number who made their millions at Amazon.com and, to a lesser extent, at RealNetworks, Visio (acquired by Microsoft), and Aldus (acquired by Adobe). Today, some Google employees who work at Google's Seattle office are joining these ranks.

The influx of this wealth had a strong impact on Seattle and the surrounding communities. One result has been the creation of a thriving industry in high-end, very expensive homes. These Microsoft and other millionaires are college educated; many were exposed to fine arts at the university. They created homes that are not just large and situated on exceedingly valuable property, but that also are appointed with the highest-quality components.

Today, if you drive through a small area just south of central Seattle, you will find a half dozen vendors of premium granite, marble, limestone, soapstone, quartzite, and other types of stone slabs within a few blocks of each other. These materials cover counters, bathrooms, and other surfaces in the new and remodeled homes of this millionaire class. The stone is quarried in Brazil, India, Italy, Turkey, and other countries and either cut at its origin or sent to Italy for cutting. Huge cut slabs, 6 feet by 10 feet, arrive at the stone vendors in south Seattle, who stock them in their warehouses.

The stone slabs vary not only in material, but also in color, veining pattern, and overall beauty. Choosing these slabs is like selecting fine art. (Visit *www.pentalonline.com* or *www.metamarble.com* to understand the premium quality of these vendors and products.)

Typically, the client (homeowner) hires an architect who either draws plans for the kitchen, bath, or other stone area as part of the overall house design or who hires a specialized kitchen architect who draws those plans. Most of these clients also hire interior decorators who help them select colors, fabrics, furniture, art, and other home furnishings. Because selecting a stone slab is like selecting art, clients usually visit the stone vendors' warehouses personally. They walk through the warehouses, often accompanied by their interior designer, and maybe also their kitchen architect, carrying little boxes into which stone vendor employees place chips of slabs in which the client expresses interest.

Usually, the team selects several stone slabs for consideration, and those are set aside for that client. The name of the client or the decorator is written in indelible ink on the side of the stone to reserve it. When the client or design team makes a final selection, the name is crossed out on the stone slabs they do not purchase. The purchased slabs are set aside for shipping.

During the construction process, the contractor will have selected a stone fabricator, who will cut the stone slab to fit the client's counters. The fabricator will also treat the stone's edges, possibly repolish the stone, and cut holes for sinks and faucets. Fabricators move the slabs from the stone vendor to their workshops, prepare the slab, and eventually install it in the client's home.

Questions

1. Identify the key actors in this scenario. Name their employer (if appropriate) and describe the role that they play. Include as a key player the operations personnel who move stones in the warehouse as well as those who load stones on the fabricators' trucks.

2. Apply the OMIS model to the stone fabricator's process. Identify at least one flaw in each measure.

3. For your proposed IS improvements, specify if they are activity, linkage, or control improvements.

4. Where are the information silos? Why did these silos develop over the years? Are there good reasons to convert to an enterprise system?

5. Draw the new process using BPMN.

"Are they out of their minds?" asks Pat Smith, the athletics director at Central Colorado State.

"I'm not sure Pat, but I will tell you the university is serious about this," replies Jenna Thurman, Pat's assistant.

"University Central Administration wants us to go through them for every purchase?"

"Well not all the purchases, but the ones above $500, yes. But they say that this new ERP software will save the university over a half million dollars in the first year."

"Did they say how?"

"Apparently, other places on campus did dumb things. You read about the fraud at the bookstore and the cost overruns with the new computers in the union. The university also mentioned our little adventure with that T-shirt maker. They say we should have known that company used child labor. Oh, and they claim we paid 50 percent more per jersey than the intramural department."

Visibly angry, Pat nearly screams, "And so the great solution is to go through purchasing for everything. Every order will take a month!"

"Well, they claim this new ERP system will shorten the time. They approve a list of all the suppliers for everyone on campus and they negotiate the prices for each item, and we're free to order through the system as we see fit."

"Wait, did I hear you say 'each item'? We order thousands of different things!!"

"They did admit this will take a while."

"Did they really say we paid more for our jerseys than intramurals?!! Do they have any idea how impossible it would be to recruit Division I players and say, 'and you'll look great in this 8-dollar jersey.'"

"But, boss, on the positive side they said that when other universities went to this system the suppliers worked harder to stay on everyone's good side because they had more to lose.

They did sort of point out that our soccer team jersey problem probably wouldn't have happened if that supplier had other contracts with the school they wanted to protect."

"So now what do we have to do?"

"They said start making lists of items you expect to buy this year. I'm invited to configuration meetings every Monday for the rest of my life. And starting in the fall we all have training sessions on the new software to look forward to."

"Thanks Jenna. And I thought keeping the boosters' club happy after last year was going to be my biggest headache."

As Jenna leaves, Pat admits to himself that the prospect of saving hundreds of thousands of dollars was too good for the administration to pass up in this time of rising tuition. The school had to save where it could. He is suspicious though; this new buying process might limit his flexibility to award contracts to suppliers who were consistent givers to the sports program or keep him from buying decent jerseys. Pat thinks the idea of a single way to buy everything on campus wouldn't be a good thing for the athletics department. He knows that no one at the university understands how different an athletics department is from other departments.

Q1. What problem does an ERP system solve?

Q2. What are the elements of an ERP system?

Q3. What are the benefits of an ERP system?

Q4. What are the challenges of implementing an ERP system?

Q5. What types of organizations use ERP?

Q6. Who are the major ERP vendors?

Q7. What makes SAP different from other ERP products?

Chapter Preview

The athletics director was right. The university has to try to save money, and using an ERP system might help achieve that objective. Clearly, ERP systems can reduce costs, but successfully installing an ERP system is exceptionally challenging. It can take years to implement and can cost hundreds of millions of dollars. These systems also require an organization to make difficult changes in the way it does things. It is a long road the university is heading down.

In the previous chapter, we looked at business from a process perspective and used the OMIS model to better understand how to make processes more efficient and effective. Here we discuss the same issue of IS and business process improvement, but from the IS point of view. More specifically, we investigate how large-scale ERP systems like the one implemented at the university can improve processes across an entire organization. To do so, we will examine the benefits and challenges of implementing an ERP system, but first we revisit the information silo problem from Chapter 5.

Q1. What Problem Does an ERP System Solve?

To appreciate the popularity of ERP systems today, consider how businesses operated before they were introduced. Businesses were much like Central Colorado State—their departments ran their own processes using their own information systems and databases. Furthermore, many of these department processes were not well designed; they were relatively ineffective and inefficient, and, to make matters worse, they were hard to integrate with processes in other departments.

Then the Web flattened the world with fiber optic cable that carried data at speeds unimaginable just years before. Reality caught up with imagination when software engineers at SAP realized that this new network and advances in database storage allowed them to create large, centralized, well-connected databases that spanned entire companies. To use this new information system, businesses would also have to adopt processes designed by SAP. These processes were based on best industry-practices and designed from the start to be easily integrated with each other. Large firms saw an opportunity to implement one IS that would help improve and integrate their many processes.

The key to ERP systems is that data are consolidated in one central database. Recall from Chapter 5 that an information silo occurs when data are isolated and replicated in separated information systems. With information silos, the data needed by one process are stored in an information system designed and used in another process. Because information silos exist in isolation from one another, they create islands of automation that can diminish the efficiency and effectiveness of processes and make process integration difficult.

The silo problem is solved by ERP systems. We explain this approach in the rest of the chapter. However, before we get there, we briefly consider another approach to the same silo problem. This second solution is a more decentralized approach called enterprise application interface (EAI). ERP and EAI systems are sometimes referred to as *enterprise systems*.

Enterprise Application Integration (EAI)

An **enterprise application integration (EAI)** system tackles the silo problem by providing layers of software that connect information systems together. EAI is software that enables information silos to communicate with each other and to share data. The layers of EAI software are shown in Figure 6-1. For example, when the accounting information system sends data to the human resources information system the EAI program intercepts the data, converts it to work in the format required by the human resources system, and then sends the converted data on to the human resources system. The reverse action is taken to send data back from the human resources system to the accounting system.

Although there is no centralized EAI database, EAI software keeps files of metadata that describe where all the organization's data are located and how the data must be transformed to work at each location. These details are hidden from users; the EAI system appears to be an integrated database to the user.

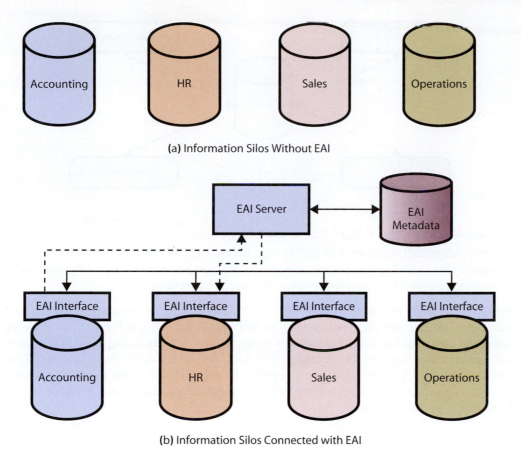

FIGURE 6-1
EAI Architecture

(a) Information Silos Without EAI

(b) Information Silos Connected with EAI

EAI does the following:

- It connects information silos via a new layer of software.
- It enables existing applications to communicate and share data.
- It provides integrated data.
- It leverages existing systems, leaving departmental information systems as is, but providing an integration layer over the top.
- It enables a gradual move to ERP.

The major benefit of the EAI connect-the-silos approach is that it enables organizations to use existing applications while eliminating many of the problems of information silos. Converting to an EAI system is not nearly as disruptive as converting to ERP, it can be less expensive, and it provides many of the benefits of ERP. Some organizations develop EAI applications as a stepping stone to complete ERP systems.

Enterprise Resource Planning (ERP)

An **enterprise resource planning (ERP)** product is a suite of software, a database, procedures and a set of processes for supporting business operations with a single, consistent, information system. These systems integrate process data from departments such as accounting, human resources, sales, and operations into a single system, as shown in Figure 6-2. ERP is so named because it attempts to integrate all the resources of an enterprise into a single information system.

The primary purpose of an ERP system is integration; an ERP system allows the "left hand of the organization to know what the right hand is doing." *ERP systems standardize processes and bring the data from a company's processes into one place so that the data can go out to many places in real time.*

Properly implemented, an ERP system consolidates data about customers, products, people, equipment, machinery, facilities, production schedules, vendors, and finances in a single database. By consolidating the data in one place, the data are always up-to-date and available in real time to be used by any process in the organization.

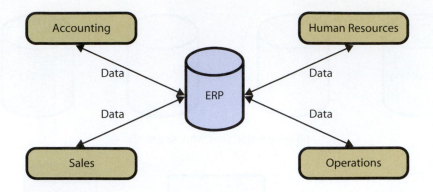

ERP Implementation: Before and After Examples

To better understand the impact of an ERP system, we will examine processes in two organizations before and after an ERP system is implemented. The first organization is the university discussed in the opening vignette, the second is a company that assembles bicycles.

EXAMPLE 1: SINGLE PROCESS—UNIVERSITY PURCHASING Compare the university's procurement process before and after implementing an ERP system, as shown in Figure 6-3. On the top half of the figure, each university department works with its own purchasing agent to buy goods and services from suppliers. In the bottom half, each department works through a centralized university purchasing agent to buy from suppliers. By consolidating all the purchasing activity in one central office, the school is better able to standardize purchasing and it is able to gain bargaining power over suppliers.

FIGURE 6-3

Procurement by University Departments Before and After ERP

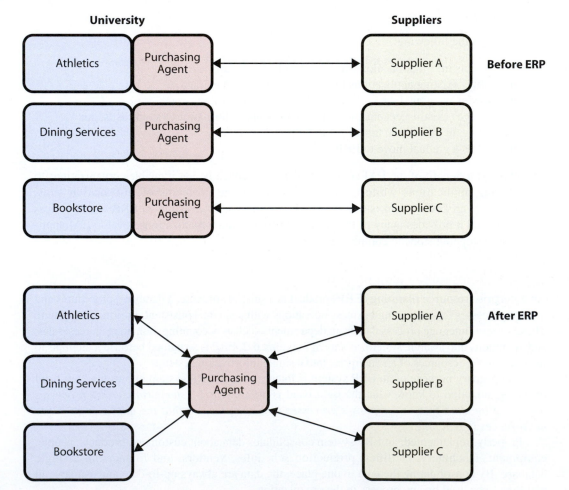

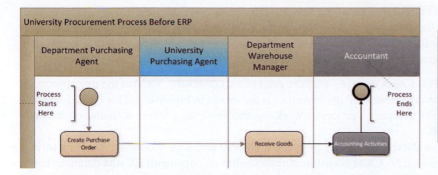

Before ERP Implementation

Objectives	Measures
Use reliable suppliers	Not specified
Use boosters (unstated)	Not specified

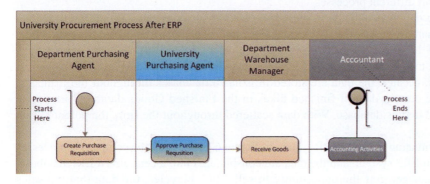

After ERP Implementation

Objectives	Measures
Reduce cost	Cost

FIGURE 6-4

Procurement by University Before and After ERP

Figure 6-3 shows the impact of an ERP system on the university. The impact of an ERP system on a department is shown in Figure 6-4. The top half shows the activities before implementing an ERP system, and the bottom half shows the activities after implementation. Before implementation, each department's procurement process had three main activities—Create Purchase Order, Receive Goods, and Accounting Activities, as shown in the top BPMN in Figure 6-4. The process was initiated by an actor in the Department Purchasing Agent role. Every department at the university had a Purchasing Agent; in the athletic department, this role was played by Jenna.

Jenna started the process by completing a Purchase Order (PO). An example PO might be an order for 500 T-shirts for summer camp. The second activity was Receive Goods. Goods were received when the T-shirts arrived on campus at the athletic warehouse where Joe, in the role of Warehouse Manager, signed for the delivery and put them on a shelf. Later, the university accounting office would get a bill from the T-shirt maker and pay it. The purchases by the athletic department were recorded in a department database (not shown for simplicity). The department databases are not shown in Figure 6-4 for simplicity. Each department on campus maintained its own purchasing database, creating information silos as a result.

The athletic department objectives for this process were to use reliable suppliers who would be able to deliver the goods on time and were reasonably priced. Jenna also had an unstated objective, which was to use suppliers who were also boosters of the athletic department. Measures for these objectives were never specified.

After implementing the ERP system, a new procurement process provided by the ERP vendor is used by every department. This new process is shown in the bottom of Figure 6-4. Now Jenna completes a Purchase Requisition. A Purchase Requisition is a PO awaiting approval. The Purchase Requisition is approved by a University Purchasing Agent as the second activity. The rest of the activities in this process remain the same. Rather than storing data in department databases, the new ERP process maintains all the procurement data in a central database. Now if any department wants to order T-shirts, all the data on T-shirt suppliers, delivery times, and prices are available in real time.

With the purchasing office now orchestrating the process, specific and clear objectives and measures have been developed for the process and shared with all purchasing agents. The university's objective with the new process is efficiency—lowering cost as measured by comparing this month's expenditures to last year's during the same month.

Although it is helpful to understand how an ERP system can improve a single process such as procurement at the university, it is perhaps more important to understand how an ERP system can improve the integration of processes for an entire organization. To see these larger-scale impacts, we shift gears to a bicycle assembly company.

EXAMPLE 2: PROCESSES AS A WHOLE—BICYCLE ASSEMBLY COMPANY Some of the main processes for the bicycle company before ERP implementation are shown in Figure 6-5. This figure illustrates how many of the bike company's processes work together, with the primary activities of the value chain across the top.

Notice the five databases shown as cylinders—Vendor, Raw Material, Manufacturing, Finished Goods, and CRM. CRM is customer relationship management; a CRM database keeps track of data about customers. These five databases are information silos, isolated from each other as they support different processes.

By not having data consolidated in one place, the bicycle company faces difficulty when data need to be shared in real time. For example, if the sales department has the unexpected opportunity to sell 1,000 bicycles, the sales manager must know if the company can produce these bikes in time to meet the delivery date. Unfortunately, the sales manager does not have all the data she needs, because the data are stored in isolated databases throughout the firm. She does not know the current data of finished bikes in the Finished Goods database or of bike parts in the Raw Materials database. With data scattered throughout the firm, the potential sale is in jeopardy.

Contrast this situation with the ERP system in Figure 6-6. Here, all the company's processes are supported by an ERP system, and the data are consolidated into a centralized ERP database. When the sales manager gets the opportunity to sell 1,000 bicycles, the data that the sales manager needs to confirm the order is readily available in the ERP system. From her desk, the sales manager can see how many bikes are finished and ready to sell and how many bikes will be

FIGURE 6-5

Pre-ERP Information Systems for Bicycle Company

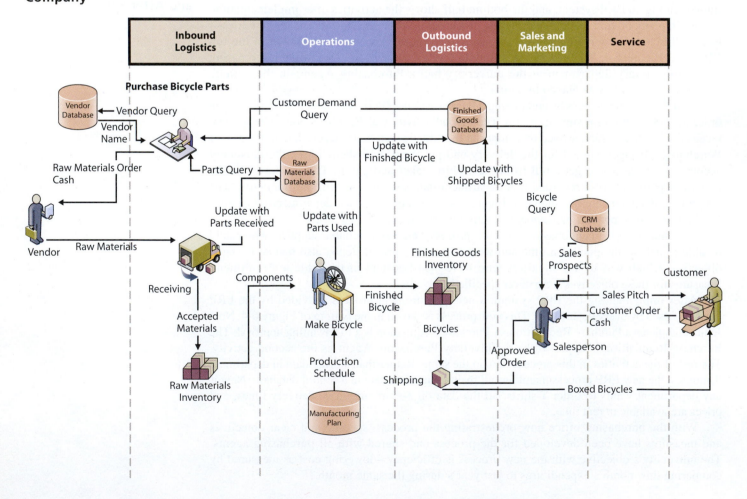

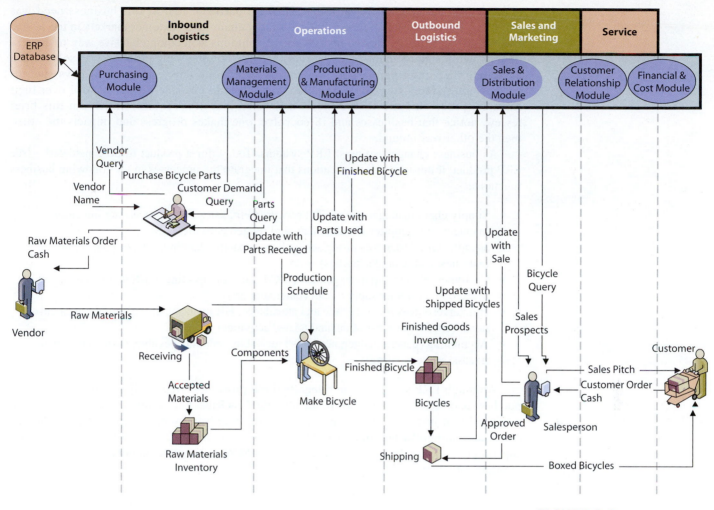

FIGURE 6-6

ERP System for Bicycle Company

produced in the coming days. Further, the ERP system can show the sales manager that if this current inventory is not quite enough the company can double production next week, but that the cost of the bikes will go up 40 percent.

If the sales manager decides to proceed with the sale and production must double, the ERP system notifies managers in inbound logistics, operations, and outbound logistics with supply and production schedules. By consolidating the data in one place, the impact of the sale can be shared in real time with all affected processes.

Q2. What Are the Elements of an ERP System?

To better understand the components of current ERP systems, consider their evolution. Current ERP systems are particularly strong in the areas in which they were first developed, such as manufacturing and supply processes.

Although the term *ERP* is relatively new, businesses have been using IS to support their processes for 50 years, well before the Internet. In the 1960s, a business could use a dedicated phone line, a computer card reader, and punch cards to send inventory orders to a supplier. By the 1970s, businesses began to buy their own mainframe computers and manufacturing companies began to use software called **material requirements planning (MRP)** to efficiently manage inventory, production, and labor. As computing power became cheaper, **manufacturing resource planning (MRPII)** was developed that added financial-tracking capabilities as well as the opportunity to schedule equipment and facilities.

The business environment continued to evolve with the advent of **just in time (JIT)** delivery. JIT synchronizes manufacturing and supply—manufacturing occurs just as raw materials arrive. To execute JIT, tight supplier relationships were needed. These relationships depended on unimpeded flows of data between partners. Just as this business need was emerging, Internet technologies globalized supply chains and customer markets in the 1990s. Businesses began to see newly emerging ERP solutions as a comprehensive way to address their growing supply chain needs, ensure that the looming Y2K problem was solved, and overcome their information silo problem. A short time later, new federal laws such as the **Sarbanes-Oxley Act (SOX)** required companies to exercise greater control over their financial processes, and ERP systems addressed that new requirement. From this brief review, notice that businesses and IS coevolve; one makes progress and impacts the other, then the other way around.

As business changes, so must ERP systems. Today, for a product to be considered a true ERP product, it must include applications that integrate the processes in the following business functions:[1]

- Supply chain management (SCM; procurement, sales order processing, inventory management, supplier management, and related activities)
- Manufacturing (manufacturing scheduling, capacity planning, quality control, bill of materials, and related activities)
- Customer relationship management (CRM; sales prospecting, customer management, marketing, customer support, call center support)
- Human resources (payroll, time and attendance, HR management, commission calculations, benefits administration, and related activities)
- Accounting (general ledger, accounts receivable, accounts payable, cash management, fixed-asset accounting)

Although ERP solutions can integrate these processes, frequently an organization will purchase and implement just parts of the total ERP package. For example, a defense contractor might rely on just SCM and manufacturing, and a university may only install the human resources and purchasing functions. The most common partial implementations are CRM to support promotion, sales, and service processes or SCM to integrate supply chain processes and promote data sharing with supply chain partners.

The Five Components of an ERP System: Software, Hardware, Data, Procedures, and People

As mentioned, an ERP product (like SAP) includes three of the five components of an IS. It includes software, databases, and procedures. To create an ERP product, an organization installs the software and databases on hardware and trains its people to use the procedures. Consider each component:

ERP SOFTWARE ERP software accomplishes interprocess data integration. The software typically resides on servers and on client machines in the company. The software can be customized to meet customer requirements without changing program code. This customization is called **configuration**.

This process of configuring the software is similar to the configuration you do when you install an e-mail system. During installation of an e-mail system, you might make 10 to 20 decisions, such as how long old e-mail is retained, what folders are available, and what names are used for address books. In the same way, a company will make over 8,000 configuration decisions to customize the ERP system to its needs. For example, an hourly payroll application is configured to specify the number of hours in the standard workweek, the hourly wages for different job categories, the wage adjustments for overtime and holiday work, and so forth. At the university, the software must be configured with spending limits for each department, warehouse addresses, bank accounts, and many other details.

Of course, there are limits to how much configuration can be done. If a new ERP customer has requirements that cannot be met via configuration, then the customer either needs to adapt its business to what the software can do or write application code to meet its requirements.

[1] ERP101, "The ERP Go To Guide." Available at *www.erpsoftware360.com/erp-101.htm*. Accessed June 2011.

For example, the athletics department has some of its own money given by boosters for particular items such as greens fees for the golf team. As it turns out, the university could not figure out how to configure the ERP system to display these funds appropriately. As a result, the university had to write its own code and add it to the ERP software.

Code can be added to any ERP implementation using specific application languages such as Java. The most common use of this application code is to create company-unique reports from ERP data.

The university could also pay another vendor to write this custom software for it. Custom software is expensive both initially and in long-term maintenance costs because it is not guaranteed to work with newer versions of ERP software. Thus, avoiding customization by choosing an ERP product that has applications that function close to the organization's requirements is critically important to success.

ERP DATABASES   An ERP solution includes a gigantic, but largely unpopulated, database; a database design; and initial configuration data. It does not, of course, contain the company's actual operational data. Operational data are entered during development and use.

If your only experience with databases is creating a few tables in Microsoft Access, then you probably underestimate the value and importance of ERP database design. Good database design is essential, because an ERP database can contain over 25,000 tables. The design includes the metadata for those tables, as well as their relationships to each other, and rules and constraints about how the data in some tables must relate to data in other tables.

One of the key characteristics of relational databases is that they are modular. Being modular means that tables can be added or removed without significant impact on the overall structure. An ERP implementation may only use some of the 25,000 tables initially and then later seamlessly add new tables as more of the ERP database is used.

Databases used by ERP systems include IBM DB2, Oracle Database, and Microsoft SQL Server. In Chapter 3, a distinction was made between the DBMS that creates and maintains the database and the database itself. Figure 6-7 shows this relationship. An ERP system is the DBMS, and when the ERP system is installed, a database, often made by a different company than the ERP system, is also licensed and installed.

PROCEDURES   IS procedures are instructions and methods for users to interact with the application. Training the employees of a business on how to interact with an ERP system can be a time-consuming and costly operation. To support this need, ERP vendors have developed extensive training classes and training curricula to enable users to learn the ERP system. ERP vendors typically conduct classes on site prior, during, and after implementation. To reduce expenses, the vendors sometimes train the organization's users to become in-house trainers in training sessions called **train the trainer**. Even with this approach, the training bill is very large; a firm will budget a third of the total cost of the implementation on training and consulting fees. ERP vendors also provide on-site consulting for implementing and using the ERP system. Additionally, a small industry of ERP consultants also support the training needs of new ERP customers.

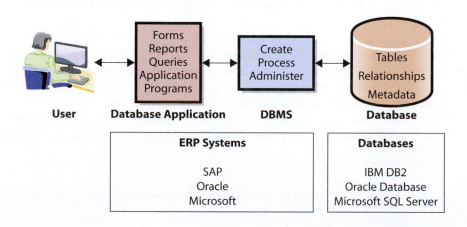

FIGURE 6-7

DBMS and Database

One other note on procedures is useful to students new to ERP systems. Each actor in a process only needs access to a limited set of ERP data and software. For example, Jenna only needs a few ERP menu options and on-screen forms to act as a Purchasing Agent. The University Purchasing Agent who approves Jenna's requisitions only needs a few other options and screens. When an ERP system is fully implemented, access to system functionality and data is limited by the role an employee plays. This important control feature of the system is often not apparent to new students who see the entire suite of functionality and data.

HARDWARE   Each ERP implementation requires a wide variety of hardware, including disk storage, servers, clients, printers, scanners, network devices, and cables. To determine the necessary levels for each of these hardware devices, an organization first estimates the number of users, the processes supported, and the volume of data for the intended system. With these estimates, hardware sizing can be accomplished.

Currently, organizations are facing an ERP hardware dilemma. Employees are increasingly using smartphones to accomplish business activities and processes, including processes that interact with the company's ERP system. The dilemma: Should the firm allow individuals to use their private smartphones with installed company apps to interact with the ERP products or should they purchase company smartphones for its employees? With the latter option, employees would then have the opportunity to use their work phone for private use.

This smartphone issue is just the latest in a long list of hardware issues brought about by new hardware. Another is cloud computing. Currently, most ERP products are purchased and installed on company hardware. With the cloud, ERP systems may be rented with a much lower upfront cost, stored on cloud vendor hardware, and paid for by use. This move by ERP firms toward hosted implementations and away from on-premises solutions will continue. Ellison's NetSuite offers accounting and financial systems for large international organizations in the cloud. SAP's NetWeaver also provides a hosted solution, and SAP may be able to gradually move its large installed base to it.

All ERP solutions are designed and implemented on hardware that soon becomes dated. New hardware makes ERP systems more useful, but integrating the new hardware is often expensive and challenging.

PEOPLE   The people involved with an ERP system fall into three roles. *Users* are the employees of the firm implementing the system. **Analysts**, also called *systems analysts* or *business analysts*, are also employees. Analysts have specialized training or education that enables them to support, maintain, and adapt the system after it has been implemented. Many analysts have a background or education in MIS or IT. A third role is *consultant*. A consultant works for the ERP vendor or a different company, called a *third party*, and helps budget, plan, train, configure, and implement the system. These consultants may work at the implementing firm for a period before, during, and after the implementation.

Although job titles and descriptions vary, a short list of the most common ERP positions is presented in Figure 6-8. Salary estimates are provided, although they vary widely by experience and location. Like an increasing number of IS jobs, success in these positions is based less on technical skill and more on process understanding and an ability to work with people. According to the Bureau of Labor Statistics, job opportunities in ERP and IS in general are expected to grow by 30 percent from 2008–2018.[2]

INHERENT BUSINESS PROCESSES   ERP systems are more than an IS. They also specify processes for the implementing organization. These processes are called **inherent processes**. For the implementing organization, some of the changes it must make from existing processes to ERP processes are minor and hardly noticed, but some changes can be significant.

ERP systems include hundreds, or even thousands, of processes and activities. Some ERP vendors call these inherent processes **process blueprints**. Organizations implementing an ERP

[2] Bureau of Labor Statistics, "Career Guide to Industries, 2010–11 Edition: Software Publishers," December 17, 2009. Available at *www.bls.gov/oco/cg/cgs051.htm*.

Title	Job Description	Salary (in U.S. dollars)
Consultant	Employed by firm other than implementing company or ERP vendor, can perform any of the following roles during implementation	60,000–100,000
Systems analyst	Understands technical aspects of ERP; helps plan, configure, and implement ERP system for company use	70,000–90,000
Developer	Writes additional code where necessary for implementing ERP systems	76,000–92,000
Project manager	Defines objectives; organizes, plans, and leads team that implements ERP solution	70,000–110,000
Business analyst	Understands process aspects; helps plan, configure, and implement ERP system for company use	75,000–95,000
Architect	High-level planner of IS at an organization; ensures compatibility of technology and directs technology toward strategic goals	90,000–130,000
Trainer	Trains end users on how ERP system operates, explains their roles, and trains trainers	65,000–78,000

FIGURE 6-8

ERP Job Titles, Descriptions, and Salary Estimates

system must either adapt to the predefined inherent processes or design new ones. In the latter case, the design of a new process may necessitate changes to software and database structures, all of which mean great expense!

Q3. What Are the Benefits of an ERP System?

In the previous chapter, we said that an IS can improve a process by improving activities, improving the links among activities, and improving the control of the process. Although improvements to a particular process are certainly beneficial, an ERP system also provides benefits to the organization as a whole. These organizational benefits are listed in Figure 6-9.

One benefit of an ERP system for the organization is converting its processes to the vendor's inherent, best-practice processes that are appropriate for that company's strategy. For example, at the university, best practices are now a part of the university procurement process. These practices include buying in bulk, negotiating prices prior to purchase, and a centralized procurement requisition approval activity. Prior to implementing the ERP system, the separate university departments purchased individually and not in bulk, they had little opportunity to negotiate price, and if a delivery was late or of poor quality the department had little training or expertise in making things right.

A second benefit is that real-time data sharing allows managers to see trends as they are occurring and to respond appropriately. For example, the purchasing office at the university can see up-to-the-minute totals for each department's purchases. As a result, if food prices rise

• Implements processes that are industry best practices.
• Data sharing occurs in real time.
• Management can be more insightful and provide better oversight.
• The information silo problem is solved.

FIGURE 6-9

Benefits of Using an ERP Solution

FIGURE 6-10

Example Measures of the
Benefits of ERP

Objective	Measure
Reduce inventory	Inventory costs were 25% of sales, now 15%
Reduce costs	Costs of raw materials 10% less than before
Reduce returns	Reduce number of returns by 10%
Reduce end-of-year closing time	Closing time in days was 14, now 4
Volume of cross-selling	Cross-selling revenues double

The cost of a new system can be determined in a number of ways. For a discussion of a few of the ethical issues relating to cost estimates, see the Ethics Guide on pages 178–179.

significantly, the purchasing office can help dining services reallocate funds from other dining services accounts or change upcoming orders. Similarly, if an academic department is approaching its enrollment limit on a class the ERP system can notify the department chair and if deliveries are running late a warehouse can be kept open late.

A third benefit for the organization is that an effective ERP system can lead to better management as more managers have visibility to more data. For example, if the athletics director wants to check on the status of an order before meeting with a coach, that data is only seconds away. Similarly, the university purchasing department can easily total all the purchases from a particular vendor and renegotiate prices.

Finally, as was discussed earlier, another significant benefit of an ERP system is solving the information silo problem. This means that at the university the different departments no longer create and maintain their own purchasing databases.

Although the general benefits are compelling, it is also useful to examine how these ERP benefits are measured. A sampling of these measures, along with typical objectives, is shown in Figure 6-10.

Q4. What Are the Challenges of Implementing an ERP System?

The process of converting an organization like the one shown in Figure 6-5 to an ERP-supported organization like that in Figure 6-6 is daunting and expensive. In fact, the *Wall Street Journal* calls ERP implementation the "corporate equivalent of a root canal."[3] If not done well, the losses are often very significant. Well-known firms like Kmart and Hershey's lost over $100 million implementing ERP systems. In another debacle, the Los Angeles school district's ERP system issued 30,000 erroneous checks.[4]

Before implementation can even begin, users must be trained on the new processes, procedures, and use of the ERP system's features and function. Additionally, the company needs to conduct a simulation test of the new system to identify problems. Then, during implementation, the organization must convert its data, procedures, and personnel to the new ERP system. All of this happens while the business continues to run on the old system.

Implementing an ERP system is much easier for an organization that has implemented some type of enterprise system in the past. Often a firm will implement a full ERP using a pilot implementation strategy. Using this approach, the organization will first implement an ERP on a smaller scale, in one division or function. The most common initial processes are in the financial or human relations functions.

[3] *Wall Street Journal*, March 14, 1997, p. 1.
[4] Traci Barker and Mark N. Frolick, "ERP Implementation Failure: A Case Study," *Information Systems Management*, Volume 20, Issue 4, 2003, pp. 43–49.

MIS InClass 6

Building a Model

The purpose of this exercise is to better understand the impacts of an ERP on the organization. In this exercise, student teams will build replicas of a model that is hidden from their sight.

Before class, the instructor constructed a model that is now hidden from view. The goal of the student team is to build a model identical to that one. The model is concealed in the hallway immediately outside the classroom. The class is divided into teams, and each person on the team is assigned one of four roles. Each team is composed of between four and six students with the following roles:

Source: Andresr/Shutterstock.

- **Looker:** The looker looks at the instructor's model and remains in the hallway. The looker cannot write anything down. The looker explains to the messenger how to assemble the model.

- **Messenger:** The messenger listens to the looker's description. The messenger relays these verbal instructions to the builders in the room. The messenger cannot look at either the instructor's model or the team's model as it is being assembled.

- **Feedbacker:** The feedbacker can look at the instructor's model and the team's model. The feedbacker can say only "yes" or "no" to questions asked by any other team member.

- **Builders:** The rest of the team is made up of builders. Builders construct the replica of the instructor's model. They acquire the pieces from a supplier who supplies all the teams.

The game begins with the lookers in the hallway each giving their messenger an initial set of instructions. Play the game until the last team has built the replica.

After the game, discuss the following:

1. Do the roles in the game correspond to business roles?

2. Describe your team's building process and its objectives. Use the looker–messenger exchange as the first activity and assembling pieces as the last activity.

3. How did your process evolve from the first iteration of the process to the last? How did you learn to use the feedbacker? If the feedbacker is considered a simple IS, how does this IS lead to process improvement? If so, was that improvement to an activity, a linkage, or a control?

4. Communication standards enable effective communication. What are the communication standards your team needed to make progress?

5. There is no (computer) IS in this game. If your team had some money to spend on an IS, what would you buy?

6. Would the purchase of that IS improve an activity, a linkage, or a control?

7. After spending money on an IS, which player's job would change? In the real world, would this change create stress?

8. With the process used at the end of the game, how much time would it take to construct the next model?

Implementation Decisions

For a successful implementation, the devil is in the details, and there are a lot of details. For a large organization, there can be tens of thousands of configuration details to decide. To make matters even more challenging, many of the most important decisions require a wide understanding of both the business and the ERP system. As a result, teams of experts are needed. With teamwork, additional challenges emerge, such as building effective collaboration, communication, commitment, and responsibility.

Earlier in this chapter, the configuration decisions about wages were introduced. Figure 6-11 lists a sample of the other kinds of configuration decisions implementation teams must make. One configuration challenge is item identifiers. Does the company want to identify or track every item in an incoming and outgoing shipment or just the shipment itself? Further, does it want to track material as it is being assembled or only when it is finished?

Another set of configuration decisions requires the company to specify resupply times. For each and every item in the company's supply chain, resupply times must be calculated.

FIGURE 6-11

A Sample of Configuration Decisions

What do we select as our item identifier?
How long are resupply times?
What will be our order sizes?
Which BOM format should we use?
Who approves customer credit (and how)?
Who approves production capacity (and how)?
Who approves schedule and terms (and how)?
What actions need to be taken if the customer modifies the order?
How does management obtain oversight on sales activity?

These times are based on how long it takes to process the order, the time the supplier needs to ship it after an order is received, and the transportation times.

Another set of issues is order size. More specifically, the organization must specify the number of items in a standard order. At one extreme is to order continuously in small amounts to reduce inventory. However, using that approach, transportation and ordering costs become a problem. At the other extreme, order sizes that are larger require warehouse space and tie up substantial capital.

Another source of detail challenge is the structure of the **bill of material (BOM)**. The BOM is like a recipe, it specifies the raw materials, quantities, and subassemblies needed to create a final product. Most large organizations have a wide variety of BOM structures in place for making their products. Deciding on one BOM standard can be challenging, particularly when the organization makes different types of products in different divisions.

For each of these decisions, implementation teams must decide among choices offered by the ERP vendor. But there is another option in addition to the vendor's options for each choice. This is the option to purchase custom software, as mentioned on page 165. However, this choice presents yet another challenge. ERP vendors periodically update their software, and the custom software may not be compatible with the new ERP software. The custom software code would then have to be rewritten, retested, and reinstalled. A number of companies overcame the other implementation challenges only to fail at this one. They unwittingly created a monster of custom software that they must rewrite every time the ERP system changes.

People Issues

In addition to the challenge of sorting through all these decisions, the actions and attitudes of the people in the implementing organization can make the situation even more challenging. This challenge is aptly summarized by the saying, "All our problems wear shoes." Although this may overlook the technical ERP challenges, the saying wisely indentifies the biggest challenge to successful implementation. These people-related issues are listed in Figure 6-12.

FIGURE 6-12

People-Related Implementation Challenges

Work is changed
Top management involvement after initial decision to implement
Top management oversells capabilities
Perceived threat to department autonomy
Failure to specify objectives and measures for new processes

ERP implementations change the way work is done in the organization. People tend to resist change even when the benefits of the change are well known. One reason is that the change often does not directly benefit the individual who has to change his or her work. The benefits occur for the organization. For example, Jenna's work doesn't get much easier at the athletics department after the ERP system is implemented, but the organization benefits by the change.

Another common problem is that top management believes that the hard part of the implementation process is the decision to implement. Once that decision is made, they believe that they can move on. Instead, they need to stay involved, monitor implementation progress, devote appropriate resources, and share a vision with their employees about why this system will be helpful.

A second top management problem is overselling the vision of what the system will do. Often management can be blinded by the benefits of the promised system and not look carefully at the assumptions behind the promises. This can lead top management to buy more features than they need or that the organization can implement successfully. Employees who may be more familiar with the assumptions and the necessary change quickly become jaded when the "grand solution" runs into inevitable implementation problems.

Another problem can arise when a manager views the ERP solution as a threat to his or her department's autonomy, to his or her way of doing things. For example, the athletics director at the university in the opening case was concerned that the new procurement system would limit his ability to do things to support the unique needs of the athletics department.

Finally, management may fail to specify how their grand vision of this ERP system translates into day-to-day operations. More specifically, they fail to specify objectives and measures for the new processes. Management must develop specific objectives and measures for processes appropriate to the company's strategy. For example, if the university strategy is to be the low-cost leader in higher education, then Jenna's procurement process should have objectives such as reducing time and cost of procurement and use measures such as labor hours saved and cost savings.

Q5. What Types of Organizations Use ERP?

ERP systems are used by many organizations. Use depends on many factors. Two important factors—the organization's industry and the organization's size—are examined next.

ERP by Industry Type

The first major ERP customers were large manufacturers in the aerospace, automotive, industrial equipment, and other industries. Given success in manufacturing, it was natural for ERP vendors to go up the supply chain and sell ERP solutions to those industries that supplied the manufacturers—distributors, raw materials extractors and processors, and the petroleum industry. At the same time, health care was becoming more complex, and hospitals were changing from a service to a profit orientation and began to adopt ERP solutions.

Over time, ERP use spread to companies and organizations in other industries, such as those listed in Figure 6-13. Today, ERP systems are used by governments and utilities, in the retail industry, and in education.

ERP by Organization Size

ERP, as stated, was initially adopted by large manufacturing organizations that had complex process problems that needed ERP solutions. Those large organizations also had the resources and skilled personnel needed to accomplish and manage an ERP implementation. Over time, as ERP implementation improved, other smaller organizations were able to implement ERP. Today, ERP is used in organizations with yearly revenues as low as $5 million.

Value chains and basic business processes are not different in character between small and large organizations. To quote F. Scott Fitzgerald, "The rich are no different from you and me, they just have more money." The steps required to check credit, verify product availability, and

FIGURE 6-13

ERP by Industry

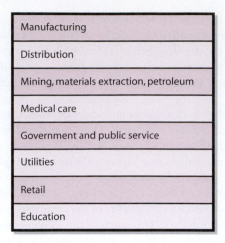

| Manufacturing |
| Distribution |
| Mining, materials extraction, petroleum |
| Medical care |
| Government and public service |
| Utilities |
| Retail |
| Education |

approve terms are no different for order processing at Amazon.com than they are at Phil's muffler shop. An excellent sales process for a multimillion-dollar company is very helpful to midsize companies. They differ in scale, but not in character.

However, companies of different sizes have one very important difference that has a major impact on ERP: the availability of skilled business and IT analysts. Small organizations employ only one or two IT analysts who not only manage the ERP system, but also manage the entire IS department. They are spread very thin and often are in over their heads during an ERP implementation. Smaller, simpler ERP solutions are common among these companies.

Midsize organizations expand IT from one person to a small staff, but frequently this staff is isolated from senior-level management. Such isolation can create misunderstandings and distrust. Because of the expense, organizational disruption, and length of ERP projects, senior management must be committed to the ERP solution. When IT management is isolated, such commitment is difficult to obtain and may not be strong. This issue is problematic enough that many ERP consultants say the first step for these firms in moving toward ERP is to obtain deep senior-level commitment to the project.

Large organizations have a full IT staff that is headed by the chief information officer (CIO), who is a business and IT professional who sits on the executive board and is an active participant in organizational strategic planning. ERP implementation will be part of that strategic process and, when begun, will have the full backing of the entire executive group.

International ERP

One way that the needs of large organizations do differ in character from those of small organizations is international presence. Most billion-dollar companies operate in many countries, and the ERP application programs must be available in many languages and currencies. Some companies can declare a single "company language" and force all company transactions to use that language (usually English). Other companies must accommodate multiple languages in their ERP solution.

Once implemented, ERP brings huge benefits to multinational organizations. International ERP solutions are designed to work with multiple currencies, manage international transfers of goods in inventories, and work effectively with international supply chains. Even more important, ERP solutions provide a worldwide consolidation of financial statements on a timely basis. As a result, they can produce one set of financial reports, better analyze where costs could be saved, and identify where production can be optimized.

Q6. Who Are the Major ERP Vendors?

Although over 100 companies advertise ERP products, not all of those products meet the minimal ERP criteria in Q2. Even of those that do, the bulk of the market is held by the five vendors shown in Figure 6-14.

Company	ERP Market Rank	Remarks	Future
Epicor	5	Strong industry-specific solutions, especially retail.	Epicor 9 designed for flexibility (SOA). Highly configurable ERP. Lower cost.
Microsoft Dynamics	4	Four products acquired by acquisition: AX, Nav, GP, and Solomon. AX and Nav more comprehensive. Solomon on the way out? Large VAR channel.	Products not well integrated with Office. Not integrated at all with Microsoft development languages. Product direction uncertain. Watch for Microsoft ERP announcement on the cloud (Azure).
Infor	3	Privately held corporation that has acquired an ERP product named Baan, along with more than 20 others.	Span larger small companies to smaller large companies. Has many solutions.
Oracle	2	Combination of in-house and acquired (PeopleSoft, Siebel) products.	Intensely competitive company with strong technology base. Large customer base. Flexible SOA architecture. Expensive. Oracle CEO Ellison owns 70% of NetSuite.
SAP	1	Led ERP success. Largest vendor, most comprehensive solutions. Largest customers.	Technology older. Expensive and seriously challenged by less expensive alternatives. Huge customer base. Future growth uncertain.

FIGURE 6-14

Characteristics of Top Vendors

ERP Vendor Market Share

In 2011, SAP had the largest market share, with over 35 percent of the market. Oracle was second, Microsoft a distant third, and Infor and Epicor were fourth and fifth, respectively. Over the last several years, SAP's market share has decreased slightly as smaller vendors such as Infor and Epicor have gained market share. Most of these changes can be attributed to the growth in the small-to-medium market and the maturity of ERP systems in large organizations.

ERP Products

Figure 6-15 shows how the ERP products from each of these companies relate to the size of their customers. Both Epicor and Microsoft Dynamics address the needs of small and midsize organizations. Infor has a product for almost everyone, as you will see. Oracle and SAP currently serve the largest organizations and are seeking to expand their offerings to medium and smaller-sized organizations.

EPICOR Epicor is known primarily for its retail-oriented ERP software, although it is broadening its penetration in other industry segments. Its lead ERP product, called Epicor 9, is based on a modern software development design pattern called service oriented architecture (SOA). SOA, as described in Chapter 5, enables cost-effective application flexibility and allows organizations to connect their application programs with Epicor 9 in highly customizable ways. Epicor's products are lower in cost than products from other companies.

INFOR Infor has pursued an acquisition strategy to consolidate many product offerings under one sales and marketing organization. Infor has acquired more than 20 companies, and today it sells an ERP product for just about any type of firm in just about any industry. As you might imagine, the products vary in purpose, scope, and quality. They span the midrange as well as higher-end small companies and lower-end large companies.

MICROSOFT DYNAMICS Microsoft Dynamics is composed of four ERP products, all obtained via acquisition: AX, Nav, GP, and SL. AX and Nav have the most capabilities; GP is smaller and easier to use. Although Dynamics has over 80,000 installations, the future of SL

FIGURE 6-15

Vendors and Company Size

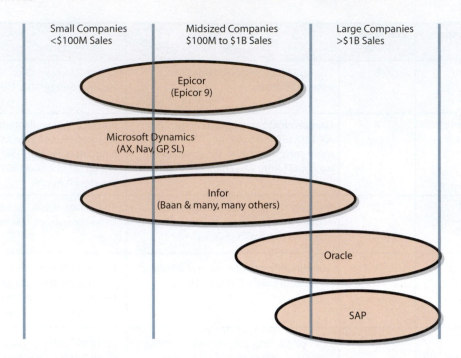

is particularly cloudy; Microsoft outsources the maintenance of the code to provide continuing support to existing customers. Each product is particularly capable in different business functions.

None of these products is well integrated with Microsoft Office, none of them uses SOA, and none of them is integrated at all with Microsoft's development languages. In fact, Microsoft's ERP direction is difficult to determine. It seems to have four horses headed in different directions, and none of them is attached to the primary Microsoft coach. Possibly, it will make an ERP announcement for a new ERP product in the cloud. Or maybe, as long as these products meet most of the needs of its customers, Microsoft executives are just too busy to care.

ORACLE Oracle is an intensely competitive company with a deep base of technology and high-quality technical staff. Oracle developed some of its ERP products in-house and has complemented those products with others obtained through its acquisition of PeopleSoft (high-quality HR products) and Siebel (high-quality CRM products).

Because they are designed according to SOA principles, Oracle's ERP is adaptable and customizable. Beginning with its first DBMS product release, Oracle has never been known to create easy-to-use products. It is known, however, for producing fully featured products with superior performance. They are also expensive.

Oracle CEO Larry Ellison owns 70 percent of NetSuite, a company that offers a cloud-based solution for integrated financial reporting for large, international organizations. It would not be unusual for Oracle to acquire that company as part of a future ERP product in the cloud.

SAP SAP is the gold standard of ERP products. SAP is used by midsized and large companies and offers the most expensive of the ERP products. In Q7, we elaborate more on SAP than the other ERP products, because we will use it in the next two chapters to explain the procurement and sales processes and how an ERP system improves those processes.

Q7. What Makes SAP Different from Other ERP Products?

SAP is a product of **SAP AG**, a German firm. The core business of SAP AG is selling licenses for software solutions and related services. In addition, it offers consulting, training, and other services for its software solutions. Founded in 1972 by 5 former IBM employees, SAP AG has grown to become the third largest software company in the world, with about 50,000 employees, 100,000 customers, and 10 million users in over 100 countries.

The stated goal of SAP software is to help companies make their business processes more efficient and agile. To do this, it relies on a database of over 25,000 tables. It is pronounced as three letters, S-A-P, not as the word *sap*. The letters are an abbreviation for "Systems, Applications, Products," which in German is "*Systeme, Anwendungen, Produkte.*" Detractors humorously claim it might also stand for "Stop All Progress" or "Start And Pray," titles that hint at the challenges of using SAP and of its importance to the company.

Over 80 percent of *Fortune* 500 companies use SAP, including Coke, Caterpillar, Exxon Mobile, Procter & Gamble, IBM, Marathon Oil, General Motors, Nike, and General Electric. To install SAP today, those companies might spend $100 million or more. Of this total cost, hardware may account for 20 to 25 percent, software 20 to 25 percent, and "human ware" (training, consulting, and implementation) 50 to 60 percent. Training, consulting, and implementation of SAP products has become a career for many in IT, and it is easy to see why—companies need technical people who understand the business and business processes and can make SAP work for them.

The prices mentioned above vary, because getting SAP up and running in a company varies—in some cases the process can take years. One time-consuming process is answering the over 8,000 configuration decisions mentioned earlier. To speed up the configuration process, SAP produces and sells **industry-specific platforms**. An industry-specific platform is like a suit before it is tailored; it is a preconfiguration platform that is appropriate for a particular industry, such as retail, manufacturing, or health care. All SAP implementations start with an SAP industry-specific platform and are further configured to a particular company with the configuration choices mentioned earlier. A second lengthy and expensive process is training employees of all levels how to use the system.

A common way to view SAP is as a collection of interconnected and interdependent modules, some of which are listed in Figure 6-16. A **module** is a distinct and logical grouping of processes. For example, SD, the Sales and Distribution module, is a collection of processes supervised by the marketing department. These processes record customer data, sales data, and pricing data. Not every module is implemented in every installation of SAP. Companies that install SAP choose modules for their implementation.

SAP Inputs and Outputs

An example SAP screen is shown in Figure 6-17. When the screen first loads, it is largely empty. On a screen like this, Jenna enters a vendor number in the box numbered 1 and the material in box number 2. After clicking the check icon, marked as 3, SAP populates the screen as shown with data about the company, payment options, and pricing choices for Jenna.

The screen shown in Figure 6-17 is called the Create Purchase Order: Overview screen. When SAP is implemented and configured at a particular organization, this screen is made available only to approved purchasing agents in each department. Different roles in the organization give people access to different screens and different data; accountants would have access to their screens, warehouse people their screens, and so on.

FIGURE 6-16
SAP Modules

QM	Quality Management	PP	Production Planning
FI	Financial Accounting	CO	Controlling
PM	Plant Maintenance	SD*	Sales and Distribution
HR	Human Resource	MM**	Materials Management
PS	Project Systems	BI	Business Intelligence

*SD   includes sales processes, the topic of Chapter 8.
**MM includes procurement processes, the topic of Chapter 7.

FIGURE 6-17

**Procurement Example
Screen**

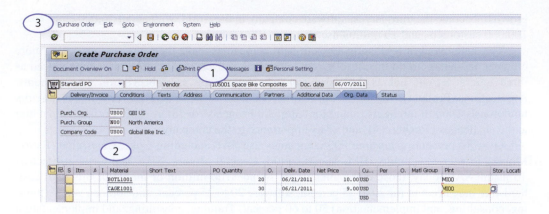

Although it is difficult to tell from this example, Jenna does not have the option to permanently delete a purchase order once it has been saved. SAP is designed to preclude deleting saved records. This control makes auditing and supervision of the transactions more complete and reduces the risk of fraud. Other controls limit the data the salesperson can enter. For example, items sold must already be in inventory, zip codes must match cities, and delivery locations to a warehouse must be specified.

SAP Software

SAP was the first ERP software designed to work at different companies. Prior to SAP, early ERP programs were customized products—companies wrote their own programs to support their own processes. When SAP was launched, its first effort was to consolidate data for financial, accounting, inventory, and production-planning processes. Personnel and plant management modules were developed in the 1980s.

One of the more well-known versions of SAP is called **R/3**. The R/3 program (where R means "real time") was the first truly integrated system that was able to support most of an organization's major operational processes. Built in the 1990s, the R/3 platform uses client-server architecture. It experienced runaway growth in the 1990s and was installed in 17,000 organizations. Ironically, this past success creates a problem today. SAP R/3 uses classic, thick-client, client-server architecture, rather than a browser-based approach that would be easier to use on a wide range of devices, such as smartphones and other thin clients.

Because of this large installed base, SAP has lagged the competitions' rapid move to thin-client, SOA, cloud-based solutions. Instead, it must focus resources and attention on the needs of its current customers (and the attendant, large revenue stream from their maintenance contracts). SAP has the twin challenge of building a stable single platform that makes company processes efficient today, but at the same time providing a platform that will adapt to take advantage of new IT developments. SAP overcame its early dependence on mainframe architecture, now it must do so again to overcome its dependence on client-server architecture.

To this end, SAP has rebranded its R/3 software as the **SAP Business Suite**. The SAP Business Suite runs on a program called an *application platform*. The SAP application platform is NetWeaver. NetWeaver is like the operating system in your computer. Recall from Chapter 3 that an operating system helps connect programs, printers, and other devices. Similarly, **NetWeaver** connects SAP to hardware, third-party software, and output devices. NetWeaver also has SOA capabilities that help it integrate SAP with non-SAP applications. These features enable the Business Suite/NetWeaver approach to be more adaptive to new IT developments compared to R/3. **ABAP** is SAP's high-level application language that is used to enhance the functionality of an SAP implementation.

Helping your future company, whether large or small, make wise use of ERP systems will be one of the challenges you will face during your business career. You will be hired initially into a department based on your experience and education, but all businesses want integrated processes. As a result, you will be asked to think about how your department's processes can be improved with the ERP system and how they can be integrated with other processes in the firm. This will take some of the skills mentioned in Chapter 1—the ability to experiment, collaborate, think about systems, and use abstract reasoning.

Employers seek new hires who have mastered some of the aspects of ERP systems. So take time to command the vocabulary in these next several chapters. Learn how the procurement and sales processes work in Chapters 7 and 8 and how an ERP system supports those processes. If you have access to SAP, accomplish the SAP exercises at the end of the next two chapters and, once complete, start over and deliberately make mistakes, try new things, and see how SAP acts. Learn beyond the book; later you'll be glad you did.

Ethics Guide

ERP Estimation

Todd Douglas Jones was the director of IT at Central Colorado State when the ERP system was implemented. He was a big advocate of the ERP system because he had seen such systems work elsewhere and was convinced it would work well at the university.

Todd was charged with the task of determining the costs and benefits for the new system. After some preliminary research on the topic he decided that cost should primarily be measured in the price of the product and the number of hours of training for the users of the system. Benefits will be determined by the reduction in operating costs.

In order to help the university's president and staff see that the benefits of purchasing and implementing an ERP solution outweighed the costs, Todd shaded the facts in order to make the ERP choice look more promising. Todd did a number of questionable things:

a. He researched 10 schools that had implemented a similar system. He could have used the cost and labor of all 10 schools as estimates for his school. However, in his opinion, three of the schools mismanaged the implementation, and he chose not to include those schools in his estimate, resulting in a lower cost estimate for his university.

b. He estimated that end-user training would be 750 hours, although he expected at least 1,000 hours would be needed. He planned to fund the other 250 hours from his IT training budget for next year.

c. To calculate cost savings, Todd used a different set of 10 schools than he used in item a. He believed that these 10 schools were closer in size to his own school and were more representative of his university, and they made the cost savings look better than the 10 other schools.

Six months after the very successful implementation, Todd was hailed as a visionary. The university is saving thousands of dollars a month. Seven months after the implementation, an auditor discovered the three questionable activities listed above.

You are Todd. Your boss knows what you did. You look into your own motivations and with a clear conscience you tell yourself:

I did not tell a lie. I knew that the system would be a tremendous success, and if I did not help the boss come to see that I would have let a great opportunity pass us by. I did what was best for the most people. I did not directly profit from this. If I were the boss, I would want my IT manager to help me reach the right conclusion, too. And look how it turned out—that alone shows I did the right thing.

DISCUSSION QUESTIONS

1. Of the ethical lapses listed, which one was the most serious?
2. What would you do if you were Todd's boss? How does this change your management of Todd in the future?
3. What is the difference between inappropriate rationalization and justification?
4. How do you know when you are rationalizing inappropriately?
5. Do you agree with Todd's last statement? Does a good result always indicate a good process or a good decision?

Active Review

Use this Active Review to verify that you understand the material in the chapter. You can read the entire chapter and then perform the tasks in this review, or you can read the text material for just one question and perform the tasks in this review for that question before moving on to the next one.

Q1. What problem does an ERP system solve?

Explain how businesses used IS before ERP systems. Identify the problem solved by an enterprise system. Explain information silos. State the differences between the two enterprise systems—EAI and ERP. Define *EAI* and describe how EAI works. Explain how metadata is used by EAI. Give several reasons why a firm might want to use an EAI rather than ERP. Name the components of an ERP. Describe the primary purpose of an ERP.

Q2. What are the elements of an ERP system?

Explain how businesses used computers for inventory purposes before the Internet. Explain the difference between MRP and MRPII. Explain how business and IS have coevolved. Name several of the business functions integrated by ERP. Explain why an ERP implementation might not install all these functions. Describe why a company might create a custom program for its ERP implementation. Define *configuration*. Describe the relationship between ERP systems and databases. Describe a new hardware dilemma and how it impacts ERP. Explain several ERP jobs. Describe inherent processes and explain why they are a part of ERP.

Q3. What are the benefits of an ERP system?

Explain why it is not accurate to say that ERP improves existing processes. Describe the advantages of the real-time data benefit of ERP systems. Explain how ERP benefits management. Give examples of how the benefits of an ERP implementation could be measured.

Q4. What are the challenges of implementing an ERP system?

Why is implementing an ERP solution easier for some organizations? Describe the challenges common to all teams, not just implementation teams. Give several examples of the types of decisions a firm must make to implement an ERP system. Explain the general options the implementation team has for each decision. Explain the disadvantages of using custom software with ERP. Describe how management can make implementation more difficult than necessary.

Q5. What types of organizations use ERP?

Explain how the type of firm that uses ERP has changed over time. How can the size of the organization impact ERP success? What ERP needs are unique to large organizations?

Q6. Who are the major ERP vendors?

How do the top ERP vendors differ? Name four or five of the top vendors and explain how they are unique. Identify the relative market share of each. Explain which ERP vendors serve small and midsized organizations and which serve large organizations.

Q7. What makes SAP different from other ERP products?

Describe SAP AG. Break down the expenses for implementing SAP. Define *module* and give examples of SAP modules. Explain how access to SAP screens can be controlled and how SAP limits or controls data inputs. Describe SAP's NetWeaver. Explain the important characteristics of R/3.

Key Terms and Concepts

ABAP *176*
Analysts *166*
Bill of material (BOM) *170*
Configuration *164*
Enterprise application integration
    (EAI) *158*
Enterprise resource planning (ERP) *159*
Epicor *173*
Industry-specific platform *175*

Infor *173*
Inherent processes *166*
Just in time (JIT) *163*
Manufacturing resource planning
    (MRPII) *163*
Material requirements planning
    (MRP) *163*
Microsoft Dynamics *173*
Module *175*

NetWeaver *176*
Process blueprints *166*
R/3 *176*
SAP AG *174*
SAP Business Suite *176*
Sarbanes-Oxley Act (SOX) *164*
Train the trainer *165*

Using Your Knowledge

1. Give two examples of organizations you know that have information silos. Would either of these organizations choose an EAI solution over an ERP solution? Explain. Using Figure 6-15, what size category are these organizations and which vendors have a possible ERP solution to offer?

2. What would happen next fall if the freshman class is unexpectedly 20 percent larger than this year's class? Which campus organizations need to know that data early? Do you think your university has a way to share this data efficiently?

3. An ERP can create a digital dashboard of important statistics and measures. What data would you like on your dashboard if you were the athletics director? Are they all measures of process objectives? What data would you like if you were the president of the university? Who else at the university could use a dashboard to do their work more effectively?

4. What does this MIS class do differently than other classes? Maybe the assignments are a bit different, maybe the instructor does some things a little differently. What if a university instructional ERP system was invented that featured inherent processes that removed these unique elements? Would that make the school's teaching process more efficient and effective? How could you measure that improvement. Would it be worth it?

5. The athletics director buys sports equipment from a supplier with a well-implemented ERP. What advantages are there for your school to buy from a supplier with an ERP system? You might expect to see an advertising claim from that company like, "We can meet customer orders in 20 percent less time than the industry average." Create a list of two or three measures you would expect to hear from a supplier with an effective ERP system and two or three measures that an ERP system might not improve.

6. To have a successful ERP system, a sports equipment supplier will have made a variety of good configuration decisions. Give examples of what you think might be the company's item identifiers, resupply times, and order sizes. Also, who do you think approves customer credit and production capacity increases? What actions need to be taken if a customer modifies an order?

7. Assume that a sports equipment supplier chose SAP and is an equipment wholesaler and does not produce the equipment that it sells to universities. As a wholesaler, which module in Figure 6-16 might the supplier not purchase from SAP?

8. Figure 6-4 shows the procurement process now used at the university and the objectives and measures used by the athletics department. If you worked as the purchasing agent for food services, buying all the food served in campus dining halls, what would be the objectives and measures of your procurement process?

Collaboration Exercise 6

Collaborate with a group of fellow students to answer the following questions. For this exercise do not meet face to face. Your task will be easier if you coordinate your work with SharePoint, Office 365, Google Docs with Google+ or equivalent collaboration tools. (See Chapter 9 for a discussion of collaboration tools and processes.) Your answers should reflect the thinking of the entire group, and not just that of one or two individuals.

1. Using your local hospital as an example, answer the following questions:
   a. Where might information silos exist if an ERP system is not being used?
   b. Should the hospital pursue more efficient processes or more effective ones? Does it matter if you are a patient?
   c. Using your answer to item b, what measures might be used to assess the benefits of an ERP system at the hospital? (See Figure 6-10 on page 168 for example measures).
   d. Of the implementation decisions listed in Figure 6-11, which ones apply to the hospital?
   e. Which ERP vendor would you suggest for the hospital? Explain your selection.
   f. Assign each person on your team the task of diagramming a different hospital process using BPMN. Then merge your diagrams and reduce the detail in each of the individual processes so that the overall process diagram has about the same number of activities as the individual processes did before merging.

2. Using your university or college as an example, answer the following questions:
   a. Where might information silos exist if an ERP system is not being used?
   b. Will using an ERP system improve the efficiency or effectiveness of processes? What are the objectives of the process(es) being improved?
   c. Using your answer to item b, what measures might be used to assess the benefits of an ERP system at the university? (See Figure 6-10 on page 168 for example measures.)
   d. Of the implementation decisions listed in Figure 6-11, which ones apply to the university?
   e. Which ERP vendor would you suggest for the university? Explain your selection.

3. The exercise in MIS InClass 6 was designed to help you see important aspects of processes and enterprise systems:
   a. What lessons from the chapter did you learn by playing the game?
   b. What other lessons from the chapter could have been learned but seemed to have been missed by your class?
   c. Rewrite the instructions to improve the game.
   d. Could this game be used in other business school classes? What learning objectives could this game deliver?

CASE STUDY 6

The Sudden End of the U.S. Air Force[5]

"Why does the country need an independent Air Force?" This question is now being asked by the top brass and the civilian leadership at the Pentagon. Many other agencies—local, state, and federal—are asking similar types of questions. New enterprise systems available to government agencies are making them question old ways of doing things and old processes. The need for intelligence agencies to overcome their information silos and share data on potential terrorist threats is constantly in the news. The same information silo problem exists with your local police and fire departments and with many other government agencies at all levels. The Air Force issue is a classic case of what happens when a new IS and information silos meet.

The military still needs airplanes, but what it needs more are integrated end-to-end processes that connect soldiers fighting on the ground with airplanes supporting them. Military airplanes provide two important services—they collect data about the war zone and they drop ordinance on targets. In both cases, these are just activities within larger processes, processes that until now had to be done by different departments using their own isolated databases.

---

[5] Based on: Greg Jaffe, "Combat Generation: Drone Operators Climb on Winds of Change in the Air Force," *Washington Post,* February 28, 2010.

One process is the Collect Battlefield Intelligence (BI) process. Troops currently fighting and managers planning the fighting both need BI. In both cases, the process starts as a Department of the Army request for intelligence. This request is passed to the Department of the Air Force, which then schedules the flight, assigns pilots, specifies locations, and collects the data. After the flight, the data is then sent back to the Army. The delivery of ordinance goes through exactly the same interdepartmental process; the only difference is that when the trigger is pulled in the airplane a bomb goes out rather than data comes in.

These processes have worked this way for about 50 years. Recently, pilotless drones have been developed that do the work that manned airplanes did in the past. These drones have much in common with information systems. The plane, the hardware, is controlled by the software that flies the plane. Data is collected by the drone, and the drone has a database of GPS coordinates and data on the height of every obstacle near it. People operate the drone to drop ordinance and collect BI using well-established procedures.

These flying information systems, these drones, have changed many of the old processes used by the organization in much the same way ERP changes processes. Because they can be much smaller than manned airplanes, and much cheaper, drones can be assigned to the Army units doing the fighting. As a result, the process to drop ordinance or gather BI is accomplished much more quickly. Instead of information silos that separated Air Force and Army data, now the drone can quickly respond to the request and the data can be made available in real time to the Army units that need it. If these new processes are completely adopted, there may be no need for an independent Air Force.

Questions

1. Using BPMN documentation, diagram the Collect Battlefield Intelligence process before and after the use of drones. Some activities are Request for Intelligence, Schedule Airplane, and Transmit Data. Resources include the Army database and the Air Force database. Roles include Warfighter, Planner, and Airplane Scheduler. Actors can be Airplane and Drone.

2. Will the new process have the same objectives as the old process? Are the new objectives focused on effectiveness or efficiency, or both? What measures should be used to prove efficiency and effectiveness?

3. Beyond the two processes mentioned here, if the Department of Defense implemented an ERP system, which of the benefits in Figure 6-9 could it expect to attain?

4. Again, if one ERP system is used in the future, what are the most significant challenges the Department of Defense will encounter?

5. Pick another government agency that you understand well. Explain what existing processes would be replaced, what the benefits of an ERP system would be, and the challenges faced.

"Tell me, Wally, what was the hardest part of your job as a warehouse manager?" asks Jerry Pizzi. The two are huddled around a small table in a warehouse at Chuck's Bikes, Inc. (CBI),[1] a small bicycle company that buys frames, tires, and accessories and then assembles bikes that it then sells to retailers. They are discussing Wally's pending retirement.

"It was probably dealing with people. Suppliers would only tell me half the story when my orders were going to be late, and our salespeople seem to think I should be able to read their minds," says Wally.

"And, by the way, this job description doesn't describe what I do," says Wally, pointing to an updated version of his job description.

"Wally, you are one of a kind. We can't replace you, but we can be specific about the skills we need," Jerry replies. Jerry, the head of human resources at CBI, and Wally are tweaking a draft job description to hire Wally's replacement.

"Wally, do you see anything we missed?"

"Nothing is missing, but this description makes my job sound like you need to be a statistics and computer whiz just to apply. I never thought the job was that complicated—just figure out what you need to order, what you have, what is available, and when you need everything. This year's orders are like last year's orders. You keep a little of everything."

"Wally, you made that work. I wish we could hire you. But since we can't, we'll change the job and make sure the new person can use the new SAP system well."

"You know that system is not as easy to use as was advertised."

"That's an understatement. I'm still getting used to it. Some days I wish I were the one retiring."

After they work on some details, Jerry thanks Wally for his help and sees him out. Later, Jerry and Wally's boss, Tim, discuss the job description.

"Wally was the best warehouse manager Chuck's Bikes ever had," Tim says.

[1] At the request of the SAP University Alliance, we did not make any changes or extensions to the Global Bike, Inc. (GBI) case. Instead, we have created a company that is different, a competitor, for which we can add characters without compromising the GBI SAP materials but that is close enough to enable students to be able to use the GBI SAP simulation, if appropriate.

"But, he's also one reason the new system doesn't run well," adds Jerry. "His skill set was well matched to that job as it was about 15 years ago."

"I know, but I'm still glad he took our offer to retire early. You're right, he hasn't adapted to the SAP system very well."

"I don't think it was just the new system. His job was already becoming more complex. Wally was great until we expanded the product line a couple of years ago."

"Wally did mention that he thought this new description overemphasizes math and computer skills."

"I see his point. I think we should balance those with team skills and communication. The new position will require more communication with the other warehouses and departments here."

"I'll add those. But look at this description now. Doesn't it seem odd that someone who we both think was terrific at one time couldn't win his own job today."

"It does seem like a new day."

Q1. What are the fundamentals of a Procurement process?

Q2. How did the Procurement process at CBI work before SAP?

Q3. What were the problems with the Procurement process before SAP?

Q4. How does CBI implement SAP?

Q5. How does the Procurement process work at CBI after SAP?

Q6. How can SAP improve the integration of supply chain processes at CBI?

Q7. How does the use of SAP change CBI?

Chapter Preview

In this chapter, we look into the Procurement process that Wally supervised before and after the implementation of SAP. We are interested in how SAP made that process and other processes at his company better.

In the previous two chapters, we introduced processes and ERP systems. Here and in the next chapter we show how the general ideas about processes and ERP systems from those two chapters can be applied to two common business processes. We will see the benefits of standardizing processes and bringing the data from CBI's processes into one place so that the data can be used throughout the company in real time. In this chapter, we examine the Procurement process. In Chapter 8, we examine the Sales process.

We begin by considering how CBI accomplished procurement before implementing SAP. We then examine how SAP improved CBI's Procurement process. Although most of the chapter concerns the Procurement process, toward the end of the chapter we will broaden our discussion to other processes in CBI's supply chain. Certainly the Procurement process can be made more effective with SAP, but the impacts of SAP on a firm's supply chain are even more significant.

Q1. What Are the Fundamentals of a Procurement Process?

Before discussing the Procurement process at CBI, a short review of procurement will set the stage for understanding this process at CBI. **Procurement** is the process of obtaining goods and services. Examples of these goods are raw materials, machine spare parts, and cafeteria services. Procurement is an operational process executed hundreds or thousands of times a day in a large organization. The three main procurement activities are Order, Receive, and Pay, as shown in Figure 7-1. These three activities are performed by actors in different departments and were briefly introduced in Chapter 6 with the example of procurement at a university.

Procurement is the most common organizational process. Every organization, from single-employee startups to Walmart, from county to federal governments, relies on its Procurement process. Even college students have to procure items: You order books and movies online, and you buy clothes and food. Everything you own, you procured in some way. And, like procurement at an organization, your process has objectives—you do not want to buy inferior goods and you do not want to waste time or money.

Many organizations have similar procurement objectives, the most common of which are saving time and money. According to some estimates, a well-managed procurement process can spend half as much as a poorly managed procurement process to acquire the same goods.[2]

FIGURE 7-1

Main Procurement Process Activities and Roles

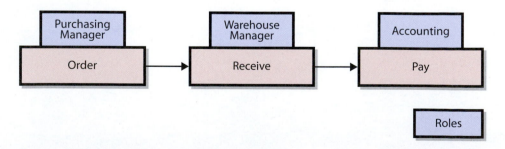

[2] High performance through procurement Accenture 2007. https://microsite.accenture.com/supplychainmastery/Insights/Documents/Achieving%20High%20Performance%20through%20Procurement%20Mastery.pdf

Primary Activity	Description	Process and Chapter
Inbound logistics	Receiving, storing, and disseminating inputs to products	Procurement, Chapter 7
Operations	Transforming inputs into final products	
Outbound logistics	Collecting, storing, and physically distributing products to buyers	
Sales and marketing	Inducing buyers to purchase products and providing the means for them to do so	Sales, Chapter 8
Customer service	Assisting customers use of products and thus maintaining and enhancing the products' value	

FIGURE 7-2

Procurement Process Within the Value Chain of CBI

The state of Pennsylvania has saved $360 million a year by restructuring its procurement process; other states have saved 10 to 25 percent of their purchasing budgets.[3] Another reason why procurement is an important process is that when firms grow by acquisition, procurement is one of the only processes that spans the entire new organization. By combining procurement into one process, the new larger firm can leverage the quantity of the items ordered to gain lower prices. Many states are combining the procurement processes at their various universities and prisons to obtain lower prices from suppliers.

In this chapter, we consider the portion of procurement that supports the inbound logistics process in the value chain. In this role, procurement obtains the raw material needed for subsequent assembly in the production process of the operations activity in the value chain, as shown in Figure 7-2. Other value chain activities also develop and execute procurement processes to obtain things other than raw materials, such as legal services, machine parts, and transportation services.

The activities in the Procurement process at CBI are shown in Figure 7-3. To better understand the activities in Figure 7-3, consider how CBI acquires tires for its bikes. The first activity is to find qualified suppliers who make tires. Once these firms have been identified as potential suppliers, CBI asks each supplier to specify the price it would charge for each type of tire and order quantity. Using this price data, CBI creates a **purchase order (PO)**, a written document requesting delivery of a specified quantity of a product or service in return for payment. At CBI the

FIGURE 7-3

Main Procurement Process Activities, Subactivities, and Actors at CBI

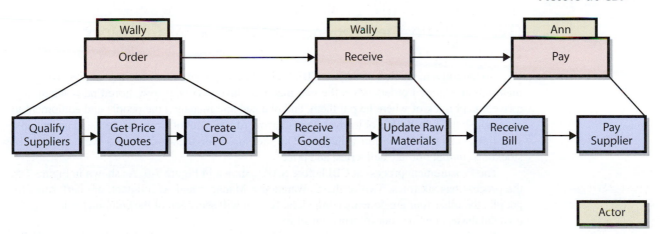

[3] David Yarkin, "Saving States the Sam's Club Way," *New York Times*, February 28, 2011, p. A23.

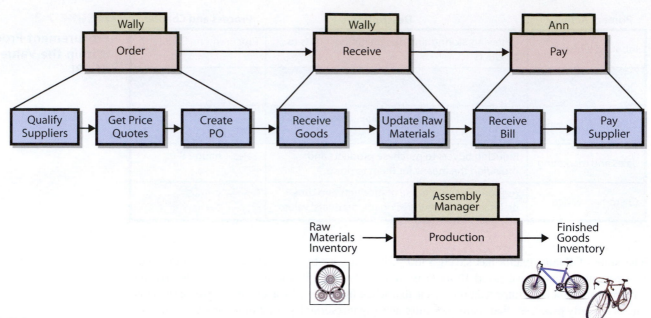

FIGURE 7-4

Main Procurement Process Activities, Subactivities, Production Process, and Inventories

Purchase Order specifies a supplier, the tire part number, quantities of tires, and delivery dates. The tires are then received from the supplier in one of CBI's warehouses. Once the tires are received, CBI updates its Raw Materials Inventory database. Soon after, a bill arrives from the supplier and the supplier is paid.

A key term in the Procurement process is inventory. CBI maintains two types of inventory, as shown in Figure 7-4. At the top of Figure 7-4, the Procurement process acquires raw materials, whereas the Production process, shown on the bottom, converts the raw materials into finished goods. **Raw materials inventory** stores components like bicycle tires and other goods procured from suppliers. These raw materials must be on hand for assembly operations to occur in the Production process. At CBI, raw materials inventory includes bike frames, wheels, and seats. **Finished goods inventory** is the completed products awaiting delivery to customers. At CBI, finished goods inventory is the assembled bikes and accessories. Before SAP was implemented, CBI stored records of both inventories in its Inventory database.

Q2. How Did the Procurement Process at CBI Work Before SAP?

Prior to the implementation of SAP at CBI, Wally was responsible for ordering and receiving raw materials. He issued orders when the raw materials inventory was low, stored parts when they arrived, kept track of where he put them, and planned and managed the people and equipment to accomplish those tasks. His objectives were to avoid running out of a raw materials, to use reliable suppliers, and to stay within a budget. The measures for these objectives were number of stockouts, number of late deliveries, and price.

The Procurement process at CBI before SAP is shown in Figure 7-5. As shown in Figure 7-5, the process has six roles. Two of these, Warehouse Manager and Accountant, are performed by people; the other four are done by computers. As you will see, each of the computer roles uses its own database, creating four information silos.

The first activity in the process shown in Figure 7-5 is Pre-Order Actions. In this step, Wally, in his role as Warehouse Manager, would notice that an item was below its reorder point, look over previous purchases for these items to discover a good supplier, and determine his order quantity. He would often log in to the Sales database to see if that item would be needed in the

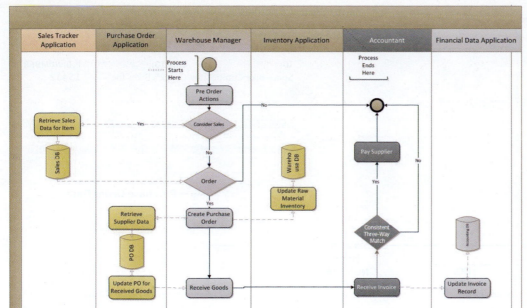

FIGURE 7-5

Procurement Process at CBI Before SAP

next few days to fulfill recent sales. If he decided to order at the Order decision node, he would start the Create Purchase Order activity and log in to his Purchase Order database to obtain supplier data needed to complete the Purchase Order. Wally would use the purchase order form shown in Figure 7-6. In this example, he ordered 15 Deluxe Road Bike frames from Space Bike Composites of Houston, Texas.

Later, when the items arrive at the warehouse, the Receive Goods activity occurs. In this activity, a warehouse worker unpacks the box, counts the items, and updates the raw material inventory quantity in the Warehouse database. At the end of the day, Wally updates the Purchase Order database to reflect all the purchase orders that were received that day.

Several days later, an **invoice**, or itemized bill, is received from the supplier. The data on the invoice—the amount due and the purchase order number for that invoice—are entered into the Accounting database. Before the accountants pay the bill, they make sure that the data on the invoice matches the data in the purchase order and the goods receipt (see Figure 7-7). If the data in this **three-way match** are consistent, a payment is made and the payment data are posted to the Accounting database. In the entire Procurement process at CBI, four databases are used—one in sales, two in the warehouse, and one in accounting. Each of these databases was constructed to serve the needs of different departments; over the years, they have resulted in information silos.

CBI BICYCLES   PURCHASE ORDER

FIGURE 7-6

Wally's Purchase Order in Paper Form

TO:	SHIP TO:	P.O. NUMBER:
Space Bike Composites	Chuck's Bikes Inc	**15432**

P.O DATE	REQUISITIONER	SHIPPED VIA	F.O.B. POINT	TERMS
1/14/2012	Wally Jones	Truck	Midpoint	

QTY	UNIT	DESCRIPTION	UNIT PRICE	TOTAL
15	PQ131	Deluxe Road Bikes	$120	1800

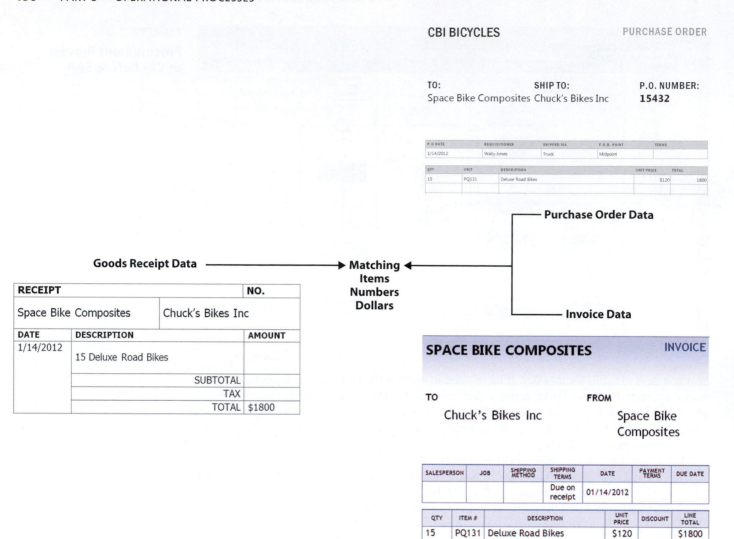

FIGURE 7-7

Three-Way Match

Q3. What Were the Problems with the Procurement Process Before SAP?

The problems with the Procurement process before SAP were well known at CBI. They are listed in Figure 7-8.

Warehouse Problems

In the years preceding SAP implementation, CBI had expanded its sales and product line. It had also adopted a strategy of quick response to changes in customer demand. It wanted to be the

FIGURE 7-8

Problems at CBI with Procurement Before SAP

Role	Problems
Warehouse	Growth in finished goods inventory reduces warehouse space for raw material inventory. Warehouse manager does not have data on sales price discounts.
Accounting	Three-way match discrepancies take time to correct. Accounting data are not real time.
Purchasing	Purchasing agents not centralized; training experience and motivation difference. Weak internal controls lead to limited scrutiny of purchases.

company that bike retailers could count on to supply popular new bike models and accessories. As a result, CBI wanted to hold a wide variety of finished goods so that it could quickly respond to changes in customer demands. As it turns out, the finished goods inventory and the raw material inventory share the same warehouse, so more finished goods meant that there was less room for raw materials. Less room for raw materials and more types of raw materials for the wider variety of finished goods created a perfect storm in Wally's warehouse. He was increasingly running out of raw materials.

Another problem was that Wally was blind to sales price data. Wally could log into the Sales database to see what bikes and accessories CBI sold each day, but that database did not include price discounts. He did not know if a sudden increase in sales of one bike was due to a deep price discount or whether the product was being bundled with something else that was selling well. The sudden increase might be due to these marketing campaigns, or it might be the first sign of a big spike in popularity for that bicycle. Wally was always the last to find out. As a result, Wally frequently ordered too few or too many bike components.

Accounting Problems

In accounting, Ann supervised the payment activities. Most of Ann's challenges occurred at the end of the Procurement process. One of her activities was to ensure that the three-way match was correct. When discrepancies occurred, the accounting department had to begin a costly and labor-intensive process that required several e-mails to the warehouse and the supplier to resolve. For example, if the warehouse miscounted or if the supplier shipped the wrong components, Ann would have to access various databases, compare results, and e-mail suppliers to confirm the results of her inquiry.

The other accounting problem was that accounting reports always lagged; they were never up-to-the-minute. Actually, they were never up-to-the-day. This was a result of not sharing real-time accounting data throughout the organization. Instead, accounting reports were produced at the end of the month. It took the accountants several days to **roll up**, or compile and summarize, the accounting transactions into balance sheets and income statements. This was a problem, because other firms that competed with CBI had begun to rely on ERP systems to produce real-time accounting data. With more current data, managers at these other firms could notice problems sooner and respond to customers more quickly.

Purchasing Problems

CBI had no purchasing department, a fact that created numerous problems. First, the purchasing agents, like Wally, were scattered throughout the firm. They had diverse training, experience, and motivation. As a result, they produced a variety of mistakes on the purchase orders. Further, they had little knowledge about what was happening in other parts of the organization. For example, CBI's repair shop had recently found several very good suppliers of bike parts that Wally in the warehouse would have used, too, but he was not aware of them. These suppliers would have granted CBI lower prices if both Wally and the repair shop combined their purchases. The old Procurement process at CBI required each of its purchasing agents to be meticulous record keepers. However, Wally and other purchasing agents sometimes forgot to transcribe data from the handwritten purchase order to the database, used wrong addresses for suppliers, or entered incorrect totals. Doing their primary jobs was their passion; the procurement paperwork was a much lower priority. Further, it was hard to train these dispersed purchasing agents because they were scattered throughout the organization and had great differences in training needs and expectations from their bosses.

A final problem with the old process was that the upper management at CBI was under pressure from the board of directors to exercise more control over financial processes. A lack of financial control was at the root of Enron and WorldCom's financial meltdowns, which led to new federal government financial requirements, such as the Sarbanes-Oxley Act. The Sarbanes-Oxley Act of 2002 imposed new regulations on how corporations govern themselves, requiring them to set higher standards for the control of their financial operations. Wally and his colleagues could make costly mistakes, favor suppliers for the wrong reasons, or succumb to the temptation to procure items based on their own interests and not the firm's. By bringing all the purchasing to one office in the company, CBI could exercise much better oversight.

The true cost of a system is rarely known before full implementation. Read the Ethics Guide on pages 206–207 to examine the ethical dilemmas in procuring a system.

This improved oversight is an example of **internal control**. Internal controls systematically limit the actions and behaviors of employees, processes, and systems within the organization to safeguard assets and to achieve objectives. One of the key benefits of ERP systems and IS in general are improved internal controls of financial data.

Q4. How Does CBI Implement SAP?

CBI wanted to use SAP not only to overcome these problems but also to better achieve its competitive strategy. Thus, CBI began the SAP project by examining and focusing its strategy. They could then use the revised strategy to guide its managers when making various SAP configuration decisions. For CBI, the strategy examination process has three activities:

- Determine industry structure.
- Commit to a specific competitive strategy.
- Develop objectives and measures for processes to support the competitive strategy.

CBI initiated its planning process by using Porter's Five Forces model to determine the structure of its industry, as shown in Figure 7-9. CBI determined that the bike wholesale industry has strong rivalry and that customers have low switching costs. Because of low switching costs, a bike retailer could easily switch from one bike maker to another.

To survive and flourish in such an industry, CBI decided to pursue a competitive strategy that focused on high-end bikes and a differentiation strategy of responsiveness to retailers. This competitive strategy is shown in the bottom-right quadrant of Figure 7-10. The high-end bike industry segment includes very lightweight racing bikes and touring bikes with composite frames and sophisticated gear-shifting systems. Responsiveness means that orders from retailers are fulfilled rapidly; a retailer could order a wide range of products, and new hot-selling items would be available. While CBI pursues this competitive strategy, it also seeks to reduce its own internal costs, particularly in procurement and sales.

As stated, CBI wanted to use SAP to help it achieve this strategy. In particular, CBI believed that SAP would help focus its processes on responsiveness to customers while holding costs down. To help it implement SAP to support this strategy, CBI hired an IS consulting firm that specialized in SAP implementation. Matt, the lead consultant, organized managers into teams to create objectives and measures for each of CBI's processes. Matt's firm also provided each team a project manager and a systems analyst to help create the objectives and measures. Wally participated on the team that created the objectives and measures for the Procurement process. This team decided on the four objectives as shown in Figure 7-11.

Wally's team decided on two efficiency objectives—smaller finished goods inventory and fewer errors. To assess the less inventory objective, the team chose to keep track of **inventory turnover**, which is the number of times inventory is sold over a given period, most commonly a year. CBI also decided to measure the total cost of the inventory on hand. To assess the fewer errors objective, CBI decided to record three-way match errors.

On the effectiveness side, the team decided on two measures for better financial controls and three for responsiveness to customers. Financial controls will be better if the rollup time at the end of the month is shorter and if more managers make requests for financial reports. To evaluate

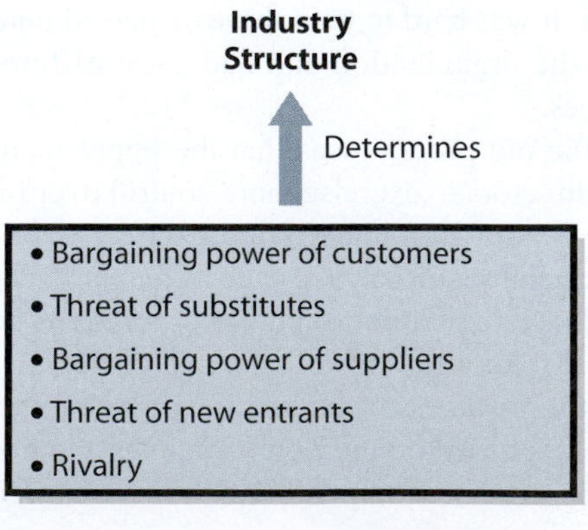

FIGURE 7-9

Determine Industry Structure with Five Forces Model

Industry Structure

↑ Determines

- Bargaining power of customers
- Threat of substitutes
- Bargaining power of suppliers
- Threat of new entrants
- Rivalry

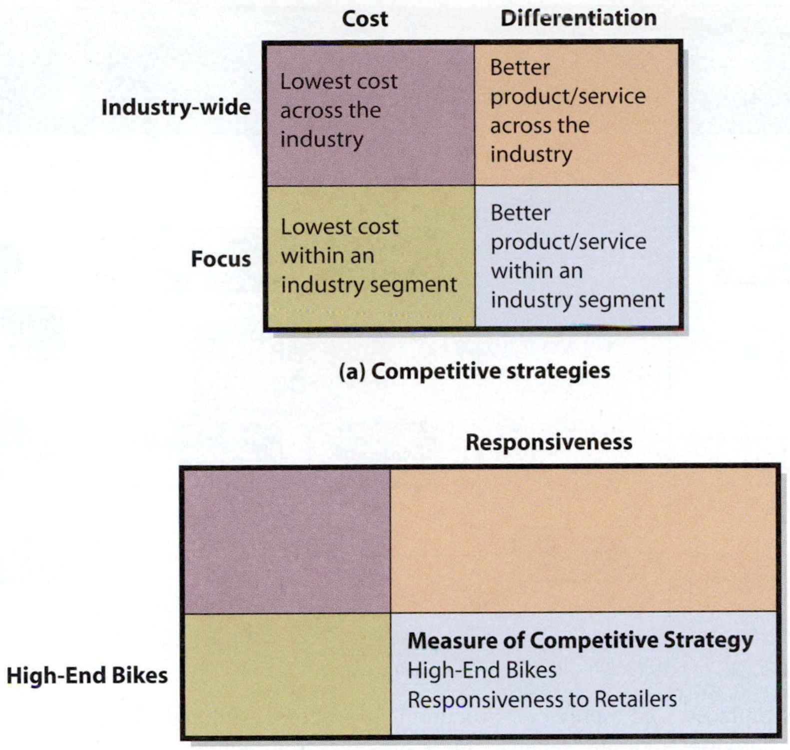
Cost
Differentiation
Industry-wide
Lowest cost across the industry
Better product/service across the industry
Focus
Lowest cost within an industry segment
Better product/service within an industry segment
(a) Competitive strategies
Responsiveness
High-End Bikes
Measure of Competitive Strategy
High-End Bikes
Responsiveness to Retailers

(b) Competitive Strategy chosen by CBI of High-End Bikes; Customer Responsiveness Differentiation

FIGURE 7-10
Four Competitive Strategy Options and CBI's Competitive Strategy

Objective	Measure
Efficiency	
Smaller finished goods inventory	Inventory turnover Total cost of inventory on hand
Fewer errors	Number of three-way match errors
Effectiveness	
Better financial control	Time required for end of period rollup Number of managers requesting financial reports
More responsive to customers	Order fulfillment time Number of products to sell Stockouts of new, hot-selling products

FIGURE 7-11
Objectives and Measures for the New Procurement Process

responsiveness, the team picked order fulfillment time; number of products to sell; and stockouts of new, hot-selling products.

As you read this, understand that these details at CBI are not the major point. The major point is that *before implementing any ERP system, an organization must first use its strategy to set objectives and measures for major business processes.*

Q5. How Does the Procurement Process Work at CBI After SAP?

Let's fast-forward 2 years. CBI has now fully implemented SAP, and Wally, as first introduced in the opening vignette to this chapter, is approaching retirement. The SAP inherent Procurement

FIGURE 7-12

Procurement Process at CBI After SAP

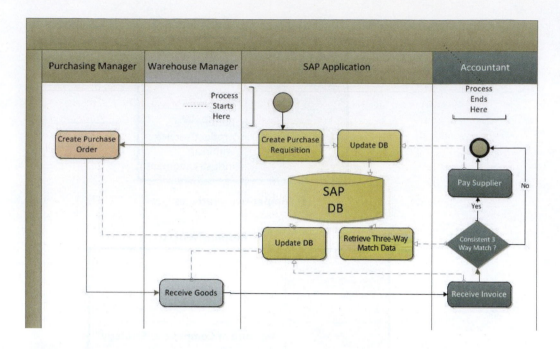

process has replaced CBI's previous Procurement process. Although the new process has the same major activities—Order, Receive, and Pay—the Order activity has changed significantly. See Figure 7-12 for a BPMN diagram of the new SAP-based Procurement process.

The Order activity in the new Procurement process begins with the Create Purchase Requisition activity. A **purchase requisition (PR)** is an internal company document that issues a request for a purchase. This activity is automated at CBI; a computer is the actor, not a human. For example, a PR is automatically generated when the amount of raw material inventory goes below the reorder point. In the example that follows, the PR is for 20 water bottles and 30 water bottle cages.

Purchasing

In the new purchasing department, if Maria, the purchasing manager, approves of the purchase, she converts the PR into a purchase order (PO). Whereas the automatically generated PR is a CBI document, the PO is a document that CBI shares with its suppliers and, if accepted, is a legally binding contract. In this example, when the PO is completed and accepted, the supplier, Space Bike Composites, has agreed to deliver the goods.

Maria logs into SAP and navigates to one of her screens, the Create Purchase Order screen, which is shown in Figure 7-13. We will return to Maria in a moment, but first a few words about the SAP screens you will see here and in the next chapter. Tens of thousands of such screens exist

FIGURE 7-13

Purchase Order Screen in SAP

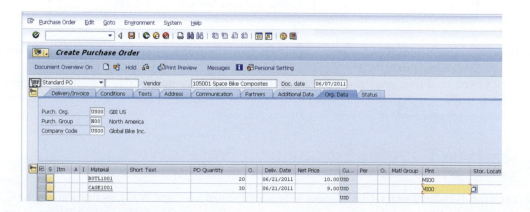

in SAP, so learning the particulars of a few of them is not of great value. Rather, we want you to learn the reoccurring features of an SAP screen, the data typed in by employees, and how the Procurement activity flows from one screen to the next. These skills will be useful for you no matter which ERP screens or process you work with.

Every screen has a title. Here, that title is Create Purchase Order and is shown on the top left. Immediately above the screen title is a drop-down menu (Purchase Order, Edit, GoTo, etc.) and a series of icons for navigating, saving, and getting help. Most of these menu items and icons are the same for almost all SAP screens. Below the title is a header section where Maria must input some data. We pick up her story again at this point.

In this example, the header includes three identifying data items that Maria must input. The header's three boxes—Purch. Org., Purch. Group, and Company Code—are used to identify a particular CBI warehouse.[4] Other inputs would identify CBI's other divisions and warehouse locations. Below the header is the items section that allows Maria to specify for this PO the Material (bottles and cages), PO Quantity (20 and 30), Delivery Date (06/21/2011), Net Price (10.00 and 9.00), and Plant (MI00 for Miami). Each PO can have many of these item lines. Maria finishes the PO by specifying Space Bike Composites (105001) as the vendor in the box in the center of the screen above the header section.

Once Maria saves this PO, SAP records the data in the database. At that point, Maria might move on to entering another PO or log out. After each PO is saved, SAP accomplishes several other tasks. SAP creates a unique PO number and displays this number on Maria's screen. SAP notifies Space Bike Composites via e-mail, a Web service, or an electronic message of the PO details. SAP also calculates the shipment's total weight and total cost and updates the inbound raw material inventory table in the database.

Warehouse

Once the PO is saved and transmitted to Space Bike Composites, the next activity at CBI is Receive Goods when the shipment arrives. Let's move the clock forward 7 days from when the PO was sent. The bottles and cages have arrived in a box delivered to Wally's warehouse. On the outside of the box, Space Bike Composites has printed the PO number and the contents of the box. Wally notes the PO number, opens the box, and counts and inspects the contents. He then goes to his computer and logs into SAP and the Goods Receipt screen. This screen is shown in Figure 7-14.

The title of this screen, near the top, is Goods Receipt Purchase Order. The header includes a Document Date of 06/07/2011, the Vendor (Space Bike Composites), and other data that Wally types in. He counts the quantity of bottles and cages in the box and discovers that 20 bottles and 30 cages were shipped. He moves to the item section and checks the two OK boxes (the OK column is shortened in the Figure to O). in the item area to confirm that the material arrived in acceptable condition. Wally then enters 20 and 30 for the quantities that arrived. For larger orders, several shipments may be required. Here one PO has one goods receipt. He clicks Save and exits SAP.

FIGURE 7-14

Goods Receipt Screen in SAP

---

[4] Note that the figures refer to Global Bike Inc. (GBI), not CBI. Again, CBI is used in this textbook; GBI is the dataset provided by SAP to University Alliance members.

Once Wally saves the goods receipt, SAP creates a document number for this particular goods receipt. In addition, it updates records in the Raw Material Inventory table in the database to reflect the addition of these new bottles and cages. Because CBI now owns the goods, SAP posts a debit to the raw materials inventory account. Finally, an entry is made in the PO record to show that a goods receipt occurred that corresponds to that PO.

Accounting

The next activity, Receive Invoice, occurs when Space Bike Composites sends CBI an invoice for the material. Ann in accounting receives the invoice the day after the material arrives. To record the arrival of the invoice, she opens the Enter Incoming Invoice screen, shown in Figure 7-15.

In the header section, she enters the date of the invoice (06/07/2011), the Amount ($470.00), and the Purchase Order number (4500000172). After she enters this data, the system finds other data about the PO and displays it on the screen. This data includes the vendor name and address and the two items that were ordered, each on its own row in the items section. When Ann saves this data, SAP records the invoice, displays a new document number for the invoice, and updates the accounting data records to reflect the arrival of the invoice.

The final activity, Pay Supplier, posts an outgoing payment to Space Bike Composites. This is the electronic equivalent of writing a check. Before she posts the payment, Ann performs a three-way check. She compares the data on the PO, the goods receipt, and the invoice to make sure that all three agree on items, numbers, and dollar amounts.

Once payment is made, Ann opens the final SAP screen, Post Outgoing Payment, shown in Figure 7-16. Here she specifies the date of the payment (06/07/2011), the bank Account (100000), and the Amount (470.00). She also must specify an existing vendor in the Account box at the bottom of the screen (the vendor number for Space Bike Composites is 105001). She clicks the Process Open Items icon in the upper-left side of the screen and then saves the transaction. A document number is again created, and an accounting update is made to reflect the outgoing payment.

As you can see, each actor—Maria, Wally, and Ann—interacts with SAP using different screens. Each actor has access to only a limited number of SAP screens. This access is based on each actor's role in the process.

The Benefits of SAP for the CBI Procurement Process

By bringing all the data into one place for use in real time, SAP helps overcome the problems of the old Procurement process listed in Figure 7-8. For example, in the warehouse, Wally now knows prices charged to customers. In accounting, there are fewer three-way mismatches, because SAP reduces errors made by the purchasing agents and the financial data are now always current. By centralizing purchasing, the new process improves the scrutiny of purchases, because all the procurement data for the organization is in one central database.

FIGURE 7-15

Enter Incoming Invoice Screen in SAP

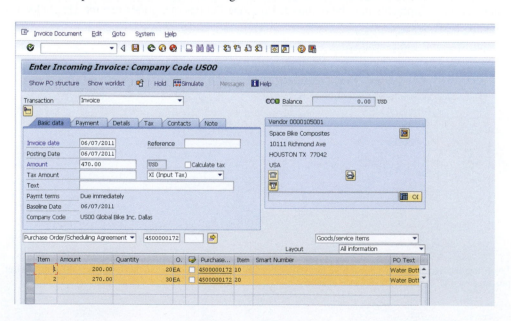

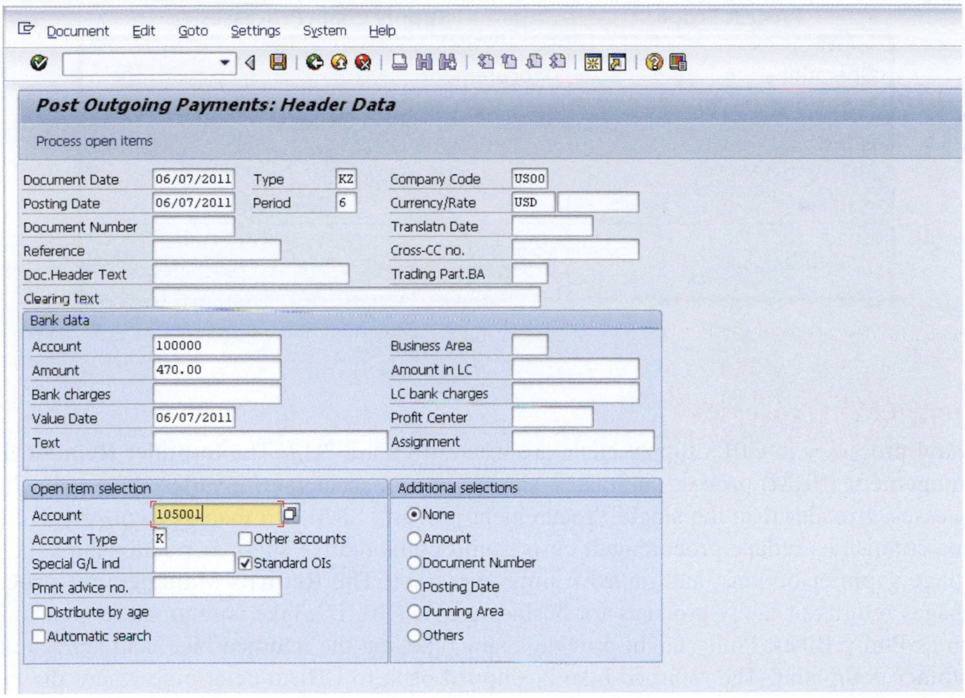

FIGURE 7-16

Post Outgoing Payments Screen in SAP

As stated, CBI implemented SAP to not only overcome problems, but to pursue its particular strategy. This strategy and the Procurement process objectives that support it were listed earlier in Figure 7-11. The new Procurement process is more efficient than before, because SAP reduces inventory. By implementing SAP, CBI has automated several of the Procurement activities and subactivities. Because the process is now faster, resupply times have been reduced; as a result, less raw material inventory for every item can be held. With less inventory, the time raw materials sit in inventory before it is used in production is reduced.

A second objective of the new process was to reduce errors. Fewer errors now occur because the data are entered into only one database, and controls on inputs reduce input mistakes. For example, before SAP Wally had to enter supplier data in both the PO database and the Inventory database. If he mistyped data in either system, that error would not be caught. The number of three-way mismatches is less with the new process.

The new process is also more effective because financial controls have been improved. The objective of improved financial control can be seen by the faster rollup times at the end of the month now that the data are consolidated. With more current data, CBI managers now request more financial reports and use them more frequently.

Finally, SAP helped CBI's Procurement process become more responsive to customer demands. CBI uses SAP to share sales and sale forecast data with its suppliers. As a result of having more data, forecasts for each supplier in the chain are more accurate. The improved supply chain helps CBI reduce order fulfillment times, increase product variety, and improve sales of new products.

Q6. How Can SAP Improve the Integration of Supply Chain Processes at CBI?

Clearly, SAP can help improve the Procurement process for CBI. However, procurement is just one of many processes SAP can support within the company's supply chain. The real benefit of SAP is integration of many individual processes.

Many companies have a well-run procurement process before implementing ERP. However, the SAP Procurement process is just one of a family of inherent processes that SAP designed to run well together. As a result, process integration is much more easily achieved with SAP than by attempting to cobble together processes designed independently.

FIGURE 7-17

Sample of Supply Chain Processes

Process Scope	Supply Chain Processes
Operational	Procurement
Managerial	Supplier Relationship Management (SRM) Returns Management
Strategic	Supplier Evaluation

Supply Chain Processes

Several processes in CBI's supply chain are listed in Figure 7-17. The **Supplier Relationship Management (SRM) process** automates, simplifies, and accelerates a variety of supply chain processes. Broader than the single Procurement process, SRM is a management process that helps companies reduce procurement costs, build collaborative supplier relationships, better manage supplier options, and improve time to market. The **Returns Management process** manages returns of faulty products for businesses. At CBI, if a bike is returned to a customer such as Philly Bikes, Philly might provide a new bike, tag the returned bike, and annotate the customer complaint. The returned bike is shipped back to CBI to determine where the fault occurred. Efficiently getting the defect to the right supplier and charging the right cost to each company in the supply chain are the goals of the Returns Management process. The **Supplier Evaluation process** determines the criteria for supplier selection and adds and removes suppliers from the list of approved suppliers.

Supply Chain Process Integration

Although CBI would like to improve each of these processes, CBI would also like to integrate them. The integration of supply chain processes is called **supply chain management (SCM)**. More specifically, SCM is the design, planning, execution, and integration of all supply chain processes.[5] SCM uses a collection of tools, techniques, and management activities to help businesses develop integrated supply chains that support organizational strategy. SAP offers SCM capabilities and can help CBI to integrate these processes.

The integration of processes is improved by sharing data between processes and increasing process synergy. Integration of processes is the same idea as linkages among activities that was introduced in Chapter 5. There we said that linkages occur when one activity impacts another. Here, process integration occurs when one process impacts another. In the following paragraphs, we will see how sharing data and increasing process synergy, two techniques for integrating processes, can lead to benefits for CBI and its supply chain partners.

Improving Supply Chain Process Integration by Sharing Data

Process integration is improved when processes share data. Figure 7-18 shows two examples where processes are improved by sharing data. For example, data from the Returns Management process about defective bicycle parts should be shared with the Supplier Evaluation process to ensure that suppliers with high defect rates are removed from the list of approved suppliers.

Not only can SAP help integrate CBI's supply processes, it can also help integrate CBI's processes with its supply partners by sharing data. Before CBI and its suppliers shared data, CBI's raw material inventories were quite large. For example, CBI maintained a large quantity of tires and other raw materials to feed its production lines. In those days, procuring raw materials could take weeks, so running out of a raw material could shut down production for days. One reason that procurement was a slow process was that CBI's suppliers only produced raw materials when orders arrived. Today, CBI shares its sales data with its suppliers in real time. As a result, suppliers can anticipate CBI's orders and make raw

[5] Association for Operations Management, *APICS Dictionary*, 13th ed. (Chicago: 2011).

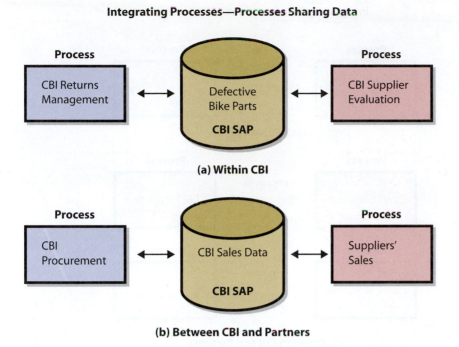

Integrating Processes—Processes Sharing Data

(a) Within CBI

(b) Between CBI and Partners

FIGURE 7-18

Examples of Process Integration by Sharing Data

materials in anticipation of orders. By sharing more data and sharing this data rapidly, raw material inventory at CBI could shrink as suppliers become better informed of and more responsive to changes in CBI's sales. Inventories shrink and customer responsiveness improves as more and more data are shared.

Integrating supply chain processes not only reduces raw material inventory at CBI, it helps to reduce the bullwhip effect in the supply chain. The **bullwhip effect** occurs when companies order more supplies than are needed due to a sudden change in demand. For example, if a spike in sales occurred in the old days, CBI would increase its orders to its suppliers. However, in the old days it might be several days after the initial spike for the order to arrive at the supplier. By this time, if sales keep up, CBI could be facing a critical shortage and its order would increase. This type of delay in ordering would also occur for CBI's supplier, the frame manufacturer. While the middle man, the frame maker, was waiting for parts from its supplier, CBI might increase its demand still more as it sees even stronger retailer demand and grow increasingly impatient. If the frame manufacturer was pressed by CBI and others it sells to, the frame manufacturer may raise its order to its suppliers, too. By the time upstream suppliers crank up supply for parts for the new bike frame, demand from customers may recede, leaving the frame manufacturer or CBI holding extra inventory that cannot be sold. This effect can be diminished by real-time sharing of sales order data among collaborating firms in the supply chain.

Improving Supply Chain Process Integration by Increasing Process Synergy

As mentioned previously, a second way to improve process integration is to increase process synergy. Process synergy occurs when processes are mutually supportive; that is, when one process is done well, the objectives of another process are supported. Examples of synergy among processes are shown in Figure 7-19. You synergize your dating and studying processes when you study with your significant other. You synergize your shopping and your banking by doing both on one trip.

One example of process synergy occurs at CBI between the Returns Management process and the Production process. One of the objectives of production is to reduce defective bikes. The Returns Management process collects data on defective returns from retailers of CBI bikes and accessories. The final step of the Returns Management process is to analyze how to improve the Production process to create fewer defects and thus fewer returns. When the Returns Management process is done well, an objective of the Production process is supported.

FIGURE 7-19

Examples of Process Integration by Process Synergy

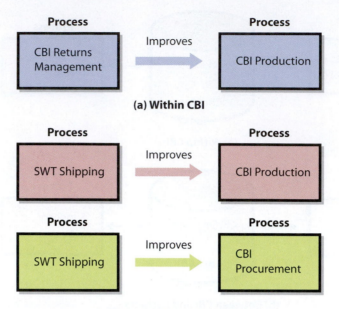

Integrating Processes—Process Synergy

(a) Within CBI

(b) Between CBI and Partners

Increasing process synergy can also be seen in CBI's supply chain. If retailer demand shifts suddenly, CBI and its suppliers can quickly shift production lines to meet the new demand. CBI and its suppliers rely on the SW Trucking Company to deliver raw materials. In the old days without process synergy, SW Trucking had no excess capacity to support the extra shipping needed to move the bike parts from suppliers to CBI to retailers. SW Trucking was a bottleneck. A **bottleneck** occurs when a limited resource greatly reduces the output of an integrated series of activities or processes. SW Trucking decided to improve its Shipping process by keeping excess capacity available. As a result, the Production process at CBI was improved, because one of its objectives was being responsive to customer demand. Not only did this improve production at CBI, it also improved procurement, because the additional shipping capacity meant that CBI's Procurement process could better achieve its objective of reducing raw material inventory.

SAP Integration Problems with Emerging Technologies

Before we wrap up this question, you should understand that SAP is just one way to improve procurement processes and integration. Some companies want to use other, newer information systems technologies like those listed in Figure 7-20. If they do so, they will need to integrate those new capabilities with SAP. Such integration may be expensive, but to preserve the benefits of SAP, it must be done.

FIGURE 7-20

IS That Impact Supply Chain Processes

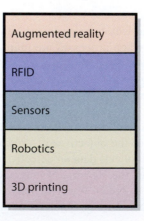

Augmented reality

RFID

Sensors

Robotics

3D printing

Source: Kazuhiro Nogi/Getty Images, Inc. AFP.

FIGURE 7-21
Augmented Reality

With **augmented reality (AR)**, computer data or graphics are overlaid onto the physical environment. An example of augmented reality is shown in Figure 7-21. Using AR, warehouse workers at CBI can look at video images of the warehouse and see overlaid on top of the image data about the location of a product they are looking for, the arrival date of the next shipment of a particular item, or the weight of a container. By augmenting reality with procurement data, CBI can save time looking for items and make other procurement and production activities more efficient.

Radio-frequency identification (RFID) technology, as shown in Figure 7-22, can be used to identify and track items in the supply chain. As small and as cheap as a grain of rice, RFID chips broadcast data to receivers that can display and record the data. In the supply chain domain, suppliers put RFID chips on the outside of boxes and shipping pallets so that when those boxes get to their destination the receiving company can know the contents of the box without opening it. This makes tracking inventory faster and cheaper for all collaborating companies in a supply chain.

CBI and its supplier partners can outfit their trucks with sensors and tracking devices to make the Transportation activity of the Procurement process more efficient. Transportation is one of the highest-cost activities in the Procurement process, and equipping every truck with two-way data exchange can lower costs by optimizing routes to avoid traffic jams, using onboard sensors to better plan vehicle maintenance, and alerting warehouse personnel when delivery trucks are approaching a warehouse.

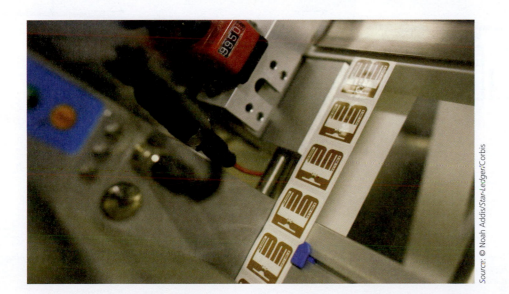

Source: © Noah Addis/Star-Ledger/Corbis

FIGURE 7-22
RFID Chip

MIS InClass 7

The Bicycle Supply Game[6]

The purpose of this exercise is to better understand how supply chains are affected by information systems. In this game, the class will form supply chains and attempt to be the most efficient supplier.

The four links in each chain are retailer, distributor, wholesaler, and frame maker. The game is played for a period of 50 weeks. Each week each of the four teams in the supply chain orders bikes from its supplier and each team fulfils the orders from its customer. Pennies represent bicycles as the sole item in the supply chain, drinking cups are used to transport pennies between stations, and Post-it notes are used to make orders.

The goal is for each supplier in the chain to have the most efficient procurement process; that is, minimizing inventory and back orders.

Set up as many identical supply chains as needed, as shown in Figure 7-23. Notice that the supply chains are constructed with delays between the ordering of bicycles and their arrival. Each supplier is comprised of a team of one to three students. Each

Source: Dmitry Yashkin/Shutterstock.

supplier records its orders, inventory, and backlog on a form like the one shown in Figure 7-24.

The retailers perform the same actions as the other groups, except their orders come from a stack of 3 × 5 cards that contain

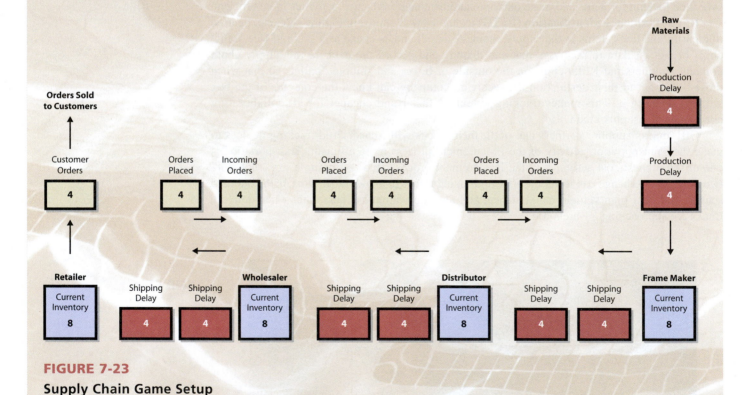

FIGURE 7-23

Supply Chain Game Setup

(continued)

---

[6] See the "MIT Beer Game" in Chapter 3 of Peter Senge's *The Fifth Discipline: The Art & Practice of The Learning Organization,* rev. ed. (New York: Random House, 2006). Also see Wikipedia, "Beer Distribution Game," *http://en.wikipedia.org/wiki/MIT_Beer_Game.*

Game Record

FIGURE 7-24

Supply Chain Game Form

Position:_____   Team Member Names:_____

Week	Inventory	Backlog	Total Cost for Week
1.	4	0	$ 2.00
2.			
3.			
4.			
5.			

prerecorded orders that specify customer demand for the 50 weeks. Students are not to look at incoming orders, prerecorded orders, or supplies until that activity and then they may look at only that week's order and supply.

Each week follows the same process with these five activities:

1. Receive inventory and advance the shipping delay.
2. Receive incoming orders and advance the order delay.
3. Fill the order.
4. Record inventory or backlog.
5. Place and record orders.

When the game is played, follow these activities as the instructor directs so that every team has accomplished each activity before any team moves on to the next. The game begins with a balanced condition in the supply chain; that is, every existing order is for four pennies, every delivery cup is filled with four pennies, and every supplier begins with eight pennies in inventory.

At the end of the game each supplier calculates its overall costs.

Cost = .50 (inventory) + 1.00 (backlog)

A backlog occurs when an order is made that cannot be fulfilled. This backlog accumulates from week to week until it is paid off completely. The supplier with the lowest value is the winner.

At the end of the game discuss the following:

1. Describe the order pattern from the customers to the retailer every week.
2. Why did the ordering pattern between the suppliers in the supply chain evolve the way it did?
3. What are the objectives and measures for each team's procurement process?
4. Where is the IS? What would more data allow? What data are most needed?
5. If you spent money on an IS, would it improve an activity, a linkage, or a control?
6. Create a BPMN diagram of your team's weekly procurement process.

Advances in robotics are leading to more widespread use of robotic forklifts in warehouses. At CBI and other warehouses, pallets of raw material inventory are moved from inbound delivery trucks to storage locations and then to outbound trucks using robotic forklifts. These forklifts rely on RFID chips on pallets to locate the pallet in the warehouse and to be directed to where the pallet is to go. Although the initial costs are significant, robots can reduce inventory costs markedly for CBI and other firms.

Three-dimensional (3D) printing technologies will also impact CBI's Procurement process. With **3D printing**, also called *additive manufacturing*, objects are manufactured through the deposition of successive layers of material, as shown in Figure 7-25. Just as two-dimensional printers deposit ink in two dimensions, 3D printers deposit material in three dimensions, layering material in the third dimension as it dries. Rather than rely on suppliers for all its raw materials, CBI may choose to "print" some raw materials in house. This will impact several supply chain processes and is an example of improving process synergy.

These IS are impacting procurement now, and other, new IS technologies are on the way. As companies continue to pursue their strategies, new technologies will be absorbed into

FIGURE 7-25

3D Printing

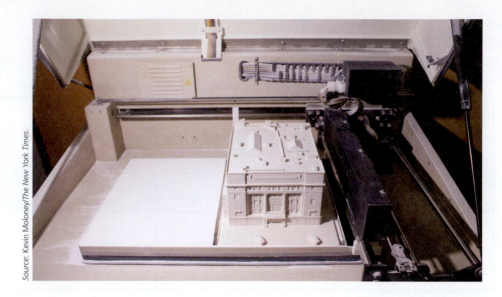

Source: Kevin Moloney/The New York Times.

the companies' processes. SAP will chose to adapt its applications to some of these new technologies, but for the rest, organizations will need to develop their own patches of the new technology into SAP. The bottom line: SAP and other new IS can significantly improve the Procurement process but they will need to work together.

Q7. How Does the Use of SAP Change CBI?

While pursuing a better Procurement process with SAP, companies like CBI are inevitably changed. Some of these changes are listed in Figure 7-26, and a few of them are quite significant. Some changes can be anticipated and are clear from the beginning. For example, CBI employees knew that SAP would require a new purchasing department to accomplish the Procurement process.

Other changes are more subtle, such as the new sets of skills necessary to optimize a supply chain. For example, with more data being produced and saved, CBI will hire more people with abstract reasoning and analytical skills to look for patterns in the data that will lead to new ways to improve processes. Another change that can be expected is that CBI will become more process focused; that is, it will increasingly focus on the inputs and outputs of its processes to connect with partner firms. Pressures from suppliers and customers to share more and more data will lead CBI to be more open with company data than in the past. Finally, the adoption of SAP may lead CBI to use more outsourcing. Many firms outsource parts of their production to take advantage of other firms that can produce a subassembly or service cheaper than they can.

In the CBI warehouse, Wally has seen these organizational and technological changes in the past few years. One result is that CBI is doing less production of bicycles and instead is purchasing more finished bicycles. CBI believes this will help it reduce costs by shifting production to suppliers who can do the work at a lower cost. CBI is also lowering costs by using more full truck shipments rather than partial loads. Because of these large shipments, storage of the finished goods is optimized across CBI's worldwide system and is not done locally. The inventory system dictates where in the warehouse each item is stored; in fact, at Wally's warehouse the SAP system now dictates an item's location to the robot forklifts. Another recent change is that much more data are produced by the new system and shared with CBI customers and suppliers than was ever done in the past. This willingness to share inventory and pricing data gives CBI customers the opportunity to compare prices.

Finally, one more change is significant for Wally and the other warehouse managers at other locations. Before SAP, they were the ones who decided what was purchased. They would notice low raw material levels and then use their experience to decide if, when, and how many parts or

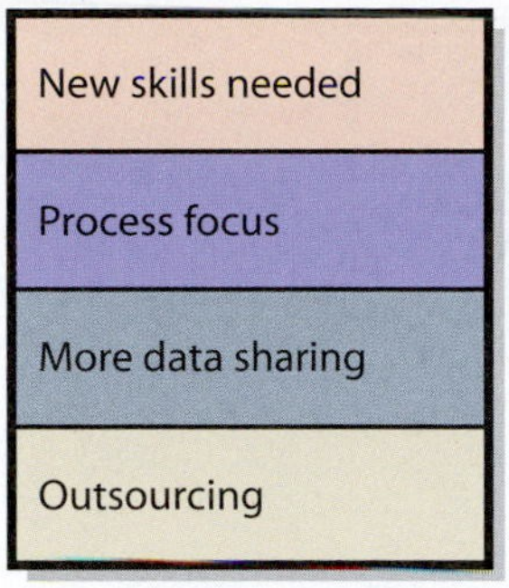

FIGURE 7-26

Impacts of SAP on Organizations

New skills needed
Process focus
More data sharing
Outsourcing

bikes were ordered. Now, the system automatically tracks raw material inventory and generates purchase requisitions when reorder levels are reached.

Wally's Job Change

These changes have taken a toll on Wally. Before the installation of SAP, Wally's job was to manage the inventory levels in the warehouse. And he was good at it. Using Excel spreadsheets, some freeware programs he found on the Internet, and his fax machine, Wally did the job well. When the new company-wide SAP system was announced, he could see that it was a good idea, and the only way for the firm to stay in business. Although helping to implement the system in the warehouse was a time-consuming challenge, Wally looked forward to seeing the project through. He took on the responsibility of scheduling training classes for everyone at the warehouse. However, he encountered his first disappointment when he noticed that the budget for these classes was much less than was planned for earlier, apparently a victim of cost overruns in other parts of the implementation.

As the system went online he helped sell the system to frustrated and disgruntled workers. Some of his people were not able to see the big picture and resisted the changes the new processes brought about. He could understand their frustration with this new technology. Data that was easy to find now seemed needlessly hidden, reports were different and not as informative as before, and the error messages were very confusing. Data was spread out and not as easy to cobble together as before. Wally faithfully helped triage the complaints for upper management and for the IT staff, who appreciated his support and ability to keep things working during a difficult implementation.

As time went on, other problems left him wondering about his future. Most of the jobs in the warehouse were redesigned. A few people had to be let go, others found work elsewhere in the company. Overall, a third of the staff was quickly gone. The substitution of robots for forklift drivers was the most obvious job change. But other changes were also noticeable. Much more of everyone's time was spent entering data into the system, checking and producing reports, or responding to questions from the system or from other offices in the company he had never heard of. His particular job changed quite a lot. He was no longer the purchasing agent, instead he monitored the purchase requisitions the system kicked out every day. At first he thought the system was making purchase requisitions erratically, but as he raised doubts he noticed that management was satisfied with most of the requisitions and he was told the system was operating correctly. Recently, he came to realize that he missed being more involved. He wanted to use his wits and experience rather than watch numbers on a screen. He decided to take an early retirement, and go find his old job.

Wally's experiences are not uncommon. They are included here to present some of the human challenges when ERP systems are implemented. ERP implementations change the type of work many people do. Change, a constant in IT and in business, can be hard on the people experiencing it. And although change is hard on people, it is necessary for businesses to stay competitive. Jack Welch, the CEO of General Electric once said that if change is happening on the outside of a company faster than on the inside, the end that company is in sight.

Procurement Ethics

Buy-in is a term that refers to selling a product or system for less than its true price. An example for CBI would be if a consultant proposed $15,000 to provide some software code when good estimating techniques indicate that the price should be at least $35,000. If the contract for the system or product is written for "time and materials," CBI will ultimately pay the $35,000 for the code or it will cancel the acquisition once the true cost is known. However, if the contract for the system or product is written for a fixed cost, then the developer will absorb those extra costs. The latter strategy is used if the contract opens up other business opportunities that are worth the $20,000 loss.

Buy-ins always involve deceit. Most would agree that it is unethical or wrong for the consultant in this case to offer a time-and-materials project with the intent of sticking CBI with the full cost later. Opinions vary on buying in on a fixed-priced contract. Some would say that buying in is always deceitful and should be avoided. Others say that it is just one of many different business strategies.

What about in-house projects? Do the ethics change if an in-house development team is building a system for use in-house? If team members know that there is only $50,000 in the budget for the new system, should they start the project if they think its true cost is $75,000? If they do start, at some point senior management will either have to admit

a mistake and cancel the project or find the additional $25,000.

These issues become even stickier if the team members disagree about how much the project will cost. Suppose one faction of the team believes the new system will cost $35,000, another faction estimates $50,000, and a third thinks $65,000. Can the project sponsors justify taking the average? Or, should they describe the cost as the range of estimates to senior management?

Other buy-ins are more subtle. Suppose you are a project manager of an exciting new project that is possibly a career-maker for you. You are incredibly busy, working 6 days a week and long hours each day. Your team has developed an estimate for $50,000 for your project. A little voice in the back of your mind says that maybe not all the costs for every aspect of the project are included in that estimate. You mean to follow up on that thought, but more pressing matters in your schedule take precedence. Soon you find yourself in front of management presenting the $50,000 estimate. You probably should have found the time to investigate the estimate, but you didn't. Is your behavior unethical?

Or, suppose you approach a more senior manager with your dilemma: "I think there may be other costs, but I know that $50,000 is all we've got. What should I do?" Suppose the senior manager says something like, "Well, let's go forward. You don't know of anything else, and we can always find more money in the budget elsewhere if we have to." How do you respond?

You can buy in on schedule as well as cost. If the marketing department says, "We have to have the new product for the trade show," do you agree, even if you know it's highly unlikely? What if marketing says, "If we don't have it by then, we should just cancel the project." Suppose it's not impossible to make that schedule, it's just highly unlikely. How do you respond?

DISCUSSION QUESTIONS

1. Do you agree that buying in on a time-and-materials project is always unethical? Explain your reasoning. Are there circumstances in which it could be illegal?

2. Suppose you learn through the grapevine that your opponents in a competitive bid are buying in on a time-and-materials contract. Does this change your answer to question 1?

3. Suppose you are a project manager who is preparing a request for proposal on a time-and-materials systems development project. What can you do to prevent buy-ins?

4. Under what circumstances do you think buying in on a fixed-price contract is ethical? What are the dangers of this strategy?

5. Explain why in-house development projects are always time-and-materials projects.

6. Given your answer to question 5, is buying in on an in-house project always unethical? Under what circumstances do you think it is ethical? Under what circumstances do you think it is justifiable, even if it is unethical?

7. Suppose you ask a senior manager for advice, as described in the guide. Does the manager's response absolve you of guilt? Suppose you ask the manager and then do not follow her guidance. What problems result?

8. Explain how you can buy in on schedule as well as costs.

9. For an in-house project, how do you respond to the marketing manager who says that the project should be cancelled if it will not be ready for the trade show? In your answer, suppose that you disagree with this opinion—suppose you know the system has value regardless of whether it is done by the trade show.

Source: Shutterstock

Active Review

Use this Active Review to verify that you understand the material in the chapter. You can read the entire chapter and then perform the tasks in this review, or you can read the text material for just one question and perform the tasks in this review for that question before moving on to the next one.

Q1. What are the fundamentals of a Procurement process?

Define *procurement* and explain its three main activities. Name the value chain activity in which the Procurement process, as addressed in this chapter, operates. Explain the common subactivities in the Procurement process. Explain how raw material and finished goods inventories differ.

Q2. How did the Procurement process at CBI work before SAP?

Explain the Procurement process at CBI before SAP. Describe the Pre-Order Actions activity, particularly with regards to the Sales database. Describe what data are stored in the four different databases. Explain what an invoice is, who sends it, and what happens when it arrives. Describe which data must match for a three-way match.

Q3. What were the problems with the Procurement process before SAP?

Explain the problems at CBI in the warehouse, in accounting, and in purchasing prior to the implementation of SAP. Describe the conflict between raw material inventory and finished goods inventory at CBI. Explain how not having price data impacts the Procurement process. Describe why a company might want to restrict purchasing to just one department and not scatter it throughout the organization. Explain what the Sarbanes-Oxley Act requires and how ERP systems address that requirement.

Q4. How does CBI implement SAP?

Describe the activities in CBI's strategy process. Explain the competitive strategy chosen by CBI. Explain the objectives and measures selected by CBI for the Procurement process.

Q5. How does the Procurement process work at CBI after SAP?

Describe the Procurement process after the implementation of SAP. Explain the difference between a purchase requisition and a purchase order. Describe the main sections of an SAP screen. Explain the actions that automatically occur after a purchase order is saved and after a goods receipt is saved. Describe how the new Procurement process with SAP is both more efficient and effective.

Q6. How can SAP improve the integration of supply chain processes at CBI?

Describe the processes of Supplier Relationship Management, Returns Management, and Supplier Evaluation. Define supply chain management (SCM) and explain the benefits of effective SCM. Explain the two ways processes can be integrated and give an example of each. Explain the bullwhip effect and bottlenecks and explain how they occur. Also describe how integrated processes can alleviate these situations. Explain how AR, RFID, and 3D printing can impact supply chain processes.

Q7. How does the use of SAP change CBI?

Explain some of the new skills needed at CBI after SAP is implemented. Describe why CBI is becoming more process focused after implementing SAP. How does the adoption of SAP lead CBI to share more data with suppliers and customers? Explain the advantages of outsourcing. Explain some of the changes at CBI due to SAP. Explain how Wally accomplished his Procurement process before SAP. Describe some of the actions Wally took to support a smooth transition to SAP. Describe how Wally's job changed.

Key Terms and Concepts

3D printing   *203*
Augmented reality (AR)   *201*
Bottleneck   *200*
Bullwhip effect   *199*
Buy-in   *206*
Finished goods inventory   *188*
Internal control   *192*
Inventory turnover   *192*

Invoice   *189*
Procurement   *186*
Purchase order (PO)   *187*
Purchase requisition (PR)   *194*
Radio-frequency identification
   (RFID)   *201*
Raw materials inventory   *188*
Returns Management process   *198*

Roll up   *191*
Supplier evaluation process   *198*
Supplier Relationship Management
   (SRM) process   *198*
Supply chain management
   (SCM)   *198*
Three-way match   *189*

Using Your Knowledge

1. Two supply chain processes introduced in this chapter are Returns Management and Supplier Evaluation.
   a. Create a BPMN diagram of each of these processes.
   b. Specify efficiency and effectiveness objectives for each process and identify measures appropriate for CBI.
   c. What new information system technologies could be used by CBI to improve these processes, as specified by your measures in part b? Can AR, RFID, or 3D printing be used to improve these processes?

2. Which of the four nonroutine cognitive skills identified in Chapter 1 (i.e., abstract reasoning, systems thinking, collaboration, and experimentation) did you use to answer the previous question?

3. Which of the four skills in Exercise 2 would be most important for Wally's replacement?

4. The Procurement process in this chapter is an inbound logistics operational process. Name two other operational processes at CBI. Describe two inbound logistics managerial processes and two strategic processes.

5. If a warehouse worker opens a box and the contents are broken, those items will be returned to the supplier. Add this activity to the BPMN diagram of the Procurement process (Figure 7-12).

6. SAP generates a document number for many of the activities in the Procurement process to aid in order tracking and auditing. Which activities generate a document number?

7. For the Procurement process after SAP implementation, what are the triggers for each activity to start? For example, what action (trigger) initiates the Create PO activity?

8. What kinds of errors can Wally, Maria, and Ann make that are not captured by SAP? One example is that Wally might count 20 bottles and 30 cages but mistakenly enter 20 cages and 30 bottles. Describe a particularly harmful mistake that each can make and how the process could be changed to prevent that error.

9. How does a pizza shop's Procurement process differ from CBI's? What do you believe is the corporate strategy of your favorite pizza franchise? What are the objectives and measures of its Procurement process to support this strategy?

Collaboration Exercise 7

Collaborate with a group of fellow students to answer the following questions. For this exercise do not meet face to face. Your task will be easier if you coordinate your work with SharePoint, Office 365, Google Docs with Google+ or equivalent collaboration tools. (See Chapter 9 for a discussion of collaboration tools and processes.) Your answers should reflect the thinking of the entire group, and not just that of one or two individuals.

In Chapter 6, a university implemented an SAP system. One of the changes is that most purchases must now be approved by a new university purchasing office. The athletics director is concerned that centralizing the purchasing at the university will impose difficulties on the athletics department.

1. Figure 7-8 lists problems with the Procurement process at CBI. Which of these would apply to the university?

Which would not? What are some procurement problems that might be unique to an athletics department?

2. Figure 7-11 lists objectives and measures that the managers at CBI determined for the Procurement process. What objectives and measures would you suggest for the university? What objectives and measures would you expect the athletics director to suggest?

3. Figure 7-26 lists the impacts of SAP on an organization. Which of these impacts would affect the athletics department?

4. Chapter 1 explained four nonroutine cognitive skills: abstract reasoning, systems thinking, collaboration, and ability to experiment. Explain how implementing the new Procurement process at CBI will require each of these skills from the members of the SAP implementation team.

ACTIVE CASE 7: SAP PROCUREMENT PROCESS TUTORIAL

A tutorial for a Procurement process using SAP is located in the appendix to this chapter. That tutorial leads the student through a Procurement process that orders, receives, and pays for 20 bicycle water bottles and 30 water bottle cages. Once the tutorial is complete, students should answer the following questions.

Questions

1. Describe your first impressions of SAP.
2. What types of skills seem to be necessary to use this system?
3. Create a screen capture of an SAP screen. Underneath the image, provide an answer to each of the following questions:
   a. In which of the activities does this screen occur?
   b. What is the name of this screen?
   c. What is the name of the screen that precedes it? What screen comes after it?
   d. What actor accomplishes this activity?
   e. Describe an error that this actor may do on this screen that SAP will prevent.
4. Make an informal diagram of the four main actors: Supplier (Composite Bikes), Purchasing (Maria), Warehouse (Wally), and Accounting (Ann). Draw arrows that show the data that flows among the actors during this process. Number the arrows and include on each arrow what data are included in the message.
5. Using the same four main actors as in question 4, this time show with the arrows how the material (the water bottles and cages) moves.
6. One concern of a business is fraud. One fraud technique is to create suppliers who are not suppliers but are coconspirators. The conspirator inside the business accepts invoices for non-existent deliveries. For this fraud scheme to work, who at CBI has to take part? How can SAP processes decrease the chance of this type of fraud?
7. Select any of the main activities or subactivities in the Procurement process.
   a. What event triggers this activity?
   b. What activity follows this activity?
   c. For one data entry item for this activity, describe what would happen in the rest of the process if that entry was erroneous.
   d. For one data entry item for this activity, describe what limits (controls) you would put in place on the data to prevent the type of error described in item c.

APPENDIX 7—SAP PROCUREMENT TUTORIAL

FIGURE 7A-1

Procurement Process and SAP Steps

This tutorial follows the Procurement process shown in Figure 7A-1. The top of Figure 7A-1 appears in Chapter 7 as Figure 7-3. This top figure shows the three main Procurement activities—Order, Receive, and Pay, and the subactivities (Qualify Suppliers, etc.). At the bottom of Figure 7A-1, we have added the six SAP steps included in this tutorial. These six steps were chosen to keep this tutorial simple. To further simplify the process we begin with step 3, Create Purchase Order. As shown in Figure 7A-1, you will play the roles of Wally and Ann.

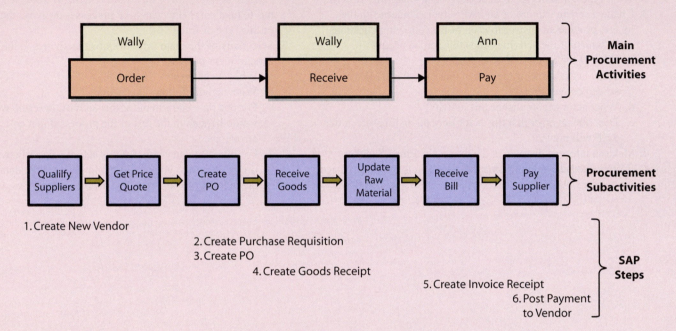

Navigate to the SAP Welcome screen (Figure 7A-2).

FIGURE 7A-2

Welcome Screen

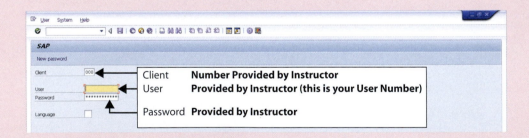

In this first exercise, we will purchase 20 water bottles and 30 water bottle cages from an existing vendor called Space Bike Composites. The bottles cost $10.00 and the cages $9.00. While our company in this tutorial is Global Bike, Inc., our actors—Wally and Ann—and our Procurement process are from Chuck's Bikes.[1] The three digits at the end of your User ID will be used throughout this tutorial. For example if your User ID is GBI-123, then 123 is your User Number. In this tutorial 001 is used as the User Number.

1 Create New Vendor
Skipped—does not apply to this first exercise, it is introduced later.

---

[1] All tutorials in this text use Global Bike 2 (6.04), IS8 System ID, and IDES SAP ERP ECC 6.04 SAPGUI Description.

2   Create Purchase Requisition

Skipped—does not apply to this first exercise, it is introduced later.

3   Create Purchase Order

As a warehouse manager like Wally, your first step is to create a Purchase Order. From the SAP Easy Access screen (Figure 7A-3), navigate to the Purchase Order screen by selecting:

Logistics > Materials Management > Purchasing > Purchase Order > Create > Vendor/Supplying Plant Known

FIGURE 7A-3

SAP Easy Access Screen

A purchase order, when received and accepted by a vendor, creates a legally binding contract between two parties. The first screen is the Create Purchase Order screen (Figure 7A-4).

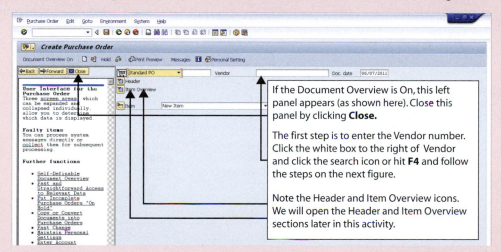

FIGURE 7A-4

Create Purchase Order Screen

The next screen is the Vendor Search screen (Figure 7A-5). We need to find the vendor number for Space Bike Composites to complete the Purchase Order. While Wally might have this number memorized, we want to search in order to demonstrate how searching is done within SAP. Please note that where 001 appears in Figure 7A-5 you will type in your User Number.

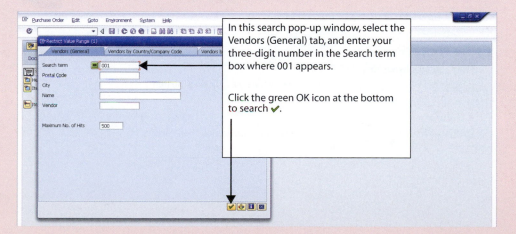

FIGURE 7A-5

Vendor Search Screen

The Vendor List screen (Figure 7A-6) now loads.

FIGURE 7A-6

Vendor List Screen

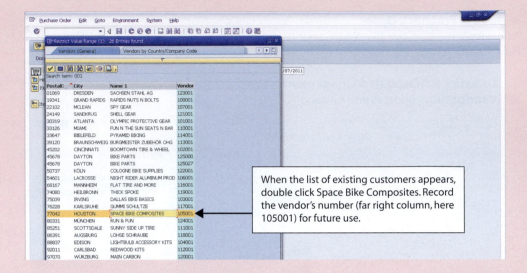

After double-clicking on Space Bike Composites, the system returns to the Create Purchase Order screen. On the next screen (Figure 7A-7), you will enter three inputs for Purch. Org., Purch. Group, and Company Code, the last two digits of each of the inputs is a zero, not the letter "O." These three inputs specify which office at Global Bikes is making the order.

FIGURE 7A-7

Create Purchase Order with Vendor Screen

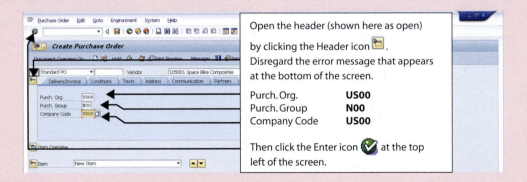

After clicking Enter, the system loads more data on the screen. Next we will enter data about the Material (the water bottles and cages) we are purchasing (Figures 7A-8 through 7A-11).

FIGURE 7A-8

Create Purchase Order with Item Overview On Screen

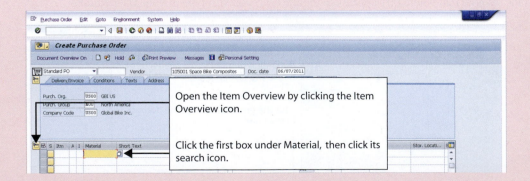

This will load the Material Search screen (Figure 7A-9) that will help us find the Material numbers we need for the Purchase Order.

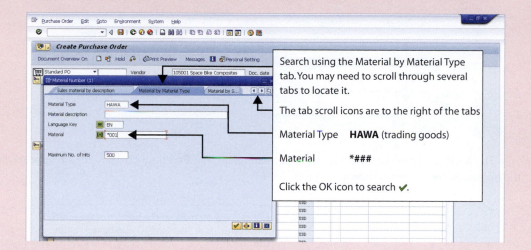

FIGURE 7A-9
Material Search Screen

HAWA is the code used by SAP to identify trading goods. The next screen (Figure 7A-10) will show the trading goods you can order.

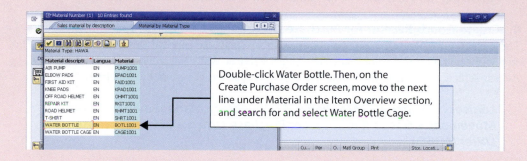

FIGURE 7A-10
Material List Screen

When you return to the Create Purchase Order screen after selecting Water Bottle, complete the following inputs (as shown in Figure 7A-11). Then to complete the second line, you can search for *Water Bottle Cages* or simply type in *Cage1###* (where ### is your User Number). On the following screen (Figure 7A-11), you will enter a date (for the delivery date). To enter date data, use the convenient Search button located to the right of the date input box. Also note, the plant (Plnt on the screen) is MI00, not M100 .

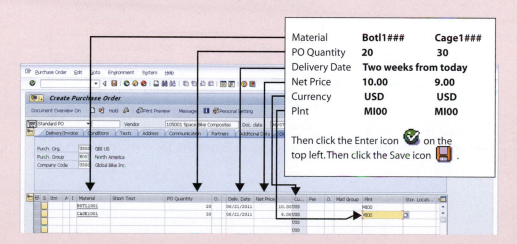

FIGURE 7A-11
Create Purchase Order with Material Screen

A pop up box appears (Figure 7A-12), click the Save button.

FIGURE 7A-12

Create Purchase Order Save Screen

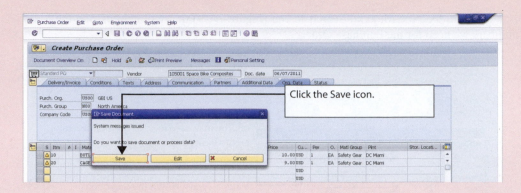

The SAP database now updates and when complete, the Purchase Order screen reappears, the bottom of the screen is shown in Figure 7A-13.

FIGURE 7A-13

Purchase Order Number Screen

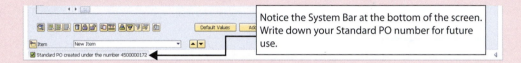

Return to the SAP Easy Access menu by clicking the yellow circle Exit icon near the top of the screen. This icon is located on the same ribbon as the Enter and Save icons.

4 Create Goods Receipt for Purchase Order

The next step for Wally and for you is to create a Goods Receipt for this Purchase Order. This step will occur after the water bottles and cages arrive at Wally's warehouse. From the SAP Easy Access screen, navigate to the Goods Receipt Purchase Order screen by selecting:

> **Logistics > Materials Management > Inventory Management > Goods Movement > Goods Receipt > For Purchase Order > GR for Purchase Order (MIGO)**

A goods receipt is recognition that the goods ordered in the PO have arrived. Once the goods receipt has been created, inventory for these items is increased and accounts payable is increased (Figure 7A-14).

FIGURE 7A-14

Goods Receipt Screen

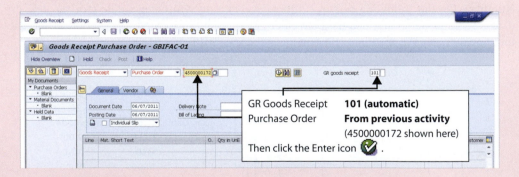

The system loads data from the PO, as shown in Figure 7A-15.

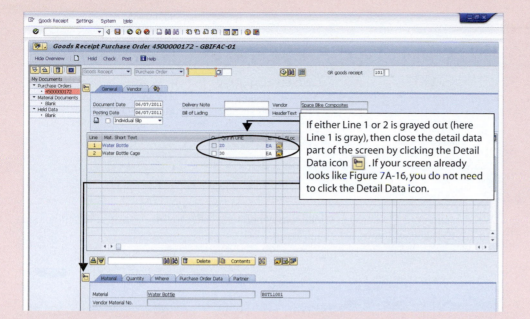

FIGURE 7A-15

Goods Receipt with Detail On Screen

By closing the detail data part of the screen, your screen will look like Figure 7A-16. The reason the Water Bottle line was grayed out in 7A-15 is that the Detail Data section was open at the bottom of the screen. Notice in 7A-16 the Detail Data section is closed.

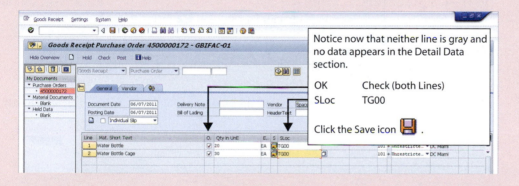

FIGURE 7A-16

Goods Receipt with Detail Off Screen

By checking OK, you are verifying that 20 water bottles and 30 cages were delivered (Figure 7A-17). If not, you would not check OK and would instead enter the quantity that did arrive. Figure 7A-16 shows this column header as O. instead of O.K., which can be shown by adjusting the column width.

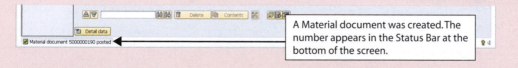

FIGURE 7A-17

Goods Receipt Material Document Screen

Return to the SAP Easy Access menu by clicking the Exit icon.

5   Create Invoice Receipt from Vendor

An accountant, like Ann, would accomplish the final two steps—Creating an Invoice and Paying the Vendor. From the SAP Easy Access screen, navigate to the Enter Incoming Invoice screen by selecting:

Logistics > Materials Management > Logistics Invoice Verification > Document Entry > Enter Invoice

Shortly after the goods arrived, the vendor has sent us a bill for $470 for the bottles and cages, and here we record this bill in our system (Figure 7A-18). Note, in Figure 7A-18 that the Tax Amount is entered via a drop-down box, which is the rightmost input box for Tax Amount.

FIGURE 7A-18

Create Invoice Screen

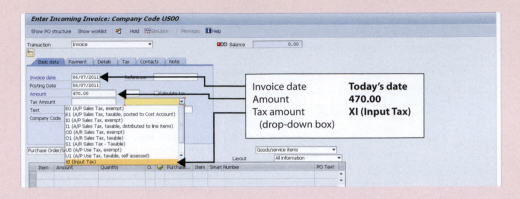

We also enter our PO number, which was generated earlier in this process at the end of step 3 (Figure 7A-13). This is shown below in Figure 7A-19.

FIGURE 7A-19

Create Invoice with PO Number Screen

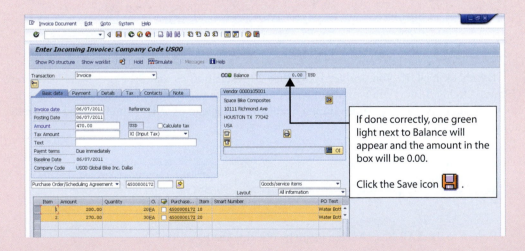

The system loads vendor data and displays the updated Incoming Invoice screen (Figure 7A-20).

FIGURE 7A-20

Create Invoice Final Screen

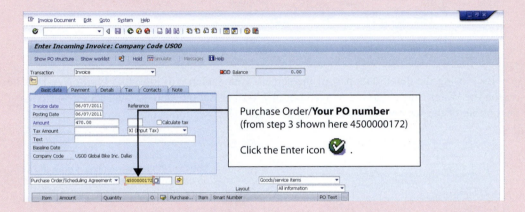

If there are no errors, a document number is produced on the bottom of the next screen (Figure 7A-21).

FIGURE 7A-21

Create Invoice Document Number Screen

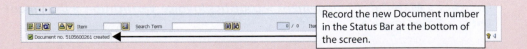

Return to the SAP Easy Access menu by clicking the Exit icon.

6   Post Payment to the Vendor

The final step occurs when you or Ann pays the vendor. This payment may be made immediately upon receipt of the invoice or shortly thereafter. From the SAP Easy Access screen, navigate to the Post Outgoing Payments screen by selecting:

Accounting > Financial Accounting > Accounts Payable > Document Entry > Outgoing Payment > Post

In this activity, we record our payment to the vendor for $470.00 (Figure 7A-22). A journal entry is made to decrease accounts payable.

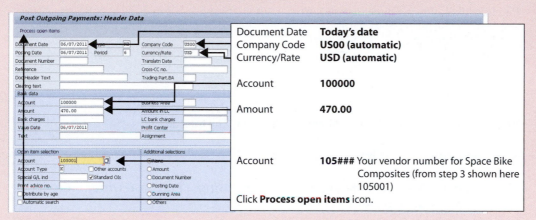

FIGURE 7A-22

Post Outgoing Payments Screen

Document Date	**Today's date**
Company Code	**US00 (automatic)**
Currency/Rate	**USD (automatic)**
Account	**100000**
Amount	**470.00**
Account	**105###** Your vendor number for Space Bike Composites (from step 3 shown here 105001)

Click **Process open items** icon.

If you have to search for your vendor number in the bottom Account text box, select the Vendors (General) tab in the search pop-up window and use ### as the search term. Once you click on Process open items, the Post Outgoing Payments Process open items screen appears (Figure 7A-23).

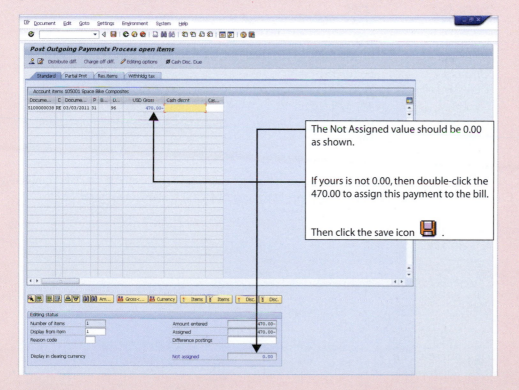

FIGURE 7A-23

Post Outgoing Payments Final Screen

The Not Assigned value should be 0.00 as shown.

If yours is not 0.00, then double-click the 470.00 to assign this payment to the bill.

Then click the save icon.

The SAP database is again updated and the Post Payment Document Number screen (Figure 7A-24) appears.

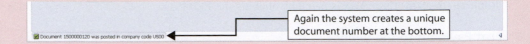

> Again the system creates a unique document number at the bottom.

Record the document number that once again appears on the Status bar. Return to the SAP Easy Access screen by clicking the Exit icon. This will generate a pop-up window that is misleading. There is no data to be lost at this point, so click Yes.

You have finished the first exercise.

You Try It 1

Purchase the following three materials from a different vendor—Rapids Nuts N Bolts:

5	Air Pumps	$14 each
10	Elbow Pads	$375 each
15	First Aid Kits	$20 each

Request delivery in 2 weeks. Use Miami for the plant. The total amount is $4120.00.

3   Create Purchase Order

Logistics > Materials Management > Purchasing > Purchase Order > Create > Vendor/Supplying Plant Known

Data needed:

Vendor	**108### (Your Rapids Nuts N Bolts vendor number based on your User Number)**
Purch. Org.	**US00**
Purch. Group	**N00**
Company Code	**US00**
Material	**PUMP1###, EPAD1###, FAID1### (These are Trading Goods)**
Quantity	**5, 10, 15**
Delivery Date	**Two weeks from today**
Net Price	**14, 375, 20**
Currency	**USD**
Plnt	**MI00**

Not every screen is shown here. Refer to the first exercise to see each screen. The completed Create Purchase Order screen as it appears at the *end* of step 3 is shown in Figure 7A-25.

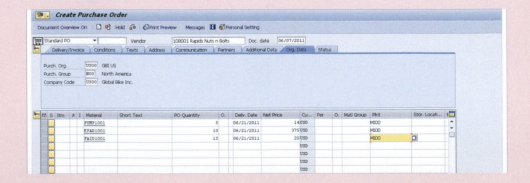

Click the Save icon. Record the PO number at the bottom of the screen. Return to the SAP Easy Access menu by clicking the Exit icon.

4   Create Goods Receipt for Purchase Order

Logistics > Materials Management > Inventory Management > Goods Movement > Goods Receipt > For Purchase Order > GR for Purchase Order (MIGO)

Data needed:

Gr Goods Receipt	**101**
Purchase Order	**From previous step (4500000173 shown here)**
OK	**Three check marks**
SLoc	**TG00 (Trading Goods)**

The completed Goods Receipt screen is shown in Figure 7A-26.

FIGURE 7A-26

Goods Receipt Final Screen

Click the Save icon. Return to the SAP Easy Access menu by clicking the Exit icon.

5   Create Invoice Receipt from Vendor

Logistics > Materials Management > Logistics Invoice Verification > Document Entry > Enter Invoice

Data needed:

Invoice Date	**Today's date**
Amount	**4120.00**
Tax Amount	**XI (Input Tax)**
Purchase Order	**Your PO number (4500000173 shown here)**

Once these four items have been entered and the Enter icon has been clicked, the Enter Incoming Invoice screen will appear, as shown in Figure 7A-27. If done correctly, the Balance box in the upper right-hand corner should indicate 0.00.

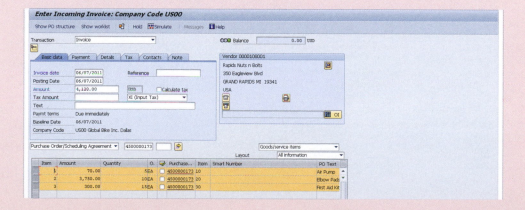

FIGURE 7A-27

Create Invoice Final Screen

Click the Save icon. Return to the SAP Easy Access menu by clicking the Exit icon.

6   Post Payment to the Vendor

Accounting > Financial Accounting > Accounts Payable > Document Entry >
Outgoing Payment > Post

Data needed:

Document Date	**Today's date**
Company Code	**US00 (automatic)**
Currency/Rate	**USD (automatic)**
Account	**100000**
Amount	**4120.00**
Account	**108### (Rapids Nuts N Bolts vendor number based on your User Number)**

Before clicking Process Open Items, the Post Outgoing Payments screen appears as shown in Figure 7A-28:

FIGURE 7A-28

Post Outgoing Payments Header Screen

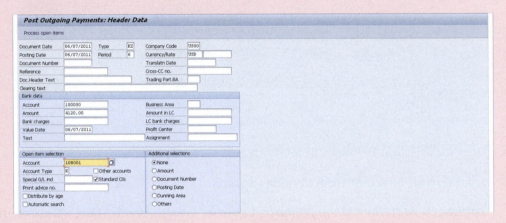

After clicking Process Open Items, the screen appears as shown in Figure 7A-29. If correct, the Not Assigned at the bottom-right corner will be 0.00. Then click the Save icon.

FIGURE 7A-29

Post Outgoing Payments Final Screen

You are now finished with You Try It 1. Return to the SAP Easy Access menu by clicking the Exit icon.

You Try It 2

In step 1 of You Try It 2, you will create a new vendor called Bike Parts. Then, in step 2, Creating a Purchase Requisition, you will request a price quote for 10 repair kits. In step 3, you will once again create a PO; however, this time the PO is based on the purchase requisition you created in step 2.

1   Create New Vendor

Logistics > Materials Management > Purchasing > Master Data > Vendor > Central > Create

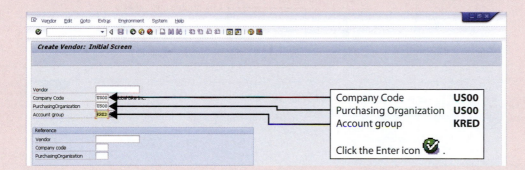

FIGURE 7A-30

Create Vendor Initial Screen

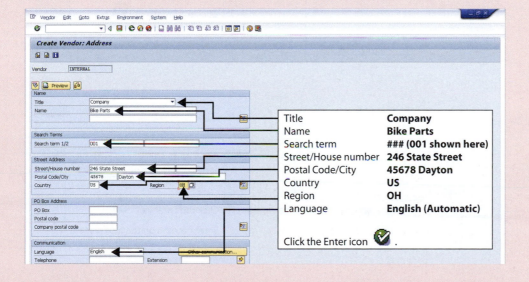

FIGURE 7A-31

Create Vendor Address Screen

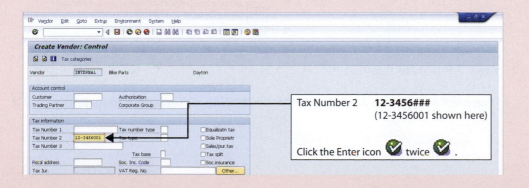

FIGURE 7A-32

Create Vendor Tax Screen

FIGURE 7A-33

Create Vendor Accounting Screen

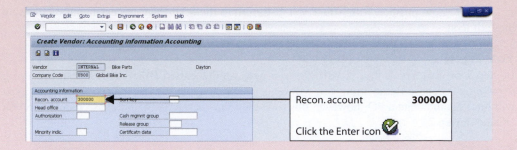

FIGURE 7A-34

Create Vendor Payment Screen

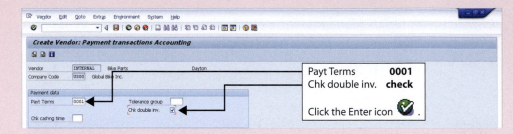

FIGURE 7A-35

Create Vendor Correspondence Screen

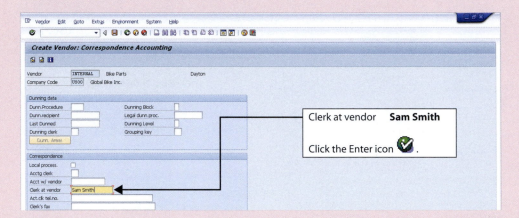

FIGURE 7A-36

Create Vendor Purchasing Screen

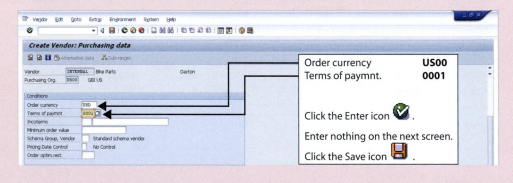

FIGURE 7A-37

Create Vendor Number Screen

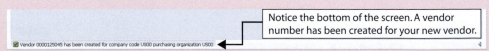

2   Create Purchase Requisition

Logistics > Materials Management > Purchasing > Purchase Requisition > Create

FIGURE 7A-38

Purchase Requisition Screen

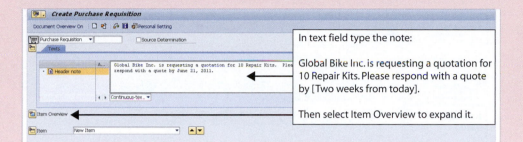

FIGURE 7A-39

Purchase Requisition Text Screen

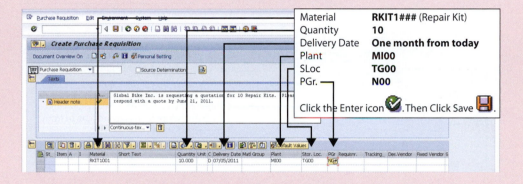

FIGURE 7A-40

Purchase Requisition Item Screen

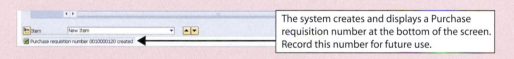

FIGURE 7A-41

Purchase Requisition Number Screen

3 Create Purchase Order (now from Requisition)

Logistics > Materials Management > Purchasing > Purchase Order > Create > Vendor/Supplying Plant Known

Step 3 was completed in the first exercise and in You Try It 1. This time you are creating the PO from the purchase requisition you created in step 2.

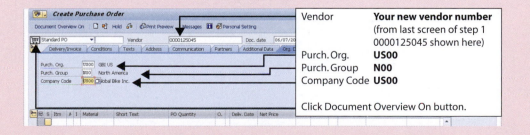

FIGURE 7A-42

Purchase Order Screen

FIGURE 7A-43

Purchase Order from Purchase Requisition Screen

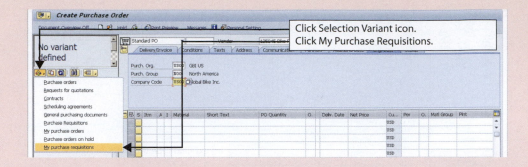

Click Selection Variant icon.
Click My Purchase Requisitions.

FIGURE 7A-44

Purchase Order from Purchase Requisition Selection Screen

Your Purchase Requisition (from step 2) should be displayed (10000120 shown here).

FIGURE 7A-45

Purchase Order Adopt from Purchase Requisition Screen

Highlight your Purchase Requisition and click the Adopt icon (second icon in from the left).

FIGURE 7A-46

Purchase Order Price Screen

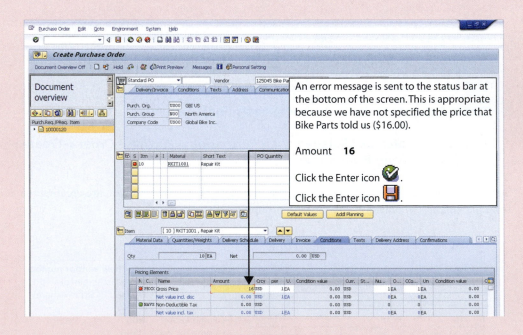

An error message is sent to the status bar at the bottom of the screen. This is appropriate because we have not specified the price that Bike Parts told us ($16.00).

Amount   **16**

Click the Enter icon.

Click the Enter icon.

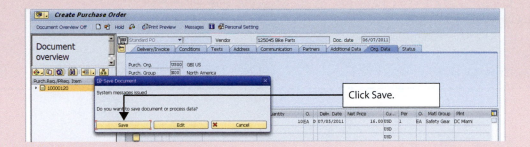

FIGURE 7A-47

Purchase Order Save Screen

FIGURE 7A-48

Purchase Order Number Screen

You have finished You Try It 2.

"Our best client! And we lost the sale!" Sue's exasperated as she talks to Doug in sales.

"Nothing you could have done, Sue. You can't sell bikes that we don't have and couldn't get."

"But Doug, why, why, why does this keep happening??? Don't they know we're losing sales left and right? And now Heartland, our biggest customer!"

"I guess this won't happen with the new SAP system. It will give us up-to-the-minute inventory figures."

"I hope CBI is still in business by the time we get the system."

Sue later hears the full story from Ann in accounting.

"Ann, when I looked at the inventory I saw that we had 55 of the bikes they wanted, and I only needed 50 for the sale."

"Yeah, it did show that. But what it didn't show is that Doug had sold 10 of them earlier that day."

"So, when I thought we had 55, which is what the computer showed, we actually had 45?"

"Right."

"But, Ann, Doug sold those bikes to that little outfit in Kansas City. Those guys are small potatoes compared to Heartland. Why didn't we cancel their order instead of Heartland's?"

"That makes sense, but we've never done that."

"Even worse, Ann, Heartland didn't want the bikes until next month. Couldn't we order the frames and parts and put them together in the next 2 weeks or so? We've done that before to save sales."

"Wouldn't work. Space Bike Composites is our only supplier of that frame and they've discontinued it."

"Why wasn't the sales department told?"

"We thought another supplier was going to come through with the frame, but that was a dead end."

"We've got to find a way to keep the sales reps in the loop. We're going to lose Heartland if I have to cancel more orders."

"I agree, but how? There are hundreds of items we sell and hundreds of suppliers, and the suppliers have suppliers. Would sales reps read hundreds of e-mails about possible problems? Nobody reads that security stuff the IT people send out every day, and that's just one paragraph."

"Fine. That doesn't do anything about Heartland, though . . . or my commission check."

Q1. What are the fundamentals of a Sales process?

Q2. How did the Sales process at CBI work before SAP?

Q3. What were the problems with the Sales process before SAP?

Q4. How does CBI implement SAP?

Q5. How does the Sales process work at CBI after SAP?

Q6. How can SAP improve the integration of customer-facing processes at CBI?

Q7. How does e-commerce integrate firms in an industry?

Chapter Preview

In this chapter, we examine sales. More specifically, the Sales process at a small bicycle company called Chuck's Bikes, Inc. before and after the implementation of SAP. To accomplish this, we will examine the same questions we used in Chapter 7 when we discussed the Procurement process. It is not coincidence that our approach here is the same as in Chapter 7. One of the most valuable aspects of a process perspective is that once its lessons are learned, they apply to all business processes.

We begin by examining the Sales process at CBI before SAP and learning how SAP ultimately improved it. We conclude the chapter by considering other processes that involve customers and how SAP and IS can be used to improve and integrate them.

As with the procurement discussion, it is easy to get lost in the details. Keep in mind that sales is all about building relationships with customers. As you will see, SAP can help.

Q1. What Are the Fundamentals of a Sales Process?

Sue made, and lost, a large sale to CBI's best customer. CBI is a bicycle company that buys frames, tires, and accessories and assembles bikes that are then sold to retailers. Before we rush to find fault at CBI, let's make sure we understand the activities involved in a sale. The business definition of a **sale** is an exchange of goods or services for money. More precisely, a sale is revenue from delivery of merchandise or a service where payment may be made in cash or other compensation. The Sales process is an operational process with three main activities—Sell, Ship, and Payment—as shown in Figure 8-1.

The sales activities—Sell, Ship, and Payment—are accomplished by actors playing the Sales Agent, Warehouse Manager, and Accountant roles. The Sales process is located within the value chain in the sales and marketing primary activity shown in Figure 8-2.

FIGURE 8-1

Main Sales Process Activities and Roles

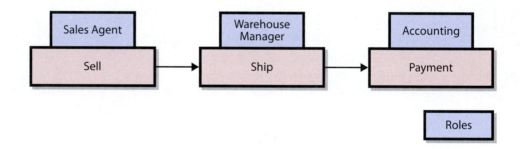

FIGURE 8-2

Sales Process Within the Value Chain of CBI

Primary Activity	Description	Process & Chapter
Inbound logistics	Receiving, storing, and disseminating inputs to products	Procurement, Chapter 7
Operations	Transforming inputs into final products	
Outbound logistics	Collecting, storing, and physically distributing products to buyers	
Sales and marketing	Inducing buyers to purchase products and providing the means for them to do so	Sales, Chapter 8
Customer service	Assisting customers' use of products thus maintaining and enhancing the products' value	

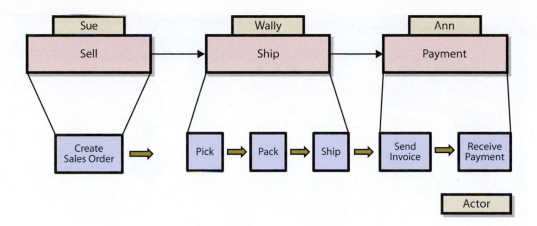

FIGURE 8-3

Main Sales Process Activities, Subactivities, and Actors

For a business, sales is the most important process. Without sales, no one gets paid and buildings go dark. Although sales is a complex and difficult process, it is also governed by a simple overriding principle: Satisfy the customer. Peter Drucker, one of the fathers of modern management theory, once said that there are no results that matter inside the company, the only result that matters is a satisfied customer.[1]

The online sale of flowers provides a good example of the Sales process. Online florists use effective sales processes to build long-term, mutually beneficial relationships with customers. For example, when you send flowers to your mother for her birthday and include a birthday greeting, the flower company keeps track of this transaction and will send you a reminder e-mail a few days before her birthday. If you regularly send flowers to a particular person and then lapse, the company may again send a reminder: "It's been two months since you last sent Debbie flowers." The florist may also suggest a particular arrangement or offer you a discounted price to retain you as a frequent customer.

The florist would like to retain good customers. Acquiring new customers can cost 5 to 10 times as much as retaining existing ones. To retain customers, the florist needs to know things about its customers, like buying preferences and important dates. The more the company knows about its customers and their needs, the better the chance it has to sell them flowers in the future.

Let's consider the Sales process at CBI in the chapter opening scenario. Figure 8-3 shows the main sales activities and subactivities. The first subactivity is to create a sales order that specifies that Heartland wants 50 bikes in 2 weeks. Later, on the planned shipping date, Wally, the warehouse manager, ensures that the bicycles from finished goods inventory are picked, packed in a box, and shipped to Heartland. Shortly thereafter, Ann in accounting sends Heartland an invoice. When Heartland's payment arrives, Ann posts the payment to a bank account.

We make two simplifications to the Sales process in this chapter. First, we address sales from one business to another rather than from a business to its consumers. These **business-to-business (B2B)** sales are much more common than **business-to-consumer (B2C)** sales like the florist example just given. This is because each B2C sale typically requires many B2B sales within the supply chain to acquire and assemble the product. A second simplification is that this chapter primarily addresses the sale of products, not services.

Q2. How Did the Sales Process at CBI Work Before SAP?

Before we can appreciate the benefits of using SAP, we will start with the lost sale described earlier. To understand why Sue's sale was cancelled, consider the Sales process for CBI. The significant activities in this process are shown in Figure 8-4. This process has six roles, three performed by human actors—Sue, Wally, and Ann—and three by computer. Each computer actor is served by its own database, creating three information silos.

The Ethics Guide on pages 248–249 demonstrates how one person's actions can affect a process and an entire company.

---

[1] *Forbes ASAP,* August 29, 1994, p. 104.

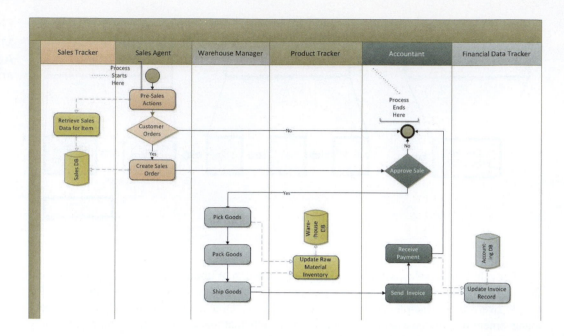

The first activity in Figure 8-4 is Pre-Sales Actions. In this activity, Sue and other sales reps contact customers, give price quotes, verify that products are available, check on special terms, and confirm delivery options.

If the customer decides to order, the next activity is Create Sales Order. An example of a sales order (SO) is shown in Figure 8-5. On the example shown, Sue is selling Heartland Bikes 50 Stream bikes at $300 each for a total price of $15,000.

Once complete, the SO is sent to accounting for approval. To approve the SO, Ann in accounting gets price data from the Sales database, customer data from the Accounting database, and inventory data from the Warehouse database. These data flows to Ann are not shown in Figure 8-4 for sake of simplicity. For existing customers, Ann uses data in the Accounting database to determine the history of payments by the customer, Heartland, in this case, before approving the sale. If this sale is for a new customer, there would be no customer data in the Accounting database, and Ann would add the new customer to that database and determine the risk of selling to this customer.

Sales Order

03/21/2012

TO	Heartland Bike	SHIP TO	Heartland Bike

Salesperson	Job	Shipping Method	Shipping Terms	Delivery Date	Payment Terms	Due Date
Sue					Due on receipt	

Qty	Item #	Description	Unit Price	Discount	Line Total
50	TXTR1001	Stream N3 28	$300		$15,000

During this activity, Ann also accesses data in the Warehouse database to make sure there is sufficient inventory to sell. If there is not enough inventory, the sale is usually disapproved. However, as in the case of Sue's sale to Heartland, if the delivery for the sale is delayed at the customer's request, Ann will call the warehouse to ask if future deliveries are expected that will replenish the inventory in time.

If approved by accounting, the SO is passed onto the warehouse where Wally and his staff will collect (or "pick") and ship the bicycles on the correct day. These activities in the Sales process diagram are labeled Pick Goods, Pack Goods, and Ship Goods. Once the bikes are shipped by the warehouse, Wally sends a notice to accounting that the goods have shipped so that accounting can send Heartland the invoice. The final activity, Receive Payment, occurs when Heartland sends a payment to CBI for the sale.

This process rejected Sue's sale for two reasons. Recall that the inventory data in the Warehouse database lags by a day. When Sue made the sale, the database indicated the inventory at the beginning of the day—55 Stream bikes. However, 10 of those bikes were sold before Sue's sale to a little retailer in Kansas City. When the SO of 50 bikes arrived at accounting, there were only 45 Streams available to sell. As mentioned in the introduction, Ann in accounting will coordinate to get an additional shipment of bike frames if the delivery of the sale provides enough time. However, in this case, Ann discovers that the supplier is discontinuing the frame. She contacted Heartland to ask if they would change their order and accept the 45 bikes instead of the desired 50, but when Heartland declined she had to cancel the sale.

Q3. What Were the Problems with the Sales Process Before SAP?

The pre-SAP Sales process has led to a number of problems that have plagued CBI over the years. These problems are shown in Figure 8-6.

Sales Problems

Starting with the Sales role, the inventory data visible to salespeople in the Warehouse database lags by one day. Currently, Wally updates his finished goods inventory data in the Warehouse database at the end of the day. The updated inventory data are sent to the salespeople overnight so that when CBI opens in the morning the salespeople know which bikes are available in inventory. At times, as in the opening scenario, this has led to the sale of bicycles no longer in inventory. Although the bicycles are in the inventory at the warehouse at the beginning of the day, those bicycles have already been sold. As a result, salespeople promise bikes and delivery dates to customers that cannot be met.

Input errors can also occur. Sue and other salespeople have at times written down the wrong address for a customer, incorrectly calculated a price discount, or created multiple versions of the same customer or same order. These errors take time to discover and correct.

Warehouse Problems

In the warehouse, Wally and his crew also have their share of problems. When a sale is made to a new customer, the warehouse picks and packs the order before receiving final permission to ship. The New Customer Order process is set up this way to reduce the time from order to delivery for

Role	Problems
Sales	No current inventory data Input errors
Warehouse	Pick and pack for new customers is inefficient if sale is cancelled No way to share production or supply issues and delays
Accounting	Time spent on invoice and other errors New customer delays

FIGURE 8-6

Problems at CBI with Sales Before SAP

new customers. If the warehouse waited until accounting approved the sale to start the pick-and-pack activities, many of the promised delivery times would not be met and some of the new customer order inventory might be shipped in other orders. Because of this process, when new customers are disapproved by accounting, Wally and his crew must unpack and return the products to the shelves and update the inventory data in the Warehouse database.

A second issue is that Wally does not have any way to communicate with salespeople about upcoming supply disruptions. Wally knew that the Stream bike frame supplier had decided not to produce any additional frames for the Stream bikes Sue wanted to sell to Heartland.

Accounting Problems

Things are not much better in accounting. Ann supervises a staff of very careful accountants who make the occasional data entry and arithmetic errors. Some problems are unique to the Accounting role. Her office occasionally receives payments from customers with incorrect or missing invoices. The staff may also credit the wrong account or make other update errors. These infrequent errors can take hours to sort out and damage customer relations.

Delays also occur in checking the credit of new customers. This step has created a number of unwarranted shipment delays when credit checks run long or when ambiguous credit scores are found.

These problems have cost CBI sales and customers over the years, and as industry competition increased CBI had to change or it would go out of business. CBI believed that SAP would help correct these Sales process deficiencies.

Q4. How Does CBI Implement SAP?

Many of these problems with the current Sales process can be overcome with an effective ERP system like SAP. However, as mentioned in Chapter 7, ERP systems are implemented not only to overcome problems, but also to achieve strategy. To implement SAP successfully, top management reexamined CBI's strategy and committed to a competitive strategy that focused on a particular industry segment—high-end bikes—and a differentiation on responsiveness to retailers.

CBI then selected the SAP Sales process most appropriate for this strategy. SAP provides a variety of Sales processes to its customers. CBI, like other SAP customers, selected the Sales process it believed was best suited to its strategy. CBI then configured this process to its sales objectives. Sales managers decided on one efficiency objective and two effectiveness objectives, which are shown in Figure 8-7.

The efficiency objective—fewer cancelled sales—will be measured by the percentage of sales that are cancelled. A cancelled sale is one that is made but subsequently disapproved, as in the example at the beginning of the chapter.

The first effectiveness objective—faster customer response—will be measured by the time from sales order agreement to the arrival of ordered products. A second measure will be the percentage of sales of first-year products. CBI offers new bikes and accessories based on customer input. If these new products are being purchased by retailers, this is a sign that CBI is

FIGURE 8-7

Objectives and Measures for the New Sales Process

Objective	Measure
Efficiency	
Fewer cancelled sales	Percentage of cancelled sales
Effectiveness	
Faster customer response	Elapsed time for order to arrival Percentage of sales of first-year products
Reduce cancelled sales to top customers	Cancelled sales to top 20 retailers

responding well to customer wants. A second effectiveness objective is to reduce lost revenue from cancelled sales to their best customers. CBI wants to be able to cancel lower revenue sales when they conflict with higher revenue sales.

Q5. How Does the Sales Process Work at CBI After SAP?

Now consider the situation two years later. CBI has implemented the SAP system, and every employee knows how to use it. Figure 8-8 shows the SAP inherent Sales process implemented at CBI.

Sales

The new Sales process features the same three actors as the previous Sales process—Sue, Wally, and Ann. However the three computer actors are reduced to the single SAP system that tracks all the sales data. For comparative purposes, we will trace the same Sales process as before. This is the sale of 50 Stream bikes to Heartland when only 45 are available.

The Pre-Sales Actions activity is the same with one exception. The inventory and price data are now current. Sue can see that 55 bikes are available and that 10 of the 55 have been sold. She can see that the 10 bikes have not been shipped, and that her customer will have priority. As we pick up Sue's story, she has just made the sale and is sitting down in her office to input the sales data into SAP in the Create Sales Order activity. As she logs into the system, her Sales Order screen looks like Figure 8-9 before data have been added to it.

The Sales Order screen has many of the same features as the Procurement process screens in Chapter 7. The title, at the top left in this case, is Create Standard Order: Overview. In the header section, Sue enters Heartland's customer number (25056), the date of the transaction (PO date of 06/20/2011), and the transaction number (PO Number 05432). The PO Number is determined by Heartland's numbering system. The PO date for Heartland is the sales date for

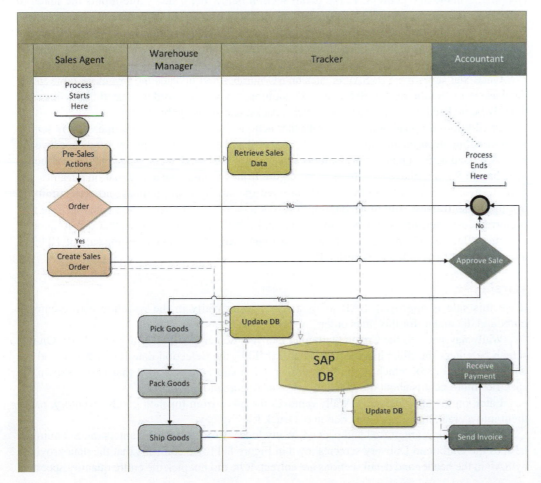

FIGURE 8-8

Sales Process at CBI After SAP

FIGURE 8-9

Sales Order Screen in SAP of 50 Stream Bikes to Heartland

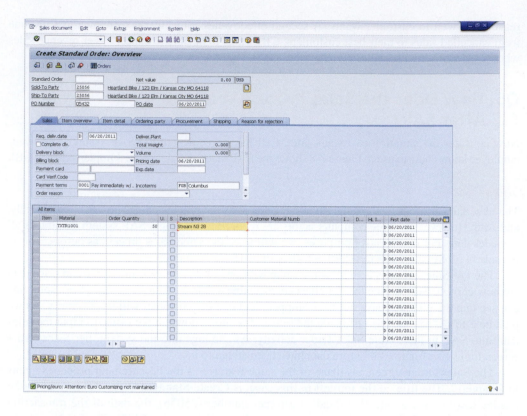

CBI—the date the sale was made. Once Sue enters these three data elements, SAP retrieves the customer's name and address. In the detail section below the header, Sue inputs the material number for Stream bikes (TXTR1001) and the number ordered (50). Her screen now looks like Figure 8-9. If the sale had more than one item, these additional items would be included on lines below the Stream bikes. Sue then saves the information and enters another sale or exits the system.

Once Sue saves the SO, SAP creates an SO number and updates the inventory table in the database to reflect the sale of 50 Streams. In addition, a new SO record is created that will subsequently be updated when the warehouse picks, packs, and ships the bikes.

In addition to updating data, several other actions are triggered. First, a message is sent to the accounting department requesting credit approval and a decision to approve or disapprove the sale. A second action updates the assembly schedule for CBI. SAP recognizes that the warehouse only has 45 Stream bikes, and attempts to acquire from suppliers the additional bike frames and parts to assemble. When automated responses in the supply chain indicate no opportunity to acquire these frames, Ann in accounting receives a message. She sees Sue's pending sale to a preferred customer, the 45 bikes in inventory, and the 10 bikes sold earlier that day to another customer. Because Heartland is a preferred customer, Ann is able to cancel the sale of 10 bikes and move 5 of these bikes to Heartland.

Warehouse

Once this sale is approved, SAP sends a message to Wally in the warehouse to create an outbound document for this sales order.

Wally navigates to the Create Outbound Delivery screen, as shown in Figure 8-10. On this screen he enters the Shipping point as Miami (MI00), the Selection date (6/27/2011), and the Order number (185), which is the SO number. On a subsequent screen that is not shown, he specifies more details about the sale and saves the document.

Later, on the appointed day, Wally removes the bikes from finished goods inventory, packs them into a crate, and places the crate in the truck loading bay.

Once the bikes are picked and packed, Wally logs into SAP. After he enters the SO number, he sees the Outbound Delivery screen shown in Figure 8-11. He confirms that the data provided by SAP in the header and detail sections are correct. If he did not pick the entire quantity specified

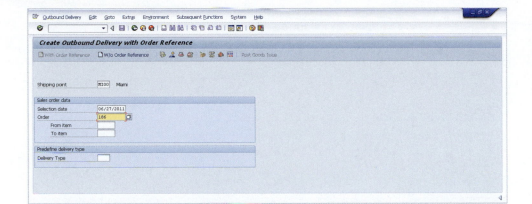

FIGURE 8-10
**Outbound Delivery
Screen in SAP**

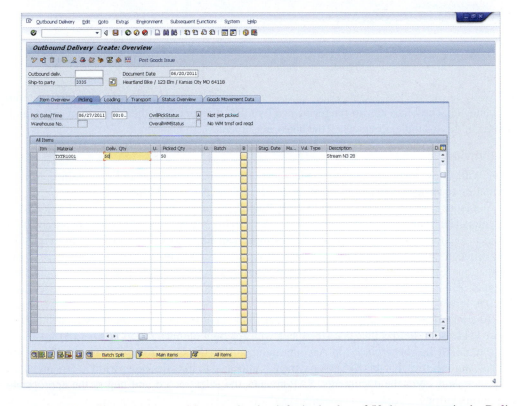

FIGURE 8-11
Picking Screen in SAP

in the sale, 50 in this case, he would overwrite the defaulted value of 50 that appears in the Deliv. Qty column. Once he saves this data, the inventory table is updated and the sales record is edited to reflect that the Stream bikes have now been picked and packed.

The Ship Goods activity occurs when the delivery truck leaves the warehouse with the shipment. Again, Wally navigates to the Outbound Delivery screen shown in Figure 8-12. Because this sales order has been picked and packed, the screen is now labeled Change Outbound Delivery

FIGURE 8-12
Posting Screen in SAP

FIGURE 8-13

**Maintain Billing Due List
Screen in SAP**

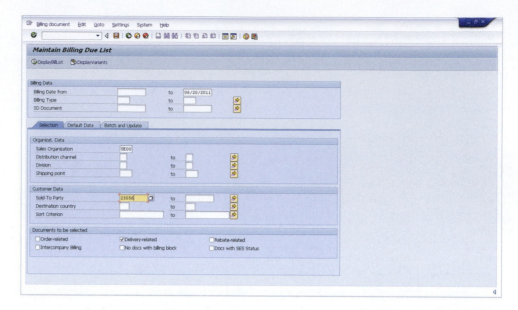

and Wally selects the Post Goods Issue button. **Posting** means that legal ownership of the material has changed. The bikes are no longer owned by CBI; they are now the property of Heartland. Posting in this example occurs when the bikes are shipped.

Accounting

After Wally has posted the goods issue and the bicycles have changed ownership, Ann in accounting receives a message that she can bill Heartland for the 50 Streams.

She logs into SAP and navigates to the Billing Due List screen that is shown in Figure 8-13. She enters Heartland's number in the Sold-To Party field (25056) and selects the DisplayBillList icon near the top of the screen. On the following screen (not shown), Ann selects from a list of sales orders to Heartland, adds the sales order for the 50 Stream bikes, and clicks the Save icon. This action triggers SAP to send a message to Heartland Bike Company. The message is the bill, which is also called an invoice, for the 50 bikes. A week later, Ann in accounting receives a check in the mail for the 50 Streams.

To credit Heartland's account, she navigates to the Post Incoming Payments screen shown in Figure 8-14. Here she specifies that Heartland, with Account number 25056, has paid $15,000 and that the money has been placed in Account number 100000. On a following screen that is not shown, Ann specifies that this $15,000 payment is allocated to the sales order with 50 Stream bikes.

Once Ann saves the documents, SAP updates the sales record and makes the appropriate accounting entries.

FIGURE 8-14

**Post Incoming Payments
Screen in SAP**

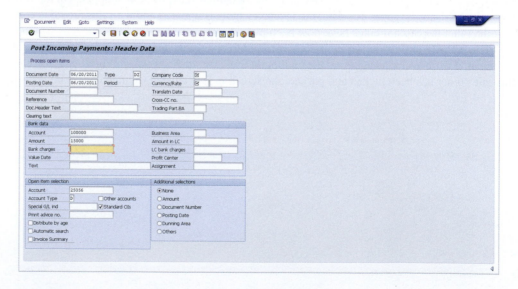

The Benefits of SAP for the CBI Sales Process

Several general benefits of the new SAP system at CBI are immediately evident. Sales reps have access to the most current data in the one SAP database. The New Customer Approval activity is quicker, and, as a result, the warehouse no longer packs new customer orders before approval. Data on significant supply chain disruptions is made available to all in the organization.

Although these are very helpful improvements, CBI implemented SAP to help it achieve a specific strategy. Earlier in the chapter the objectives and measures for the Sales process appropriate for this strategy were specified in Figure 8-7.

The implementation of SAP helps CBI achieve its efficiency objective. With more accurate and up-to-date pricing and inventory data, there are fewer cancelled sales.

One of the effectiveness objectives was faster customer response. With SAP, more of the sales activities and subactivities are automated, so the process is faster. The measurement used at CBI, time from sale until arrival, is reduced. Also, the sale of first-year products has increased with SAP. With SAP, sales reps have more accurate data on inventory levels of the new products throughout the supply chain. Prior to SAP, these new products would not appear as inventory in the Warehouse database for potential sale until the day they arrived. Now sales reps can see when these new products will be available and have accurate data on pending sales of these new items.

The second effectiveness objective of reducing cancelled sales to the best customers is also achieved. SAP helps achieve this by allowing the accounting department to give priority to its better customers when products are limited.

Having considered the benefits of SAP on the Sales process, we now broaden the processes under consideration. These other processes, such as the Customer Service process and the Promotion process, involve CBI's customers. These processes are called customer-facing processes.

MIS InClass 8

Phones and Processes

Divide the class into small groups according to each student's cell phone platform (Android, iPhone, etc.). Some popular platforms may have multiple groups. Each group should address the following questions. A team spokesperson should then explain the group's answers to the class or the team can submit its answers to the instructor.

Source: Robert Kneschke/Shutterstock.

1. Why did you pick the cell phone that you have? Are you a satisfied customer? Why or why not? What positive and negative experiences have you had with your phone?
2. What features about your phone are most important to you? Which of your personal processes do these features support? (Socializing, coordinating, scheduling, etc.)
3. Pretend to be your parents or someone their age. Answer items 1 and 2 from their perspective.
4. Where do you interact with your platform provider, and what data does it collect? What data should it collect?
5. Which processes of your platform's provider (Apple, Samsung, etc.) does data from your phone help to improve?
6. Now consider your phone's carrier (AT&T, Verizon, etc.). Which processes of your cell phone carrier does data from your phone help to improve?
7. Are you a customer your phone company would want to retain on the next contract? Explain why or why not.
8. Assume that you are working at a company in the area of your choice. Which business processes do professionals in that job use their cell phones to support? What are the objectives and measures of that process? How does using a cell phone improve that process?

FIGURE 8-15

Sample of Customer-
Facing Processes

Process Scope	Customer-Facing Processes
Operational	Promotion Sales Service
Managerial	Promotional Discounting Service Trends
Strategic	New Product Launch Promotion Evaluation

Q6. How Can SAP Improve the Integration of Customer-Facing Processes at CBI?

We have examined how SAP can improve CBI's Sales process. However, the Sales process is just one of many customer-facing processes that SAP can support. These processes are listed in Figure 8-15. The Promotion process is designed to increase sales, stimulate demand, or improve product availability over a predetermined limited time. The Sales process, defined earlier, is the exchange of goods or services for money. The Service process, first defined in Chapter 5, provides after-sales support to enhance or maintain the value of a product.

Integration of Customer-Facing Processes

Although supporting each of these processes is helpful, the real value of SAP is integrating these processes. Integrating these customer-facing processes and managing all the interactions with customers is called **customer relationship management (CRM)**. The relationship of the Sales process to other customer-facing processes and CRM is the same as the Procurement process, other supply chain processes, and supply chain management (SCM), as shown in Figure 8-16. Like integration of processes across the supply chain, the integration of customer-facing processes is improved by sharing data and increasing process synergy.

Improving Customer-Facing Process Integration by Sharing Data

Process integration is improved when processes share data. To see how this works, consider your process of returning merchandise to a retailer. It is easier for you to return your merchandise if you have a receipt. If this receipt was e-mailed to you, it may be easier to find than a printed receipt. By using electronic receipts, your retailer's Sales process has made your returns process easier. Rather than issue paper receipts, which are more costly and more frequently lost, many retailers are sharing receipt data with customers electronically by sending an e-mail or a message to a customer's smartphone. Not only does this reduce sales costs, an objective of the retailer's Sales process, it also improves the customer's Returns process, because customers can find their receipts more frequently.

FIGURE 8-16

CRM and SCM
Processes

CRM Processes—Chapter 8	SCM Processes—Chapter 7
Front Office-Customer Facing	**Back Office-Supply Chain**
Sales	Procurement
Service	Demand Management
Promotion	Returns Management
Other Processes	Other Processes

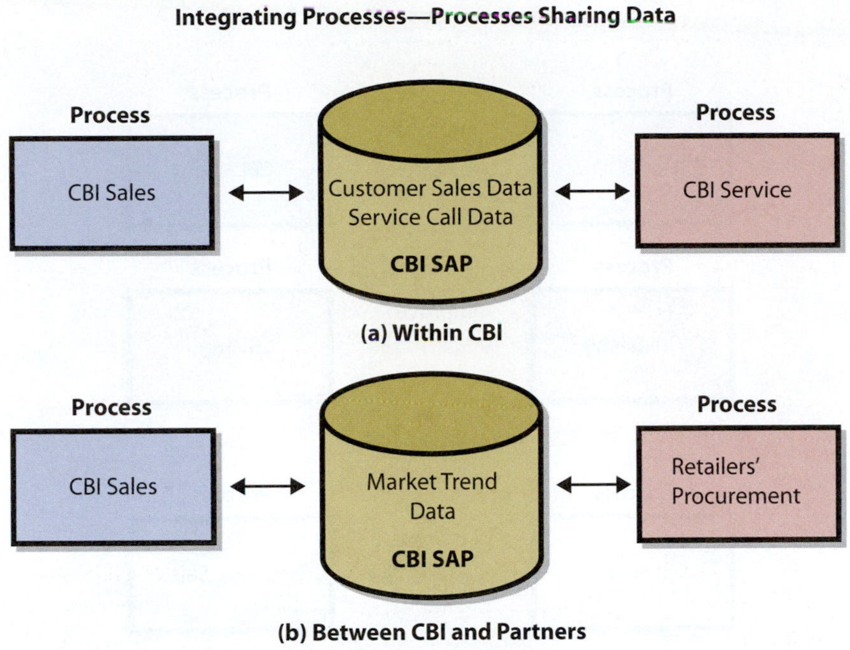

Integrating Processes—Processes Sharing Data

FIGURE 8-17

Examples of Data Sharing

Process — CBI Sales ⟷ Customer Sales Data / Service Call Data / **CBI SAP** ⟷ Process — CBI Service

(a) Within CBI

Process — CBI Sales ⟷ Market Trend Data / **CBI SAP** ⟷ Process — Retailers' Procurement

(b) Between CBI and Partners

Examples of integration of processes by data sharing at CBI are shown in Figure 8-17. Both sales and service are improved when they share customer data. By having access to customer sales data, CBI service is improved. For example, when a customer calls for service about a problem with a particular shipment, the service agent at CBI knows the sales data for that shipment and all shipments to that customer. By having the sales data, the agent is better informed about the customer's situation. Likewise, the Sales process is improved with customer service call data. A sales representative can review service data from a customer before initiating a sales call. That way the sales representative can offer to the customer products that were not the subject of a service call.

By sharing data, the Sales process of CBI can be integrated with the Procurement processes of its customer retailers. For example, CBI sells to many small outlets. These small retailers do not have the resources to collect data on market trends. CBI does. CBI can share its market trend data with retailers, who can then make better procurement decisions about what bikes to buy from CBI. Both firms win when CBI's Sales process and the small retailer's Procurement process share this market trend data, because they both sell more bikes.

These are not isolated examples. SAP helps CBI integrate all its processes by consolidating data in one database. This standardizes the data, overcomes information silos, and enables sharing data in real time with all processes.

Improving Customer-Facing Process Integration by Increasing Process Synergy

The second way to improve process integration is to increase process synergy. Process synergy occurs when processes are mutually supportive—when one process is done well, then the objectives of another process are supported. Synergy between sales and procurement is evident in your personal life. Amazon.com recognizes the synergy between its Sales process and your personal Procurement process. When people want to buy something, they want to do it quickly. Therefore, it can be said that people have a Procurement process objective of not wasting time. Amazon.com has found that online sales revenue increases 1 percent for every one-tenth of a second decrease in load time.[2] As a result, it makes download time an objective of its Sales process.

Examples of increasing synergy at CBI are shown in Figure 8-18. At CBI the Production process can support the objectives of the Sales process. If the Production process times are consistent, the delivery of a sale is rarely late. As a result, customers are satisfied and opportunities

[2] Jolie O'Dell, "Why Web Sites Are Slow and Why Speed Really Matters," *Mashable*, April 6, 2011. Available at: *http://mashable.com/2011/04/06/site-speed/*.

FIGURE 8-18

Examples of Process Synergy

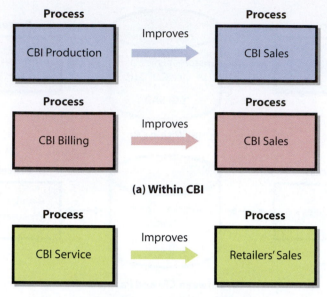

Integrating Processes—Process Synergy

(a) Within CBI

(b) Between CBI and Partners

for future sales are improved. The objective of the Sales process, repeat customers, is supported by the Production process.

A second example of process synergy is the support of the Sales process by the Billing process. When an accountant at CBI is contacted by a customer or the accountant contacts a customer to clarify a bill, the Billing process requires the accountant to share current pricing of products with the customer. More specifically, the accountant shares prices on products if the new price is better than the price on the bill, which, in turn, leads to future sales.

To improve process synergy with retailers, CBI can use its Service process to support the Sales processes of its customer retailers. For example, when a defective bike is returned to CBI from one of its retailers, the CBI Service process uses overnight shipping to give the retailer a new bike within 24 hours. As a result, the retailer's Sales process is improved, because each of CBI's retailers can promise customers 24-hour replacements.

SAP helps CBI achieve process synergy. SAP achieves process synergy by designing processes to work together. In the examples just given, the SAP Production process is designed to provide consistent production process times. The SAP Billing process can be configured to show current pricing data to billing agents. By using SAP processes, CBI can use a coherent set of processes that have been developed explicitly for mutual support. This is in contrast to CBI's previous processes, which were designed over time within different departments. These processes evolved using isolated databases, and each process was designed to achieve only its own objectives.

SAP Integration Problems with Emerging Technologies

Earlier we said that the integration of customer-facing processes is called customer relationship management (CRM). When SAP is used to integrate customer processes, this module is called SAP CRM. However, SAP is not the only IS that supports customer process integration. Other emerging technologies that SAP must learn to integrate with include social CRM and cloud-based CRM.

SOCIAL CRM As mentioned previously, one way customer processes are integrated is by sharing data. **Social CRM** is an information system that helps a company collect customer data from social media and share it among its customer-facing processes.

In today's social media environment, the vendor–customer relationship is complex and is not controlled by the vendor. Businesses offer many different customer touch points, and customers craft their own relationship with the business by their use of those touch points.

FIGURE 8-19

**Salesforce.com
Homepage**

Social CRM data is collected through interactions on Facebook, Twitter, wikis, blogs, discussion lists, frequently asked questions, sites for user reviews, and other social media. Social CRM systems collect and distribute this data to a variety of customer processes.

CLOUD-BASED CRM: SALESFORCE.COM **Salesforce.com** is the preeminent cloud-based CRM vendor. Rather than purchasing CRM software and installing it on site, companies utilize a pay-as-you-go plan to use the online software and run it off site at Salesforce.com. This payment arrangement is also called *software as a service*. With over 80,000 customer firms, Salesforce.com is growing rapidly, particularly with small to medium-sized firms. The Salesforce.com homepage is shown in Figure 8-19.

Salesforce.com helps a company integrate its customer processes in several ways. First, by keeping data in the cloud with Salesforce.com, a small company's data is stored in a format that is compatible with a wide variety of software. Because of the universal format, it is easier for the company to share this data among its various customer processes. Second, the software is scalable. A company can conduct a small-scale trial of the CRM software at one office to test the integration of its customer processes at one location before rolling it out to the whole company. Finally, start-up costs are zero; firms pay as they use the service without a big up-front contract. A company can therefore conduct its integration trial at one location without significant investment.

Integration Challenges and Lessons

Although it is clear that SAP, social CRM, and cloud-based CRM can help integrate customer-facing processes, making integration a reality is challenging. First, with customer-facing processes, the measures of success are difficult to determine and can be debated. For example, you might ask what percentage of the increase in sales this year is due to integrated processes last year and what percentage of the increase is due to the economy, or having better products, or the new sales promotion?

Second, SAP and other CRM systems can be seen as a distraction by sales representatives. These representatives may see their job as building relationships with customers. They may view time spent with technology as time they could use to make commissions. Although a reasonable concern, it represents a common problem with information systems. Oftentimes the people who implement and use a system do not share in all the benefits they bring.

PROCESS INTEGRATION CHALLENGES As we close this discussion on integration of customer-facing processes, let's step back from sales integration and look at the bigger picture. Why is integrating any set of business processes hard?

FIGURE 8-20

**Process Integration
Lessons**

To integrate processes:

Make the goals and measures of the integrating processes explicit.

Data must flow from process to process.

Businesspeople must understand other parts of the business.

One source of difficulty is that each process impacts many other processes. If sales only impacted service and not a host of other processes, integration would be much easier. However, the Sales process also impacts the processes that hire salespeople, train them, and promote them. The objectives of each process can conflict with the objectives of other processes. For example, the objectives of one process might be to save money, whereas another tries to grow sales. Now broaden this. When the Sales process impacts 10 or 15 other processes, and each process has multiple objectives, conflicts multiply. Trying to support the objectives of all the other processes simultaneously can be like finding one movie to go to that 10 friends will all like.

A second challenge is that all of the processes are in a state of change. Processes change, as we have mentioned in earlier chapters, due to technology changes, strategy changes, and product changes. Keeping all these processes working well together while they all change is difficult.

These challenges are not new. Ever since Henry Ford developed his assembly line the dream of process integration has been pursued, but with limited success. ERP systems give organizations a new way to tackle the challenges of process integration.

Process Integration Lessons

Creating integrated processes is difficult, but some lessons have emerged. These are listed in Figure 8-20.

One lesson is that integration requires explicit objectives and measures of the integrating processes. If the objectives and measures of a process are not well known, integration is difficult. If you and your friends are trying to decide among restaurants or movies but no one shares their measures about what makes a good restaurant or movie, the challenge of picking a mutually satisfying solution becomes even harder. That is why for the last four chapters we have tried to be explicit about the objectives and measures of each process.

A second lesson is that integration requires data sharing. The key to flowing data is making the data compatible with a variety of software. If inventory data are stored in a database, and the salespeople want it on their smartphone, then the database must be compatible with the phone. If CBI wants to share sales forecast data with a wide variety of its retailers, it must make its data compatible with the software used in the industry. Although businesspeople do not need to know how to make data compatible, they should be able to ask compatibility questions.

A third lesson is that integration can occur when processes support other process objectives. This can only happen when businesspeople understand other parts of the business. Just as salespeople must know their customers' businesses and procurement processes in order to sell and integrate with them, they must also know how lead times are determined in their own firm's procurement process and how payments are processed in accounting in order to integrate with these other processes. When you are in business, make sure you know the objectives and measures for your company's processes.

Q7. How Does E-Commerce Integrate Firms in an Industry?

In the past two chapters, we have discussed integration of processes between CBI and its partners. For example, in the last chapter CBI's Procurement process was integrated with its suppliers' Sales processes; here we considered CBI's Sales process and its customers' Procurement processes. However, process integration occurs on a larger scale and between all types of firms

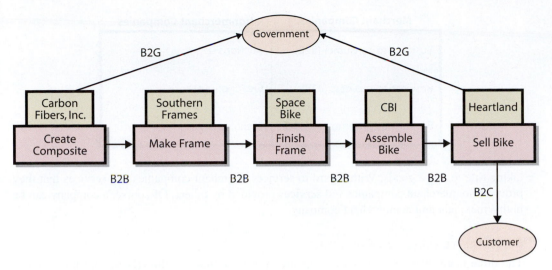

FIGURE 8-21

E-Commerce Integration

and between firms and customers. In fact, the chain of organizations from the firm that creates the raw material to the firm that makes the final customer sale can be considered an integrated process, as shown in Figure 8-21. This integration of processes is achieved using e-commerce.

More specifically, **e-commerce** is a multifirm process of buying and selling goods and services using Internet technologies. Processes are also integrated when data are exchanged among firms on a private network, but here we focus on the public Internet and the open market it creates.

In Figure 8-21, composites, which are raw material for bike frames, are created by Carbon Fibers, Inc. The composites are sold to a frame manufacturer, Southern Frames, who makes the bicycle frames. The frames are sold to a frame wholesaler, Space Bike Composites in this scenario, where the frames are finished. CBI assembles the bikes and sells the finished product to retailers such as Heartland who, in turn, sells to a final customer.

The collection of these five firms and the five activities accomplished at each can be viewed as a process. Recall that a process is a series of activities accomplished by actors playing roles. In this example, a different enterprise plays each role in the E-commerce process.

In this process, and in all e-commerce, there is no unified or explicit strategy, because no one manager has the authority to specify a competitive strategy for the whole process. As a result, the e-commerce process has no universal objective. That said, most industries and participating firms pursue an implicit strategy and objective of reducing costs.

With each individual firm acting in its own best interest, an efficient supply chain emerges. **emergence** is the way a complex system like an efficient supply chain emerges from the interaction of a large number of simple interactions. Computer simulations, the Web, social media, the stock market, and national elections also display emergent patterns from a large number of simple interactions.

This interorganizational e-commerce process is supported by **interorganizational IS**, which interact with each other via the public Internet. Interorganizational IS are IS used by more than one firm. Just as IS can improve intraorganizational process, IS can also improve interorganizational processes by improving their integration. Integration is achieved by sharing data. For example, each firm in Figure 8-21 might use an ERP system, and these systems may share purchase order, sales order, and inventory data. Another interorganizational system, say, in the health care industry, might share patient data in the form of electronic health care records; an interorganizational system in the defense industry might share classified military data.

By shifting our process focus beyond CBI and its partners to interorganizational e-commerce, we can better understand industry and market issues, such as merchant types, types of transactions, pricing, and disintermediation.

Figure 8-22 lists categories of companies that participate in e-commerce. The U.S. Census Bureau, which publishes statistics on e-commerce activity, defines **merchant companies** as those that own the goods they sell. They buy goods and resell them. It defines **nonmerchant companies** as those that arrange for the purchase and sale of goods without ever owning or

FIGURE 8-22

Merchant and
Nonmerchant List

Merchant Companies	Nonmerchant Companies
Business-to-consumer (B2C)	Auctions
Business-to-business (B2B)	Clearinghouses
Business-to-government (B2G)	Exchanges

taking title to those goods. With regard to services, merchant companies sell services that they provide; nonmerchant companies sell services provided by others. Of course, a company can be both a merchant and nonmerchant company.

E-Commerce Merchant Companies

The three main types of merchant companies are those that sell directly to consumers, those that sell to companies, and those that sell to government. Each uses slightly different IS in the course of doing business. B2C e-commerce concerns sales between a supplier and a retail customer (the consumer). IS that support the Sales process of B2C companies are typically **Web storefronts** that customers use to enter and manage their orders. Amazon.com, REI.com, and LLBean.com are examples of companies that use Web storefronts.

B2B e-commerce refers to sales between companies. As Figure 8-21 shows, raw materials suppliers and other firms use interorganizational IS like ERP systems to integrate B2B supply chains.

B2G, or **business-to-government** merchants, sell to governmental organizations. In Figure 8-21, the composite raw material supplier and the bike retailer might sell their products to government agencies.

Nonmerchant E-Commerce

The most common nonmerchant e-commerce companies are auctions and clearinghouses. **Auctions** match buyers and sellers by using an IS version of a standard auction. This application enables the auction company to offer goods for sale and to support a competitive-bidding process. The best-known auction company is eBay, but many other auction companies exist; many serve particular industries.

Clearinghouses provide goods and services at a stated price and arrange for the delivery of the goods, but they never take title. One division of Amazon.com, for example, operates as a nonmerchant clearinghouse, allowing individuals and used bookstores to sell used books on the Amazon.com Web site. As a clearinghouse, Amazon.com uses its Web site as an IS to match the seller and the buyer and then takes payment from the buyer and transfers the payment to the seller, minus a commission.

Another type of clearinghouse is an **electronic exchange** that matches buyers and sellers, similar to that of a stock exchange. Sellers offer goods at a given price through the electronic exchange, and buyers make offers to purchase over the same exchange. Price matches result in transactions from which the exchange takes a commission. Priceline.com is an example of an exchange used by consumers.

How Does E-Commerce Improve Market Efficiency?

E-commerce improves market efficiency in a number of different ways. For one, e-commerce leads to **disintermediation**, which is the elimination of middle layers of distributors and suppliers. You can buy a bicycle from a typical " bricks-and-mortar" retailer like Heartland, or you can use CBI's Web site and purchase the bike directly from CBI. If you take the latter route, you eliminate the retailer. The product is shipped directly from CBI's finished goods inventory to you. You eliminate the retailer's inventory-carrying costs, and you eliminate shipping overhead and handling activity. Because the retailer and associated inventories have become unnecessary waste, disintermediation increases market efficiency.

E-commerce also improves the flow of price data. As a consumer, you can go to any number of Web sites that offer product price comparisons. You can search for the bike you want and sort the results by price and vendor reputation. You can find vendors that avoid your state sales tax or that omit or reduce shipping charges. The improved distribution of data about price and terms enables you to pay the lowest possible cost and serves ultimately to remove inefficient vendors. The market as a whole becomes more efficient.

From the seller's side, e-commerce produces data about price elasticity that has not been available before. **Price elasticity** measures the amount that demand rises or falls with changes in price. Using an auction, a company can learn not just what the top price for an item is, but also the second, third, and other prices from the losing bids. In this way, the company can determine the shape of the price elasticity curve.

Similarly, e-commerce companies can learn price elasticity directly from experiments on customers. For example, in one experiment, Amazon.com created three groups of similar books. It raised the price of one group 10 percent, lowered the price of the second group 10 percent, and left the price of the third group unchanged.

Customers provided feedback to these changes by deciding whether to buy books at the offered prices. Amazon.com measured the total revenue (quantity times price) of each group and took the action (raise, lower, or maintain prices) on all books that maximized revenue. Amazon.com repeated the process until it reached the point at which the best action was to maintain current prices.

Managing prices by direct interaction with the customer yields better data than managing prices by watching competitors' pricing. By experimenting, companies learn how customers have internalized competitors' pricing, advertising, and messaging. It might be that customers do not know about a competitor's lower prices, in which case there is no need for a price reduction. Or, it may be that the competitor is using a price that, if lowered, would increase demand sufficiently to increase total revenue.

Process Integration and Your Business Future

One of the goals of this textbook is to help you become comfortable with processes and how they integrate. We first explained processes and then discussed how processes integrate a supply chain and the customer-facing processes within one firm. We also applied integration concepts to processes between firms. Our goal all along was to get to the following conclusion: *Process integration is essential to business.* As a result, it is essential to your future. In every job you will have, in every company large and small, you will play a role in many processes. If you are an accountant, your accounting classes will prepare you well to do those roles; if you are in sales, your marketing courses will get you ready for your roles as a salesperson. But in every job and in every role you play, you will be more effective if you keep the big picture, the process integration picture, in mind.

Process thinking will help you better understand your role in any process. Further, it will help you ask questions about process objectives and measures. It will also help make you aware of how the data from your process is used elsewhere and how your process supports the objectives of other processes. Finally, thinking about processes will help you see how IS can improve these processes.

In Chapter 1, we suggested four skills will be valuable to you in your career: reasoning, collaboration, experimentation, and systems thinking. Recall from that chapter that a systems thinker is one who understands how the inputs and outputs of processes relate. Here we can express that in a more specific way. A systems thinker is a process thinker. A process thinker considers how the change in one process output impacts other processes.

Where there are business processes there is likely to be an ERP system. Whether you are an accounting, supply chain, marketing, or finance student, chances are that you will work with SAP or another ERP system on your very first job after college. As an accountant you will post payments and configure SAP to allow different payment schedules and to create automatic price discounts. As a salesperson, you may record every customer interaction in your CRM module, post and edit sales, and invent new reports that will help your company identify new trends and opportunities. These activities will impact other processes outside of your office. You and your employer will be pleased if by the time you start you have mastered some aspects of SAP so you can anticipate these impacts. So take this time to master the vocabulary in these chapters. Learn how to navigate to different screens and to move around within the screens. Think about processes and how ERP systems change and improve processes. If you can, do the tutorials in the Appendix, make mistakes, start over—learn beyond the book.

Ethics Guide

Are My Ethics for Sale?

Suppose you are a salesperson at CBI. CBI's sales forecasting system predicts that your quarterly sales will be substantially under quota. You call your best customers to increase sales, but no one is willing to buy more.

Your boss says that it has been a bad quarter for all of the salespeople. It's so bad, in fact, that the vice president of sales has authorized a 20 percent discount on new orders. The only stipulation is that customers must take delivery prior to the end of the quarter so that accounting can book the order. "Start dialing for dollars," she says, "and get what you can. Be creative."

Using CBI's CRM system, you identify your top customers and present the discount offer to them. The first customer balks at increasing her inventory, "I just don't think we can sell that much."

"Well," you respond, "how about if we agree to take back any inventory you don't sell next quarter?" (By doing this, you increase your current sales and commission, and you also help CBI make its quarterly sales projections. The additional product is likely to come back next quarter, but you think, "Hey that's then and this is now.")

"OK," she says, "but I want you to stipulate the return option on the purchase order."

You know that you cannot write that on the purchase order because accounting won't book all of the order if you do. So you tell her that you'll send her an e-mail with that stipulation. She increases her order, and accounting books the full amount.

With another customer, you try a second strategy. Instead of offering the discount, you offer the bikes and accessories at full price, but agree to pay a 20-percent credit in the next quarter. That way you can book the full price now. You pitch this offer as follows: "Our marketing department analyzed past sales using our fancy new CRM system, and we know that increasing advertising will cause additional sales. So, if you order more product now, next quarter we'll give you 20 percent of the order back to pay for advertising."

In truth, you doubt the customer will spend the money on advertising. Instead, they'll just take the credit and sit on a bigger inventory. That will kill your sales to them next quarter, but you'll solve that problem then.

Even with these additional orders, you're still under quota. In desperation, you decide to sell product to a fictitious company that is "owned" by your brother-in-law. You set up a new account, and when accounting calls your brother-in-law for a credit check, he cooperates with your scheme. You then sell $40,000 of product to the fictitious company and ship the bikes to your brother-in-law's garage. Accounting books the revenue in the quarter, and you have finally made quota. A week into the next quarter, your brother-in-law returns the merchandise.

Meanwhile, unknown to you, SAP is scheduling bike assemblies. The assembly schedule reflects the sales from your activities (and those of the other salespeople), which indicate a sharp increase in product demand. Accordingly, it generates a schedule that calls for substantial assembly increases and schedules workers for the assemblies. SAP also increases the procurement of parts and frames from suppliers to meet the increased demand.

DISCUSSION QUESTIONS

1. Is it ethical for you to write the e-mail agreeing to take the product back? If the e-mail comes to light later, what do you think your boss will say?
2. Is it ethical for you to offer the "advertising" discount? What effect does that discount have on your company's balance sheet?
3. Is it ethical for you to ship to the fictitious company? Is it legal?
4. Describe the impact of your activities on next quarter's inventories.

Active Review

Use this Active Review to verify that you understand the material in the chapter. You can read the entire chapter and then perform the tasks in this review, or you can read the text material for just one question and perform the tasks in this review for that question before moving on to the next one.

Q1. What are the fundamentals of a Sales process?

Define *sale* and explain the activities and subactivities in the Sales process. Explain the overriding principle of sales. Locate the Sales process within the value chain.

Q2. How did the Sales process at CBI work before SAP?

Explain the major activities in the Sales process at CBI before SAP and identify the actor who accomplishes each activity and what data are used. Explain how the Sales process is different at CBI for new customers. Identify the two reasons that Sue's sale was disapproved.

Q3. What were the problems with the Sales process before SAP?

Explain the problems in the Sales process for sales, the warehouse, and accounting.

Q4. How does CBI implement SAP?

State CBI's competitive strategy. Describe the efficiency objective and how it will be measured. Identify the two effectiveness objectives and the measures used to assess each one.

Q5. How does the Sales process work at CBI after SAP?

How is the Pre-Sales Action activity different after SAP is implemented? Explain the major activities in the Sales process after SAP. Specify what data each actor supplies for each activity and what SAP does once each actor saves the data on his or her screen. Explain the general benefits of SAP's new Sales process for CBI. Describe how the new process improves the effectiveness and efficiency objectives.

Q6. How can SAP improve the integration of customer-facing processes at CBI?

Describe CRM. Explain the Promotion and Service customer-facing processes. Describe how the Sales process can be integrated with other processes by sharing data and by process synergy. Explain social CRM and how it can be used to improve a company's sales. Describe the advantages of using Salesforce.com or another cloud-based CRM vendor. Why is integrating customer-facing processes a challenge? Explain the two main challenges to integrating business processes and the lessons learned about process integration.

Q7. How does e-commerce integrate firms in an industry?

Define *e-commerce*. What makes the E-commerce process different from a process within a business? Explain emergence and give an example. Describe an interorganizational IS. How do merchant and nonmerchant companies differ? Explain the three types of nonmerchant companies. Describe how e-commerce can lead to disintermediation and to price elasticity data. Explain how process integration impacts your business future.

Key Terms and Concepts

Auction *246*
Business-to-business (B2B) *231*
Business-to-consumer (B2C) *231*
Business-to-government (B2G) *246*
Clearinghouse *246*
Customer relationship
   management (CRM) *240*

Disintermediation *246*
E-commerce *245*
Electronic exchange *246*
Emergence *245*
Interorganizational IS *245*
Merchant company *245*
Nonmerchant company *245*

Posting *238*
Price elasticity *247*
Sales *230*
Salesforce.com *243*
Social CRM *242*
Web storefront *246*

Using Your Knowledge

1. This chapter introduced the Service process and the Promotion process:
   a. Diagram each process with a BPMN.
   b. For each process, specify efficiency and effectiveness objectives and measures appropriate for CBI.
   c. What new IS technologies could CBI use to improve these processes, as specified by your measures in item b?
   d. How can these two processes be integrated with each other?
2. Which of the four nonroutine cognitive skills discussed in Chapter 1 (abstract reasoning, systems thinking, collaboration, or experimentation) did you use to accomplish exercise 1?
3. Even after SAP is implemented, input errors can still be made. What kinds of errors can Wally, Sue, and Ann still make? Describe a particularly harmful

mistake that each can make and how the process could be changed to prevent that error.
4. Think of a company that you buy a product or service from. Specify the touch points you share with that company. Do you believe the company does a good job collecting data from these encounters?
5. Think of another company who you purchase from and that you are disappointed with. Identify the customer-facing process that may be at fault. Specify how that process could be improved.
6. Using the example of a fast-food restaurant or coffee shop, identify three processes that must integrate well for the outlet to run smoothly. Specify what data the processes must share or which processes can support the objectives of other processes. Give an example of how the processes not integrating well would be apparent to you, as a customer.

Collaboration Exercise 8

Collaborate with a group of fellow students to answer the following questions. For this exercise do not meet face to face. Your task will be easier if you coordinate your work with SharePoint, Office 365, Google Docs with Google+ or equivalent collaboration tools. (See Chapter 9 for a discussion of collaboration tools and processes.) Your answers should reflect the thinking of the entire group, and not just that of one or two individuals.

Groupon offers a "Daily Deal" through its Web site *www.groupon.com*. Groupon originated in Chicago in 2008 and quickly spread to other cities in North America and then around the world. Groupon offers a Daily Deal in each of its geographic areas each day. If a specified minimum number of customers accept the deal, the deal becomes available to everyone who signed up. The coupon for each deal is made available to participating customers the day following its announcement. If the minimum number of customers is not met, the deal is cancelled for all.

For example, a popular health spa may offer through Groupon a $50 savings on a $125 weekend pass. If the minimum number of customers was set at 500 and, for purposes of this example, 800 accept the offer, then the 800 are notified that "The deal is on." Groupon charges each customer's credit card for $75. Groupon stores customers' credit card data so that customers can accept and participate in deals with minimal fuss. By charging the credit cards for each customer, Groupon receives cash up front. The next day, each of the 800 customers who purchased the Groupon can log into Groupon, navigate to their list of Groupons, and print their $125 voucher. They take the voucher to the spa and redeem it on arrival.

Participating firms, such as the spa, do not pay Groupon up front. Groupon takes a percentage of the $75 for each customer and pays the spa the rest. Visit Groupon at *www.groupon.com* to read more about the process.

As a team, complete the following:

1. Create a process diagram in BPMN to show this process *within* Groupon.
2. Create a process diagram in BPMN for the spa that shows activities from contacting Groupon for the first time through the end of the spa's promotion.
3. What are the objectives of each process? Label each as either an effective or efficient objective.
4. What measures should both firms use to assess accomplishment of the objectives identified in step 3?
5. Describe how Groupon's IS support this process.
6. Groupon's Procurement process integrates with the spa's Sales process. How is this integration accomplished?
7. Groupon's Sales process integrates with a customer's Procurement process. How is this integration accomplished?
8. What other IS (social media, smartphones, etc.) could Groupon use to improve its Promotion or Sales process?

ACTIVE CASE 8: SAP SALES PROCESS TUTORIAL

A tutorial for the Sales process using SAP is included in the appendix to this chapter, Appendix 8. The tutorial leads the student through a Sales process that sells 5 bicycles to a customer called Philly Bikes. Once the tutorial is complete, students should answer the following questions.

Here are the questions at the end of the exercise.

Questions

1. If you completed the Case Study/Tutorial in Chapter 7, how is the Sales process in SAP similar to the Procurement process in SAP? In what important ways are they different?

2. Create a screen capture of an SAP screen. Underneath the image, provide an answer to each of the following questions:
   a. In which of the activities does this screen occur?
   b. What is the name of the screen?
   c. What is the name of the screen that precedes it? What screen comes after it?
   d. What actor accomplishes this activity?
   e. Describe an error that this actor could make on this screen that SAP will prevent.

3. Make an informal diagram of the four main actors—the Customer (Philly Bikes), Sales (Sue), the Warehouse (Wally), and Accounting (Ann). Draw arrows that show the data that flows between each of the actors during this process. Number the arrows and include on each arrow what data are included in the message.

4. Using the same four main actors, this time show with the arrows how the material (the bikes) moves.

5. One concern of a business is fraud. One fraud technique is to create customers who are not customers but who are coconspirators. The conspirator inside the business credits the account of the coconspirator for payments that were never actually received. For this fraud scheme to work, who at CBI has to take part? How can SAP processes decrease the chance of this type of fraud?

6. Select any of the main activities or subactivities in the Sales process and:
   a. Specify what event triggers this activity to occur.
   b. Identify what activity follows this activity.
   c. For one data entry item, describe what would happen in the rest of the process if that entry was erroneous.
   d. For one data entry item, describe what limits (controls) you would put in place on the data to prevent the type of error described in item c.

7. Having completed one or both tutorials, make two suggestions about how:
   a. SAP could make their software easier to use.
   b. the tutorial(s) could be improved to help new students learn about processes and SAP.

APPENDIX 8—SAP SALES TUTORIAL

This tutorial follows the Sales process shown in Figure 8A-1. The top of this diagram appears in Chapter 8 as Figure 8-3. This top figure shows the three main Sales activities—Sell, Ship, and Payment, and the subactivities (Create Sales Order, etc.). At the bottom of Figure 8A-1, we have added the eight steps included in this tutorial. To keep this tutorial simple, we begin with step 3, Create a Sales Order.

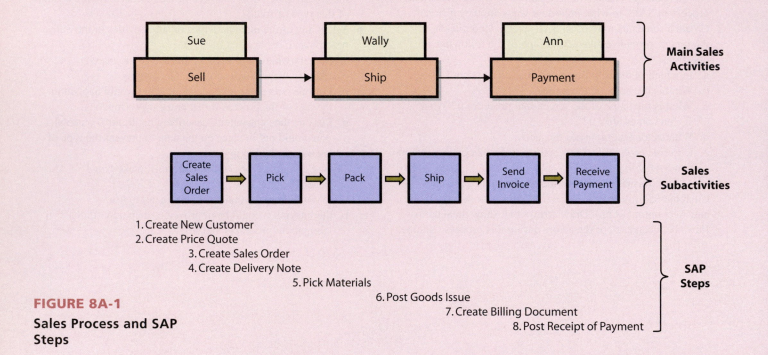

FIGURE 8A-1

Sales Process and SAP Steps

First Exercise
In this first exercise, we will sell five black Deluxe Touring bicycles to Philly Bikes. While our company in this tutorial is Global Bike, Inc., our actors—Sue, Wally, and Ann—and our Sales process are from Chuck's Bikes. Log in using data provided by your instructor (see Figure 7A-2).

1   Create New Customer
Skipped—does not apply to this first exercise, it is introduced later.

2   Create Price Quote
Skipped—does not apply to this first exercise, it is introduced later.

3   Create Sales Order
This first step, creating a sales order, is accomplished by a salesperson, at CBI, this is Sue. From the SAP Easy Access screen (Figure 8A-2), navigate to the Sales Order page by selecting:

Logistics > Sales and Distribution > Sales > Order > Create

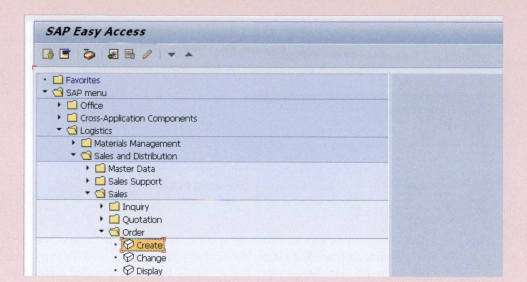

When you double-click Create, the next screen to appear is the Create Sales Order: Initial screen (Figure 8A-3). As in the tutorial in Chapter 7, the last two digits in Sales Organization in Figure 8A-3 are zeros, not the letter "O."

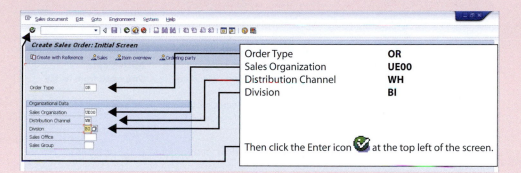

The next screen to appear is the Create Standard Order: Overview screen (Figure 8A-4). This screen may look familiar; it is Figure 8.9 from Chapter 8.

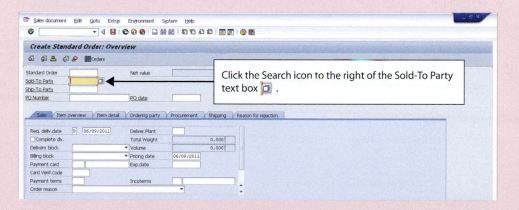

This will produce the pop-up search window shown in Figure 8A-5.

A list of potential customers is shown (Figure 8A-6).

FIGURE 8A-6

Customer List Screen

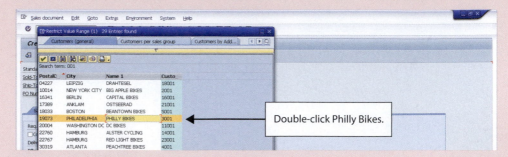

After you select Philly Bikes, you are returned to the Create Standard Order: Overview screen (Figure 8A-7). Notice that the Philly Bikes ID number appears in the Sold-To Party box. The PO number (65430 in this exercise) was specified by Philly Bikes and included in the sales order to provide the link between their purchase order and our sales order.

FIGURE 8A-7

Create Standard Order: Overview Screen

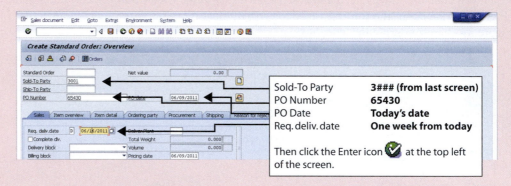

Click the Enter icon, and a warning pop-up window is displayed (Figure 8A-8).

FIGURE 8A-8

Pop-up Warning Screen

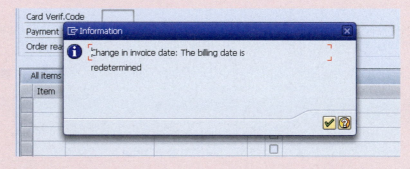

Click the Enter icon to continue. The system retrieves data about the Philly Bikes customer and displays an updated Create Standard Order: Overview screen (Figure 8A-9).

FIGURE 8A-9

Create Standard Order: Overview Screen

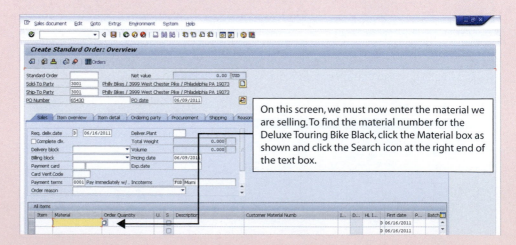

This will load the material search pop-up screen (Figure 8A-10).

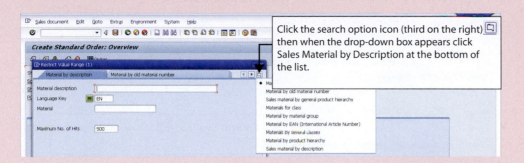

FIGURE 8A-10
Material Search Screen

This will reload a new search pop-up screen (Figure 8A-11).

FIGURE 8A-11
Material Search Screen

This will show you the sales material you can sell (Figure 8A-12).

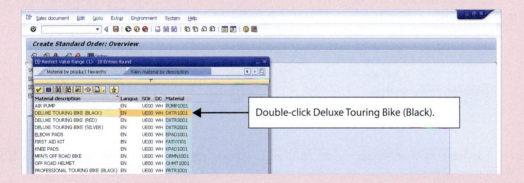

FIGURE 8A-12
Material List Screen

This returns you to the Create Standard Order: Overview screen. The material number for the Deluxe Touring Bike (Black) is now displayed in the Material column (Figure 8A-13).

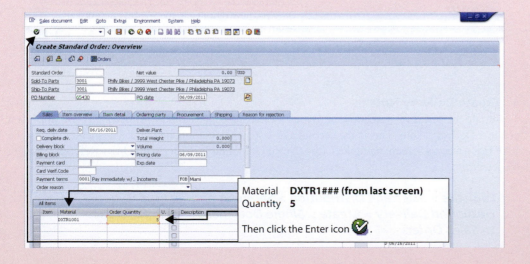

FIGURE 8A-13
Create Standard Order: Overview Screen

The system will check availability and retrieve Item Number, Total Weight, Net Value, and other data to complete your sales order, as shown in Figure 8A-14.

FIGURE 8A-14

Create Standard Order: Overview Screen

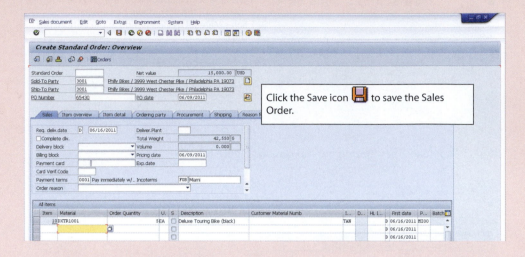

FIGURE 8A-15

Standard Order Number Screen

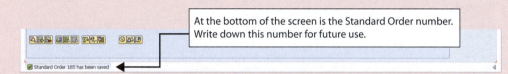

The sales order is now complete. To return to the SAP Easy Access Screen click on the exit icon as shown in Figure 8A-16.

FIGURE 8A-16

Toolbar Screen

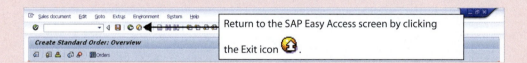

The Easy Access Screen can be returned to its original structure by clicking on the SAP Menu icon (Figure 8A-17).

FIGURE 8A-17

Easy Access Screen

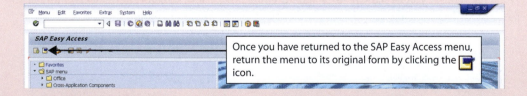

4   Create Delivery Note

To initiate the series of warehouse activities—Pick and Ship (called Post in SAP)—we must first create a Delivery Note. This is the second and last step accomplished by a salesperson. From the SAP Easy Access screen, navigate to the Create Outbound Delivery with Order Reference screen by selecting:

> *Logistics > Sales and Distribution > Shipping and Transportation >*
> *Outbound Delivery > Create > Single Document > With Reference*
> *to Sales Order*

When the Create Outbound Delivery with Order Reference screen appears (Figure 8A-18), the Order number should automatically load, and it should correspond to the number you just created in the Sales Order step. Note that our Shipping point is our Miami plant, and the second digit is the letter "I," not the number 1.

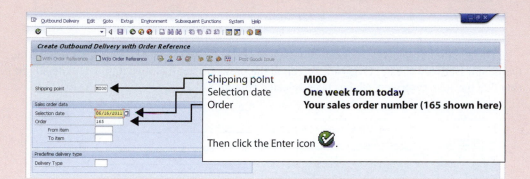

FIGURE 8A-18

**Create Outbound
Delivery Screen**

The Create Outbound Delivery screen is displayed containing the data from the sales order (Figure 8A-19).

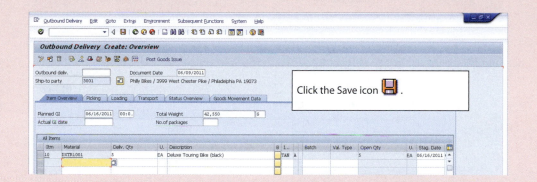

FIGURE 8A-19

**Create Outbound
Delivery Screen**

By saving the document, the SAP system ensures that the material is available and can meet the specified delivery date. The SAP system assigns a unique number to this delivery document and displays it at the lower-left corner of the Status bar (Figure 8A-20).

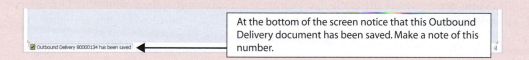

FIGURE 8A-20

**Outbound Delivery
Number Screen**

Return to the SAP Easy Access screen by clicking the Exit icon.

5 Pick Materials

Logistics > Sales and Distribution > Shipping and Transportation > Outbound Delivery > Change > Single Document

When a sales order is picked, the material is moved from its storage location and moved to its packing area. This picking step and the next step, posting, is accomplished by the warehouse manager, at CBI this is Wally. To do this, we must change the delivery document. The first screen in this step is the Change Outbound Delivery screen (Figure 8A-21).

FIGURE 8A-21

Change Outbound Delivery Screen

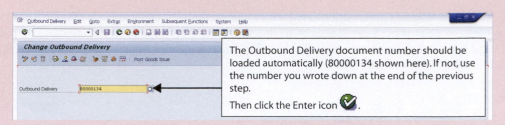

The Outbound Delivery document number should be loaded automatically (80000134 shown here). If not, use the number you wrote down at the end of the previous step.

Then click the Enter icon ✓.

The Outbound Delivery Change: Overview screen will appear (it is very similar to the Outbound Delivery Create: Overview screen in the previous step). Notice in the item detail section that the Item Overview tab has been selected (Figure 8A-22).

FIGURE 8A-22

Outbound Delivery Change Screen

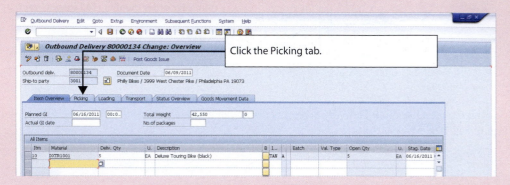

Click the Picking tab.

On this screen, Storage location (SLoc) may appear as a very narrow column with its visible heading shortened as "S . . ." (Figure 8A-23).

FIGURE 8A-23

Outbound Delivery Change Screen

SLoc   FG00
Picked Qty   5

Then click the Save icon 💾.

Again, a message in the Status bar appears that confirms that the outbound delivery document is once again saved. It is the same document number you created in step 4. Return to the SAP Easy Access screen by clicking the Exit icon.

6   Post Goods Issue

Logistics > Sales and Distribution > Shipping and Transportation > Outbound Delivery > Change > Single Document

When posting occurs, possession of the material transfers from Global Bike to Philly and inventory at Global Bike is reduced. Legal ownership of the material also changes hands. The first screen that appears in this step, Change Outbound Delivery (Figure 8A-24), is the same as the first and last screen in the previous step (Figure 8A-21).

FIGURE 8A-24

Change Outbound Delivery Screen

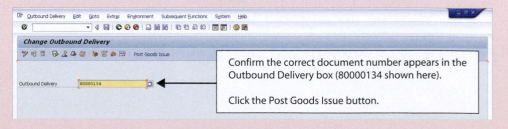

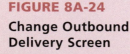

Confirm the correct document number appears in the Outbound Delivery box (80000134 shown here).

Click the Post Goods Issue button.

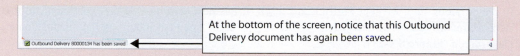

Return to the SAP Easy Access screen by clicking the Exit icon.

7   Create Billing Document for Customer

*Logistics > Sales and Distribution > Billing > Billing Document >
Process Billing Due List*

This step creates an invoice for the bikes that have been shipped. This invoice is sent to the customer. This step, and the final step, posting receipt of the payment, is done by an accountant, at CBI this is accomplished by Ann. The first screen is the Maintain Billing Due List screen (Figures 8A-26).

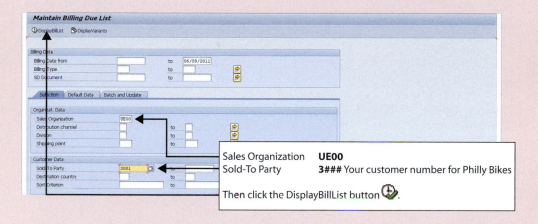

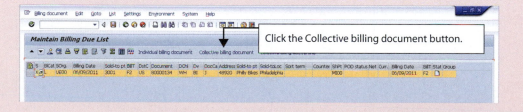

Click the Collective Billing Document icon, and the background color of this row will disappear.

This completes the Billing step, you do not need to click Enter or Save. Return to the SAP Easy Access screen by clicking the Exit icon twice.

8   Post Receipt of Customer Payment

*Accounting > Financial Accounting > Accountants Receivable >
Document Entry > Incoming Payments*

In the previous step, we sent Philly Bikes a bill. It has now sent us a $15,000 payment. In this step, we record receipt of that payment. The first screen is the Post Incoming Payments: Header Data screen (Figure 8A-29).

FIGURE 8A-29

Post Incoming Payments Screen

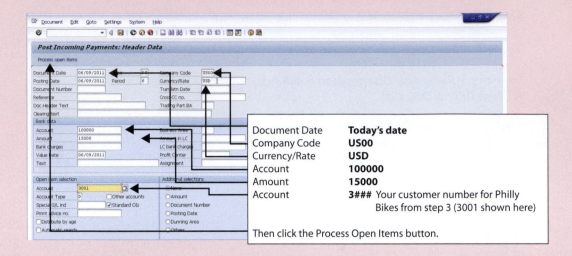

FIGURE 8A-30

Post Incoming Payments Process Open Items Screen

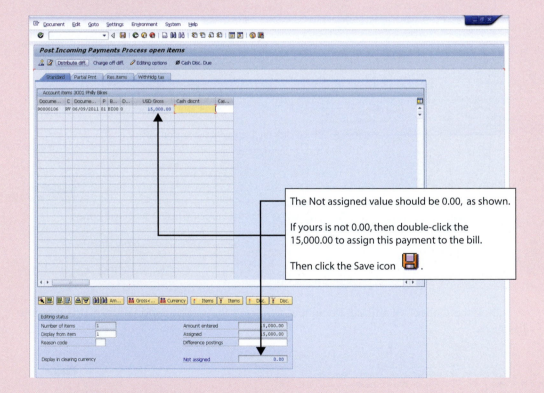

FIGURE 8A-31

Payment Document Screen

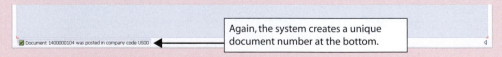

Return to the SAP Easy Access screen by clicking the Exit icon. This will generate a pop-up window that is misleading (Figure 8A-32). There is no data to be lost at this point, so click Yes. You are finished with the first exercise.

FIGURE 8A-32

Pop-up Warning Screen

You Try It 1

You will sell 10 Professional Touring Black Bikes to Philly. All the data necessary is included before each step.

This is PO 65431, the PO date is today, and the requested delivery date is 1 week from today. Ship the order a week from today. Use Miami as the shipping point. The total price is $32,000.

3   Create Sales Order

Logistics > Sales and Distribution > Sales > Order > Create

Data needed:

Order Type	**OR**
Sales Organization	**UE00**
Distribution Channel	**WH**
Division	**BI**

When these four inputs have been made, your screen will look like Figure 8A-33.

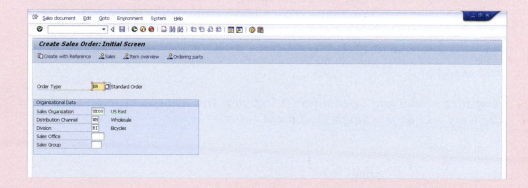

FIGURE 8A-33

Create Sales Order Screen

Data needed:

Sold-To Party	**3### (3001 shown here)**
PO Number	**65431**
PO date	**Today's date**
Req. delv.date	**One week from today**

After entering these four data items, click the Enter icon and then click the check icon on the pop-up warning message. The Create Standard Order: Overview screen appears, as shown in Figure 8A-34.

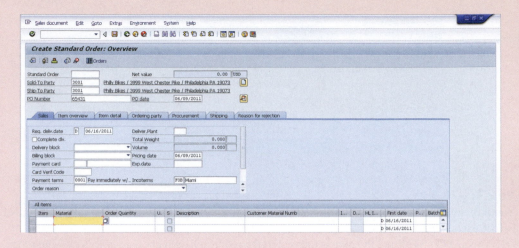

Enter the material data:

Material	**PRTR1###**
Order Quantity	**10**

After entering these two data items, click the Enter icon and then the Save icon.

4 Create Delivery Note

*Logistics > Sales and Distribution > Shipping and Transportation >
Outbound Delivery > Create > Single Document > With Reference
to Sales Order*

Data needed:

Shipping point	**MI00**
Selection date	**One week from today**
Order	**Your sales order number (automatic, from step 3)**

Same screens as the first exercise.

5 Pick Materials

*Logistics > Sales and Distribution > Shipping and Transportation > Outbound
Delivery > Change > Single Document*

Data needed:

SLoc	**FG00**
Picked Qty	**10**

After you have made these two inputs, your screen will look like Figure 8A-35.

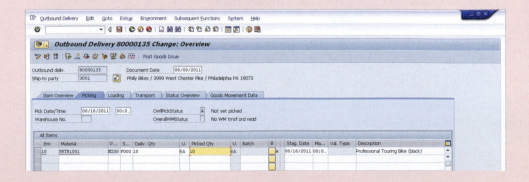

6   Post Goods Issue

Logistics > Sales and Distribution > Shipping and Transportation > Outbound Delivery > Change > Single Document

Same screens as the first exercise.

7   Create Billing Document for Customer

Logistics > Sales and Distribution > Billing > Billing Document > Process Billing Due List

Data Needed:

Sales Organization	**UE00**
Sold-To Party	**3### Your customer number for Philly Bikes**

After clicking the Display Bill List button and the Collective Billing Document button, the Maintain Billing Due List screen appears, as shown in Figure 8A-36.

FIGURE 8A-36

Maintain Billing Due List Screen

8   Post Receipt of Customer Payment

Accounting > Financial Accounting > Accountants Receivable > Document Entry > Incoming Payments

Data needed:

Document Date	**Today's date**
Company Code	**US00**
Currency/Rate	**USD**
Account	**100000**
Amount	**32000**
Account	**3### (3001 shown here)**

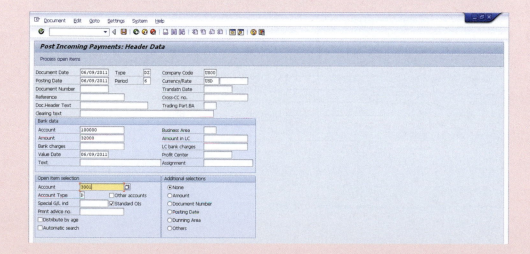

FIGURE 8A-37

Post Incoming Payments Screen

After clicking the Process Open Items button, the Post Incoming Payments Process Open Items screen will appear as shown in Figure 8A-38.

FIGURE 8A-38

Post Incoming Payments Process Open Items Screen

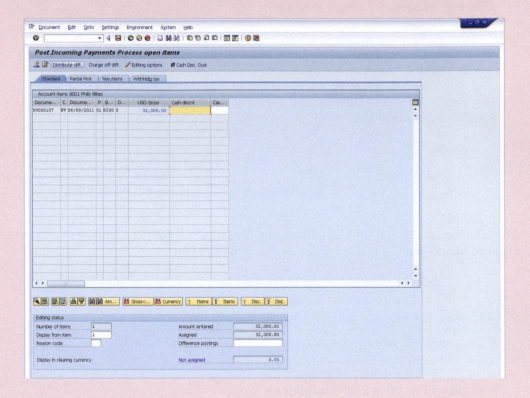

You Try It 2

Sell three Deluxe Touring Black Bikes to a new customer—Cycle Works—and give it a price quote. The Cycle Works data can be found on the following New Customer screens (Figures 8A-39 through 8A-45).

1   Create New Customer

Logistics > Sales and Distribution > Master Data > Business Partner > Customer > Create > Complete

FIGURE 8A-39

Customer Create: Initial Screen

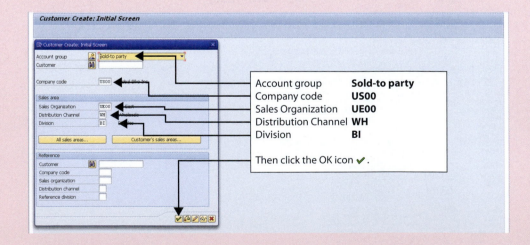

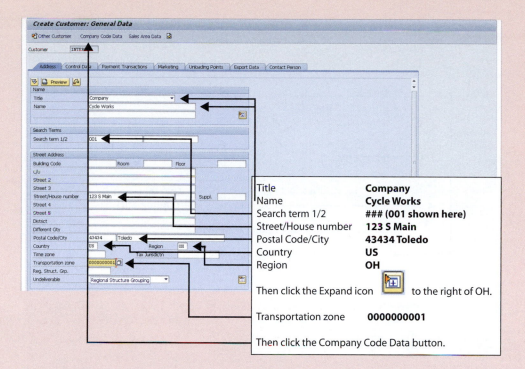

FIGURE 8A-40

Create Customer: General Data Screen

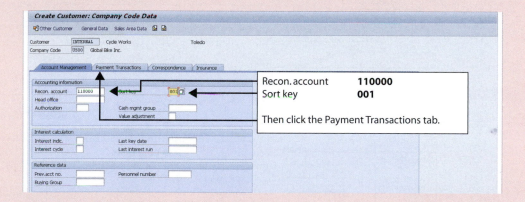

FIGURE 8A-41

Create Customer: Company Code Data Screen

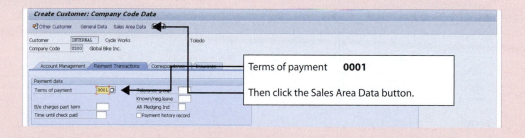

FIGURE 8A-42

Create Customer: Company Code Data Screen

FIGURE 8A-43

Create Customer: Sales Area Data Screen

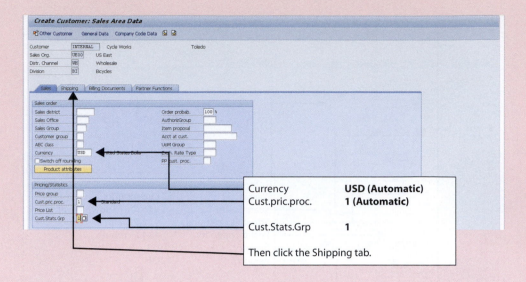

FIGURE 8A-44

Create Customer: Sales Area Data Screen

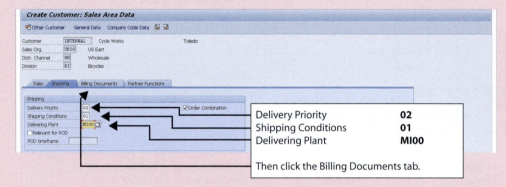

FIGURE 8A-45

Create Customer: Sales Area Data Screen

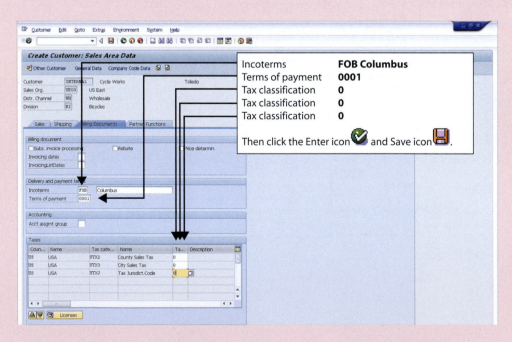

A new customer is created (Figure 8A-46).

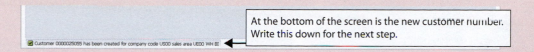

At the bottom of the screen is the new customer number. Write this down for the next step.

2   Create Price Quote

Logistics > Sales and Distribution > Sales > Quotation > Create

Cycle Works, our new customer, has asked for a price quote on Deluxe Black Bikes (Figures 8A-47 and 8A-48). Bikes you will sell to them in step 3.

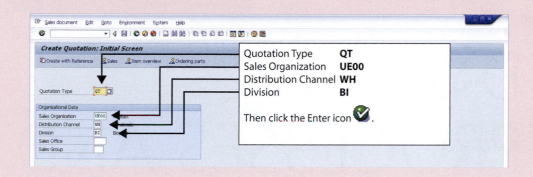

Quotation Type   **QT**
Sales Organization   **UE00**
Distribution Channel **WH**
Division   **BI**

Then click the Enter icon .

FIGURE 8A-47

Create Quotation Screen

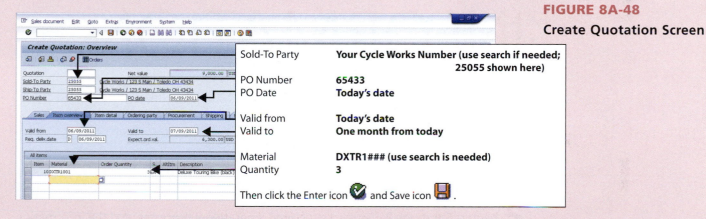

Sold-To Party   **Your Cycle Works Number (use search if needed; 25055 shown here)**

PO Number   **65433**
PO Date   **Today's date**

Valid from   **Today's date**
Valid to   **One month from today**

Material   **DXTR1### (use search is needed)**
Quantity   **3**

Then click the Enter icon and Save icon .

FIGURE 8A-48

Create Quotation Screen

3   Create Sales Order

In this step, create a sales order to sell the three Deluxe Touring Black Bikes to Cycle Works. The PO is 65433, the date is today, and ship a week from today. The total price is $9,000. All the other data is the same as in the first exercise.

DYNAMIC PROCESSES AND INFORMATION SYSTEMS

Chapters 5 through 8 discussed structured, operational processes, and the information systems that support them. The three chapters in this part continue the discussion of processes and systems, but for less structured, more dynamic processes. Chapter 9 discusses collaboration processes and systems that support decision making, problem solving, and project management. It also explains how you can use Microsoft SharePoint for your own student projects. Chapter 10 addresses social processes and systems. Such social processes include those based on Web 2.0, social networking, and Enterprise 2.0.

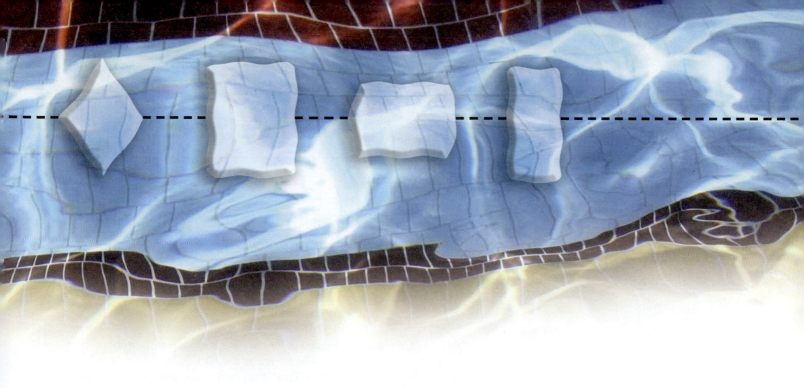

Finally, Chapter 11 presents business intelligence (BI) processes and systems. In it, we discuss the purpose of BI systems and the reporting and data mining processes that these systems support.

Unlike the procurement and sales processes that you studied in Chapters 7 and 8, dynamic processes are neither predefined nor fixed. That does not mean, however, that they are unstructured. Dynamic processes are structured, but their structure is fluid and frequently changed, and they often include a lot of backtracking and repetition. Although specifying objectives and measures are as important to improving dynamic processes as they are to structured operational processes, dynamic processes typically have fewer well-accepted objectives and measures. Further, dynamic processes do have activities in which particular objectives are achieved, but the means by which those goals are achieved vary widely. Finally, formal diagramming techniques such as BPMN are not as useful for dynamic processes as for structured processes. As you will see in Chapter 9, when we do use such techniques, the activities become very high level and generic, such as "analyze data."

"**N**o, Felix! Not again! Over, and over, and over! We decide something one meeting and then go over it again the next meeting and again the next. What a waste!" Tara is part of a working team at FlexTime.

"What do you mean, Tara? I think it's important we get this right."

"Well, Felix, if that's the case, why don't you come to the meetings?"

"I just missed a couple."

"Right. Last week we met here for, oh, 2, maybe 3, hours and we decided to look for ways to save costs without changing who we are as a studio."

"But Tara, if we could raise revenue, we wouldn't have to save costs. I think I have a couple of good ideas on how to do that."

"Felix! Last week we discussed that and decided it was too risky . . . we wouldn't see results in time. Plus, that's not what Kelly asked us to do."

"Look, Tara, Kelly just wants the studio to be profitable. Sales are down and costs aren't. All we need to do is raise sales."

"Right. But how do you do it? And what's the cost of raising sales? Come on, Felix, you're driving me nuts. We discussed this *ad nauseam* last week. Let's make some progress. Why don't some of you other guys help me! Jan, what do you think?"

"Felix, Tara is right. We did have a long discussion on what we're doing—and we did agree to focus on saving money."

"Well, Jan, I think it's a mistake. Why didn't anyone tell me? I put a lot of time into developing my sales plan."

"Did you read the e-mail?" Jan asks tentatively.

"What e-mail?"

"The meeting summary e-mail that Jan sends out each week."

"I got the e-mail but I couldn't download the attachment. Something weird about a virus checker couldn't access a gizmo or something like that . . ."

Tara can't stand that excuse, "Here, Felix, take a look at mine. I'll underline the part where we concluded that we'd focus on sales so you can be sure to see it."

"Tara, there's no reason to get snippy about this. I thought I had a good idea."

"OK, so we're agreed—*again this week*—that we're going to look for ways of reducing costs. Now, we've wasted enough time covering old ground. Let's get some new thinking going."

Felix slumps back into his chair and looks down at his cell phone.

"Oh, no, I missed a call from Mapplethorpe. Ahhhh."

"Felix, what are you talking about?"

"Mapplethorpe, my best client. Wants to change his PT appointment this afternoon. I'm sorry, but I've got to call him. I'll be back in a few minutes."

Felix leaves the room.

Tara looks at the three team members who are left.

"Now what?" she asks. "If we go forward we'll have to rediscuss everything we do when Felix comes back. Maybe we should just take a break?"

Jan shakes her head. "Tara, let's not. It's tough for me to get to these meetings. I don't have a class until tonight, so I drove down here just for this. I've got to pick up Simone from day care. We haven't done anything yet. Let's just ignore Felix."

"OK, Jan, but it isn't easy to ignore Felix."

The door opens and Kelly, FlexTime's co-owner, walks in.

"Hi everyone! How's it going? OK if I sit in on your meeting?"

Q1. What makes for effective collaboration?

Q2. What are characteristics of fundamental collaboration processes?

Q3. How can collaboration systems improve team communication?

Q4. How can collaboration systems manage content?

Q5. How can you use Microsoft SharePoint for student team projects?

Q6. How can collaboration systems control workflow?

Chapter Preview

FlexTime has a problem: Revenue is down and it needs to reduce costs. Kelly, one of FlexTime's partners, knows this and wants her employees and contractors to recommend ways of reducing costs in such a way that FlexTime maintains its competitive strategy. Or, as Tara puts it, "without changing who we are as a studio."

But before addressing the cost savings problem, this team has another problem to solve: They need to agree on the work processes they will use. They need answers to questions like: How and when will they meet? How can they make it easy for team members to participate while maintaining their professional and personal lives? How will they share documents with one another? How will they ensure that they're making progress on a timely basis?

Those questions concern team processes. Not processes like those in Chapters 7 and 8, where the output of one activity is fed in a standardized way as an input into other activities, but, in a more general sense, how will the team do its work? How will it collaborate?

This chapter has two major themes: first, in Q1 and Q2, we discuss the nature of collaboration and collaboration *processes*. Then, in questions Q3 through Q6, we discuss how *information systems* support those processes. You are already using some of the tools, like texting and Skype, that we will discuss. The point here is for you to understand how those and other tools are used in professional collaborations.

The knowledge you gain from this chapter is practical and useful. You can apply it as soon as tonight. Almost every one of your business school classes involves a team project of some sort, and you will improve the quality of your work if you apply this knowledge to your projects. You will also have a more satisfying collaboration experience.

As you read this chapter, keep in mind that collaboration is one of the four critical skills that Robert Reich identified for twenty-first-century workers (Chapter 1). As you will see, the ability to use collaboration information systems is a key part of modern collaboration skills.

Q1. What Makes for Effective Collaboration?

To answer this question, we need first to distinguish between cooperative and collaborative teams.

A **cooperative team** is a group that works together to accomplish something, but each person works independently to accomplish his or her portion of the work. A team of painters working on a building is a cooperative team. Each is given a portion of the building to paint and works on his or her own.

Many, perhaps most, student teams are cooperative teams. Given a group project, the team meets and divides the work into sections that are assigned to team members. An hour before the project is due the team members meet again to assemble their independent pieces into a whole.

Such cooperative teams are useful because they shorten the time required to achieve a result; five painters can paint the building faster than one. However, the work product of a cooperative team is not better than that of a single individual working alone. It is just faster.

A **collaborative team** is a group that works together using feedback and iteration. With a collaborative team, one person produces something, others review it, and the originator or others make revisions. The work proceeds in a sequence of steps or iterations of feedback and rework. With collaborative teams, members learn from each other, and, as a result, the team can often produce a result that is better in quality than any team member could have produced on his or her own, in any amount of time. Your student projects will result in much higher quality if you choose to work as a collaborative team.

Kelly, the co-owner of FlexTime, gave her team an important assignment: suggest how to reduce costs without compromising FlexTime's competitive strategy. No single employee or contractor on that team has the best solution. The best solution will evolve from feedback and iteration among team members.

Warning!

If you are like most undergraduate business students, especially freshmen or sophomores, your life experience is prohibiting you from understanding collaboration. So far, almost everyone you know has the same experience as you and, more or less, thinks like you. Your friends and associates have the same educational background, scored more or less the same on standardized tests, and have the same orientation toward success. So, why collaborate? Most of you think the same way, anyway. "What does the professor want and what's the easiest, fastest way to get it to her?"

So, consider this thought experiment. Your company is planning to build a new facility that is critical for the success of a new product line and will create 300 new jobs. The county government will not issue a building permit because the site is prone to landslides. Your engineers believe your design overcomes that hazard, but your chief financial officer (CFO) is concerned about Sarbanes-Oxley ramifications in the event there is a problem. Your corporate counsel is investigating the best way to overcome the county's objections while limiting liability. Meanwhile, a local community group is protesting your site because it believes it is too close to an eagle's nest. Your public relations director is meeting with local environmental groups.

Do you proceed with the project?

To decide, you convene a meeting of the chief engineer, the CFO, your legal counsel, and the PR director. Each of those people has different education and expertise, different life experiences, and different values. In fact, the only thing they have in common is that they are paid by your company. That team will participate collaboratively in ways that are far different from your experiences so far. So, keep this example in mind as you read this chapter.

What Are Critical Collaboration Skills?

Most students know what is required to be an effective member of a cooperative team: Come to meetings, be timely, communicate well, do your fair share of the work, and do it when you say you will. Although those characteristics are important for all kinds of teamwork, they are not enough for collaborative teams.

The power of collaboration arises from feedback. So in addition to the characteristics just listed, key skills for collaborative workers involve the ability to give and receive feedback and, in particular, the ability to give and receive *critical* feedback. Positive feedback is nice; it builds goodwill and engenders positive feelings. It does not help the work product one iota, however. Or, as Darwin John, the world's first chief information officer (CIO), stated, "If two of you have the same exact opinion, then we have no need for one of you."[1]

Critical feedback is essential for improving work product and team knowledge. Researchers Ditkoff, Allen, Moore, and Pollard surveyed 108 business professionals on the qualities, attitudes, and skills that make a good collaborator.[2] Figure 9-1 lists the most and least important characteristics reported in the survey. Most students are surprised to learn that 5 of the top 12 characteristics involve disagreement (highlighted in blue in Figure 9-1). Most students believe that "we should all get along" and more or less have the same idea and opinions about team matters. Although it is important for the team to be social enough to work together, this research indicates that it is also important for team members to have different ideas and opinions and to express them to each other. The respondents seem to be saying, "You can be negative, as long as you care about what we're doing."

The characteristics rated *not relevant* are also revealing. Experience as a collaborator or in business does not seem to matter. Being popular also is not important. A big surprise, however, is that being well organized was rated 31st out of 39 characteristics. Perhaps the respondents were recognizing that collaboration is a dynamic and not well-organized process.

---

[1] Personal conversation with the author.
[2] Dave Pollard, "The Ideal Collaborative Team." Available at: *http://www.ideachampions.com/downloads/collaborationresults.pdf* (accessed December 2010).

FIGURE 9-1

Importance of Collaboration Characteristics

Source: Based on http://www.ideachampions.com/downloads/collaborationresults.pdf.

Twelve Most Important Characteristics for an Effective Collaborator

1. Is enthusiastic about the subject of our collaboration.

2. Is open-minded and curious.

3. Speaks their mind even if it's an unpopular viewpoint.

4. Gets back to me and others in a timely way.

5. Is willing to enter into difficult conversations.

6. Is a perceptive listener.

7. Is skillful at giving/receiving negative feedback.

8. Is willing to put forward unpopular ideas.

9. Is self-managing and requires "low maintenance."

10. Is known for following through on commitments.

11. Is willing to dig into the topic with zeal.

12. Thinks differently than I do/brings different perspectives.

Nine Least Important Characteristics for an Effective Collaborator

31. Is well organized.

32. Is someone I immediately liked. The chemistry is good.

33. Has already earned my trust.

34. Has experience as a collaborator.

35. Is a skilled and persuasive presenter.

36. Is gregarious and dynamic.

37. Is someone I knew beforehand.

38. Has an established reputation in field of our collaboration.

39. Is an experienced businessperson.

What Is a Successful Collaborative Team?

Richard Hackman has studied teams and teamwork for many years and is the author of numerous articles and books on leading teams.[3] Hackman has identified three criteria for judging the success of a team:

- Successful outcome
- Growth in team capability
- Meaningful and satisfying experience

Most of us assume the first criteria. The team needs to accomplish its goal: solve a problem, make a decision, or create a work product. Whatever the objective is, the first success criterion is, "Did we do it?" As well as, "Did we do it within the time and budget allowed?"

The other two criteria may surprise you. Over time, did the team get better? Did it become more efficient? More effective? You can apply what you learned about processes in Chapters 5 through 8 to these questions. Did the team develop better work processes? Did it combine or eliminate activities? Were new linkages among activities established? Does the team have

---

[3] J. Richard Hackman, *Leading Teams* (Boston: Harvard Business School Press, 2002).

measures for their processes? Do the students try to integrate team processes with other processes; that is, do they learn class material in their role as a team member that they can use to make their individual study process more effective? Also, did individual performance improve? Did team members teach and otherwise help one another?

The third element of team success is that team members have a meaningful and satisfying experience. Of course, the nature of team goals is a major factor in making work meaningful. But few have the opportunity to develop a life-saving cancer vaccine. For most business professionals, it is a matter of making the product, creating the shipment, accounting for the payment, finding the prospects, and so on.

So, in the more mundane world, what makes work meaningful? One common thread in Hackman's book is that work is perceived as meaningful *by the team*. Updating the inventory database may not be the most exciting work, but if that activity is perceived by the team as important, it will become meaningful. This effect is redoubled if team members receive recognition for their work.

As a student, think about these three criteria on your next team. In addition to accomplishing the activity, did the team improve? Did the team members have a meaningful and satisfying experience?

Q2. What Are Characteristics of Fundamental Collaboration Processes?

Businesses use collaborative teams for three primary purposes:

- Make decisions
- Solve problems
- Manage projects

In this question, we will consider the processes that underlie each of these purposes and describe requirements for information systems that support them. These processes are dynamic; we will examine a general template of each, but understand that particular instance will evolve depending on the unique situation. For example, deciding on a restaurant for dinner with your friends and deciding on an airplane model for an airline share a similar decision-process template, but the particulars are vastly different. Do not look for fixed, predefined processes like those for procurement and sales.

Decision-Making Collaboration

Collaboration is used for some types of decision making, but not all. Consequently, to understand the role for collaboration we must begin with an analysis of decision making. Decisions are made at all three of the levels of process: *operational, managerial,* and *strategic* (see Figure 9-2).

OPERATIONAL DECISIONS **Operational decisions** are decisions that support operational processes concerning day-to-day activities. Typical operational decisions are: How many widgets should we order from vendor A? Should we extend credit to vendor B? Which invoices should we pay today?

Few operational decisions require collaboration. Deciding, for example, how much of product A to order from vendor B does not require the feedback and iteration among members that typifies collaboration. Although the process of generating the order might require the coordinated work of people in purchasing, accounting, and manufacturing, there is seldom a need for one person to comment on someone else's work. In fact, involving collaboration in routine, structured decisions is expensive, wasteful, and frustrating. "Do we have to have a

FIGURE 9-2

Hierarchy of Decisions

meeting about everything?" is a common lament. In most cases, operational decisions are supported by information systems like ERP.

MANAGERIAL DECISIONS   As stated in Chapter 5, managerial processes concern the allocation and utilization of resources. Typical decisions that support managerial processes are: How much should we budget for computer hardware and programs for department A next year? How many engineers should we assign to project B? How many square feet of warehouse space do we need for the coming year?

In general, if a managerial decision requires consideration of different perspectives, then it will benefit from collaboration. For example, consider the decision of whether to increase employee pay in the coming year. No single individual has the answer. The decision depends on an analysis of inflation, industry trends, the organization's profitability, the influence of unions, and other factors. Senior managers, accountants, human resources personnel, labor relationship managers, and others will each bring a different perspective to the decision. They will produce a work product for the decision, evaluate that product, and make revisions in an iterative fashion—the essence of collaboration.

STRATEGIC DECISIONS   **Strategic decisions** are decisions that support strategic processes concerning broad-scope, organizational issues. Typical decisions at the strategic level are: Should we start a new product line? Should we open a centralized warehouse in Tennessee? Should we acquire company A?

Strategic decisions are almost always collaborative. Consider a decision about whether to move manufacturing operations to China. This decision affects every employee in the organization, the organization's suppliers, its customers, and its shareholders. Many factors and many perspectives on each of those factors must be considered.

To summarize, few operational decisions require collaboration; many managerial decisions do; and most, if not all, strategic decisions do. Further, when deciding whether a decision will benefit from collaboration, the key factor is whether feedback and iteration are required.

By the way, collaborative decision making does not necessarily mean that the team makes the final decision. Rather, it means that iteration and feedback were involved in some way during the decision process. The team may have generated data, performed analyses, and created recommendations in a collaborative fashion, but the final decision may have been made by an individual. If so, we would consider this a collaborative decision process even though an individual made the final decision.

Decision-Making Collaboration Processes

Figure 9-3 presents a template for decision-making collaboration processes. Although this process is shown in BPMN format, the activities and data flows are very general. We use BPMN here only because it is a convenient way of expressing process structure.

The need for a decision arises from the organization's environment. For example, the marketing department may need to decide how much of its advertising budget to allocate to a given product, or the IS department may need to decide what type and characteristics of computer hardware to buy for users.

TEAM RULES   Given the need, the decision maker, who can be an individual or a group, forms the collaborative team. The first activity for the team is to establish team rules, including:

- Team purpose, objectives, and authority
- Team member roles and expectations
- Team membership
- Work methods
- Collaboration information systems

The decision maker may have set the team's purpose, objectives, and authority; if not, the team should do so at the onset. Other rules include member roles, expectations for those roles, a statement as to who is on the team, work methods to be employed, information systems to be used, and so forth. These may be informal or they may be formally documented. If the latter, they will be included in the team's data repository.

GATHER DATA   The second activity in the decision-making process template is to gather data. The specifics depend entirely on the decision to be made. As you will learn in Chapter 11, many

FIGURE 9-3

Process Template for Decision-Making Collaboration

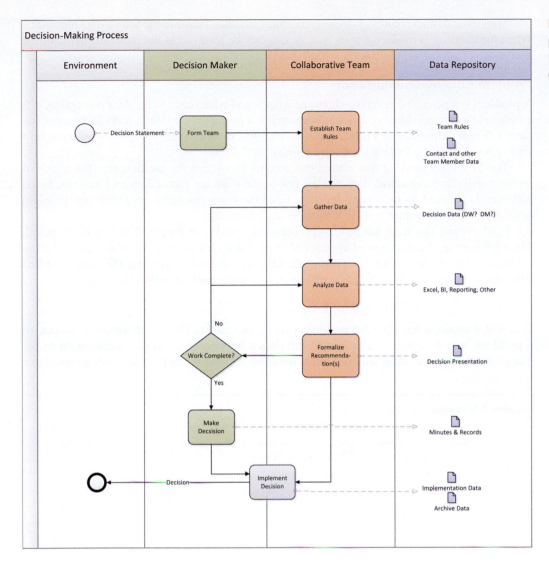

decisions rely on data stored in data warehouses. Feedback is important in this activity because members will have different ideas on what data are needed for the decision and different knowledge on what data are available and where within the organization.

ANALYZE DATA Data analysis is the third activity in this process. Here, the team may use tools like Microsoft Excel or business intelligence tools to process decision data. Again, it is impossible to state specific activities here because this is a template for many decisions. However, consider how important feedback is. Team members will have different perspectives on what analysis is needed, how complete the analysis is, what the results imply about the decision to be made, and so forth. Providing effective critical feedback can dramatically improve the resulting decision.

FORMULIZE RECOMMENDATION(S) In this activity, results of the team's efforts are documented and made ready for presentation to the decision maker. Many different tools are used for such presentations, but you can be sure that, for the foreseeable future, you can add a great deal of value to teams on which you work if you obtain advanced-level Microsoft PowerPoint skills.

DECISION OR REWORK? The decision maker may or may not consider the team's work to be complete. In some cases, decision makers do not like the choices they have been given and direct the team to do further work, either by considering other data or making other analyses. This diagram shows only one such backward loop. In truth, in dynamic processes flow from any of the activities can loop back to any prior activity. Such loops were omitted from Figure 9-3 to reduce diagram clutter.

Minutes and other records of decision meetings are often stored in the team's data repository. When the decision is made, the team may or may not be involved in the implementation of the decision.

Problem-Solving Collaboration

A **problem** is a perceived difference between what is and what ought to be. As a perception, it is a view held by an individual or a group. Because it is a perception, different users and groups can have different definitions of a problem. Often the most difficult part of solving a problem isn't finding a solution, it is finding a common problem definition.

The FlexTime meeting that started this chapter illustrates the inefficiency that a lack of problem definition can cause. Tara and the rest of the team are focused on cost savings. Felix, however, is focused on increasing revenue. Until the team can agree on a common problem definition, the collaboration will be ineffective and frustrating.

Furthermore, this team has process problems in addition to the problem that Kelly posed. The team does not have an agreed upon set of rules, it does not have an effective way of sharing documents, and it does not have a realistic schedule or medium for meetings. The team must first solve these process problems before it will be able to define and solve FlexTime's problem.

Problem-Solving Collaboration Processes

Figure 9-4 shows a template for problem-solving processes. The environment gives rise to a problem, which, again, is a perceived difference between what is and what ought to be. The problem owner or some authority forms the team. As shown, the first members assigned to a

FIGURE 9-4

Process Template for Problem-Solving Collaboration

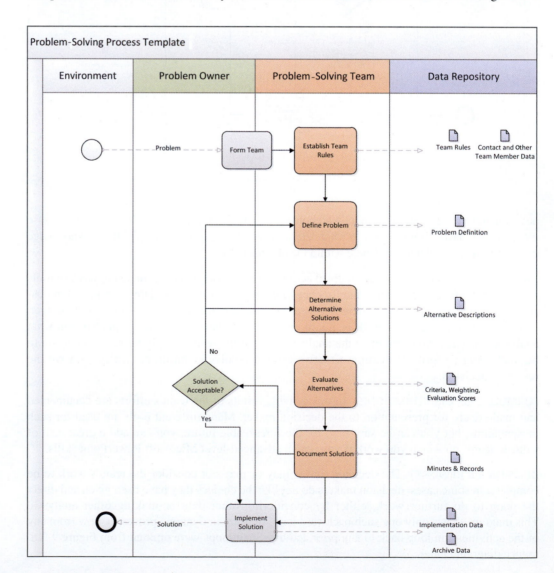

team may be involved in selecting other team members. The activity of establishing team rules has the same tasks as described for decision-making collaboration.

DEFINE PROBLEM As stated earlier, a problem is a perception. Different team members will have different ideas about what is and also about what should be. Obtaining a commonly understood and accepted definition of the problem to be solved is crucial. Once that definition is achieved, the team should document it in some fashion and store the documentation in the team's data repository.

Problem definitions and documentation can be extensive. Consider, for example, the need to fix problems in operational processes like procurement or sales. In this case, the problem definition will consist of both as-is and ought-to-be process documentation.

DETERMINE ALTERNATIVES The third activity shown in Figure 9-4 is to determine alternative solutions. Reflect on the nature of the work to be done and you can see why feedback and iteration are vital. One team member will have alternatives that will spark the thinking of other team members. The ability to give and receive critical feedback is essential.

EVALUATE ALTERNATIVES Once alternatives are specified, the next step is for the team to evaluate them. Of course, to make an evaluation, the team must agree on a set of criteria and their relative importance. Those criteria as well as the results of analysis are stored in the team's data repository.

As a dynamic process, any of these activities can result in a loop backwards to repeat earlier work. While evaluating alternatives, the team may decide that the set of proposed alternatives is insufficient, or the team may identify one or more other alternatives to consider. Or, at any stage, the team may decide that it has inaccurately defined the problem. At FlexTime, Felix might have been right.

DOCUMENT SOLUTION Once the alternatives have been evaluated, the next step is to document the solution. The process template in Figure 9-4 indicates that the problem-solving team evaluates alternatives and selects a solution without the assistance of the problem holder. However, it would be rare for an organization to proceed to implement a solution without some involvement of the problem holder. Figure 9-4 shows this involvement as a decision that the problem holder makes about whether the proposed solution is acceptable.

This aspect of Figure 9-4 is a crude summary of many different possibilities. If the problem owner has more power than the team, then the owner may be considerably more involved in the solution than indicated here. However, if the problem owner has little power, the solution may be implemented over the problem holder's objections.

IMPLEMENT SOLUTION The last activity shown in Figure 9-4 is to implement the solution. This activity appears on the line between the Problem Owner and Problem-Solving Team roles because either or both roles can be involved in the solution.

Before moving on, examine Figure 9-4 again and consider the ways that feedback and iteration will be important throughout the problem-solving process. Also, think about information systems that could be used for the data repository. Can you see a role for e-mail? IM? File sharing? We will consider these alternatives and others in the next question.

Project Management Collaboration Processes

Project management is a rich and complicated subject. Hackman and others have written extensively about it. The Project Management Institute (*www.pmi.org*), an international nonprofit organization, specializes in documenting and training best-of-breed project management techniques. It publishes the *PMBOK* (*Project Management Body of Knowledge*) *Guide*, which is a rich compendium of project management techniques.

Unfortunately, we do not have space or time to delve deeply into project management in this text. We will present a project management process template here and discuss the role of collaboration information systems for project management later in this chapter. We will also discuss project management for systems development in Chapter 12.

Because project management is complicated and a wildly varied topic, rather than attempt to produce a template like those in Figures 9-3 and 9-4, we will instead consider the sub-activities and data in four basic activities of a project's lifetime: starting, planning, doing, and wrapping-up. See Figure 9-5 and consider each activity.

FIGURE 9-5

Project Management Activities and Data

Activity	Sub-Activities	Data for Repository
Starting	Set team authority Set project scope and initial budget Form team Establish team roles, responsibilities, and authorities Establish team rules	Team member data start-up documents
Planning	Determine activities and dependencies Assign activities Determine schedule Revise budget	Project plan, budget, and other documents
Doing	Manage activities and budget Solve problems Reschedule activities as necessary Document and report progress	Updated project schedule Updated project budget
Wrapping Up	Determine completion Prepare archival documents Disband team	Archival documents

STARTING ACTIVITY The fundamental purpose of the starting activity is to set the ground rules for the project and the team. In industry, teams need to determine or understand what authority they have. Is the project given to the team? Or, is part of the team's activity to identify what the project is? Is the team free to determine team membership, or is membership given? Can the team devise its own methods for accomplishing the project, or is a particular method required? Student teams differ from those in industry because the team's authority and membership are set by the instructor. However, although student teams do not have the authority to define the project, they do have the authority to determine how that project will be accomplished.

Other activities during the starting activity are to set the scope of the project and to establish an initial budget. Often this budget is preliminary and is revised after the project has been planned. An initial team is formed during this activity with the understanding that team membership may change as the project progresses. It is important to set team member expectations at the onset. What role will each team member play, and what responsibilities and authority will he or she have? Team rules are also established, as discussed under decision making.

PLANNING ACTIVITY The purpose of the planning activity is to determine "who will do what and by when." Work activities are defined, and resources like personnel, budget, and equipment are assigned to them. As you will learn when we discuss project management in Chapter 12, activities can depend on one other. For example, you cannot evaluate alternatives until you have created a list of alternatives to evaluate. In this case, we say that there is a *activity dependency* between the activity *evaluate alternatives* and the activity *create a list of alternatives*. The *evaluate alternatives* activity cannot begin until the completion of the *create alternative list* activity.

Once activities and resources have been assigned, it is possible to determine the project schedule. If the schedule is unacceptable, more resources can be added to the project or the project scope can be reduced. Risks and complications arise here, however, as discussed in Chapter 12. The project budget is usually revised at this point as well.

DOING ACTIVITY Tasks are accomplished during the doing activity. The key management challenge here is to ensure that activities are accomplished on time and, if not, to identify schedule problems as early as possible. As work progresses, it is often necessary to add or delete activities, change activity assignments, add or remove activity labor or other resources, and so forth. Another important activity is to document and report project progress.

WRAPPING-UP ACTIVITY Are we done? This question is an important and sometimes difficult one to answer. If work is not finished, the team needs to define more tasks and continue the doing

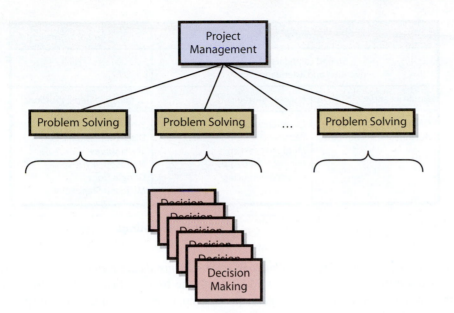

FIGURE 9-6

Collaboration Process Hierarchy

activity. If the answer is yes, then the team needs to document its results, document information for future teams, close down the project, and disband the team.

Each of these activities generates and uses data in a team repository, as shown in the rightmost column of Figure 9-5.

THE COLLABORATION HIERARCHY Before we discuss information systems for collaboration, consider the relationship of the three collaboration processes just discussed. As shown in Figure 9-6, project management involves solving problems. Hence, any information system that you use for problem solving will add benefit and utility to project management. Similarly, problem solving always involves decision making. Hence, any information system that you use to benefit decision making will also benefit problem solving (and project management).

Q3. How Can Collaboration Systems Improve Team Communication?

For the balance of this chapter, we will discuss how you can use information systems to facilitate collaboration processes. Specifically, we will address how information systems support communication, content management, and workflow control.

If teams truly *collaborate*—if the team members create work products (such as documents), encourage others to criticize those products, and revise those products in accordance with the criticism—then clearly communication is essential. As stated, one element of good communication is the skills of the team members. The second, which we address here, are the information systems used to communicate.

Figure 9-7 summarizes technology available to facilitate communication. **Synchronous communication** occurs when all team members meet at the same time, such as with conference calls or face-to-face meetings. **Asynchronous communication** occurs when team members do not meet at the same time. Employees who work different shifts at the same location or team members who work in different time zones around the world typically meet asynchronously.

Most student teams attempt to meet face-to-face, at least at first. Arranging such meetings is always difficult, however, because student schedules and responsibilities differ. If you are going to arrange such meetings, consider creating an online group calendar in which team members post their availability, week by week. Also, use the meeting facilities in Microsoft Outlook to issue invitations and gather RSVPs. If you do not have Outlook, use an Internet site such as Evite (*www.evite.com*) for this purpose. For face-to-face meetings, you will need little other technology beyond standard Office applications such as Word and PowerPoint.

The Ethics Guide on pages 302–303 addresses some of the ethical challenges that arise when teams hold virtual meetings.

FIGURE 9-7

Technology Used for Communication

Synchronous		Asynchronous
Shared calendars Invitation and attendance		
Single location	Multiple locations	Single or multiple locations
Office applications such as Word and PowerPoint	Conference calls Webinars Multiparty text chat Microsoft Web Apps Videoconferencing	E-mail Discussion forums Team surveys Microsoft SkyDrive Google Docs Microsoft SharePoint

Virtual meetings

Given today's communication technology, most students should forgo face-to-face meetings. They are too difficult to arrange and seldom worth the trouble. Instead, learn to use **virtual meetings**, which are meetings in which participants do not meet in the same place, and possibly not at the same time.

In business, more and more meetings are conducted online. Business travel is time consuming, expensive, and quickly becomes a stressful hassle. Most businesspeople are quite happy to stay at their home location and use some form of online meeting.

If the virtual meeting is synchronous (all meet at the same time), teams use **conference calls**, **webinars**, or **multiparty text chat**. A webinar is a virtual meeting in which attendees view one of the attendee's computer screens. **WebEx** (*www.webex.com*) is a popular commercial webinar application used in virtual sales presentations. **SharedView** is a Microsoft product for sharing a computer screen that you can download for free at *www.connect.microsoft.com/site/sitehome.aspx?SiteID=94*. Microsoft Web Apps can also be used to share content, as explained in the next question.

If everyone on your team has a camera on his or her computer, you can also do **videoconferencing**. The user in Figure 9-8 is videoconferencing with **Microsoft Lync**, a communication tool that provides IM, audio, videoconferencing, a shared whiteboard for team members to write upon, and other capabilities. Google provides **Google Talk**, which also has videoconferencing capabilities. Some students use Skype (now Microsoft Skype) as well.

In some business and class situations, synchronous meetings, even virtual ones, are impossible to arrange. You just cannot get everyone together at the same time. In this circumstance, when the team must meet asynchronously, many teams try to communicate via e-mail.

FIGURE 9-8

Example Use of Lync

The problem with e-mail is that there is too much freedom. Not everyone will participate, because it is easy to hide from e-mail. (Did Felix, in the opening scenario, really not get the attachment?) Discussion threads become disorganized and disconnected. After the fact, it is difficult to find particular e-mails, comments, or attachments.

Discussion forums are an alternative. Here, one group member posts an entry, perhaps an idea, a comment, or a question, and other group members respond. Such forums are better than e-mail because it is harder for the discussion to get off track. However, it remains easy for some team members not to participate.

Team surveys are another form of communication technology. With these, one team member creates a list of questions and other team members respond. Surveys are an effective way to obtain team opinions; they are generally easy to complete, so most team members will participate. Both discussion forums and surveys provide documentation of members' views and opinions, which can be important later in a project.

Q4. How Can Collaboration Systems Manage Content?

The second driver of collaboration performance is **content management**. Feedback and iteration are possible only if content is shared. Such content includes all of the team data and documents in the data repositories in Figures 9-3 through 9-5 as well as other content used by the team such as documents, illustrations, spreadsheets, PowerPoint presentations, video, and other data.

Information systems used for sharing content depend on the degree of control that team members want. Figure 9-9 lists three categories of content-management control: no control, version management, and version control. Consider each.

Shared Content with No Control

The most primitive way to share content is via e-mail attachments. It is easy to share content this way, but e-mail attachments have numerous problems. For one, there is always the danger that someone does not receive an e-mail, does not notice it in his or her inbox, or does not bother to save the attachments. Then, too, if three users obtain the same document as an e-mail attachment, each changes it, and each sends back the changed document via e-mail, different, incompatible versions of that document will be floating around. So, although e-mail is simple, easy, and readily available, it will not suffice for collaborations in which there are many document versions or for which there is a desire for content control.

Another way to share content is to place it on a shared **file server**, which is simply a computer that stores files just like the disk in your local computer. If your team has access to a file server, you can put documents on the server and others can download them, make changes, and upload them back onto the server using FTP (discussed in Chapter 3).

Storing documents on servers is better than using e-mail attachments because documents have a single storage location. They are not scattered in different team members' e-mail boxes. Team members have a known location for finding documents.

However, without any additional control it is possible for team members to interfere with one another's work. For example, suppose team members A and B download a document and edit it, but without knowing about the other's edits. Person A stores his version back on the server and then person B stores her version back on the server. In this scenario, person A's changes will be lost.

Alternatives for Sharing Content		
No Control	Version Management	Version Control
E-mail with attachments Shared files on a server	Wikis Google Docs Microsoft SkyDrive	Microsoft SharePoint

Increasing degree of content control

FIGURE 9-9

Information Technology for Sharing Content

Furthermore, without any version management it will be impossible to know who changed the document and when. Neither person A nor person B will know whose version of the document is on the server. To avoid such problems, some form of version management is recommended.

Shared Content with Version Management

Systems that provide **version management** track changes to documents and provide features and functions to accommodate concurrent work. The means by which this is done depends on the particular system used. In this section, we consider three systems that you should consider for your team's work: wikis, Google Docs, and Microsoft SkyDrive. Microsoft SharePoint, the premier content-sharing system from Microsoft, can also be used for version management. We will not discuss SharePoint here, but will show its use for version control in the next section and then show how you can use it for your teams in Q5.

WIKIS   The simplest version-management systems are wikis. A **wiki** (pronounced *we-key*) is a shared knowledge base in which the content is contributed and managed by the wiki's users. The most famous wiki is Wikipedia, a general encyclopedia available to the public.

Collaborative teams can use wiki technology to create and maintain private wikis that serve as a repository of team knowledge. When a user contributes a wiki entry, the system tracks who created the entry and the date of creation. As others modify the entry, the wiki software tracks the identity of the modifier, the date, and possibly other data. Some users are given permission to delete wiki entries.

GOOGLE DOCS   **Google Docs** is a collaboration application for sharing documents, presentations, spreadsheets, drawings, and other data. Google Docs is rapidly evolving; by the time you read this, Google may have added additional file types or changed the system from what is described here. Figure 9-10 shows the types of data that can be shared as of December 2010. You can google the name *Google Docs* to obtain the latest information about the application.

With Google Docs, anyone who edits a document must have a Google account. (A Google account is not the same as a Gmail account.) You can establish a Google account using a Hotmail, a university, or any other e-mail account. Your Google account will be affiliated with whatever e-mail account you provide.

To create a shared Google file, go to *http://docs.google.com* (note there is no *www* in this address). Sign into (or create) your Google account. From that point on, you can upload documents and spreadsheets, share them with others, and download them to common file formats.

You can then make the document available to others by entering their e-mail addresses (which need not be Google accounts). Those users are notified that the document exists and are given a link by which they can access it. If they have (or create) a Google account, they can edit the document as well.

FIGURE 9-10

Types of Google Docs

Source: Google Docs & Spreadsheets™. Google is a trademark of Google Inc.

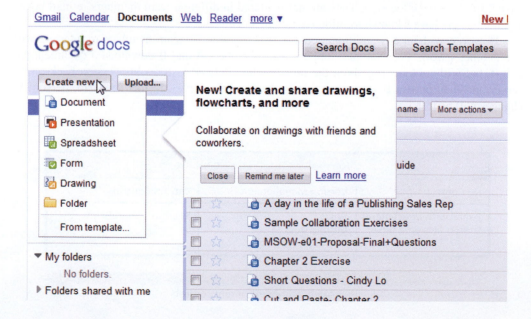

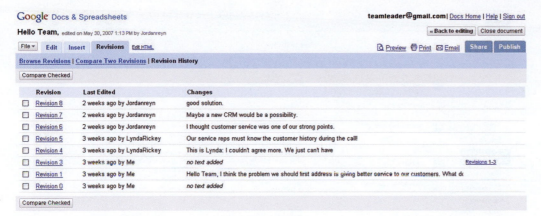

FIGURE 9-11

Google Docs Library

Source: Google Docs & Spreadsheets™. Google is a trademark of Google Inc.

With Google Docs, documents are stored on a Google server. Users can access the documents from Google and with partners, simultaneously see and edit documents. In the background, Google merges the users' activities into a single document. You are notified that other users are editing a document at the same time as you are, and with many browsers you can readily see changes by clicking on the edit flag that appears when changes are made by others. Google tracks document revisions, with brief summaries of changes made. Figure 9-11 shows a sample revision for a sample document that has been shared among three users.

Google Docs is free, and all documents must be processed by Google programs on its servers. A Microsoft Word or Excel document can be uploaded to a Google Docs & Spreadsheets server, but the document must be edited by Google programs. Documents can be saved in Word, Excel, or other common file formats.

MICROSOFT SKYDRIVE **Microsoft SkyDrive** is Microsoft's answer to Google Docs. It provides the ability to store and share Office documents and other files and offers free storage of up to 25 GB. Additionally, SkyDrive includes license-free Web application versions of Word, Excel, PowerPoint, and OneNote that are called **Office Web Apps**. These applications run in the browser and are quite easy to use. Figure 9-12 shows an instance of the Word Web App. These programs have less functionality than desktop Office programs, but they are free and readily accessed on the Web.

In addition to Office Web Apps, the desktop Office 2010 applications are tightly integrated with SkyDrive. You can open and save documents directly from and to SkyDrive from inside Microsoft Office products, as shown in Figure 9-13.

To set up a SkyDrive, you need a Windows Live ID. If you have either a Hotmail or MSN e-mail account, that account is your Windows Live ID. If you do not have a Hotmail or MSN e-mail account, you can create a Windows Live ID with some other e-mail account, or you can create a new Hotmail account, which is free.

Once you have a Windows Live ID, go to *www.skydrive.com* and sign in. You will be given 25 GB of storage. You can create file folders and files and use either Office or Web Apps as well.

FIGURE 9-12

Example Use of Word Web App

FIGURE 9-13

Saving a Word 2010 Document to a SkyDrive Account

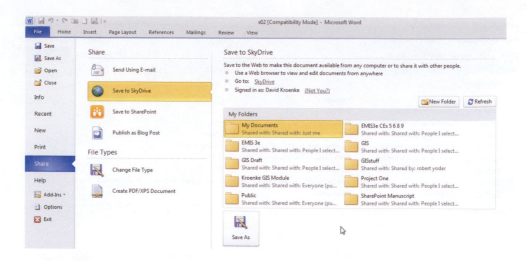

Like Google accounts, you can share folders with others by entering their Office Live IDs or their e-mail accounts. Users who have an Office Live ID can view and edit documents; users who do not have an Office Live ID can only view documents.

Only one user at a time can open SkyDrive documents for editing. If you attempt to open a document that someone else is editing, you will receive the message shown in Figure 9-14. When the user who is editing that document finishes, you will receive a message offering to merge your work with the latest copy of the document that has just been returned.

Microsoft has developed a Facebook application for processing SkyDrive directories. That application, called Docs (not to be confused with Google Docs), works just as described here, it has just been given the look and feel of a Facebook application.

Both Google Docs and Microsoft SkyDrive are free and very easy to use. They are both far superior to exchanging documents via e-mail or via a file server. If you are not using one of these two products, you should. Go to *http://docs.google.com* or *www.skydrive.com* and check them out. You will find easy-to-understand demos if you need additional instruction.

Shared Content with Version Control

Version-management systems improve the tracking of shared content and potentially eliminate problems caused by concurrent document access. They do not, however, provide **version control**. They do not limit the actions that can be taken by any particular user, and they do not give control over the changes to documents to particular users.

With version-control systems, each team member is given an account with a set of permissions. Shared documents are placed into shared directories, sometimes called **libraries**. For example, on a shared site with four libraries, a particular user might be given read-only permission for library 1; read and edit permission for library 2; read, edit, and delete permission for library 3; and no permission even to see library 4.

Furthermore, document directories can be set up so that users are required to check out documents before they can modify them. When a document is checked out, no other user can obtain it for the purpose of editing it. Once the document has been checked in, other users can obtain it for editing.

FIGURE 9-14

SkyDrive Options for Opening a Document Locked by Another User

> **File In Use**   [?] [X]
>
> This file is locked for editing by Don Nilson
> Do you want to:
>
> ● View a *r*ead-only copy
> ○ Edit the file and *m*erge your changes with the server file when it becomes available
> ☑ Receive a *n*otification when the server file is available
>
> Why can't I edit the server file?
>
>   [OK]   [Cancel]

FIGURE 9-15

Checking Out a Document in SharePoint

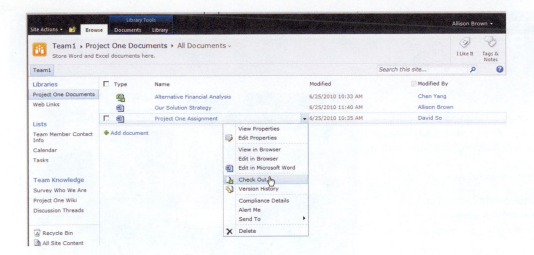

Figure 9-15 shows a screen for a user of Microsoft SharePoint 2010. The user, Allison Brown (shown in the upper right-hand corner of the screen), is checking out a document named Problem One Assignment. Once she has it checked out, she can edit it and return it to this library.

As described so far, this locking capability is similar to that of Google Docs and Microsoft SkyDrive. The only difference is that users have explicit control over checking documents out and in. However, in addition to checkout/check-in capabilities, version-control systems maintain version histories like the SharePoint document history shown in Figure 9-16. This history shows the version number and check-in date of that version, as well as the name of the user, the size of the document when checked in, and comments that the user wrote when he or she checked the document in.

FIGURE 9-16

Document Version History

Version History

Delete All Versions

No. ↓	Modified	Modified By	Size	Comments
5.0	6/25/2010 11:40 AM	Allison Brown	18.4 KB	Made suggestions for the way we address competitive advantage.
4.0	6/25/2010 11:40 AM	Allison Brown	18.4 KB	Made suggestions for the way we address competitive advantage.
3.0	6/25/2010 11:38 AM	Julian Isla	18.4 KB	Included suggestions on changing our financial analysis
2.0	6/25/2010 11:37 AM	David So	18.3 KB	I added my comments to Corrina's.
1.0	6/25/2010 10:31 AM	Corinna Bolender	17.9 KB	

MIS InClass 9

Virtual Practice!

In this contest, you and a group of your classmates will compete against other teams in a short collaborative project. Every member of your team will need access to a networked computer with a browser in order to participate.

The ground rules of this contest are as follows:

a. This contest tests, in part, your ability to meet virtually. Consequently, in Phase 2 you are not allowed to meet and communicate face-to-face with your team members.

b. You will be assigned the use of either Google Docs or Microsoft SkyDrive. You must use your assigned product, along with e-mail or texting, for all of your work.

c. Your work will be judged in terms of the speed with which you can create results as well as on the quality of your team's work product.

The contest is divided into two phases, as described below.

Source: Goodshoot Getty Images–Thinkstock.

Phase 1

1. Your team has been assigned the use of either Google Docs or Microsoft SkyDrive. Each of your team members needs to obtain an account that will enable him or her to edit documents using the collaborative tool you have been assigned. Meet with your team members and determine what each person needs to do to make that happen. Agree on the methods by which your team will work. Assign one person as the team leader.

2. Each team member should:
   a. Obtain any account necessary from either Google or Microsoft.
   b. Share the name of your account with your teammates.
   c. Create a document that contains your name, contact data for this exercise, your home town, and your hobbies. Store this document on Google Docs or SkyDrive, depending on which you are assigned.
   d. Share the stored document with your teammates.

3. Consolidate all of your documents into a single document. Your team leader can determine how best to do that and communicate the technique to be used to the rest of the team.

4. When you have completed this activity, your team leader should send a link to your consolidated document to your instructor so that he or she can verify that you have accomplished this activity. Your instructor will only need read access to your document. Your team will score points based upon how quickly it has accomplished this activity.

5. Review Phase 2 with your teammates to be certain that everyone understands what is required.

6. After this point, no face-to-face communication is allowed.

Phase 2

Suppose you made a serious mistake when scheduling your classes and you discover that you are not enrolled in a class that you must take this term in order to graduate. Unfortunately, all sections of that class are full. In this phase, your team will work collaboratively to determine the best strategy that your team can conceive for getting into this needed, but closed, class.

1. Working as an individual:
   a. Create a document that describes your best idea for getting into the class.
   b. Use Google Docs or Microsoft SkyDrive to share your documents with your team.

2. Have one team member combine all of the team members' documents into a single document.

3. Working as an individual:
   a. Review the consolidated document and edit it as you think appropriate.
   b. Add new ideas, raise issues about existing ideas, or resolve problems.
   c. Leave evidence in the document that you have contributed.
   d. When you are satisfied with your team's answer, leave a statement to that effect, with your name, in the document.

4. When all team members have indicated that they are satisfied with the answer, the team leader should send a link to the document to your instructor. Your team will score points based on the speed and quality of your work.

5. Present your document to the rest of the class.

Numerous version-control applications exist. For general business use, SharePoint is the most popular; we will discuss it in Q6. Other document-control systems include MasterControl (*www.mastercontrol.com*) and Document Locator (*www.documentlocator.com*). Software development teams use applications such as CVS (*www.nongnu.org/cvs*) or Subversion (*http://subversion.apache.org*) to control versions of software code, test plans, and product documentation.

Q5. How Can You Use Microsoft SharePoint for Student Team Projects?

Microsoft SharePoint is a comprehensive platform for creating, operating, and administrating Web sites. It is most widely known as a platform for creating and managing collaboration sites, and we will consider it in the collaboration context here. However, SharePoint can also be used as the backbone of more general purpose Web sites. For example, the New Zealand tourism Web site *www.kiwiexperience.com* is based on SharePoint.

Basic-level SharePoint is part of Windows Server, but it is beyond the scope of this course for you to install it and set it up. Instead, your professor can ask Pearson, this text's publisher, to set up SharePoint on behalf of your university. **Office 365**, a new program from Microsoft, includes Lync, Exchange (e-mail), and SharePoint. If your university participates in this program, you will have access to all of those products. Or, possibly, your IS department may have set up SharePoint for use by your class. In any case, to use it your group will need access to a SharePoint server.

With a few basic skills, it is quite easy to create a SharePoint collaboration site and to set it up for use on student projects. That site can then be customized using SharePoint tools in your browser. For additional customization, you can use Microsoft Office SharePoint Designer, a tool specifically designed to tailor the look and feel of SharePoint sites. For even greater customization and control, developers can use Microsoft Visual Studio.

In this question, we will discuss some of the SharePoint features that are useful for student projects. We will not discuss how to create those features, however. If you want to learn more about how to create and customize SharePoint sites, see *SharePoint for Students*.[4]

SharePoint Features Recommended for Student Teams

To begin, a **SharePoint site** is a collection of resources that are created and managed via SharePoint and accessed using HTTP, HTML, and related protocols. In our case, the resources are used for collaboration, but, as noted earlier, they can be used for general-purpose Web sites as well. A SharePoint site can contain one or more subsites, which are fully featured SharePoint sites in their own right.

Figure 9-17 shows a SharePoint site that has been created for use by a student team. The name of the site is *Team 1,* as you can tell from the upper left-hand corner of the figure. The Team 1 site contains many different pages; the notation Team 1 → Home means this figure is showing the Home page of the Team 1 site. The left-hand column is called the **Quick Launch**

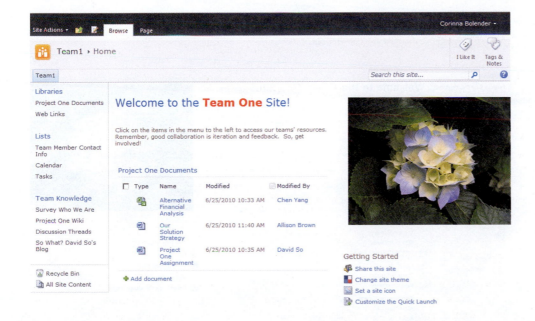

FIGURE 9-17

Example Student Team Site

---

[4] Carey Cole, Steve Fox, and David Kroenke, *SharePoint for Students* (Upper Saddle River, NJ: Pearson Education, 2012).

FIGURE 9-18

**Example Web Links
Library**

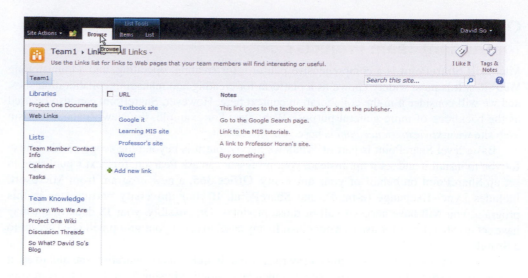

menu, and it is a partial list of resources contained within the site. If the user clicks, say, *Web Links*, SharePoint will display a list of links to additional Web sites, as shown in Figure 9-18.

The center of the Home page in Figure 9-17 contains the contents of the list named *Project One Documents*. Any of the lists in Quick Launch could be shown in this same position or in some other position on the Home page. The team that uses this site thought the most important list is this document library, so they chose to place it here in the center of the Home page.

In most cases, a team would replace the picture of the flower with a picture of the team members or of something related to the team's assignment. Finally, the list in the bottom right-hand corner has links to other actions team members might take on this site.

Fundamentally, SharePoint is a list manager. Each of the items in Quick Launch is a list of items of some type. For example, *Project One Documents* is a list of documents for team members to share. *Web Links* is a list of Web links, as shown in Figure 9-18. *Team Member Contact Info is* a list of team members, their e-mail addresses, phone numbers, and so forth. *Calendar* is a list of events shown in the calendar; *Tasks* is a list of team tasks; and so forth.

The actions that can be taken on the elements in a list depend on the type of list. Project One Documents is a document list; the actions available for documents are shown in Figure 9-19. If the user clicks *View in Browser* or *Edit in Browser*, SharePoint will open the document in the

FIGURE 9-19

**SharePoint Document
Actions**

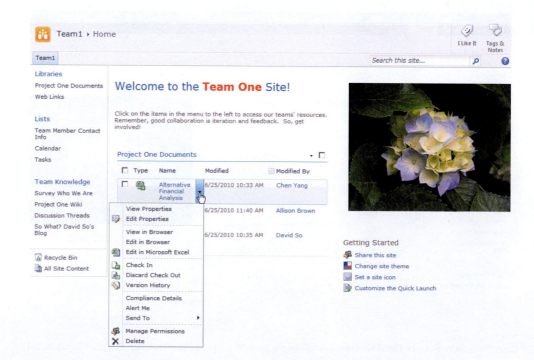

FIGURE 9-20

SharePoint Team Calendar

Microsoft Word Web App (discussed under SkyDrive). Other options include checking out and checking in, producing a version history, and other options, including Delete.

One option is particularly useful for team work. If you click *Alert Me*, SharePoint will send you an e-mail any time anyone changes the document. This is particularly useful for lists that have the latest breaking news, such as an Announcement list (not shown here).

Figure 9-20 shows a Calendar list. An event has already been scheduled for November 10, and the user is in the process of adding a new event on November 8. You can change the calendar format to weekly and daily as well.

SharePoint provides a special type of list called a *Tasks list*. Figure 9-21 shows an example Tasks list with three tasks. Notice that the task is assigned to a particular person and that each task has Status, Due Date, and %Complete metadata. If the task has predecessor tasks that must be completed before that task, those predecessors can also be added to the Tasks list. SharePoint can produce a Gantt diagram of tasks, if desired (not shown).

SharePoint surveys are easy to create and use. Figure 9-22 shows a page for completing an example survey.

Teams can readily create wiki libraries using SharePoint. Figure 9-23 shows the top-level page called *Project One Wiki*. By default, team members can easily change the text on each page, but SharePoint permissions can be set to allow only certain members to edit entries, if desired. Note in this figure that Project 1 and Project 1 Grade are links to other wiki pages, as are the three phrases at the bottom of this figure. The links Project 2 and Project 3 have been entered into this page, but underlining of the link names indicates that those pages have not yet been created.

The last resource we will discuss on this site is a blog created and managed by one of the team members, David So. Look back to Figure 9-19. If the user clicks *So What? David So's Blog* in Quick Launch, SharePoint will display the current page of David So's blog, as

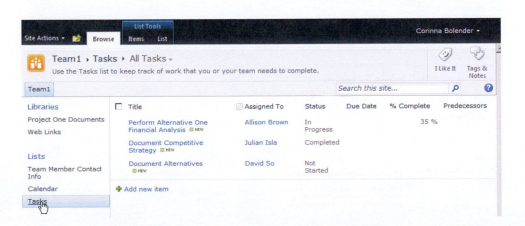

FIGURE 9-21

SharePoint Tasks List

FIGURE 9-22

Taking a SharePoint Survey

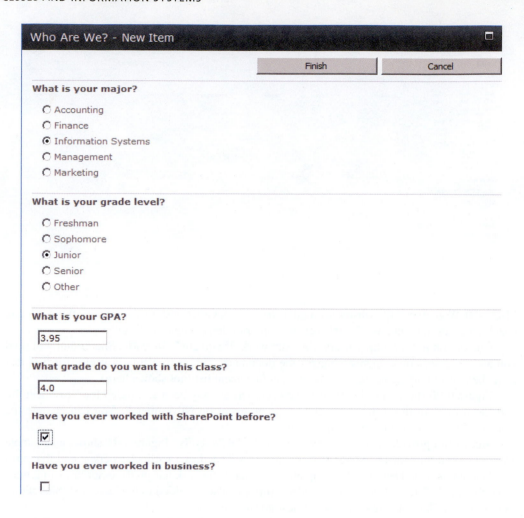

shown in Figure 9-24. David So can add entries. Team members can submit entries for David So's approval. If he approves them, they will be added to the blog. Any team member can make a comment to a blog entry, but David So can remove it if he wants.

What Are Recommended Uses for Particular SharePoint Tools?

SharePoint provides many different tools for teams to use. To decide which might be appropriate for you, consider Figure 9-25, which lists common SharePoint collaboration tools and recommends potential applications for them.

FIGURE 9-23

Example SharePoint Wiki Page

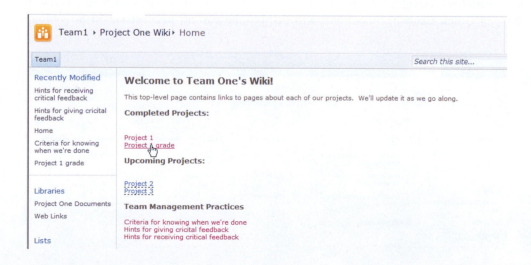

FIGURE 9-24

Example SharePoint Blog

Document libraries serve as a repository for team documents. You might have different libraries for different aspects of the project. For example, if your project involves cost assessments, you might have a library that has all the documents concerning costs. Or, you might put all the Word documents in one library, all the Excel documents in a second, and so forth. Document libraries can be set up to require check out and check in as well as to have version histories.

Lists are good for tracking anything. SharePoint provides default lists for events (calendar lists), tasks, and contacts. You can also create a custom list type for tracking the characteristics of any resource.

Surveys are good for getting to know your teammates, for verifying understanding of project goals and other topics, and for deciding when to wrap up the project. The team can use wikis to create a team glossary, to show the relationships among defined terms, and to document the team's knowledge.

Discussion forums provide a means to asynchronously discuss any issue—and to track the comments made by different authors. They can also be used to share knowledge. Finally, one or more team members (or groups) can publish blogs using the built-in SharePoint blogging capability.

SharePoint Feature	Use
Document library	Single repository of team documents Can have multiple libraries Can require check out/check in Can ask SharePoint to maintain version history
Lists	Track events, tasks, contacts Create a general-purpose list for tracking any resource
Survey	Introduce team members Verify understanding of goals and other topics Wrap up project
Wiki	Share and document team knowledge
Discussion forums	Discuss one or more topics
Blog	Publish opinions and get feedback on them

FIGURE 9-25

Potential Uses of SharePoint Features

By all means, if you have an opportunity to use SharePoint while in school, do so. It is an easily learned and very powerful product. And, as mentioned, SharePoint skills are highly marketable today.

Q6. How Can Collaboration Systems Control Workflow?

In Q3 and Q4, you learned how information systems can be used to facilitate team communication and manage content, two of the three critical collaboration drivers. **Workflow control**, the third driver, is the process of ensuring that business processes are properly executed. Although the term could legitimately be applied to any business process, it is normally used in conjunction with processes that involve collaborative teamwork. SharePoint provides automated support for workflow control via a set of features called *workflows*. A **workflow** is a sequence of activities that is managed and logged by SharePoint.

Microsoft SharePoint workflows can manage workflows over documents, lists, and other types of content. SharePoint ships with several built-in workflows; we will illustrate one of them here. In addition, business analysts can create custom workflows using a graphical interface in SharePoint Designer. It is also possible to create workflows using Visio and then import them into SharePoint Designer. Finally, those with computer programming skills can create highly customized workflows using Visual Studio and development languages such as C# or Visual Basic.

The Workflow Problem Requirements

To illustrate document workflow control, suppose that a departmental manager wants two people to review all documents that are submitted to a particular SharePoint **document library**, which is a named collection of documents in SharePoint. Whenever a document is added to the document library, the manager wants the document to be reviewed first by employee Joseph Schumpeter and then by employee Adam Smith. Such an arrangement is called a **sequential workflow** because the review activities occur in sequence. In a **parallel workflow**, the reviews would occur simultaneously. Numerous other types of workflows are possible, but we will not consider them here.[5]

You *can* manage a workflow like this manually, sending e-mails, checking to see if the reviews are done, sending reminder e-mails, etc. However, doing so often (usually?) results in an administrative nightmare, and these are the sorts of tasks that information systems do well. Using SharePoint will reduce administrative costs and improve reliability.

Figure 9-26 illustrates the application of the Gather Feedback workflow, one of the workflows that is built in to SharePoint. With it, when a document creator submits a document to a particular SharePoint library (labeled *Data Repository* in Figure 9-26), SharePoint starts a workflow. It sends an e-mail announcing the start of the workflow to the product manager as well as an e-mail to Joseph Schumpeter telling him that he has been requested to review the document. SharePoint workflow also inserts an activity for Schumpeter into a SharePoint Tasks list.

Schumpeter reviews the document (he will need to obtain it from the data repository, but this arrow has been omitted from Figure 9-26 for clarity). After he has made his review, he will store his comments in the task and mark it as completed. At that point, SharePoint sends an e-mail to the next reviewer, Adam Smith, and creates a task for Smith in the Tasks list. After Smith has completed his review, he stores his comments in the Tasks list and marks his task as completed. At this point, SharePoint sends a Workflow Completed e-mail to the product manager.

---

[5] For more information about workflows and the Windows Workflow Foundation, see Mark J. Collins, *Office 2010 Workflow* (New York: Apress, 2010).

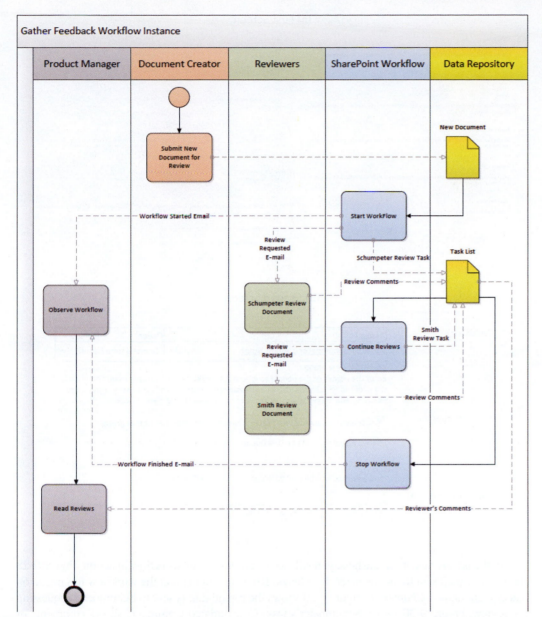

FIGURE 9-26

**Gather Feedback
Workflow**

Implementing the Workflow

Figure 9-27 shows how the product manager creates the workflow. She would go to the document library that is to have the workflow and select Create Workflow. SharePoint would display the screen shown in Figure 9-27(a). Here, she specifies the Collect Feedback workflow type, names the workflow, specifies a list to store the tasks, and creates a list to contain a history of the workflow's action. A variety of Start Options are possible; here she allows the workflow to be started manually and also requests that SharePoint automatically start it when a new document is added to the library.

On the next screen, shown in Figure 9-27(b), she names Schumpeter and Smith as reviewers and types the text that will be sent in the request e-mail (ignore the Expand Groups entry). Finally, she provides a due date for completion of all the tasks.

From this point forward, any time anyone creates a new document in this library, SharePoint will run this workflow on that document.

FIGURE 9-27

Creating a Collect Feedback Workflow

(a) First Screen

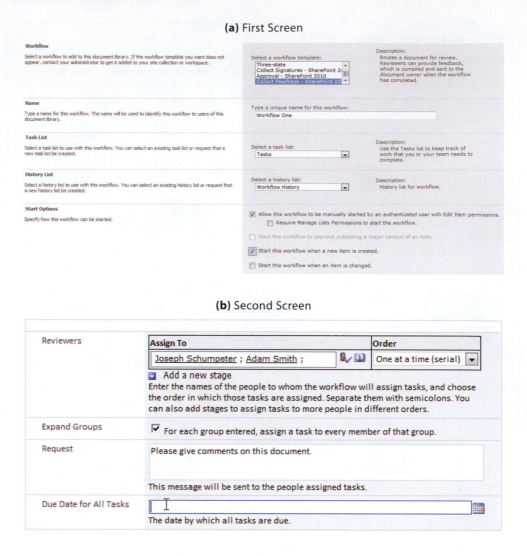

(b) Second Screen

In the next series of screenshots, you will see examples of this workflow in action. Figure 9-28 shows the e-mail sent to the manager (here David Kroenke) stating that the workflow has begun on a document named *Chapter_1*. Figure 9-29 shows the e-mail that is sent to Schumpeter requesting the review. Figure 9-30 shows Schumpeter's task. Consolidated Comments shows comments of prior reviewers; here there are none. Schumpeter types his comments into the Comments field.

FIGURE 9-28

Workflow Started E-Mail to Project Manager

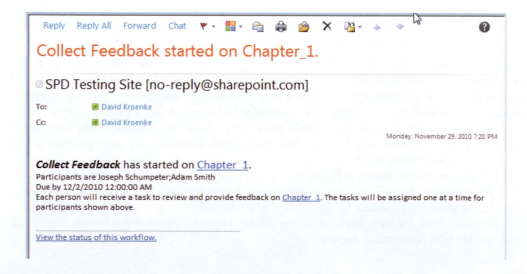

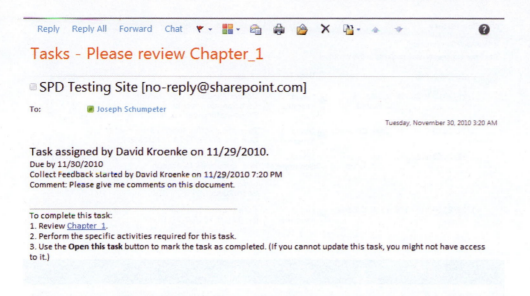

FIGURE 9-29

Review Request E-Mail Sent to Schumpeter

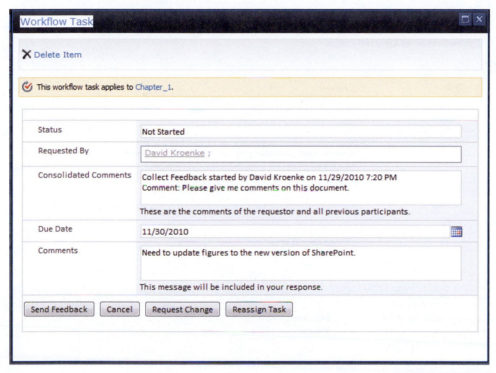

FIGURE 9-30

Task Given to Schumpeter

Figure 9-31 shows the Tasks list after Schumpeter's review. Notice that Schumpeter's task is marked as complete and that SharePoint has created a new task for Adam Smith that has not yet been started. Figure 9-32 shows the history of this workflow after Schumpeter's review but before Smith's review.

When Smith completes his review, he will type his comments in the Tasks list form shown in Figure 9-33. Notice that he can read Schumpeter's comment in this form as he types his own remarks in the Comments list. Figure 9-34 shows one of the reports available to depict the status

FIGURE 9-31

Tasks List After Schumpeter's Review

FIGURE 9-32

Workflow History List After Schumpeter Review

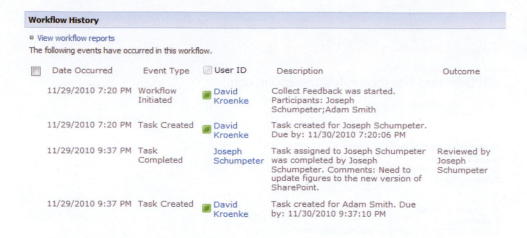

FIGURE 9-33

Task Given to Adam Smith

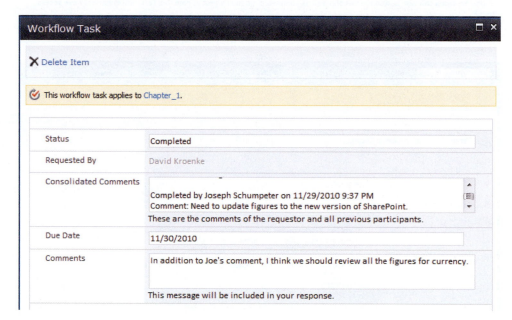

FIGURE 9-34

Workflow After Smith's Review

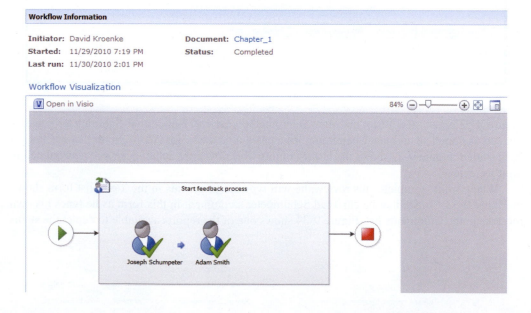

FIGURE 9-35

Workflow History After Smith's Review

of the workflow. This report, which could possibly be quite complex for a different workflow, can be opened with Visio as well.

Figure 9-35 shows the final workflow history, and Figure 9-36 shows the Workflow Completed e-mail sent to the product manager. Notice that all of the reviewer's comments are included in this e-mail.

If either of the reviewers does not complete his review on time, SharePoint will send reminder e-mails to the reviewer as well as the manager. This will continue until either the review is completed or the workflow is cancelled.

Workflow control is powerful, and like any powerful tool needs to be used with care. If hundreds of documents are added to the library, the manager and reviewer's e-mail inboxes will be inundated with requests and status notices. Also, multiple workflows can operate at the same time, and unending loops are possible. For example, if one workflow makes changes to a library that has a second workflow, and if that second workflow makes changes to the library that has the first, the two workflows will get into an infinite loop, spewing e-mails all over the organization! See Windischman et al. for more cautions regarding workflows.[6]

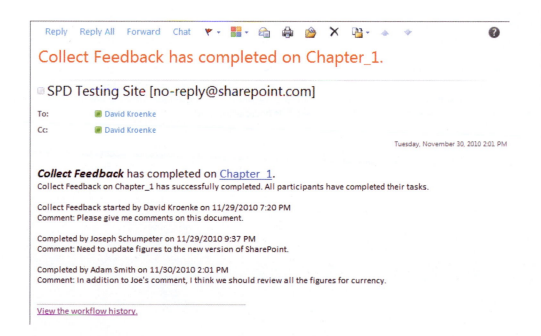

FIGURE 9-36

E-Mail to Product Manager at Workflow Completion

---

[6] Woodrow W. Windischman, Asif Rehamani, Bryan Phillips, Marcy Kellar, *Beginning SharePoint Designer 2010* (Indianapolis: Wiley, 2011), pp. 378, 379.

Ethics Guide

Virtual Ethics?

The term *virtual* means something that appears to exist but does not exist in fact. A *virtual private network (VPN)* is a computer network that appears to be private, but in fact operates on a public network The term *virtual meeting* describes a meeting in which everyone is present, but via an information system and not face-to-face.

However, and it is a big *however*, "Is everyone present?" Is the person who signed on as David So truly David So? Or is it someone else? Or is it David So with a staff of seven people, all of whom are anonymous to the rest of the group? Figures 9-16 through 9-19 show a SharePoint site used by Allison Brown, Corinna Bolender, and David So. What if none of them was really involved? What if, in fact, those contributions were really made by Ashley, Haley, and Jordan, but none of them knew the others were *spoofing* (pretending to be someone they are not)? What if Haley was actually Corinna's daughter sitting in her organizational behavior class at college, making casual contributions, while Corinna played golf?

Suppose you run a consulting company and you want to send less experienced consultants out on jobs. During an initial meeting (held electronically, using text chat) with a potential client, you tell the client that he is meeting with Drew Suenas, a new and inexperienced employee. But, the meeting actually includes Drew and Eleanor Jackson, your most experienced and senior consultant. During the meeting, all of the remarks attributed to Drew were actually made by Eleanor. The client is most impressed with what it thinks are Drew's perceptive comments about its situation and agrees to hire Drew, even though he is inexperienced. You keep using Eleanor this way, spoofing several of your young associates to get jobs for them. You justify this by saying, "Well, if they get into trouble, we'll send Eleanor out to fix the problem."

Or, suppose you have an archrival, Ashley. You and Ashley compete for a future promotion, and you just cannot stand the idea of her moving ahead of you. So you set up a sequence of virtual meetings, but you never invite Ashley. Then, just before a crucial meeting, one that involves senior members of your organization, you invite Ashley to be your silent helper. You tell her you do not have the authority to invite her, but you want her to have a chance to express her thoughts. So you attend the meeting and you incorporate Ashley's thinking into your chat comments. People think you are the sole author of those ideas and are impressed. Ashley's work is never attributed to her.

Consider another possibility. Suppose David So is an independent consultant who has been hired to write the blog in Figure 9-24. David, who is very busy, hires Charlotte to write the blog for him. David bills his time for $110 an hour and pays Charlotte $45, keeping the difference. And, he has free time for more paid work. David reviews her work, but he does none of it himself. The client never knows that it's Charlotte, not David, who writes the blog.

Or, let's bring it closer to home. Suppose you take online tests as part of your class. What keeps you from taking the test with your brother, who happens to work for Google as a product manager for Google Docs? Suppose you take the test by yourself, but you believe others are taking their tests with silent helpers. Given that belief, are you justified in finding your own helper?

What do you think? Are your ethics virtual?

Discussion Questions

1. Is it *illegal* to spoof someone? Does it matter whether you have that person's permission to spoof them?

2. Is it *ethical* to spoof someone? Does it matter whether you have that person's permission?

3. Under what circumstances do you believe it is ethical to spoof someone?

4. Consider the SharePoint site in which everyone was spoofing and no one knew it. What are the consequences to the organization of having such a site?

5. Considering Eleanor's spoofing of young associates, what is different between text chat and a speaker phone? Haven't we always had these problems, except Eleanor was passing notes and making comments while the phone was muted? What behavior should you follow when talking with someone who is on a speaker phone? How does the videoconferencing capability of products like Lync change this situation?

6. Is it ethical for David So to hire someone to write the blog for him? As long as the client is satisfied with the blog, does it matter? After all, David reviews all of her work.

7. Is it cheating to have a helper on an online test? Are you justified if everyone else is doing it? What control is possible for online tests? Should such tests be used at all?

Active Review

Use this Active Review to verify that you understand the material in the chapter. You can read the entire chapter and then perform the tasks in this review, or you can read the text material for just one question and perform the tasks in this review for that question before moving on to the next one.

Q1. What makes for effective collaboration?

Distinguish between cooperative and collaborative teams and give an example of each. Explain the importance of feedback and iteration. List critical collaboration skills. State three criteria for judging a team's success.

Q2. What are characteristics of fundamental collaboration processes?

Name the three primary applications of collaboration in business. Explain which types of decisions require collaboration and explain why. Explain why a decision that is made by a sole individual can still be collaborative. Summarize the activities in Figure 9-3 and describe the content of a decision-making data repository. Define *problem*. State what is often the most difficult part of solving a problem and explain why. Summarize the activities in Figure 9-4 and describe the content of a problem-solving data repository. List the four activities of the project management process. Explain activities for each and define the content of a project management repository.

Q3. How can collaboration systems improve team communication?

Explain why communication is important to student collaborations. Define *synchronous* and *asynchronous communication* and explain when each is used. Name two collaboration tools that can be used to help set up synchronous meetings. Describe

collaboration tools that can be used for face-to-face meetings. Describe tools that can be used for virtual, synchronous meetings. Describe tools that can be used for virtual, asynchronous meetings. Compare and contrast the advantages of e-mail, discussion forums, and team surveys.

Q4. How can collaboration systems manage content?

Describe two ways that content is shared with no control and explain the problems that can occur. Explain how control is provided by the following collaboration tools: wikis, Google Docs, and Microsoft SkyDrive. Explain the difference between version management and version control. Describe how user accounts, passwords, and libraries are used to control user activity. Explain how check in/check out works.

Q5. How can you use Microsoft SharePoint for student team projects?

Define *SharePoint* and explain its broader role as well as the role discussed here. Summarize three ways of customizing a SharePoint site. Define *SharePoint site* and explain what a subsite is. Explain the role of Quick Launch. Describe what happens when the user clicks each of the items in the Quick Launch menu shown in Figure 9-14. Summarize the features, functions, and roles for SharePoint.

Q6. How can collaboration systems control workflow?

Describe reasons why a team might want to use a tool like SharePoint to manage workflows. Explain the difference between a sequential workflow and a parallel workflow. Using Figure 9-26 as a guide, explain how SharePoint uses e-mail and Tasks lists to manage a workflow.

Key Terms and Concepts

Asynchronous communication   *283*
Collaborative team   *274*
Conference calls   *284*
Content management   *285*
Cooperative team   *274*

Discussion forums   *285*
Document library   *296*
Dogfooding   *307*
File server   *285*
Google Docs   *286*

Google Talk   *284*
Libraries   *288*
Microsoft Lync   *284*
Microsoft SharePoint   *291*
Microsoft SkyDrive   *287*

Multiparty text chat *284*
Office 365 *291*
Office Web Apps *287*
Operational decisions *277*
Parallel workflow *296*
Problem *280*
Quick Launch *291*
Sequential workflow *296*

SharedView *284*
SharePoint site *291*
Strategic decisions *278*
Synchronous communication *283*
Team surveys *285*
Version control *288*
Version management *286*
Videoconferencing *284*

Virtual meetings *284*
WebEx *284*
Webinars *284*
Wiki *286*
Workflow control *296*
Workflow *296*

Using Your Knowledge

1. Suppose your university's varsity football team has had a losing season for the past 3 years. (If you don't like football, choose any other varsity sport.) Using Figure 9-3 as a guide, summarize the process your university should use in deciding whether to fire the head coach. Specify the objectives and measures of this process (the objectives may include complete the process on time, fairness, completeness, etc.). Be as specific as possible; make assumptions and justify them, if necessary.

2. Suppose that during your college's review process with the AACSB (the agency that accredits colleges of business), your college is told that it needs to reduce the average grade given in business classes. Suppose that the dean of your college believes that this directive cannot be ignored. Using Figure 9-4 as a guide, summarize the process your college should use to solve this problem. Be as specific as possible; make assumptions and justify them, if necessary.

3. Reflect on your experience working on teams in previous classes as well as on collaborative teams in other settings, such as a campus committee. To what extent was your team collaborative? Did it involve feedback and iteration? If so, how? How did you use collaborative information systems, if at all? If you did not use collaborative information systems, describe how you think such systems might have improved your work methods and results. If you did use collaborative information systems, explain how you could improve on that use, given the knowledge you have gained from this chapter.

4. This exercise requires you to experiment with Google Docs. You will need two Google accounts to complete this exercise. If you have two different e-mail addresses, then set up two Google accounts using those addresses. Otherwise, use your school e-mail address and set up a Google Gmail account. A Gmail account will automatically give you a Google account.
   a. Using Microsoft Word, write a memo to yourself. In the memo, explain the nature of the communication collaboration driver. Go to *http://docs.google.com* and sign in with one of your Google accounts. Upload your memo using Google Docs. Save your uploaded document and share your document with the e-mail in your second Google account. Sign out of your first Google account.
      (If you have access to two computers situated close to each other, use both of them for this exercise. You will see more of the Google Docs functionality by using two computers. If you have two computers, do not sign out of your Google account. Perform step b and all actions for the second account on that second computer. If you are using two computers, ignore the instructions in the following steps to sign out of the Google accounts.)
   b. Open a new window in your browser. Access *http://docs.google.com* from that second window and sign in using your second Google account. Open the document that you shared in step a.
   c. Change the memo by adding a brief description of the content-management driver. Save the document from your second account. If you are using just one computer, sign out from your second account.
   d. Sign in on your first account. Open the most recent version of the memo and add a description of the role of version histories. Save the document. (If you are using two computers, notice how Google warns you that another user is editing the document at the same time. Click *Refresh* to see what happens.) If you are using just one computer, sign out from your first account.
   e. Sign in on your second account. Reopen the shared document. From the File menu, save the document as a Word document. Describe how Google processed the changes to your document.

5. This exercise requires you to experiment with Microsoft SkyDrive. You will need two Office Live IDs to complete this exercise. The easiest way to do it is to work with a classmate. If that is not possible, set up two Office Live accounts using two different Hotmail addresses.
   a. Go to *www.skydrive.com* and sign in with one of your accounts. Create a memo about collaboration

tools using the Word Web App. Save your memo. Share your document with the e-mail in your second Office Live account. Sign out of your first account.

(If you have access to two computers situated close to each other, use both of them for this exercise. If you have two computers, do not sign out of your Office Live account. Perform step b and all actions for the second account on that second computer. If you are using two computers, ignore the instructions in the following steps to sign out of the Office Live accounts.)

b. Open a new window in your browser. Access *www.skydrive.com* from that second window and sign in using your second Office Live account. Open the document that you shared in step a.

c. Change the memo by adding a brief description of content management. Do not save the document yet. If you are using just one computer, sign out from your second account.

d. Sign in on your first account. Attempt to open the memo and note what occurs. Sign out of your first account and sign back in with your second account. Save the document. Now, sign out of your second account and sign back in with the first account. Now attempt to open the memo. (If you are using two computers, perform these same actions on the two different computers.)

e. Sign in on your second account. Reopen the shared document. From the File menu, save the document as a Word document. Describe how Microsoft SkyDrive processed the changes to your document.

Collaboration Exercise 9

The purpose of this exercise is for you and a team of your fellow students to improve your collaboration skills. It has three activities. During the first, you are asked to reflect on ways that you can improve your collaboration skills. During the second, your team will use collaboration to solve a problem. During the last activity, you will have a chance to reflect on what you have done. Use Google Docs, Microsoft SkyDrive, SharePoint, Office 365, or some other collaboration system to conduct your meetings.

Activity 1: Set Goals for Improving Collaboration Skills

a. With your team, discuss the collaboration skills presented in Figure 9-1. Create your own ranking of what you believe to be the most important collaboration skills. Justify any differences between your team's conclusion and the results of the survey in Figure 9-1.

b. As a team, choose the two highest skills in your list in Figure 9-1 that your team believes it needs to improve. Explain your choice. Use feedback and iteration as much as possible.

c. For the two skills you choose in item b, identify specific ways in which you can improve. State goals both for individuals and for your team.

Activity 2: Solve the Problem at the Start of Chapter 2

In this activity, you will solve the problem presented at the start of Chapter 2. For your solution, assume that the intramural league has a full-time director, Dawn Jenkins; a full-time office manager, Mary Anne (see introduction to Chapter 4); and 11 part-time student employees.

a. Examine the problem-solution process in Figure 9-4. Discuss this process as a team and decide if you want to change it. If so, describe your changes. If not, explain why not.

b. Follow the process you developed in item a. Be certain that you employ feedback and iteration, particularly critical feedback, in your solution.

c. Document your solution as directed by your instructor.

Activity 3: Reflect

a. As individual team members, evaluate how well you did in accomplishing your goals in activity 1. Summarize how well your team did as a whole in accomplishing those goals. Document your opinions as individuals.

b. Meet as a team and develop a team evaluation of how well you did with your goals in activity 1. Use feedback and iteration in this process.

c. Submit your individual response to item a and your team's response in item b, as directed by your instructor.

CASE STUDY 9

Eating Our Own Dog Food

Dogfooding is the process of using a product or idea that you have developed or promoted. The term arose in the 1980s in the software industry when someone observed that their company wasn't using the product they had developed, or, "they weren't eating their own dog food." Wikipedia attributes the term to Brian Valentine, test manager for Microsoft LAN Manager in 1988, but the authors of this text recall using the term before that date. Whatever its origin, if, of their own accord, employees choose to dogfood their own product or idea, many believe that product or idea is likely to succeed.

You may be asking, "So what?" Well, this text was developed by a collaborative team using Office 365 and many of the techniques described in this chapter. We dogfooded the ideas and products in this chapter.

To see how, first consider Figure 9-37, which summarizes the major processes for a textbook between its inception and your purchase of it. During concept development, authors prepare descriptive material and sample chapters and submit them to the publisher. If the publisher's acquisition editor sees merit in the project, it is sent out for review assessment by potential professor users. If the reviews are positive, the project is approved and the authors write draft chapters, which are also reviewed. When the acquisition editor deems all of the chapters ready for production, the text enters the second major process, text development.

During this activity, the book is designed, chapter text is improved by a copy editor, the art and chapter figures are prepared, and eventually PDF pages are produced, approved, and used to print the book. The last two processes, sales and order fulfillment, do not concern us here.

Figure 9-38 shows a BPMN diagram of the process that transforms a draft chapter in Word, PowerPoint, and PNG image format into PDF pages. During this process, the authors work closely with the developmental editor, who ensures that the text is complete and complies with the market requirements, as specified by the acquisitions editor. We need not delve into this process in detail here; just observe that many different versions of chapter text and chapter art are created as people playing the various roles edit and approve and adjust edits.

(By the way, this BPMN diagram is a bit deceiving because it makes this process appear to be structured rather than dynamic. In fact, the process is not nearly so well structured. Sometimes authors are involved in reviewing art, sometimes not. Sometimes the acquisition editor is involved in reviewing

Process	Major Activities
Concept development	Authors develop concept documentation Acquisition editor reviews Potential using professors' review Go/no go decision Authors develop first draft Additional professor reviews Authors revise as needed
Text development	Book design Authors prepare chapter drafts for production Preproduction chapter editing Copyediting Art creation PDF pages produced PDF pages reviewed Copies printed
Sales	Sales force learns purpose and strengths of text Sales force calls on professors
Order fulfillment	Bookstores order Students buy

FIGURE 9-37
Textbook Processes

FIGURE 9-38

Chapter PDF Development Process

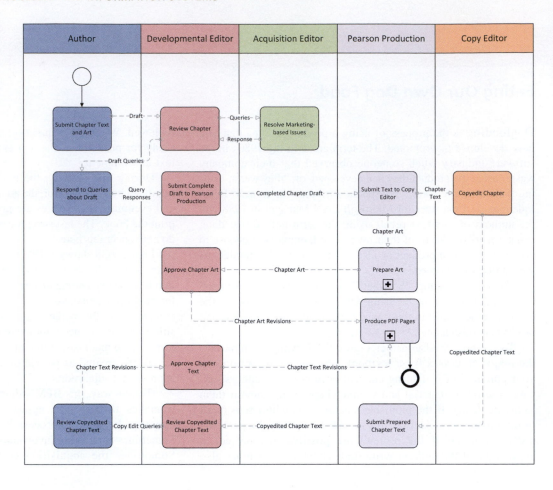

chapter text, sometimes not. Take this diagram as the gist, the overall nature of this process, and not as a literal, only-to-be-done this way diagram.)

Face-to-face meetings are normally impossible because the people fulfilling the roles in Figure 9-38 usually live in different geographic locations. In the past, the developmental process was conducted using e-mail and an FTP server. As you can imagine, considerable confusion can ensue with the hundreds of documents, art exhibits, and multiple reviewed copies of each. Furthermore, task requests that are delivered via e-mail are easily lost. Dropped tasks and incorrect versions of documents and art are not common, but they do occur.

The authors of this text decided to eat their own dogfood and use Microsoft Office 365 for the production of this text. Each week, the two authors and the developmental editor, Laura Town, would meet via Lync. Figure 9-39 shows a typical Lync meeting. Notice that the three actors in this process are sharing a common whiteboard. Each can write or draw on that whiteboard. In the second screenshot in Figure 9-39, each actor placed his or her name above the text they entered. At the end of the meeting, the whiteboards were saved and placed on the team's SharePoint site to be used as minutes of the meeting.

Figure 9-40 shows the team's SharePoint site. The left side displays a menu, called Quick Launch, that has links to important content on the site. The center portion has tasks that have a value other than Completed for Status. The right-hand section has a library of saved whiteboards from team meetings.

The team set up alerts so that when new tasks were created in the Tasks list, SharePoint would send an e-mail to the person who had been assigned that task. Figure 9-41 shows an e-mail that was sent to David Kroenke when Laura added a task to the Tasks list.

All documents and figures were stored and managed in SharePoint libraries. Figure 9-42 shows the library that contains the figures for this chapter. With so many figures and so much review and editing, it is easy to confuse figures and versions. By storing them in SharePoint, the team took advantage of library version tracking. Figure 9-43 shows the version history of the text of this chapter. As you can see, David has created numerous versions; Earl has reviewed just one of them in the middle of the chapter's evolution. Earl needs to review the final chapter version, so a task should be created asking him to do so. That new task will spawn an e-mail to him like the e-mail in Figure 9-41. I (David) will create that task just as soon as I finish this sentence! That's dogfooding!

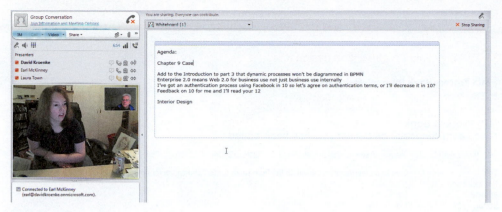

FIGURE 9-39

Lync Weekly Meeting

FIGURE 9-40

SharePoint Team Home Page

FIGURE 9-41

Task Alert E-Mail

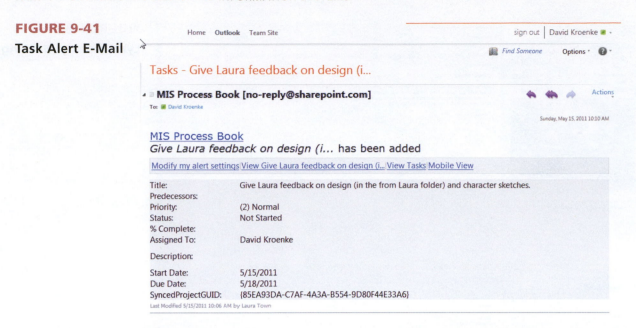

FIGURE 9-42

Chapter 9 Figure Library

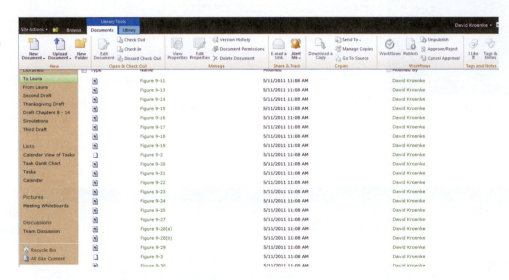

FIGURE 9-43

Chapter 9 Version History

Questions

1. In your own words, define *dogfooding*. Do you think dogfooding is likely to predict product success? Why or why not? When would dogfooding not predict product success?

2. Is dogfooding a structured or a dynamic process? List possible objectives of dogfooding processes.

3. Examine Figure 9-38 and list three to five objectives and measures of those objectives that you think would be appropriate for this process.

4. If the diagram in Figure 9-38 is only a structured approximation to an unstructured process, does it have any value? Why or why not?

5. Explain how this team uses the shared whiteboard to generate minutes. What are the advantages of this technique?

6. Explain how this team uses alerts. Summarize the advantages of using alerts.

7. Summarize the advantages to this team of using Lync.

8. Summarize the advantages to this team of using SharePoint.

9. Explain how you think Office 365 contributes to the objectives you identified in your answer to question 2.

10. Which aspects of Office 365 described here could have value to you when accomplishing student team projects? Explain why they add value compared to what you are currently doing.

"I would totally recommend the University Golf Course for your wedding reception if you want to be told to disinvite your close friends and family. I wanted to have my wedding reception there because it is a close drive from the wedding, the facilities are perfect and the views are perfect . . . little did I know that they were TOTAL liars who planned renovations DURING my wedding reception—told me to cut 35 people from my guest list!! What is the point of having your reception if the people you love aren't there to enjoy it with you!!?? They are just so disorganized they couldn't organize a picnic!! Whatever you do, don't ever work with the University Golf Course!!!!!"

—Posting on the Central Colorado State Golf Course Facebook Page

"She said WHAT?" asks Nia Lloyd, general manager of the university golf course.

"She said we couldn't organize a picnic," Ashley responds.

"On our Facebook page????" Nia is incredulous.

"Yup."

"Well, delete it then. That shouldn't be too hard."

Nia turns to look out the window at the golfers headed to the first tee.

"Nia, we can do that, but I think we should be careful here," Ashley offers this opinion cautiously.

"No, of course, let's leave it out there. Let's tell the whole world that you and I can't organize a wedding." Sarcasm drips from her voice.

"Well, Nia, here's the deal. You don't want to enrage the connected . . . they have power. Remember what happened to Nestlé?"

"No, what? Are they disorganized, too?"

"They got some bad PR on their site and just deleted it. Bingo, the criticisms came back, a thousandfold. Worse, someone at Nestlé got high-handed and posted a criticism of the commenters; it was like pouring gas on a raging fire."

"OK I get it. Tell me what we CAN do!"

"Be open. The key is open, honest communication. We fix the problem—get the maintenance done ahead of schedule or delay, I don't care. Then, we tell our upset and nervous bride that we fixed it . . . maybe ask her, gently, to write that on our page. Possibly we follow up with our side of the story, briefly and not defensively."

"Too passive for me. Let's sue her for defamation." Nia's sarcasm turns to anger.

"No, Nia. No. That's not the way. Do you have any idea of the comments we'd get?"

"A lot."

Nia stares at the golfers out the window, "Weddings. Why did I think weddings were a good idea? What's the matter with golf? It's a good business . . . you water the grass, put out the flags, move the tees around. . . ."

Q1. What are Web 2.0 and social media?

Q2. How can Web 2.0 improve business processes?

Q3. How can social media improve business processes?

Q4. How can Web 2.0 improve the process of building social capital?

Q5. What are the challenges for businesses using Web 2.0?

Q6. What is on the horizon that will have a significant impact on Web 2.0?

Chapter Preview

The Web is changing. Applications like Twitter, Facebook, Wikipedia, and YouTube change what we do on the Web. Not long ago, the Web was a one-way street, and we could only read on the Web. But recently a remarkable change occurred. The Web became a two-way street, and we now contribute tweets, wall posts, videos, votes, reviews, blogs, and other content. While this has made the Web much more engaging for us, businesses are noticing this new way of doing things and are getting in on the act. But businesses, like the university golf course, are discovering that Web 2.0 comes with its own surprises, as the techniques for using these new media are not well established.

There is an old saying in the new field of MIS that technique follows technology. It means that often a new technology appears on the scene for a time before people figure out the right technique for its use. So it is with these new Web 2.0 technologies. The technology is here, but the technique to apply it to business is still a work in progress.

To us, the right technique will involve applying these new technologies to processes. It is easy to get mesmerized by the latest new technology, and Web 2.0 is no exception. But to be useful in business the latest new thing needs to pay off. Technology is useful to business only if it improves business processes.

Just as we did in earlier chapters where we demonstrated the impact of SAP on procurement and sales, here we suggest ways to use Web 2.0 to make business processes more effective or efficient. While the operational processes of procurement and sales were fairly predefined and fixed, the processes that Web 2.0 supports tend to be dynamic.

We begin the chapter by defining Web 2.0 and social media, and then we investigate how these technologies are being applied to business processes. We wrap up by considering some of the challenges and near-term prospects for Web 2.0 and social media.

Q1. What Are Web 2.0 and Social Media?

In the 1990s, Yahoo!, Amazon.com, AOL, and Netscape built the first wave of applications for the Web; applications we now call traditional applications. Today, we are in the middle of a second wave—Web 2.0. In this chapter, we examine what makes the Web 2.0 family—Google, Facebook, Twitter, Wikipedia, and others—different, and what makes its youngest child, social media, so attractive to business.

Web 2.0

Web 2.0 generally refers to a loose grouping of capabilities, technologies, business models, and philosophies. Web 2.0 software is free and constantly changing Web-based software designed to support the sharing of user-generated content. It began to emerge early in the 2000s as network technologies rapidly matured. Network speed, interconnectivity, and reliability were all significantly improving—and businesses noticed. Businesses also observed that users were changing what they did on their computers. For example, young people were no longer just using instant messaging, they were making profiles and sharing pictures and content on Facebook and then-popular MySpace. The trickle of communication among young people using texting and instant messaging was soon a torrent of images, blogs, and videos.

During this time, as networks matured, the center of software activity began to shift from desktop applications to Web applications. With faster and more reliable networks, software that once could only run on a desktop could now be used on the Web. For example, in the 1990s desktop software like Microsoft Office dominated the landscape, now Web apps like Google Docs and Microsoft Office 365 are more common. These advancements have not only changed how people create documents and do their work, they have also changed how businesses and customers relate to each other.

Search engines in the mid '90s were the first tool to demonstrate the new possibilities of Web 2.0. This type of Web app was a complete novelty, and it was free. At about the same time, Amazon.com started collecting and sharing customer reports on products, again for free. For the first time, customers could read a review of a product written by fellow customers on the same Web site they used to buy the product. Other new sites also emerged. Wikipedia provided a constantly updated encyclopedia, and new blogging products provided a platform for a stunning variety of stories, commentary, and news about a wide range of topics. Portals and RSS readers by Google and MSN gave users the opportunity to configure their own Web sites with their choice of content. Web 2.0 had arrived.

Just as users were getting used to this new way of interacting with free software, Facebook, Twitter, and other social media platforms sprang to life. These social media applications are examples of Web 2.0 that emphasize user-generated content. We will explain more about social media platforms after we take a moment to be more specific about the details of Web 2.0.

Figure 10-1 outlines the most significant characteristics of Web 2.0 applications and how they differ from their predecessors. Web 2.0 applications are free, and their interfaces change frequently. They are designed to support two-way communication and user-generated content. Curiously, while the term *Web 2.0* is the shorthand for these new platforms, the term *Web 1.0* is rarely used to describe the previous generation. Most major software applications now use Web 2.0 principles; however, the continued use of traditional applications such as Microsoft Office, antivirus products, and individual tax software shows that traditional applications can still work, at least in the short term.

SOFTWARE: FREE WITH FREQUENT RELEASES Traditional software is licensed as a product. Examples of licensed software include Microsoft Office 2010. ERP software, accounting and tax software, and software that helps businesses design and manufacture products. These software programs run on-site, on servers and desktops owned by the business that purchases the software licenses. Releases are made in a very controlled fashion, and extensive testing precedes every release.

Web 2.0 applications from Google, eBay, and Twitter exemplify Web 2.0. These companies do not sell software licenses; their software is not sold. Instead of software license fees, the Web 2.0 business model relies on advertising or other revenue that results as users employ the software as a free service. A small part of the software runs on-site; most of it is executed on the software company's servers.

INTERFACE: CONSTANT CHANGE *Interfaces,* the point of interaction between the user and the computer, change often in Web 2.0. For example, Google releases new versions of its programs frequently. New features are added with little notice or fanfare. Web 2.0 users are accustomed to, and even expect, frequent updates to their menu license-free software.

In contrast, new versions of traditional applications are released infrequently. Between 1993 and 2010, for example, Microsoft released a new version of Office once every 3 to 4 years. The traditional software model carefully controls the users' experience. The interface is static, changing very infrequently. For example, the menu ribbon in Word, as well as in PowerPoint and in Excel, does not change unless new software is purchased.

Characteristic	Web 2.0 Applications	Traditional Applications
Software	Free	Software as a product for sale
Interface	Constant change; frequent updates change the user interface	Few interface changes
Goal	Support interaction and communication	Problem solving, productivity, no user participation
Content	Users and providers contribute content	Providers contribute and control all content
Examples	Google, Facebook, Twitter, Wikipedia	Microsoft Office, TurboTax, Encyclopedia Britannica

FIGURE 10-1

Web 2.0 and Traditional Web Applications

Not only do Web 2.0 interfaces change frequently, users can also change the interface. Web 2.0 apps encourage **mashups** that combine the output from two or more Web sites into a single user experience. In the process, a mashup changes the user interface. Google's My Maps, shown in Figure 10-2, is an excellent example of a mashup. Google publishes Google Maps and provides tools for users to add their own data to make custom interfaces to those maps. Thus, users mash the Google Map product with their own data. For example, one user demonstrated the growth of gang activity to the local police by mapping new graffiti sites on Google Maps. Other users share their experiences or photos of hiking trips or other travel on Google Maps.

GOAL: SUPPORT INTERACTION AND COMMUNICATION   The aim of the traditional software is to support individual goals—to assist the user in creating documents, performing analyses, monitoring finances, making presentations, keeping track of things, managing projects, and designing products. In contrast, Web 2.0 is about participation. The software still supports user goals, but the method to support these goals is through two-way communication and interaction. Two-way communication occurs as users send and receive messages. With Web 2.0 applications, users provide reviews, map content, discuss responses, create blog entries, and so forth. Amazon.com's customer reviews are an example of two-way communication and interaction among customers.

CONTENT: USERS INCREASINGLY SUPPLY CONTENT   Traditional site owners produce and control all content. Web 2.0 sites allow users to contribute content. This content might be a simple yes/no vote or a discussion board at the end of a news article. Users who contribute to the site are called **prosumers**. More than just consuming the data on the site, prosumers take an active role and produce data for other consumers to read. Facebook, YouTube, and Twitter are all based on user content, as is blogging.

Social Media

With the arrival of Facebook and Twitter at the end of the last decade, the term *social media* was created. **Social media** is any Web application that depends on **user-generated content (UGC)**. User-generated content is publically available content created by end users. This makes social media a type of Web 2.0 application. Social media also shares the other elements

FIGURE 10-2
My Maps Mashup

Source: © 2011 Google.

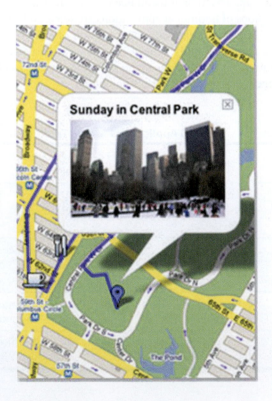

of Web 2.0—free, constantly changing, and designed to support interaction and two-way communication. But what makes these social media applications unique is that they rely 100 percent on user-generated content.

The power of user-generated content has made social media very attractive to business. Users who generate and share content create networks of consumers and prosumers. Businesses love consumer networks because nothing draws a crowd like a crowd. If a network of consumers is buzzing about a product, the network itself draws an even bigger crowd. Social media sites can help businesses encourage customers to talk about their products and services and share this conversation with other customers. A free network that draws a crowd is a tantalizing opportunity few businesses can afford to ignore.

Facebook, Twitter, blogs, LinkedIn, and wikis are the most popular current examples of social media. While you may have personal experience using these, in this chapter we focus on how businesses can use social media tools and other Web 2.0 software to improve their processes.

To begin, we start by examining the three general categories of social media, shown in Figure 10-3. While the landscape of social media can change rapidly, the general categories in Figure 10-3 have been fairly constant.

Sharing social media sites such as blogs, Twitter, and YouTube emphasize contributions in the form of messages and videos. Compared to the networking and collaborating applications, this type of social media supports the user's need to send messages. In this type of media, the recipient of the message is often unknown to the sender.

Networking media such as Facebook, LinkedIn, and foursquare are used to connect individuals. Rather than sending messages to unfamiliar recipients, here the emphasis, and the attraction, is on belonging. Messages are sent to other known users and received from them. For example, **foursquare**, a mobile Web application, allows registered users to connect with friends and share their location.

The final category, *collaborating media*, includes a wide range of platforms such as Wikipedia, StumbleUpon, Digg, Delicious, Google Docs, and Quora. Collaboration, which was defined in Chapter 9, is a group process where work is accomplished through feedback and iteration. The focus of this type of social media is to support the user's collaboration processes. For example, **Digg** allows users to share votes on Web articles with other users, and **Delicious** enables users to tag Web sites, create lists of sites, and share those lists with other users.

Wikipedia, Google, eBay, and Facebook are all Web 2.0 organizations that have pioneered Web 2.0 applications and techniques to their benefit. In this chapter, we consider how these applications might be used by non-Internet organizations. How might Alaska Airlines, Procter & Gamble, FlexTime, Central Colorado State, and CBI use Web 2.0? Organizations sense the value here to do new and possibly very profitable things. In fact, the term **Enterprise 2.0** was coined to label the business use of Web 2.0. But businesses are a bit wary of flashy new information technologies. A good deal of money was lost on the first wave of Internet exuberance that ended with the dot-com bust shortly after 2000. Today's managers do not want to be fooled a second time. As a result, even though many businesses are plunging into Web 2.0, business managers are insisting that this time the applications show a payoff. We feel the best way to demonstrate the potential payoff is to show how Web 2.0 and social media can improve business processes.

Category	Examples
Sharing	Blogs and microblogs, Twitter, and YouTube
Networking	Facebook, LinkedIn, and foursquare
Collaborating	Wikis, Stumbleupon, Digg, Google Docs

FIGURE 10-3

Major Categories of Social Media

FIGURE 10-4

Examples of Existing Business Processes Impacted by Web 2.0 and Social Media

Existing Process	Web 2.0	Social Media		
		Sharing	Networking	Collaborating
Promotion	✓	✓	✓	✓
Online Advertising Sales	✓			
Market Research	✓			
B2C Sales	✓			
Customer Communication		✓		✓
Hiring			✓	

Q2. How Can Web 2.0 Improve Business Processes?

In this question, we examine the impact of Web 2.0 applications on dynamic business processes. In the next question, we address the impact of social media. While Web 2.0 and social media have impacts on many business processes, we include here only a sample of those processes. The four examples of processes improved with Web 2.0 and the six examples of processes improved by social media are shown in Figure 10-4.

The processes supported by Web 2.0 and social media are typically dynamic processes. Although operational processes such as sales and procurement can also be supported by these new information systems, these systems are still somewhat experimental and change their software frequently. Because they are experimental, low cost, easy to use, and flexible, their first uses in business tends to be in support of dynamic processes.

Figure 10-5 shows examples of processes improved by Web 2.0 and how these improvements can be measured. Recall the OMIS model discussed in Chapter 5. Every process has objectives that are measured, and the impact of an IS on the process can be observed using these measures. We examine each of these processes and the impact of Web 2.0, in turn.

The Promotion Process

One of the primary objectives of the Promotion process is to influence the purchasing decisions of potential customers. Consider an Oracle promotional ad that might appear in the print version of the *Wall Street Journal*. Oracle has no control over who reads that ad, nor does it know much about the people who do (just that they fit the general demographic of *Wall Street Journal* readers). On any particular day, 10,000 qualified buyers for Oracle products might happen to read the ad, or then again, perhaps only 1,000 qualified buyers read it. Neither Oracle nor the *Wall Street Journal* knows the number, but Oracle pays the same amount for the ad, regardless of the number of readers or who they are. In the Web 2.0 world, advertising is specific to user interests. Someone who searches online for "Oracle software" is likely an IT person (or a student) who has a strong interest in Oracle and its competing products. Oracle would like to advertise to that person.

Google pioneered Web 2.0 advertising with its **AdWords** software. AdWords is Google's popular pay-per-click advertising product. With AdWords companies pay a predetermined price for particular search words. For example, the university golf course might agree to pay $2 for the words *golf*

FIGURE 10-5

Processes Improved by Web 2.0

Process	Objective	Measure
Promotion	Better accountability	Counts of responses or Web site visits
Online Advertising Sales	Reduce time spent managing Web site	Employee hours per week
Market Research	Research time for new product research and development	Calendar days
B2C Sales	Increase B2C sales	Conversion rate

and *Colorado*. When a customer uses Google to search for those terms, Google will display a link to the university golf course Web site. If the user clicks that link (and *only* if the user clicks that link), Google charges the golf course account $2. The golf course pays nothing if the user does not click. AdWords supports the objectives of the Promotion process at the golf course. One of the objectives of the university golf course's Promotion process was a more targeted marketing approach, the success of which is measured by how many people responded to the promotion and visited the Web site.

The Online Advertising Sales Process

Some organizations sell advertising space on their Web sites. Others would like to sell space if the cost of finding advertisers could be reduced. On the traditional Web, banner ads and pop-up ads were the favored method of advertising. Organizations with Web site space had to find advertisers and work out the details of the advertising agreement. This can be a time-consuming process of agreeing to terms, providing images and text, and tracking page loads for each agreement. A Web 2.0 application that makes this process of buying and selling advertisements more efficient is Google's AdSense.

AdSense searches an organization's Web site and inserts ads that match content on that site. When users click those ads, Google pays the Web site owner a fee. The organization that owns the site does not have to maintain a process of finding advertisers. AdSense supports the objectives of the Online Advertising Sales process. One of these objectives is to spend less time managing the Web advertising process as measured by hours of employee time per week.

The Market Research Process

Web 2.0 applications can help a company make its process of market research more efficient. Before Web 2.0 this process required employees to search the Web for relevant topics. For example, a software company employee conducting research on current computer security issues would visit various security Web sites to read relevant articles. Now with Web 2.0 applications such as RSS feeds and discussion boards the process of finding relevant content is more automated. An example of an RSS reader is shown in Figure 10-6. The RSS reader shown in Figure 10-6 receives *New York Times* articles about the Internet as well as articles from SearchSecurity and TechCrunch.

A pharmaceutical company employee can use an RSS reader to set up an RSS feed that displays articles on her reader of eye diseases that appear on medical Web sites. Her RSS reader is automatically updated when the medical Web site is updated. One of the pharmaceutical company's objectives was to reduce the time for new product market research as measured in calendar days.

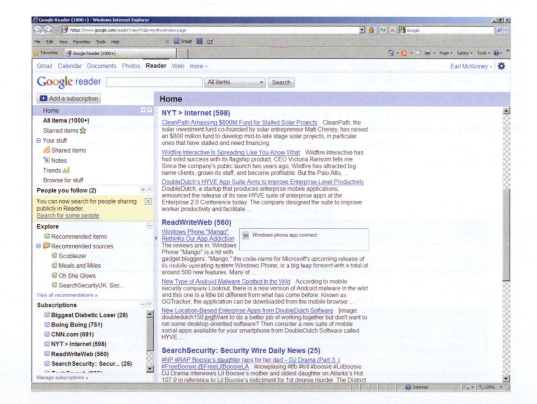

FIGURE 10-6

RSS Reader

Source: © 2011 Google.

The B2C Sales Process

Retailers can improve the B2C Sales process with Web 2.0 applications. A key activity of the B2C Sales process is collecting customer data. This data might include which browser the visitor is using, the visitor's IP address, and if the user eventually purchased from the site. Before Web 2.0, B2C businesses had to write their own code to collect this type of data. Enter **Google Analytics**. Now, B2C sites can download free Google Analytics software to collect Web traffic data. This data includes the data mentioned earlier—where the customer came from (from a search engine, another site, etc.), where the customer visited in the site, and the **conversion rate**, which is the ratio of the number of customers who eventually purchased divided by the number who visited. Analysts can examine this type of data and make changes to the site with the objective of increasing conversion rates. Installed on over a half million of the most popular Web sites, Google Analytics helps companies improve their B2C Sales process as measured by conversion rates.

Supporting New Processes with Web 2.0

Web 2.0 applications not only improve existing processes, they support new ones. Suppose you are watching a hit movie and you would like to buy the jewelry, dress, or watch worn by the leading actress. Suppose that Nordstrom sells all those items. With Web 2.0 technology, the movie's producer and Nordstrom can mash their content together so that you, watching the movie on a DVD at home, can click the item you like and be directed to Nordstrom's Web site to purchase the item. For Nordstrom, Web 2.0 has provided support for a new Entertainment-Sales process.

Process Integration with Web 2.0

In earlier chapters, we showed how ERP systems can not only improve one process, but, more importantly, improve the integration of processes. Web 2.0 is no different. For example, Google Analytics can help improve the integration of the B2C Sales process and the Promotion process. As Google Analytics helps improve the conversion rate of visitors in the Sales process, it will also provide data on where the best customers come from, which improves the Promotion process. The university golf course currently uses AdWords to place links to the golf course on Web searches. Google Analytics might reveal a higher conversion rate for visitors who come to the university golf course Web site from searches that use the words *Colorado* and *Golf* than from searches that use *Central Colorado State* and *Golf*. As a result, the Promotion process is improved by spending more on the more productive paid search terms.

Q3. How Can Social Media Improve Business Processes?

Like other Web 2.0 applications, social media can impact business processes in a variety of ways. Although the applications vary, the largest number of them are customer-facing processes—processes that promote, sell, or service products. Here we present a sample of the applications organized into the three types of social media mentioned earlier—sharing, networking, and collaborating. Figures 10-7, 10-8, and 10-10 show the three categories of social media platforms and the objectives of the processes supported. These figures also show the measures used to assess the objectives.

FIGURE 10-7

Processes Improved by Sharing Social Media

The Promotion Process

Objective	Measure
Increase awareness of product or service	Counts of likes, retweets, downloads

The Customer Communication Process

Objective	Measure
Increasing communication to and from customers	Counts of messages, tweets, blog followers

Sharing Social Media

Sharing social media such as blogs and microblogs, Twitter, and YouTube can be used to support a variety of existing and new business processes. Figure 10-7 shows examples of existing processes supported by these apps.

THE PROMOTION PROCESS Perhaps the most immediate and profitable way that social media help business is by supporting the process of promotion. Notice in the four examples that follow the variety of products promoted and how the results of the promotions are measured.

- A food blender manufacturer created a series of inexpensive "Will it Blend" videos for YouTube. These videos featured its CEO blending marbles in his company's blender. Later, it produced videos showing him blending a tiki torch, hockey pucks, and iPhones. The videos went **viral**—shared and promoted by individuals on social media outlets—and after millions of views, the YouTube series was credited with helping boost the company's blender sales by over 40 percent.[1]
- In the entertainment industry, the Black Eyed Peas were early proponents of social media. The group has used Twitter to solicit song requests at concerts. They have used social media outlets to increase fan awareness and participation in public appearances, and they use social media tools to increase downloads of their music.
- Stride Gum funded a YouTube video of Matt Harding dancing around the world in 42 different countries. At the end of this upbeat video, a Stride Gum announcement appears identifying Stride Gum as the video's sponsor. The Dancing Matt video was viewed 33 million times in its first 2 years. The clip is credited with increasing sales by 8 percent and moving Stride Gum to fifth in the sugarless gum industry.[2]
- A small New York City day spa promoted its anti-aging facial treatment with a YouTube video entitled "The Bird Poop Facial." The video resulted in wide viewership and marked increase in both buzz about the spa and demand for its facials.

These Promotion processes have a variety of objectives. One common objective is increasing awareness of the product or service. Possible measures for this objective are counts of likes, retweets, and downloads.

THE CUSTOMER COMMUNICATION PROCESS Government agencies have learned to use social media tools to communicate with particular population centers facing natural dangers. For example, police and fire officials tweet about dangerous weather and forest fire movement to help keep local residents informed.

A number of companies are turning to social media to improve communication with potential customers, particularly in the aftermath of an organizational crisis. In recent years, BP, Toyota, and Johnson & Johnson have faced public concern about their products and have turned to social media to provide an outlet to explain their perspective and to explain the steps that they were taking to prevent future crises.

Many companies lurk on sharing social media platforms to better communicate with customers. Examples include:

- The maker of WD-40, a lubrication and cleaning compound, discovered that its product easily and safely removes bugs from car fenders by reading social media customer posts about its product.
- Walmart's IT department in Arkansas discovered a developing problem with a store's checkout registers by listening to customer complaints on Twitter. The department was already working on a solution when the store called to report the problem.
- A customer on a Virgin Atlantic cross-country flight tweeted that he was offended by a fellow traveler's odor. Within minutes, Virgin Atlantic customer service had read the tweet, determined which flight most likely generated it, and notified the flight attendant. The flight attendant then strolled the aisle asking casually if anyone would like to move seats to another location in the plane.

[1] SociaLens Case Study. Available at *www.socialens.com/wpcontent/uploads/2009/04/20090127_case_blendtec11.pdf* (accessed July 2011).
[2] Available at *www.adrants.com/mt335/mt-search.cgi?IncludeBlogs=1&search=nokia.*

One objective of Customer Communication processes may be as simple as increasing the communication to or from customers. The corresponding measures can be counts of messages, tweets, or blog followers.

Networking Social Media

Networking social media such as Facebook, LinkedIn, and foursquare are used to support a variety of processes, some of which are the same as those supported by sharing social media. Examples of processes supported by networking social media are shown in Figure 10-8.

THE PROMOTION PROCESS Businesses can use Facebook groups to strengthen their promotions. For example, the university golf course could create an invitation group for each wedding to use as its wedding Web site. The bride then invites everyone on the guest list to join the group. Prior to the wedding, the bride and groom could place photos and videos of their relationship and engagement on the group site. The happy couple could provide links to gift registries, directions to the golf course, weather forecasts, and any other information of interest to the wedding attendees. They could also start a discussion list. Further, if the golf course can convince wedding parties to use its groups, it can form relationships with the wedding invitees, and as a result enhance the golf course brand.

A number of firms are using networking social media to enhance their brands in promotional campaigns:

- The Discovery Channel used a Facebook app on its Facebook page to promote the network's popular Shark Week series. When a visitor clicked on the app, the Discovery Channel created a mashup of data and pictures from the visitor's Facebook site with Shark Week video footage. The result shows the user being attacked by sharks, with an authentic looking press release that included contrived comments from actual friends on Facebook. The video was easy to post on the visitor's Facebook wall, creating a viral hook.[3]

- JCPenney used Facebook Connect to create a series of "doghouse" videos to generate online sales. Individuals could "send" loved ones to the doghouse—a penalty for purchasing thoughtless gifts such as vacuum cleaners for anniversaries and diet books for birthdays. The only way out of the doghouse was to purchase a considerate gift from the JCPenney Web site. The doghouse sender and sendee could communicate via Facebook wall posts in front of friends, thereby raising awareness of the promotion and JCPenney.[4]

- Many car manufacturers provide Web visitors a convenient option to download images of their products directly to the visitor's Facebook page. Once the image appears on the Facebook wall, the visitor can invite friends to comment on plans to purchase the product. These apps by the Discovery Channel, JCPenney, and car manufacturers take advantage

FIGURE 10-8

Processes Improved by Networking Social Media

The Promotion Process

Objective	Measure
Enhance the brand	Counts of wall posts, invitations

The Hiring Process

Objective	Measure
Increase valid data collected on applicants	Number of media or data sources used

[3] Josh Catone, "10 Impressive New Applications of Facebook Connect," Mashable, July 21, 2009. Available at: *http://mashable.com/2009/07/21/facebook-connect-new/*.
[4] Creativity Online, "JCPenney: Beware of the Doghouse." Available at: *http://creativity-online.com/work/jc-penney-beware-of-the-doghouse/14501*.

of a user's social graph. A **social graph** is a network of personal interdependencies, such as friendships, common interests, or kinship, on a social media application.

- Foursquare is a networking social app that provides restaurants and bars a convenient way to use social media to create competitions, reward frequent visitors, and invite friends of frequent visitors. Foursquare restaurants can promote competition among visitors for rewards and status. This location-based social media is one of the first to mashup location data and users' social graphs. Figure 10-9 shows a foursquare site.

Promotional objectives vary from firm to firm. One common objective may be to enhance the brand. One indication of a strong brand is a brand that a customer is willing to pass on to a friend. Therefore, a measure of brand enhancement might be counts of Facebook wall mentions, foursquare invitations between friends, and counts of invitations from one customer to another to visit an online promotion.

THE HIRING PROCESS Another use of this category of social media is to gather intelligence about potential employees in support of the firm's Hiring process. LinkedIn is the most popular professional networking social media site. On the site, users maintain a resume-like profile and a list of connections—people they know. Through LinkedIn, many firms are lowering costs and shortening times needed to post jobs, find candidates, collect recommendations, and make hiring decisions.

Facebook is also being used in the hiring process. In 2009, Mashable reported that some NFL teams used fictitious Facebook profiles to follow potential draft choices.[5] The unsuspecting draft choices who friended these accounts believed the accounts belonged to attractive young ladies. While many would question the ethics of this particular approach, many other companies collect data from social media sites in less controversial ways to make their hiring process more effective.

FIGURE 10-9

Foursquare Web Site

Source: Used with permission of FourSquare.com.

---

[5] Mashable. Available at *http://mashable.com/2009/04/10/nfl-draft-facebook//* (accessed July 2011).

FIGURE 10-10

Processes Improved by
Collaborating Social
Media

The Promotion Process

Objective	Measure
Reduce product returns	Frequency or value of returned products

The Customer Communication Process

Objective	Measure
Increasing communication among customers	Counts of wiki page edits or additions, number or length of customer reviews, or the number of participants

An objective of a Hiring process may be to increase the valid data collected on job candidates. The measure of this objective could be the number of media used or the number of data sources per candidate.

Collaboration Social Media

Collaboration social media such as wikis, StumbleUpon, Google Docs, and Digg support business processes much like the sharing and networking examples just mentioned. Figure 10-10 shows examples of existing processes supported by collaboration social media.

THE PROMOTION PROCESS On collaborative social media sites, users contribute text, votes, documents, questions, answers, and lists in order to work together in both formal and informal groups.

As mentioned earlier, Amazon.com jumpstarted the customer collaboration concept with user reviews of its products. Amazon.com collected millions of product reviews and made these reviews available to customers. Borrowing this concept, PETCO used customer dissatisfaction data to decide which product not to promote on its Web site. This approach is called **crowdsourcing**, the outsourcing of a task that traditionally was done by an employee to a large, undefined group of people.

Many news sites allow readers to rate and comment on articles and offer readers a convenient button to tweet or Digg articles. Social media sites like Digg collect these ratings and create collaborative lists of popular articles and sites by topic. These collaboratively edited lists give businesses a convenient way to follow and assess customer trends and changing interests. One objective of these promotions might be to use crowdsourcing to reduce product returns. A measure that can be used to assess this objective is the frequency or value of returned goods.

THE CUSTOMER COMMUNICATION PROCESS A number of organizations, both in business and government, use wikis to help customers find online help about their products. Pitney Bowes maintains a wiki forum for customers to ask questions. Often a customer question will be answered by another customer. The wiki has reduced service center calls by 30,000, saving the company $300,000.

Some universities pay students to communicate with prospective students on social media. Prospective students can use these social media contacts to find out how to get questions answered, to read about student life, and to connect to other students before arriving. Government agencies have used social media to track the outbreak and spread of the flu. Google can track flu searches by location. As more users in an area conduct searches on *flu* and related terms, Google can pinpoint flu outbreaks geographically.[6]

Healthcare providers are increasingly aware of the role social media are playing in patient education. Hospitals and healthcare specialists recommend particular discussion sites where reliable answers are given to patient questions. A number of recent studies refer to this interaction as Health 2.0 and suggest that patients who can collaborate with providers and other patients on diagnosis and treatment report a greater level of satisfaction with their care.[7]

[6] Erik Qualman, *Socialnomics* (Hoboken, NJ: Wiley, 2009).
[7] *The Economist*. April 16, 2009. Health 2.0. Available at *http://www.economist.com/node/13437940*.

One objective of a Customer Communication process might be to increase communication among customers. The measures might be counts of additions or edits to a wiki site or the number or length of customer reviews or the number of participants.

Supporting New Processes with Social Media

To this point, we have shown how social media can improve existing processes. Most of our examples have addressed processes that link organizations to their customers. However, social media, like Web 2.0 and other IS, can support the emergence of new processes within the organization. Businesses can use Web 2.0 to create internal company wikis, to store knowledge, and to find expertise. Locating an expert in the organization in the past was an informal process. Now, firms have developed specific processes to collect and share expertise. For example, when software engineers join a company like Microsoft they input their areas of knowledge, such as SQL Server, SharePoint, or fluency in Greek, into a SharePoint-supported internal blog site. Later, if someone at Microsoft needs to find a Greek-speaking, SharePoint expert to help on a project for a company in Greece, the contact data for employees that match that description are available.

Another new process might be labeled *social media content generation*. One challenge of using social media is to provide consistently new and fresh ideas. Consider CBI, the bicycle wholesaler used in earlier chapters. The company wants to use blogs and Twitter to promote its new line of bicycles. Sue, the sales manager has launched a blog and Twitter account and populated them with content from sales reps, bike enthusiasts, and managers, asking each to make one post a day to the blog. Sue has also hired a professional to summarize the blogs once a week. She has directed an assistant to generate tweets from the blogs and to retweet relevant tweets made by others. She has connected her sales reps to particularly useful blogs with tweets. These activities constitute a new Content Generation process supported by social media, and Sue continues to refine it.

Process Integration with Social Media

The value of social media is heightened when businesses use it to help integrate processes. Central Colorado State uses student blogs in support of its Recruitment process. Current students blog and tweet about campus life and opportunities in support of Recruiting process objectives. During the summer, the blogging and tweeting shift to topics such as an upcoming orientation weekend, class registration tips, and other new student topics to support the school's New Student Registration process. During the year, the blog shifts again to help students plan for upcoming semesters, supporting the Freshman Retention process.

Tips for Conducting Social Media Promotions

As we close this section on how social media can improve business processes, note that many of the examples involved improving promotion. Creating a successful promotional campaign on social media can be a challenge. Early studies of successful campaigns suggest that there are four keys to success, as shown in Figure 10-11. First, stay involved. Create a plan about how the promotion will be updated, and stay active with the promotion by including new content daily. Second, motivate your early consumers to contribute to the promotion. These early supporters might be willing to make a positive post, write a good review, or retweet your Twitter messages. Third, develop a reward mechanism to give status to contributors. You might award icons to screen names that are frequent posters, or you might generate rankings of customer reviews. Contributors will post more frequently if they notice positive feedback from you about their content and if they build an identity with your promotion. Finally, do not underestimate the time required. Promotions can be very time consuming.

Stay Involved—have a plan to update the promotion daily
Motivate early prosumers to contribute
Develop a reward mechanism
Don't underestimate time required

FIGURE 10-11

Social Media Promotion Keys to Success

Q4. How Can Web 2.0 Improve the Process of Building Social Capital?

Web 2.0 and social media can help a business build social capital. **Social capital** is the investment in social relations with the expectation of benefits in the marketplace. Building social capital is a dynamic process that is vital to the firm. Here we explain the process of building social capital and then explore how social media helps this process. In the previous two questions, we considered how Web 2.0 and social media impact business processes. Most of the measures used to show process improvement were fairly immediate. However, with social capital the measures used to demonstrate process improvement take more time to accrue. Another aspect of this process that is unique is that the benefits of social capital spill over to other processes. Businesses invest in social capital like other capital, to apply it profitably to other projects and processes down the road.

What Is Social Capital?

Karl Marx described **capital** as the investment of resources for future profit. Capital is like the money you put in a bank account. Capital accumulates for later use. Business literature defines three types of capital. **Traditional capital** refers to investments into resources such as factories, machines, manufacturing equipment, and the like. **Human capital** is the investment in human knowledge and skills for future profit. By taking this class, you are investing in your own human capital. Finally, social capital, defined earlier, is an investment in social relationships.

Social capital has three benefits for a business.[8] Relationships in social networks can provide a business with *data* about opportunities, alternatives, problems, and other factors important to business professionals. They also provide an opportunity to *influence* decision makers and to increase the influence of the organization in the industry. Third, being linked to a network of highly regarded contacts is a form of *social credential*. Others will be more inclined to work with you if they believe critical personnel are standing with you and may provide resources to support you.

When you attend a business function for the purpose of meeting people and reinforcing relationships, you are in the process of building social capital. Similarly, when you join LinkedIn or contribute to Facebook, you are investing in your social capital.

Businesses and individuals working in those businesses seek to accumulate social capital. A business may encourage employees to create their own blog or to tweet, or the business may have its own social media accounts. Both individual and business social capital pay dividends for the firm.

Building social capital is a process. That process has three objectives:

1. Increase the number of relationships in a social network (measure is the number of relations).
2. Increase the strength of those relationships (measure is the frequency of favors).
3. Connect to those with more assets (measure is dollar value).

You build social capital by adding more friends and by strengthening the relationships you have with existing friends. Further, you gain more social capital by adding friends and strengthening relationships with people who control resources that are important to you. Such calculations may seem cold, impersonal, phony, and self-serving. When applied to the recreational use of social media, they may be. But when you use social media for professional purposes, keep in mind that social capital flows both ways. Professionals in other organizations seek out relationships with you as investments in their social capital.

How an Organization Can Use Social Media to Increase the Number of Relationships

As shown in Figure 10-12, in a traditional business relationship clients (you) have some experience with a business, such as a local restaurant. Traditionally, you may express your opinions about that experience by word-of-mouth to your social network (here denoted by

---

[8] Nan Lin, Karen S. Cook, Ronald S. Burt, *Social Capital: Theory and Research* (New Brunswick, NJ: Transaction Publishers, 2001).

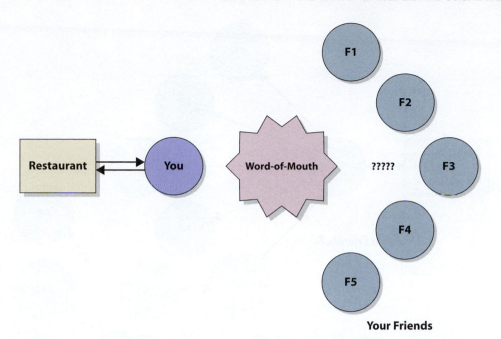

FIGURE 10-12

Traditional Marketing Network

friends F1, F2, etc.). However, such communication is unreliable and brief: You are more likely to say something to your friends if the experience was particularly good or bad; but, even then, you are likely only to say something to those friends whom you encounter while the experience is still recent. And once you have said something, that's it; your words don't live on for days or weeks.

Social media facilitates interactions on a social network. Social media have numerous characteristics, one of which is that they make the transmission of your opinions more reliable and longer lasting. For example, suppose the restaurant establishes a presence using social media, maybe it has a page on Facebook. The nature of the presence is unimportant here.

When you mention the restaurant on your social media outlet, something about that business will be broadcast to your friends, as shown in Figure 10-13. That messaging is automatic; "I just had the Sunday brunch at this restaurant, Yummm!" will be reliably broadcast to all of your friends and, unlike word-of-mouth, that message will last for hours, even days. That, in itself, is a powerful marketing program.

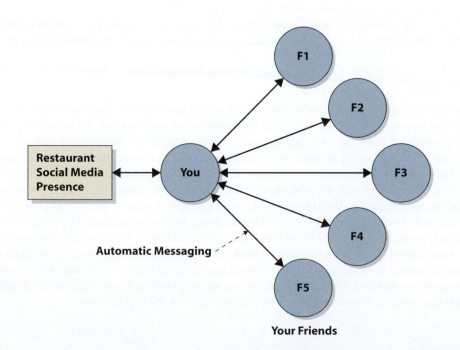

FIGURE 10-13

Social Media Marketing Network

FIGURE 10-14

Viral Social Media Marketing Network

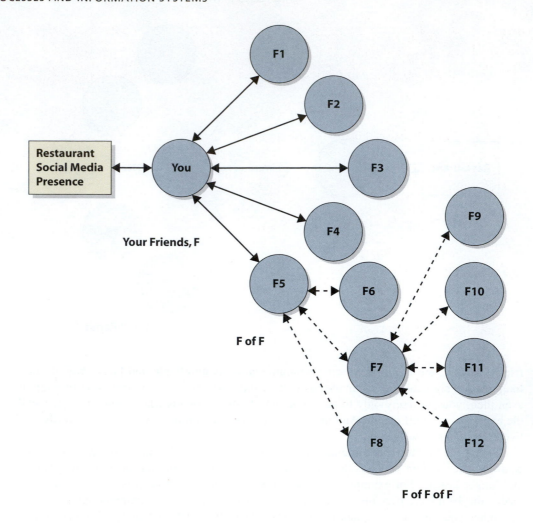

However, social media provides even greater possibilities. As shown in Figure 10-14, you have friends (OK, you have more than five friends, but space is limited), and your friends have friends, and those friends have friends. If something about your message, induces F5 (for example) to broadcast about the restaurant to her friends, and if that message induces F7 to broadcast about the restaurant to his friends, and so forth, the messaging will be viral.

In sum, the restaurant is using a particular social media presence on Facebook to improve its process of building social capital. The restaurant expects this social capital to lead to future revenues.

How an Organization Can Use Social Media to Increase the Strength of Relationships

To an organization, the **strength of a relationship** is the likelihood that a person or other organization in the relationship will do something that benefits the organization. An organization has a strong relationship with you if you buy its products, write positive reviews about it, post pictures of you using the organization's products or services, and so on. As stated earlier, social media provide three forms of value: data, influence, and social credentials. If an organization can induce those in its relationships to provide more of any of those factors, it has strengthened that relationship.

In his autobiography, Benjamin Franklin said that if you want to strengthen your relationship with someone in power, ask them to do you a favor. Before he invented the public library, he would ask powerful strangers to lend him their expensive books. In that same sense, organizations have learned that they can strengthen their relationships with you by asking you to do them a favor. Customer reviews, passing job announcements to qualified candidates, and retweeting are common examples of what a company can ask an individual to do on social media. When you provide that favor, it also strengthens your relationship with the organization.

When posting information about yourself online, what ethical guidelines should you follow? Read the Ethics Guide on pages 334–335 and consider how online activity is fraught with ethical questions.

MIS InClass 10

Using Twitter to Support the Class Discussion Process

Prior to class, your instructor will decide on a unique hashtag to use for this exercise. During class, use your Twitter account and create tweets that include this hashtag. Tweets can include observations about class ideas or questions about the day's topic. At the end of the class, you will discuss the tweets.

If you do not have a Twitter account, obtain one at the beginning of class.

As an alternative, rather than send tweets to the public twittersphere, you can use Twitter's direct message feature to send private tweets to a class Twitter account. To use this approach, your instructor must first create the class Twitter account. Prior to sending a direct message to that account, each student must follow the class account. The teacher can log in and display the direct messages at the end of class.

At the end of the class, discuss the following:

1. How well does Twitter support the Class Discussion process?
2. What are the objectives and measures of the Class Discussion process?

Source: Annette Shaff/Shutterstock.

3. What other educational processes can Twitter support? What are the objectives of these processes, and how does Twitter help achieve them?
4. Can in-class use of Twitter be used to integrate educational processes? These processes might include student assessment, student collaboration, technology use, as well as class discussion.

Frequent interactions strengthen relationships and hence increase social capital. The more you interact with a company, the stronger your commitment and allegiance. Social media like posts on a wall, new content by other users, and games give organizations new opportunities for frequent interactions. But continued frequent interactions occur only when both parties see value in continuing the relationship. Thus, at some point, the organization must do something to make it worth your while to continue to do them a favor.

How an Organization Can Use Social Media to Connect to Those with More Assets

The third objective of the process of building social capital is to connect with people who control more assets. In addition to the financial assets of these people, an organization's social capital is also partly a function of the social capital of those to whom it relates. The most visible measure of social capital is the number of relationships. Someone with 1,000 loyal Twitter followers is usually more valuable than someone with 10. But the calculation is more subtle than that; if those 1,000 followers are college students, and if the organization's product is adult diapers, the value of the relationship to the followers is low. A relationship with 10 Twitter followers who are in retirement homes would be more valuable.

There is no formula for computing social capital, but the three factors would seem to be more multiplicative than additive. Or, stated in other terms, the value of social capital is more in the form of

$$SocialCapital = NumberRelationships \times RelationshipStrength \times EntityResources$$

Than it is:

$$SocialCapital = NumberRelationships + RelationshipStrength + EntityResources$$

Again, do not take these equations literally; take them in the sense of the interaction of the three factors. The multiplicative nature of social capital means that a huge network of relationships to people who have few resources may be lower than that of a smaller network with people with substantial resources. Furthermore, those resources must be relevant to the organization. Students with pocket change are relevant to Pizza Hut; they are irrelevant to a BMW dealership.

Bottom line, social media can improve the organization's process of building social capital. As mentioned previously, the organization expects that this investment will have benefits in the long run. These payoffs may be increased sales, better business intelligence, influence with suppliers and buyers, or greater prestige will attract better talent.

Q5. What Are the Challenges for Businesses Using Web 2.0?

Businesses using Web 2.0 face two types of challenges. These are management problems and user-content problems. We examine each, in turn.

Management Problems

One of the management challenges with Web 2.0 applications is that their labor requirements are difficult to estimate. As with any new technology, few guidelines are available to estimate the time required to use them effectively. Another challenge is to create useful measures. It can be difficult to determine how to measure the usefulness of a new technology. Of course, increasing the bottom line or increasing sales would be a welcome measure, but there may be benefits to a Web 2.0 initiative that are hard to measure or that may only unfold over many years. For example, even if a Web 2.0 campaign has little apparent impact on sales or profits, perhaps the positive word-of-mouth, buzz, or customer satisfaction may be valuable but difficult to measure. Also, the team that conducted the campaign may have learned many lessons that can be used on upcoming projects, lessons like how to estimate labor and manage such projects—payoffs that are hard to measure.

Another set of problems with Web 2.0 and social media in particular are associated with customer privacy. *Every improvement to a business process involving customers using social media data comes at a price of less privacy.* If the healthcare industry wants to improve patient collaboration among patients with a similar disease, this can only happen if the participants give up private data about their health. Businesses built on social media and those businesses using this media must anticipate privacy concerns by users and privacy laws by governments that will restrict the use of social media data.

Also note that Web 2.0 applications may not appropriate for many processes. A number of processes require IS support that is more consistent and controlled than flexible and changing. Any IS that deals with assets, whether financial or material, requires a high level of control. You probably do not want your credit card transactions to emerge in user-generated content, nor do you want them mashed up on a map that is shared with the world. As CFO, you probably do not want your accounts payable or general ledger system to have an emergent user interface; in fact, the Sarbanes-Oxley Act prohibits that possibility.

User Content Problems

Web 2.0 can be like Pandora's box, once a company opens itself to user content, it can be difficult to undo the damage. Before a business plunges headlong into any commercial application of Web 2.0, it should be aware of the risks that these tools entail. Some of the major risks are:

- Junk and crackpots
- Inappropriate content
- Unfavorable reviews
- Mutinous movements
- Dependency on the social media vendor

Crackpots may use the site as a way of expressing passionately held views about unrelated topics, such as UFOs, government cover-ups, weird conspiracy theories, and so forth. Because of the possibility of such content, employees of the hosting business must regularly monitor the site and remove objectionable material immediately. Companies like Bazaarvoice offer services not only to collect and manage ratings and reviews, but also to monitor a site for irrelevant content.

Unfavorable reviews are another risk. Research indicates that customers are sophisticated enough to know that few, if any, products are perfect. Most customers want to know the disadvantages of a product before purchasing it so they can determine if those disadvantages are important for their application. Customers expect both positive and negative comments; it is better to be perceived as honest and genuine than as old fashioned and a hype machine. However, if every review is bad, if the product is rated 1 star out of 5, then the company is using Web 2.0 technology to needlessly publish its problems.

Mutinous movements are an extension of bad reviews where prosumers revolt and use an organization's site in damaging ways. The campaign Web site *www.my.barackobama.com* had a strong social media component, and when then-Senator Obama changed his position on immunity for telecoms engaged in national security work 22,000 members of his site joined a spontaneous group to object. Hundreds of members posted very critical comments of Obama, on his own site! This was an unexpected backlash to a campaign that had enjoyed unprecedented success raising money from small donors via social media.

Although it is possible for organizations to develop their own social media capability, many organizations use social media vendors such as Facebook and Twitter. Those organizations are vulnerable to the success and policies of Facebook, Twitter, and others. These social media vendors are new companies with unproven business models; they may not survive. Also, using a social media vendor for a business purpose makes the business vulnerable to the reliability and performance the vendor provides.

The vulnerability is real, but the choices are limited. As stated, companies can create their own social media capability, but doing so is expensive and requires highly skilled employees and frequent and expensive updates. And, having developed its own capability, no company will have the popularity and mindshare of Facebook or Twitter.

Responding to User Content Problems

Some social media campaigns are launched well with strong funding and support, but over the course of the campaign fail to update sufficiently and the campaign grinds to a halt, leaving the impression of a poorly conceived plan. Social media campaigns are like parties. It takes effort to plan and launch them, but no host ever leaves a party in the middle of it or the guests will quickly lose interest and leave the scene a mess.

While the party is ongoing, the host must know what to do with inappropriate behavior by a guest. The same applies to social media campaigns. What will it do with problematic content?

If the problematic content represents reasonable criticism of the organization's products or services, the best response may be to leave it where it is. Such criticism indicates that the site is not just a shill for the organization, but contains legitimate user content. Such criticism also serves as a free source of product reviews, which can be useful for product development. To be useful, the development team needs to know about the criticism, so systems to ensure that it is found and communicated to the development team are important.

A second response is to respond to the problematic content. This response is, however, dangerous. If the response could be construed, in any way, as patronizing or insulting to the content contributor, the response can enrage the user community and generate a strong backlash. Also, if the response appears defensive, it can become a strong public relations negative. In most cases, responses are best reserved for when the problematic content has caused the organization to do something positive as a result. For example, suppose a user publishes that he or she was required to hold for customer support for 45 minutes. If the organization has done something to reduce wait times, then an effective response to the criticism is to recognize it as valid and state, nondefensively, what has been done to reduce wait times.

Deleting content should be reserved for contributions that are inappropriate because they are contributed by crackpots, because they have nothing to do with the site, or because they contain obscene or otherwise inappropriate content. However, deleting legitimate negative comments can result in a strong user backlash. As Ashley mentioned in the opening scenario, Nestlé created a PR nightmare on its Facebook account with its response to criticism it received about its use of palm oil. Someone altered the Nestlé logo, and in response Nestlé decided to delete all Facebook contributions that used that altered logo, and in doing so appeared arrogant and heavy-handed. The result was a negative firestorm on Twitter.

A sound principle in business is to never ask a question to which you do not want the answer. We can extend that principle to social media: Never set up a site that will generate content for which you have no effective response!

Q6. What Is on the Horizon That Will Have a Significant Impact on Web 2.0?

So much change is in the air: new Google apps, new uses of Twitter, widespread smartphone use, and moving apps to the cloud, to name just a few. Is there a Web 3.0 around the corner? We don't know. However, new devices and technologies will continue to change how businesses use the Web.

Recently, in Brazil, Unilever placed GPS devices in 50 packages of its Omo detergent. The GPS devices were activated when customers removed the package from the shelf. The devices then reported the customers' home location back to Unilever. Unilever employees then contacted the customers at home and gave them a free pocket video cameras. The point? A new kind of promotion. But what's next?

One area of development may be the fusion of social media and **location-based marketing**. Location-based marketing integrates customer location data into marketing activities. Imagine walking in your nearby downtown and receiving a tweet from one of your favorite restaurants for a half-priced dinner or a text message from a good friend who just received deep discounts to a movie starting 10 minutes from now down the street. Businesses like restaurants, movie theaters, flower shops, hotels, and fresh-food outlets sell goods that expire, products that cannot be sold after a short time. Further, most of these businesses have already paid most of their costs for the product—there are few expenses for adding last-minute customers. Firms with this type of perishable inventory can use location-based social media to help manage their inventory. Improving perishable inventory management with social media is similar to how Amazon.com revolutionized online inventory management.

A second emerging issue is **social media monitoring**. With the proliferation of social media options, many firms are turning to these listening platforms to help monitor and track mentions of their products and brands on social media platforms. For example, the tweets and wall posts of some firms are retweeted and reposted much more frequently than others, creating more buzz, a greater footprint, and stronger brand identity with customers. As business use of social media increases, these monitoring tools will become more essential to justifying and validating social media use. Examples of these monitoring tools include KLOUT, Radian6, and Sysomos.

Another developing area for social media is authenticating users on the Web. One ongoing challenge for businesses on the Web is to accurately and efficiently **authenticate** that users are who they say they are. B2C sites, banking sites, and university portals are examples of the wide range of online sites that require user authentication. Currently, it is every business for themselves—each site has its own process and its own usernames and passwords. Because individuals store so many personal items and photos on Facebook, it might become possible for Facebook to use these data items to authenticate users for online businesses. For example, to log into your university system you might first be redirected by the university login page to a Facebook login page. If you can successfully log in to Facebook, you are redirected back to the university, bypassing its login page. Social media sites like Facebook know more about you than anywhere else online. Facebook might use this advantage to develop a third-party Authentication process.

What are the new management principles for the Web 2.0 world? We don't yet know. As we said in the beginning of the chapter, technique follows technology. Web 2.0 and social media are potentially disruptive technologies. Only companies that can develop techniques for applying these technologies to processes will be able to reap the benefits. You will manage in very interesting and dynamic times.

These new Web 2.0 and social media systems are still in their infancy. Because of their low cost, ease of use, and flexibility, many firms will be experimenting with them in the coming years. Your generation was the first to use these tools for personal use, and because of this experience you will be instrumental in helping firms understand how they can be used to support their processes.

Ethics Guide

Ethics, Social Media, and Stretching the Truth

No one is going to publish their ugliest picture on their Facebook page, but how far should you go to create a positive impression? If your hips and legs are not your best features, is it unethical to stand behind your sexy car in your photo? If you've been to one event with someone very popular in your crowd, is it unethical to publish photos that imply you meet as an everyday occurrence?

Surely there is no obligation to publish pictures of yourself at boring events with unpopular people just to balance the scale for those photos in which you appear unrealistically attractive and overly popular. As long as all of this occurs on a Facebook or Google+ account that you use for personal relationships, well, what goes around comes around. But consider social media in the business arena.

a. Suppose that a river-rafting company starts a group on a social media site for promoting rafting trips. Graham is a 15-year-old high school student and a potential customer. He wants to be more grownup than he is, so he posts a picture of a handsome 22-year-old male as a picture of himself. He also writes witty and clever comments on the site photos and claims to play the guitar and be an accomplished masseuse. Are his actions unethical? Suppose someone decided to go on the rafting trip, in part because of Graham's postings, and was disappointed with the truth about Graham. Would the rafting company have any responsibility to refund that person's fees?

b. Suppose you own and manage the rafting company. Is it unethical for you to encourage your employees to write positive reviews about your company?

Does your assessment change if you ask your employees to use an e-mail address other than the one they have at work?

c. Again, suppose you own and manage the rafting company and that you pay your employees a bonus for every client they bring to a rafting trip. Without specifying any particular technique, you encourage your employees to be creative in how they obtain clients. One employee invites his Facebook friends to a party at which he shows photos of prior rafting trips. On the way to the party, one of the friends has an automobile accident and dies. His spouse sues your company. Should your company be held accountable? Does it matter if you knew about the presentation? Would it matter if you had not encouraged your employees to be creative?

d. Suppose your rafting company has a Web site for customer reviews. In spite of your best efforts at camp cleanliness, on one trip (out of dozens) your staff accidentally served contaminated food and everyone became ill with food-poisoning. One of those clients from that trip writes a poor review because of that experience. Is it ethical for you to delete that review from your site?

e. Instead of owner, suppose you were at one time employed by this rafting company and you were, undeservedly you think, terminated. To get even, you use Facebook to spread rumors to your friends (many of whom are river guides) about the safety of the company's trips. Are your actions unethical? Are they illegal? Do you see any ethical distinctions between this situation and that in item d?

f. Again, suppose that you were at one time employed by the rafting company and were undeservedly terminated. You notice that the company's owner does not have a Facebook account, so you create one for her. You've known her for many years and have dozens of photos of her, some of which were taken at parties and are unflattering and revealing. You post those photos along with critical comments that she made about clients or employees. Most of the comments were made when she was tired or frustrated, and they are hurtful, but because of her wit, also humorous. You send friend invitations to people whom she knows, many of whom are the target of her biting and critical remarks. Are your actions unethical?

g. Assume you have a professor who has written a popular textbook. You are upset with the grade you received in his class, so you write a scandalously poor review of that professor's book on Amazon.com. Are your actions ethical?

Active Review

Use this Active Review to verify that you understand the material in the chapter. You can read the entire chapter and then perform the tasks in this review, or you can read the text material for just one question and perform the tasks in this review for that question before moving on to the next one.

Q1. What are Web 2.0 and social media?

Give examples of the companies that dominated the software industry in the 1990s and give examples of Web 2.0 companies. Explain the changes in network technologies that enabled the emergence of Web 2.0. Describe how software was sold before Web 2.0. Explain how interface updates differ with Web 2.0 apps. Give an example of a mashup. Define the term *prosumer*. Why do businesses find social media attractive? Describe the three major categories of social media and give an example of a popular social media app in each category.

Q2. How can Web 2.0 improve business processes?

Explain the purpose of a promotional process. Describe how AdWords supports that process. Explain AdSense and a business process it supports. Similarly, explain RSS and a process it supports. Describe Google Analytics and the type of business process it is designed to improve. Give an example of a new business process and a Web 2.0 app that supports it. Explain how Web 2.0 can help integrate business processes and give an example.

Q3. How can social media improve business processes?

Describe a social media app, a business process it supports, and a measure that can be used to assess its impact. Do this for each of the three categories of social media—sharing, networking, and collaboration. Define the terms *viral* and *social graph*. Explain how social media can help integrate business processes and give an example. Explain the keys to success for a social media promotion.

Q4. How can Web 2.0 improve the process of building social capital?

Explain capital and describe the three types of capital. Describe the possible benefits of social capital for business. Identify and explain the three objectives of the process of building social capital. Provide an example of how social media supports each of these three objectives.

Q5. What are the challenges for businesses using Web 2.0?

Give an example of a potential management problem for businesses using Web 2.0. Explain the relationship between privacy and business customer process improvement. Describe the types of processes for which Web 2.0 apps are inappropriate. Explain several of the content problems that a business may experience and offer possible solutions for those problems.

Q6. What is on the horizon that will have a significant impact on Web 2.0?

Describe a location-based marketing example and explain how Web 2.0 apps be used to support location-based marketing. Explain why businesses need social media monitoring platforms. Describe the purpose of authentication. Explain why Facebook or other social media could be used in authentication. Explain why the phrase "technique follows technology" can be used to describe the current Web 2.0 environment.

Key Terms and Concepts

AdSense   *319*
AdWords   *318*
Authenticate   *332*
Capital   *326*
Conversion rate   *320*
Crowdsourcing   *324*
Delicious   *317*
Digg   *317*
Enterprise 2.0   *317*

Foursquare   *317*
Google Analytics   *320*
Human capital   *326*
Location-based marketing   *332*
Mashup   *316*
Mutinous movement   *331*
Prosumer   *316*
Social capital   *326*
Social graph   *323*

Social media   *316*
Social media monitoring   *332*
Strength of a relationship   *328*
Traditional capital   *326*
User-generated content   *316*
Viral   *321*
Web 2.0   *314*

Using Your Knowledge

1. Visit Zillow at *www.zillow.com*. Enter the address of someone's home (your parents' perhaps) and obtain an appraisal of it. Check out the appraised values of the neighbors' homes. Do you think this site violates anyone's privacy? Why or why not? Find and describe features that demonstrate that this is a Web 2.0 app. Explain why this site might be considered a threat by traditional real estate companies. How might real estate agents use this site to market their services? How can real estate brokers (those who own agencies) use this site to their advantage?

2. Suppose you are in charge of designing the university golf course's Facebook page. Describe three features that the golf course could put on its page (e.g., a link to tee time reservations). Explain what process would be improved at the golf course with each new feature and specify a measure you would use to assess this improvement.

3. Whereas the golf course deals directly with consumers, CBI, the bicycle wholesaler, deals with retailers who then sell to consumers. How does this change the way CBI uses social media? Specify processes at CBI that can be supported by social media and measures that will assess improvements.

4. Go to Wikipedia. Read the About Wikipedia page and the Collaborative Writing page. Make a diagram that shows the process of creating and updating a Wikipedia page. Is page creation and editing a process with an effectiveness goal or efficiency goal?

What measures could be used to assess improvement in the process?

5. Search the Web using the words *Google My Maps* and follow the links to learn how to make your own maps. Then create a map of your own. Does My Maps have all the features of a Web 2.0 app?

6. Visit Digg, Delicious, and Quora. Prepare a report or presentation to the class that explains the site, which Web 2.0 characteristics are evident, and what personal or business processes the site can support.

7. Search the Web using the words *Office 365* and read about this Microsoft product. Which Web 2.0 characteristics are evident? Do you think this approach will be successful for Microsoft?

8. Assess your own stock of social capital. What activities around campus would help you increase your social capital? What social media apps could you use to increase your social capital?

9. Become a prosumer. Find a cause or group on Facebook that you believe in and contribute in ways that you do not typically contribute. Does the organization value your help in an encouraging way? If you were in charge of the site, how would you reward prosumers?

10. Join LinkedIn if you have not done so already. Start a resume and connect to people you know. Investigate job opportunities in your area of study. Locate organizations and research a few as you would if you had an upcoming job interview.

Collaboration Exercise 10

Collaborate with a group of fellow students to answer the following questions. For this exercise do not meet face to face. Your task will be easier if you coordinate your work with SharePoint, Office 365, Google Docs with Google+ or equivalent collaboration tools. (See Chapter 9 for a discussion of collaboration tools and processes.) Your answers should reflect the thinking of the entire group, and not just that of one or two individuals.

With a group of classmates, propose and carry out a small marketing promotional initiative for an organization using social media. The organization may be a business, nonprofit, university program, student activity group, or other suitable entity. Run the promotion for several weeks.

Your criteria for success include usefulness to the client (i.e., how successful it is), thoroughness, and professionalism. To better understand how to promote your product or service, consult any introductory marketing textbook or online resource and

search for *promotion* or *social media promotion*. You should also reread the keys to success for a social media campaign at the end of Q3 in this chapter before you begin. To better understand social media promotions, you might visit Mashable (*www.mashable. com*), a leading online social media site, or Technorati to search the blogosphere for guidance on social media use.

To begin, your team should discuss and specify:

1. Your target audience (you may have more than one)
2. The benefit offered by your product/service
3. The objective of your promotional activity (e.g., provide information, increase demand, differentiate, etc.)
4. Your initial design, message(s), or content
5. How success will be measured

At the end of your promotion, present to the class your plan, your experiences during the promotion, and what you would do differently next time.

CASE STUDY 10

Tourism Holdings Limited (THL)

Note: Because this case involves concepts from both this chapter and from Chapter 11, it is continued at the end of that chapter.

Tourism Holdings Limited (THL) is a publicly listed New Zealand corporation that owns multiple brands and businesses in the tourism industry. Principal holdings of THL include:

- New Zealand tourist attractions such as Waitomo Black Water Rafting and Waitomo Glowworm Caves
- Kiwi Experience and Feejee Experience, hop-on, hop-off tourist bus services
- Four brands of holiday rental vehicles
- Ci Munro, a van customization manufacturing facility

In 2009, THL earned $5 million in profit before interest and taxes on $170 million in revenue. It operates in New Zealand, Australia, and Fiji and has sales offices in Germany and the United Kingdom as well.

THL originated as The Helicopter Line, a corporation that provided scenic helicopter flights over New Zealand. Over the years, THL sold the helicopter business and has since owned and operated numerous different tourism organizations and brands. THL continues to frequently buy and sell tourism businesses. For the current list of businesses, visit *www.thlonline.com/THLBusinesses*.

According to Grant Webster, THL's CEO, "THL is a house of brands and not a branded house." Thus, in the holiday rental business, THL owns and operates four different van rental brands: Maui, Britz, backbacker, and ExploreMore. These brands are differentiated on price; Maui is the most expensive line, whereas ExploreMore appeals to the most budget-conscious traveler. Britz is the next step down in price from Maui, and backpacker falls between Britz and ExploreMore.

Tourism Market

In 2008, an estimated 866 million international visitors toured the world. That number is expected to grow to more than 1.6 billion visitors by 2020, according to *Tourism Business Magazine*. In 2008, travel and tourism was the world's largest business sector, accounting for 230 million jobs and over 10 percent of the world's GDP.[9]

Despite these long-term growth prospects, international tourism contracted recently, following the financial crisis in the Fall of 2008. As of June 2009, 1.15 million international travelers visited New Zealand annually,[10] a decrease of 5 percent from the year before, and 5.5 million international travelers visited Australia, a decline of 2 percent.[11]

According to Webster, "While we believe the long-term prospects of tourism in our traditional markets of New Zealand, Australia, and Fiji will remain strong, THL's substantial growth opportunities will be achieved by expanding to other countries, possibly the United States, or Europe."

Investment in Information Systems

THL considers information systems and technology as a core component of its business value and has invested in a variety of innovative information systems and Web 2.0 technologies. Webster, the CEO, speaks knowledgeably about information technologies, including SharePoint, OLAP, and data mining (discussed in Chapter 11).

Because of its acquisition of multiple brands and companies, THL accumulated a disparate set of information systems, based on a variety of different technologies. These disparate technologies created excessive software maintenance activity and costs. To reduce costs and simplify IS management, THL converted its customer-facing Web sites to use Microsoft SharePoint. "Having a single development platform reduced our maintenance expenses and enabled us to focus management attention, development, and personnel training on a single set of technologies," according to Steve Pickering, Manager of Interactive Information Systems.

THL uses SharePoint not for collaboration, but rather as a development and hosting platform for sophisticated, highly interactive Web sites. You can find an example of such sophisticated capabilities at *www.kiwiexperience.com*. Click "Design Your Own Trip . . ." and the Web site will display a map of New Zealand as well as a menu of instructions. You can then select different locations, experiences, and sites from the menu, and the Web site will recommend particular tours, as shown in the right-hand pane in Figure 10-15. Visit the site to get a sense of the interactivity and sophistication of processing.

Web 2.0 and social media enable the tourism industry to disintermediate sales channels. According to the New Zealand Ministry of Tourism, the Internet was used by 49 percent of international travelers to research travel options in 2006. That percentage has increased dramatically, and it is likely well over 50 percent today.

As with all disintermediation, when THL sells directly to the consumer, it saves substantial distribution costs. To facilitate direct sales, THL actively uses Google AdWords and is a key consumer of Google Analytics. THL is also experimenting with online chat, both voice and video. "A camper rental can cost $5,000 to $10,000 or more, and we believe our customers want a trusted relationship with a salesperson in order to commit," according to Webster. "We think that video online chat might give us that relationship with our customers."

---

[9] *Tourism Business Magazine,* November 2009, p. 20. Visit *www.tourismbusinessmag.co.nz* for more information.
[10] New Zealand Ministry of Tourism. Available at: *www.tourismresearch.govt.nz*.
[11] Tourism of Australia. Available at: *www.tourism.australia.com*.

FIGURE 10-15

Interactive Map of New Zealand at www.KiwiExperience.com

Source: Used with permission of Tourism Holdings Limited.

Questions

1. This case implies that the frequent acquisition and disposition of tourism brands poses problems for information systems. Summarize what you think those problems might be. Consider all five components of an information system. To what extent does standardizing on a single development platform solve those problems? Which of the five components does such standardization help the most?

2. Visit *www.kiwiexperience.com* and click Design Your Own Trip. Select a variety of locations in the Adrenalin, Nature, and Kiwi Culture places. Select several locations in each category and then select a pass that fits your destinations.
   a. Evaluate this user interface. Describe its strengths and weaknesses.
   b. Evaluate the Map Instructions. Do you find these instructions adequate? Explain why or why not.
   c. Summarize the ways in which this site uses social media.
   d. Explain why this site is an example of a mashup.

3. From the *www.kiwiexperience.com*, click Community and then Social Media and explore the site's social media page (this page may have moved, so you may have to look elsewhere on the site to see its use of social media).
   a. What are you initial reactions? Does the layout and concept invite you to participate and provide your own content?
   b. This Web site, and this social media page in particular, supports the Promotion process for THL. What other THL processes do the Web site and page support?
   c. Process improvement requires specific objectives and adequate measures. For example, one promotional objective might be to increase user interaction. The measure could be the number of clicks. What are two other possible promotional objectives for THL? Specify a measure for each.
   d. Will THL's current use of social media support the objectives and measures you specified in the previous item? How might it improve its use of social media so that it will better support your objectives for its Promotion process?

In a windowless office deep inside the corporate office of CBI, Ann, the manager of the accounting department, and Cody, the director of IT, are looking intently at a monitor.

"Ann, we use this program to determine which computers are downloading music and video files," explains Cody.

"What do we do when people abuse our system?"

"We let them know. Usually that takes care of it. But not with your man Shawn. We sent him our standard 'Don't abuse our system' e-mails, but nothing changed. Maybe it's time you do the supervisor thing and chat with him."

"Is he downloading illegally or is it from iTunes or YouTube?"

"We don't look that closely. In either case, it slows our network."

"What else?"

With a mischievous glint, Cody shows Ann a screen that displays a line with each employee name and columns for popular applications like Facebook, Google, and Outlook. "We collect data on millions of packets of Internet traffic flowing in and out of CBI every day and we sort them by IP address. This screen shows the IP address of each employee, their name, and how often they use each application."

As Ann struggles to find a measured response, Cody rambles on, "We track how often employees log in to Facebook. We also track when employees log in and out of the company network, and what types of apps they use—e-mail, video, the new ERP system. Those kinds of things."

"I don't remember being told that someone is recording my keystrokes!"

"I thought HR put out a policy letter. A lot of companies are doing it. HR says this will help them someday determine who is productive, and who is not."

"So if I log in and out of my ERP system a lot does that mean I'm more productive than if I left it open? What if I use texting instead of e-mail, is that good or bad? Do we have any reliable measures or are we just guessing what the numbers might mean? Maybe people are using texting to get their job done faster than using e-mail?"

"I know Fred purchased like a terabyte of data from SPYIT to compare how people use our network to other companies. They have some pretty sophisticated statistics. But I really don't know how it works."

Q1. Why do organizations need business intelligence (BI)?

Q2. How does BI support the Informing process?

Q3. What are examples of the Reporting process?

Q4. What are examples of the Data Mining process?

Q5. What are the components of a BI system?

Q6. What are the potential problems with BI systems?

Q7. What future technological advances will affect BI use?

Q8. Who are the key BI vendors and how does SAP accomplish BI?

Chapter Preview

The Sales and Procurement operational processes described in Chapters 7 and 8 generate significant amounts of data. In addition, the dynamic processes associated with collaboration and social media in Chapters 9 and 10 can also spin off mountains of data. But these are just a few of the many processes generating data at an organization. All this data includes useful patterns, relationships, and insights, but it is hidden, like a needle in a haystack. Finding these useful patterns is the goal of business intelligence (BI).

In this chapter, we investigate how companies like CBI use BI systems to support their processes. The chapter begins by explaining why BI is vital for business. We then explain the processes a BI system supports and describe the components of a BI system. We discuss the challenges of using BI systems and explore new BI developments. The chapter closes with a discussion of BI vendors and how SAP enables BI.

Q1. Why Do Organizations Need Business Intelligence (BI)?

Organizations need business intelligence is to make processes more effective and efficient. A **business intelligence system** is an information system that supports business processes by consolidating and analyzing data in a large database to help users create information. Consider the recent business examples listed in Figure 11-1.

Progressive, an insurance company, used BI to discover that people who do not pay their bills on time are much more likely to be involved in car accidents than those who do pay their bills on time. As a result, Progressive was able to more accurately predict the likelihood that a potential customer would be involved in an accident. Therefore, its Rate Quote process is now more accurate. The objective of the Rate Quote process is to offer lower premiums to customers who pay their bills on time (and therefore are less likely to be in an accident) in order to attract their business. In addition, this insight enables Progressive to offer high rates to potential customers who have a greater likelihood of an accident. These high-risk drivers then accept lower rates offered by other insurance companies. These other insurance companies, unaware of the risk, may offer low rates to high-risk drivers, offers that may cost these companies in the long run.

Netflix used BI to pursue its objective of improving its Movie Recommendation process. If Netflix is better than its competitors at the Movie Recommendation process, you will probably rent more from Netflix than from its competitors. Why would you go to a rental store or another cable or Web-based movie service if it cannot help you sift through thousands of movie choices as successfully as Netflix?

As depicted in the movie *Moneyball*, the Oakland Athletics baseball team wins more games than other teams with similar resources. Using BI, the Athletics improved its Player Assessment process. The team creates and uses superior statistics in its Player Assessment process so that it can be better informed about player talent. But the Athletics' secret is out. The Boston Red Sox, another baseball team, has hired its own BI wizard to help the team make better personnel decisions. This improved Player Assessment process contributed to the Red Sox winning two World Series, ending an 86-year period with no titles. Baseball is not the only sport to use BI; the New England Patriots

Data mining and other business intelligence systems have their merits as demonstrated by the examples in this chapter, but they are not without problems, as discussed in the Guide on pages 366–367.

FIGURE 11-1

Examples of BI

Company	Industry	Process	Objective	Measure
Progressive	Insurance	Rate quote	Insure safer drivers	More accurate rate quote
Netflix	Movie rental	Movie recommendation	Better prediction of next movie	Predictive accuracy
Oakland A's	Sports	Player assessment	Improve assessment of players	More informed decision making

NFL team also uses BI to support its Player Assessment process. The Patriots won three Super Bowls in four years, in part by using BI to improve its Player Assessment process. In each of these settings, a company used BI to spot patterns in vast databases and then used this intelligence to improve its processes.

Proponents believe that BI, also called *business analytics,* or simply *analytics,* will do for businesses what search engines have done for individuals. When you use a search engine, that information system analyzes its vast database of Web sites to present to you a list of Web sites that will help you create the information you need. Just as a search engine helps you find a needle in an Internet haystack, BI helps businesspeople find patterns in mountains of data.

Although businesses have been searching for patterns in data for a very long time, today the volume of data available and the tools to analyze it have made BI increasingly common and indispensible. Not only are businesses in on the act, but governments use BI to spot tax evasion and fight terrorism, and healthcare agencies are using BI to better understand diseases and to analyze the human genome.

The explosion in data and data sharing can be traced to several factors. BI is improving because new tools like SOA and XML make data sharing easier, widespread ERP use makes data collection easier, and the declining cost of storage makes data storage more affordable. These factors have led to a staggering increase in the data created and stored. Recent estimates show that each year 70 exabytes of data are generated; that is, 12,000 gigabytes per person of data, worldwide; 70 exabytes is equivalent to 14 times the total number of words ever spoken by humans. As the amount of data has grown, so has spending on BI, which has tripled in the past 12 years.[1] Not only is there more data than ever, users now have at their disposal many more software tools. In the past, only highly trained analysts could use BI, now business users with much less training can search databases to uncover patterns.

As more and more data become available and BI systems continue to improve, more patterns will emerge. This unrelenting growth in data and the human potential to spot patterns in it is a synergy aptly summarized by the statement: "Computers are incredibly fast, accurate, and stupid. Humans are incredibly slow, inaccurate, and brilliant. Together, they are powerful beyond imagination." BI is an excellent example of this synergy.

Q2. How Does BI Support the Informing Process?

Most generally, BI is the IS that supports a process called Informing. In the Informing process, an actor, typically a person, seeks to become informed. An Informing process is integrated with another process and supports the other processes (as shown in Figure 11-2). It is a process within a process, as shown at the bottom of the figure. For example, the Informing process could be added to the Procurement process to help a company reduce costs in its supply chain.

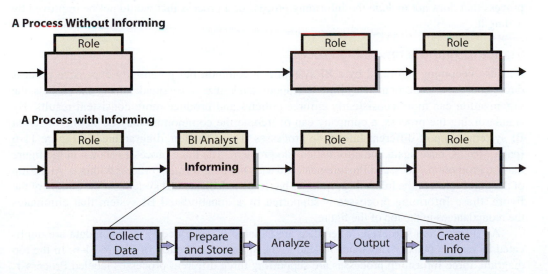

A Process Without Informing

A Process with Informing

[1] From Gartner: Available at *www.gartner.com/it/page.jsp?id=1642714.*

FIGURE 11-2

An Example Process Without and with an Informing Process

FIGURE 11-3

Main Activities and Roles in the Informing Process

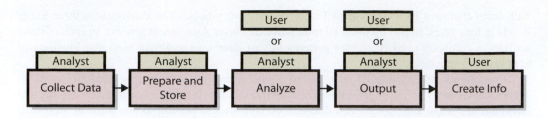

The objectives of the Informing process are typically to provide insight to users and to improve the quality of their information. In this chapter, the Informing process always relies on a BI system; however, in practice, it does not require BI. Many times, a business actor will become informed without using BI. For example, the Informing process also occurs when an actor reads, looks up data in a spreadsheet, and discusses ideas with colleagues.

Figure 11-3 shows the main activities and roles of the Informing process. In the first activity, a BI analyst collects data. This data may come from one source or several data sources. The data are then prepared and stored in a data warehouse before it is analyzed and an output is created. Preparing data might include filtering the data and transforming it into a consistent and usable format. In the final activity, an end user conceives information from the data in the output. As indicated in Figure 11-3, the end user may do the Analysis and Output activities, the analyst may do them, or they might collaborate. In the opening scenario, Ann is playing the role of end user and Cody the role of analyst.

BI Analysts have specialized training or education that enables them to support, maintain, and adapt BI systems. Many BI analysts have a background or education in MIS or statistics or both.

The Informing Process in the Sales Process

In Chapters 5 through 10, we discussed a wide range of business processes and we simplified them. One simplification we made was hiding the Informing process that occurs in many of the processes. Informing is particularly common in processes with decisions. For example, in Chapter 8 the Sales process begins with the Pre-Sales Actions and Create Sales Order activities. This Sales process is reproduced in Figure 11-4. In Figure 11-5 (page 346), we indicate that the salesperson will accomplish the Informing activity after Pre-Sales Actions and before Create Sales Order. To become informed, the salesperson analyzes data about a particular customer or product in order to decide how to approach a potential customer.

Although Figures 11-4 and 11-5 show how the Informing process can support an operational process, the Informing process also supports dynamic processes. One example of a dynamic process is the Promotional process. Managers assessing the success of a promotion will frequently become informed from Web site conversion rates or social media monitoring metrics. The process has been supported by the Informing process. In fact, it is hard to imagine a business process that does not include the Informing process or a process that would not be improved by adding it.

Standardizing the Informing Process

Because becoming informed by a BI system is a common but potentially expensive process throughout the organization, many firms attempt to standardize it. By standardizing the process, the organization can more consistently enforce policies and produce more consistent results. By standardizing the process, a company can overcome the common malady of having different BI systems support different Informing processes. This situation, diagrammed in Figure 11-6 (page 346), is, once again, the information silo problem. The three processes shown in the figure may be Promotion, Sales, and Procurement, and each has an Informing process within it. At the top of the figure, each of the Informing processes has its own dedicated BI system. At the bottom of the figure, these Informing processes is supported by a consolidated BI system that eliminates the redundancies in the top of the figure.

An information silo exists when data are isolated in separated IS or when data are duplicated in various places. This tends to lead to the situation at the top of Figure 11-6. In the top diagram, three Informing processes are supporting three different processes labeled Process 1, Process 2, and Process 3. In each, the Informing process has its own dedicated BI system.

FIGURE 11-4
The Sales Process
Without Informing

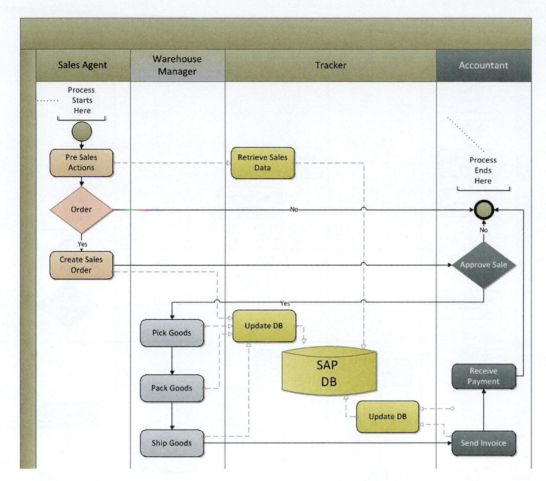

Clearly, consolidating BI data in one location, as shown at the bottom of Figure 11-6, can help standardize the Informing process. Consolidating BI data is one beneficial byproduct of implementing an ERP system.

An example of a common IS that supports various Informing processes is your smartphone. Your smartphone is like the consolidated BI at the bottom of Figure 11-6. Your smartphone is an IS that helps you become informed to improve a variety of different processes, such as finding an address, texting a friend, or reading a Web site. The value of the smartphone is that this one BI system makes you more effective and efficient in many of these processes, not just one. Imagine how impractical it would be to have to carry several smartphones with you because each only supports a single process.

Versions of the Informing Processes

For simplicity, we have treated informing as one process. In reality, informing can be split into two main types of processes: Reporting processes and Data Mining processes. These processes are summarized in Figure 11-7 (page 347).

THE REPORTING PROCESS The **Reporting process** creates structured reports and delivers those reports to users. The analysis of the data is simple: Data are sorted and grouped, and simple totals and averages are calculated using operations such as sorting, grouping, and summing. The objective of the Reporting process is most often better assessment. *Assessment* means to evaluate what is happening. It is used to address questions like: What type of customer is buying this product? How well is this product selling? Most often, reporting can be accomplished with just operational data within the organization. An example of reporting is the process used by the professional sports teams to assess player talent. The Oakland Athletics mentioned earlier grouped and sorted baseball data in new ways. Another, from the opening scenario, is Cody's process at CBI that tracks and reports IP addresses and applications. The Reporting process is explained more completely in Q3.

FIGURE 11-5

The Sales Process with Informing

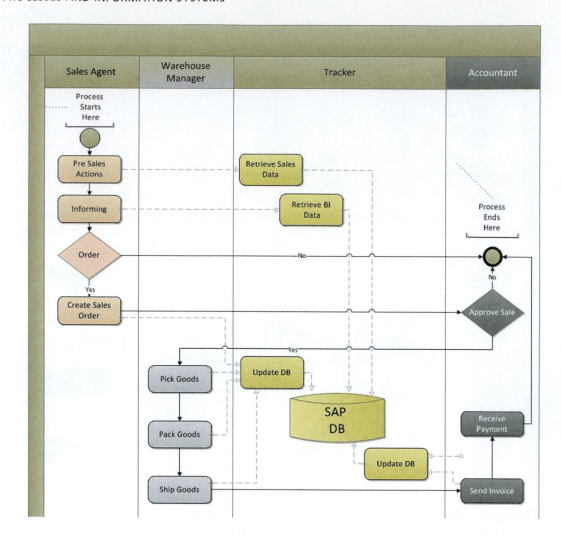

FIGURE 11-6

BI in Silos and BI without Silos

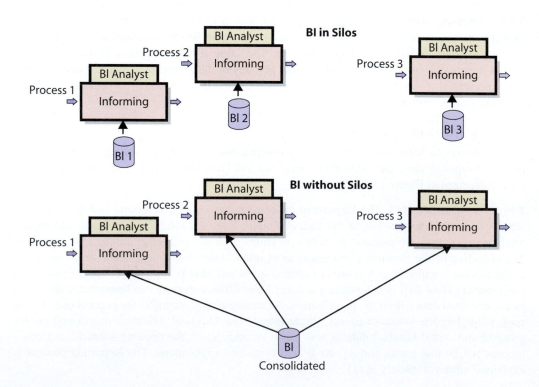

Informing Version	Common Type of Objective	Company in Figure 11-1	Common Analysis	Types
Reporting	Assessment	Oakland A's	Simple—summing, totaling	Noninteractive—RFM Interactive—OLAP
Data mining	Prediction	Progressive Netflix	Advanced statistics	Cluster Regression Market basket Decision tree Others

FIGURE 11-7
Two Types of Informing Processes: Reporting and Data Mining

THE DATA MINING PROCESS The **Data Mining process** has the same activities as the Reporting process. However, in the Analysis activity the statistics used are much more sophisticated and complex. In most cases, the objective of data mining is better *prediction.* For example, the Data Mining process used by Progressive generates predictions about the likelihood of a motor vehicle accident. Another example of the Data Mining process predicts products that tend to be purchased together. In one famous example, a data mining process determined that customers who buy diapers are likely to buy beer. The analysis required sophisticated statistical techniques beyond simple grouping and sorting that controlled for day of the week, customer gender, and price. This insight prompted store managers to locate beer and diapers near each other in store displays. The Data Mining process is explained more completely in Q4.

Q3. What Are Examples of the Reporting Process?

Examples of how the Reporting process supports other processes occur throughout CBI. For example, when a customer calls Sue in sales, she uses a Reporting process to see every recorded transaction with that customer. She uses this process to become more informed about the prices she can offer the customer. For example, if the customer has purchased in greater amounts in the past but has reduced purchases lately, Sue may try to entice them with a significant bulk discount. Ann in accounting uses a Reporting process to group accounts to show profit for each bicycle accessory, sorting them in order of profitability and grouping them by type of accessory.

As shown in Figure 11-8, the Reporting process has the same activities as the Informing process. Figure 11-8 also shows some of the options for the activities in the Reporting process.

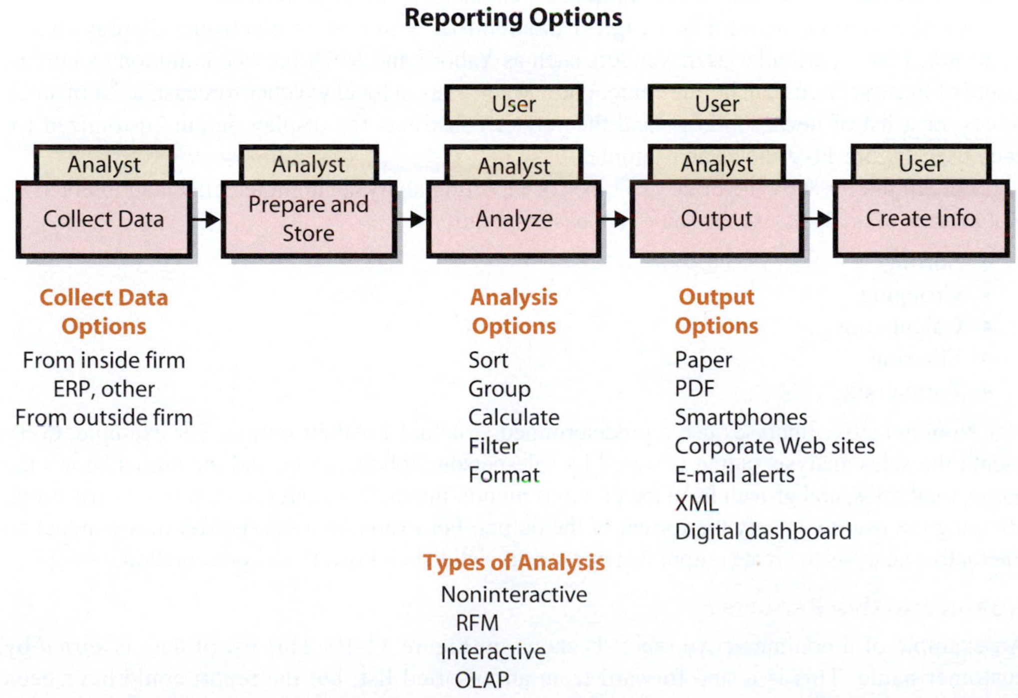

Reporting Options
User
User
Analyst
Analyst
Analyst
Analyst
User
Collect Data
Prepare and Store
Analyze
Output
Create Info
Collect Data Options
From inside firm
ERP, other
From outside firm
Analysis Options
Sort
Group
Calculate
Filter
Format
Output Options
Paper
PDF
Smartphones
Corporate Web sites
E-mail alerts
XML
Digital dashboard
Types of Analysis
Noninteractive
RFM
Interactive
OLAP

FIGURE 11-8
Activities and Options in the Reporting Process

FIGURE 11-9

Digital Dashboard Example

Data are collected from a variety of sources, including operational databases; an ERP database; and external databases, such as those containing customer purchasing data. The data are then prepared and stored in a repository called a *data warehouse*, which is a special type of database configured for BI applications. We will skip the Analyze activity for a moment and consider the various output options next. Report output options include a variety of media. Some output is printed on paper; other output is generated in formats such as PDF files that can be printed or viewed electronically. Output can also be delivered to computer screens and smartphones. Additionally, companies sometimes place output on internal corporate Web sites for employees to access. For example, an organization might place the output of its latest sales analysis on the sales department's Web site or the output on customers serviced on the customer service department's Web site. Output can be delivered in e-mail alerts or in XML format.

Another output medium is a **digital dashboard**, which is an electronic display that is customized for a particular user. Vendors such as Yahoo! and MSN provide common examples. Users of these services can define content they want—say, a local weather forecast, a list of stock prices, or a list of news sources—and the vendor constructs the display output customized for each user. Figure 11-9 shows an example.

For simplicity, we categorize two types of reporting analysis: noninteractive and interactive. Both forms of analysis use the same five basic operations:

- Sorting
- Grouping
- Calculating
- Filtering
- Formatting

Noninteractive analyses use a predetermined structure for their output. For example, every month the sales analysis output is sorted by salesperson alphabetically, and the output shows the name, total sales, and growth from the previous month. Interactive analyses are more unstructured, allowing the user to specify the format of the output. For example, a salesperson may conduct an interactive analysis to create output that appears as a slide in a PowerPoint presentation.

Noninteractive Reports

An example of a noninteractive report is shown in Figure 11-10. This list of data is *sorted* by customer name. This is a step forward from an unsorted list, but the report could have been designed to *group* the orders, producing another noninteractive report, as shown in Figure 11-11.

CustomerName	CustomerEmail	DateOfSale	Amount
Ashley, Jane	JA@somewhere.com	5/5/2011	$110.00
Corning,Sandra	KD@somewhereelse.com	7/7/2011	$375.00
Ching, Kam Hoong	KHC@somewhere.com	5/17/2011	$55.00
Rikki, Nicole	GC@righthere.com	6/19/2009	$155.00
Corning,Sandra	SC@somewhereelse.com	2/4/2010	$195.00
Scott, Rex	RS@somewhere.com	7/15/2011	$56.00
Corovic,Jose	JC@somewhere.com	11/12/2011	$55.00
McGovern, Adrian	BL@righthere.com	11/12/2009	$47.00
Wei, Guang	GW@ourcompany.com	11/28/2010	$385.00
Dixon,Eleonor	ED@somewhere.com	5/17/2011	$108.00
Lee,Brandon	BL@somewhereelse.com	5/5/2009	$74.00
Duong,Linda	LD@righthere.com	5/17/2010	$485.00
Dixon, James T	JTD@somewhere.com	4/3/2010	$285.00
La Pierre,Anna	SG@righthere.com	9/22/2011	$120.00
La Pierre,Anna	WS@somewhere.com	3/14/2010	$47.50
La Pierre,Anna	TR@righthere.com	9/22/2010	$580.00
Ryan, Mark	MR@somewhereelse.com	11/3/2010	$42.00
Rikki, Nicole	MR@righthere.com	3/14/2011	$175.00
Scott, Bryan	BS@somewhere.com	3/17/2010	$145.00
Warrem, Jason	JW@ourcompany.com	5/12/2011	$160.00
La Pierre,Anna	ALP@somewhereelse.com	3/15/2010	$52.00
Angel, Kathy	KA@righthere.com	9/15/2011	$195.00
La Pierre,Anna	JQ@somewhere.com	4/12/2011	$44.00
Casimiro, Amanda	AC@somewhere.com	12/7/2010	$52.00
McGovern, Adrian	AM@ourcompany.com	3/17/2010	$52.00
Menstell,Lori Lee	LLM@ourcompany.com	10/18/2011	$72.00
La Pierre,Anna	DJ@righthere.com	12/7/2010	$175.00
Nurul,Nicole	NN@somewhere.com	10/12/2011	$84.00
Menstell,Lori Lee	VB@ourcompany.com	9/24/2011	$120.00

FIGURE 11-10

Noninteractive Report of Raw Sales Data

CustomerName	CustomerEmail	DateOfSale	Amount
Adams, James	JA3@somewhere.com	1/15/2011	$145.00
Angel, Kathy	KA@righthere.com	9/15/2011	$195.00
Ashley, Jane	JA@somewhere.com	5/5/2011	$110.00
Austin, James	JA7@somewhere.com	1/15/2010	$55.00
Bernard, Steven	SB@ourcompany.com	9/17/2011	$78.00
Casimiro, Amanda	AC@somewhere.com	12/7/2010	$52.00
Ching, Kam Hoong	KHC@somewhere.com	5/17/2011	$55.00
Corning,Sandra	KD@somewhereelse.com	7/7/2011	$375.00
Corning,Sandra	SC@somewhereelse.com	2/4/2010	$195.00
Corovic,Jose	JC@somewhere.com	11/12/2011	$55.00
Daniel, James	JD@somewhere.com	1/18/2011	$52.00
Dixon, James T	JTD@somewhere.com	4/3/2010	$285.00
Dixon,Eleonor	ED@somewhere.com	5/17/2011	$108.00
Drew, Richard	RD@righthere.com	10/3/2010	$42.00
Duong,Linda	LD@righthere.com	5/17/2010	$485.00
Garrett, James	JG@ourcompany.com	3/14/2011	$38.00
Jordan, Matthew	MJ@righthere.com	3/14/2010	$645.00
La Pierre,Anna	DJ@righthere.com	12/7/2010	$175.00
La Pierre,Anna	SG@righthere.com	9/22/2011	$120.00
La Pierre,Anna	TR@righthere.com	9/22/2010	$580.00
La Pierre,Anna	ALP@somewhereelse.com	3/15/2010	$52.00
La Pierre,Anna	JQ@somewhere.com	4/12/2011	$44.00
La Pierre,Anna	WS@somewhere.com	3/14/2010	$47.50
Lee,Brandon	BL@somewhereelse.com	5/5/2009	$74.00
Lunden,Haley	HL@somewhere.com	11/17/2008	$52.00
McGovern, Adrian	BL@righthere.com	11/12/2009	$47.00
McGovern, Adrian	AM@ourcompany.com	3/17/2010	$52.00
Menstell,Lori Lee	LLM@ourcompany.com	10/18/2011	$72.00
Menstell,Lori Lee	VB@ourcompany.com	9/24/2011	$120.00

FIGURE 11-11

Noninteractive Sales Data, Sorted by Customer Name

FIGURE 11-12

Noninteractive Sales Data, Sorted by Customer Name and Grouped by Orders and Purchase Amount

CustomerName ▾	NumOrders ▾	TotalPurcha: ▾
Adams, James	1	$145.00
Angel, Kathy	1	$195.00
Ashley, Jane	1	$110.00
Austin, James	1	$55.00
Bernard, Steven	1	$78.00
Casimiro, Amanda	1	$52.00
Ching, Kam Hoong	1	$55.00
Corning,Sandra	2	$570.00
Corovic,Jose	1	$55.00
Daniel, James	1	$52.00
Dixon, James T	1	$285.00
Dixon,Eleonor	1	$108.00
Drew, Richard	1	$42.00
Duong,Linda	1	$485.00
Garrett, James	1	$38.00
Jordan, Matthew	1	$645.00
La Pierre,Anna	6	$1,018.50
Lee,Brandon	1	$74.00
Lunden,Haley	1	$52.00
McGovern, Adrian	2	$99.00
Menstell,Lori Lee	2	$192.00
Nurul,Nicole	1	$84.00
Pham,Mary	1	$38.00
Redmond, Louise	1	$140.00
Rikki, Nicole	2	$330.00
Ryan, Mark	1	$42.00
Scott, Bryan	1	$145.00
Scott, Rex	1	$56.00
UTran,Diem Thi	1	$275.00
Warrem, Jason	1	$160.00

Suppose the user is interested in repeat customers. If so, the report could have been designed to *filter* the groups of orders to select only those customers that have two or more orders. The results of these operations are shown in Figure 11-12. Notice that the report not only grouped the orders but also *calculated* the number of orders for each customer and the total purchase amount per customer. This report is considered noninteractive because the output is in the same format each month; the analyst does not look at the output and return to the analysis step.

The five operations just discussed may seem too simple to produce important results, but this is not the case. Reporting can produce incredibly interesting and useful results. For example, in the opening scenario Cody and Ann were looking at a noninteractive report on users and applications. Another common type of noninteractive report is an RFM analysis.

An **RFM analysis** analyzes and ranks customers according to their purchasing patterns. RFM considers how *recently* (R) a customer has ordered, how *frequently* (F) a customer has ordered, and how much *money* (M) the customer has spent, as shown in Figure 11-13.

To produce an RFM score, the RFM analysis first sorts customer purchase records by the date of their most recent (R) purchase. A common form of this analysis divides the customers into five groups and gives customers in each group a score of 1 to 5. The 20 percent of the customers having the most recent orders are given an R score of 1, the 20 percent of the customers having the next most recent orders are given an R score of 2, and so forth, down to the last 20 percent, who are given an R score of 5.

FIGURE 11-13

Example of RFM Data

Customer	RFM Score
Ajax	1 1 3
Bloominghams	5 1 1
Caruthers	5 4 5

The RFM analysis then re-sorts the customers on the basis of how frequently they order. The 20 percent of the customers who order most frequently are given an F score of 1, the next 20 percent of most frequently ordering customers are given a score of 2, and so forth, down to the least frequently ordering customers, who are given an F score of 5.

Finally, the analysis sorts the customers again according to the amount spent on their orders. The 20 percent who have ordered the most expensive items are given an M score of 1, the next 20 percent are given an M score of 2, and so forth, down to the 20 percent who spend the least, who are given an M score of 5.

Figure 11-13 shows sample RFM results. The first customer, Ajax, has ordered recently and orders frequently. Ajax's M score of 3 indicates, however, that it does not order the most expensive goods. From this report, the sales team can conclude that Ajax is a good, regular customer, and that they should attempt to up-sell more-expensive goods to Ajax.

The second customer in Figure 11-13 could represent a problem. Bloominghams has not ordered in some time, but when it did order in the past it ordered frequently, and its orders were of the highest monetary value. This data suggests that Bloominghams might have taken its business to another vendor. Someone from the sales team should contact this customer immediately.

No one on the sales team should even think about the third customer, Caruthers. This company has not ordered for some time; it did not order frequently; and, when it did order, it bought the least-expensive items, and not many of them. Let Caruthers go to the competition; the loss will be minimal.

Interactive Reports

Interactive analyses use the same basic analysis operations of sorting, grouping, and filtering, but, as the name implies, allows the user to use these operations interactively; that is, the user or analyst can experiment with one method of analysis, interpret the output, and then go back and reanalyze the data. Interactive options allow the end user to change both the analysis and the structure of the output. A diagram of an interactive Reporting process is shown in Figure 11-14. A simple example of an interactive report would be a user querying a database in Access, interpreting the output from the query, and then changing the query.

The most common term used for interactive reporting is **online analytical processing (OLAP)**. OLAP provides the ability to analyze the data using the basic operations—sorting, grouping, calculating, filtering, and formatting—in an interactive structure. An OLAP report is similar to interacting with a search engine. A search engine groups Web sites based on the words you type in. More important, a search engine is interactive. You can alter what the search engine is looking for by changing your terms. You can also change the format of the

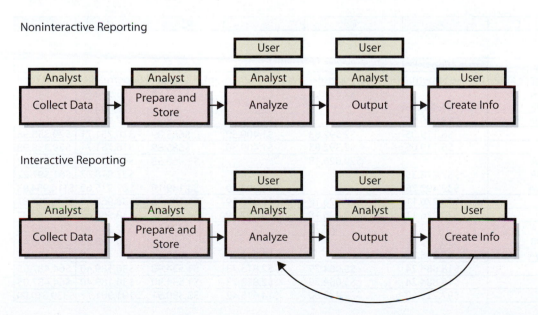

FIGURE 11-14

Main Activities in Noninteractive and an Interactive Reporting Process

	A	B	C	D	E	F	G
1							
2							
3	Store Sales Net	Store Type ▼					
4	Product Family ▼	Deluxe Supermarket	Gourmet Supermarket	Mid-Size Grocery	Small Grocery	Supermarket	Grand Total
5	Drink	$8,119.05	$2,392.83	$1,409.50	$685.89	$16,751.71	$29,358.98
6	Food	$70,276.11	$20,026.18	$10,392.19	$6,109.72	$138,960.67	$245,764.87
7	Non-Consumable	$18,884.24	$5,064.79	$2,813.73	$1,534.90	$36,189.40	$64,487.05
8	Grand Total	$97,279.40	$27,483.80	$14,615.42	$8,330.51	$191,901.77	$339,610.90

FIGURE 11-15

OLAP Product Family and Store Type

output—you can change the number of Web sites displayed on the screen; you can sort by different choices; and, if you are using Google, you can even display the output in a wheel format using its Wonder Wheel.

An OLAP report has measures and dimensions. An **OLAP measure** is the data item of interest. It is the item that is to be summed or averaged or otherwise processed in the OLAP report. Total sales, average sales, and average cost are examples of measures. An **OLAP dimension** is a characteristic or attribute of a measure. Purchase date, customer type, customer location, and sales region are all examples of dimensions.

Figure 11-15 shows a typical OLAP report. Here, the OLAP measure is *Net Store Sales*, and the dimensions are *Product Family* and *Store Type*. This report shows how net store sales vary by product family and store type. For example, stores of type *Supermarket* sold a net of $36,189 worth of Non-Consumable goods.

A presentation like that in Figure 11-15 is often called an **OLAP cube**, or sometimes simply a *cube*. The reason for this term is that some reports show these displays using three dimensions, like a cube in geometry.

As stated earlier, the distinguishing characteristic of an interactive report is that the user can alter the analysis and output. Figure 11-16 shows such an alteration. Here, the user added another dimension, *Store Country* and *Store State*, to the horizontal display. Product-family sales are now differentiated only by store location. Observe that the sample data only includes stores in the United States, and only in the western states of California, Oregon, and Washington.

With an OLAP report, it is possible to **drill down** into the data. This term means to further divide the data into more detail. In Figure 11-17, for example, the user has drilled down into the stores located in California; the OLAP report now shows sales data for the four cities in California that have stores.

FIGURE 11-16

OLAP Product Family and Store Location by Store Type

	A	B	C	D	E	F	G	H	I
1									
2									
3	Store Sales Net			Store Type ▼					
4	Product Family ▼	Store ▼	Store State	Deluxe Superma	Gourmet Supermar	Mid-Size Groce	Small Grocery	Supermarket	Grand Total
5	Drink	USA	CA		$2,392.83		$227.38	$5,920.76	$8,540.97
6			OR	$4,438.49				$2,862.45	$7,300.94
7			WA	$3,680.56		$1,409.50	$458.51	$7,968.50	$13,517.07
8		USA Total		$8,119.05	$2,392.83	$1,409.50	$685.89	$16,751.71	$29,358.98
9	Drink Total			$8,119.05	$2,392.83	$1,409.50	$685.89	$16,751.71	$29,358.98
10	Food	USA	CA		$20,026.18		$1,960.53	$47,226.11	$69,212.82
11			OR	$37,778.35				$23,818.87	$61,597.22
12			WA	$32,497.76		$10,392.19	$4,149.19	$67,915.69	$114,954.83
13		USA Total		$70,276.11	$20,026.18	$10,392.19	$6,109.72	$138,960.67	$245,764.87
14	Food Total			$70,276.11	$20,026.18	$10,392.19	$6,109.72	$138,960.67	$245,764.87
15	Non-Consumable	USA	CA		$5,064.79		$474.35	$12,344.49	$17,883.63
16			OR	$10,177.89				$6,428.53	$16,606.41
17			WA	$8,706.36		$2,813.73	$1,060.54	$17,416.38	$29,997.01
18		USA Total		$18,884.24	$5,064.79	$2,813.73	$1,534.90	$36,189.40	$64,487.05
19	Non-Consumable Total			$18,884.24	$5,064.79	$2,813.73	$1,534.90	$36,189.40	$64,487.05
20	Grand Total			$97,279.40	$27,483.80	$14,615.42	$8,330.51	$191,901.77	$339,610.90

	A	B	C	D	E	F	G	H	I	J
1										
2										
3	Store Sales Net				Store Type					
4	Store Country	Store Sta	Store City	Product Family	Deluxe Super	Gourmet Supermar	Mid-Size Groce	Small Grocery	Supermarket	Grand Total
5	USA	CA	Beverly Hills	Drink		$2,392.83				$2,392.83
6				Food		$20,026.18				$20,026.18
7				Non-Consumable		$5,064.79				$5,064.79
8			Beverly Hills Total			$27,483.80				$27,483.80
9			Los Angeles	Drink					$2,870.33	$2,870.33
10				Food					$23,598.28	$23,598.28
11				Non-Consumable					$6,305.14	$6,305.14
12			Los Angeles Total						$32,773.74	$32,773.74
13			San Diego	Drink					$3,050.43	$3,050.43
14				Food					$23,627.83	$23,627.83
15				Non-Consumable					$6,039.34	$6,039.34
16			San Diego Total						$32,717.61	$32,717.61
17			San Francisco	Drink				$227.38		$227.38
18				Food				$1,960.53		$1,960.53
19				Non-Consumable				$474.35		$474.35
20			San Francisco Total					$2,662.26		$2,662.26
21		CA Total				$27,483.80		$2,662.26	$65,491.35	$95,637.41
22		OR		Drink	$4,438.49				$2,862.45	$7,300.94
23				Food	$37,778.35				$23,818.87	$61,597.22
24				Non-Consumable	$10,177.89				$6,428.53	$16,606.41
25		OR Total			$52,394.72				$33,109.85	$85,504.57
26		WA		Drink	$3,680.56		$1,409.50	$458.51	$7,968.50	$13,517.07
27				Food	$32,497.76		$10,392.19	$4,149.19	$67,915.69	$114,954.83
28				Non-Consumable	$8,706.36		$2,813.73	$1,060.54	$17,416.38	$29,997.01
29		WA Total			$44,884.68		$14,615.42	$5,668.24	$93,300.57	$158,468.91
30	USA Total				$97,279.40	$27,483.80	$14,615.42	$8,330.51	$191,901.77	$339,610.90
31	Grand Total				$97,279.40	$27,483.80	$14,615.42	$8,330.51	$191,901.77	$339,610.90

FIGURE 11-17

OLAP Product Family and Store Location by Store Type Drilled Down to Show Stores in California

Notice another difference between Figures 11-16 and 11-17. The user has not only drilled down, she has also changed the order of the dimensions. Figure 11-16 shows *Product Family* and then store location within *Product Family*. Figure 11-17 shows store location and then *Product Family* within store location.

To summarize, the Informing process has two types. One type of Informing process is the Reporting process just discussed. Reporting also has two basic versions: noninteractive and interactive. As shown earlier in Figure 11-7, the objective of both versions of the Reporting process is typically assessment, to evaluate what is happening. The Data Mining process, discussed next, also involves a very large database. However, the objective of the Data Mining process is to predict patterns and relationships in the data.

Q4. What Are Examples of the Data Mining Process?

The Data Mining process uses advanced statistical techniques to find patterns and relationships among data for classification and prediction. As shown in Figure 11-18, data mining resulted from a convergence of disciplines. Data mining emerged from statistics and mathematics and from artificial intelligence and machine-learning fields in computer science. Like interactive reporting with OLAP, all data mining analyses are interactive. An example of the Data Mining process is the process used by Netflix to recommend a movie. The eventual recommendation analysis is the result of hundreds, if not thousands, of iterations by the programming team using very advanced statistical techniques. At each iteration, the team examined the predictive results of the analysis and then added or subtracted variables as they tweaked their analysis to improve its results.

One reason CBI implemented the BI component of SAP was to conduct data mining. One example of the usefulness of data mining at CBI was that it improved the Outbound Delivery process. CBI outfitted its fleet of delivery trucks with sensors to track truck location and used the output of the Data Mining process to suggest smart routes to follow to avoid construction, traffic, and stop lights. In another application, CBI partnered with its retail customers to gain access to their sales data. The Data Mining process consolidates this customer data from the various retail outlets into a single data warehouse. Once combined, the data are mined with advanced statistical techniques to spot unusual buying patterns across the industry. These predictive buying patterns help CBI salespeople adjust future delivery dates and delivery options in order to save both the retailer and CBI money.

Just as the Reporting process had two different types of analysis—noninteractive and interactive—the Data Mining process also features a variety of analyses. In the following sections, we present four examples. These are shown in Figure 11-19.

Cluster Analysis

One common form of analysis is **cluster analysis**. With it, statistical techniques identify groups of entities that have similar characteristics. A common use for cluster analysis is to find groups of similar customers from customer order and demographic data. For example, a cluster analysis might discover two very different customer groups: One group has an average age of 33,

FIGURE 11-18

Convergent Disciplines for Data Mining

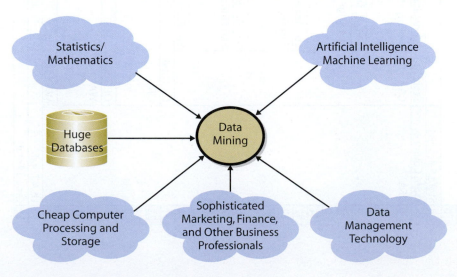

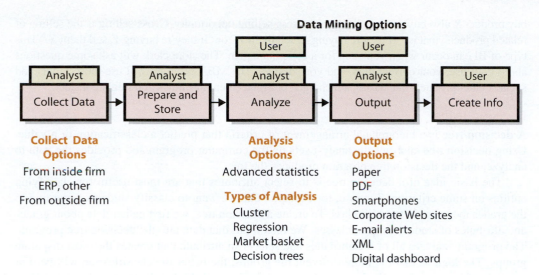

FIGURE 11-19

Activities and Options In the Data Mining Process

owns two iPhones, has an expensive home entertainment system, drives a Lexus SUV, and tends to buy expensive children's play equipment. The second group has an average age of 64, owns Arizona vacation property, plays golf, and buys expensive wines. A marketing company that is promoting children's play equipment may decide to advertise in consumer technology media such as *Wired* magazine and music download platforms to communicate with the cluster of consumers who buy play equipment.

Regression Analysis

Another type of data mining analysis, which measures the impact of a set of variables on another variable, is called a **regression analysis**. For example, suppose marketing experts in a communications company believe that cell phone usage on weekends is determined by the age of the customer and the number of months the customer has had the cell phone account. A sample regression result for the cell phone example is:

$$CellphoneWeekendMinutes = 12 + (17.5 * CustomerAge) + (23.7 * NumberMonthsOfAccount)$$

Using this equation, analysts can predict the number of minutes of weekend cell phone use by summing 12, plus 17.5 times the customer's age, plus 23.7 times the number of months of the account.

As you will learn in your statistics classes, considerable skill is required to interpret the quality of such a model. The regression software will create an equation, such as the one shown. Whether that equation is a good predictor of future cell phone usage depends on statistical factors. Factors you will learn in a statistics class such as *t* values, confidence intervals, and related statistical measures.

Regression analysis is often used in sports to predict future performance. One reason is that when a game is played, consistent statistics are recorded and so are wins and losses. Regression allows the analyst to experiment with a range of statistics to determine which variables better predict wins and losses.

Market Basket Analysis

Suppose you run a dive shop, and one day you realize that one of your salespeople is much better than others at up-selling your customers. Any of your sales associates can fill a customer's order, but this one salesperson is especially good at selling customers items *in addition to* those for which they ask. One day, you ask him how he does it.

"It's simple," he says. "I just ask myself what is the next product they would want to buy. If someone buys a dive computer, I don't try to sell her fins. If she's buying a dive computer, she's already a diver and she already has fins. But, these dive computer displays are hard to read. A better mask makes it easier to read the display and get the full benefit from the dive computer."

A **market basket analysis (MBA)** determines sales patterns. Such an analysis shows the products that customers tend to buy together. In marketing transactions, the fact that customers who buy product *X* also buy product *Y* creates a cross-selling opportunity. **Cross-selling** is the selling of related products; that is, "If they're buying *X*, sell them *Y*" or "If they're buying *Y*, sell them *X*." This type of BI can occur when you shop for a cell phone plan. The store clerk will ask some questions about your use, your current plan, and your desires. The MBA program will use those inputs and suggest other products like a case, a recharger, or replacement insurance you might consider.

Decision Trees

A **decision tree** is a hierarchical arrangement of criteria that predict a classification or a value. Using decision tree analyses the analyst sets up the computer program and provides the data to analyze, and the decision tree program produces the tree.

The basic idea of a decision tree is to select attributes that are most useful for classifying entities on some criterion. Suppose, for example, that we want to classify students according to the grades they earn in the MIS class. To create a decision tree, we first gather data about grades and attributes of students in past classes. We then input that data into the decision tree program. The program analyzes all of the attributes and selects an attribute that creates the most disparate groups. The logic is that the more different the groups, the better the classification will be. For example, if every student who lived off campus earned a grade higher than 3.0, and every student who lived on campus earned a grade lower than 3.0, then the program would use the variable *live-off-campus* or *live-on-campus* to classify students. In this unrealistic example, the program would be a perfect classifier, because each group is pure, with no misclassifications.

More realistically, consider Figure 11-20, which shows a hypothetical decision tree analysis of MIS class grades. Again, assume we are classifying students depending on whether their grade was greater than 3.0 or less than or equal to 3.0.

The decision tree software that created this tree examined student characteristics such as students' class (junior or senior), their major, their employment, their age, their club affiliations, and other student characteristics. It then used values of those characteristics to create groups that were as different as possible on the classification grade above or below 3.0.

For the results shown here, the decision tree program determined that the best first criterion is whether the students are juniors or seniors. In this case, the classification was imperfect, as shown by the fact that neither of the senior nor the junior groups consisted only of students with GPAs above or below 3.0. Still, it did create groups that were less mixed than in the *All Students* group.

Next, the program examined other criteria to further subdivide *Seniors* and *Juniors* so as to create even more groups. The program divided the senior group into subgroups: those who are

FIGURE 11-20

Grades of Students from Past MIS Class

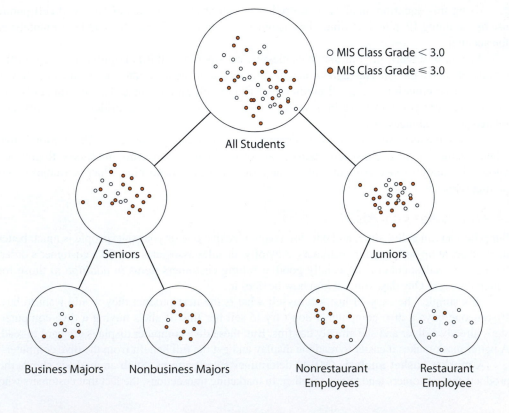

business majors and those who are not. The program's analysis of the junior data, however, determined that the difference between majors is not significant. Instead, the best classifier (the one that generated the most different groups) is whether the junior worked in a restaurant. Decision tree analysis is also called *recursive partitioning,* because at each step the analysis partitions itself into groups.

Examining this data, we see that junior restaurant employees do well in the class, but junior nonrestaurant employees and senior nonbusiness majors do poorly. Performance in the other senior group is mixed.

A decision tree like the one in Figure 11-20 can be transformed into a set of decision rules having the format, If . . . then . . . . Decision rules for this example are:

- If student is a junior and works in a restaurant, then predict grade > 3.0.
- If student is a senior and is a nonbusiness major, then predict grade ≤ 3.0.
- If student is a junior and does not work in a restaurant, then predict grade ≤ 3.0.
- If student is a senior and is a business major, then make no prediction.

Most data mining software is sophisticated and can be difficult to use well. However, because data mining is valuable, some business professionals, especially those in finance and marketing, have become expert in their use. In fact, today there are many interesting and rewarding careers for business professionals who are knowledgeable about data mining techniques.

These four examples of Data Mining processes are just a sample of the available analysis options. Other data mining options include neural networks, text and Web mining, sensitivity analysis, what-if analysis, Bayesean methods, fuzzy logic, and multicriteria decision analysis.

MIS InClass 11

I Know That, I Think

Set a lower and an upper bound for each of the following 10 questions. For example, if the question was "What is the age of President Obama?" you might think the answer is about 45, so you would set a lower bound of 40 and an upper bound of 50. Make these bounds wide enough so that you get 9 out of the 10 questions correct.

Source: Laurence Gough/Fotolia, LLC–Royalty Free.

	Lower Bound	Upper Bound	Question
1.	_____	_____	What is the height of the Empire State Building?
2.	_____	_____	In what year was former President Reagan born?
3.	_____	_____	What is the length of the longest overland tunnel in the world?
4.	_____	_____	What is the current national circulation of the *Wall Street Journal*?
5.	_____	_____	What is the population of Australia?
6.	_____	_____	What is the distance between Atlanta and Dallas?
7.	_____	_____	How many books are in the Library of Congress?
8.	_____	_____	How many countries are there in the world?
9.	_____	_____	How many steps does the Washington Monument have?
10.	_____	_____	What year did Julius Caesar die?

Also, make your lower and upper bounds reasonable estimates. You are not allowed to use any help on this exercise.

Once you have answered these questions, your instructor will tell you the correct answers.

As a class, discuss the following questions:

1. Why did you set your boundaries where you did?
2. What does your score on this exercise suggest?
3. Which Informing process (Reporting or Data Mining) would have improved your answers?

Supervised and Unsupervised Data Mining Analysis

Data mining analysis can be categorized as unsupervised and supervised. With **unsupervised data mining**, analysts do not create a model or hypothesis before running the analysis. Instead, they apply the data mining software to the data and observe the results. With this method, analysts create hypotheses *after the analysis* in order to explain the patterns found. Another term for unsupervised analysis is *data-driven analysis*. An example of an unsupervised data mining is postelection analysis. Analysts may run hundreds of data mining analyses—who carried the soccer mom demographic, who got the vote of independents, what percentage of precincts with less than 60 percent of college educated registered voters went for the incumbent. The analyst then looks over the results and creates a hypothesis: "The winner did better than expected with two groups, which carried the winner over the top; these two were . . ." Cluster analysis, MBA, and decision trees are examples of unsupervised data mining.

With **supervised data mining**, analysts develop a model *prior to the analysis* and apply statistical analyses to the data to estimate parameters of the model. Regression analysis is an example of supervised data mining. For example, in the cell phone example given earlier the analyst first develops the model that weekend cell phone use is determined by customer and account age, then the regression analysis is done.

Q5. What Are the Components of a BI System?

Having considered Informing processes supported by BI systems, we now shift our attention away from the processes supported by BI to consider the BI system and its components. Like any other information system, a BI system has five components.

Prior to this recent explosion in data and software tools, BI systems used to analyze data were often called **decision support systems (DSS)**. A DSS is an information system used in support of decision making. It is still a term used today when the supported process is decision making. We consider DSS to be a subset of BI.

Hardware

The key piece of hardware in a BI system is a BI server. A BI server is used by an analyst to analyze the data and produce the output. A BI server can deliver output in the variety of formats, listed earlier in Figures 11-8 and 11-19. For example, at CBI the BI server can push the results of an RFM analysis on operational sales data to Sue's smartphone.

Software

BI software also varies based on the analysis method used. Most special-purpose BI software packages can support either reporting or data mining analysis. Some general-purpose software, such as Excel, can also be used for either reporting or data mining. Some specialized BI software might do just one or the other.

Data

Data can be collected for a BI system in two ways. First, the data may come from an **operational database** that contains the data from the operational processes in a company. Second, data may come from other sources that are then combined with operational process data. In either case, once the data are collected they are then prepared and stored in a **data warehouse**, a repository for the organization's BI data. BI data are kept in a data warehouse because a data warehouse is specially designed to make sorting and retrieving large volumes of data efficient. Operational databases, in contrast, are designed to make data inputs and updates efficient.

Before data can be stored in a data warehouse, programs first read operational and other data and then extract, filter, clean, and, if necessary, transform the data for storage. These data may be stored in a data warehouse database using a data warehouse DBMS, which can be different from the organization's operational DBMS. For example, an organization might use Oracle for its operational processing and SQL Server for its data warehouse.

FIGURE 11-21
Available Consumer Data

- Name, address, phone
- Age
- Gender
- Ethnicity
- Religion
- Income
- Education
- Voter registration
- Home ownership
- Vehicles
- Magazine subscriptions
- Hobbies
- Catalog orders
- Marital status, life stage
- Height, weight, hair and eye color
- Spouse name, birth date
- Children's names and birth dates

Data warehouses often include data that are purchased from outside sources. A common example is customer credit data. Figure 11-21 lists some of the consumer data that can be purchased from commercial vendors today. An amazing and frightening amount of data is available.

Recall, metadata is data about other data. BI metadata is data about the source of the data, its format, its assumptions and constraints, and other facts about the data. Metadata are kept in a data warehouse. For example, metadata for sales data might specify the format of the date field as *dd-mm-yyyy*.

Procedures

BI users follow a variety of procedures or instructions. These methods of interactions depend on the user's objectives, his or her knowledge and experience, and the nature of the BI system. In general, however, BI systems tend to be flexible and interactive, supporting users engaged in nonstructured, nonroutine work. In such an environment, procedures are limited to basic operational instructions, such as how to obtain a user account, how to subscribe to a particular BI product, how to obtain a result, and how to conduct a particular analysis.

People

There is no BI, no informing, without people. Moreover, two organizations could have very similar data, hardware, software, and procedures, but different people, and therefore have vastly different success. It is like having a rocket scientist and a high school student looking for propulsion insights in a vast public library. The rocket scientist will able to find more useful patterns in the literature than the student.

Two groups of people interact with a BI system: end users and analysts. In the opening scenario, Ann is an example of a user and Cody is an analyst. Users interact with the output to find patterns in the data. Finding patterns is creating information. Analysts can assist in this process by creating useful reports and developing sound procedures for users to follow. However, in the end the end users must inform themselves.

Q6. What Are the Potential Problems with BI Systems?

Although the discussion in this chapter may have helped clarify the benefits of using a BI system to become informed, some of its problems may not be easy to see. Each of the BI components can have problems, and here we focus on two: problems with the data and problems with people.

Data Problems

Unfortunately, most operational and purchased data have problems that inhibit their usefulness. Figure 11-22 lists the major problem categories.

When using operational data, some data may be incomplete and must be prepared before it can be analyzed. Operational data that are critical, such as order prices and quantities, are very accurate and complete; other data that are only marginally necessary need not be. For example, some systems gather demographic data in the ordering process. But, because such data are not needed to fill, ship, and bill orders, their quality suffers. Problematic data are termed **dirty data**.

FIGURE 11-22

Common Data Problems in BI

> Dirty data
>
> Missing values
>
> Inconsistent data
>
> Data not integrated
>
> Wrong granularity
>
> Too much data

Examples are a value of *B* for customer gender and of *213* for customer age. These values can be problematic for BI purposes.

Purchased data often contain *missing* elements. Most data vendors state the percentage of missing values for each attribute in the data they sell. An organization buys such data because for some uses some data are better than no data at all. This is especially true for data items whose values are difficult to obtain, such as the number of adults in a household, household income, dwelling type, and the education of the primary income earner. For BI applications, though, a few missing or erroneous data points can be worse than no data at all because they bias the analysis.

Inconsistent data, the third problem in Figure 11-22, is particularly common for data that have been gathered over time. When an area code changes, for example, the phone number for a given customer before the change will not match the customer's number after the change. Likewise, part codes can change, as can sales territories. Before such data can be used, they must be recoded for consistency over the period of the study.

Another problem is *nonintegrated data*. Suppose, for example, that an organization wants to perform an RFM analysis but wants to consider customer payment behavior as well. The organization wants to add a fourth factor (which we will call *P*), and scale it from 1 to 5 on the basis of how quickly a customer pays. Unfortunately, however, the organization records such payment data in an Oracle financial management database that is separate from the Microsoft CRM database that has the order data. Before the organization can perform the analysis, the data must somehow be integrated.

Data can also have the wrong **granularity**. Granularity is the level of detail of the data, and it can be too fine or too coarse. For the former, suppose we want to analyze the placement of graphics and controls on an order entry Web page. It is possible to capture the customers' clicking behavior in what is termed **clickstream data**. Those data, however, include everything the customer does at the Web site. In the middle of the clickstream are data for clicks on the news, e-mail, instant chat, and a weather check. Although all of that data may be useful for a study of consumer computer behavior, it will be overwhelming if all we want to know is how customers respond to an ad located differently on the screen. To proceed, the data analysts must throw away millions and millions of clicks.

Data can also be too coarse. For example, a file of order totals cannot be used for a market basket analysis. For market basket analysis, we need to know which items were purchased with which others. This does not mean the order-total data are useless. They can be adequate for an RFM analysis, for example; they just will not do for a market basket analysis. In general, it is better to have too fine a granularity than too coarse. If the granularity is too fine, the data can be made coarser by summing and grouping. Only analysts' labor and computer processing are required. If the granularity is too coarse, however, there is no way to separate the data into constituent parts.

People Problems

People problems fall into three categories: users, analysts, and leaders, as shown in Figure 11-23.

User resistance is a common malady of all information systems, and BI is no exception. Users resist BI systems for a wide range of reasons. People resist BI use because the system may change their job. The system might also require knowledge the user does not have or is unmotivated to attain. The BI system might be tried and found difficult or not valuable. If a salesperson tries to use the system in the course of interacting with clients, but finds the data too hard to use, too slow, or not worthwhile, that salesperson may resist future use of this or other BI systems.

Category	Output Problem
Users	User resistance, must have knowledge to produce information, underestimate cost of reports
Analysts	Limited process knowledge, no stopping point, asking wrong questions, mistake data for information, underestimate variety of user needs
Leaders	Unspecified scope, inadequate funding or staffing, limited statistical understanding, overselling results

FIGURE 11-23

BI People Problems: Users, Analysts, and Leaders

A common problem is to assume the BI system creates information that is the same for all users. Recall from our definition in Chapter 2 that information is any difference that makes a difference. Therefore, information is unique to each user, while the data on which each user creates information may be common to all. The hardware and software do not create information; they create the data for users to create information. One implication of this is that the person must have knowledge in order to create information. For example, the user must have knowledge about depreciation to create depreciation information from data. Therefore, a more knowledgeable user will create more information from data than a less knowledgeable user examining the same data. The usefulness of BI data is therefore completely dependent on the knowledge of the businessperson examining it. With BI, the adage "one size fits all" is often not true; it might be more appropriate to say "one size fits one."

A third type of user problem is that users may underestimate the cost of producing a BI report or data mining project. It is difficult to identify accurately all the costs associated with a BI project. As a result, one or two users may consume too much of the BI analyst's time. They may believe that a particular dashboard or analysis is essential, but may change their mind if accurate cost data were available.

BI analysts also contribute their own share of problems. The most consistent problem is that analysts often know much more about the BI system than the processes it is supporting. For example, if the analyst is using BI to develop a list of best customers, the analyst must know about sales in order to generate a valid list. The analyst must have extensive knowledge about the domain in order to know what the data mean, which data are valuable, and how to probe the data with appropriate questions.

Analysts also have a hard time saying, "Enough." Many BI projects have no obvious or convenient stopping point. Rather, the analyst might think, "Just one more week of experimenting with this data or one more run with this new model, and I'll have it." While engaged on the project it is very hard to know if the project will turn out to be a resource black hole or an informational holy grail. Analysts are understandably reluctant to give up on a project that they believed in strongly when it started.

Another problem with BI systems is asking the wrong questions. Clearly some of the questions being asked at CBI in the opening scenario about worker productivity are not good questions. Oftentimes, the poor questions are more subtle and are due to a lack of understanding of the process by the analyst. Poor-quality questions lead to poor-quality results. However, every BI success involves valuable questions. A wise person once said that questions are more important than answers. Nowhere is this more evident than with BI systems.

The last group of people we consider here are the leaders of the organization. Leaders may not provide adequate objectives to BI projects, they may inadequately fund them, and they may not adequately staff them. Another problem is that they may not understand the statistics used in the analysis or the assumptions that the analyst had to make, causing the leaders to misinterpret or overstate the results. Leaders can also contribute to BI pushback by overselling the potential of a BI system. BI will not often transform a business with a shocking finding. More often, BI confirms intuition and leads to steady improvements in processes. Clever BI examples, including the ones at the beginning of this chapter, can distract from accomplishing steady and mundane process improvements, such as packing trucks more efficiently, rescheduling robot forklifts, and tweaking pricing algorithms.

Q7. What Future Technological Advances Will Affect BI Use?

We expect BI use to grow. Advances in technology will create more opportunities for BI analysis. Further, we expect that as business customers expand their use of social media, even more data will become available for BI use. BI systems that spot patterns in the rapidly expanding universe of Facebook, Twitter, and blogs will help companies better understand their customers.

Technology

BI use will continue to expand as display technologies improve. We begin by examining three recent advances: visualization, augmented reality, and smartphones. These output options will have a positive impact on the use of BI because they provide new opportunities to display BI results. Two other technologies—RFID tags and social media—are two new sources of BI data.

Visualization is the creation of images or diagrams that communicate a message. Simple examples include bar charts and infographics. Advances in visualization technologies that enable user interaction and animation will expand the use of BI. For example, an output of sales data by different product groups can be animated to show trends over time.

In a similar way, **augmented reality** will also lead to more widespread use of BI. Augmented reality is the live or indirect view of the real world augmented by computer-based data. It is a mashup of the real world supplemented by data about the objects in that world. For example, you can superimpose walking directions on your smartphone's camera view. Superimposed green arrows are displayed on top of the real-world image so that you can follow directions to a building, see the distance to a building, and display a host of other data about the building and the surrounding area. Also, paramedics, upon finding your unconscious body, will soon be able to identify you with facial recognition software and then superimpose your health-care data on a live video display of your image.

A third technology that will impact BI is the trend in business toward mobile devices. BI was born in the era of laptop and desktop machines. As mobile devices grow in output sophistication and computing power, BI will increasingly be done on smartphones and tablets. For example, smartphones equipped with a cheap hardware appliance can evaluate blood samples in field clinics. The mobile device can conduct sophisticated statistical analysis of the blood and provide users interactive diagnostic tools if the blood sample has anomalies.

Not only will mobile devices be used to analyze and display results, they will also create enormous volumes of location data for businesses and governments to analyze. By evaluating text messages and phone locations, BI researchers are already able to pinpoint flu outbreaks, the movement of political ideas, the loneliness of individuals, and the eating habits of users.[2]

Two other technologies will also generate large volumes of data for BI applications: RFID tags and Web 2.0. Some experts have said that soon anything big enough to have an RFID tag on it will. As a result, hundreds of millions of objects with tags on them will generate data about the object, where it is, and how it has moved. In addition, the user-generated content from billions of Facebook posts, tweets, and blogs will also provide terabytes of data and new opportunities for BI analysis.

However, the most significant impact on BI use may be cloud computing. As firms move more and more data storage into the cloud, cloud-based vendors that offer BI as a service will be increasingly attractive. We will revisit this topic later when we discuss emerging vendors in the BI market in Q8.

Technology Backlash

Technology changes will impact BI, but they may also impact consumers' willingness to use credit cards and social media. As more data are collected on customers by credit card companies and by social media sites, the usefulness of BI will continue to grow. This anticipated growth in data about individual financial and personal behavior may lead to a privacy backlash.

---

[2] Robert Hotz, "The Really Smart Phone," *Wall Street Journal*, April 23, 2011.

For example, suppose you never buy expensive jewelry on your credit card. If you travel to South America and attempt to buy a $5,000 diamond bracelet using that credit card, watch what happens! Especially if you make the attempt on a credit card other than the one for which you paid for the travel. A reporting process integrated into the credit card agency's purchase-approval process will detect the unusual pattern, on the spot, and require you to personally verify the purchase on the telephone or in some other way before it will accept the charge. Such applications are exceedingly accurate because they are well designed and implemented by some of the world's best BI developers.

In fact, credit card companies already know a lot. If you use your card to purchase "second-hand clothing, retread tires, bail bond services, massages, or for gambling activities,"[3] you alert the credit card company of potential financial problems and, as a result, it may cancel your card or reduce your credit limit. This practice raised enough concern that the U.S. Congress passed a credit card reform law that requires the Federal Trade Commission (FTC) to investigate BI use by credit card companies.

In November 2009, the United States passed the Personal Data Privacy and Security Act, which gives consumers more privacy rights in terms of the data collected and distributed by commercial data brokers. However, despite the law's passage companies are still looking for new ways to gain access to data on consumers. The San Francisco BI firm, Rapleaf, for example, monitors social media such as Facebook, Twitter, and MySpace and then makes a prediction based on who your friends are whether you are a worthy credit risk. Joel Jewitt, the vice president of Rapleaf says, "Who you hang around with has empirical implications with how you behave."[4]

Should there be limits on companies purchasing data? Suppose several of your friends on Facebook switch cell phone companies. Recent data mining studies have shown that people often reconsider their cell phone plan when people they know switch providers. Would it be appropriate for cell phone companies to purchase data from social media sites in order to contact friends of people who recently switched?

This intelligence is sure to be very useful for a number of businesses. But exactly how this data will be used and how it will be used legally has yet to be worked out. Business intelligence and privacy may be on a collision course. Finding common ground will be a constant challenge. You and your classmates will have a chance to develop innovative applications for it during your careers. It should be fascinating!

Q8. Who Are the Key BI Vendors and How Does SAP Accomplish BI?

ERP vendors make BI modules to accompany their ERP systems. These ERP BI modules can support both reporting and data mining. However, while ERP systems do an admirable job of consolidating operational data into one database, their BI systems are not as good at getting that data out.

Vendors

The current BI vendors share a $6 billion a year industry. One way to organize the vendors is shown in Figure 11-24. At the top are the large, diverse software firms. These four—SAP, Oracle, IBM, and Microsoft—sell and service a wide range of BI products. This group owns two-thirds of the BI market. Their advantage is that companies may already use their ERP or database products, so adding BI takes advantage of a quicker learning curve and reduces data compatibility issues.

The next group is pure-play BI companies; that is, software companies that make and service only BI products. These are companies like SAS, Information Builders, and MicroStrategy. These companies have developed statistical software and BI systems for over 35 years and do not offer other software products.

---

[3] MSN.com, "Can Lifestyle Hurt Your Credit?" *http://articles.moneycentral.msn.com/Banking/FinancialPrivacy/can-your-lifestyle-hurt-your-credit.aspx* (accessed August 2009).
[4] Lucas Conley, "How Rapleaf Is Data-Mining Your Friend Lists to Predict Your Credit Risk," *Fast Company,* November 16, 2009. Available at: *www.fastcompany.com/blog/lucas-conley/advertising-branding-and-marketing/company-we-keep.*

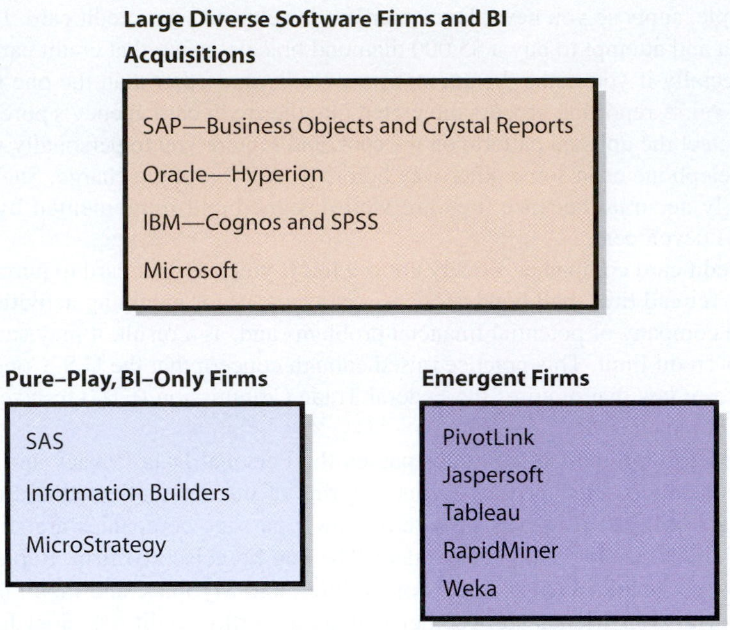

FIGURE 11-24
Major BI Vendors

Large Diverse Software Firms and BI Acquisitions

SAP—Business Objects and Crystal Reports

Oracle—Hyperion

IBM—Cognos and SPSS

Microsoft

Pure–Play, BI–Only Firms

SAS

Information Builders

MicroStrategy

Emergent Firms

PivotLink

Jaspersoft

Tableau

RapidMiner

Weka

FIGURE 11-24
Major BI Vendors

A final group will be interesting to watch. These small and emerging organizations are pursuing a variety of strategies, but many leverage the cloud concept. Several of these, including RapidMiner and Weka, are open source online tools that are available for free. Their pitch, shown in Figure 11-25, capitalizes on cloud attributes of flexibility, efficiency, ease of use, and low startup costs.

SAP BI

Like all ERP systems, SAP consolidates a vast database of operational data in one place. It calls this collection of operational process data **online transactional processing (OLTP)**. The term *transactional processing* is equivalent to *operational processing*. SAP makes a distinction between this OLTP data and the analysis on that data with OLAP.

SAP analysis of the data is called OLAP. The SAP software that analyzes the data is called **Business Objects (BO)**. Business Objects was an independent software firm until its acquisition by SAP. An example output from BO is shown in Figure 11-26. In Figure 11-26, a pie chart of yearly sales by country occupies the top pane. After clicking on Belgium in the pie, the bottom pane shows the drill down data of yearly sales in Belgium.

A company that implements SAP can also choose to write program code to accomplish specific tasks that SAP does not provide. Approximately 95 percent of all this program code is devoted to creating company-specific BI reports.

FIGURE 11-25
Cloud BI Pitch

"You want our solution, for your growing business. You don't want to be tied down to your ERP provider if you have one, they are good at processes and storing the data. We're better at getting it out. And that's what you want. Our BI products are cloud compliant—actually they were born in the cloud and can be designed to be used on data stored there, not in big clumsy ERP on-site databases. What's best about our product is that we've made them easy to learn. We don't have expensive consultants like our big brothers, we change only when you use our product, so we made them easy for you and your employees to use. They are the ones that know what they want, don't make them go through your IT staff, put the power in their hands!"

FIGURE 11-26

SAP Business Objects Report Example

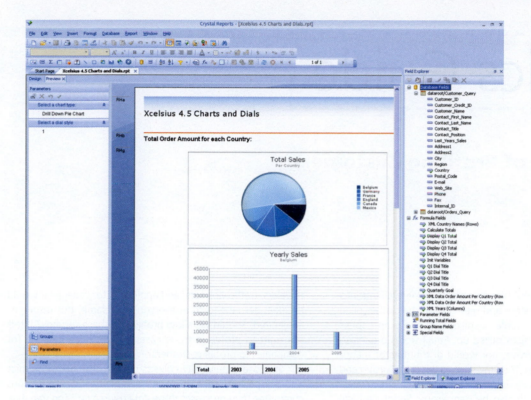

SAP and the other ERP vendors also make it possible to analyze data with software from other companies. One common method is to download data from SAP into an Excel file and then use Excel to analyze the data. This process of exporting to Excel to analyze data will be explained more fully in the case study at the end of the chapter.

If Ann at CBI wants to be able to analyze the financial transactions in the SAP database, she has three general options. As just mentioned, she can learn to download data to Excel and conduct the analysis herself. She could also analyze the data using BO software provided by SAP, or she could request from Cody and the IT department a specific report that summarizes the data as she specifies.

Ethics Guide

The Ethics of Profiling Customers

Classification is a useful human skill. Imagine walking into your favorite clothing store and seeing all of the clothes piled together on a center table. T-shirts and pants and socks intermingle, with the sizes mixed up. Retail stores organized like this would not survive, nor would distributors or manufacturers who managed their inventories this way. Sorting and classifying are necessary, important, and essential activities. But those activities can also be dangerous. Serious ethical issues arise when we classify people. What makes someone a good or bad "prospect"? If we're talking about classifying customers in order to prioritize our sales calls, then the ethical issue may not be too serious. But what about profiling airline travelers, traffic violators, and applicants for college? It would be ideal perhaps to treat everyone the same, but resources are limited. Should we allow profiling in these settings? If it is not right to profile in these cases, why is it permissible for companies to profile customers?

Suppose a university collects data on the demographics and the performance of all of its students. The admissions committee then processes these data using a decision tree data mining program. Assume the analysis is conducted properly and the tool uses statistically valid measures to obtain statistically valid results. Thus, the following resulting tree accurately represents and explains patterns found in the data.

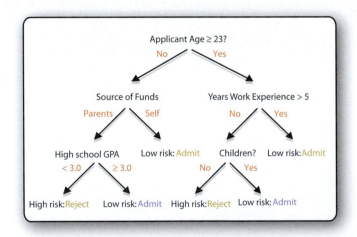

DISCUSSION QUESTIONS

1. Explain what conditions in the data could have caused this particular structure to emerge. For example, what conditions may have existed for self-funding students under the age of 23 to be classified as low risk (low risk of failing to complete the program)? Explain how you think the three other branches in this tree may have come about.

2. How would you expect the following individuals to react to this tree:

   a. A 23-year-old woman whose job experience is 3 years as a successful Wall Street financial analyst.

   b. A 28-year-old gay male with 4 years' job experience who has no children and pays his own college education.

   c. The university fund-raising committee that wants to raise money from parent donations.

   d. A student who was seriously ill while attending a topnotch high school but managed to graduate with a GPA of 2.9 by working independently on her classes from her hospital room.

3. Suppose you work in admissions and your university's public relations department asks you to meet with the local press for an article they are preparing regarding your admittance policy. How do you prepare for the press meeting?

4. Would your answer to question 3 change if you work at a private rather than public institution? Would it change if you work at a small liberal arts college rather than a large engineering-oriented university?

5. What conclusions do you make regarding the use of decision trees for categorizing student applicants?

6. What conclusions do you make regarding the use of decision trees for profiling individuals in general?

Source: Luba V Ne/Shutterstock.

Active Review

Use this Active Review to verify that you understand the material in the chapter. You can read the entire chapter and then perform the tasks in this review, or you can read the text material for just one question and perform the tasks in this review for that question before moving on to the next one.

Q1. Why do organizations need business intelligence (BI)?

Explain why organizations seek to use business intelligence. Give an example of a firm that uses BI, the process it improves, and the measure used to show that improvement. Define *business intelligence* (BI). Describe how government and healthcare agencies are using BI. Explain why the use of BI is increasing.

Q2. How does BI support the Informing process?

Explain the Informing process. Describe a process and how the Informing process might improve it. Explain the major activities in the Informing process. Describe the key differences between the Reporting and Data Mining processes.

Q3. What are examples of the Reporting process?

Explain the main options in the Reporting process. What are the two types of analysis and how do they differ? Give an example of a noninteractive analysis and an interactive analysis. Explain how an RFM analysis is performed. Describe the main elements of an OLAP analysis. Give an example of drilling down.

Q4. What are examples of the Data Mining process?

Explain the main options in the Data Mining process. Describe how data mining differs from reporting. What is the result of cluster analysis? What does a regression equation identify? Explain why a firm might use market basket analysis. Once a decision tree analysis has been conducted,

explain how the results can be transformed into the If . . . then . . . format. Describe the difference between unsupervised and supervised data mining and give a BI application example of each.

Q5. What are the components of a BI system?

Explain the role of a BI server. What is a data warehouse and how does it differ from an operational database? Describe what might be necessary before data can be stored in the warehouse. What is an example of metadata? Explain why people are the most important component of a BI system. Where is information in the BI system created?

Q6. What are the potential problems with BI systems?

What are the two categories of BI problems? Give examples of dirty, missing, inconsistent, and nonintegrated data. Describe data granularity and explain how it can be a problem for BI. Explain how users, analysts, and leaders can cause problems. Explain why the expression "one size fits one" is appropriate for BI. Why are questions more important than answers?

Q7. What future technological advances will affect BI use?

Explain and give examples of visualization and augmented reality. How will mobile devices impact BI? Describe two other new technologies that will generate large volumes of BI data. Describe an example of how a credit card company might misuse your purchasing data.

Q8. Who are the key BI vendors and how does SAP accomplish BI?

Name the four large diverse software firms that sell BI software. What are the three categories of BI vendors? What makes BI in the cloud attractive to businesses? What are some of the differences between OLTP and OLAP data? What are the three options available for users to analyze BI data using SAP?

Key Terms and Concepts

Augmented reality *362*
Business intelligence system *342*
Business Objects *364*
Clickstream data *360*
Cluster analysis *354*
Cross-selling *356*
Data mining process *347*
Data warehouse *358*
Decision support systems (DSS) *358*
Decision tree *356*

Digital dashboard *348*
Dirty data *359*
Drill down *352*
Granularity *360*
Market basket analysis (MBA) *355*
OLAP cube *352*
OLAP dimension *352*
OLAP measure *352*
Online analytical processing
   (OLAP) *351*

Online transactional processing
   (OLTP) *364*
Operational database *358*
Regression analysis *355*
Reporting process *345*
RFM analysis *350*
Supervised data mining *358*
Unsupervised data
   mining *358*
Visualization *362*

Using Your Knowledge

1. Reread the three examples at the beginning of the chapter that involved Progressive, Netflix, and the Oakland Athletics. Specify the process that BI improves at each firm and a second process that BI could support. Explain the measures you would use to demonstrate how the BI example would improve the effectiveness or efficiency of the process.

2. Create a BPMN diagram of a Managerial process that can be supported by the Informing process. As in question 1, specify objectives and measures for that Managerial process and explain how the Informing process will improve those measures.

3. Reflect on the differences between the Reporting process and the Data Mining process. What are their similarities and differences? How do their costs differ? What benefits does each offer? How would an organization choose between these two processes?

4. Suppose you are a member of the Audubon Society, and the board of the local chapter asks you to help it analyze its member data. The group wants to analyze the demographics of its membership against members' activity, including events attended, classes attended, volunteer activities, and donations. Describe two different reporting examples and one data mining example that it might develop.

5. You are the director of student activities at your university. Recently, some students have charged that your department misallocates its resources. They claim the allocation is based on outdated student preferences. Funds are given to activities that few students find attractive, and insufficient funds are allocated to new activities in which students do want to participate.

Describe how you could use reporting and/or data mining to assess this claim.

6. In this chapter, we say that questions are more important than answers. Look at Figures 11-15, 11-16, and 11-17 and write down questions you have that might reveal patterns in the data shown in these figures.

7. Reread the opening scenario. CBI owns the computers, and workers should be productive with their time, but how did you react to the story? Do you think that CBI should know how employees use the network? Is it ethical to snoop on employee behavior? Assume that CBI wants to collect data on network misuse. Suggest measures that CBI could use to assess network misuse.

8. The following sayings about data and information are often used in business to convey an important idea. As you read these, select three and write down how they could be used to convey an idea from this chapter:

> "If you torture numbers long enough, they'll confess to anything."
> "If you want a green suit, turn on a green light."
> "You don't fatten the pig by weighing it."
> "Not everything that counts can be counted, and not everything that can be counted counts."
> "Statistics are no substitute for judgment . . . and vice versa."
> "Data don't speak to strangers."
> "Without data, you're just another person with an opinion."
> "It ain't so much the things we know that get us in trouble, it's the things we know that just ain't so."

Collaboration Exercise 11

Collaborate with a group of fellow students to answer the following questions. For this exercise do not meet face to face. Your task will be easier if you coordinate your work with SharePoint, Office 365, Google Docs with Google+ or equivalent collaboration tools. (See Chapter 9 for a discussion of collaboration tools and processes.) Your answers should reflect the thinking of the entire group, and not just that of one or two individuals.

Mary Keeling owns and operates Carbon Creek Gardens, a retailer of trees, garden plants, perennial and annual flowers, and bulbs. "The Gardens," as her customers call it, also sells bags of soil, fertilizer, small garden tools, and garden sculptures. Mary started the business 16 years ago when she bought a section of land that, because of water drainage, was unsuited for residential development. With hard work and perseverance, Mary has created a warm and inviting environment with a unique and carefully selected inventory of plants. The Gardens has become a favorite nursery for serious gardeners in her community.

"The problem," she says, "is that I've grown so large, I've lost track of my customers. The other day, I ran into Tootsie Swan at the grocery store, and I realized I hadn't seen her in ages. I said something like, 'Hi, Tootsie, I haven't seen you for a while,' and that statement unleashed an angry torrent from her. It turns out that she'd been in over a year ago and had wanted to return a plant. One of my part-time employees waited on her and had apparently insulted her, or at least didn't give her the service she wanted. So, she decided not to come back to The Gardens.

"Tootsie was one of my best customers. I'd lost her, and I didn't even know it! That really frustrates me. Is it inevitable that as I get bigger, I lose track of my customers? I don't think so. Somehow, I have to find out when regular customers aren't coming around. Had I known Tootsie had stopped shopping with us, I'd have called her to see what was going on. I need customers like her.

"I've got all sorts of data in my sales database. It seems like the insight I need is in there, but how do I get it out?"

In this exercise, you will apply the knowledge of this chapter to Mary Keeling's problem.

1. Mary wants to know when she's lost a customer. One way to help her would be to produce a report, say in PDF format, showing the top 50 customers from the prior year. Mary could print that report or place it on a private section of her Web site so that she can download it from wherever she happens to be.

   Periodically—say, once a week—Mary could request a report that shows the top buyers for that week. That report could also be in PDF format, or it could just be produced onscreen. Mary could compare the two reports to determine who is missing. If she wonders whether a customer such as Tootsie has been ordering, she could request a query report on Tootsie's activities. Describe the advantages and disadvantages of this solution.

2. Describe the best possible application of an OLAP tool at Carbon Creek. Can it be used to solve the lost customer problem? Why or why not? What is the best way, if any, for Mary to use OLAP at Carbon Creek? If none, explain why.

3. Describe the best possible application of decision tree analysis at Carbon Creek. Can it be used to solve the lost customer problem? Why or why not? What is the best way, if any, for Mary to use decision tree analysis at Carbon Creek? If none, explain why.

4. Describe the best possible application of RFM analysis at Carbon Creek. Can it be used to solve the lost customer problem? Why or why not? What is the best way, if any, for Mary to use RFM at Carbon Creek? If none, explain why.

5. Describe the best possible application of market basket analysis at Carbon Creek. Can it be used to solve the lost customer problem? Why or why not? What is the best way, if any, for Mary to use market basket analysis at Carbon Creek? If none, explain why.

6. Which of the Informing analysis options in this exercise will provide Mary the best value? If you owned Carbon Creek Gardens and you were going to implement just one of these analysis options, which would you choose? Why?

CASE STUDY 11

Tourism Holdings Limited (THL) (continued)

Before proceeding, reread Case 10, page 338, which introduces THL, Tourism Holdings Limited, a New Zealand–based company that owns and operates multiple businesses. In this case, we will examine how THL uses information systems to support vehicle leasing in its four camper-leasing business lines.

Leasing camper vehicles to customers has three fundamental phases:

1. Matching customer requirements with vehicle availability
2. Reserving vehicles and operations support
3. Billing and customer service

Online Reservations Systems

Customers access a Web site for whichever brand of vehicle they wish to rent. On that site, they specify the dates and locations from which they want to rent and return a vehicle. THL information systems access the vehicle inventory to determine which vehicles might be available.

That determination is complex. THL may not have the wanted vehicle in the desired location, but it might have a higher-priced vehicle available and choose to offer the customer a free upgrade. Or, it might have the desired vehicle in a different city and choose to move the vehicle to that location. However, moving the vehicle might impact prior reservations for that vehicle, making such movement infeasible. Finally, this complexity is compounded because certain vehicles are not to be rented from particular locations. (Two-wheel drive standard vehicles cannot be rented for the Australian outback, for example). And, of course, vehicles undergo both scheduled and unscheduled maintenance.

Pricing is another complicated decision in the reservation process. Like hotels and airlines, THL engages in flex pricing, whereby prices are determined not only by the vehicle and rental period, but also by customer demand.

To accommodate this complexity, THL developed a rule-based availability information system known as Aurora. Business analysts create business rules like those shown in Figure 11-27. Figure 11-27 shows an example of rules that block vehicles from rental; Figure 11-28 shows a screen that is used to set up or modify a rule. All rules are stored in a SQL Server database, a database that also contains all of the vehicle reservation data. Application programs in the Aurora system access and process the business rules when determining vehicle availability. Because rules are set up and managed with easy-to-use interfaces like that in Figure 11-28, nonprogrammer business analysts are able to change reservation policy without the assistance of technical personnel.

THL also operates information systems for vehicle check-in and customer billing. The Aurora reservation system off-loads data to a second SQL Server database that operates a report server (see Figure 11-29). By off-loading the data, THL produces numerous sophisticated reports without impacting the performance of the online reservation system.

Reports from the server guide both operational and managerial processes. One report, for example, shows the vehicles that are to be checked out and returned to each rental location. Other reports show which vehicles need to be transferred to other locations, which vehicles are to be sent for maintenance, which vehicles are to be retired from the fleet, and so forth.

BI Systems

"We know our operational data contains a wealth of information about our customers, their rental needs, trends in rental activity and vehicle needs, and other key business drivers," Grant Webster, THL's CEO, stated. "We've already developed numerous OLAP cubes and we're working on other types of business intelligence applications."

As shown in Figure 11-29, data from the report server is downloaded to a third server that provides OLAP services. Operational data are processed, and OLAP cubes are created on a weekly basis. Figure 11-30 shows a cube that displays revenue earned from vehicle sales in 2005 (THL is, naturally, reluctant to publish current versions of such private data).

OLAP analysis is interactive. In Figure 11-30, the user could, for example, change the brand and geographic market columns, and the totals would be adjusted accordingly. Excel Pivot charts are an example of an OLAP output. The difference is that THL's report server produces output based on thousands of transactions; such volume would be very difficult to process in Excel.

FIGURE 11-27

Example Rental Rules

Source: © Tourism Holdings Limited. Used with permission.

FIGURE 11-28

Setting Up a Blocking Rule

Source: © Tourism Holdings Limited. Used with permission.

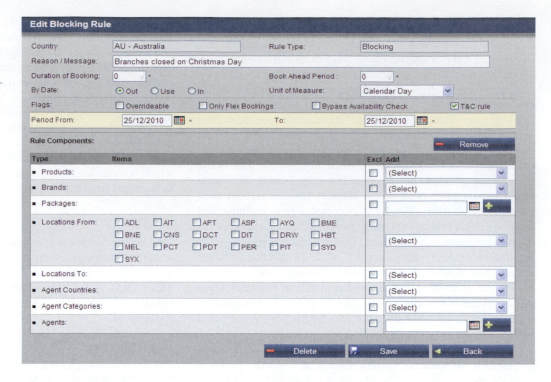

FIGURE 11-29

THL Information Systems

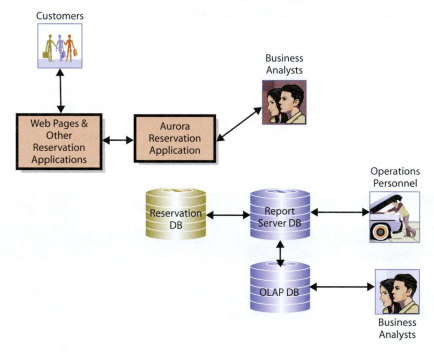

Questions

1. Considering the rule-based reservation system:
   a. Summarize the benefits of having policy determined by rules rather than by computer code.
   b. What are the consequences of someone entering an incorrect rule? Offer both mundane and drastic examples.

   c. Considering your answer to item b, if you managed the reservation system at THL what process would you use for the modification of rules?

2. Examine the OLAP report in Figure 11-30. The values in this output (or cube) are sums of rental revenue of vehicles.

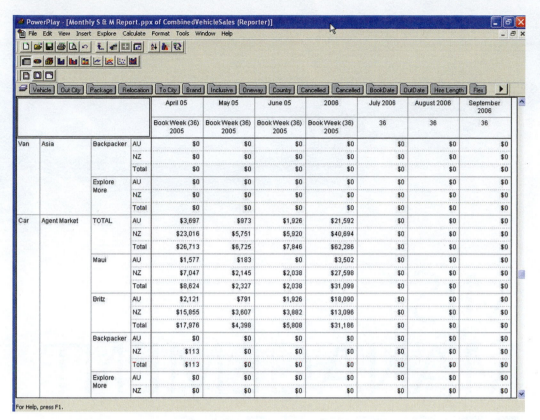

FIGURE 11-30
THL OLAP Report

Source: © Tourism Holdings Limited.
Used with permission.

a. Using your intuition and business knowledge, what information do you create from the output $3,697? From $1,587 and $2,121?

b. State three conclusions that you can make from the data in Figure 11-30.

c. The principal advantage of OLAP is that columns and rows can be switched and the output values will be recalculated automatically. Explain what would happen if the user of this output were to switch the second column (geographic area) with the third column (brand). You do not have sufficient data to compute values, but explain in words what will happen.

3. This OLAP Reporting process is not conducted for its own purposes. Rather, like all Informing processes, it supports a business process for THL. What process is being supported? Specify an objective for that process.

4. Considering customer reservation data, describe an example of what a market basket analysis might include.

5. Suppose that THL decides to start a van rental business in the United States. Suppose that it is considering opening operations in Alaska, California, Arizona, New Mexico, or Florida.

a. Given the nature of THL's current camper-vehicle rental activities, which of those states do you think would be best? Justify your decision. Consider potential competition, market size, applicability of THL's experience, and other factors you deem relevant.

b. Summarize THL's competitive strengths for this new operation.

c. Summarize THL's competitive vulnerabilities for this new operation.

d. Describe how its reservation system adds value to this new operation.

e. Summarize the problems that you think THL might have in running a business 7,500 miles (or more) from its headquarters.

MIS MANAGEMENT PROCESSES

MIS, like all business endeavors, accomplishes work via processes. The typical IS department has processes for planning, developing, maintaining, and operating enterprise and interenterprise systems. The IS department is involved in the support of other departments and end users as well.

Most of these IS processes are beyond the scope of this book. However, in this last part, and last chapter, we will consider three MIS management processes that are likely to involve you as a future business professional. They are processes for managing other business processes, processes for developing information systems, and processes for protecting IS.

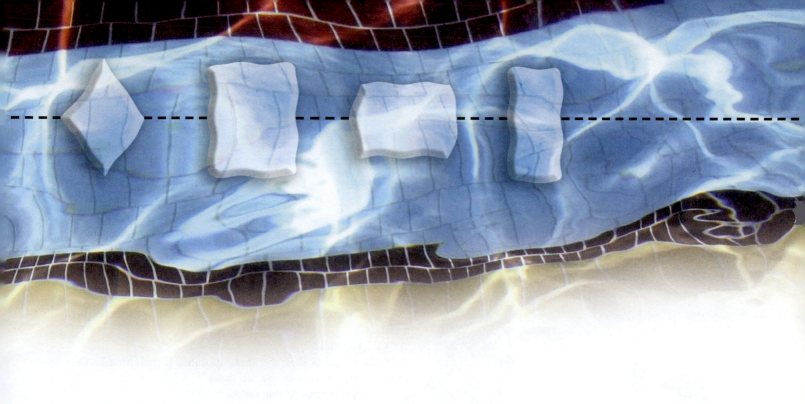

You should know about the first two of these processes because you may be asked to participate. End users are the primary source of requirements for processes and systems management, and they are often called upon to provide feedback on processes and systems structures and features. You should know about IS security for three reasons. First, you need to know the major dimensions of IS security for your organization. This includes knowing the kinds of security safeguards that should be in place. Second, if those safeguards are not in place, you need to know how to argue effectively for their creation. Third, you will have responsibilities and roles to play in protecting the information systems that you use. As a business professional, you need to understand the rationale for those responsibilities and have sufficient knowledge to fulfill roles that you are assigned.

"Neil, I don't like it."

"What do you mean, Kelly? Our members are demanding that they be able to enroll in exercise classes online!"

"Maybe so, but think about renewals."

"What do you mean?"

"Look, someone comes to the front desk and wants to enroll in a class."

"OK, so what?"

"Well, we check their membership status. If their membership expires during the class, we sell them."

"So, we can do that online."

"You think so?"

"Sure."

"I don't know. I like to meet them face-to-face. I like to have a chance to talk with them, find out their issues, maybe suggest a different class, a personal trainer. . . ."

"We can do that online."

"I doubt it. Someone's online, they try to enroll, and some computer tells them they can't???"

"Look, we're not going to give them some stupid error message, like 'Operation invalid. Renew your membership.'"

"No, then what will you do?"

"I won't do anything. The system will gently remind them that they need to renew and take them to our renewal page."

"And if they don't renew?"

"Well, then they don't get into the class."

"And 4 months from now, we notice our membership is down 10 percent? Great idea."

"Look, the system will give us a report, whenever we want, on member renewals. We can check it to find out when people don't renew."

"That means we need to change all of our processes. The staff won't like it."

"Well, maybe not. But, we've got to do it."

"Why? The current system works!"

"Well, for one, the competition is doing it, and our younger members are used to 24/7 online access. We're vulnerable to losing them. And, there's something else . . ."

"What's that?"

"Scalability. We can scale up. We won't be so dependent on you or people you've trained to make the sale. Lack of trained people won't keep us from opening other locations."

"If we have any members left, that is."

Q1. What are the activities of business process management?

Q2. What are the activities in the systems development life cycle (SDLC) development process?

Q3. Which comes first: process or systems development?

Q4. What is information systems security?

Q5. What are the components of an organization's security program?

Q6. What technical safeguards are available?

Q7. What human security safeguards are available?

Chapter Preview

FlexTime, like every organization today, needs to adapt to new technologies and new opportunities. Organizations that do not adapt cannot thrive, and they may not even be able to survive.

To understand how organizations adapt, recall the definition of MIS: the management and use of processes, information systems, and information to help organizations achieve their strategy. Organizations can adapt by changing their strategy or, if the strategy remains the same, technology opportunities may require changes in processes or systems.

To help you help your organization to adapt, we will consider two MIS management processes in this chapter: business process management, which is a process for managing other processes, and systems development, which is a process for creating and maintaining information systems. We discuss these processes in questions Q1 through Q3.

The balance of this chapter concerns IS security. You need only open your browser to today's news to see why IS security is so important. Sony, Apple, the U.S. government, and other large organizations have suffered serious customer and client data breaches in 2011. Any organization for which you work is subject to the same security vulnerabilities and threats as they are. As you will see, you have important roles to play in implementing safeguards to protect your organization.

Q1. What Are the Activities of Business Process Management?

As we have stated repeatedly, business processes provide the key means by which businesses accomplish work. Because this is so, it is not surprising that businesses use a process to manage processes. The most important of such processes is known as *business process management (BPM)*. Here we will describe the primary activities of the BPM process and illustrate their use at FlexTime.

Figure 12-1 shows the four basic activities in **business process management (BPM)**, a recurring process for systematically monitoring, modeling, creating, and implementing business

FIGURE 12-1

Four Activities in the BPM Process

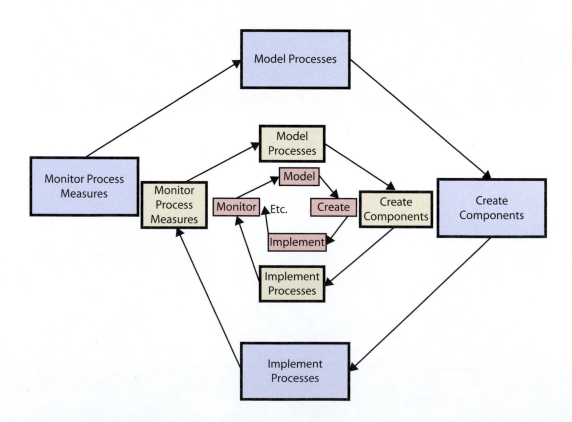

processes. In Figure 12-1, note how the activities of monitor/model/create/implement repeat. As each activity is completed, it feeds into the next activity.

During the monitoring activity managers evaluate process measures against their objectives and respond to changes in the business climate, as described below. Next, models and other forms of requirements for changes in the business process are created. Components for implementing those requirements are then created, and the process changes are then implemented. That implementation activity leads to the monitoring activity of the next cycle. Consider each activity in more detail.

The BPM Monitoring Activity

Organizations are dynamic, and processes within organizations need to be adapted. The need for process change arises from two sources:

- The process does not consistently meet its objectives.
- Changes in the business environment.

Managers can learn that a process needs to be adapted in one of two ways. They can ignore the process and possible need for change until disaster ensues, or they can continually monitor the process and proactively make changes before problems occur.

Organizations that engage in process management take the latter approach. To do so, they create targets for process objectives and they frequently, sometimes continuously, measure the process against those objectives.

MONITORING PROCESS PERFORMANCE ON ITS OBJECTIVES As you have learned, process objectives are either effective or efficient. Effectiveness assesses how well the process helps the organization achieve its strategy. For example, the shipping department of an organization that differentiates based on high-quality service will set high objectives for the percent of orders shipped on time, the percent of orders that are accurate, and the percent of orders that are delivered to the correct address. If the process consistently underperforms on those objectives, the process needs to be changed.

Measures of effectiveness objectives for dynamic processes are more abstract than those for operational processes like shipping, but they still exist. For example, effectiveness measures for a collaboration process include how well the team accomplished its objectives, the degree to which the team grew as a working unit, and the growth in individuals' skills and abilities during the team's functioning.

Concerning the use of information systems to support business processes, the Information Systems Audit and Control Association has created a set of standard practices called **COBIT (Control Objectives for Information and related Technology)** that can be used to assess effectiveness of information systems. Explaining these standards is beyond the scope of this discussion, but you should know that they exist. See *www.isaca.org/cobit* for more explanation.

Measures of efficiency objectives determine how well the process uses its resources. For shipping, efficiency measures include the average cost of preparing a shipment, the number of trucks required to deliver shipments, the cost per item of packaging, and so forth. For dynamic processes, efficiency measures might include the number of employee hours required to make a decision or to complete a project or the cost of those hours.

MONITORING FOR CHANGES IN THE PROCESS ENVIRONMENT FlexTime has a process for enrolling people in classes and for selling memberships to new members and to customers whose memberships have expired. Let us suppose that the process meets its objectives. Even so, as you saw at the start of this chapter, changes in technology or business fundamentals can require that the process be adapted.

Thus, business processes need to be monitored against changes in technology. For example, portable devices such as the iSomethings and their copycats give customers new ways of accessing FlexTime. As Neil says in the opening vignette, customers want to be able to enroll in classes online, via devices such as smartphones or even browsers on personal computers. As you learned in Chapter 10, businesses are constantly adapting to use new social media such as Facebook, Twitter, and foursquare.

A second source of change in a process's environment is the business itself. A substantial change in any of the following factors can mean a need to modify business processes:

- Market (e.g., new customer category, change in customer characteristics)
- Product lines
- Supply chain
- Company policy
- Company organization (e.g., merger or acquisition)
- Internationalization
- Business environment

To understand the implications of such changes, suppose FlexTime opens two additional locations and decides to create two classes of memberships: global memberships that are valid at any FlexTime location and specific memberships that are valid only at a particular FlexTime facility. The process in Figure 12-1 will need to be adjusted to ensure that customers are enrolling in classes at locations for which their membership is valid.

Or, FlexTime might create a new kind of membership, one that is valid for the purpose of taking a particular class. The processes of selling memberships and of enrolling customers in classes will need to be adjusted to accommodate that new membership type.

The BPM Modeling Activity

At some point, either because a process is not meeting its performance objectives or because of changes in the business environment, processes will need to be changed. As stated in Chapter 5, three types of process change are possible: increase or decrease the resources available to a process, usually by adding or removing people from process roles; change the structure of the process; or change both the process's resources and structure, as is done when changing the way that information systems support processes.

If the process change involves only alterations in human resources, then no new process modeling is necessary. However, if the structure of the process is altered or if information systems are used in a new way, then process modeling is required. During this activity, business users who have expertise and are involved in the process (this could be you!) adjust and evaluate those models. Usually teams build an **as-is model** that documents the current situation and then changes that model to make adjustments necessary to solve process problems.

Figure 12-2 shows an as-is model for the class enrollment process at FlexTime. The process currently has four roles: Customer and Desk Clerk, which are roles filled by humans, and Membership Sales and Class Scheduler, which are roles filled by computers. Notice that if a customer's membership has expired, when that customer attempts to enroll in a new class the desk clerk sells a membership renewal. Also, notice that if a class is full or otherwise unavailable, the clerk attempts to sell a different class. It is these human sales activities that Kelly is concerned will be lost if FlexTime converts to an automated system.

After constructing the as-is model, the process management team then models alternatives. Figure 12-3 shows one possible alternative in which the Sales Clerk role is replaced by a Web Application role, a role that will be filled by a computer-based application. The logic of this proposed change in process is the same as in Figure 12-2, but notice that the sales activities are to be done by a Web application, with flashy graphics and easy renewal forms.

Because Kelly and others at FlexTime are concerned to know the successfulness of those automated sales activities, customer responses are recorded in the Membership and Scheduled Class databases. Periodically, sales managers can request reports of those data, as shown in Figure 12-4.

The diagrams shown in Figures 12-2 through 12-4 are typical of those that would be created during the modeling activity. If management decides to implement these changes, the team proceeds to the next activity, create components.

The BPM Create Components Activity

The third major BPM activity is to create process components. For example, at FlexTime, the Web application that members use to enroll online would be developed at this activity. As in information system, all five components need to be created: a server or cloud service needs to be

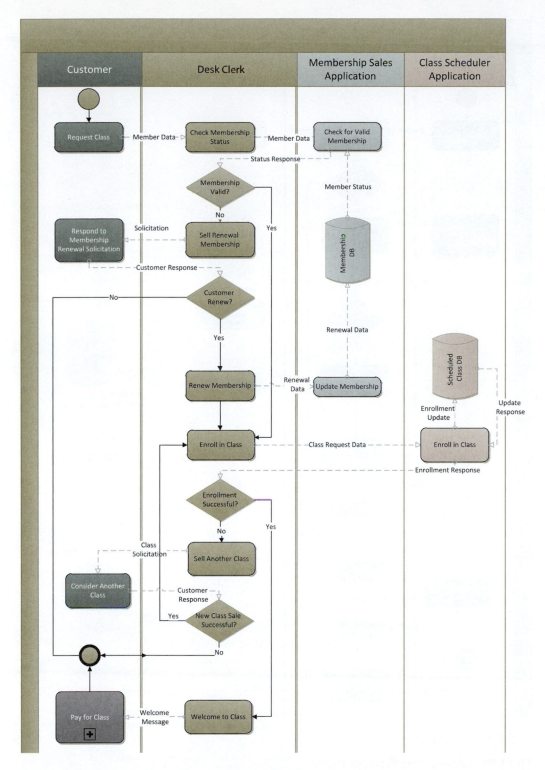

FIGURE 12-2

FlexTime As-Is Class Enrollment Process

identified, software created, databases changed for storing response data, procedures implemented, and employees trained to use the new system. We will say more about this when we discuss the systems development life cycle in Q2.

In addition to IS components, procedures and training for activities that do not involve information systems need to be developed as well. At FlexTime, procedures need to be created for the evaluation activities in Figure 12-4. FlexTime's new online system involves modest process changes. For new and more elaborate process developments, considerable efforts will need to be invested in creating new procedures.

FIGURE 12-3

FlexTime Proposed Web Application Class Enrollment Process

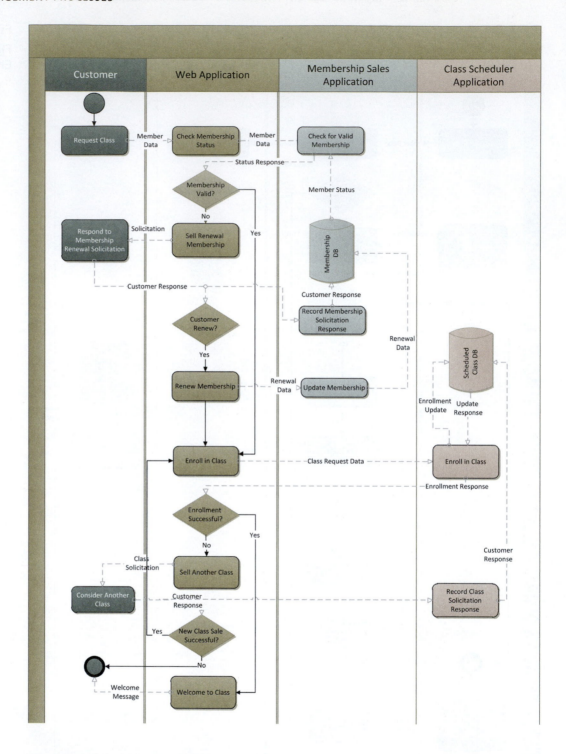

The BPM Implement Process Activity

Implementation activities make process changes operational. Activities to perform here are similar to implementation activities for the systems development life cycle (SDLC), and we will defer discussion of them to the SDLC discussion in Q2.

For processes, however, note that if the new version of the business process involves considerable change for employees, there is likely to be resistance to the new system. We discussed this in Chapters 5 through 8, and we won't repeat that discussion here. It is important to remember the need for addressing change resistance, however.

FIGURE 12-4

**FlexTime Sales
Management/Sales
Evaluation Process**

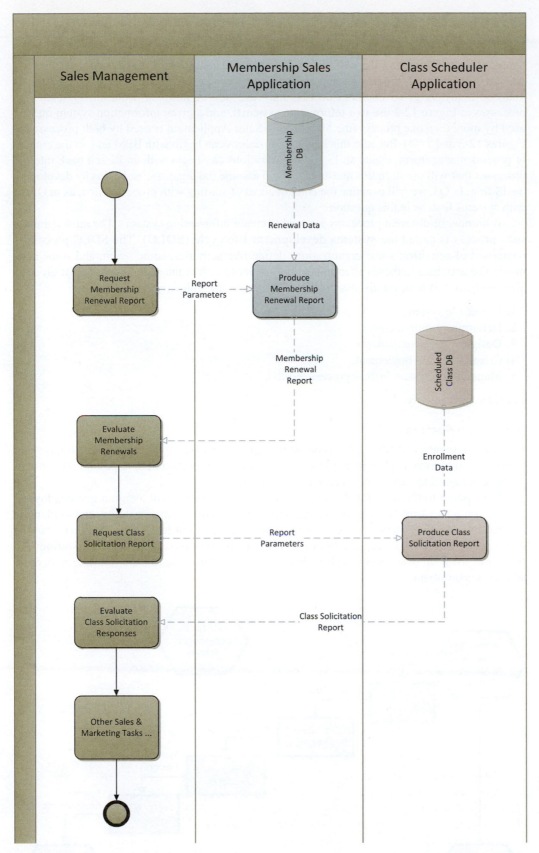

Q2. What Are the Activities of the Systems Development Life Cycle (SDLC) Development Process?

Systems development is the process of creating and maintaining an information system. As stated in Chapter 2, the relationship between a business process and an information system is many-to-many. A given business process may use one or more information systems (the processes in Figure 12-2 use two information systems), and a given information system may be used by more than one process (the Membership Sales Application is used by both processes in Figures 12-3 and 12-4). Because this is so, organizations can begin with BPM and, in the context of process management, create an IS. Or, organizations can begin with an IS and back into the processes that will use it. In this question, we will assume the organization begins by developing the IS first. In Q3, we will examine the consequences of starting with processes first, as in Q1, or with systems first, as in this question.

A number of different processes are used to create information systems. The most common such process is called the **systems development life cycle (SDLC)**. The SDLC process is composed of activities; some organizations define five activities, some seven, and some even more. The activities in these different versions are more or less the same; they are just grouped differently. In this text, we discuss the SDLC as having the following five activities:

1. Define the system.
2. Determine requirements.
3. Design system components.
4. Create, test, and implement.
5. Maintain the system (assess process results).

Consider each activity:

Define the System

As shown in Figure 12-5, the SDLC is begun in response to a need for a new information system; perhaps from a strategic plan, perhaps from senior management direction, or possibly because of the need for an IS to support new or adapting processes.

In response to the need for the new system, the organization will assign a few employees, possibly on a part-time basis, to define the new system, to assess its feasibility, and to plan the project. In a large organization, someone from the IS department leads the initial team, but the members of that initial team are both users and IS professionals. For an organization like FlexTime, the team would most likely be led by someone with some IS expertise, like Neil, or by an outside consultant.

FIGURE 12-5

BPM Provides Requirements for Systems Development

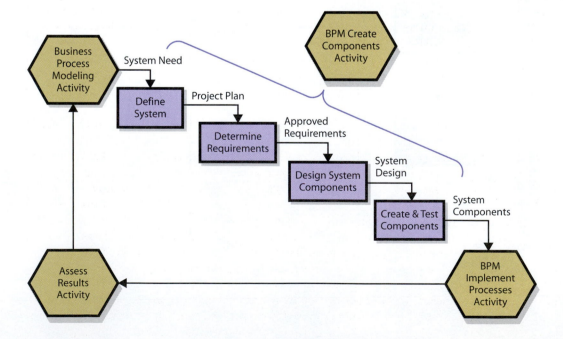

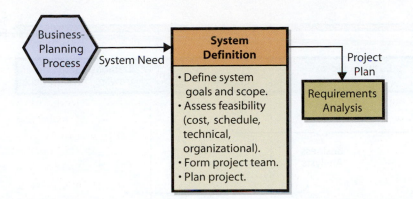

FIGURE 12-6

SDLC: System Definition Activity

DEFINE SYSTEM GOALS AND SCOPE As shown in Figure 12-6, the first step is to define the goals and scope of the new information system. Is the goal of the new system to support one or two processes, or is the new system broader in scope? Using the FlexTime example, should the new Web application concern only class enrollments and membership renewals, or should it include scheduling of personal trainers and other FlexTime facilities? These questions are asked and answered as part of the definition activity.

ASSESS FEASIBILITY Given the goals and scope of the new system, the next task is to assess feasibility. "Does this project make sense?" The aim here is to eliminate obviously nonsensical projects before forming a project development team and investing significant labor.

Feasibility has four dimensions: **cost**, **schedule**, **technical**, and **organizational feasibility**. Because IS development projects are difficult to budget and schedule, cost and schedule feasibility can be only an approximate, back-of-the-envelope analysis. The purpose is to eliminate any obviously infeasible ideas as soon as possible.

Technical feasibility refers to whether existing information technology is likely to be able to meet the needs of the new system. The new Web-based enrollment system at FlexTime is well within the capabilities of existing technology. For more advanced systems, this is not always the case.

Finally, *organizational feasibility* concerns whether the new system fits within the organization's customs, culture, charter, or legal requirements. At FlexTime, for example, is the idea of online sales and solicitation appropriate? Will customers object to sales pitches for other classes when their first choice class is full? Will that solicitation be considered "not in the spirit of FlexTime"?

FORM A PROJECT TEAM If the defined project is determined to be feasible, the next step is to form the project team. Normally, the team consists of both IT personnel and user representatives. Typical personnel on a development team are a manager (or managers for larger projects), business analysts, systems analysts, programmers, software testers, and users.

As stated in Chapter 6, a **business analyst** is someone who is well versed in the Porter models, organizational strategy, systems alignment theory such as COBIT, and who also understands the proper role for technology. As shown in Figure 12-7, business analysts work primarily with business processes, but they are also involved in systems development.

Systems analysts are IS professionals who understand both business and technology. They are active throughout the systems development process and play a key role in moving the project through the systems development process. Systems analysts integrate the work of the programmers, testers, and users. Depending on the nature of the project, the team may also include hardware and communications specialists, database designers and administrators, and other IT specialists. As shown in Figure 12-7, systems analysts work with process design as well, but their primary focus is information systems development.

The team composition changes over time. During requirements definition, the team will be heavy with business and systems analysts. During design and implementation, it will be heavy with programmers, testers, and database designers. During integrated testing and conversion, the team will be augmented with testers and business users.

User involvement is critical throughout the system development process. Depending on the size and nature of the project, users are assigned to the project either full or part time. Sometimes

FIGURE 12-7

Focus of Personnel Involved in BPM and Systems Development

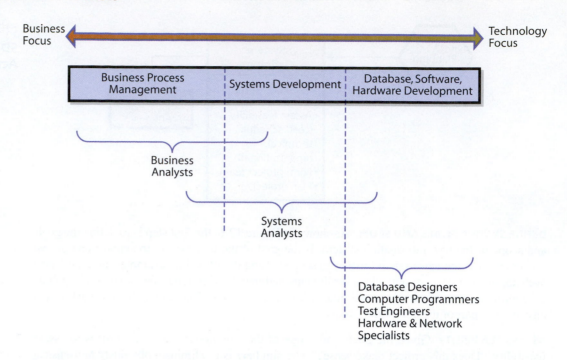

users are assigned to review and oversight committees that meet periodically, especially at the completion of project phases and other milestones. Users are involved in many different ways. *The important point is for users to have active involvement and to take ownership of the project throughout the entire development process.*

The first major task for the assembled project team is to plan the project. Members of the project team specify tasks to be accomplished, assign personnel, determine task dependencies, and set schedules.

Determine Requirements

Determining the system's requirements is the most important activity in the systems development process. If the requirements are wrong, the system will be wrong. If the requirements are determined completely and correctly, then design and implementation will be easier and more likely to result in success.

Examples of requirements in Figures 12-4 and 12-5 are the data items that members need to enter to request a class, the means by which solicitations for membership renewals and alternate classes will be made, and (not shown in these figures) how members will pay for renewals and classes. For example, it is possible to accept payment over the Web, but that will involve specifying important security requirements. Or, FlexTime could decide to collect payment when the member appears for the class. Other alternatives are also possible. Whichever is chosen, the particulars of that choice are specified during the requirements activity.

If you take a course in systems analysis and design, you will spend weeks on techniques for determining requirements. Here, we will just summarize that process. Typically, systems analysts interview users and record the results in some consistent manner. Good interviewing skills are crucial; users are notorious for being unable to describe what they want and need. Users also tend to focus on the tasks they are performing at the time of the interview. Tasks performed at the end of the quarter or end of the year are forgotten if the interview takes place mid-quarter. Seasoned and experienced systems analysts know how to conduct interviews to bring such requirements to light.

As listed in Figure 12-8, sources of requirements include existing systems as well as the forms, reports, queries, and application features and functions desired in the new system. Security is another important category of requirements.

If the new system involves a new database or substantial changes to an existing database, then the development team will create a data model. As you learned in Chapter 4, that model must reflect the users' perspective on their business and business activities. Thus, the data model is constructed on the basis of user interviews and must be validated by those users.

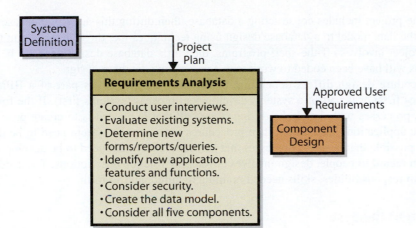

FIGURE 12-8

SDLC: Requirements Analysis Activity

Sometimes the requirements determination is so focused on the software and data components that other components are forgotten. Experienced project managers ensure consideration of requirements for all five IS components, not just for software and data. Regarding hardware, the team might ask: Are there special needs or restrictions on hardware? Is there an organizational standard governing what kinds of hardware can, or cannot, be used? Must the new system use existing hardware? What requirements are there for communications and network hardware?

Similarly, the team should consider requirements for procedures and personnel: Do accounting controls require procedures that separate duties and authorities? Are there restrictions that some actions can be taken only by certain departments or specific personnel? Are there policy requirements or union rules that restrict activities to certain categories of employees? Will the system need to interface with information systems from other companies and organizations? In short, requirements need to be considered for all of the components of the new information system.

These questions are examples of the kinds of questions that must be asked and answered during requirements analysis.

Design Components

Each of the five components is designed in this activity. Typically, the team designs each component by developing alternatives, evaluating each of those alternatives against the requirements, and then selecting from among those alternatives. Accurate requirements are critical here; if they are incomplete or wrong, then they will be poor guides for evaluation.

Figure 12-9 shows that design tasks pertain to each of the five IS components. For hardware, the team determines specifications for the hardware that they want to acquire. (The team is not designing hardware in the sense of building a CPU or a disk drive.) Program design depends on the source of the programs. For off-the-shelf software, the team must determine candidate products and evaluate them against the requirements. For off-the-shelf with alteration programs, the team identifies products to be acquired off-the-shelf and then determines the alterations required. For custom-developed programs, the team produces design documentation for writing program code.

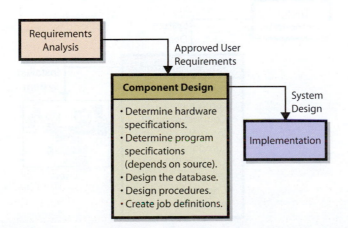

FIGURE 12-9

SDLC: Component Design Activity

If the project includes constructing a database, then during this activity database designers convert the data model to a database design using techniques like those described in Chapter 4. If the project involves off-the-shelf programs, then little database design needs to be done; the programs will have been coded to work with a preexisting database design.

Procedure design differs depending on whether the project is part of a BPM process (processes first) or is part of a systems development process (systems first). If the former, then business processes will already be designed, and all that is needed is to create procedures for using the application. If the latter, then procedures for using the system need to be developed, and it is possible that business processes that surround the system need to be developed as well.

With regard to people, design involves developing role job descriptions. These descriptions will detail responsibilities, skills needed, training required, and so forth.

Implement the System

The term *implementation* has two meanings for us. It could mean to implement the information systems components, only, or it could mean to implement the information system and the business processes that use the information system. As you read the following task descriptions, keep in mind that the tasks can apply to both interpretations of implementation.

Tasks in the implementation activity are to build and test system components and to convert users to the new system and possibly new business processes (see Figure 12-10). Developers construct each of the components independently. They obtain, install, and test hardware. They license and install off-the-shelf programs; they write adaptations and custom programs, as necessary. They construct a database and fill it with data. They document, review, and test procedures, and they create training programs. Finally, the organization hires and trains needed personnel.

Testing the system is important, time consuming, and expensive. A **test plan**, which is a formal description of the system's response to use and misuse scenarios, is written. Professional test engineers, called Product Quality Assurance (PQA) test engineers are hired for this task. Often teams of professional test engineers are augmented by users as well.

SYSTEM CONVERSION Once the system has passed testing, the organization installs the new system. The term **system conversion** is often used for this activity because it implies the process of *converting* business activity from the old system to the new. Again, conversion can be to the new system, only, or it can be to the new system, including new business processes.

Four types of conversion are possible: pilot, phased, parallel, and plunge. Any of the first three can be effective. In most cases, companies should avoid "taking the plunge"!

With **pilot installation**, the organization implements the entire system/business processes on a limited portion of the business. An example would be for FlexTime to use the online enrollment system for a few customers, perhaps as a special "beta program" benefit for long-time members. The advantage of pilot implementation is that if the system fails, the failure is contained within a limited boundary.

FIGURE 12-10

SDLC: Implementation Activity

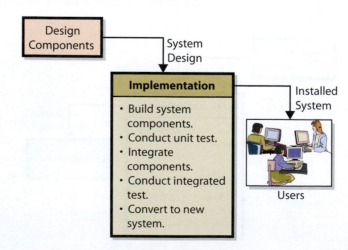

	Hardware	Software	Data	Procedures	People
Design	Determine hardware specifications.	Select off-the-shelf programs. Design alterations and custom programs as necessary.	Design database and related structures.	Design user and operations procedures.	Develop user and operations job descriptions.
Implementation	Obtain, install, and test hardware.	License and install off-the-shelf programs. Write alterations and custom programs. Test programs.	Create database. Fill with data. Test data.	Document procedures. Create training programs. Review and test procedures.	Hire and train personnel.
	Integrated Test and Conversion				

Unit test each component

Note: Cells shaded tan represent software development.

FIGURE 12-11

Design and Implementation for the Five Components

As the name implies, with **phased installation** the new system/business process is installed in phases across the organization(s). Once a given piece works, then the organization installs and tests another piece of the system, until the entire system has been installed. Some systems are so tightly integrated that they cannot be installed in phased pieces. Such systems must be installed using one of the other techniques.

With **parallel installation**, the new system/business process runs in parallel with the old one until the new system is tested and fully operational. Parallel installation is expensive, because the organization incurs the costs of running both existing and new systems/business process. Users must work double-time, if you will, to run both systems. Then, considerable work is needed to reconcile results of the new with the old.

The final style of conversion is **plunge installation** (sometimes called *direct installation*). With it, the organization shuts off the old system/business process and starts the new one. If the new system/process fails, the organization is in trouble: Nothing can be done until either the new system/process is fixed or the old system/process is reinstalled. Because of the risk, organizations should avoid this conversion style if possible. The one exception is if the new system is providing a new capability that will not disrupt the operation of the organization if it fails.

Figure 12-11 summarizes the tasks for each of the five components during the design and implementation activities. Use this figure to test your knowledge of the tasks in each activity.

Maintain the System

The term **maintenance** is a misnomer; the work done during this activity is either to *fix* the system so that it works correctly or to *adapt* it to changes in requirements.

Figure 12-12 shows tasks during the maintenance activity. First, there needs to be a means for tracking both failures[1] and requests for enhancements to meet new requirements. For small systems, organizations can track failures and enhancements using word-processing documents. As systems become larger, however, and as the number of failure and enhancement requests increases, many organizations find it necessary to develop a tracking database. Such a database contains a description of the failure or enhancement. It also records who reported the problem, who will make the fix or enhancement, what the status of that work is, and whether the fix or enhancement has been tested and verified by the originator.

---

[1] A *failure* is a difference between what the system does and what it is supposed to do. Sometimes you will hear the term *bug* used instead of failure. As a future user, call failures *failures*, because that's what they are. Don't have a *bugs* list, have a *failures* list. Don't have an *unresolved bug*, have an *unresolved failure*. A few months of managing an organization that is coping with a serious failure will show you the importance of this difference in terms.

FIGURE 12-12

**SDLC: System
Maintenance Activity**

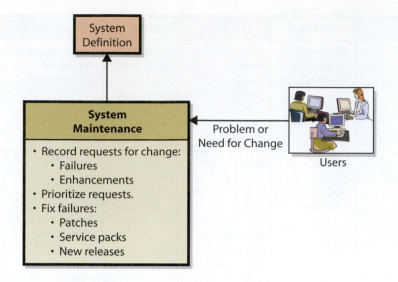

Typically, IS personnel prioritize system problems according to their severity. They fix high-priority items as soon as possible, and they fix low-priority items as time and resources become available.

Because an enhancement is an adaptation to new requirements, developers usually prioritize enhancement requests separate from failures. The decision to make an enhancement includes a business decision that the enhancement will generate an acceptable rate of return.

Q3. Which Comes First: Process or Systems Development?

The many-to-many relationship between business processes and information systems poses a dilemma when it comes time to build or redesign them. Which should we do first? Should we specify one or more business processes and then build the information systems that they require? Or, do we attempt to determine, in the abstract, all of the ways that someone might use an information system, build it, and then construct the business processes around it?

If you reflect on this situation, you can see why ERP systems, which promise to do everything, are both wonderful and terrible. They are wonderful because they include all the business processes and all the system components that an organization will need, at least as determined by the ERP vendor. They are terrible because to implement ERP an organization must attempt to do everything at once.

But, for non-ERP business processes and information systems, and for small organizations like FlexTime, which should come first? Consider the alternatives.

Business Processes First

Suppose we decide to design business processes first, and then build IS components as a consequence of that process design. If we take this approach, we will have a development process that looks like that in Figure 12-13. The organization will engage in business process management, and construct system components in the create components activity of the BPM cycle.

This approach works well for the business processes that are being constructed, because the requirements for that system are taken from those processes. But, what about other processes in the future? For example, examine the Membership Sales and Class Scheduler applications in Figure 12-4. The database structures and reporting programs are constructed to meet the needs of the Sales Evaluation process for membership renewals and class solicitations. But, suppose in a few months, FlexTime wants to evaluate other types of sales. Those applications will not work for those other types and will need to be redone at extra expense and effort.

Thus, starting from processes and working toward information systems is likely to work well for the business processes under consideration, but will cause problems later for other processes that could use that same information system. So, what if we start with the information system, first?

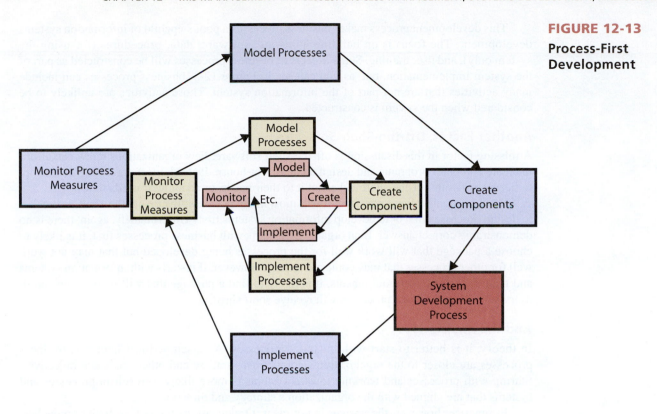

FIGURE 12-13
Process-First Development

Information System First

Suppose we decide to start with the information system first. To do so, a development team would talk with representative future users of the system and attempt to determine all of the ways that someone at FlexTime might want do online enrollment. From those requirements, they would then design components and construct the system.

If we develop information systems first, we will have a development process like the systems development life cycle, which has the five steps shown in Figure 12-14. A high-level business planning process determines that a system is needed for some function; at FlexTime that function would be to evaluate sales. Given that system need, the development team would then refine the system definition, determine requirements, design system components, and then implement the system.

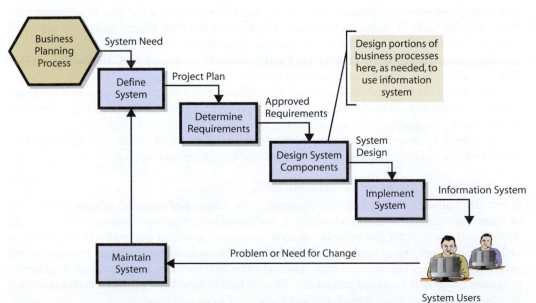

FIGURE 12-14

Classic Five-Step Systems Development Life Cycle

This development process makes business processes a poor stepchild of information systems development. The focus is on building hardware, software, data, procedures (for using the system only), and user training. Some aspects of business processes will be constructed as part of the system implementation, but, as you can see in Figure 12-3, business processes can include many activities that are not part of the information system. Those activities are unlikely to be considered when the system is constructed.

Another Factor: Off-the-Shelf Software

A missing factor in this discussion is off-the-shelf software. Few organizations today can afford to create computer programs and design databases in-house. Instead, most organizations attempt to license software off-the-shelf and adapt it to their needs, or adapt their needs to it.

So, if an organization knows that it will most likely license software off-the-shelf, is it better to design processes first or to develop information systems first? Unfortunately, again, there is no demonstrably correct answer. If an organization starts with business processes first, it is likely to choose a package that will work well for the processes being developed but that may not work well for other processes that may come along later. However, if it starts with information systems and then collects all the requirements, it is likely to find a package that will work better for all users, but, again, business processes will receive short shrift.

And the Answer Is . . .

In theory, it is better to start with business processes. As discussed in Chapter 1, business processes are closer to the organization's competitive strategy and other goals and objectives. Staring with processes and working toward systems is more likely to result in processes and systems that are aligned with the organization's strategy and direction.

In practice, however, the answer is not clear. Organizations today take both approaches. Sometimes the same organization takes one approach with one set of processes and systems and a second approach with a different set.

As you can imagine, much more can be said and learned about processes for developing business processes and information systems. If you want to learn more, take a course in systems development. For now, we need to move on to another important MIS management process: information security.

Q4. What Is Information Systems Security?

Information systems security is the process of protecting information systems *vulnerabilities* from *threats* by creating appropriate *safeguards*. We will illustrate each of the italicized key terms in this and the next section.

Before we do so, understand that information systems security is crucial. Every organization that employs an information system should implement IS security in a way that is appropriate for its strategy. In 2011, 77 million users of Sony PlayStations had their names, addresses, and credit card data compromised because of lax security procedures. Not to be outdone, Apple and Facebook also compromised security via the iPhone and Facebook pages. Undoubtedly, other disasters will have occurred by the time you read this.

Because of the financial and reputation costs of such problems, no organization should wait to consider security until after a security incident has occurred. Instead, organizations today must create security programs, as we will discuss in Q5.

We begin by describing security vulnerabilities. We will first summarize the sources of vulnerabilities and then describe specific threats that arise from each source.

What Are the Sources of Vulnerabilities?

A **security vulnerability** is a potential challenge to the integrity of information systems from one of three sources: human error and mistakes, malicious human activity, and natural events and disasters. *Human errors and mistakes* include accidental problems caused by both employees and nonemployees. An example is an employee who misunderstands operating procedures and accidentally deletes customer records. This category also includes poorly written application programs and poorly designed procedures. Finally, human errors and mistakes include physical accidents, such as driving a forklift through the wall of a computer room.

The second source of security problems is *malicious human activity*. This category includes employees and former employees who intentionally destroy data or other system components. It also includes hackers who break into a system and virus and worm writers who infect computer systems. Malicious human activity also includes outside criminals who break into a system to steal for financial gain, and it also includes terrorism.

Natural events and disasters are the third source of security problems. This category includes fires, floods, hurricanes, earthquakes, tsunamis, avalanches, and other acts of nature. Problems in this category include not only the initial loss of capability and service, but also losses stemming from actions to recover from the initial problem.

What Are the Types of Security Threats?

A **threat** is a challenge to information systems security. Four types of threat are listed in Figure 12-15: unauthorized data disclosure, incorrect data modification, denial of service, and loss of infrastructure. We will consider each type.

UNAUTHORIZED DATA DISCLOSURE *Unauthorized data disclosure* can occur by human error when someone inadvertently releases data in violation of policy. An example at a university would be a new department administrator who posts student names, numbers, and grades in a public place, when the releasing of names and grades violates state law. Another example is employees who unknowingly or carelessly release proprietary data to competitors or to the media.

The popularity and efficacy of search engines has created another source of inadvertent disclosure. Employees who place restricted data on Web sites that can be reached by search engines might mistakenly publish proprietary or restricted data over the Web.

Of course, proprietary and personal data can also be released maliciously. **Social engineering** is a category of threats that involve manipulating a person or group to unknowingly release confidential information. **Pretexting** is social engineering in which someone deceives by pretending to be someone else. A common scam involves a telephone caller who pretends to be from a credit card company and claims to be checking the validity of credit card numbers: "I'm checking your MasterCard number; it begins 5491. Can you verify the rest of the number?" All MasterCard numbers start with 5491; the caller is attempting to steal a valid number.

Phishing is another social engineering technique for obtaining unauthorized data via e-mail pretexting. The *phisher* pretends to be a legitimate company and sends an e-mail requesting confidential data, such as account numbers, Social Security numbers, account passwords, and so forth. Phishing compromises legitimate brands and trademarks. See MIS InClass 12 on page 395.

FIGURE 12-15

Security Threats and Source

		Source		
		Human Error	**Malicious Activity**	**Natural Disasters**
Threat	**Unauthorized data disclosure**	Procedural mistakes	Pretexting Phishing Spoofing Sniffing Computer crime	Disclosure during recovery
	Incorrect data modification	Procedural mistakes Incorrect procedures Ineffective accounting controls System errors	Hacking Computer crime	Incorrect data recovery
	Denial of service (DOS)	Accidents	DOS attacks	Service interruption
	Loss of infrastructure	Accidents	Theft Terrorist activity	Property loss

Spoofing is another term for someone pretending to be someone else. If you pretend to be your professor, you are spoofing your professor. **IP spoofing** occurs when an intruder uses another site's IP address as if it were that other site. **E-mail spoofing** is a synonym for phishing.

Social engineering always involves the people component of an IS. Other types of unauthorized data disclosure involve hardware and software. **Sniffing** is a technique for intercepting computer communications. With wired networks, sniffing requires a physical connection to the network. With wireless networks, no such connection is required: **Drive-by sniffers** simply take computers with wireless connections through an area and search for unprotected wireless networks. They can monitor and intercept wireless traffic at will. Even protected wireless networks are vulnerable, as you will learn. Spyware and adware are two other sniffing techniques discussed later in this chapter.

Other forms of computer crime include breaking into networks to steal data such as customer lists, product inventory data, employee data, and other proprietary and confidential data.

Finally, people might inadvertently disclose data during recovery from a natural disaster. During a recovery, everyone is so focused on restoring system capability that they might ignore normal security safeguards. A request like "I need a copy of the customer database backup" will receive far less scrutiny during disaster recovery than at other times.

INCORRECT DATA MODIFICATION The second threat category in Figure 12-15 is *incorrect data modification*. Examples include incorrectly increasing a customer's discount or incorrectly modifying an employee's salary, earned days of vacation, or annual bonus. Other examples include placing incorrect information, such as incorrect price changes, on the company's Web site or company portal.

Incorrect data modification can occur through human error when employees follow procedures incorrectly or when procedures have been designed incorrectly. For proper internal control on systems that process financial data or that control inventories of assets, such as products and equipment, companies should ensure separation of duties and authorities and have multiple checks and balances in place.

A final type of incorrect data modification caused by human error includes *system errors*. An example is the lost update problem discussed in Chapter 4 (page 102).

Hacking occurs when a person gains unauthorized access to a computer system. Although some people hack for the sheer joy of doing it, other hackers invade systems for the malicious purpose of stealing or modifying data. **Computer criminals** invade computer networks to obtain critical data or to manipulate the system for financial gain. Examples are reducing account balances or causing the shipment of goods to unauthorized locations and customers. It is also possible to use social engineering.

Finally, faulty recovery actions after a disaster can result in incorrect data changes. The faulty actions can be unintentional or malicious.

DENIAL OF SERVICE Human error in following procedures or a lack of procedures can result in **denial of service**. For example, humans can inadvertently shut down a Web server or corporate gateway router by starting a computationally intensive application. An OLAP application that uses the operational DBMS can consume so many DBMS resources that order-entry transactions cannot get through.

Denial-of-service attacks can be launched maliciously. A malicious hacker can flood a Web server, for example, with millions of bogus service requests that so occupy the server that it cannot service legitimate requests. For example, computer worms can infiltrate a network with so much artificial traffic that legitimate traffic cannot get through. Finally, natural disasters may cause systems to fail, resulting in denial of service.

LOSS OF INFRASTRUCTURE Human accidents can cause *loss of infrastructure*. Examples are a bull-dozer cutting a conduit of fiber-optic cables and the floor buffer crashing into a rack of Web servers.

Theft and terrorist events also cause loss of infrastructure. A disgruntled, terminated employee can walk off with corporate data servers, routers, or other crucial equipment. Terrorist events also can cause the loss of physical plants and equipment.

Natural disasters present the largest risk for infrastructure loss. A fire, flood, earthquake, or similar event can destroy data centers and all they contain. The devastation in Japan from the tsunami in March 2011 as well as that caused by the tornados in the U.S. Midwest in 2011 are potent examples of the risks to infrastructure from natural causes.

MIS InClass 12

Phishing for Credit Cards, Identifying Numbers, and Bank Accounts

A **phisher** is an individual or organization that spoofs legitimate companies in an attempt to illegally capture personal data such as credit card numbers, e-mail accounts, and driver's license numbers. Some phishers install malicious program code on users' computers as well.

Phishing is usually initiated via e-mail. Phishers steal legitimate logos and trademarks and use official sounding words in an attempt to fools users into revealing personal data or clicking a link. Phishers do not bother with laws about trademark use. They place names and logos like Visa, MasterCard, Discover, and American Express on their Web pages and use them as bait. In some cases, phishers copy the entire look and feel of a legitimate company's Web site.

In this exercise, you and a group of your fellow students will be asked to investigate phishing attacks. If you search the Web for *phishing*, be aware that your search may bring the attention of an active phisher. Therefore, do not give any data to any site that you visit as part of this exercise!

1. To learn phishing fundamentals, visit *www.microsoft.com/protect/fraud/phishing/symptoms.aspx*. To see recent examples of phishing attacks, visit *www.fraudwatchinternational.com/phishing/*.
   a. Using examples from these links, describe how phishing works.
   b. Explain why a link that appears to be legitimate, such as *www.microsoft.mysite.com*, may, in fact, be a link to a phisher's site.
   c. List five indicators of a phishing attack.
   d. Write an e-mail that you could send to a nontechnical friend or relative that explains what phishing is and how your friend or relative can avoid it.

Source: Brian A Jackson/Shutterstock.

2. Suppose you received the e-mail in Figure 12-16 and mistakenly clicked See more details here. When you did so, you were taken to the Web page shown in Figure 12-17. List every phishing symptom that you find in these figures and explain why it is a symptom.
3. Suppose you work for an organization that is being phished.
   a. How would you learn that your organization is being attacked?
   b. What steps should your organization take in response to the attack?
   c. What liability, if any, do you think your organization has for damages to customers that result from a phishing attack that carries your brand and trademarks?
4. Summarize why phishing is a serious problem to commerce today.
5. Describe actions that industry organizations, companies, governments, and individuals can take to help to reduce phishing.

Your Order 1D: "17152492"
Order Date: "09/07/12"
Product Purchased: "Two First Class Tickets to Cozumel"
Your card type: "CREDIT"
Total Price: "$349.00"
Hello, when you purchased your tickets you provided an incorrect mailing address.
See more details here
Please follow the link and modify your mailing address or cancel your order. If you have questions, feel free to contact us account@usefulbill.com

FIGURE 12-16

Fake Phishing E-Mail

FIGURE 12-17

Fake Phishing Screen

FIGURE 12-18

CSI Computer Crime and Security Survey, 2009

Source: Based on *http://www. pathmaker.biz/whitepapers/CSI Survey2009.pdf*.

Type	Percent of Respondents
Malware infection	64%
Laptop or mobile device theft	42%
Spoofed by phishing	34%
Denial of service	29%
Bots within organization	23%
Financial fraud	20%

You may be wondering why Figure 12-15 does not include viruses, worms, and Trojan horses. The answer is that viruses, worms, and Trojan horses are *techniques* for causing some of the threats in the figure. They can cause a denial-of-service attack, or they can be used to cause malicious, unauthorized data access, or data loss.

The Computer Security Institute annually conducts a survey of computer crime. Figure 12-18 summarizes the most common crimes from the 2009 survey, which provides the most recent publicly accessible data. As you will learn in the next question, you have a direct role in preventing three of these top six crimes: You can reduce the likelihood of malware by running malware protection software; you can protect your laptop and mobile devices from theft; and you can follow systems procedures to prevent financial fraud.

Q5. What Are the Components of an Organization's Security Program?

All of the threats listed in Figure 12-15 are real and as serious as they sound. Accordingly, organizations must address security in a systematic way. A **security program**[2] has three components: senior-management involvement, safeguards of various kinds, and incident response.

The first component, *senior-management involvement*, has two critical security functions: First, senior management must establish the security policy. This policy sets the stage for the organization's response to security vulnerabilities. However, because no security program is perfect, there is always risk. Management's second function, therefore, is to manage risk by balancing the costs and benefits of the security program.

Safeguards are protections against security vulnerabilities. A good way to view safeguards is in terms of the five components of an information system, as shown in Figure 12-19. Some of the safeguards involve computer hardware and software. Some involve data; others involve procedures and people. In addition to these safeguards, organizations must also consider disaster-recovery safeguards. An effective security program consists of a balance of safeguards of all these types.

Management sets security policies to ensure compliance with security policy, as discussed in the Ethics Guide on pages 410–411.

FIGURE 12-19

Security Safeguards as They Relate to the Five IS Components

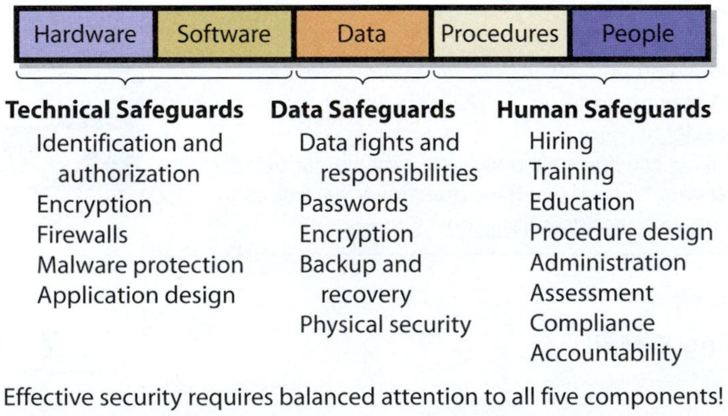

Hardware	Software	Data	Procedures	People

Technical Safeguards	**Data Safeguards**	**Human Safeguards**
Identification and authorization	Data rights and responsibilities	Hiring
Encryption	Passwords	Training
Firewalls	Encryption	Education
Malware protection	Backup and recovery	Procedure design
Application design	Physical security	Administration
		Assessment
		Compliance
		Accountability

Effective security requires balanced attention to all five components!

[2] Note that the word *program* is used here in the sense of a management program that includes objectives, policies, procedures, directives, and so forth. Do not confuse this term with a computer program.

The final component of a security program consists of the organization's *planned response to security incidents.* Clearly, the time to think about what to do is *not* when the computers are crashing all around the organization. We begin the discussion of the security program with the responsibilities of senior management.

What Is Management's Security Role?

Management has a crucial role in information systems security. Management sets the security policy, and only management can balance the costs of a security system against the risk of security vulnerabilities. The National Institute of Standards and Technology (NIST) published an excellent security handbook that addresses management's responsibility. It is available online at *http://csrc.nist.gov/publications/nistpubs/800-12/handbook.pdf.* We will follow its discussion in this section.

The *NIST Handbook* of Security Elements

Figure 12-20 lists elements of computer security described in the *NIST Handbook*. First, computer security must support the organization's strategy. There is no "one size fits all" solution to security threats. Security systems for a diamond mine and security systems for a wheat farm will differ.

According to the second point in Figure 12-20, when you manage a department you have a responsibility for information security in that department, even if no one tells you that you do. Do appropriate safeguards exist? Are your employees properly trained? Will your department know how to respond when the computer system fails? If these issues are not addressed in your department, raise the issue to higher levels of management.

Security can be expensive. Therefore, as shown in the third principle of Figure 12-20, computer security should have an appropriate cost-benefit ratio. Costs can be direct, such as labor costs, and they can be intangible, such as employee or customer frustration. Organizations such as FlexTime cannot afford to provide the same level of security as Pearson Education or the IRS provide. All the same, they should pay attention to security and manage security risk, as described in the next section.

According to the fourth principle in Figure 12-20, security responsibilities and accountabilities must be explicit. General statements like "everyone in the department must adequately safeguard company assets" are too broad to be useful. Instead, managers should assign specific tasks to specific people or specific job functions.

Because information systems integrate the processing of many departments, security threats originating in your department can have far-reaching consequences. If one of your employees neglects procedures and enters product prices incorrectly on your Web storefront, the consequences will extend to other departments, other companies, and your customers.

Understanding that computer system owners have security responsibilities outside their own departments and organizations is the fifth principle of computer security.

As the sixth principle in Figure 12-20 implies, there is no magic bullet for security. No single safeguard, such as a firewall, a virus-protection program, or increased employee training, will provide effective security. The threats described in Figure 12-15 require an integrated security program.

FIGURE 12-20

Elements of Computer Security

1. Computer security should support the mission of the organization.
2. Computer security is an integral element of sound management.
3. Computer security should be cost-effective.
4. Computer security responsibilities and accountability should be made explicit.
5. System owners have computer security responsibilities outside their own organizations.
6. Computer security requires a comprehensive and integrated approach.
7. Computer security should be periodically reassessed.
8. Computer security is constrained by societal factors.

Once a security program is in place, the company cannot simply forget about it. As the seventh principle in Figure 12-20 indicates, security is a continuing need, and every company must periodically evaluate its security program.

Finally, social factors put some limits on security programs. Employees resent physical searches when arriving at and departing from work. Customers do not want to have their retinas scanned before they can place an order. Computer security conflicts with personal privacy, and a balance may be hard to achieve.

Q6. What Technical Safeguards Are Available?

Technical safeguards involve the hardware, software, and data components of an information system. Figure 12-21 lists primary technical safeguards; we will consider each.

Identification and Authentication

Every information system today should require users to sign on with a user name and password. The user name *identifies* the user (the process of **identification**), and the password *authenticates* that user (the process of **authentication**).

PASSWORDS Passwords are a critical component of information systems security, and yet many users are casual about creating and using passwords. John Pozadzides, an Internet Security expert, claims he could break 20 percent of all users' passwords within minutes using a few simple rules.[3]

According to Microsoft, an appropriate password does not include any word in any dictionary and contains both upper- and lowercase letters, numbers, and special characters, such as $, %, and &. Even with that, passwords should be long. According to Posadzides, any seven character password can be broken in a little more than 2 hours by a determined hacker armed with an average-capability PC. However, a password with 11 characters would require over a century, and one with 14 characters would take more than 2,000 years.

Despite repeated warnings to the contrary, many users are careless in their use of passwords. For example, you can find yellow sticky notes holding written passwords adorning the computers in many companies. In addition, users tend to be free in sharing their passwords with others. These deficiencies can be reduced using smart cards and biometric authentication, but good security begins with appropriate, long passwords.

SMART CARDS A **smart card** is a plastic card similar to a credit card. Unlike credit, debit, and ATM cards, which have a magnetic strip, smart cards have a microchip. The microchip, which holds far more data than a magnetic strip, is loaded with identifying data. Users of smart cards are required to enter a **personal identification number (PIN)** to be authenticated.

BIOMETRIC AUTHENTICATION **Biometric authentication** uses personal physical characteristics such as fingerprints, facial features, and retinal scans to authenticate users. Biometric authentication provides strong authentication, but the required equipment is expensive. Often, too, users resist biometric identification because they feel it is invasive.

FIGURE 12-21

Technical Safeguards

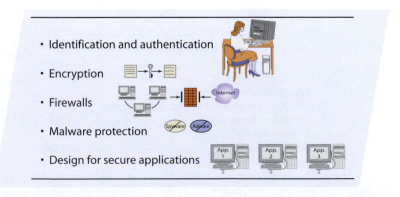

- Identification and authentication
- Encryption
- Firewalls
- Malware protection
- Design for secure applications

---

[3] John Pozadzides, "How I'd Hack Your Passwords," MSN Money. Available at: *http://money.msn.com/identity-theft/how-i-would-hack-your-passwords.aspx*.

Biometric authentication is in the early stages of adoption. Because of its strength, it likely will see increased usage in the future. It is also likely that legislators will pass laws governing the use, storage, and protection requirements for biometric data.

You can remember authentication methods by understanding they fall into three categories: what you know (password or PIN), what you have (smart card), and what you are (biometric).

Encryption

The second technical safeguard in Figure 12-21 is encryption. **Encryption** is the process of transforming clear text into coded, unintelligible text for secure storage or communication. Considerable research has gone into developing **encryption algorithms** (procedures for encrypting data) that are difficult to break. Commonly used methods are DES, 3DES, and AES; search the Web for these terms if you want to know more about them. Figure 12-22 summarizes five encryption techniques.

A **key** is a number used to encrypt the data. It is called a *key* because it unlocks a message, but it is a number used with an encryption algorithm and not a physical thing like the key to your apartment.

To encode a message, a computer program uses the encryption method with the key to convert a noncoded message into a coded message. The resulting coded message looks like gibberish. Decoding (decrypting) a message is similar; a key is applied to the coded message to recover the original text. In **symmetric encryption**, the same key (again, a number) is used to encode and to decode. With **asymmetric encryption**, two keys are used; one key encodes the message, and the other key decodes the message. Symmetric encryption is simpler and much faster than asymmetric encryption.

Technique	How It Works	Characteristics
Symmetric	Sender and receiver transmit message using the same key.	Fast, but difficult to get the same key to both parties.
Asymmetric	Sender and receiver transmit message using two keys, one public and one private. Message encrypted with one of the keys can be decrypted with the other.	Public key can be openly transmitted, but needs certificate authority (see below). Slower than symmetric.
SSL/TLS	Works between Levels 4 and 5 of the TCP-OSI architecture. Sender uses public/private key to transmit symmetric key, which both parties use for symmetric encryption—for a limited, brief period.	Used by most Internet applications. A useful and workable hybrid of symmetric and asymmetric.
Digital signatures	Sender hashes message, and uses private key to "sign" a message digest, creating digital signature; sender transmits plaintext message and digital signature. Receiver rehashes the plaintext message and decrypts the digital signature with the user's public key. If the message digests match, receiver knows that message has not been altered.	Ingenious technique for ensuring plaintext has not been altered.
Digital certificates	A trusted third party, the certificate authority (CA), supplies the public key and a digital certificate. Receiver decrypts message with public key (from CA), signed with CA's digital signature.	Eliminates spoofing of public keys. Requires browser to have CA's public key.

FIGURE 12-22

Basic Encryption Techniques

A special version of asymmetric encryption, **public key/private key**, is used on the Internet. With this method, each site has a public key for encoding messages and a private key for decoding them. Before we explain how that works, consider an analogy:

Suppose you send a friend an open combination lock (like you have on your gym locker). Suppose you are the only one who knows the combination to that lock. Now, suppose your friend puts something in a box and locks the lock. Now, neither they nor anyone else can open that box. They send the locked box to you, and you apply the combination to open the box.

A public key is like the combination lock and the private key is like the combination. Your friend uses the public key to code the message (lock the box), and you use the private key to decode the message (use the combination to open the lock).

Now, suppose we have two generic computers, A and B. Suppose A wants to send an encrypted message to B. To do so, A sends B its public key (in our analogy, A sends B an open combination lock). Now B applies A's public key to the message and sends the resulting coded message back to A. At that point, neither B nor anyone other than A can decode that message. It is like the box with a locked combination lock. When A receives the coded message, A applies its private key (the combination in our analogy) to unlock or decrypt the message.

Again, public keys are like open combination locks. A will send a lock to anyone who asks for one. But A never sends its private key (the combination) to anyone. Private keys stay private.

Most secure communication over the Internet uses a protocol called **HTTPS**. With HTTPS, data are encrypted using a protocol called the **Secure Socket Layer (SSL)**, also known as **Transport Layer Security (TLS)**. SSL/TLS uses a combination of public key/private key and symmetric encryption.

The basic idea is this: Symmetric encryption is fast and is preferred. But, the two parties (say you and a Web site) don't share a symmetric key. So, the two of you use public/private encryption to share the same symmetric key. Once you both have that key, you use symmetric encryption.

Figure 12-23 summarizes how SSL/TLS works when you communicate securely with a Web site:

1. Your computer obtains the public key of the Web site to which it will connect.
2. Your computer generates a key for symmetric encryption.
3. Your computer encodes that key using the Web site's public key. It sends the encrypted symmetric key to the Web site.
4. The Web site then decodes the symmetric key using its private key.
5. From that point forward, your computer and the Web site communicate using symmetric encryption.

At the end of the session, your computer and the secure site discard the keys. Using this strategy, the bulk of the secure communication occurs using the faster symmetric encryption. Also, because keys are used for short intervals, there is less likelihood they can be discovered.

Use of SSL/TLS makes it safer to send sensitive data such as credit card numbers and bank balances. Just be certain that you see *https//:* in your browser and not just *http://*.

FIGURE 12-23

The Essence of HTTPS (SSL or TLS)

1. Your computer obtains public key of Web site.

Web Site Public Key

2. Your computer generates key for symmetric encryption.

You

3. Your computer encrypts symmetric key using Web site's public key.

Web Site

Symmetric Key Encrypted Using Web Site's Public Key

4. Web site decodes your message using its private key. Obtains key for symmetric encryption.

Communications Using Symmetric Encryption

5. All communications between you and Web site use symmetric encryption.

Warning: Under normal circumstances, neither e-mail nor instant messaging (IM) uses encryption. It would be quite easy for one of your classmates or your professor to read any e-mail or IM that you send over a wireless network in your classroom, in the student lounge, at a coffee shop, or in any other wireless setting. Let the sender beware!

The last two encryption techniques in Figure 12-22, digital signatures and digital certificates are beyond the scope of this text. You should know, however, that the purpose of **digital signatures** is to ensure that nonencrypted, plain text is not altered during transmission. **Digital certificates** are an encryption technique that is used to protect against spoofing of public keys.

Firewalls

Firewalls are the third technical safeguard listed in Figure 12-21. A firewall is a computing device that prevents unauthorized network access. A firewall can be a special-purpose computer or it can be a program on a general-purpose computer or on a router. Firewalls are built into Windows and Macintosh operating systems, and those firewalls are augmented by other firewall devices that protect most organizational networks. A discussion of firewall technology is beyond the scope of this book.

Malware Protection

The next technical safeguard in our list in Figure 12-21 is malware. The term **malware** has several definitions. Here we will use the broadest one: *Malware* is viruses, worms, Trojan horses, spyware, and adware.

VIRUSES, TROJAN HORSES, AND WORMS A **virus** is a computer program that replicates itself. Unchecked replication is like computer cancer; ultimately, the virus consumes the computer's resources. Furthermore, many viruses also take unwanted and harmful actions.

The program code that causes unwanted activity is called the **payload**. The payload can delete programs or data or, even worse, modify data in undetected ways. Imagine the impact of a virus that changed the credit rating of all customers. Some viruses publish data in harmful ways—for example, sending out files of credit card data to unauthorized sites.

There are many different virus types. **Trojan horses** are viruses that masquerade as useful programs or files. The name refers to the gigantic mock-up of a horse that was filled with soldiers and moved into Troy during the Trojan War. A typical Trojan horse appears to be a computer game, an MP3 music file, or some other useful innocuous program.

A **worm** is a virus that propagates using the Internet or other computer network. Worms spread faster than other virus types because they are specifically programmed to spread. Unlike nonworm viruses, which must wait for the user to share a file with a second computer, worms actively use the network to spread. Sometimes, worms so choke a network that it becomes unusable.

SPYWARE AND ADWARE **Spyware** programs are installed on the user's computer without the user's knowledge or permission. Spyware resides in the background and, unknown to the user, observes the user's actions and keystrokes, monitors computer activity, and reports the user's activities to sponsoring organizations. Some malicious spyware captures keystrokes to obtain user names, passwords, account numbers, and other sensitive information. Other spyware supports marketing analyses, observing what users do, Web sites visited, products examined and purchased, and so forth.

Adware is similar to spyware in that it is installed without the user's permission and that it resides in the background and observes user behavior. Most adware is benign in that it does not perform malicious acts or steal data. It does, however, watch user activity and produce pop-up ads. Adware can also change the user's default window or modify search results and switch the user's search engine. For the most part, it is just annoying, but users should be concerned any time they have unknown programs on their computers that perform unknown functions.

Figure 12-24 lists some of the symptoms of adware and spyware. Sometimes these symptoms develop slowly over time as more and more malware components are installed. Should these symptoms occur on your computer, remove the spyware or adware using antimalware programs.

FIGURE 12-24

Spyware and Adware Symptoms

- Slow system start up
- Sluggish system performance
- Many pop-up advertisements
- Suspicious browser homepage changes
- Suspicious changes to the taskbar and other system interfaces
- Unusual hard-disk activity

MALWARE SAFEGUARDS Fortunately, it is possible to avoid most malware using the following malware safeguards:

1. **Install antivirus and antispyware programs on your computer.** Your IS department will have a list of recommended (perhaps required) programs for this purpose. If you choose a program for yourself, choose one from a reputable vendor. Check reviews of antimalware software on the Web before purchasing.

2. **Set up your antimalware programs to scan your computer frequently.** You should scan your computer at least once a week and possibly more. When you detect malware code, use the antimalware software to remove them. If the code cannot be removed, contact your IS department or antimalware vendor.

3. **Update malware definitions. Malware definitions**—patterns that exist in malware code—should be downloaded frequently. Antimalware vendors update these definitions continuously, and you should install these updates as they become available.

4. **Open e-mail attachments only from known sources.** Also, even when opening attachments from known sources, do so with great care. According to professor and security expert Ray Panko, about 90 percent of all viruses are spread by e-mail attachments.[4] This statistic is not surprising, because most organizations are protected by firewalls. With a properly configured firewall, e-mail is the only outside-initiated traffic that can reach user computers.

    Most antimalware programs check e-mail attachments for malware code. However, all users should form the habit of *never* opening an e-mail attachment from an unknown source. Also, if you receive an unexpected e-mail from a known source or an e-mail from a known source that has a suspicious subject, odd spelling, or poor grammar, do not open the attachment without first verifying with the known source that the attachment is legitimate.

5. **Promptly install software updates from legitimate sources.** Unfortunately, all programs are chock full of security holes; vendors are fixing them as rapidly as they are discovered, but the practice is inexact. Install patches to the operating system and application programs promptly.

6. **Browse only in reputable Internet neighborhoods.** It is possible for some malware to install itself when you do nothing more than open a Web page. Don't go there!

BOTS, BOTNETS, AND BOT HERDERS Recently, new terms have been introduced into the computer security vocabulary. A **bot** is a computer program that is surreptitiously installed and that takes actions unknown and uncontrolled by the computer's owner or administrator. The term *bot* is a new catch-all term that refers to any type of virus, worm, Trojan Horse, spyware, adware, or other program not installed and controlled by the computer's owner or manager. Some bots are very dangerous and malicious; some steal credit card data, banking data, and e-mail addresses. Others cause denial-of-service attacks and still others just produce pop-ups and other annoyances.

A **botnet** is a network of bots that is created and managed by the individual or organization that infected the network with the bot program. The individual or organization that controls the botnet is called a **bot herder**. Botnets and bot herders are potentially serious problems not only to commerce, but also to national security. It is believed that a unit of the North Korean Army

[4] Ray Panko, *Corporate Computer and Network Security* (Upper Saddle River, NJ: Prentice Hall, 2004), p. 165.

FIGURE 12-25
Data Safeguards

- Data rights and responsibilities
- Rights enforced by user accounts authenticated by passwords
- Data encryption
- Backup and recovery procedures
- Physical security

served as a bot herder for a botnet that caused denial-of-service attacks on Web servers in South Korea and in the United States in July 2009.

The safeguards discussed for malware are the best protection against bots. Stay tuned, however; the end of the bot story has not yet been written.

Design Secure Applications

The final technical safeguard in Figure 12-21 concerns the design of applications. As an example of the importance of this safeguard, if Web pages are improperly designed, it is possible to gain unauthorized access and permissions using techniques known as **code injection**. The essence of these techniques involves entering program code instead of data into Web page text boxes. Database data can be comprised using **SQL injection attacks**, in which SQL code is unknowingly processed by a Web page. **Cross-site scripting (XSS)** is a similar technique most common on discussion boards and other user forums that is used to inject Web page scripting into the server or on to the computers of users who access the server. Both types of code injection are readily prevented if the applications are properly design.

As a user of information systems, you will not design programs yourself. However, you should ensure that any information system developed for you and your department includes security as one of the application requirements.

Data Safeguards

Data safeguards are measures used to protect databases and other organizational data. Figure 12-25 summarizes some important data safeguards. First, the organization should specify user data rights and responsibilities. Second, those rights should be enforced by user accounts that are authenticated at least by passwords.

The organization should protect sensitive data by storing it in encrypted form. Such encryption uses one or more keys in ways similar to that described for data communication encryption. One potential problem with stored data, however, is that the key might be lost or that disgruntled or terminated employees might destroy it. Because of this possibility, when data are encrypted, a trusted party should have a copy of the encryption key. This safety procedure is sometimes called **key escrow**.

Another data safeguard is to periodically create backup copies of database contents. The organization should store at least some of these backups off premises, possibly in a remote location. Additionally, IT personnel should periodically practice recovery, to ensure that the backups are valid and that effective recovery procedures exist. Do not assume that just because a backup is made the database is protected.

Physical security is another data safeguard. The computers that run the DBMS and all devices that store database data should reside in locked, controlled-access facilities. If not, they are subject not only to theft, but also to damage. For better security, the organization should keep a log showing who entered the facility, when, and for what purpose.

Q7. What Human Security Safeguards Are Available?

Human safeguards involve the people and procedure components of information systems. In this section we consider four such safeguards:

- Human resources
- Account administration
- Systems procedures
- Security monitoring

Human Resources

Human resources safeguards are summarized in Figure 12-26. These safeguards apply to both employee and nonemployee, part-time or contract personnel.

POSITION DEFINITIONS It is impossible to have effective human safeguards unless job tasks and responsibilities are clearly defined for each position. In general, job descriptions should provide a separation of duties and authorities. For example, no single individual should be allowed to approve expenses, write checks, and account for the disbursement. Instead, one person should approve expenses, another person pay them, and a third account for the transaction. Similarly, in inventory, no single person should be allowed to authorize an inventory withdrawal, remove the items from inventory, and account for the removal.

Given appropriate job descriptions, users' computer accounts should give users the least possible privilege necessary to perform their jobs. For example, users whose job description does not include modifying data should be given accounts with read-only privilege. Similarly, user accounts should prohibit users from accessing data they do not need.

Finally, the security sensitivity should be documented for each position. Some jobs involve highly sensitive data (e.g., employee compensation, salesperson quotas, and proprietary marketing or technical data). Other positions involve no sensitive data. Documenting *position sensitivity* enables security personnel to prioritize their activities in accordance with the possible risk and loss.

HIRING AND SCREENING PROCESSES Security considerations should be part of the hiring process. Of course, if the position involves no sensitive data and no access to information systems, then screening for information systems security purposes will be minimal. When hiring for high-sensitivity positions, however, extensive interviews, references, and background investigations are appropriate. Note, too, that security screening applies not only to new employees, but also to employees who are promoted into sensitive positions.

FIGURE 12-26

Human Resource Safeguards

- Position definition
  - Separate duties and authorities.
  - Determine least privilege.
  - Document position sensitivity.

"OK to pay this"

- Hiring processes

"Where did you last work?"

- Dissemination and enforcement (responsibility, accountability, compliance)

"Let's talk security..."

- Termination processes
  - Friendly

"Congratulations on your new job"

  - Unfriendly

"We've closed your accounts. Good-bye"

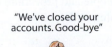

DISSEMINATION AND ENFORCEMENT Obviously, employees cannot be expected to follow security procedures if they do not know about them. Therefore, employees need to be trained on security policies, procedures, and the responsibilities they will have.

Employee security training begins during new-employee training, with the explanation of general security policies and procedures. That general training must be amplified in accordance with the position's sensitivity and responsibilities. Promoted employees should receive security training that is appropriate to their new positions. The company should not provide user accounts and passwords until employees have completed required security training.

Enforcement consists of three interdependent factors: responsibility, accountability, and compliance. First, the company should clearly define the security *responsibilities* of each position. The design of the security program should be such that employees can be held *accountable* for security violations. Procedures should exist so that when critical data are lost it is possible to determine how the loss occurred and who is accountable. Finally, the security program should encourage security *compliance*. Employee activities should regularly be monitored for compliance, and management should specify disciplinary action to be taken in light of noncompliance.

Management attitude is crucial: Employee compliance is greater when management demonstrates, both in word and deed, a serious concern for security. If managers write passwords on staff bulletin boards, shout passwords down hallways, or ignore physical security procedures, then employee security attitudes and employee security compliance will suffer. Note, too, that effective security is a continuing management responsibility. Regular reminders about security are essential.

TERMINATION PROCESSES Companies also must establish security policies and procedures for the termination of employees. Most job terminations are friendly and occur as the result of the completion of work tasks by part-time employees, or when employees are promoted, retire, or resign to take other positions. Standard human resources policies should ensure that system administrators receive notification in advance of the person's last day, so that they can remove accounts and passwords. Procedures for recovering keys for encrypted data and any other security assets must be part of the employee's out-processing.

Unfriendly termination is more difficult because personnel, especially disgruntled employees, may be tempted to take malicious or harmful actions. In such a case, system administrators might need to remove user accounts and passwords prior to notifying the employee of her termination. Other actions may be needed to protect the company's information assets. A terminated sales employee, for example, might attempt to take the company's confidential customer and sales-prospect data for future use at another company. The terminating employer should take steps to protect those data prior to the termination.

The human resources department should be aware of the importance of giving IS administrators early notification of employee termination. No blanket policy exists; the information systems department must assess each case on an individual basis.

Account Administration

The second human safeguard is account administration. The administration of user accounts, passwords, and help-desk policies and procedures are important components of the security system.

ACCOUNT MANAGEMENT Account management concerns the creation of new user accounts, the modification of existing account permissions, and the removal of unneeded accounts. Information system administrators perform all of these tasks, but account users have the responsibility to notify the administrators of the need for these actions. The IS department should create standard procedures for this purpose. As a future user, you can improve your relationship with IS personnel by providing early and timely notification of the need for account changes.

The existence of accounts that are no longer necessary is a serious security vulnerability. IS administrators cannot know when an account should be removed; it is up to users and managers to give such notification.

PASSWORD MANAGEMENT Passwords are the primary means of authentication. They are important not just for access to the user's computer, but also for authentication to other networks and servers to which the user may have access. Because of the importance of passwords, NIST recommends that employees be required to sign statements similar to that shown in Figure 12-27.

FIGURE 12-27

Sample Account Acknowledgment Form

Source: National Institute of Standards and Technology, *Introduction to Computer Security: The NIST Handbook*, Publication 800-12, p. 114.

I hereby acknowledge personal receipt of the system password(s) associated with the user IDs listed below. I understand that I am responsible for protecting the password(s), will comply with all applicable system security standards, and will not divulge my password(s) to any person. I further understand that I must report to the Information Systems Security Officer any problem I encounter in the use of the password(s) or when I have reason to believe that the private nature of my password(s) has been compromised.

When an account is created, users should immediately change the password they are given to a password of their own. In fact, well-constructed systems require the user to change the password on first use.

Additionally, users should change passwords frequently thereafter. Some systems will require a password change every 3 months or perhaps more frequently. Users grumble at the nuisance of making such changes, but frequent password changes reduce not only the risk of password loss, but also the extent of damage if an existing password is compromised.

Some users create two passwords and switch back and forth between those two. This strategy results in poor security, and some password systems do not allow the user to reuse recently used passwords. Again, users may view this policy as a nuisance, but it is important.

HELP-DESK POLICIES In the past, help desks have been a serious security risk. A user who had forgotten his password would call the help desk and plead for the help-desk representative to tell him his password or to reset the password to something else. "I can't get this report out without it!" was (and is) a common lament.

The problem for help-desk representatives is, of course, that they have no way of determining that they are talking with the true user and not someone spoofing a true user. But, they are in a bind: If they do not help in some way, the help desk is perceived to be the "unhelpful desk."

To resolve such problems, many systems give the help-desk representative a means of authenticating the user. Typically, the help-desk information system has answers to questions that only the true user would know, such as the user's birthplace, mother's maiden name, or last four digits of an important account number. Often, too, the method by which the new password can be obtained is sent to the user in an e-mail. E-mail, as you learned, is sent as plaintext, however, so the new password itself ought not to be e-mailed. If you ever receive notification that your password was reset when you did not request such a reset, immediately contact IS security. Someone has compromised your account.

All such help-desk measures reduce the strength of the security system, and, if the employee's position is sufficiently sensitive, they might create too large a vulnerability. In such a case, the user may just be out of luck. The account will be deleted, and the user must repeat the account-application process.

Systems Procedures

Procedures are a third human safeguard. Figure 12-28 shows a grid of procedure types: normal operation, backup, and recovery. Procedures of each type should exist for each information system. For example, the order-entry system will have procedures of each of these types, as will the Web storefront, the inventory system, and so forth. The definition and use of standardized procedures reduces the likelihood of computer crime and other malicious activity by insiders. It also ensures that the system's security policy is enforced.

Procedures exist for both users and operations personnel. For each type of user, the company should develop procedures for normal, backup, and recovery operations. As a future user, you will be primarily concerned with user procedures. Normal-use procedures should provide safeguards appropriate to the sensitivity of the information system.

Backup procedures concern the creation of backup data to be used in the event of failure. Whereas operations personnel have the responsibility for backing up system databases and other systems data, departmental personnel have the need to back up data on their own computers. Good questions to ponder are, "What would happen if I lost my computer or iPhone tomorrow?"

FIGURE 12-28
Systems Procedures

	System Users	**Operations Personnel**
Normal Operation	Use the system to perform job tasks, with security appropriate to sensitivity.	Operate data center equipment, manage networks, run Web servers, and related operational tasks.
Backup	Prepare for loss of system functionality.	Back up Web site resources, databases, administrative data, account and password data, and other data.
Recovery	Accomplish job tasks during failure. Know tasks to do during system recovery.	Recover systems from backed up data. Role of help desk during recovery.

"What would happen if someone dropped my computer during an airport security inspection?" "What would happen if my computer were stolen?" Employees should ensure that they back up critical business data on their computers to a safe repository such as Microsoft SharePoint. The IS department can help in this effort by designing backup procedures and making backup facilities available.

Finally, systems analysts should develop procedures for system recovery. First, how will the department manage its affairs when a critical system is unavailable? Customers will want to order, and manufacturing will want to remove items from inventory even though a critical information system is unavailable. How will the department respond? Once the system is returned to service, how will records of business activities during the outage be entered into the system? How will service be resumed? The system developers should ask and answer these questions and others like them and develop procedures accordingly.

Security Monitoring

Security monitoring is the last of the human safeguards we will consider. Important monitoring functions are activity log analyses, security testing, and investigating and learning from security incidents.

Many information system programs produce *activity logs*. Firewalls produce logs of their activities, including lists of all dropped packets, infiltration attempts, and unauthorized access attempts from within the firewall. DBMS products produce logs of successful and failed log-ins. Web servers produce voluminous logs of Web activities. The operating systems in personal computers can produce logs of log-ins and firewall activities.

None of these logs add any value to an organization unless someone looks at them. Accordingly, an important security function is to analyze these logs for vulnerability patterns, successful and unsuccessful attacks, and evidence of security vulnerabilities.

Additionally, companies should test their security programs. Both in-house personnel and outside security consultants should conduct such testing.

Another important monitoring function is to investigate security incidents. How did the problem occur? Have safeguards been created to prevent a recurrence of such problems? Does the incident indicate vulnerabilities in other portions of the security system? What else can be learned from the incident?

Security systems reside in a dynamic environment. Organization structures change. Companies are acquired or sold; mergers occur. New systems require new security measures. New technology changes the security landscape, and new vulnerabilities arise. Security personnel must constantly monitor the situation and determine if the existing security policy and safeguards are adequate. If changes are needed, security personnel need to take appropriate action.

Security, like quality, is an ongoing process. There is no final state that represents a secure system or company. Instead, companies must monitor security on a continuing basis.

Organizational Response to Security Incidents

Every organization needs to be prepared for security incidents. Publicly traded companies are required by the Sarbanes-Oxley Act to do so. Other organizations should do so as a matter of good management. When an incident occurs, whether from an act of nature or from a human vulnerability, time is of the essence. Employees need to know what to do and how to do it. In this section we will consider backup and recovery sites and incident response plans.

DISASTER-RECOVERY BACKUP SITES A computer *disaster* is a substantial loss of computing infrastructure caused by acts of nature, crime, or terrorist activity. As stated several times, the best way to solve a problem is not to have it. The best safeguard against a natural disaster is appropriate location. If possible, place computing centers, Web farms, and other computer facilities in locations not prone to floods, earthquakes, hurricanes, tornados, or avalanches. Even in those locations, place infrastructure in unobtrusive buildings, basements, backrooms, and similar locations well within the physical perimeter of the organization. Also, locate computing infrastructure in fire-resistant buildings designed to house expensive and critical equipment.

However, sometimes business requirements necessitate locating the computing infrastructure in undesirable locations. Also, even at a good location, disasters do occur. Therefore, many businesses prepare backup processing centers in locations geographically removed from the primary processing site.

Figure 12-29 lists major disaster-preparedness tasks. After choosing a safe location for the computing infrastructure, the organization should identify all mission-critical applications. These are applications without which the organization cannot carry on and which, if lost for any period of time, could cause the organization's failure. The next step is to identify all resources necessary to run those systems. Such resources include computers, operating systems, application programs, databases, administrative data, procedure documentation, and trained personnel.

Next, the organization creates backups for the critical resources at the remote processing center. A **hot site** is a utility company that can take over another company's processing with no forewarning. Hot sites are expensive; organizations pay $250,000 or more per month for such services. **Cold sites**, in contrast, provide computers and office space. They are cheaper to lease, but customers install and manage systems themselves. The total cost of a cold side, including all customer labor and other expenses, might not necessarily be less than the cost of a hot site.

Once the organization has backups in place, it must train and rehearse cutover of operations from the primary center to the backup. In the case of a hot site, employees must know how to ensure the handoff occurred without a problem, how to run systems while the hot site is active, and how to recover processing when the primary site is again operational. For cold sites, employees must know how to apply backups, how to start systems, and how to run systems from the cold site location. As with all emergency procedures, periodic refresher rehearsals are mandatory.

Backup facilities are expensive; however, the costs of establishing and maintaining that facility are a form of insurance. Senior management must make the decision to prepare such a facility, by balancing the risks, benefits, and costs.

One of the key advantages of working with reputable cloud vendors, by the way, is that the cloud vendor will have the responsibility for data center disaster planning and recovery. Microsoft, for example, provides automatic backup and recovery of all Office 365 sites.

INCIDENT-RESPONSE PLAN The last component of a security plan that we will consider is incident response. Figure 12-30 lists the major factors. First, every organization should have an incident-response plan as part of the security program. No organization should wait until some asset has been lost or compromised before deciding what to do. The plan should include how employees are to respond to security problems, whom they should contact, the reports they should make, and steps they can take to reduce further loss.

FIGURE 12-29

Disaster Preparedness Tasks

- Locate infrastructure in safe location.
- Identify mission-critical systems.
- Identify resources needed to run those systems.
- Prepare remote backup facilities.
- Train and rehearse.

FIGURE 12-30

Factors in Incident Response

- Have plan in place
- Centralized reporting
- Specific responses
  - Speed
  - Preparation pays
  - Don't make problem worse
- Practice!

Consider, for example, a virus. An incident-response plan will stipulate what an employee should do when he notices the virus. It should specify whom to contact and what to do. It may stipulate that the employee should turn off his computer and physically disconnect from the network. The plan should also indicate what users with wireless computers should do.

The plan should provide centralized reporting of all security incidents. Such reporting will enable an organization to determine if it is under systematic attack or whether an incident is isolated. Centralized reporting also allows the organization to learn about security vulnerabilities, take consistent actions in response, and apply specialized expertise to all security problems.

When an incident does occur, speed is of the essence. Viruses and worms can spread very quickly across an organization's networks, and a fast response will help to mitigate the consequences—both to the organization and to others outside the organization. Because of the need for speed, preparation pays. The incident-response plan should identify critical personnel and their off-hours contact information. These personnel should be trained on where to go and what to do when they get there. Without adequate preparation, there is substantial risk that the actions of well-meaning people will make the problem worse. Also, the rumor mill will be alive with all sorts of nutty ideas about what to do. A cadre of well-informed, trained personnel will serve to dampen such rumors.

Finally, organizations should periodically practice incident response. Without such practice, personnel will be poorly informed on the response plan, and the plan itself might have flaws that become apparent only during a drill.

Ethics Guide

Security Privacy

Some organizations have legal requirements to protect the customer data they collect and store, but the laws may be more limited than you think. The **Gramm-Leach-Bliley (GLB) Act**, passed by Congress in 1999, protects consumer financial data stored by financial institutions, which are defined as banks, securities firms, insurance companies, and organizations that provide financial advice, prepare tax returns, and provide similar financial services.

The **Privacy Act of 1974** provides protections to individuals regarding records maintained by the U.S. government, and the privacy provisions of the **Health Insurance Portability and Accountability Act (HIPAA)** of 1996 gives individuals the right to access health data created by doctors and other healthcare providers. HIPAA also sets rules and limits on who can read and receive your health information.

The law is stronger in other countries. In Australia, for example, the Privacy Principles of the Australian Privacy Act of 1988 govern not only government and healthcare data, but also records maintained by businesses with revenues in excess of AU$3 million.

To understand the importance of the limitations, consider online retailers that routinely store customer credit card data. Do Dell, Amazon.com, the airlines, and other e-commerce businesses have a legal requirement to protect their customers' credit card data? Apparently not—at least not in the United States. The activities of such organizations are not governed by the GLB, the Privacy Act of 1974, or HIPAA.

Most consumers would say, however, that online retailers have an ethical requirement to protect a customer's credit card and other data, and most online retailers would agree. Or at least the retailers would agree that they have a strong business reason to protect that data. A substantial loss of credit card data by any large online retailer would have detrimental effects on both sales and brand reputation.

Data aggregators further complicate the risk to individuals because they develop a complete profile of households and individuals. And no federal law prohibits the U.S. government from buying information products from the data accumulators.

But, let's bring the discussion closer to home. What requirements does your university have on the data it maintains about you? State law or university policy may govern those records, but no federal law does. Most universities consider it their responsibility to provide public access to graduation records. Anyone can determine when you graduated, your degree, and your major. (Keep this service in mind when you write your resume.)

Most professors endeavor to publish grades by student number and not by name, and there may be a state law that requires that separation. But what about your work? What about the papers you write, the answers you give on exams? What about the e-mails you send to your professor? The data are not protected by federal law, and they are probably not protected by state law. If your professor chooses to cite your work in research, she will be subject to copyright law, but not privacy law. What you write is no longer your personal data; it belongs to the academic community. You can ask your professor what she intends to do with your coursework, e-mails, and office conversations, but none of that data is protected by law.

The bottom line: Be careful with your personal data. Large, reputable organizations are likely to endorse ethical privacy policy and to have strong and effective safeguards to effectuate that policy, but individuals and small organizations might not. If in doubt, ask.

DISCUSSION QUESTIONS

1. When you order from an online retailer, the data you provide is not protected by U.S. privacy law. Does this fact cause you to reconsider setting up an account with a stored credit card number? What is the advantage of storing the credit card number? Do you think the advantage is worth the risk? Are you more willing to take the risk with some companies than with others? Why or why not?

2. Suppose you are the treasurer of a student club, and you store records of club members' payments in a database. In the past, members have disputed payment amounts; therefore, when you receive a payment, you scan an image of the check or credit card invoice and store the scanned image in a database.

   One day, you are using your computer in a local wireless coffee shop and a malicious student breaks into your computer over the wireless network and steals the club database. You know nothing about this until the next day, when a club member complains that a popular student Web site has published the names, bank names, and bank account numbers for everyone who has given you a check.

What liability do you have in this matter? Could you be classified as a financial institution because you are taking students' money? (You can find the GLB at *www.ftc.gov/privacy/privacyinitiatives/glbact.html*.) If so, what liability do you have? If not, do you have any other liability? Does the coffee shop have a liability?

3. Suppose you are asked to fill out a study questionnaire that requires you to enter identifying data as well as answers to personal questions. You hesitate to provide the data, but the top part of the questionnaire states, "All responses will be strictly confidential." So, you fill out the questionnaire.

   Unfortunately, the person who is conducting the study visits the same wireless coffee shop that you visited (in question 2), and the same malicious student breaks in and steals the study results. Your name and all of your responses appear on that same student Web site. Did the person conducting the study violate a law? Does the confidentiality assurance on the form increase that person's requirement to protect your data? Does your answer change if the person conducting the study is (a) a student, (b) a professor of music, or (c) a professor of computer security?

4. In truth, only a very talented and motivated hacker could steal databases from computers using a public wireless network. Such losses, although possible, are unlikely. However, any e-mail you send or files you download can readily be sniffed at a public wireless facility. Knowing this, describe good practice for computer use at public wireless facilities.

5. Considering your answers to the above questions, state three to five general principles to guide your actions as you disseminate and store data.

Source: Max Krasnov/Shutterstock.

Active Review

Use this Active Review to verify that you understand the material in the chapter. You can read the entire chapter and then perform the tasks in this review, or you can read the text material for just one question and perform the tasks in this review for that question before moving on to the next one.

Q1. What are the activities of business process management?

Describe the need for business process management (BPM) and explain why it is a cycle. Name the four activities of the BPM process and summarize the tasks in each. Explain the role of COBIT. Summarize three reasons that processes need to be changed and give an example of each. Explain how Figures 12-3 and 12-4 address the need to allow employees to enroll in classes online while addressing Kelly's concerns expressed at the start of this chapter.

Q2. What are the activities in the systems development life cycle (SDLC) development process?

Name five basic systems development activities. Explain how they pertain whether developing processes first or information systems first. Describe tasks required for the definition, requirements, and design steps. Explain the role of business analysts and systems analysts. Explain the tasks required to implement and maintain the system and assess the process. Describe four types of process/system conversion. Describe how activities in these last two steps differ depending on whether the processes or systems are developed first.

Q3. Which comes first: process or systems development?

Explain how information systems and business processes differ. Give an example, other than one in this text, of a business process that uses two or more information systems. Give an example, other than one in this text, of an information system that is part of two or more business processes. Explain the problems that occur if we develop business processes first, with IS as a component. Explain the problems that occur if we develop information systems first, with business processes as a component. Explain the differences between Figures 12-13 and 12-14. Summarize the issues to address when answering which comes first.

Q4. What is information systems security?

Define *information systems security* and explain the meaning of each of its three key terms. List four threats and describe each. Give one example of each of the 12 vulnerabilities shown in Figure 12-15.

Q5. What are the components of an organization's security program?

Broadly describe senior management's security role. Explain how safeguard types relate to the five components of an information system. Explain the meaning of each element in Figure 12-19. Name and describe the three components of an organization's security program.

Q6. What technical safeguards are available?

Define *technical safeguard* and explain which of the five components are involved in such safeguards. Summarize each of the safeguards in Figure 12-20. Explain the use of identification and authentication and describe three types of authentication. Describe symmetric and asymmetric encryption and explain how they are used for SSL/TLS. Explain the purpose of digital signatures and certificate authorities. Define *firewall*. Name the five types of malware as defined in this text and briefly describe each. Describe the six antimalware techniques presented. Define *bot, botnets,* and *bot herders*. Define *data safeguards* and give four examples. Explain each.

Q7. What human security safeguards are available?

Name the components involved in human safeguards. Name and describe four human resources safeguards Summarize account administration safeguards. Describe six types of procedures for system users and system operations personnel. Explain three security monitoring functions. Explain why organizations need to prepare for security incidents ahead of time. Describe ways of avoiding natural disasters; explain the role for remote processing. Define *hot site* and *cold site* and explain the difference. Describe the advantages of using a reputable cloud vendor. Explain the importance of an incident-response plan and the need for centralized reporting. Explain why a rapid, but controlled, incident response is needed and why practice is important.

Key Terms and Concepts

Adware   *401*
As-is model   *380*
Asymmetric encryption   *399*
Authentication   *398*
Biometric authentication   *398*
Bot   *402*
Bot herder   *402*
Botnet   *402*
Business analyst   *385*
Business process management
   (BPM)   *378*
COBIT (Control Objectives for
   Information and related
   Technology)   *379*
Code injection   *403*
Cold site   *408*
Computer criminals   *394*
Cost feasibility   *385*
Cross-site scripting (XSS)   *403*
Denial of service   *394*
Digital certificate   *401*
Digital signature   *401*
Drive-by sniffers   *394*
E-mail spoofing   *394*
Encryption   *399*
Encryption algorithm   *399*

Gramm-Leach Bliley Act   *410*
Hacking   *394*
Health Insurance Portability and
   Accountability Act (HIPAA)   *410*
Hot site   *408*
HTTPS   *400*
Identification   *398*
Information systems security   *392*
IP spoofing   *394*
Key   *399*
Key escrow   *403*
Maintenance   *389*
Malware   *401*
Malware definitions   *402*
Organizational feasibility   *385*
Parallel installation   *389*
Payload   *401*
Personal identification number
   (PIN)   *398*
Phased installation   *389*
Phisher   *395*
Phishing   *393*
Pilot installation   *388*
Plunge installation   *389*
Pretexting   *393*
Privacy Act of 1974   *410*

Public key/private key   *400*
Schedule feasibility   *385*
Secure Socket Layer (SSL)   *400*
Security program   *396*
Security vulnerability   *392*
Smart card   *398*
Sniffing   *394*
Social engineering   *393*
Spoofing   *394*
Spyware   *401*
SQL injection attack   *403*
Symmetric encryption   *399*
System conversion   *388*
Systems analysts   *385*
Systems development   *384*
Systems development life cycle
   (SDLC)   *384*
Technical feasibility   *385*
Technical safeguards   *398*
Test plan   *388*
Threat   *393*
Transport Layer Security
   (TLS)   *400*
Trojan horse   *401*
Virus   *401*
Worm   *401*

Using Your Knowledge

1. Search Google or Bing for the phrase "what is a business analyst." Investigate several of the links that you find and answer the following questions:
   a. What are the primary job responsibilities of a business analyst?
   b. What knowledge do business analysts need?
   c. What skills/personal traits do business analysts need?
   d. Would a career as a business analyst be interesting to you? Explain why or why not.
2. Reread the chapter's opening vignette and review Figures 12-2, 12-3, and 12-4.

   a. Summarize Kelly's concerns about having members make their own class reservations over the Web.
   b. Do you think those concerns are realistic?
   c. Summarize how the processes in Figures 12-3 and 12-4 address her concerns.
   d. Create a mockup of a report that the system in Figure 12-4 should create. Explain how Kelly and other analysts can use the features of your report to address her concern.
   e. In your opinion, does the proposed system adequately address her concerns? Why or why not?
3. Reread the opening vignettes regarding CBI at the beginning of Chapters 7 and 8. Using that information

as background, generate a two- to three-page document that summarizes the security management activities that CBI should practice. Consider each of the vulnerabilities in Figure 12-15. As you write the document, keep in mind that CBI must strike a balance between comprehensive security management and cost. Explain what it means for CBI to manage risk. Describe the difference between not creating a security safeguard because CBI never thought about it and not creating a safeguard because of a risk management decision.

4. Consider the 12 categories of vulnerability in Figure 12-15. Describe the three most serious vulnerabilities to each of the following businesses:
   a. CBI
   b. Your university
   c. A neighborhood accounting firm

5. Describe a potential technical safeguard for each of the vulnerabilities you identified in your answer to question 4.

6. Describe a potential data safeguard for each of the vulnerabilities you identified in your answer to question 4. If no data safeguard is appropriate to a business, explain why.

7. Describe a potential human safeguard for each of the vulnerabilities you identified in your answer to question 4.

8. Describe how each of the organizations in question 4 should prepare for security incidents.

9. How likely are the vulnerabilities you identified in question 4? If you were the owner or a senior manager in these organizations, which of the items you described in questions 4 through 8 would you implement? Justify your answer.

Collaboration Exercise 12

Collaborate with a group of fellow students to answer the following questions. For this exercise do not meet face to face. Your task will be easier if you coordinate your work with SharePoint, Office 365, Google Docs with Google+ or equivalent collaboration tools. (See Chapter 9 for a discussion of collaboration tools and processes.) Your answers should reflect the thinking of the entire group, and not just that of one or two individuals.

Wilma Baker, Jerry Barker, and Chris Bickel met in June 2012 at a convention of resort owners and tourism operators. They sat next to each other by chance while waiting for a presentation; after introducing themselves and laughing at the odd sound of their three names, they were surprised to learn that they managed similar businesses. Wilma Baker lives in Santa Fe, New Mexico, and specializes in renting homes and apartments to visitors to Santa Fe. Jerry Barker lives in Whistler Village, British Columbia, and specializes in renting condos to skiers and other visitors to the Whistler/Blackcomb Resort. Chris Bickel lives in Chatham, Massachusetts, and specializes in renting homes and condos to vacationers to Cape Cod.

The three agreed to have lunch after the presentation. During lunch, they shared frustrations about the difficulty of obtaining new customers, especially in the current economic downturn. Barker was especially concerned about finding customers to fill the facilities constructed to host the 2010 Olympics.

As the conversation developed, they began to wonder if there was some way to combine forces (i.e., they were seeking a competitive advantage from an alliance). So, they decided to skip one of the next day's presentations and meet to discuss ways to form an alliance. Ideas they wanted to discuss further were sharing customer data, developing a joint reservation service, and exchanging property listings.

As they talked, it became clear they had no interest in merging their businesses; each wanted to stay independent. They also discovered that each was very concerned, even paranoid, about protecting their existing customer base from poaching. Still, the conflict was not as bad as it first seemed. Barker's business was primarily the ski trade, and winter was his busiest season; Bickel's business was mostly Cape Cod vacations, and she was busiest during the summer. Baker's high season was the summer and fall. So, it seemed there was enough difference in their high seasons that they would not necessarily cannibalize their businesses by selling the others' offerings to their own customers.

The question then became how to proceed. Given their desire to protect their own customers, they did not want to develop a common customer database. The best idea seemed to be to share data about properties. That way they could keep control of their customers but still have an opportunity to sell time at the others' properties.

They discussed several alternatives. Each could develop her or his own property database, and the three could then share those databases over the Internet. Or, they could develop a centralized property database that they would all use. Or, they could find some other way to share property listings.

Because we do not know Baker, Barker, and Bickel's detailed requirements, you cannot develop a plan for a specific system. In general, however, they first need to decide how elaborate an information system they want to construct. Consider the following two alternatives:

a. They could build a simple system centered on e-mail. With it, each company sends property descriptions to the others via e-mail. Each independent company then forwards these descriptions to its own customers, also using e-mail. When a customer makes a reservation for a property, that request is then forwarded back to the property manager via e-mail.

b. They could construct a more complex system using a Web-based, shared database that contains data on all their properties and reservations. Because reservations tracking is a common business task, it is likely that

they can license an existing application with this capability.

In your answers to questions 1 and 2, use Microsoft Visio and BPMN templates to construct your diagrams. If you don't have those templates, use the cross-functional and basic flowchart templates. If you do not have access to Visio, use PowerPoint instead.

1. Create a process diagram for alternative a using Figure 12-3 as a guide. Each company will need to have a role for determining its available properties and sending e-mails to the other companies that describe them. They will also need to have a role for receiving e-mails and a role for renting properties to customers. Assume the companies have from three to five agents who can fulfill these roles. Create a role for the e-mail system if you think it is appropriate. Specify roles, activities, repositories, and data flows.

2. Create a process diagram for alternative b using Figure 12-2 as a guide. Each company will need to have a role for determining its available properties and adding them to the reservation database. They will also need a role for renting properties that accesses the shared database. Assume the companies have from three to five agents who can fulfill these roles. Create a role for the property database application. Specify roles, activities, repositories, and data flows.

3. Compare and contrast your answers in questions 1 and 2. Which is likely to be more effective in generating rental income? Which is likely to be more expensive to develop? Which is likely to be more expensive to operate?

4. If you were a consultant to Baker, Barker, and Bickel, which alternative would you recommend? Justify your recommendation.

CASE STUDY 12

Slow Learners, or What?

Way back, in ancient IS history, in 1974, Colorado State University conducted a study of the causes of information systems failures. The study team interviewed personnel on several dozen projects and collected survey data on another 50 projects. The analysis of the data revealed that the single most important factor in IS failure was a lack of user involvement. The second major factor was unclear, incomplete, and inconsistent requirements.

During one study interview, a large sugar producer had attempted to implement a new system for paying sugar-beet farmers. The new system was to be implemented at some 20 different sugar-beet collection sites, which were located in small farming communities, adjacent to rail yards. One of the benefits of the new system was significant cost savings, and a major share of those savings occurred because the new system eliminated the need for local comptrollers. The new system was expected to eliminate the jobs of 20 or so senior people.

The comptrollers, however, had been paying local farmers for decades; they were popular leaders not just within the company, but in their communities as well. They were well liked, highly respected, important people. A system that caused the elimination of their jobs was, using a term from this chapter, *organizationally infeasible*, to say the least.

Nonetheless, the system was constructed, but an IS professional involved stated, "Somehow, that new system just never seemed to work. The data were not entered on a timely basis, or they were in error, or incomplete; sometimes the data were not entered at all. Our operations were falling apart during the key harvesting season, and we finally backed off and returned to the old system." Active involvement of system users would have identified this organizational infeasibility long before the system was implemented.

That's ancient history, you say. Maybe, but in 1994 the Standish Group published a now famous study on IS failures. Entitled "The CHAOS Report," the study indicated that the leading causes of IS failure are, in descending order: (1) lack of user input, (2) incomplete requirements and specifications, and (3) changing requirements and specifications.[5] That study was completed some 20 years after our study.

In 2004, Professor Joseph Kasser and his students at the University of Maryland analyzed 19 system failures to determine their cause. They then correlated their analysis of the cause with the opinions of the professionals involved in the failures. The correlated results indicate the first-priority cause of system failure was "Poor requirements"; the second-priority cause was "Failure to communicate with the customer." (Google or Bing *Joseph Kasser* to learn more about this work.)

In 2003, the IRS Oversight Board concluded the first cause of a massive, expensive failure in the development of a new information system for the IRS was "inadequate business unit ownership and sponsorship of projects. This resulted in unrealistic business cases and continuous project scope 'creep.'"[6]

For nearly 40 years, studies have consistently shown that leading causes of system failures are a lack of user involvement and incomplete and changing requirements. Yet failures from these very failures continue to mount.

Questions

1. Using the knowledge you have gained from this chapter, summarize the roles that you think users should take during an information systems development project. What responsibilities do users have? How closely should they work with the IS team? Who is responsible for stating requirements and constraints? Who is responsible for managing requirements?

2. If you ask users why they did not participate in requirements specification, some of the common responses are the following:
   a. "I wasn't asked."
   b. "I didn't have time."
   c. "They were talking about a system that would be here in 18 months, and I'm just worried about getting the order out the door today."
   d. "I didn't know what they wanted."
   e. "I didn't know what they were talking about."
   f. "I didn't work here when they started the project."
   g. "The whole situation has changed since they were here; that was 18 months ago!"

   Comment on each of these statements. What strategies do they suggest to you as a future user and as a future manager of users?

3. If you ask IS professionals why they did not obtain a complete and accurate list of requirements, common responses are:
   a. "It was nearly impossible to get on the users' calendars. They were always too busy."
   b. "The users wouldn't regularly attend our meetings. As a result, one meeting would be dominated by the needs of one group, and another meeting would be dominated by the needs of another group."
   c. "Users didn't take the requirement process seriously. They wouldn't thoroughly review the requirements statements before review meetings."

---

[5] The "CHAOS Report" and yearly updates are available at *www.standishgroup.com*.
[6] IRS Oversight Board, "Independent Analysis of IRS Systems Modernization," December 2003. Available at *www.treas.gov/irsob/reports/special_report1203.pdf*.

d. "Users kept changing. We'd meet with one person one time and another person a second time, and they'd want different things."

e. "We didn't have enough time."

f. "The requirements kept changing."

Comment on each of these statements. What strategies do they suggest to you as a future user and a future manager of users?

4. If it is widely understood that one of the principal causes of IS failures is a lack of user involvement, and if this factor continues to be a problem after 30+ years of experience, does this mean that the problem cannot be solved? For example, everyone knows that you can maximize your gains by buying stocks at their annual low price and selling them at their annual high price, but doing so is very difficult. Is it equally true that although everyone knows that users should be involved in requirements specification, and that requirements should be complete, it just cannot be done? Why or why not?

Application Exercises

Please note all exercise files can be found on the following web site: *www.pearsonhighered.com/kroenke.*

PART 1

Chapter 1

1-1. **X** Figure AE-1 shows an Excel spreadsheet that the resort bicycle rental business shown in Figure 1-9, page 18 uses to value and analyze its bicycle inventory. Examine this figure to understand the meaning of the data. Now use Excel to create a similar spreadsheet. Note the following:

- The top heading is in 20-point Calibri font. It is centered in the spreadsheet. Cells A1 through H1 have been merged.
- The second heading, *Bicycle Inventory Valuation*, is in 18-point Calibri, italics. It is centered in Cells A2 through H2, which have been merged.
- The column headings are set in 11-point Calibri, bold. They are centered in their cells, and the text wraps in the cells.

a. Make the first two rows of your spreadsheet similar to that in Figure AE-1. Choose your own colors for background and type, however.

b. Place the current date so that it is centered in cells C3, C4, and C5, which must be merged.

c. Outline the cells as shown in the figure.

d. Figure AE-1 uses the following formulas:

> **Cost of Current Inventory = Bike Cost × Number on Hand**
> **Revenue per Bike = Total Rental Revenue/Number on Hand**
> **Revenue as a Percent of Cost of Inventory = Total Rental Revenue/Cost of Current Inventory**

Please use these formulas in your spreadsheet, as shown in Figure AE-1.

e. Format the cells in the columns, as shown.

f. Give three examples of decisions that management of the bike rental agency might make from this data.

g. What other calculation could you make from this data that would be useful to the bike rental management? Create a second version of this spreadsheet in your worksheet document that has this calculation.

1-2. **A** In this exercise, you will learn how to create a query based on data that a user enters and how to use that query to create a data entry form.

a. Download the Microsoft Access file **Ch01Ex02**. Open the file and familiarize yourself with the data in the Customer table.

b. Click *Create* in the Access ribbon. On the far right, select *Query Design*. Select the *Customer* table as the basis for the query. Drag Customer Name, Customer Email,

		Resort Bicycle Rental					
		Bicycle Inventory Valuation					
		Thursday, July 28, 2011					
Make of Bike	**Bike Cost**	**Number on Hand**	**Cost of Current Inventory**	**Number of Rentals**	**Total Rental Revenue**	**Revenue per Bike**	**Revenue as Percent of Cost of Inventory**
Wonder Bike	$325	12	$3,900	85	$6,375	$531	163.5%
Wonder Bike II	$385	4	$1,540	34	$4,570	$1,143	296.8%
Wonder Bike Supreme	$475	8	$3,800	44	$5,200	$650	136.8%
LiteLift Pro	$655	8	$5,240	25	$2,480	$310	47.3%
LiteLift Ladies	$655	4	$2,620	40	$6,710	$1,678	256.1%
LiteLift Racer	$795	3	$2,385	37	$5,900	$1,967	247.4%

FIGURE AE-1

Date Of Last Rental, Bike Last Rented, Total Number Of Rentals, and Total Rental Revenue into the columns of the query results pane (the table at the bottom of the query design window).

c. In the CustomerName column, in the row labeled Criteria, place the following text:

[Enter Name of Customer:]

Type this exactly as shown, including the square brackets. This notation tells Access to ask you for a customer name to query.

d. In the ribbon, click the red exclamation mark labeled *Run*. Access will display a dialog box with the text "Enter Name of Customer:" (the text you entered in the query Criteria row). Enter the value *Scott, Rex* and click OK.

e. Save your query with the name *Parameter Query*.

f. Click the Home tab on the ribbon and click the Design View (upper left-hand button on the Home ribbon). Replace the text in the Criteria column of the CustomerName column with the following text. Type it exactly as shown:

Like "*" & [Enter part of Customer Name to search by:] & "*"

g. Run the query by clicking Run in the ribbon. Enter *Scott* when prompted *Enter part of Customer Name to search by*. Notice that the two customers who have the name Scott are displayed. If you have any problems, ensure that you have typed the phrase above *exactly* as shown into the Criteria row of the CustomerName column of your query.

h. Save your query again under the name *Parameter Query*. Close the query window.

i. Click *Create* in the Access ribbon. Under the Forms group, select the down arrow to the right of More Forms. Choose *Form Wizard*. In the dialog that opens, in the Tables/Queries box, click the down arrow. Select *Parameter Query*. Click the double chevron (>>) symbol and all of the columns in the query will move to the Selected Fields area.

j. Click *Next* three times. In the box under *What title do you want for your form?* enter *Customer Query Form* and click *Finish*.

k. Enter *Scott* in the dialog box that appears. Access will open a form with the values for Scott, Rex. At the bottom of the form, click the right-facing arrow and the data for Scott, Bryan will appear.

l. Close the form. Select *Object Type* and *Forms* in the Access Navigation Pane. Double-click on Customer Query Form and enter the value *James*. Access will display data for all six customers having the value James in their name.

Chapter 2

2-1.   The spreadsheet in Microsoft Excel file **Ch02Ex01** contains records of employee activity on special projects. Open this workbook and examine the data that you find in the three spreadsheets it contains. Assess the accuracy, relevancy, and sufficiency of this data to the following people and problems.

a. You manage the Denver plant, and you want to know how much time your employees are spending on special projects.

b. You manage the Reno plant, and you want to know how much time your employees are spending on special projects.

c. You manage the Quota Computation project in Chicago, and you want to know how much time your employees have spent on that project.

d. You manage the Quota Computation project for all three plants, and you want to know the total time employees have spent on your project.

e. You manage the Quota Computation project for all three plants, and you want to know the total labor cost for all employees on your project.

f. You manage the Quota Computation project for all three plants, and you want to know how the labor-hour total for your project compares to the labor-hour totals for the other special projects.

g. What conclusions can you make from this exercise?

2-2. The database in the Microsoft Access file **Ch02Ex02** contains the same records of employee activity on special projects as in Application Exercise 2-1. Before proceeding, open that database and view the records in the *Employee Hours* table.

a. Seven queries have been created that process this data in different ways. Using the criteria of accuracy, relevancy, and sufficiency, select the single query that is most appropriate for the information requirements in Application Exercise 2-1, parts a–f. If no query meets the need, explain why.

b. What conclusions can you make from this exercise?

c. Comparing your experiences on these two projects, what are the advantages and disadvantages of spreadsheets and databases?

PART 2

Chapter 3

3-1. Sometimes you will have data in one Office application and want to move it to another Office application without rekeying it. Often this occurs when data were created for one purpose but then are used for a second purpose. For example, Figure AE-2 presents a portion of an Excel spreadsheet that shows the assignment of computers to employees. Neil, at FlexTime, might use such a spreadsheet to track who has which equipment.

Suppose that you (or Neil) want to use this data to help you assess how to upgrade computers. Let's say, for example, that you want to upgrade all of the computers' operating systems to Windows 7. Furthermore, you want to first upgrade the computers that most need upgrading, but suppose you have a limited budget. To address this situation, you would like to query the data in Figure AE-2 to find all computers that do not have Windows 7, and then select those with slower CPUs or smaller memory as candidates for upgrading. To do this, you need to move the data from Excel and into Access.

Once you have analyzed the data and determined the computers to upgrade, you want to produce a report. In that case, you may want to move the data from Access and back to Excel, or perhaps into Word. In this exercise, you will learn how to perform these tasks.

a. To begin, download the Excel file **Ch03Ex01** into one of your directories. We will import the data in this file into Access, but before we do so familiarize yourself with the data by opening it in Excel. Notice that there are three worksheets in this workbook. Close the Excel file.

b. Create a blank Access database. Name the database *Ch03Ex01_Answer*. Place it in some directory; it may be the same directory into which you have placed the Excel file, but it need not be. Close the default table that Access creates and delete it.

FIGURE AE-2

Job Title	Number of Employees	Computer System Required	Computer Type
Product manager	8	B	Laptop
Telesales	12	A	Desktop
Department administrator	2	A	Desktop
Marketing communications manager	4	B	Laptop
Marketing analyst	4	C (desktop) B (desktop)	Both, a desktop and laptop for each analyst
Marketing programs manager	6	B	Desktop
You	1	???	???

c. Now, we will import the data from the three worksheets in the Excel file **Ch03Ex01** into a single table in your Access database. In the ribbon, select *External Data* and *Import from Excel*. Start the import. For the first worksheet (Denver), you should select *Import the source data into a new table in the current database*. Be sure to click *First Row Contains Column Headings* when Access presents your data. You can use the default Field types and let Access add the primary key. Name your table *Employees* and click *Finish*. There is no need to save your import script.

For the second and third worksheets, again click *External Data, Import Excel*, but this time select *Append a copy of the records to the table Employees*. Import all data.

d. Open the *Employee* table and examine the data. Notice that Access has erroneously imported a blank line and the Primary Contact data into rows at the end of each data set. This data is not part of the employee records, and you should delete it (in three places—once for each worksheet). The *Employee* table should have a total of 40 records.

e. Now, create a parameterized query on this data. Place all of the columns except *ID* into the query. In the *OS* column, set the criteria to select rows for which the value is not *Windows 7*. In the *CPU (GHz)* column, enter the criterion: <=[Enter cutoff value for CPU]. In the *Memory* (GB) column, enter the criterion: <=[Enter cutoff value for Memory]. Test your query. For example, run your query and enter a value of 2 for both CPU and memory. Verify that the correct rows are produced.

f. Use your query to find values of CPU and memory that give you as close to a maximum of 15 computers to upgrade as possible.

g. When you have found values of CPU and memory that give you 15, or nearly 15, computers to upgrade, leave your query open. Now, click *External data, Word*, and create a Word document that contains the results of your query. Adjust the column widths of the created table so that it fits on the page. Write a memo based on this table explaining that these are the computers that you believe should be upgraded.

3-2. Assume that you have been asked to create a spreadsheet to help make a buy-versus-lease decision for the servers on your organization's Web farm. Assume that you are considering the servers for a 5-year period, but you do not know exactly how many servers you will need. Initially, you know you will need 5 servers, but you might need as many as 50, depending on the success of your organization's e-commerce activity.

a. For the buy-alternative calculations, set up your spreadsheet so that you can enter the base price of the server hardware, the price of all software, and a maintenance expense that is some percentage of the hardware price. Assume that the percent you enter covers both hardware and software maintenance. Also assume that each server has a 3-year life, after which it has no value. Assume straight-line depreciation for computers used less than 3 years, and that at the end of the 5 years you can sell the computers you have used for less than 3 years for their depreciated value. Also assume that your organization pays 2 percent interest on capital expenses. Assume the servers cost $5,000 each, and the needed software costs $750. Assume that the maintenance expense varies from 2 to 7 percent.

b. For the lease-alternative calculations, assume that the leasing vendor will lease the same computer hardware as you can purchase. The lease includes all the software you need as well as all maintenance. Set up your spreadsheet so that you can enter various lease costs, which vary according to the number of years of the lease (1, 2, or 3). Assume the cost of a 3-year lease is $285 per machine per month, a 2-year lease is $335 per machine per month, and a 1-year lease is $415 per machine per month. Also, the lessor offers a 5 percent discount if you lease from 20 to 30 computers and a 10 percent discount if you lease from 31 to 50 computers.

c. Using your spreadsheet, compare the costs of buy versus lease under the following situations. (Assume you either buy or lease. You cannot lease some and buy some.) Make assumptions, as necessary, and state those assumptions.

   (1) Your organization requires 20 servers for 5 years.

   (2) Your organization requires 20 servers for the first 2 years and 40 servers for the next 3 years.

Type	Topology	Transmission Line	Transmission Speed	Equipment Used	Protocol Commonly Used	Remarks
Local area network	Local area network	UTP or optical fiber	Common: 10/100/1000 Mbps Possible: 1 Gbps	Switch NIC UTP or optical	IEEE 802.3 (Ethernet)	Switches connect devices, multiple switches on all but small LANs.
	Local area network with wireless	UTP or optical for non-wireless connections	Up to 600 Mbps	Wireless access point Wireless NIC	IEEE 802.11n	Access point transforms wired LAN (802.3) to wireless LAN (802.11).
Connections to the Internet	DSL modem to ISP	DSL telephone	Personal: Upstream to 1 Mbps downstream to 40 Mbps (max 10 likely in most areas)	DSL modem DSL-capable telephone line	DSL	Can have computer and phone use simultaneously. Always connected.
	Cable modem to ISP	Cable TV lines to optical cable	Upstream to 1 Mbps Downstream 300 Kbs to 10 Mbps	Cable modem Cable TV cable	Cable	Capacity is shared with other sites; performance varies depending on others' use.
	WAN wireless	Wireless connection to WAN	500 Kbps to 1 Mbps	Wireless WAN modem	One of several wireless standards.	Sophisticated protocol enables several devices to use the same wireless frequency.

FIGURE AE-3

(3) Your organization requires 20 servers for the first 2 years, 40 servers for the next 2 years, and 50 servers for the last year.

(4) Your organization requires 10 servers the first year, 20 servers the second year, 30 servers the third year, 40 servers the fourth year, and 50 servers the last year.

(5) For the previous case, does the cheaper alternative change if the cost of the servers is $4,000? If it is $8,000?

3-3. Numerous Web sites are available that will test your Internet data communications speed. A good one is available at *www.speakeasy.net/speedtest/*. (If that site is no longer active, Google or Bing "What is my Internet speed?" to find another speed-testing site. Use it.)

a. While connected to your university's network, go to Speakeasy and test your speed against servers in Seattle, New York City, and Atlanta. Compute your average upload and download speeds. Compare your speed to the speeds listed in Figure AE-3.

b. Go home, or to a public wireless site, and run the Speakeasy test again. Compute your average upload and download speeds. Compare your speed to those listed in Figure AE-3. If you are performing this test at home, are you getting the performance you are paying for?

c. Contact a friend or relative in another state. Ask him or her to run the Speakeasy test against those same three cities.

d. Compare the results in parts a, b, and c. What conclusion, if any, can you make from these tests?

Chapter 4

4-1. A common scenario in business is to combine the processing of Microsoft Access and Excel. A typical scenario is for users to process relational data with Access, import some of the data into Excel, and use Excel's tools for creating professional looking charts and graphs. You will do exactly that in this exercise.

Download the Access file **Ch04Ex01**. Open the database, select *Database Tools/ Relationships*. As you can see, there are three tables: *Product, Vendor Product Inventory,* and *Vendor*. Open each table individually to familiarize yourself with the data.

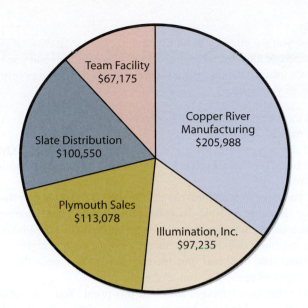

For this problem, we will define *Inventory Cost* as the product of *Industry Standard Cost* and *Quantity On Hand*. The query *Inventory Cost* computes these values for every item in inventory for every vendor. Open that query and view the data to be certain you understand this computation. Open the other queries as well so that you understand the data they produce.

a. Sum this data by vendor and display it in a pie chart like that shown in Figure AE-4. Proceed as follows:

(1) Open Excel and create a new spreadsheet.

(2) Click *Data* on the ribbon and select *Access* in the *Get External Data* ribbon category.

(3) Navigate to the location in which you have stored the Access file **Ch04Ex01**.

(4) Select the query that contains the data you need for this pie chart.

(5) Import the data into a table.

(6) Format the appropriate data as currency.

(7) Select the range that contains the data, press the function key, and proceed from there to create the pie chart. Name the data and pie chart worksheets appropriately.

b. Follow a similar procedure to create the bar chart shown in Figure AE-5. Place the data and the chart in separate worksheets and name them appropriately.

FIGURE AE-5

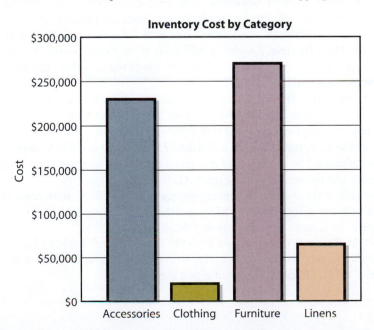

4-2. Suppose you are hired by an auto dealer to create a database of customers and their interests. Salespeople have been keeping data in a spreadsheet, and you have been asked to convert that data into a database. Because the dealer's data is so poorly structured, it will be a challenge, as you will see.

a. Download the Excel file named **Ch04Ex02**. Open the spreadsheet and examine the data. It's a mess!

b. Download the Access file with the same name, **Ch04Ex02**. Open the database, select Database Tools, and click Relationships. Examine the four tables and their relationships.

c. Somehow, you have to transform the data in the spreadsheet into the table structure in the database. Because so little discipline was shown when creating the spreadsheet, this will be a labor-intensive task. To begin, import the spreadsheet data into a new table in the database; call that table Sheet1 or some other name.

d. Copy the *Name* data in *Sheet1* onto the clipboard. Then, open the *Customer* table and paste the column of name data into that table.

e. Unfortunately, the task becomes messy at this point. You can copy the *Car Interests* column into *Make or Model of Auto*, but then you will need to straighten out the values by hand. Phone numbers will need to be copied one at a time.

f. Open the *Customer* form and manually add any remaining data from the spreadsheet into each customer record. Connect the customer to his or her auto interests.

g. The data in the finished database has much more structure than that in the spreadsheet. Explain why that is both an advantage and a disadvantage. Under what circumstances is the database more appropriate? Less appropriate?

4-3. In this exercise, you will create a two-table database, define relationships, create a form and a report, and use them to enter data and view results.

a. Download the Excel file **Ch04Ex03**. Open the spreadsheet and review the data in the *Employee* and *Computer* worksheets.

b. Create a new Access database with the name *Ch04Ex03_Solution*. Close the table that Access automatically creates and delete it.

c. Import the data from the Excel spreadsheet into your database. Import the *Employee* worksheet into a table named *Employee*. Be sure to check *First Row Contains Column Headings*. Select *Choose my own primary key* and use the ID field as that key.

d. Import the *Computer* worksheet into a table named *Computer*. Check *First Row Contains Column Headings*, but let Access create the primary key.

e. Open the relationships window and add both *Employee* and *Computer* to the design space. Drag ID from *Employee* and drop it on *EmployeeID* in *Computer*. Check *Enforce Referential Integrity* and the two checkmarks below. Ensure that you know what these actions mean.

f. Open the Form Wizard dialog box (under *Create, More Forms*) and add all of the columns for each of your tables to your form. Select *View your data by Customer*. Title your form *Employee* and your subform *Computer*.

g. Open the *Computer* subform and delete *EmployeeID* and *ComputerID*. These values are maintained by Access, and it is just a distraction to keep them. Your form should appear like the one shown in Figure AE-6.

h. Use your form to add two new computers to *Jane Ashley*. Both computers are Dells, and both use Vista; one costs $750, and the second costs $1,400.

i. Delete the Lenovo computer for Rex Scott.

j. Use the Report Wizard (under *Create*) to create a report having all data from both the *Employee* and *Computer* tables. Play with the report design until you find a design you like. Correct the label alignment if you need to.

Employee

ID	2
First Name	Jane
Last Name	Ashley
Department	Mkt

Computer

Serial Number	Brand	Purchase Cost	Operating System
100	Dell	$1,750	Vista
800	HP	$750	Windows XP
*			

Record: 1 of 2   No Filter   Search

Record: 1 of 6   No Filter   Search

PART 3

Chapter 5

5-1. Assume that you have been hired to develop an Access database for a facilities reservation system at FlexTime, the workout studio introduced in Chapter 3. You have been given the following design for implementation:

FACILITY   (FacilityID, FacilityName, Description, StandardRentalFee)

RESERVATION (ReservationNumber, *FacilityID,* Date, StartTime, EndTime)

Where FacilityID and ReservationNumber are AutoNumber primary keys. RESERVATION. FacilityID is a foreign key to FACILITY. Use the appropriate data types for the other columns.

a. Create these tables in Access.
b. Create the appropriate relationship in Access.
c. Import the data in the file **Ch05Ex01.txt** into the FACILITY table.
d. Create a reservation form for creating and viewing specific reservations.
e. Create a parameterized query for finding a reservation by value of ReservationNumber.
f. Create a report that shows all of the reservations for all facilities.
g. Create a parameterized report that shows all of the reservations for a particular date.

5-2. You are the manager of the pizza shop near Central Colorado State University where Sarah works. Recently you provided handheld GPS devices with real-time traffic data to your drivers. The owner of the franchise has asked you to give a presentation to the other pizza shop managers about the usefulness of the devices. To make your case, you collected data on 50 deliveries before and 50 deliveries after installing the devices at the end of June 2012. The data is located in the file **Ch05Ex02**.

In this spreadsheet you have made two main sections. On the left is data from before the GPS were added, on the right is data after the GPS were added. There are four drivers, and each makes deliveries to four zones—A, B, C, and D. Zone A is comprised of students in dorms at the campus; the other three zones are located in different geographic regions around the town. Also included in each of the two sections are time for delivery and the price of the delivery.

a. Format the labels at the top of each section using font size and color, fill color, and cell merging to make your spreadsheet look more professional.

b. Format the price data in currency format.

c. Calculate the average time and price before and after the GPS were used.

d. Calculate the average time and price before and after the GPS were used for zone A (dorm students).

e. How much time did the GPS save overall (all four zones combined)?

f. How much time did the GPS save per order for nonstudent deliveries?

g. If you are one of the managers considering adopting GPS, what factors might be different between your restaurant and the restaurant in this exercise that might impact your willingness to invest in the GPS?

Chapter 6

6-1.   Central Colorado State is considering consolidating all purchasing functions into one central office. To assess the cost savings of such a move, the university collected data about the purchasing costs in three departments. This data is shown in the file **Ch06Ex01**.

   The data show the number of orders and the total price of the orders for each of the three departments. The file also includes data on the monthly fixed costs of operating a purchasing office. Fixed costs include the cost of the purchasing agent(s) for that month; the estimated cost of the office space; and the approximate cost of other fixed costs, such as insurance and supervision. These three departments were chosen for data collection because they represent typical small, medium, and large purchasing offices.

a. If each purchasing agent costs the university $7,500 per month, calculate the total fixed cost for each of the offices.

b. Calculate the average fixed cost per order for each of the three departments.

c. Create a bar chart with appropriate labels and titles that shows the average fixed cost per order for each of the three departments.

d. The university estimates that it has 15 small, 5 medium, and 3 large departments. If each of these departments has the same number and price of orders as the three departments shown in the file, calculate the total number and total price for the entire university.

e. The university estimates that the fixed cost data for these other departments will be the same as the three departments shown in the file; that is, each small department will have the same data as the Athletics department, each medium department is like the Student Services department, and each large one is like the Bookstore. Calculate the total fixed costs for the entire university.

f. The university assumes that when purchasing is consolidated in one office, the average cost per order will be about the same as the Bookstore's average cost per order. Using the total number of orders for the university from part d and the average fixed cost per order of a large department from part b, how much will the university save if it consolidates purchasing in one location?

6-2.   Figure AE-7 is a sample bill of materials, a form that shows the components and parts used to construct a product. In this example, the product is a child's wagon. Such bills of materials are an essential part of manufacturing functional applications as well as ERP applications.

   This particular example is a form produced using Microsoft Access. Producing such a form is a bit tricky, so this exercise will guide you through the steps required. You can then apply what you learn to produce a similar report. You can also use Access to experiment on extensions of this form.

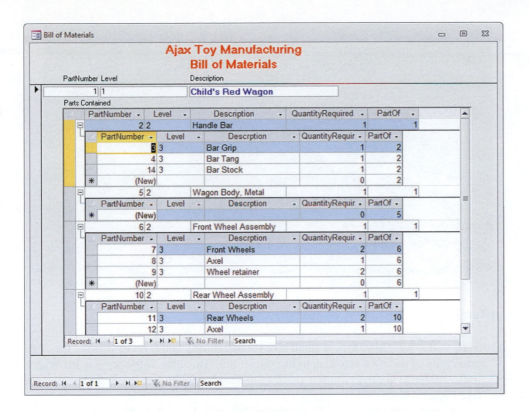

a. Create a table named *PART* with columns *Part Number, Level, Description, QuantityRequired,* and *PartOf. Description* and *Level* should be text, *PartNumber* should be AutoNumber, and *Quantity Required* and *PartOf* should be numeric, long integer. Add the *PART* data shown in Figure AE-7 to your table.

b. Create a query that has all columns of *PART*. Restrict the view to rows having a value of 1 for *Level*. Name your query *Level1*.

c. Create two more queries that are restricted to rows having values of 2 or 3 for *Level*. Name your queries *Level2* and *Level3*, respectively.

d. Create a form that contains *PartNumber, Level,* and *Description* from *Level1*. You can use a wizard for this if you want. Name the form *Bill of Materials*.

e. Using the subform tool in the Toolbox, create a subform in your form in part d. Set the data on this form to be all of the columns of *Level2*. After you have created the subform, ensure that the Link Child Fields property is set to *PartOf* and that the Link Master Fields property is set to *PartNumber*. Close the *Bill of Materials* form.

f. Open the subform created in part e and create a subform on it. Set the data on this subform to be all of the columns of *Level3*. After you have created the subform, ensure that the Link Child Fields property is set to *PartOf* and that the Link Master Fields property is set to *PartNumber*. Close the *Bill of Materials* form.

g. Open the *Bill of Materials* form. It should appear as in Figure AE-7. Open and close the form and add new data. Using this form, add sample BOM data for a product of your own choosing.

h. Following the process similar to that just described, create a *Bill of Materials Report* that lists the data for all of your products.

i. **(Optional, challenging extension)** Each part in the BOM in Figure AE-7 can be used in at most one assembly (there is space to show just one *PartOf* value). You can change your design to allow a part to be used in more than one assembly as follows: First, remove *PartOf* from PART. Next, create a second table that has two columns: *AssemblyPartNumber* and *ComponentPart Number*. The first contains a part number of an assembly and the second a part number of a component. Every component of a part will have a row in this table. Extend the views described previously to use this second table and to produce a display similar to Figure AE-7.

FIGURE AE-8
3rd Wheel

Source: Jim West/Alamy Images.

Chapter 7

7-1. **X SAP** Your firm, a small bike manufacturing outfit, is considering the possibility of adding a new item to its product line. This bike accessory is a 3rd Wheel, a trailer designed to carry children, or, in a different configuration, goods and equipment (see Figure AE-8).

Your firm will procure and build the 3rd Wheel in-house if the labor costs for assembly are sufficiently less than the cost of procuring the 3rd Wheel already assembled. You are asked to estimate the labor cost of producing this new accessory. You have downloaded labor cost data from your ERP system into an Excel spreadsheet. This data file is **Ch07Ex01**. (To see how to download the data directly from SAP, see the end of this exercise.)

At each plant there are six hourly wage rates for assembly workers, and there are two possible assembly plants—East and West—where the bikes could be assembled. To assemble the 3rd Wheel, the engineering department has developed several options. Each of the options requires a different set of hours for the pay scales, as shown below:

	Labor Hours		
Pay Scale	Option A	Option B	Option C
0	5	3	7
1	3	4	2
2	2	2	1
3	2	1	2

Finally, there are two types of employees: union and nonunion. Nonunion employee data is shown at the top of the file, union data at the bottom. Local 112 is East, Local 83 is West.

a. Calculate the total labor cost for options A, B, and C for East and West plants with nonunion workers. Which option is lowest cost?

b. Calculate the total labor cost for options A, B, and C for East and West plants with union workers. Which option is lowest cost?

c. Create a chart with appropriate labels and titles that shows all 12 options in the previous two parts.

d. Another option for your firm is to outsource the payscale 0 work. If the bottom payscale work is removed, does the lowest cost option change?

e. The analysis in part d is a common one. This interactive analysis is also called "what-if" analysis. In part d you were asked, "What if payscale 0 work is outsourced?" If you expect to do "what-if" analysis on a spreadsheet, how does that change how you set up the original spreadsheet, its data, functions, and equations?

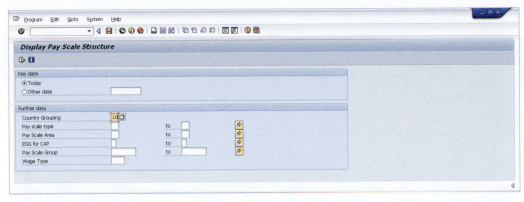

To download the data directly from SAP:[1]

(1) Log in to SAP as before.

(2) On the SAP Easy Access Screen Select:

> *Information Systems > General Report Selection > Human Resources > Personal Management > Compensation Management > Pay Structure > Display Pay Scale Structure*

(3) Enter *10* in Country Grouping (for USA), then click the *Execute* icon above Key date, as shown in Figure AE-9.

(4) On the Display Pay Scale Structure screen, click the *Local* file icon (ninth icon from left) and specify a file name and location for the file to be saved on the local machine, as shown in Figure AE-10.

(5) Open Excel. Navigate to the downloaded Excel file and open it. Inspect your spreadsheet. It should look like Figure AE-11.

[1] This example uses the Global Bike Inc SAP client set. See Appendix 7 for instructions on how to access this client set.

FIGURE AE-11

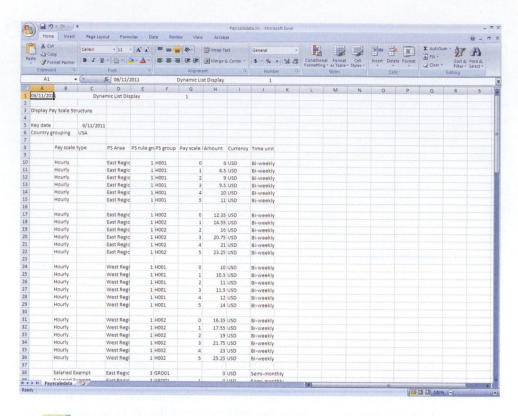

7-2. Assume that you have been given the task of compiling evaluations that your company's purchasing agents make of their e-commerce vendors. Each month, every purchasing agent evaluates all of the vendors that he or she has ordered from in the past month on three factors: price, quality, and responsiveness. Assume the ratings are from 1 to 5, with 5 being the best. Because your company has hundreds of vendors and dozens of purchasing agents, you decide to use Access to compile the results.

a. Create a database with three tables: VENDOR (*VendorNumber, Name, Contact*), PURCHASER (*EmpNumber, Name, Email*), and RATING (*EmpNumber, VendorNumber, Month, Year, Price Rating, QualityRating, ResponsivenessRating*). Assume that *VendorNumber* and *EmpNumber* are the keys of VENDOR and PURCHASER, respectively. Decide what you think is the appropriate key for RATING.

b. Create appropriate relationships.

c. Import the data in the Excel file **Ch07Ex02**. Note that data for Vendor, Purchaser, and Rating are stored in three separate worksheets.

d. Create a query that shows the names of all vendors and their average scores.

e. Create a query that shows the names of all employees and their average scores. *Hint:* In this and in part f, you will need to use the *Group By* function in your query.

f. Create a parameterized query that you can use to obtain the minimum, maximum, and average ratings on each criterion for a particular vendor. Assume you will enter *VendorName* as the parameter.

g. Using the data created by your queries, what conclusions can you make about vendors or purchasers?

Chapter 8

8-1. Suppose your manager asks you to create a spreadsheet to compute a production schedule. Your schedule should stipulate a production quantity for seven products that is based on sales projections made by three regional managers at your company's three sales regions.

a. Create a separate worksheet for each sales region. Use the data in the Word file **Ch08Ex01**. This file contains each manager's monthly sales projections for the past year, actual sales results for those same months, and projections for sales for each month in the coming quarter.

b. Create a separate worksheet for each manager's data. Import the data from Word into Excel.

c. On each of the worksheets, use the data from the prior four quarters to compute the discrepancy between the actual sales and the sales projections. This discrepancy can be computed in several ways: You could calculate an overall average, or you could calculate an average per quarter or per month. You could also weight recent discrepancies more heavily than earlier ones. Choose a method that you think is most appropriate. Explain why you chose the method you did.

d. Modify your worksheets to use the discrepancy factors to compute an adjusted forecast for the coming quarter. Thus, each of your spreadsheets will show the raw forecast and the adjusted forecast for each month in the coming quarter.

e. Create a fourth worksheet that totals sales projections for all of the regions. Show both the unadjusted forecast and the adjusted forecast for each region and for the company overall. Show month and quarter totals.

f. Create a bar graph showing total monthly production. Display the unadjusted and adjusted forecasts using different colored bars.

8-2.   Do Application Exercise 5-1, if you have not already done so.

a. Add a Status column to the RESERVATION table, where Status can have values of *Not Confirmed*, *Confirmed*, or *Cancelled*. A reservation guarantees a customer a locker and access to all equipment. Explain why FlexTime might wish to track cancelled reservations.

b. Create a data entry form that would be appropriate to make a reservation at a facility.

c. Create a data entry form that would be appropriate to confirm a reservation at a facility.

d. Create a Daily Facility Use Report. Assume the report has a parameterized query to produce all reservations for a given date.

e. Input data and test your database. Use the Windows 7 Snipping Tool or some other tool to capture screen shots of your data entry screens and your report.

PART 4

Chapter 9

9-1.   Suppose that you have been asked to assist in the managerial decision about how much to increase pay in the next year. Assume you are given a list of the departments in your company, along with the average salary for employees in that department for major companies in your industry. Additionally, you are given the names and salaries of 10 people in each of three departments in your company.

Assume you have been asked to create a spreadsheet that shows the names of the 10 employees in each department, their current salary, the difference between their current salary and the industry average salary for their department, and the percent their salary would need to be increased to meet the industry average. Your spreadsheet should also compute the average increase needed to meet the industry average for each department and the average increase, company-wide, to meet industry averages.

a. Use the data in the file **Ch09Ex01.doc** and create the spreadsheet.

b. How can you use this analysis to contribute to the employee salary decision? Based on this data, what conclusions can you make?

c. Suppose other team members want to use your spreadsheet. Name three ways you can share it with them and describe the advantages and disadvantages of each.

9-2.   Suppose that you have been asked to assist in the managerial decision about how much to increase pay in the next year. Specifically, you are tasked to determine if there are significant salary differences among departments in your company.

You are given an Access database with a table of employee data with the following structure:

EMPLOYEE (Name, Department, Specialty, Salary)

where *Name* is the name of an employee who works in a department, *Department* is the department name, *Specialty* is the name of the employee's primary skill, and *Salary* is the employee's current salary. Assume that no two employees have the same name. You have been asked to answer the following queries:

(1) List the names, department, and salary of all employees earning more than $100,000.
(2) List the names and specialties of all employees in the Marketing department.
(3) Compute the average, maximum, and minimum salary of employees in your company.
(4) Compute the average, minimum, and maximum salary of employees in the Marketing department.
(5) Compute the average, minimum, and maximum salary of employees in the Information Systems department.
(6) *Extra credit:* Compute the average salary for employees in every department. Use *Group By.*

a. Design and run Access queries to obtain the answers to these questions, using the data in the file **Ch09Ex02.mdb**.
b. Explain how the data in your answer contributes to the salary increase decision.
c. Suppose other team members want to use your Access application. Name three ways you can share it with them, and describe the advantages and disadvantages of each.

Chapter 10

10-1.   For the following exercises, tutorials and help are available from each social media platform and also by using a search engine.

a. Facebook: Use the Facebook Markup Language app to create a landing page for a local business page (you will have to first create a local business page). Use a search engine to find simple instructions for using the Facebook Mark Up Language app.
b. Twitter: Create an account and follow several of your classmates (and have them follow you). Tweet and send them a direct message. Make a tweet with a #hashtag, then use Twitter's search function to find this tweet. Find your classmates' hashtag tweets. Find and follow popular accounts or accounts of individuals or organizations in an area of interest of yours.
c. LinkedIn: Create an account and begin to fill out your profile. Create or extend the data in your profile (if you already had an account). Connect to your classmates. Find and follow companies and explore the site and learn new options in Groups, Jobs, and Contacts.
d. Blogger: Create a blog about the use of social media in small business or another topic of interest to you. Embed a YouTube video in your blog. Follow other blogs.

10-2.   For the following exercises, tutorials and help are available from each social media platform and also by using a search engine.

a. Wikipedia: Create your own user account. Go to your *my talk* page and click Edit. You will be creating a page called User talk:*Yourusername*. Write a paragraph about social media. Find a classmate's user talk entry and edit his or her paragraph. Go back to your talk page and click View History to see how your page has been edited. Finally, find an entry on Wikipedia that you can contribute to and edit that page. Use a search engine and find instructions to play Wiki Races (an example is *http://wikibin.org/articles/wiki-races.html*).
b. Delicious, Digg, and StumbleUpon: Create accounts at these sites. Share your list of bookmarks in Delicious with a classmate.

    c. **Klout.com:** Go to Klout.com or another social media monitoring site. Sign in with your Twitter account name and see the impact of your tweets. Read about how your clout is determined.

    d. **Google Docs:** Create or use an existing Gmail account. Discover how to make a Google document and share that document with your classmates. Edit the document simultaneously with classmates. Navigate to the RSS reader within your Google account. Subscribe to several interesting Web sites that you would like to follow. Subscribe to your classmates' blogs, and notice that new blog entries they create will show up in your reader.

Chapter 11

11-1. OLAP cubes are very similar to Microsoft Excel pivot tables. For this exercise, assume that your organization's purchasing agents rate vendors similar to the situation described in Application Exercise 7-2.

    a. Open Excel and import the data in the worksheet named *Vendors* from the Excel file **Ch11Ex01**. The spreadsheet will have the following column names: *VendorName, EmployeeName, Date, Year*, and *Rating*.

    b. Under the *Insert* ribbon in Excel, click *Pivot Table*. A wizard will open. Select *Excel* and *Pivot table* in the first screen. Click *Next*.

    c. When asked to provide a data range, drag your mouse over the data you imported so as to select all of the data. Be sure to include the column headings. Excel will fill in the range values in the open dialog box. Place your pivot table in a separate spreadsheet.

    d. Excel will create a field list on the right-hand side of your spreadsheet. Drag and drop the field named *VendorName* onto the words "Drop Row Fields Here." Drag and drop *EmployeeName* onto the words "Drop Column Fields Here." Now drag and drop the field named *Rating* onto the words "Drop Data Items Here." Voilà! You have a pivot table.

    e. To see how the table works, drag and drop more fields onto the various sections of your pivot table. For example, drop *Year* on top of *Employee*. Then move *Year* below *Employee*. Now move *Year* below *Vendor*. All of this action is just like an OLAP cube, and, in fact, OLAP cubes are readily displayed in Excel pivot tables. The major difference is that OLAP cubes are usually based on thousands or more rows of data.

11-2. It is surprisingly easy to create a market basket report using table data in Access. To do so, however, you will need to enter SQL expressions into the Access query builder. Here, you can just copy SQL statements to type them in. If you take a database class, you will learn how to code SQL statements like those you will use here.

    a. Create an Access database with a table named *Order_Data* having columns *OrderNumber, ItemName*, and *Quantity*, with data types Number (*LongInteger*), Text (50), and Number (*LongInteger*), respectively. Define the key as the composite (*OrderNumber, ItemName*).

    b. Import the data from the Excel file **Ch11Ex02** into the *Order_Data* table.

    c. Now, to perform the market-basket analysis, you will need to enter several SQL statements into Access. To do so, click the queries tab and select *Create Query* in Design view. Click *Close* when the Show Table dialog box appears. Right-click in the gray section above the grid in the *Select Query* window. Select *SQL View*. Enter the following expression exactly as it appears here:

```
SELECT      T1.ItemName as FirstItem,
            T2.ItemName as SecondItem

FROM        Order_Data T1, Order_Data T2

WHERE       T1.OrderNumber=
            T2.OrderNumber

AND         T1.ItemName<>
            T2.ItemName;
```

Click the red exclamation point in the toolbar to run the query. Correct any typing mistakes and, once it works, save the query using the name *TwoItemBasket*.

d. Now enter a second SQL statement. Again, click the queries tab and select *Create Query* in Design view. Click *Close* when the Show Table dialog box appears. Right-click in the gray section above the grid in the *Select Query* window. Select *SQL View*. Enter the following expression exactly as it appears here:

SELECT	**TwoItemBasket.FirstItem,**
	TwoItemBasket.SecondItem,
	Count(*) AS SupportCount
FROM	**TwoItemBasket**
GROUP BY	**TwoItemBasket.FirstItem,**
	TwoItemBasket.SecondItem;

Correct any typing mistakes and, once it works, save the query using the name *SupportCount*.

e. Examine the results of the second query and verify that the two query statements have correctly calculated the number of times that two items have appeared together. Explain further calculations you need to make to compute support.

f. Explain the calculations you need to make to compute lift. Although you can make those calculations using SQL, you need more SQL knowledge to do it, and we will skip that here.

g. Explain, in your own words, what the query in part c seems to be doing. What does the query in part d seem to be doing? Again, you will need to take a database class to learn how to code such expressions, but this exercise should give you a sense of the kinds of calculations that are possible with SQL.

PART 5

Chapter 12

12-1.   Suppose you are given the task of keeping track of the number of labor hours invested in meetings for systems development projects. Assume your company uses the traditional systems-first process illustrated in Figure AE-12. Further assume that each SDLC step requires two types of meetings: *Working meetings* involve users, business analysts, systems analysts, programmers, and PQA test engineers. *Review*

FIGURE AE-12

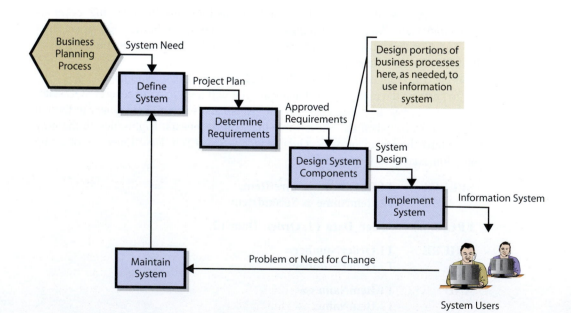

meetings involve all of those people, plus level-1 and level-2 managers of both user departments and the IS department.

a. Import the data in the Word file **Ch12Ex01** into a spreadsheet.

b. Modify your spreadsheet to compute the total labor hours invested in each phase of a project. When a meeting occurs, assume you enter the project phase, the meeting type, the start time, the end time, and the number of each type of personnel attending. Your spreadsheet should calculate the number of labor hours and should add the meeting's hours to the totals for that phase and for the project overall.

c. Modify your spreadsheet to include the budgeted number (in the source data) of labor hours for each type of employee for each phase. In your spreadsheet, show the difference between the number of hours budgeted and the number actually consumed.

d. Change your spreadsheet to include the budgeted cost and actual cost of labor. Assume that you enter, once, the average labor cost for each type of employee, as stipulated in the source data.

12-2. Use Access to develop a failure-tracking database application. Use the data in the Excel file **Ch12Ex02** for this exercise. The data includes columns for the following:

FailureNumber
DateReported
FailureDescription
ReportedBy (the name of the PQA engineer reporting the failure)
ReportedBy_email (the e-mail address of the PQA engineer reporting the failure)
FixedBy (the name of the programmer who is assigned to fix the failure)
FixedBy_email (the e-mail address of the programmer assigned to fix the failure)
DateFailureFixed
FixDescription
DateFixVerified
VerifiedBy (the name of the PQA engineer verifying the fix)
VerifiedBy_email (the e-mail address of the PQA engineer verifying the fix)

a. The data in the spreadsheet are not normalized. Normalize the data by creating a *Failure* table, a *PQA Engineer* table, and a *Programmer* table. Add other appropriate columns to each table. Create appropriate relationships.

b. Create one or more forms that can be used to report a failure, to report a failure fix, and to report a failure verification. Create the form(s) so that the user can just pull down the name of a PQA engineer or programmer from the appropriate table to fill in the *ReportedBy*, *FixedBy*, and *VerifiedBy* fields.

c. Construct a report that shows all failures sorted by reporting PQA engineer and then by *Date Reported*.

d. Construct a report that shows only fixed and verified failures.

e. Construct a report that shows only fixed but unverified failures.

12-3. Suppose you have just been appointed manager of a help desk with an IS department. You have been there for just a week, and you are amazed to find only limited information to help you manage your employees. In fact, the only data kept concerns the processing of particular issues, called *Tickets*. The following data are kept:

> **Ticket#, Date_Submitted, Date_Opened, Date_Closed, Type (new or repeat), Reporting_Employee_Name, Reporting_Employee_Division, Technician_Name Problem_System, and Problem_Description**

You can find sample Ticket data in the Excel file **Ch12Ex03**.

As a manager, you need more data. Among your needs are data that will help you learn who are your best- and worst-performing technicians, how different systems compare in terms of number of problems reported and the time required to fix those problems, how different divisions compare in terms of problems reported and the time required to fix them, which technicians are the best and worst at solving problems with particular systems, and which technicians are best and worst at solving problems from particular divisions.

a. Use either Access or Excel, or a combination of the two, to produce the information listed previously from the data in the Excel file **Ch12Ex03**. In your answer, you may use queries, formulas, reports, forms, graphs, pivot tables, pivot charts, or any other type of Access or Excel display. Choose the best display for the type of data you are producing.

b. Explain how you would use these different types of data to manage your department.

c. Specify any additional data that you would like to have produced to help you manage your department.

d. Use either Access or Excel or a combination to produce the data in part c.

12-4.   Develop a spreadsheet model of the cost of a virus attack in an organization that has three types of computers: employee workstations, data servers, and Web servers. Assume that the number of computers affected by the virus depends on the severity of the virus. For the purposes of your model, assume that there are three levels of virus severity: *Low-severity* incidents affect fewer than 30 percent of the user workstations and none of the data or Web servers. *Medium-severity* incidents affect up to 70 percent of the user workstations, up to half of the Web servers, and none of the data servers. *High-severity* incidents can affect all organizational computers.

a. Assume 50 percent of the incidents are low severity, 30 percent are medium severity, and 20 percent are high severity.

b. Assume employees can remove viruses from workstations themselves, but that specially trained technicians are required to repair the servers. The time to eliminate a virus from an infected computer depends on the computer type. Let the time to remove the virus from each type be an input into your model. Assume that when users eliminate the virus themselves, they are unproductive for twice the time required for the removal. Let the average employee hourly labor cost be an input to your model. Let the average cost of a technician also be an input into your model. Finally, let the total number of user computers, data servers, and Web servers be inputs into your model.

c. Run your simulation 10 times. Use the same inputs for each run, but draw a random number (assume a uniform distribution for all random numbers) to determine the severity type. Then, draw random numbers to determine the percentage of computers of each type affected, using the constraints detailed earlier. For example, if the attack is of medium severity, draw a random number between 0 and 70 to indicate the percentage of infected user workstations and a random number between 0 and 50 to indicate the percentage of infected Web servers.

d. For each run, calculate the total of lost employee hours, the total dollar cost of lost employee labor hours, the total hours of technicians to fix the servers, and the total cost of technician labor. Finally, compute the total overall cost. Show the results of each run. Show the average costs and hours for the 10 runs.

Glossary

3D printing. Also called *additive manufacturing*; a process of depositing successive layers of material to manufacture objects. Just as current printers deposit ink in two dimensions, 3D printing deposits material in three dimensions, layering material in the third dimension as it dries. **p. 203**

10/100/1000 Ethernet. A type of Ethernet that conforms to the IEEE 802.3 protocol and allows for transmission at a rate of 10, 100, or 1,000 Mbps (megabits per second). **p. 70**

ABAP. SAP's high-level application language that is used to enhance the functionality of an SAP implementation. It is frequently used to format the data in reports. **p. 176**

Abstract reasoning. The ability to make and manipulate models. **p. 8**

Access. A popular personal and small workgroup DBMS product from Microsoft. **p. 97**

Access point (AP). A point in a wireless network that facilitates communication among wireless devices and serves as a point of interconnection between wireless and wired networks. The access point must be able to process messages according to both the 802.3 and 802.11 standards, because it sends and receives wireless traffic using the 802.11 protocol and communicates with wired networks using the 802.3 protocol. **p. 70**

Activity. A task within a business process. **p. 132**

AdSense. A Web 2.0 product from Google. Google searches an organization's Web site and inserts ads that match content on that site; when users click those ads, Google pays the organization a fee. **p. 319**

Adware. Programs installed on the user's computer without the user's knowledge or permission that reside in the background and, unknown to the user, observe the user's actions and keystrokes, modify computer activity, and report the user's activities to sponsoring organizations. Most adware is benign in that it does not perform malicious acts or steal data. It does, however, watch user activity and produce pop-up ads. **p. 401**

AdWords. A Web 2.0 advertising product from Google. Vendors agree to pay a certain amount to Google for use of particular search words, which link to the vendor's site. **p. 318**

Analysts. Sometimes called *systems analysts* or *business analysts*, these employees have specialized training or education that enables them to support, maintain, and adapt the information systems after they are implemented. **p. 166**

Application software. Programs that perform a business function. Some application programs are general purpose, such as Excel or Word. Others are specific to a business function, such as accounts payable. **p. 64**

As-is model. A model that represents the current situation and processes. **p. 380**

Asymmetric encryption. An encryption method whereby different keys are used to encode and to decode the message; one key encodes the message, and the other key decodes the message. Symmetric encryption is simpler and much faster than asymmetric encryption. **p. 399**

Asynchronous communication. Information exchange that occurs when all members of a work team do not meet at the same time, such as those who work different shifts or in different locations. **p. 283**

Attribute. (1) A variable that provides properties for an HTML tag. Each attribute has a standard name. For example, the attribute for a hyperlink is *href*, and its value indicates which Web page is to be displayed when the user clicks the link. (2) Characteristics of an entity. Example attributes of *Order* would be *OrderNumber, OrderDate, SubTotal, Tax, Total*, and so forth. Example attributes of *Salesperson* would be *SalespersonName, Email, Phone*, and so forth. **p. 105**

Auction. Application that matches buyers and sellers by using an e-commerce version of a standard, competitive-bidding auction process. **p. 246**

Augmented reality (AR). Technology that superimposes data or graphics onto a computer-generated display of the physical environment. **p. 201**

Authentication. The process whereby an information system verifies (validates) a user. **p. 398**

Bill of material (BOM). A structure or description that specifies the raw materials, quantities, and subassemblies to create a product. **p. 170**

Biometric authentication. The use of personal physical characteristics, such as fingerprints, facial features, and retinal scans, to verify users. **p. 398**

Bits. The means by which computers represent data; also called *binary digit*. A bit is either a zero or a one. **p. 57**

Bluetooth. A common wireless protocol designed for transmitting data over short distances, replacing cables. **p. 70**

Bot. A computer program that is surreptitiously installed and that takes actions unknown and uncontrolled by the computer's owner or administrator. **p. 402**

Bot herder. The individual or organization that controls a botnet. **p. 402**

Botnet. A network of bots that is created and managed by the individual or organization that infected the network with the bot program. **p. 402**

Bottleneck. When a limited resource greatly reduces the output of an integrated series of activities or processes. **p. 200**

Bullwhip effect. Phenomenon in which the variability in the size and timing of orders increases at each stage up the supply chain, from customer to supplier. **p. 199**

Business intelligence system. An information system that supports business processes by consolidating and analyzing data in a large database to help users create information. **p. 342**

Business Objects. SAP software that analyzes business intelligence data. Business Objects was an independent software firm until its acquisition by SAP. **p. 364**

Business process. A sequence of activities for accomplishing a function. **p. 28**

Business process management (BPM). A systematic process of modeling, creating, implementing, and assessing business processes. **p. 378**

Business Process Modeling Notation (BPMN) Standard. A standard set of terms and graphical notations for documenting business processes. **p. 28**

Business-to-business (B2B). Sales between companies. **p. 231**

Business-to-consumer (B2C). Sales between a supplier and a retail customer (the consumer). **p. 231**

Business-to-government (B2G). Sales between companies and governmental organizations. **p. 246**

Buy-in. A term for selling a product or system for less than its true price. **p. 93**

Byte(s). (1) A character of data. (2) An 8-bit chunk. **p. 57**

Cable modem. A type of modem that provides high-speed data transmission using cable television lines. The cable company installs a fast, high-capacity optical fiber cable to a distribution center in each neighborhood that it serves. At the distribution center, the optical fiber cable connects to regular cable-television cables that run to subscribers' homes or businesses. Cable modems modulate in such a way that their signals do not interfere with TV signals. Like DSL lines, they are always on. **p. 72**

Capital. The investment of resources with the expectation of future returns in the marketplace. **p. 326**

Central processing unit (CPU). The CPU selects instructions, processes them, performs arithmetic and logical comparisons, and stores results of operations in memory. **p. 56**

Clearinghouse. Entity that provides goods and services at a stated price and arranges for the delivery of the goods, but never takes title to the goods. **p. 246**

Clickstream data. Web site data that describes a customer's clicking behavior. Such data includes everything the customer does at the Web site. **p. 306**

Client. A computer that provides word processing, spreadsheets, database access, and usually a network connection. **p. 59**

Client-server applications. Software applications that require code on both the client computer and the server computer. E-mail is a common example. **p. 64**

Closed source. Source code that is highly protected and only available to trusted employees and carefully vetted contractors. **p. 66**

Cloud computing. A form of hardware/software outsourcing in which organizations offer flexible plans for customers to lease hardware and software facilities. **p. 63**

Cluster analysis. Unsupervised data mining analysis that identifies groups of entities that have similar characteristics. A common use for cluster analysis is to find groups of similar customers in data about customer orders and customer demographics. **p. 354**

COBIT (Control Objectives for Information and related Technology). A set of standard practices created by the Information Systems Audit and Control Association that are used in the assessment activity of the BPM cycle to determine how well an information system complies with an organization's strategy. **p. 379**

Code injections. A technique used to gain unauthorized access to Web pages that involves entering program code instead of data into web page text boxes. **p. 403**

Cold sites. Remote processing centers that provide office space, but no computer equipment, for use by a company that needs to continue operations after a disaster. **p. 408**

Collaborative team. A group that works together using feedback and iteration. With a collaborative team, one person produces something, others review it, and the originator or others make revisions. **p. 274**

Columns. Also called *fields*, or groups of bytes. A database table has multiple columns that are used to represent the attributes of an entity. Examples are *PartNumber*, *EmployeeName*, and *SalesDate*. **p. 93**

Competitive strategy. The strategy an organization chooses as the way it will succeed in its industry. According to Porter, there are four fundamental competitive strategies: cost leadership across an industry or within a particular industry segment and product differentiation across an industry or within a particular industry segment. **p. 14**

Computer-based information system. An information system that includes a computer. **p. 32**

Computer criminals People who invade computer networks to obtain critical date or to manipulate the system for financial gain. **p. 394**

Computer hardware. Electronic components and related gadgetry that input, process, output, store, and communicate data according to the instructions encoded in computer programs or software. **p. 31**

Conference call. A synchronous virtual meeting in which participants meet at the same time via a voice-communication channel. **p. 284**

Configuration. The process of adapting ERP software to conform to customer requirements without changing program code. **p. 164**

Content management. One of the drivers of collaboration effectiveness, which enables multiple users to contribute to and change documents, schedules, task lists, assignments, and so forth, without one user's work interfering with another's. Content management also enables users to track and report who made what changes, when, and why. **p. 285**

Conversion rate. A measure of Web site traffic involving the ratio of the number of customers who eventually purchased divided by the number who visited. **p. 320**

Cooperative team. A group that works together to accomplish something, but each person works independently to accomplish his or her portion of the work. **p. 274**

Cost feasibility. Whether an information system can be developed within budget. **p. 385**

Criteria. Factors that humans use when conceiving information from data. **p. 39**

Cross-selling. The sale of related products; salespeople try to get customers who buy product *X* to also buy product *Y*. **p. 356**

Cross site scripting. A technique used to compromise database data in which Web page scripting is injected into the server. **p. 403**

Crow's foot. A line on an entity-relationship diagram that indicates a 1:N relationship betwewen two entities. **p. 107**

Crow's-foot diagram. A type of entity-relationship diagram that uses a crow's foot symbol to designate a 1:N relationship. **p. 107**

Crowdsourcing. The process by which organizations use Web 2.0 technologies such as user-generated content to outsource a task that traditionally is done by an employee to a large, undefined group of people. **p. 324**

Custom-developed software. Tailor-made software. **p. 66**

Customer relationship management (CRM). A system that integrates customer-facing processes and managing all the interactions with customers. **p. 240**

Data. Recorded facts or figures. One of the five fundamental components of an information system. **p. 31**

Data integrity problem. In a database, the situation that exists when data items disagree with one another. An example is two different names for the same customer. **p. 109**

Data mining. A type of Informing process that uses sophisticated statistical analyses to uncover patterns in a large database of data in order to improve prediction. **p. 347**

Data model. A logical representation of the data in a database that describes the data and relationships that will be stored in the database. Akin to a blueprint. **p. 104**

Data warehouses. Facilities that prepare, store, and manage data specifically for reporting and data mining. **p. 358**

Database. A self-describing collection of integrated records. **p. 93**

Database administration. The management, development, operation, and maintenance of the database so as to achieve the organization's objectives. This staff function requires balancing conflicting goals: protecting the database while maximizing its availability for authorized use. In smaller organizations, this function usually is served by a single person. Larger organizations assign several people to an office of database administration. **p. 99**

Database application. Forms, reports, queries, and application programs for processing a database. A database can be processed by many different database applications. **p. 100**

Database application system. Applications, having the standard five components, that make database data more accessible and useful. Users employ a database application that consists of forms, formatted reports, queries, and application programs. Each of these, in turn, calls on the database management system (DBMS) to process the database tables. **p. 97**

Database management systems (DBMS). A program for creating, processing, and administering a database. A DBMS is a large and complex program that is licensed like an operating system. Microsoft Access and Oracle are example DBMS products. **p. 97**

Database tier. In the three-tier architecture, the tier that runs the DBMS and receives and processes SQL requests to retrieve and store data. **p. 79**

DB2. A popular, enterprise-class DBMS product from IBM. **p. 97**

Decision support systems (DSS). An information system used in support of decision making. **p. 358**

Decision tree. Unsupervised data mining analysis that creates a hierarchical arrangement of criteria for classifying customers, items, and other business objects. **p. 356**

Delicious. A Web site that enables users to tag Web sites, create lists of sites, and share those lists with other users. **p. 317**

Denial of service (DOS). Security problem in which users are not able to access an information system; can be caused by human errors, natural disaster, or malicious activity. **p. 394**

Digg. A Web site that allows users to share votes on Web-based articles with other users. **p. 317**

Digital certificate. A document supplied by a certificate authority (CA) that contains, among other data, an entity's name and public key. **p. 401**

Digital dashboard. An electronic display that is customized for a particular user. Commonly provided by vendors like Yahoo! and MSN. **p. 348**

Digital signature. Encrypted message that uses *hashing* to ensure that plaintext messages are received without alteration. **p. 401**

Digital subscriber line (DSL). A communications line that operates on the same lines as voice telephones, but do so in such a manner that their signals do not interfere with voice telephone service. **p. 71**

Dirty data. Problematic data. Examples are a value of *B* for customer gender and a value of *213* for customer age. Other examples are a value of *999–999–9999* for a U.S. phone number, a part color of *gren*, and an e-mail address of WhyMe@GuessWhoIAM-Hah-Hah.org. All these values are problematic when data mining. **p. 359**

Discussion forum. A form of asynchronous communication in which one group member posts an entry and other group members respond. A better form of group communication than e-mail, because it is more difficult for the discussion to go off track. **p. 285**

Disintermediation. Elimination of one or more middle layers in the supply chain. **p. 246**

Document library. A named collection of documents in SharePoint. **p. 296**

Dogfooding. The process of using a product or idea that you develop or promote. The term arose in the 1980s in the software industry when someone observed that their company wasn't using the product they developed. Or, "they weren't eating their own dog food." **p. 307**

Domain name. A worldwide-unique name that is affiliated with a public IP address. The process of changing a name into its IP address is called *resolving the domain name.* **p. 76**

Drill down. With an OLAP report, to further divide the data into more detail. **p. 352**

Drive-by sniffers. People who take computers with wireless connections through an area and search for unprotected wireless networks in an attempt to gain free Internet access or to gather unauthorized data. **p. 394**

DSL (digital subscriber line) modem. A device for converting computer signals to the format needed for DSL transmission. **p. 71**

Dual processor. A computer with two CPUs. **p. 56**

Dynamic processes. A process whose structure is fluid and dynamic. Contrast with structured processes. Collaboration is a dynamic process; SAP order entry is a structured process. **p. 41**

E-commerce. A multifirm process of buying and selling goods and services using Internet technologies. **p. 245**

Effectiveness. A process objective that helps achieve organizational strategy. **p. 134**

Efficiency. A resource-oriented process objective; a process is efficient if it creates more output with the same inputs or the same output with fewer inputs. **p. 134**

Electronic exchange. Site that facilitates the matching of buyers and sellers; the business process is similar to that of a stock exchange. Sellers offer goods at a given price through the electronic exchange, and buyers make offers to purchase over the same exchange. Price matches result in transactions from which the exchange takes a commission. **p. 246**

E-mail spoofing. A synonym for *phishing*. A technique for obtaining unauthorized data that uses pretexting via e-mail. The *phisher* pretends to be a legitimate company and sends e-mail requests for confidential data, such as account numbers, Social Security numbers, account passwords, and so forth. Phishers direct traffic to their sites under the guise of a legitimate business. **p. 394**

Emergence. Attributes of a system that are not attributes of any of the system's components. For example, qualities of a supply chain, such as efficiency or throughput, that do not appear as qualities of any part. **p. 245**

Encapsulation (encapsulated). Hiding one object within another; for example, with SOA logic is encapsulated in a service. Encapsulation isolates the logic of a service from the services that use it. No service user knows nor needs to know how the service is performed. **p. 147**

Encryption. The process of transforming clear text into coded, unintelligible text for secure storage or communication. **p. 399**

Encryption algorithms. Algorithms used to transform clear text into coded, unintelligible text for secure storage or communication. Commonly used methods are DES, 3DES, and AES. **p. 399**

Enterprise 2.0. The application of Web 2.0 technologies to business use. **p. 317**

Enterprise application integration (EAI). The integration of existing systems by providing layers of software that connect applications and their data together. **p. 158**

Enterprise DBMS. A product that processes large organizational and workgroup databases. These products support many users, perhaps thousands, and many different database applications. Such DBMS products support 24/7 operations and can manage databases that span dozens of different magnetic disks with hundreds of gigabytes or more of data. IBM's DB2, Microsoft's SQL Server, and Oracle's Oracle are examples of enterprise DBMS products. **p. 103**

Enterprise resource planning (ERP) system. A suite of software, a database, and a set of inherent processes for consolidating business operations into a single, consistent, information system. **p. 159**

Entity. In the E-R data model, a representation of some thing that users want to track. Some entities represent a physical object; others represent a logical construct or transaction. **p. 105**

Entity-relationship (E-R) data model. Popular technique for creating a data model whereby developers define the things that will be stored and identify the relationships among them. **p. 105**

Entity-relationship (E-R) diagrams. A type of diagram used by database designers to document entities and their relationships to each other. **p. 106**

Epicor. A company primarily known for its retail-oriented ERP software, although it is broadening its penetration in other industry segments. **p. 173**

Ethernet. Another name for the IEEE 802.3 protocol, Ethernet is a network protocol that operates at Layers 1 and 2 of the TCP/IP–OSI architecture. Ethernet, the world's most popular LAN protocol, is used on WANs as well. **p. 70**

Exabyte. 1,024 GB. **p. 58**

Executive support systems (ESS). Information systems that support strategic processes. **p. 134**

Experimentation. A careful and reasoned analysis of an opportunity, envisioning potential products or solutions or applications of technology, and then developing those ideas that seem to have the most promise, consistent with the resources you have. **p. 9**

eXtensible Markup Language (XML). An important document standard that separates document content, structure, and presentation; eliminates problems in HTML. Used for Web Services and many other applications. **p. 82**

Fields. Also called *columns*; groups of bytes in a database table. A database table has multiple columns that are used to represent the attributes of an entity. Examples are *PartNumber*, *EmployeeName*, and *SalesDate*. **p. 93**

File. A group of similar rows or records. In a database, sometimes called a *table*. **p. 93**

File server. A computer that stores files. **p. 285**

File Transfer Protocol (FTP). A Layer-5 protocol used to copy files from one computer to another. In interorganizational transaction processing, FTP enables users to exchange large files easily. **p. 75**

Finished goods inventory. Completed products awaiting delivery to customers. **p. 188**

Five-component framework. The five fundamental components of an information system—computer hardware, software, data, procedures, and people—that are present in every information system, from the simplest to the most complex. **p. 31**

Five forces model. Model, proposed by Michael Porter, that assesses industry characteristics and profitability by means of five competitive forces—bargaining power of suppliers, threat of substitution, bargaining power of customers, rivalry among firms, and threat of new entrants. **p. 12**

Flash. An add-on to browsers that was developed by Adobe and is useful for providing animation, movies, and other advanced graphics within a browser. **p. 82**

Foreign key. A column or group of columns used to represent relationships. Values of the foreign key match values of the primary key in a different (foreign) table. **p. 96**

Form. Data entry forms are used to read, insert, modify, and delete database data. **p. 100**

Foursquare. A mobile Web application that enables registered users to connect with friends and share their location. **p. 317**

FTP (File Transfer Protocol). A Layer-5 protocol used to copy files from one computer to another. In interorganizational transaction processing, FTP enables users to exchange large files easily. **p. 75**

Gigabyte (GB). 1,024 MB. **p. 58**

Google Analytics. A Web 2.0 program from Google that enables businesses to collect Web traffic data on their Web sites. **p. 320**

Google Docs. A version-management system for sharing documents and spreadsheet data. Documents are stored on a Google server, from which users can access and simultaneously see and edit the documents. **p. 286**

Google Talk. An application by Google that also has video-conferencing capabilities. **p. 284**

Gramm-Leach-Bliley (GLB) Act. Passed by Congress in 1999, this act protects consumer financial data stored by financial institutions, which are defined as banks, securities firms, insurance companies, and organizations that provide financial advice, prepare tax returns, and provide similar financial services. **p. 410**

Granularity. The level of detail in data. Customer name and account balance is large-granularity data. Customer name, balance, and the order details and payment history of every customer order is smaller granularity. **p. 360**

Hacking. Occurs when a person gains unauthorized access to a computer system. Although some people hack for the sheer joy of doing it, other hackers invade systems for the malicious purpose of stealing or modifying data. **p. 394**

Health Insurance Portability and Accountability Act (HIPAA) The privacy provisions of this 1996 act give individuals the right to access health data created by doctors and other healthcare providers. HIPAA also sets rules and limits on who can read and receive a person's health information. **p. 410**

Hot site. A remote processing center run by a commercial disaster-recovery service that provides equipment a company would need to continue operations after a disaster. **p. 408**

HTML (Hypertext Markup Language). A language that defines structure and layout of Web page content. An HTML tag is a notation used to define a data element for display or other purposes. **p. 80**

HTTPS. A secure version of HTTP. **p. 400**

Human capital. The investment in human knowledge and skills with the expectation of future returns in the marketplace. **p. 326**

Human resources. Organizational process that assesses the motivations and skills of employees; creates job positions; investigates employee complaints; and staffs, trains, and evaluates personnel. **p. 137**

Hypertext Transfer Protocol (HTTP). A Layer-5 protocol used to process Web pages. **p. 74**

Identification. The process whereby an information system identifies a user by requiring the user to sign on with a user name and password. **p. 398**

Identifier. An attribute (or group of attributes) whose value is associated with one and only one entity instance. **p. 105**

Industry-specific platform. An ERP system configuration that is appropriate for a particular industry, such as retail, manufacturing, or health care. **p. 175**

Infor. A company that pursued an acquisition strategy to consolidate many product offerings under one sales and marketing organization. Infor sells an ERP product for just about anyone in just about any industry. **p. 173**

Information. (1) Knowledge derived from data, where *data* is defined as recorded facts or figures; (2) data presented in a meaningful context; (3) data processed by summing, ordering, averaging, grouping, comparing, or other similar operations; (4) a difference that makes a difference. **p. 36**

Information silos. Islands of automation; information systems that work in isolation from one another. **p. 143**

Information system (IS). A group of components that interact to produce information. **p. 31**

Information systems security. The process of protecting information systems vulnerabilities from threats by creating appropriate safeguards. **p. 392**

Inherent processes. Process designs included in an ERP product that may be implemented by the organization. **p. 166**

Internal control. Systematically limiting the actions and behaviors of employees, processes, and systems within the organization to safeguard assets and to achieve objectives. **p. 192**

Internet Corporation for Assigned Names and Numbers (ICANN). The organization responsible for managing the assignment of public IP addresses and domain names for use on the Internet. Each public IP address is unique across all computers on the Internet. **p. 76**

Internet service provider (ISP). An ISP provides users with Internet access. An ISP provides a user with a legitimate Internet address; it serves as the user's gateway to the Internet; and it passes communications back and forth between the user and the Internet. ISPs also pay for the Internet. They collect money from their customers and pay access fees and other charges on the users' behalf. **p. 71**

Interorganizational information system. Information systems that support processes and activities that span two or more independent organizations. **p. 245**

Inventory turnover. The number of times inventory is sold in a given period, commonly a year. **p. 192**

Invoice. An itemized bill. **p. 189**

iOS. The operating system used on the iPhone, iPad, and iPod Touch. **p. 62**

IP (Internet Protocol). A Layer-3 protocol. As the name implies, IP is used on the Internet, but it is used on many other internets as well. The chief purpose of IP is to route packets across an internet. **p. 75**

IP address. A series of dotted decimals in a format like 192.168.2.28 that identifies a unique device on a network or internet. With the IPv4 standard, IP addresses have 32 bits. With the IPv6 standard, IP addresses have 128 bits. Today, IPv4 is more common, but it will likely be supplanted by IPv6 in the future. With IPv4, the decimal between the dots can never exceed 255. **p. 76**

IP spoofing. A type of spoofing whereby an intruder uses another site's IP address as if it were that other site. **p. 76**

IPv4. The most commonly used Internet layer protocol. **p. 394**

IPv6. An Internet layer protocol created to provide for more IP addresses and other benefits. **p. 76**

Just in time (JIT). A delivery method that synchronizes manufacturing and supply so that materials arrive just as the manufacturing process requires them. **p. 163**

Key. (1) A column or group of columns that identifies a unique row in a table. Also referred to as a Primary Key. (2) A number used to encrypt data. The encryption algorithm applies the key to the original message to produce the coded message. Decoding (decrypting) a message is similar; a key is applied to the coded message to recover the original text. **p. 94**

Key escrow. A control procedure whereby a trusted party is given a copy of a key used to encrypt database data. **p. 403**

Kilobyte (K). 1,024 bytes. **p. 58**

LAN device. A computing device that includes important networking components, including a switch, a router, a DHCP server, and other elements. **p. 69**

Library. In version-control collaboration systems, a shared directory that allows access to various documents by means of permissions. **p. 288**

License. Agreement that stipulates how a program can be used. Most specify the number of computers on which the program can be installed, some specify the number of users that can connect to and use the program remotely. Such agreements also stipulate limitations on the liability of the software vendor for the consequences of errors in the software. **p. 63**

Linkages. Process interactions across value chains. Linkages are important sources of efficiencies and are readily supported by information systems. **p. 17**

Linux. A version of Unix that was developed by the open source community. The open source community owns Linux, and there is no fee to use it. Linux is a popular operating system for Web servers. **p. 62**

Local area network (LAN). A network that connects computers that reside in a single geographic location on the premises of the company that operates the LAN. The number of connected computers can range from two to several hundred. **p. 68**

Location-based marketing. The process of integrating customer location data into marketing activites. **p. 332**

Lost update problem. An issue in multiuser database processing in which two or more users try to make changes to the data but the database cannot make all those changes because it was not designed to process changes from multiple users. **p. 102**

Mac OS. An operating system developed by Apple Computer, Inc., for the Macintosh. The current version is Mac OS X. Macintosh computers are used primarily by graphic artists and

workers in the arts community. Mac OS was developed for the PowerPC, but as of 2006 runs on Intel processors as well. **p. 62**

Machine code. Code that has been compiled from source code and is ready to be processed by a computer. **p. 66**

Main memory. A set of cells in which each cell holds a byte of data or instruction; each cell has an address, and the CPU uses the addresses to identify particular data items. **p. 57**

Maintenance. In the context of information systems, (1) to fix the system to do what it was supposed to do in the first place or (2) to adapt the system to a change in requirements. **p. 389**

Malware. Viruses, worms, Trojan horses, spyware, and adware. **p. 401**

Management (of MIS). The creation, monitoring, and adapting of processes, information systems, and information. **p. 10**

Management information system (MIS). An information system that helps businesses achieve their goals and objectives. **p. 134**

Managerial processes. Processes that concern resource use; includes planning, assessing, and analyzing the resources used by the company in pursuit of its strategy. **p. 134**

Manufacturing resource planning (MRP II). A manufacturing information system that schedules equipment and facilities and provides financial tracking of activities. **p. 163**

Many-to-many (N:M) relationship. Relationships involving two entity types in which an instance of one type can relate to many instances of the second type, and an instance of the second type can relate to many instances of the first. For example, the relationship between Student and Class is N:M. One student may enroll in many classes, and one class may have many students. Contrast with *one-to-many relationships*. **p. 107**

Margin (of a business process). The difference between the value of outputs in a business process and the cost of the process. **p. 15**

Market basket analysis. An unsupervised data mining analysis that helps determine sales patterns. It shows the products that customers tend to buy together. **p. 355**

Mashup. The combining of output from two or more Web sites into a single user experience. **p. 316**

Material requirements planning (MRP). Software used to efficiently manage inventory, production, and labor. **p. 163**

Maximum cardinality. The maximum number of entities that can be involved in a relationship. Common examples of maximum cardinality are 1:N, N:M, and 1:1. **p. 107**

Measures (metrics). Quantities that are assigned to attributes; in the process context, measures help assess achievement of process objectives. **p. 138**

Megabyte (MB). 1,024 KB. **p. 58**

Memory swapping. The movement of programs and data into and out of memory. If a computer has insufficient memory for its workload, such swapping will degrade system-performance. **p. 59**

Merchant company. In e-commerce, a company that takes title to the goods it sells. The company buys goods and resells them. **p. 245**

Metadata. Data that describe data. **p. 96**

Microsoft Dynamics. A suite of ERP products licensed by Microsoft. The suite is composed of four ERP products, all obtained via acquisition: AX, Nav, GP, and SL. AX and Nav have the most capability, GP is smaller and easier to use. Although Dynamics has over 80,000 installations, the future of SL is particularly cloudy; Microsoft outsources the maintenance of the code to provide continuing support to existing customers. **p. 173**

Microsoft Lync. A communication tool that provides IM, audio and video conferencing, a shared whiteboard for team members to write on, and other shared facilities. **p. 284**

Microsoft SharePoint. A version-control application that includes many collaboration features and functions, including document check-in/checkout, surveys, discussion forums, and workflow. **p. 291**

Minimum cardinality. The minimum number of entities that must be involved in a relationship. **p. 107**

Modules. A suite of similar applications in an ERP system; examples include manufacturing and finance. **p. 175**

Moore's Law. A law, created by Gordon Moore, stating that the number of transistors per square inch on an integrated chip doubles every 18 months. Moore's prediction has proved generally accurate in the 40 years since it was made. Sometimes this law is stated that the performance of a computer doubles every 18 months. Although not strictly true, this version gives the gist of the idea. **p. 6**

Multiparty text chat. A synchronous virtual meeting in which participants meet at the same time and communicate by typing comments over a communication network. **p. 284**

Mutinous movement. An extension of bad reviews where prosumers revolt and use an organization's site in damaging ways. **p. 331**

MySQL. A popular open source DBMS product that is license-free for most applications. **p. 97**

NetWeaver. The SAP application platform that connects SAP to hardware, third-party software, and output devices. NetWeaver provides an SOA interface that eases the integration of SAP with non-SAP applications. **p. 176**

Network. A collection of computers that communicate with one another over transmission lines. **p. 68**

Network interface card (NIC). A hardware component on each device on a network (computer, printer, etc.) that connects the device's circuitry to the communications line. The NIC works together with programs in each device to implement Layers 1 and 2 of the TCP/IP–OSI hybrid protocol. **p. 69**

Nonmerchant company. An E-commerce company that arranges for the purchase and sale of goods without ever owning or taking title to those goods. **p. 245**

Nonvolatile (memory). Memory that preserves data contents even when not powered (e.g., magnetic and optical disks). With such devices, you can turn the computer off and back on, and the contents will be unchanged. **p. 59**

Normal forms. A classification of tables according to their characteristics and the kinds of problems they have. **p. 110**

Normalization. The process of converting poorly structured tables into two or more well-structured tables. **p. 108**

Object-relational database. A type of database that stores both object-oriented programming objects and relational data. Rarely used in commercial applications. **p. 96**

Objective. A goal that people in an organization have chosen to pursue. In the process context, managers develop and measure objectives for each process. Objectives fall into two categories: effectiveness and efficiency. **p. 134**

Office 365. A new Microsoft suite that includes Lync, Exchange (e-mail), SharePoint Online, and Office 2010. Office 365 is hosted as a service on Microsoft's computing infrastructure. **p. 291**

Office Web Apps. License-free Web application versions of Word, Excel, PowerPoint, and OneNote available on SkyDrive. **p. 287**

OLAP. See *Online analytical processing.* **p. 351**

OLAP cube. A presentation of an OLAP measure with associated dimensions. The reason for this term is that some products show these displays using three axes, like a cube in geometry. Same as *OLAP report.* **p. 352**

OLAP dimension. A characteristic of a measure. Purchase date, customer type, customer location, and sales region are all examples of dimensions. **p. 352**

OLAP measure. The data item of interest in an OLAP report. It is the item that is to be summed or averaged or otherwise processed. Total sales, average sales, and average cost are examples of measures. **p. 352**

OMIS model. A process to help improve business processes. The model requires that each process have explicitly stated objectives, the measures be clearly identified and improved, and information systems be considered to help achieve the objectives. **p. 137**

One-to-many (1:N) relationship. Relationships involving two entity types in which an instance of one type can relate to many instances of the second type, but an instance of the second type can relate to at most one instance of the first. For example, the relationship between *Department* and *Employee* is 1:N. A department may relate to many employees, but an employee relates to at most one department. **p. 107**

Online analytical processing (OLAP). An interactive type of reporting analysis that provides the ability to sum, count, average, and perform other simple arithmetic operations on groups of data. Such reports are interactive because users can change the format of the reports while viewing them. **p. 351**

Online Transactional Processing (OLTP). An operational process that uses an information system for the processing and reporting of day-to-day operational events. Order processing is a common OLTP example. **p. 364**

Operating system (OS). A computer program that controls the computer's resources: It manages the contents of main memory, processes keystrokes and mouse movements, sends signals to the display monitor, reads and writes disk files, and controls the processing of other programs. **p. 59**

Operational database. A data store that contains data produced and consumed by operational processes. **p. 358**

Operational decisions. Decisions that concern the day-to-day activities of an organization. **p. 277**

Operational processes. Common, routine, everyday business processes such as Procurement and Sales. **p. 134**

Optical fiber cable. A type of cable used to connect the computers, printers, switches, and other devices on a LAN. The signals on such cables are light rays, and they are reflected inside the glass core of the optical fiber cable. The core is surrounded by a *cladding* to contain the light signals, and the cladding, in turn, is wrapped with an outer layer to protect it. **p. 69**

Oracle Database. A popular, enterprise-class DBMS product from Oracle Corporation. **p. 97**

Organizational feasibility. Whether an information system fits within an organization's customer, culture, or legal requirements. **p. 385**

Ought-to-be diagram. A diagram of suggested improvements to a current process. **p. 141**

Output hardware. Hardware that displays the results of the computer's processing. Consists of video displays, printers, audio speakers, overhead projectors, and other special-purpose devices, such as large, flatbed plotters. **p. 57**

Packet. A small piece of an electronic message that has been divided into chunks that are sent separately and reassembled at their destination. **p. 75**

Parallel installation. A type of system conversion in which the new system runs in parallel with the old one for a while. Parallel installation is expensive because the organization incurs the costs of running both systems. **p. 389**

Parallel workflow. The condition that exists when two or more workers perform a task concurrently. A common example is concurrent review of a document. **p. 296**

Payload. The program codes of a virus that causes unwanted or hurtful actions, such as deleting programs or data, or even worse, modifying data in ways that are undetected by the user. **p. 401**

People. As part of the five-component framework, one of the five fundamental components of an information system; includes those who operate and service the computers, those who maintain the data, those who support the networks, and those who use the system. **p. 31**

Personal DBMS. DBMS products designed for smaller, simpler database applications. Such products are used for personal or small workgroup applications that involve fewer than 100 users, and normally fewer than 15. Today, Microsoft Access is the only prominent personal DBMS. **p. 103**

Personal identification number (PIN). A form of authentication whereby the user supplies a number that only he or she knows. **p. 398**

Petabyte. 1,024 EB. **p. 58**

Phased installation. A type of system conversion in which the new system is installed in pieces across the organization(s). Once a given piece works, then the organization installs and tests another piece of the system, until the entire system has been installed. **p. 389**

Phisher. An individual or organization that spoofs legitimate companies in an attempt to illegally capture personal data, such as credit card numbers, e-mail accounts, and driver's license numbers. **p. 395**

Phishing. A technique for obtaining unauthorized data that uses pretexting via e-mail. The *phisher* pretends to be a legitimate company and sends an e-mail requesting confidential data, such as account numbers, Social Security numbers, account passwords, and so forth. **p. 393**

Pilot installation. A type of system conversion in which the organization implements the entire system on a limited portion of the business. The advantage of pilot implementation is that if the system fails, the failure is contained within a limited boundary. This reduces exposure of the business and also protects the new system from developing a negative reputation throughout the organization(s). **p. 388**

Plunge installation. A type of system conversion in which the organization shuts off the old system and starts the new system. If the new system fails, the organization is in trouble: Nothing can be done until either the new system is fixed or the old system is reinstalled. Because of the risk, organizations should avoid this conversion style if possible. Sometimes called *direct installation*. **p. 389**

Posting. When the legal ownership of a material that has been sold is transferred from the seller to the buyer. **p. 238**

Pretexting. A technique for gathering unauthorized information in which someone pretends to be someone else. A common scam involves a telephone caller who pretends to be from a credit card company and claims to be checking the validity of credit card numbers. Phishing is also a form of pretexting. **p. 393**

Price elasticity. A measure of the sensitivity in demand to changes in price. It is the ratio of the percentage change in quantity divided by the percentage change in price. **p. 247**

Primary activities. In Porter's value chain model, the fundamental activities that create value: inbound logistics, operations, outbound logistics, marketing/sales, and service. **p. 15**

Primary Key. Also called a key. **p. 95**

Privacy Act of 1974. Legislation that provides protections to individuals regarding records maintained by the U.S. government. **p. 10**

Private IP address. A type of IP address used within private networks and internets. Private IP addresses are assigned and managed by the company that operates the private network or internet. **p. 76**

Problem. A perceived difference between what is and what ought to be. **p. 280**

Procedures. Instructions for humans. One of the five fundamental components of an information system. **p. 31**

Process blueprint. In an ERP application, a comprehensive set of inherent processes for all organizational activities, each of which is documented with diagrams that use a set of standardized symbols. **p. 166**

Procurement. Obtaining goods and services. **p. 135**

Procurement process. The operational process for acquiring goods and services. **p. 186**

Prosumers. Users who contribute to a Web site. **p. 316**

Protocol. A standardized means for coordinating an activity between two or more entities. **p. 68**

Public IP address. An IP address used on the Internet. Such IP addresses are assigned to major institutions in blocks by the

Internet Corporation for Assigned Names and Numbers (ICANN). Each IP address is unique across all computers on the Internet. **p. 76**

Public key/private key. A special version of asymmetric encryption that is popular on the Internet. With this method, each site has a public key for encoding messages and a private key for decoding them. **p. 400**

Purchase order (PO). A written document requesting delivery of a specified quantity of a product or service in return for payment. **p. 187**

Purchase requisition (PR). An internal company document that issues a request for a purchase. When accepted, data from the purchase requisition is used in the purchase order. **p. 194**

Query. A request for data from a database. **p. 101**

Quick Launch. A partial list of resources contained within a SharePoint site. **p. 291**

R/3. One of the most best known versions of SAP. It was the first truly integrated system that was able to support most of organizations' major operational processes. **p. 176**

Radio-frequency identification (RFID). Computer chips that help identify and track items. As small as, and soon to be as cheap as, a postage stamp, RFID chips broadcast data to receivers that can display and record the broadcast data. **p. 201**

RAM (random access memory). Main memory consisting of cells that hold data or instructions. Each cell has an address that the CPU uses to read or write data. Memory locations can be read or written in any order, hence the term *random access*. RAM memory is almost always volatile. **p. 57**

Raw materials inventory. A repository of parts and subassemblies procured from suppliers that are used to produce products to be stored in the finished goods inventory. **p. 188**

Record. Also called a *row*, a group of columns in a database table. **p. 93**

Regression analysis. Supervised data mining analysis that estimates the values of parameters in a linear equation. Used to determine the relative influence of variables on an outcome and also to predict future values of that outcome. **p. 355**

Relation. The more formal name for a database table. **p. 96**

Relational database. Database that carries its data in the form of tables and that represents relationships using foreign keys. **p. 96**

Relationship. An association among entities or entity instances in an E-R model or an association among rows of a table in a relational database. **p. 106**

Report. A presentation of data in a structured or meaningful context. **p. 100**

Reporting. A process that uses simple statistical analysis to uncover patterns in a large database of data in order to improve assessment. **p. 345**

Repository. A collection of records, usually implemented as a database. **p. 30**

Returns management process. A process that manages the returns of faulty products for businesses. **p. 198**

RFM analysis. A type of reporting analysis that ranks customers according to the recency, frequency, and monetary value of their purchases. **p. 350**

Role. A set of activities in a business process; resources are assigned to roles. **p. 29**

Roll up. To compile, total, and summarize data. For example, daily sales are "rolled up" into monthly sales. In accounting systems, transactions are "rolled up" into common accounting reports such as balance sheets and income statements. **p. 191**

Router. A special-purpose computer that moves network traffic from one node on a network to another. **p. 75**

Rows. Also called *records*, a group of columns in a database table. **p. 93**

Sales. An operational outbound process comprised of three main activities—Sell, Ship, and Payment. **p. 230**

Salesforce.com. The preeminent cloud-based CRM vendor. **p. 243**

SAP AG. The world's most successful ERP vendor. SAP AG is the third largest software company in the world. The core business of SAP AG is selling licenses for its SAP software solutions and related services. In addition, it offers consulting, training, and other services for its software solutions. **p. 174**

SAP Business Suite. The new name for SAP's integrated software platform. The SAP Business Suite runs on NetWeaver. **p. 176**

Sarbanes-Oxley Act (SOX). A federal law requiring companies to exercise greater control over their financial processes. **p. 164**

Schedule feasibility. Whether an information system will be able to be developed on the timetable needed. **p. 385**

Secure Socket Layer (SSL). A protocol that uses both asymmetric and symmetric encryption. SSL is a protocol layer that works between Levels 4 (transport) and 5 (application) of the TCP–OSI protocol architecture. When SSL is in use, the browser address will begin with *https://*. The most recent version of SSL is called TLS. **p. 400**

Security program. A systematic plan by which an organization addresses security issues; consists of three components: senior management involvement, safeguards of various kinds, and incident response. **p. 396**

Security vulnerability. A potential challenge to the integrity of information systems from one of three sources: human error and mistakes, malicious human activity, and natural events and disasters. **p. 392**

Sequential workflow. The condition that exists when two or more workers perform a task one at a time. A common example is the sequential review of a document. **p. 296**

Server(s). A computer that provides some type of service, such as hosting a database, running a blog, publishing a Web site, or selling goods. Server computers are faster, larger, and more powerful than client computers. **p. 60**

Server farm. A large collection of server computers that coordinates the activities of the servers, usually for commercial purposes. **p. 60**

Server tier. In the three-tier architecture, the tier that consists of computers that run Web servers to generate Web pages and other data in response to requests from browsers. Web servers also process application programs. **p. 79**

Service. In SOA, a repeatable task that a business needs to perform. **p. 144**

SharedView. A Microsoft program that enables one person to share his or her desktop with a small group of others using the Internet. Useful for online meetings. **p. 284**

SharePoint site. A workflow site, created in Microsoft's collaboration tool SharePoint, that enables team members to define workflows for their group. The software that runs the site will send e-mails to team members requesting reviews, create task lists defined for the workflow, check documents in, mark tasks as complete, e-mail the next person in the workflow, and e-mail copies of all correspondence to the workflow leader, who can use this capability to ensure that all teammates perform the work they are requested to do. **p. 291**

Silverlight. A browser add-on that was developed by Microsoft to enhance browser features to improve the user interface; to include movies, audio, animation in Web sites; and to provide greater programmer control of user activity. **p. 82**

Simple Mail Transfer Protocol (SMTP). A Layer-5 architecture used to send e-mail. Normally used in conjunction with other Layer-5 protocols (POP3, IMAP) for receiving e-mail. **p. 75**

Six Sigma. A popular strategy for process improvement that seeks to improve process outputs by removing causes of defects and minimizing variability in the process. **p. 141**

Small office/home office (SOHO). A business office with usually fewer than 10 employees; often located in the business professional's home. **p. 69**

Sniffing. A technique for intercepting computer communications. With wired networks, sniffing requires a physical connection to the network. With wireless networks, no such connection is required. **p. 394**

SOA (service-oriented architecture). A design in which every activity is modeled as an encapsulated service, and exchanges among those services are governed by standards. **p. 144**

SOA standards. Processing standards used to implement service-oriented architecture. They include XML, WSDL, SOAP, and numerous other standards. **p. 147**

Social capital. The investment in social relations with expectation of future returns in the marketplace. **p. 326**

Social CRM. An information system that helps a company collect customer data from social media and share it among their customer facing processes. **p. 242**

Social engineering. A category of threats that involve manipulating a person or group to unknowingly release confidential information. **p. 393**

Social graph. A network of personal interdependencies, such as friendships, common interests, or kinship, on a social media application. **p. 323**

Social media. Any Web application that depends on user-generated content. **p. 316**

Social media monitoring. A Web-based information system used to help monitor and track mentions of products and brands on social media platforms. **p. 332**

Source code. Computer code as written by humans and that is understandable by humans. Source code must be translated into machine code before it can be processed. **p. 66**

Spoofing. When someone pretends to be someone else with the intent of obtaining unauthorized data. If you pretend to be your professor, you are spoofing your professor. **p. 394**

Spyware. Programs installed on the user's computer without the user's knowledge or permission that reside in the background and, unknown to the user, observe the user's actions and keystrokes, modify computer activity, and report the user's activities to sponsoring organizations. Malicious spyware captures keystrokes to obtain user names, passwords, account numbers, and other sensitive information. Other spyware is used for marketing analyses, observing what users do, Web sites visited, products examined and purchased, and so forth. **p. 401**

SQL Injection Attacks. A technique used to compromise database data in which SQL code is unknowingly processed by a Web page. **p. 403**

SQL Server. A popular enterprise-class DBMS product from Microsoft. **p. 97**

Strategic decision. Decision that concerns broader-scope, organizational issues. **p. 278**

Strategic processes. Business processes that seek to resolve issues that have a long-range impact on the organization. These processes have a broad scope and impact most of the firm. **p. 134**

Strength of a relationship. In the theory of social capital, the likelihood that a person or other organization in a relationship will do something that will benefit the organization. **p. 328**

Structured processes. Formally defined, standardized processes that support day-to-day operations such as accepting a return, placing an order, computing a sales commission, and so forth. **p. 41**

Structured Query Language (SQL). An international standard language for processing database data. **p. 98**

Supervised data mining. A form of data mining in which data miners develop a model prior to the analysis and apply statistical techniques to data to estimate values of the parameters of the model. **p. 358**

Supplier evaluation. A strategic process that determines the criteria for supplier selection and adds and removes suppliers from the list of approved suppliers. **p. 198**

Supplier relationship management (SRM) process. A process that automates, simplifies, and accelerates a variety of supply chain processes. SRM is a management process that helps companies reduce procurement costs, build collaborative supplier relationships, better manage supplier options, and improve time to market. **p. 198**

Supply chain management (SCM). The design, planning, execution, and integration of all supply chain processes. SCM uses a collection of tools, techniques, and management activities to help businesses develop integrated supply chains that support organizational strategy. **p. 198**

Support activities. In Porter's value chain model, the activities that contribute indirectly to value creation: procurement, technology, human resources, and the firm's infrastructure. **p. 15**

Surrogate key Unique identifier in the DBMS. **p. 113**

Switch. A special-purpose computer that receives and transmits data across a network. **p. 69**

Symmetric encryption. An encryption method whereby the same key is used to encode and to decode the message. **p. 399**

Synchronous communication. Information exchange that occurs when all members of a work team meet at the same time, such as face-to-face meetings or conference calls. **p. 283**

System conversion. The process of converting business activity from the old system to the new. **p. 388**

Systems analysts. IS professionals who understand both business and technology. They are active throughout the systems development process and play a key role in moving the project from conception to conversion and, ultimately, maintenance. Systems analysts integrate the work of the programmers, testers, and users. **p. 385**

Systems development. The process of creating and maintaining information systems. It is sometimes called *systems analysis and design*. **p. 384**

Systems development life cycle (SDLC). The classical process used to develop information systems. These basic tasks of systems development are combined into the following phases: system definition, requirements analysis, component design, implementation, and system maintenance (fix or enhance). **p. 384**

Systems thinking. The mental process of making one or more models of the components of a system and connecting the inputs and outputs among those components into a sensible whole, one that explains the phenomenon observed. **p. 8**

Table. Also called a *file*, a group of similar rows or records in a database. **p. 93**

Tag. In markup languages such as HTML and XML, notation used to define a data element for display or other purposes. **p. 80**

Team survey. A form of asynchronous communication in which one team member creates a list of questions and other team members respond. Microsoft SharePoint has built-in survey capability. **p. 285**

Technical feasibility. Whether existing information technology will be able to meet the needs of a new information system. **p. 385**

Technical safeguard. Safeguard that involves the hardware and software components of an information system. **p. 398**

Technology development. A support activity in the value chain; includes designing, testing, and developing technology in support of the primary activities of an organization. **p. 137**

Terabyte (TB). 1,024 GB. **p. 58**

Test plan. Groups of sequences of actions that users will take when using the new system. **p. 388**

Thick client. A software application that requires programs other than just the browser on a user's computer; that is, that requires code on both client and server computers. **p. 64**

Thin client. A software application that requires nothing more than a browser and can be run on only the user's computer. **p. 64**

Threat. A challenge to information systems security. **p. 392**

Three-tier architecture. Architecture used by most e-commerce server applications. The tiers refer to three different classes of computers. The user tier consists of users' computers that have browsers that request and process Web pages. The server tier consists of computers that run Web servers and in the process generate Web pages and other data in response to requests from browsers. Web servers also process application programs. The third tier is the database tier, which runs the DBMS that processes the database. **p. 79**

Three-way match. The activity within the procurement process that ensures that the data on the invoice matches the data on the purchase order and the goods receipt. **p. 189**

Traditional capital. Investments into resources such as factories, machines, manufacturing equipment, and the like with the expectation of future returns in the market. **p. 326**

Train the trainer. Training sessions in which vendors train the organization's employees to become in-house trainers in order to improve training quality and reduce training expenses. **p. 165**

Transaction processing system (TPS). An information system that supports operational decision making. **p. 134**

Transmission Control Protocol (TCP). The most important protocol in the transport layer. One of its most easily understood functions is that TCP programs break internet traffic into pieces and send each piece along its way. This protocol works with TCP programs on other devices in the internet to ensure that all of the pieces arrive at their destination. **p. 75**

Transmission Control Protocol/Internet Protocol (TCP/IP) architecture. A protocol architecture having four layers; forms the basis for the TCP/IP–OSI architecture used by the Internet. **p. 75**

Transport Layer Security (TLS). A protocol, using both asymmetric and symmetric encryption, that works between Levels 4 (transport) and 5 (application) of the TCP–OSI protocol architecture. TLS is the new name for a later version of SSL. **p. 400**

Trojan horse. Virus that masquerades as a useful program or file. A typical Trojan horse appears to be a computer game, an MP3 music file, or some other useful, innocuous program. **p. 401**

Uniform resource locator (URL). A document's address on the Web. URLs begin on the right with a top-level domain, and, moving left, include a domain name and then are followed by optional data that locates a document within that domain. **p. 77**

Unix. An operating system developed at Bell Labs in the 1970s. It has been the workhorse of the scientific and engineering communities since then. **p. 62**

Unshielded twisted pair (UTP) cable. A type of cable used to connect the computers, printers, switches, and other devices on a LAN. A UTP cable has four pairs of twisted wire. A device called an RJ-45 connector is used to connect the UTP cable into NIC devices. **p. 69**

Unsupervised data mining. A form of data mining whereby the analysts do not create a model or hypothesis before running the analysis. Instead, they apply the data mining technique to the data and observe the results. With this method, analysts create hypotheses after the analysis to explain the patterns found. **p. 358**

User-generated content. Publicly available content created by end users. **p. 316**

User tier. In the three-tier architecture, the tier that consists of computers that have browsers that request and process Web pages. **p. 79**

Value. According to Porter, the amount of money that a customer is willing to pay for a resource, product, or service. **p. 15**

Value chain. A network of value-creating activities. **p. 15**

Version control. Use of software to control access to and configuration of documents, designs, and other electronic versions of products. **p. 288**

Version management. Tracking of changes to documents by means of features and functions that accommodate concurrent work. The means by which version management is done depends on the particular version-management system used; three such systems are wikis, Google Docs, and Windows Live SkyDrive. **p. 286**

Vertical-market application. Software that serves the needs of a specific industry. Examples of such programs are those used by dental offices to schedule appointments and bill patients, those used by auto mechanics to keep track of customer data and customers' automobile repairs, and those used by parts warehouses to track inventory, purchases, and sales. **p. 64**

Videoconferencing. Technology that combines a conference call with video cameras. **p. 284**

Viral. User-generated content, typically a video, that is shared and promoted by individuals on social media outlets in greater than expected volume. **p. 321**

Virtual. Something that appears to exist that does not in fact exist. **p. 82**

Virtual meeting. A meeting in which participants do not meet in the same place and possibly not at the same time. **p. 284**

Virtual private network (VPN). A WAN connection alternative that uses the Internet or a private internet to create the appearance of private point-to-point connections. In the IT world, the term *virtual* means something that appears to exist that does not exist in fact. Here, a VPN uses the public Internet to create the appearance of a private connection. **p. 82**

Virus. A computer program that replicates itself. **p. 401**

Visualization. The use of images, or diagrams, for communicating a message. Simple examples include bar charts and infographics. **p. 362**

Volatile (memory). Data that will be lost when the computer or device is not powered. **p. 59**

WAN wireless. A communications system that provides wireless connectivity to a wide area network. **p. 72**

Web. The Internet-based network of browsers and servers that process HTTP or HTTPS. **p. 75**

Web 2.0. A loose grouping of capabilities, technologies, business models, and philosophies that characterize new and emerging business uses of the Internet. **p. 314**

WebEx. A popular commercial webinar application used in virtual sales presentations. **p. 284**

Web farm. A facility that runs multiple Web servers. Work is distributed among the computers in a Web farm so as to maximize throughput. **p. 79**

Web page. Document encoded in HTML that is created, transmitted, and used using the World Wide Web. **p. 79**

Web server. A program that processes the HTTP protocol and transmits Web pages on demand. Web servers also process application programs. **p. 79**

Web storefront. In e-commerce, a Web-based application that enables customers to enter and manage their orders. **p. 246**

Webinar. A virtual meeting in which attendees view each other on their computer screens. **p. 284**

Wide area network (WAN). A network that connects computers located at different geographic locations. **p. 68**

Wiki. A shared knowledge base in which the content is contributed and managed by the wiki's users. **p. 286**

WiMax. An emerging technology based on the IEEE 802.16 standard. WiMax is designed to deliver the "last mile" of wireless broadband access and could ultimately replace cable and DSL for fixed applications and replace cell phones for nomadic and portable applications. **p. 72**

Windows. An operating system designed and sold by Microsoft. It is the most widely used operating system. **p. 61**

Wireless NIC (WNIC). Devices that enable wireless networks by communicating with wireless access points. Such devices can be cards that slide into the PCMA slot or they can be built-in, onboard devices. WNICs operate according to the 802.11 protocol. **p. 70**

Workflow. A process or procedure by which content is created, edited, used, and disposed. **p. 296**

Workflow control. Use of software and information systems to monitor the execution of a work team's processes; ensures that actions are taken at appropriate times and prohibits the skipping of steps or tasks. **p. 296**

Worm. A virus that propagates itself using the Internet or some other computer network. Worm code is written specifically to infect another computer as quickly as possible. **p. 401**

XML. See *eXtensible Markup Language.* **p. 82**

Index

Note: Page numbers with f indicate figures; those with n indicate footnotes.

A

ABAP, 176
Abstract reasoning, 8
Access, 9, 97, 125
Access point (AP), 70
Account administration, 405–406
  account management in, 405
  help desk policies in, 406
  password management in, 405–406, 406f
Accounting problems
  after SAP procurement process, 196
  in sales process after SAP, 238
  in sales process before SAP, 234
  before SAP procurement process, 191
Account management, 405
Activity, 28, 128, 131n
Actor, 29, 128
Additive manufacturing, 203
Adobe Acrobat, 59, 64
Adobe PageMaker, 64
Adobe Photoshop, 64
AdSense, 319
Adware, 401, 402
AdWords, 318–319
Amazon.com, 49–51, 49f
Amazon Web Services (AWS), 50
Analysts, 166
Analytics. *See* Business intelligence (BI)
Android, 62–63
Angle brackets, 80
Application platform, 176
Application software, 64–66
  acquiring, 66
  categories of, 64f
  defined, 64
  thin *vs.* thick clients and, 64–66, 65f
As-is diagram, 137
As-is model, 380, 381f
Asymmetric digital subscriber lines (ADSL), 72
Asymmetric encryption, 399
Asynchronous communication, 283
AT&T, 72, 89
Attributes, 105
Auction, 246
Augmented reality (AR), 201, 362
Authenticate, 332–333
Authentication, 398–399
Aviation Safety Network (ASN), 125, 126–127f

B

Baby Boomers, 89
Baker, Jerry, 414–415
Baker, Wilma, 414–415
Bickel, Chris, 414–415
Bill of material (BOM), 170
Binary digit (bits), 57
Biometric authentication, 398–399

Bits, 57
BlackBerry OS, 62
Black Eyed Peas, 321
Blog, SharePoint, 295f
Bluetooth, 70
Bot herders, 402–403
Botnets, 402–403
Bots, 402–403
Bottleneck, 200
Broadband, 73
Browsers, 74
B2B (business-to-business), 231
B2C (business-to-consumer), 231, 320
B2G (business-to-government), 246
Bullwhip effect, 199
Bureau of Labor Statistics, 166
Business analyst, 385, 386f
Business intelligence (BI), 340–373
  components of, 358–359
    data, 358–359, 359f
    hardware, 358
    people, 359
    procedures, 359
  informing process and, 343–347 (*See also* Data mining process)
    reporting process and, 345–346, 347f
    in sales process, 344, 345f, 346f
    standardizing, 344–345
  problems with, 359–361
    data, 359–360, 360f
    people, 360–361, 361f
  reasons for, 342–343
  reporting process and, 347–354
    activities and options in, 347–348, 348f
    digital dashboard in, 348, 348f
    interactive reports and (OLAP), 351–353f, 351–354
    noninteractive reports and, 348–351, 349–350f
    RFM analysis and, 350–351, 350f
  SAP, 364–365, 365f
  technology and, 362–363
  Tourism Holdings Limited and, 371–373
  vendors, 363–364, 364f
Business intelligence system, 342–343
Business Objects, 364–365, 365f
Business processes, 131–133
  activities in, 28
  actors in, 29
  changes in, operation of, 382
  components in, creation of, 380, 381
  concepts in, 141–142
  defined, 10, 28, 128
  examples of, 28–30, 131–133
  human resources processes, 133
  inbound logistic processes, 131
  information system's relation to, 32–35
  inherent, in ERP, 166–167
  measures in, 134, 134f
  objectives in, 133, 134f

Business processes (*continued*)
  operations processes and, 131
  outbound logistics processes and, 132
  roles in, 29
  sales and marketing processes and, 132
  service processes and, 132–133
  social media used to improve, 320–325, 320f, 322f
  standardized, 30–31
  technology development processes and, 133
  value chain and, 18–19, 131, 131f
Business process management (BPM), 378–383
  activities of, 378–383, 378f
    creation of process components, 380, 381
    modeling activity, 380
    monitoring activity, 379–380
    operation of process changes, 382
  defined, 378–379
  order of developing, 390–392, 391f
Business Process Management Notation (BPMN), 28–30, 30f
  business processes documented with, 28–30
  model, 29f
  swimlanes in, 29
  symbols, summary of, 30
Business-to-business. *See* B2B
Business-to-consumer. *See* B2C
Business-to-government. *See* B2G
Buy-in, 206
Byte, 57–58, 93

C

Cable modem, 72
Cache memory, 58
Capital, 326
Carbon Creek Gardens, 370
Central Colorado State, 178–179
Central processing unit (CPU), 56–60
  cache memory and, 58
  described, 56–57
  main memory and, 57, 58, 59
  memory swapping and, 59
  multiple, 56
  speed, function, and cost of, 57, 59
Chrome, 59, 74
Clearinghouse, 246
Clearwire, 72, 89
Clickstream data, 360
Client
  defined, 59
  vs. server, 59–60, 60f
Client-server applications, 64–66
Closed source, 66
Cloud-based CRM, 243
Cloud computing, 63
Cluster analysis, 354–355
COBIT (Control Objectives for Information and related Technology), 379
Code injection, 403
Cold site, 408
Collaboration, 9, 274–311
  communication in teams and, 283–285
  content management in, 285–290
  decision-making in, 277–280
  problem-solving in, 280–281
  project management in, 281–283, 282f

skills, 275, 276f
social media, 317, 324–325
  in customer communication process, 324–325
  in promotion process, 324
team, 274, 276–277
warning, 275
workflow controlled by, 296–301
Collaborative team, 274, 276–277
Colorado State University, 416–417
Columns, 93, 94f
Communications speeds, abbreviations used for, 70
Competitive strategy, 14–15, 192, 193f
  Porter's model of, 14–15, 14f
  value chain structure determined by, 15–18
Computer-based information system, 32
Computer criminals, 394
Computer hardware in five-component framework, 31–32, 31f, 33, 35f, 38f
Computer Security Institute, 396, 396f
Conference calls, 284
Configuration, 164–165
Consultant, 166
Content management, 285–290
  shared content with no control, 285–286, 285f
  shared content with version control, 288–289, 290
  shared content with version management, 286–288
Control, 135–136
Conversion rate, 320
Cooperative team, 274
Cost feasibility, 385
CPU. *See* Central processing unit (CPU)
Criteria
  applying to data, 39–40, 39f
  information quality and, 39
Cross-selling, 356
Cross-site scripting (XSS), 403
Crowdsourcing, 324
Crow's feet, 107
Crow's-foot diagram, 107, 107f
Custom-developed software, 66
Customer communication process
  in collaboration social media, 324–325
  in sharing social media, 321–322
Customer-facing processes, 239
Customer relationship management (CRM)
  cloud-based, 243
  defined, 240
  Oracle's, 61
  SAP, 242
  social, 242–243
Customer service processes, 132–133

D

Data
  business intelligence, 358–359, 359f
  clickstream, 360
  communications technology, 89
  computer, 57–58
    binary digits and, 57, 57f
    sizing, 57–58, 58f
  computer hardware and, 57–58
  criteria applied to, 39–40, 39f
  in decision making, 278–279

dirty, 359–360
encryption, 399
in five-component framework, 31–32, 31f, 33, 35f, 38f
incorrect modification of, 394
information quality and, factors in, 38–39
integrity problem, 109
sharing
    in integration of customer-facing processes, 240–241
    in supply chain integration, 198–199, 199f
unauthorized disclosure of, 393–394
Database, 92–97
    administering, 99, 99f
    computer disk drive represented in, 94
    contents of, 93–97
    creating, 98
    development of, user's role in, 112–113
    enterprise resource planning, 165, 165f
    improvements in, 113–117
    processing, 98–99
    purpose of, 92–93
    relational, 96
    tier, 79
    value of, 103
Database administration, 99, 99f
Database application
    components of, 100
    programs, 101, 102f
Database application system, 97–104
    administering database in, 99, 99f
    application programs in, 101, 102f
    creating database and its structures, 98
    database application in, components of, 100
    DBMS and, 97–98, 97f, 103–104
    multiuser processing in, 102
    processing database in, 98–99
    queries in, 101, 101f
    reports in, 100, 100f
Database design. *See* Data models
Database management system (DBMS), 97–98, 97f
    enterprise *vs.* personal, 103–104, 104f
Database processing, 90–127
    database application system in, 97–104
    database design in, 104–112
    database development in, 112–113
    database improvements in, 113–117
    database in, 92–97
Database tier, 79
Data communications technology, 89
Data integrity problem, 109
Data mining process, 354–358
    activities and options in, 355f
    cluster analysis and, 354–355
    convergent disciplines for, 354f
    decision trees and, 356–357
    defined, 347
    market basket analysis, 355–356
    regression analysis and, 355
    supervised and unsupervised, 358
Data models, 104–112
    database design facilitated with, 104–108
        entities and, 105, 106f
        entity-relationship data model and, 105
        relationships and, 106–108, 106f

transformed into database design, 108–112
    data integrity problem in, 109–110
    normalization, 108–110, 108f
    representing relationships in, 110–112, 111–112f
Data warehouse, 358–359
DB2, 97
Decision-making in collaboration, 277–280
    data analyzed in, 279
    data gathered in, 278–279
    incomplete, 279–280
    managerial decisions, 278
    operational decisions, 277–278
    recommendations formulized in, 279
    strategic decisions, 278
    team rules in, 278
Decision support
        systems (DSS), 358
Decision tree, 356–357, 356f
Delicious, 317
Denial of service, 394
Design secure applications, 403
Desktop programs, 64
Digg, 317
Digital certificate, 401
Digital dashboard, 348, 348f
Digital signature, 401
Digital subscriber line (DSL), 71–72
Digital warehouse, 348
Dirty data, 359–360
Disaster-recovery backup sites, 408
Discovery Channel, 322–323
Discussion forums, 285
Disintermediation, 246
Dissemination and enforcement, 405
Document library, 296
Dogfooding, 307
Doing activity, 282
Domain name, 76–77, 76f
Douglas, Todd, 178–179
Drill down, 352
Drive-by sniffers, 394
DSL line, 71
DSL modem, 71–72
Dual processor, 56
Dynamic processes
    characteristics of, 41–42
    defined, 41
    vs. structured processes, 41–42, 42f

E

E-commerce, 246–247
    defined, 245
    market efficiency improved by, 246–247
    merchant companies, 246
    nonmerchant companies, 246
    process integration and, 244–247, 245f
The Economist, 68
Effectiveness, 130
Efficiency, 130
Electronic exchange, 246
E-mail phishing, 395, 395f
E-mail spoofing, 394
Emergence, 245

Encapsulation, 143
Encryption, 399–401
Encryption algorithm, 399
Enterprise application integration (EAI), 158–159, 159f
Enterprise DBMS, 103–104, 104f
Enterprise resource planning (ERP), 156–183
  benefits of, 167–168
  components of, 164–167
    databases, 165, 165f
    hardware, 166
    inherent business processes, 166–167
    people, 166, 167f
    procedures, 165–166
    software, 164–165
  defined, 159
  elements of, 163–164
  enterprise application integration in, 158–159, 159f
  impacts of, 169
  implementation, 160–163, 160f
    decisions, 169–170
    people issues in, 170–171, 170f
    processes as a whole, 162–163, 162–163f
    single process, 160–161f, 160–162
  by industry type, 171, 172f
  international, 172
  by organization size, 171–172
  products, 173–174
  vendors in, 173–174, 173f
    company size and, 174f
    Epicor, 173
    Infor, 173
    Microsoft Dynamics, 173–174
    Oracle, 174
    SAP, 174–177
    top, 173f
Enterprise 2.0, 317
Entity, 105–106, 106f, 115–116, 116f
Entity-relationship (E-R) data model, 105
Entity-relationship (E-R) diagrams, 106–107, 107f
Epicor, 173
Ethernet, 70
Ethics
  in competitive strategy, 20–21
  in database use, 118–119
  in egocentric *vs.* empathetic thinking, 44–45
  in enterprise resource planning, 178–179
  in hardware and software vendors, 84–85
  in process improvement, 144–145
  in procurement, 206–207
  in profiling customers, 366–367
  in sales processes, 248–249
  in security privacy, 410–411
  in social media, 334–335
  virtual, 302–303
EVDO, 72, 89
Executive support system (ESS), 130
Experimentation, 9

F
Facebook
  cost-effective business applications of, 7
  information systems used in, 129, 135
  networking social media and, 322–323
  SkyDrive directories and, 288

  social CRM and, 243
  user content and, 316
  See also Social media
Failure, 389n
Feasibility, 385
Federal Trade Commission (FTC), 363
Fields, 93, 94f
File, 93, 94f
File server, 285
File Transfer Protocol (FTP), 75
Finished goods inventory, 188
Firewalls, 401
Firm infrastructure, Porter's definition of, 17
Five-component framework, 31–32, 31f, 33, 35f, 38f
Five forces model
  industry structure determined with, 192, 192f
  organizational strategy determined with, 12–14, 13f
Flash, 82
Foreign keys, 96
Form, 100
Foursquare, 323, 323f

G
Gates, Bill, 150
Getty Images, 7, 8, 24–25
Gigabyte (GB), 58
GoDaddy.com, 76–77, 76f
Google Analytics, 320
Google Docs, 9, 286–287, 286–287f, 290
Google Docs with Google+, 9
Google Maps, 316, 316f
Google Talk, 284
Gramm-Leach Bliley Act, 410
Granularity, 360
Groupon, 252

H
Hacking, 394
Hackman, Richard, 276
Harding, Matt, 321
Hardware, 56–61
  business intelligence, 358
  business professional's knowledge of, 56–61
  categories of, 56–57, 56f
  client *vs.* server and, 59–61, 60f
  computer components and, 58f
  computer data and, 57–58
  computer function and, 58–59
  defined, 56
  enterprise resource planning, 166
  input, 56, 56f
  memory and, 59
  output, 56f, 57
  processing devices and, 56–57 (*See also* Central processing unit (CPU))
  storage, 56f, 57
  vendors, ethics and, 84–85
Health Insurance Portability and Accountability Act (HIPAA), 410
Hellman & Friedman, LLC, 24–25
Help desk policies, 406
Hertz, 59
Hiring and screening processes
  in networking social media, 323–324
  security considerations in, 404
Horizontal-market application, 64

Hot site, 408
HSDPA, 72, 89
HTML (Hypertext Markup Language), 79, 80–81, 80–81f
HTML5, 82
HTTP (Hypertext Transport Protocol), 74–75
HTTPS, 74–75, 400, 400f
Human capital, 326
Human resource processes, 133
Human resources, Porter's definition of, 17
Human resources safeguards, 404–405, 404f
   dissemination and enforcement, 405
   hiring and screening processes, 404
   position definition, 404
   termination processes, 405
Human security safeguards, 403–409
   account administration, 405–406
   human resources, 404–405
   organizational response to security incidents, 407–409
   security monitoring, 407
   systems procedures, 406–407
Hyperlinks, 81

I

IBM, 63, 64, 97
ICANN (Internet Corporation for Assigned Names
   and Numbers), 76
Identification, 398
Identifier, 105
IEEE 802.3 protocol, 70
IEEE 802.11 protocol, 70, 71
IEEE 802.16 protocol, 89
IEEE 802 Committee, 70
Inbound logistic processes, 131
Incident-response plan, 408–409, 409f
Incorrect data modification, 394
Industry-specific platform, 175
Infor, 173
Information
   defined, 10, 36–37
   location of, 37–38
Information quality, 38–41, 38f
   data factors in, 38–39
   group factors in, 40–41
   human factors in, 39–40, 39f
Information silos, 139–140
   in business intelligence, 346f
   enterprise application integration and, 158–159, 159f
Information systems (IS)
   business processes' relation to, 32–35
   computer-based, 32
   defined, 10, 31
   order of developing, MIS, 391–392
   security, 392–396
     threat types in, 393–394, 396, 396f
     vulnerabilities, 392–393
   value chain used to determine, 18–19
Information technology, 52–89
   hardware and, 56–61
   Internet and, 73–77
   networks and, 68–73
   software and, 61–68
   virtual private networks and, 82–83
   Web server and, 77–82

Informing process, 343–347
   reporting process and, 345–346, 347f
   in sales process, 344, 345f, 346f
   standardizing, 344–345
   See also Data mining process
Inherent processes, 166–167
Input hardware, 56
Interactive Information Systems, 338
Interactive reports. *See* Online analytical processing (OLAP)
Internal control, 192
Internet, 73–77
   application layer protocols and, 74–75
   IP addressing and, 76–77
   as open source asset, 67
   TCP/IP architecture and, 74, 74f
   use of, example of, 73–74, 73f
   vs. internets, 68
Internet Explorer, 74
Internet service provider (ISP), 71
Internets *vs.* the Internet, 68
Interorganizational information systems, 245
Introduction to MIS (course)
   job security and, 7–8
   as most important business class, 6–7
   nonroutine skills learned through, 8–9
Inventory turnover, 192
Invoice, 189
IOS, 62, 65–66
IP (Internet Protocol), 75
IP address, 76–77
   private, 76
   public, 76–77
iPhone, 72–73
IP spoofing, 394
IPv4, 76
IPv6, 76

J

Jasc Corporation Paint Shop Pro, 64
JCPenney, 322–323
Job security, 7–8
Just in time (JIT), 163–164

K

Keeling, Mary, 370
Key
   in database, 94–96
   to encrypt data, 399
   foreign, 96
   primary, 94–96
   public key/private, 400
   surrogate, 113
Key escrow, 403
Kilobyte (K), 58
Kindle, 72
KLOUT, 332

L

LAN device, 69
Layered protocol, 68
Libraries, 288
License, 63
Linkage, 135
Linkages, 17–18

LinkedIn, 323
Linux, 62
LLBean.com, 246
Local area network (LAN), 68–71
   defined, 68
   protocols, 70–71
   SOHO, 69
   summary of, 71f
   wired, 69–70
   wireless, 70
Location-based marketing, 332
Loss of infrastructure, 394, 396
Lost update problem, 102
Lujan, Fabian I., 125

M

Machine code, 66
Mac OS, 62, 63, 65–66
Main memory, 57, 58, 59
   See also Central processing unit (CPU)
Maintenance, 389–390, 390f
Malware, 401–403
   adware, 401, 402
   bots, botnets, and bot herders, 402–403
   defined, 401
   safeguards, 402, 403f
   spyware, 401, 402
   Trojan horses, 401
   viruses, 401
   worms, 401
Management (of MIS), 10–11
Management information systems (MIS), 130
   defined, 10
   information in, 10
   information systems in, 10
   management of, 10–11
   organizational strategy and, 11–12, 12f
   processes in, 10
Management's role in security program, 397
Managerial decisions, 278
Managerial processes, 130
Manufacturing resource planning (MRPII), 163
Many-to-many (N:M) relationship, 107, 111–112, 112f
Margin, 15
Market basket analysis (MBA), 355–356
Marketing processes, 132
Market research process, Web 2.0 and, 319
Marx, Karl, 326
Mashup, 316, 316f
Material requirements planning (MRP), 163
Maximum cardinality, 107–108, 108f
McCaw, Craig, 89
Measures, 134
Megabyte (MB), 58
Memory
   cache, 58
   main, 57, 58, 59
   nonvolatile, 59
   sizes of, 59
   volatile, 59
Memory swapping, 59
Merchant company, 245–246, 246f
Metadata, 96–97, 96f

Metrics, 134
Microsoft, 15, 63, 150–151
Microsoft Academic Alliance, 28n
Microsoft Access. *See* Access
Microsoft Developer Network (MSDN) Academic Alliance (AA), 87–88
Microsoft Dynamics, 173–174
Microsoft Excel, 59, 64
Microsoft Lync, 42, 284, 284f
Microsoft Office 365. *See* Office 365
Microsoft Office 2010, 287
Microsoft PowerPoint, 64, 107
Microsoft SharedView, 284
Microsoft SharePoint, 48, 88–89, 123, 308
   blog, 295f
   Designer, 291
   document actions, 292f
   features, 291–294, 296f
   Quick Launch, 291–292
   shared content with version control and, 289, 289f, 290
   SharePoint site, 291–292, 291f
   for student team projects, 291–296
   student team site, 291f
   survey, 294f
   Tasks list, 293, 293f
   team calendar, 293f
   tools, recommended uses for, 294–296
   Web Links library, 292f
   wiki page, 294f
   for workflow, 296–301
Microsoft SkyDrive, 287–288, 287–288f, 290
Microsoft Skype, 284
Microsoft SQL Server, 97–98
Microsoft Visio, 9, 28, 107
Microsoft Visual Studio, 291
Microsoft Windows. *See* Windows
Microsoft Word, 64
Minimum cardinality, 107–108, 108f
MIS management processes
   business process management and, 378–383
   human security safeguards and, 403–409
   information systems security in, 392–396
   order of developing, 390–392
      business processes first, 390–391, 391f
      information system first, 391–392
      off-the-shelf software and, 392
      in theory *vs.* in practice, 392
   organization's security program in, 396–398
   systems development life cycle and, 384–390
   technical safeguards and, 398–403
Mobile client operating system, 62–63
Modeling activity, 380
Module, 175, 175f
Monitoring activity, 379–380
Moore's Law, 6–7
MSDN AA. *See* Microsoft Developer Network (MSDN) Academic Alliance (AA)
Multiparty text chat, 284
Mutinous movement, 331
MySQL, 97–98, 125

N

Narrowband, 73
National Institute of Standards and Technology (NIST), 397–398, 397f

Netflix, 342–343
NetWeaver, 176
Network, 68–73
　social media marketing, 327, 327f
　traditional marketing, 326–327, 327f
　viral social media marketing, 328, 328f
Networking social media, 317, 322–324
　hiring processes in, 323–324
　promotion processes in, 322–323
Network interface card (NIC), 69, 70
Networks
　Internet and internets, 73–77
　LAN, 68–71
　WAN, 71–73
New England Patriots, 342–343
New processes supported with social media, 325
New York Times, 319
New Zealand Ministry of Tourism, 338
NIST Handbook of security element, 397–398, 397f
N:M relationship (many-to-many), 107, 111–112, 112f
Nonmerchant company, 245–246, 246f
Nonmobile client operating system, 61–62
Nonroutine skills. *See* Reich's four critical skills
Nonvolatile, 59
Normal forms, 110
Normalization, 108–109, 108f
　for data integrity problem, 109–110, 109f
　summary of, 110, 110f
Normalizing the table, 110

O

Oakland Athletics, 342
Objective, 130
Object-relational database, 96n
Office 365, 9, 42, 48, 88–89, 123, 291, 308
　Lync, 42, 284, 284f
Office Web Apps, 287
OLAP cube, 352
OLAP dimension, 352
OLAP measure, 352
OMIS model, 133–134, 133f, 134f
1:N relationship (one-to-many), 110–111, 111f, 116
OneNote, 287
One-to-many (1:N) relationship, 110–111, 111f, 116
Online advertising sales process, Web 2.0 and, 319
Online analytical processing (OLAP), 351–353f, 351–354, 371–373
Online transactional processing (OLTP), 364
Open source software, 66–68
　contributing to, 67
　Internet and, 67
　as viable option, 68
Operating system (OS), 59, 61–63, 62f
　defined, 59, 61
　main memory and, 59
　mobile client, 62–63
　nonmobile client, 61–62
　server, 63
Operational database, 358
Operational decisions, 277–278
Operational processes, 124–151
　defined, 130
　examples of, 128–129, 129f
　　business processes, 131–133

　improving, 133–134
　　information systems used in, 135–138
　　non-information systems processes used in, 136–137, 136f
　　participants and diagrams in, 137–138, 137f–138f
　　process measures used in, 134, 134f
　　process objectives used in, 133, 134f
　　SOA used in, 140, 143
　information systems used in hindering, 139–140
　objectives of, 130, 130f
　scope and characteristics of, 129–130, 129f
Optical fiber cables, 69–70
Oracle, 15, 61, 174
Oracle Database, 97
Organizational feasibility, 385
Organizational response to security incidents, 407–409
Organizational strategy
　five forces model used to determine, 12–14, 13f
　MIS determined by, 11–12, 12f
Ought-to-be diagram, 137
Outbound logistics processes, 132
Output hardware, 56f, 57

P

Packet, 75
Pandora, 78
Panko, Ray, 402
Parallel installation, 389
Parallel workflow, 296
Passwords, 398, 405–406, 406f
Payload, 401
People
　in business intelligence, 359
　　problems with, 360–361, 361f
　in enterprise resource planning, 166, 167f, 170–171, 170f
　in five-component framework, 31–32, 31f, 33, 35f, 38f
Personal DBMS, 103–104, 104f
Personal identification number (PIN), 398
PETCO, 324
Phased installation, 389
Phisher, 395
Phishing, 393, 395
Phishing e-mail, 395, 395f
Phishing screen, 395f
Pickering, Steve, 338
Pilot installation, 388
Planning activity, 282
Plunge installation, 389
PMBOK (Project Management Body of Knowledge) Guide, 281
Porter, Michael, 12
　competitive strategy model and, 14–15, 14f
　five forces model and, 12–14, 192, 192f
　human resources defined by, 17
　technology defined by, 17
　value chain and, 15–19, 16f, 18f
　value defined by, 15
Position definition, 404
Posting, 238
Pozadzides, John, 398
Pretexting, 393
Price elasticity, 247
Primary activities, 15–16, 16f
Primary key, 94–96
Privacy Act of 1974, 411

Private IP address, 76
Problem, 280
Problem-solving in collaboration, 280–281
Procedures
    in business intelligence, 359
    ERP, 165–166
    in five-component framework, 31–32, 31f, 33, 35f, 38f
Process blueprints, 166–167
Process changes, operation of, 382
Process components, creation of, 380, 381
Process concepts, 141–142
Processes. *See* Business processes
Process integration
    with social media, 325
    with Web 2.0, 320
Process measures, 134, 134f
Process objectives, 133, 134f
Procurement, 186
Procurement process, 131
    after SAP, 193–196, 194f
        accounting, 196
        purchasing, 194–195, 194f
        warehouse, 195–196, 195f
    benefits of SAP, 196–197
    changes in, by using SAP, 204–205
    fundamentals of, 186–188, 187–188f
    implementing SAP, 192–193, 193f
    process activities and roles, 186f
    before SAP, 188–189, 189–190f
        accounting problems, 191
        purchasing problems, 191–192
        warehouse problems, 190–191
    SAP improvements in supply chain integration, 197–204
        by increasing process synergy, 199–200, 200f
        problems with emerging technologies and, 200–201, 200f, 203–204
        by sharing data, 198–199, 199f
    supply chain processes in, 198
    supported with SAP, 184–211
    in value chain, 187f
Product Quality Assurance (PQA), 388
Project management in collaboration, 281–283, 282f
    doing activity, 282
    planning activity, 282
    starting activity, 282
    wrapping-up activity, 282–283
Project Management Institute, 281
Project team, 385–386
Promotion process
    in collaboration social media, 324, 324f
    in networking social media, 322–323
    in sharing social media, 321
    in Web 2.0, 318–319, 318f
Prosumer, 316
Protocols
    defined, 68
    FTP, 75
    HTTP, 74–75
    IEEE 802.3 protocol, 70
    IEEE 802.11 protocol, 70, 71
    IEEE 802.16 protocol, 89
    IP (Internet Protocol), 75
    layered, 68, 74–75

SMTP, 75
    TCP, 75
Public IP address, 76–77
Public key/private key, 400
Purchase order (PO), 187–188
Purchase requisition (PR), 194
Purchasing problems
    after SAP procurement process, 194–195, 194f
    before SAP procurement process, 191–192

Q

Quad processor, 56
Query, 101, 101f
Quick Launch, 291–292

R

R/3, 176
RackSpace, 63
Radio-frequency identification (RFID), 201
RAM (random access memory), 57
Ranter, Hugo, 125
Raw materials inventory, 188
Records, 93
Recursive partitioning, 357
Regression analysis, 355
Reich, Robert, 8, 8f, 9
Reich's four critical skills, 8–9
    abstract reasoning, 8
    collaboration, 9
    experimentation, 9
    systems thinking, 8–9
Relation, 96
Relational databases, 96
Relationships, 106–108
    crow's-foot diagram, 107, 107f
    entity-relationship, 106–107, 107f
    maximum and minimum cardinalities shown, 108
    representing, in data models, 110–112, 111–112f, 116
Report, 100, 100f, 115f
Reporting process, 345–346, 347–354, 347f
    activities and options in, 347–348, 348f
    defined, 345
    digital dashboard in, 348, 348f
    interactive reports and (OLAP), 351–353f, 351–354
    noninteractive reports and, 348–351, 349–350f
    RFM analysis and, 350–351, 350f
Repository, 30
Resources, 128
Returns Management process, 198
RFM analysis, 350–351, 350f
Role, 29, 128
Roll up, 191
Router, 75
Rows, 93–96, 95f
RSS reader, 319, 319f

S

Safari, 74
Safeguards. *See* Security
Sales, 230
Salesforce.com, 243, 243f
Sales problems
    in sales process after SAP, 235–236
    in sales process before SAP, 233

Sales process, 132
    after SAP, 235–238, 235f
        accounting problems, 238
        sales problems, 235–236
        warehouse problems, 236–238
    benefits of SAP, 239
    e-commerce integration and, 244–247, 245f
    fundamentals of, 230–231
    implementing SAP, 234–235
    informing process in, 344, 345f, 346f
    before SAP, 231–234, 232f, 233f
        accounting problems, 234
        sales problems, 233
        warehouse problems, 233–234
    SAP improvements in integration of customer-facing processes,
        240–245
        challenges in, 243–244
        by increasing process synergy, 241–242, 242f
        lessons in, 244, 244f
        problems with emerging technologies and, 242–243
        by sharing data, 240–241
    supported with SAP, 228–253
SAP, 9, 41, 43, 174–177
    AG, 174
    business intelligence, 364–365, 365f
    Business Suite, 176
    CRM, 242
    Fortune 500 companies that use, 175
    industry-specific platforms sold by, 175
    inputs and outputs, 175–176, 176f
    modules, 175, 175f
    procurement process supported with, 184–211
    procurement screen, 176f
    sales process supported with, 228–253
    software, 176–177
    University Alliance, 184n
    vs. other ERP systems, 174–177
SAP procurement tutorial, 211, 212–227
    create goods receipt for purchase order, 216–217, 221
    create invoice receipt from vendor, 217–219, 221–222
    create new vendor, 212, 223–224
    create purchase order, 213–216, 220–221, 225
    create purchase order (now from requisition), 225–227
    create purchase requisition, 224–225
    post payment to vendor, 219–220, 222–223
    procurement process and SAP steps, 212f
    purchase requisition, 213
    Welcome screen, 212f
SAP sales tutorial, 254–269
    create billing document for customer, 261, 265
    create delivery note, 258–259, 264
    create new customer, 254, 266–269
    create price quote, 254, 269
    create sales order, 254–258, 263–264, 269
    pick materials, 259–260, 264
    post goods issue, 260–261, 265
    post receipt of customer payment, 261–263, 265–266
Sarbanes-Oxley Act (SOX), 164, 191
Schedule feasibility, 385
Secure Socket Layer (SSL), 400
Security
    five components of, in information system, 396f
    human security safeguards, 403–409

incidents, organizational response to, 407–409
    disaster-recovery backup sites and, 408
    incident-response plan and, 408–409, 409f
information systems security, 392–396
    security program, 396–398
    technical safeguards, 398–403
Security monitoring, 407
Security program, 396–398
    components of, 396–397
    management's role in, 397
    NIST Handbook of security elements and, 397–398, 397f
Security vulnerability, 392–393
Sequential workflow, 296
Server farm, 60–61
Server operating system, 63
Servers
    defined, 60
    vs. clients, 59–61, 60f
Server tier, 79
Service, 140
Service-oriented architecture (SOA), 140, 143, 173
    encapsulation, 143
    service, 140
    standards, 143
Service processes, 132–133
Shared content
    with no control, 285–286, 285f
    with version control, 288–289, 290
    with version management, 286–288
SharePoint. *See* Microsoft SharePoint
Sharing social media, 317, 321–322
    in customer communication process, 321–322
    in promotion process, 321
Shopping cart, 80, 80f
Silverlight, 82
Six Sigma, 137
Skype, 284
Small office/home office (SOHO), 69, 71
Smart cards, 398
SMTP (Simple Mail Transfer Protocol), 75
Sniffing, 394
SOA standards, 143
Social capital, building, 326–330
    by connecting to those with more assets, 329–330
    by increasing number of relationships, 326–328
    by increasing strengths of relationships, 328–329
Social capital, defined, 326
Social CRM, 242–243
Social engineering, 393
Social graph, 323
Social media
    business processes improved with, 320–325, 320f, 322f
    collaborating, 317, 324–325
    to connect with people with more assets, 329–330
    defined, 316–317
    marketing network, 327, 327f
    monitoring, 332
    networking, 317, 322–324
    new processes supported with, 325
    process integration with, 325
    promotions, conducting, 325, 325f
    relationships increased by, 326–328
    relationships strengthened by, 328–329

Social media (*continued*)
  sharing, 317, 321–322
  viral marketing network, 328, 328f
Software, 61–68
  application, 64–66, 64f
  business professional's knowledge of, 61–68
  categories of, 61f
  custom-developed, 66
  enterprise resource planning, 164–165
  in five-component framework, 31–32, 31f, 33, 35f, 38f
  off-the-shelf, 392
  open source, 66–68
  operating systems, 59, 61–63, 62f
  own *vs.* license, 63–64
  SAP, 176–177
  vendors, ethics and, 84–85
  Web 2.0, 315
Software as a service, 243
Sonos, 78
Source code, 66–68, 67f
Spoofing, 394
Sprint, 72, 89
Sprint Nextel, 89
Sprint ohm, 89
Spyware, 401, 402
SQL injection attack, 403
SQL Server, 97–98, 118–119
Standardized business processes, 30–31
Starting activity, 282
Strategic decisions, 278
Strategic processes, 130
Strength of relationship, 328–329
Structured processes
  characteristics of, 41
  defined, 41
  vs. dynamic processes, 41–42, 42f
Structured Query Language (SQL), 98–99
Supervised data mining, 358
Supplier evaluation process, 198
Supplier Relationship Management (SRM) process, 198
Supply chain
  effect on information systems, 202–203
  management, 198
  processes, 198, 198f
Supply chain integration, 197–204
  improved by increasing process synergy, 199–200, 200f
  improved by sharing data, 198–199, 199f
  problems with emerging technologies, 200–201, 200f, 203–204
  SAP improvements in, 197–204
    by increasing process synergy, 199–200, 200f
    problems with emerging technologies and, 200–201, 200f, 203–204
    by sharing data, 198–199, 199f
Supply chain management (SCM), 198
Support activities, 16–17
Surrogate key, 113
Swimlane, 29
Switch, 69
Symmetrical digital subscriber lines (SDSL), 72
Symmetric encryption, 399
Synchronous communication, 283
Sysomos, 332
System, defined, 31
System conversion, 388–389

Systems analysts, 385
Systems development, 384
Systems development life cycle (SDLC), 384–390
  defined, 384
  requirements for, 384–390, 384f
    define the system, 384–386, 385f
    design components, 387–388, 387f
    determine, 386–387, 387f
    implement the system, 388–389, 388–389f
    maintain the system, 389–390, 390f
Systems procedures, 406–407
Systems thinking, 8–9

T

Table, 93, 94f, 113f, 114f
Tag, 80–81
TCP (Transmission Control Protocol), 75
TCP/IP architecture, 74, 74f
Team surveys, 285
Technical feasibility, 385
Technical safeguards, 398–403
  authentication, 398–399
  biometric authentication, 398–399
  defined, 398
  design secure applications, 403
  encryption, 399–401
  firewalls, 401
  identification, 398
  malware protection, 401–403
  passwords, 398
  smart cards, 398
Technology
  business intelligence and, 362–363
  development processes, 133
  Porter's definition of, 17
10/100/1000 Ethernet, 70
Terabyte (TB), 58
Termination processes, 405
Test plan, 388
Thick client, 64–66, 65f
Thin client, 64–66, 65f
Third party, 166
Threats, 393–394, 393f, 396, 396f
  defined, 389
  denial of service, 394
  incorrect data modification, 394
  loss of infrastructure, 394, 396
  unauthorized data disclosure, 393–394
3D printing, 203
Three-tier architecture, 79–80, 79f
Three-way match, 189
T-Mobile, 72
Tourism Holdings Limited
    (THL), 338–339, 370–373
Town, Laura, 308
Traditional capital, 326
Train the trainer, 165
Transaction processing system (TPS), 130
Transport Layer Security (TLS), 400
Trojan horses, 401
Tunnel, 82
Twitter, 7, 321, 329
  See also Social media

U

Unauthorized data disclosure, 393–394
  phishing, 393, 395, 395f
  pretexting, 393
  social engineering, 393
  spoofing, 394
Unified Modeling Language (UML), 105
U.S. Air Force, 182–183
Unix, 62
Unshielded twisted pair (UTP) cable, 69–70
Unsupervised data mining, 358
URL (Uniform Resource Locator), 77
User-generated content, 316
Users, 166
User tier, 79

V

Valentine, Brian, 307
Value, Porter's definition of, 15
Value chain
  business processes and, 131, 131f
  business processes determined by, 18–19
  competitive strategy used to determine, 15–18
  defined, 15
  example of, 16f
  information systems determined by, 18–19
  linkages, 17–18
  linkages in, 135
  primary activities in, 15–16, 16f
  procurement process in, 187f
  support activities in, 16–17
Verizon, 72
Version control, 288–289, 290
Version management, 286–288
Vertical-market application, 64
Videoconferencing, 284
Viral, 321
Viral social media marketing, 328, 328f
Virtual, 82
Virtualization, 63–64
Virtual meetings, 284
Virtual private network (VPN), 82–83, 302
  connections, 83f
  defined, 82
  typical, 82f
Viruses, 401
Visualization, 362
Volatile, 59

W

Wall Street Journal, 318
WAN wireless, 72–73
Warehouse problems
  after SAP procurement process, 195–196, 195f
  in sales process after SAP, 236–238
  in sales process before SAP, 233–234
  before SAP procurement process, 190–191

Web, 75
Web 2.0, 314–316
  business processes improved
    with, 318–320, 318f
    B2C sales process, 320
    market research process, 319
    online advertising sales process, 319
    process integration with Web 2.0, 320
    promotion process, 318–319, 318f
  challenges for businesses using, 330–332
  content, 316
  defined, 314
  future impacts on, 332–333
  goals, 316
  interfaces, 315–316
  social capital and, 326–330
  software, 315
WebEx, 284
Web farm, 79
Webinars, 284
Web page, 77f, 79
Web server, 77–82
  defined, 79
  Flash and, 82
  HTML and, 79, 80–81, 80–81f
  HTML5 and, 82
  Silverlight and, 82
  three-tier architecture and, 79–80, 79f
  Web pages and, 77f, 79
  XML and, 82
Webster, Grant, 338
Web storefront, 77, 246
Wide area network (WAN), 71–73
  cable modems and, 72
  defined, 68
  DSL modems and, 71–72, 72f
  wireless, 72–73
Wikis, 286
WiMax, 72, 89
Windows, 61–62, 65–66
Windows Live ID, 287
Windows Server, 63
Wireless NIC (WNIC), 70
Work Center (WC), 141–142
Workflow, 296
Workflow control, 296–301
  implementing, 297–301
  workflow problem requirements, 296, 297f
Worms, 401
Wrapping-up activity, 282–283

X

XML (eXtensible Markup Language), 82
XOHM, 72

Y

YouTube, 7, 8, 24–25, 321